AF600527

Collected Works of Northrop Frye

VOLUME 29

Northrop Frye on Twentieth-Century Literature

The Collected Edition of the Works of Northrop Frye has been planned and is being directed by an editorial committee under the aegis of Victoria University, through its Northrop Frye Centre. The purpose of the edition is to make available authoritative texts of both published and unpublished works, based on an analysis and comparison of all available materials, and supported by scholarly apparatus, including annotation and introductions. The Northrop Frye Centre gratefully acknowledges financial support, through McMaster University, from the Michael G. DeGroote family.

Northrop Frye on Twentieth-Century Literature

VOLUME 29

Edited by Glen Robert Gill

UNIVERSITY OF TORONTO PRESS
Toronto Buffalo London

www.utorontopress.com

ISBN 978-1-4426-4053-5

Library and Archives Canada Cataloguing in Publication

Frye, Northrop, 1912–1991
Northrop Frye's writings on twentieth-century literature /
edited by Glen Robert Gill.

(Collected works of Northrop Frye ; v. 29)
Includes bibliographical references and index.
ISBN 978-1-4426-4053-5

1. English literature – 20th century – History and criticism.
2. Criticism. 3. American literature – 20th century –
History and criticism. I. Gill, Glen Robert, 1969–
II. Title. III. Series: Collected works of Northrop Frye ; v. 29

PN37.F693 2009 809 C2009-905004-8

This volume has been published with the assistance of a grant from
Victoria University.

University of Toronto Press acknowledges the financial assistance to its
publishing program of the Canada Council for the Arts and the
Ontario Arts Council.

University of Toronto Press acknowledges the financial support for its
publishing activities of the Government of Canada through the
Book Publishing Industry Development Program (BPIDP).

To my parents,
John and Arlene Gill

Contents

Preface

This volume contains Northrop Frye's writings on twentieth-century literature, which have been construed as distinct from his writings on twentieth-century culture in general, his student essays on twentieth-century authors, and his discussions of twentieth-century authors in particular relation to those of earlier literary periods. These latter writings may be found in volume 11, *Northrop Frye on Modern Culture,* volume 3, *Northrop Frye's Student Essays, 1933–1938,* and volume 10, *Northrop Frye on Literature and Society, 1936–1989,* respectively. Collected here are Frye's literary criticism, his general and thematic commentaries, and his periodical reviews of twentieth-century literature as such. This array of fifty-one items includes a book on T.S. Eliot, three essays on the work of W.B. Yeats, two on the poetics of Wallace Stevens, and two on James Joyce's *Finnegans Wake,* as well as many other critical essays and reviews, one unpublished typescript, and a brief transcribed audiotape. There is in addition one exception to the rubric: a review of a book by psychologist C.G. Jung and physicist W. Pauli, which came to light too late for inclusion in vol. 11 where it would categorically belong, and so is presented here in a less natural but still congenial context. All works were produced between 1933 and 1989, with the major essays beginning to appear in 1947. The pieces have been arranged chronologically according to date of first publication; if the item in question was originally given as a speech, however, the date is that of delivery of the speech, though the text may be taken from the printed version.

Headnotes to the individual items specify the copy-text (in the form of "from such-and-such a text"), list all known reprintings in English of the item, and also note the existence of typescripts and where they can be found in the Northrop Frye Fonds in the E.J. Pratt Library of

Victoria University. The copy-text chosen is generally the first edition, which was often the only one carefully revised and proofread by Frye himself. In some cases he did revise essays for inclusion in his own collections, such as *Fables of Identity* or *Spiritus Mundi,* and such revised versions then become the source of the authoritative text. Although this volume is a reading edition rather than a fully critical one, major variants are given in notes to each item. All substantive changes to the copy-text are noted in the list of emendations.

In preparing the text, we have followed the general practice of the Collected Works in handling published material from a variety of sources. That is to say, since the conventions of spelling, typography, and to some extent punctuation derive from the different publishers' house styles rather than from Frye, we have regularized them silently throughout the volume. For instance, Canadian spellings ending in -our have been substituted for American -or ones, commas have been added before the "and" in sequences of three, and titles of poems have been italicized.

Notes identify the source of all quotations and specific references that have been identified; short identifications, such as those for Classical works, poem titles, or the act, scene, and line of Shakespearean plays, have been placed in square brackets in the text. Biblical quotations are from the Authorized King James Version (AV). Notes provided by Frye himself are identified by [NF] following the note; the style of these has been silently changed to conform to that of the Collected Works, with additional interpolated material placed in square brackets. In the rare instances where Frye has made his own editorial insertions, in order to distinguish them from those of the volume editors his parentheses or square brackets have been replaced by braces: { }. Where the reference is to *Anatomy of Criticism, Fearful Symmetry,* or *The Great Code,* the page number of the original book is followed, after a solidus, by the page number in the Collected Works edition. References to Blake have been checked against David Erdman's *The Complete Poetry and Prose of William Blake,* revised ed. (Berkeley: University of California Press, 1982); quotations have been regularized to this edition, with accidental changes made silently and a few substantive changes listed in the Emendations. An "E" following the Blake reference gives the page number in Erdman. Authors and titles mentioned in passing are not annotated, but life dates and date of first publication of books are provided in the index.

Acknowledgments

Many generous friends and supportive colleagues aided and assisted me in the preparation of the volume, often in ways for which mere notation here provides painfully inadequate credit. Firstly, I want to thank Alvin Lee and Jean O'Grady, whose Jobian patience and persistence were central to the completion of this volume, to say nothing of their sagacious management of the Collected Works of Northrop Frye project as a whole. I am grateful to both for innumerable examples of guidance and aid, substantial and supersubstantial. Several others at the Northrop Frye Centre at Victoria University were also indispensable in the dispatch of this work, chiefly Margaret Burgess, whose general devotion to all things Frygian has made her one of the hidden movers of the Collected Works in addition to her visible role as precise and scrupulous copyeditor. The contents of the volume were originally typed or scanned by Miranda Purves. Erin Reynolds tracked down a number of important quotations for notes and citations, as did Nicholas Graham, whose company I appreciated during some long summer days while I worked at the Frye archive at the E.J. Pratt Library at Victoria University. Ward McBurney was also of great help at various points. John Court of the Centre for Addiction and Mental Health in Toronto deserves special thanks for unearthing the Jung/Pauli review in the nick of time. I am grateful to the staff of the libraries, and particularly the interlibrary loan staff, of Victoria University, the University of Toronto, McMaster University, and Montclair State University for their good work and assistance. Ron Schoeffel and Anne Laughlin of the University of Toronto Press shepherded this volume, like so many others in the Collected Works project, through the rough pastures of academic publishing, and I extend sincere thanks to them, and to the anonymous press reviewers of the manuscript, for their suggestions and professionalism.

Many others were instrumental more generally by providing me with the benefit of their expertise, experience, and energy: chief among them are Robert Denham and Michael Dolzani, who afforded me the benefit of their wide-reaching apprehension of Frye's work. Other readers and scholars of Frye, and of literature and religion in general, were of similar aid, particularly Joseph Adamson, Eleanor Cook, Nella Cotrupi, Jeffery Donaldson, Graham Forst, Troni Grande, R. B. Kershner, Garry Sherbert, Imre Salusinszky, Ian Sloan, Joseph Velaidum, and Jane Widdicombe.

Still other friends and colleagues in academia at large provided crucial moral support, including Scott Nokes, William Thompson, Jeffery Gibson, and Jean Alvares, as well as the large number of students who have welcomed my teaching of Frye's work. Lastly and most personally, I want to thank my parents, John and Arlene Gill, to whom I dedicate this volume, for supporting and respecting this work, and my wife Beth for permitting it to intrude so many times during our engagement and our first year of marriage.

Credits

We wish to acknowledge the following sources for permission to include works previously published or broadcast by them. We have not been able to determine or to contact the copyright holders of all the works included in this volume, and we welcome notice from any who have been inadvertently omitted from these acknowledgments. The dates given are those of publication or broadcast, where applicable.

American Psychiatric Association for "Nature and the Psyche" (1957)

Canadian Broadcasting Corporation for "Aldous Huxley" (1973)

Hodder Education for "The Rising of the Moon: A Study of *A Vision*" (1965)

McGill-Queen's University Press for "Henry James and the Comedy of the Occult" (1992)

University of Toronto Quarterly for "Yeats and the Language of Symbolism" (1947)

Yale University Press for "Wallace Stevens and the Variation Form" (1973)

With the exception of those listed above, all works are printed by courtesy of the Estate of Northrop Frye/Victoria University.

Abbreviations

Works are by Frye unless otherwise noted. Abbreviations of the works of Wallace Stevens are given in the headnotes of nos. 37 and 47, and abbreviations of the works of T.S. Eliot are listed the beginning of the notes for no. 41.

AC	*Anatomy of Criticism: Four Essays*. Princeton, N.J.: Princeton University Press, 1957.
AC2	*Anatomy of Criticism: Four Essays*. Ed. Robert D. Denham. CW, 22. Toronto: University of Toronto Press, 2007.
Ayre	John Ayre. *Northrop Frye: A Biography*. Toronto: Random House, 1989.
C	*Northrop Frye on Canada*. Ed. Jean O'Grady and David Staines. CW, 12. Toronto: University of Toronto Press, 2003.
CPCT	*"The Critical Path" and Other Writings on Critical Theory, 1963–1975*. Ed. Jean O'Grady and Eva Kushner. CW, 27. Toronto: University of Toronto Press, 2009.
CW	Collected Works of Northrop Frye
D	*The Diaries of Northrop Frye, 1942–1955*. Ed. Robert D. Denham. CW, 8. Toronto: University of Toronto Press, 2001.
E	*The Complete Poetry and Prose of William Blake*. Rev. ed. Ed. David Erdman. Berkeley: University of California Press, 1982.
EAC	*The Eternal Act of Creation: Essays, 1979–1990*. Ed. Robert D. Denham. Bloomington: Indiana University Press, 1993.
EICT	*The Educated Imagination and Other Writings on Critical Theory, 1933–1963*. Ed. Germaine Warkentin. CW, 21. Toronto: University of Toronto Press, 2006.

ENC *Northrop Frye's Writings on the Eighteenth and Nineteenth Centuries*. Ed. Imre Salusinszky. CW, 17. Toronto: University of Toronto Press, 2005.

FI *Fables of Identity: Studies in Poetic Mythology*. New York: Harcourt, Brace & World, 1963.

FS *Fearful Symmetry: A Study of William Blake*. Princeton, N.J.: Princeton University Press, 1947.

FS2 *Fearful Symmetry: A Study of William Blake*. Ed. Nicholas Halmi. CW, 14. Toronto: University of Toronto Press, 2004.

GC *The Great Code: The Bible and Literature*. New York: Harcourt Brace Jovanovich, 1982.

GC2 *The Great Code: The Bible and Literature*. Ed. Alvin A. Lee. CW, 19. Toronto: University of Toronto Press, 2006.

INF *Interviews with Northrop Frye*. Ed. Jean O'Grady. CW, 24. Toronto: University of Toronto Press, 2008.

LN *Northrop Frye's Late Notebooks, 1982–1990: Architecture of the Spiritual World*. Ed. Robert D. Denham. CW, 5–6. Toronto: University of Toronto Press, 2002.

LS *Northrop Frye on Literature and Society, 1936–1989*. Ed. Robert D. Denham. CW, 10. Toronto: University of Toronto Press, 2002.

M&B *Northrop Frye on Milton and Blake*. CW, 16. Toronto: University of Toronto Press, 2005.

MM *Myth and Metaphor: Selected Essays, 1974–1988*. Ed. Robert D. Denham. Charlottesville: University Press of Virginia, 1990.

NF Northrop Frye

NFC *Northrop Frye in Conversation*. Ed. David Cayley. Concord, Ont.: Anansi, 1992.

NFCL *Northrop Frye on Culture and Literature: A Collection of Review Essays*. Ed. Robert D. Denham. Chicago: University of Chicago Press, 1978.

NFF Northrop Frye Fonds, Victoria University Library

NFHK *The Correspondence of Northrop Frye and Helen Kemp, 1932–1939*. Ed. Robert D. Denham. CW, 1–2. Toronto: University of Toronto Press, 1996.

NFL The books in Frye's personal library that were annotated, now in the Victoria University Library

NFMC *Northrop Frye on Modern Culture*. Ed. Jan Gorak. CW, 11. Toronto: University of Toronto Press, 2003.

RT	*Northrop Frye's Notebooks and Lectures on the Bible and Other Religious Texts*. Ed. Robert D. Denham. CW, 13. Toronto: University of Toronto Press, 2003.
RW	*Reading the World: Selected Writings, 1935–1976*. Ed. Robert D. Denham. New York: Peter Lang Publishing, 1990.
SE	*Northrop Frye's Student Essays, 1932–1938*. Ed. Robert D. Denham. CW, 3. Toronto: University of Toronto Press, 1997.
SM	*Spiritus Mundi: Essays on Literature, Myth, and Society*. Bloomington: Indiana University Press, 1976.
StS	*The Stubborn Structure: Essays on Criticism and Society*. Ithaca, N.Y.: Cornell University Press, 1970.
WP	*Words with Power: Being a Second Study of "The Bible and Literature."* New York: Harcourt Brace Jovanovich, 1990.
WP2	*Words with Power: Being a Second Study of "The Bible and Literature."* Ed. Michael Dolzani. CW, 26. Toronto: University of Toronto Press, 2008.
WTC	*The Well-Tempered Critic*. Bloomington: Indiana University Press, 1963.

Introduction

I

Northrop Frye's towering reputation as a thinker is, unquestionably, built on the backs of his great work of literary theory *Anatomy of Criticism* and his visionary studies of the Bible, *The Great Code* and *Words with Power*. Following this, it is his books on Blake, Shakespeare, and Milton, and his works on literary genre like *The Secular Scripture*, and on literary culture like *The Critical Path*, for which he is best known. It is these influential writings that led one of his best-known critical contemporaries to label him "the foremost living student of Western literature" and "the largest and most crucial literary critic in the English language since the divine Walter [Pater] and the divine Oscar [Wilde]."[1] Next to such works, Frye's writings, on, say, Renaissance or eighteenth-century literature, on education or Canadian culture, might seem to be peripheral excursions. But as the Collected Works volumes that have re-presented such writings have shown, they are equally potent, penetrating, and of a piece with his better-known works, ramifying and underwriting them in important ways. Such is the case with Frye's writings on twentieth-century literature: in comparison to his foundational works, they may somehow appear secondary, but on closer examination they are revealed to be a definitive collection of texts in their own right and one which reflects and substantiates his overall critical project. Indeed, Frye's work in this area may be more significant than many of his other writings insofar as it represents his manifold approaches to the literature of his own time: his responses to what was appearing in print around him, his theorizations of literary modernism (and expectations of its successor, postmodernism), his observations about the academic study of modern literature, and most importantly, his criticism of the great modern writers, whose work he so often referred to in his own.

As with most branches of Frye's *oeuvre,* the reader will discover his writings on twentieth-century literature to be an evolving and developing body of work in which new priorities are constantly addressed and new critical paradigms are constantly tested. This particular corpus is probably more dynamic than many of Frye's others, in fact, as he is here digesting and responding to writers who were themselves still writing (some of whom in turn responded to him). But as is also typically the case with Frye's work, these essays proceed from a remarkably consistent position. Like many of his views, Frye's perspective on modern literature and its major contributors coalesced early, galvanized by the epiphanies and breakthroughs of his youth, only to be elaborated, reformulated, and reiterated with each new engagement over the course of his long career. The final result of this process, in this case, is a body of work that shows that Frye had an unusually broad, profound, and prescient apprehension of the literature of his day. The criticism contained here remains not only relevant, not merely effective in elucidating the authors and works in question, but taken as a whole it clarifies and contextualizes most of the defining characteristics of modern literature and criticism in relation to the field itself, to all of literature, and to the social ideologies with which literature is implicated. The fact that it took several generations of critics sequentially extending each other's work to develop what Frye understood as a simultaneous and interrelated whole (and that postmodernism has largely neglected concern for the former contexts in favour of the last), means that Frye's survey of twentieth-century literature presents us with an extraordinary opportunity: to grasp at once not only most of the particulars but the overall structure and significance of the mainstream of modern literature, as an array of texts, as a moment in the development of literature, and as a discourse with social and ideological implications. As other volumes of Frye's Collected Works have shown in relation to their purviews, this was an aspect of his genius: to see the diverse interrelations of the whole. Its operation in this case demonstrates that Northrop Frye was not just one of the great modern critics, but one of the great critics of modernism.

To appreciate this, one need only consider the way in which criticism of modern literature has developed. As Marjorie Perloff observes in her influential retrospective essay "Modernist Studies," the criticism of modern literature has proceeded through three stages. "In its earliest phases, modernist scholarship and criticism were conceived as a defense of the 'new writing,'" which primarily meant explicating modernism as "a call for rupture."[2] Implicit in this was a codification of what made the "new writing" new, a set of criteria through which modern literature ostensibly departed from the sentimentalism and emotional excesses of Romantic and Victorian literature. This included such now-familiar emphases and foci as an inner world of symbolism over external representation, the superiority of art to nature, the autonomy and depersonalization of art, symmetry and spatial form, verbal ambiguity and complexity, the fluidity of consciousness, the Freudian unconscious and dream-work, the Jungian unconscious and archetypes of myth, the ironic detachment of the individual, and the importance of the urban and the international. The presentation and explication of these qualities as innovative and distinctive was quite successful, as they remain for many scholars and students the hallmarks of modern literature.

Around 1957, however, scholarly studies began to appear that argued that modern literature was, despite or even because of these qualities, "squarely in the Romantic tradition."[3] The continuity of nineteenth- and twentieth-century literature implied in Robert Langbaum's derivation of the modern dramatic monologue from Romantic models,[4] or by the modern recurrence of what M.H. Abrams called "the greater Romantic lyric,"[5] led to speculation that modern literature was better understood as "the final phase of the great Romantic revolution."[6] The zenith of this view was probably Harold Bloom's repeated declarations in the 1970s[7] that modern poets like W.B. Yeats and Wallace Stevens were actually belated Romantics and that more consciously modernist poets like T.S. Eliot and Ezra Pound were destined for demotion. By the 1980s, as literary criticism was becoming more deeply informed by critical theory and philosophy, the argument for continuity began to be substantiated, with critics like Albert Gelpi explaining that:

> Romanticism ... rested on the assumption that meaning—and therefore expression—proceeded from the momentary gestalt, wherein subject and object not merely encountered each other but completed, or at least potentially completed each other. ... But [this] was also the source of Romantic instability and self-doubt, and so the genesis of Modernism. That epiphanic gestalt could not be invoked by the mechanics of thought or will; it could only be awaited and attended upon, and its occurrence was rare and fleeting. ... No wonder that from the beginning Romantic ecstasy was accompanied

> by Romantic angst. . . . Literature and the arts operated in a state of crisis in the nineteenth century precisely because the moment of participative insight, in which the individual and the world was sealed in a revelation of cosmic and metaphysical harmony, became steadily more difficult to attain and validate. . . . [This] deepening crisis in perception and signification, as the Romantic construct gave way through Victorian doubt to its *fin de siècle* decadence, set the agenda for Modernism . . . . The Modernists proceeded from a skeptical, experimental, relativistic, even materialistic base to seek an absolute realization and expression which internal and external circumstances seemed to rule out.[8]

Before such deductions could be thoroughly ramified, however, another shift in values marked by a "more politicized ethos"[9] brought about a third phase of modernist criticism. Driven by the complex of ideologically attuned methodologies that came to be known as new historicism or cultural studies, this critical development was distinguished by its effort to establish a "link between modernism and authoritarian politics."[10] Surveying the traditional qualities of modern literature, this critical approach interpreted them as an effort to turn away from "the reality of everyday life for a 'system of aesthetics' that might control history."[11] While this approach had been anticipated some years earlier by critics like Frank Kermode, whose *The Sense of an Ending* observed "a correlation between early modernist literature and authoritarian politics" in which "totalitarian theories of form matched or reflected . . . totalitarian politics,"[12] it became something of a consensus among modernist critics in the 1990s and, according to some accounts, still prevails. No other general approach, in any case, has emerged.

What even an itinerant reading of this volume reveals, and what seasoned readers of Frye have long realized, is that Frye's criticism of modern literature develops and interrelates these three critical approaches simultaneously, anticipating and arguably outdoing the best examples and practitioners of each phase in the process. One is hard pressed, for instance, to nominate a critic who is more consistently appreciative of the traditional qualities of modern literature; Frye was particularly interested, of course, in its expression of mythic archetypes and unconscious drives, its symbolic and formal commitments, and its verbal pyrotechnics (all of which he saw not as innovations but as conventionalizations). At the same time, Frye was very much the initiator of the reassertion of Romantic values in criticism after their reproach by figures like T.S. Eliot and T.E. Hulme: it was Frye's elucidation of the Romanticism of Blake in his first book *Fearful Symmetry* (1947) that got it all started, such that Romanticism's avenging angel Harold Bloom confessed to have "read it a hundred times" until he "intuitively memorized it" and acknowledged Frye as his "authentic precursor."[13] And if Frye is less known for the third approach, for probing the ideological and political implications of literary techniques and critical positions, that is only because he did not emphasize this aspect of his work over others. Frye was, in fact, as acutely conscious of the ideological implications of literature and criticism as any new historicist. A review of his intellectual development, in fact, reveals that amid his deepening studies in the literary and critical values of modernism and Romanticism it was his awareness of the ideological implications of both that prompted the development of what was to become the defining characteristic of his approach to modern literature: his examination of it through the lens of Romanticism to show how it is not a break with Romanticism but a progressive inversion of it, an opposite movement within a continuous cycle of literary history.

II

Born in 1912 and raised in Moncton, New Brunswick, Northrop Frye grew up in a culture that was rapidly outgrowing its Victorian attachments. His childhood absorption of the Bible and Classical mythology, however, ensured that they would always be among the tools that he would use to interpret and relate all literature, prior and subsequent to his birth. His first specifically literary experiences were the exposures his mother provided to the work of nineteenth-century giants such as Walter Scott, George Eliot, and Charles Dickens. It is interesting, therefore, that following his infamous epiphany on St. George Street, through which he dispensed with the religious fundamentalism of his childhood and acquired a measure of spiritual and intellectual freedom, his volunteer work at the Moncton public library saw him develop a fascination for George Bernard Shaw,[14] whose satires doubtless foreshadowed the scathing ironies of the major modernists. It is equally interesting that his other literary discovery at the Moncton library was the poetry of Wallace Stevens, which he came across in Louis Untermeyer's anthology *Modern American Poetry* (1921): Stevens's Romantic inclinations in the midst of literature's development toward modernism made a strong impression on Frye (*NFC*, 109/*INF*, 963), perhaps priming him for his later commitment to Blake (whom Frye as a teenager understandably found difficult).

With his move to Toronto in 1929, Frye's experience of the modernist malaise of urban alienation was counterbalanced by the city's residual Victorian gentility and the cultural vitality of the University of Toronto. He found himself similarly poised between the two periods in the classes of his teacher and mentor Pelham Edgar, who was famous for his bold (at the time) inclusion of modernists like Eliot and D.H. Lawrence on his courses and his pioneering study of Henry James, and yet was the one who in his Romantic literature class portentously commissioned Frye to study Blake (Ayre, 63). What allowed Frye to begin the process of reconciling the two literary outlooks was his epiphanic encounter in 1931 with Oswald Spengler's *The Decline of the West*, the eccentric German historian's impressionistic effort to intuit recurrent patterns of cultural development. Spengler's book, which Frye later called "not a work of history" but "a vision of history that is very close to being a work of literature" (*SM*, 187/*NFMC*, 304), exercised a huge influence on his thinking, such that he later joked of sleeping "with Spengler under my pillow for several years" (*RW*, 321/*NFMC*, 270). While Frye rejected much of the book's content, particularly its *über*-Romantic rumblings about Teutonic destiny, it stamped on his thought a methodology, a tendency to think in terms of a certain form: Spengler's penchant for cyclical structures, which he used to relate seemingly disparate and opposed movements in culture, powerfully impressed Frye. As his biographer John Ayre writes, what fascinated Frye about Spengler's use of the cyclical form in cultural theory was that it "yielded a pattern which extended to infinity and absorbed all of man's creations" (Ayre, 66). Frye would ever after avail himself of the heuristic value of cyclical paradigms in larger projects, including his connecting the seemingly opposed priorities of modernism and Romanticism.

Frye consolidated a basis for this task, and indeed of his whole career, in 1933, with the production of a sprawling essay on Romanticism for a philosophy course (*SE*, 11–83)—approximately the same time that he penned the first piece in this volume, a review of a student production of a Shaw play. It was 1934, however, that was the momentous year for Frye's modernist and Romantic studies. First, in February, came his famous epiphany about Blake, a sudden, late-night recognition of the Romantic poet's relation to his seventeenth-century precursor John Milton through their mutual reliance on the mythological framework of the

Bible: a realization which led ultimately to *Fearful Symmetry* (*NFC*, 47/*INF*, 921; Ayre, 92; *SM*, 17/*CPCT*, 322). Deeper insight into the content and function of this framework followed in or around October, when he encountered James George Frazer's *The Golden Bough* in an Old Testament class and excitedly digested the symbolism and significance of the cyclical fertility myth of the dying, rising god (*NFHK*, 1:354–5). But two other breakthroughs also occurred around this time, one which positively licensed Frye to connect modern literature to this mythological framework, and one which illustrated for him the negative effect of assuming that modernism's code was an ascent to truth rather than a vantage point on it within a cycle of literary history (and the dangers of deducing an ideological position from that assumption). Both involved the dominant figure in literary modernism, T.S. Eliot. Frye's reading around 1934 of Eliot's famous essay "Tradition and the Individual Talent" presented him with the powerful idea that "the whole of the literature of Europe from Homer . . . has a simultaneous existence and a simultaneous order":[15] a notion that enticed Frye for the rest of his career, such that his entire corpus of literary theory and criticism (especially his influential *Anatomy of Criticism*) could be seen as an effort to footnote it. But 1934 also brought forth Eliot's disturbing *After Strange Gods*, with its clear anti-Semitism and its application of a blood-and-soil argument to the American south. Frye had been warily monitoring the rightward drift in many modern writers, but Eliot's ideological missteps in this work made it clear to him that some modernists were dabbling outright in fascism and that misunderstandings about the mandate of modernism probably had something to do with it. This was the moment when Frye committed himself to moderating the priorities of modernism through Romantic humanism, and Eliot and Blake would ever after be linked in his mind as foils for each other in relation to this goal. Almost forty years later, Frye would reflect:

> There were many reasons for [my] getting interested in Blake: perhaps one may be of general interest. I am, in cultural background, what is known as a WASP, and thus belong to the only group in society which it is entirely safe to ridicule. I expected that a good deal of contemporary literature would be devoted to attacking the alleged complacency of the values and standards I had been brought up in, and I was not greatly disturbed when it did. But with the rise of Hitler in Germany, the agony of the Spanish Civil War, and the massacres and deportations of Stalinism, things began to get more

> serious. For Eliot to announce that he was Classical in literature, royalist in politics, and Anglo-Catholic in religion was all part of the game. But the feeling of personal outrage and betrayal that I felt when I opened *After Strange Gods* was something else again. And when Eliot was accompanied by Pound's admiration for Mussolini, Yeats's flirtations with the most irresponsible of Irish leaders, Wyndham Lewis's interest in Hitler, and the callow Marxism of younger writers, I felt that I could hardly get interested in any poet who was not closer to being the opposite in all respects of what Eliot thought he was. Or, if that was too specific, at least a poet who, even if dead, was still fighting for something that was alive. (*SM*, 13–14/*CPTC*, 319–20)

We should not be surprised to discover that, in the context of modern literature itself, Frye would nominate Wallace Stevens as Blake's surrogate and the poetic voice of Romantic humanism in the face of T.S. Eliot's modernism, a role the poet himself acknowledged in his candid description of himself and Eliot as "dead opposites" (see no. 47, n. 36). These, however, were not the only consequences of this breakthrough for Frye. It also brought him to one of his core critical principles: that an author could not be expected or counted upon to understand the implications of his work, hence the need for critics and criticism. "It was my becoming aware of my responsibilities as a critic," Frye would later say of this moment, "Because you couldn't trust the poets . . . . [A] poet can be any kind of damn fool and still be a poet" (*NFC*, 107–8/*INF*, 962).

From this point on, Frye would consistently strive even in his private writings to dispatch these critical responsibilities, including suggesting which poets were fools and why. Sometimes this meant defending the great poet from accusations that he was one, as when Frye reports his approbation of James Joyce's *Ulysses* in letters to his wife Helen while she was studying in England, one of which contrasts Joyce with D.H. Lawrence as a "genius who expresses his age" versus a "genius who is merely a symptom of it" (*NFHK*, 1:479). At other times, it meant acknowledging that a minor poet probably was one, as when he registers his disgust in another letter that Oxford poet Edmund Blunden, Frye's tutor while he studied at Merton College, had "[come] back from Germany full of enthusiasm for the Nazis" (*NFHK*, 2:757). But it was in his initial critical forays into modern literature that we see him fulfilling these obligations in earnest, in such works as his student paper "T.S. Eliot and Other Observations," written in 1937 (*SE*, 417–29). There, after accurately predicting that Eliot's poetic concerns following his despairing *The Waste Land* would "necessarily be concerned with portraying the advance of the individual through chaos to reintegration" (a prediction borne out by Eliot's composition of *Four Quartets*), Frye not only voices his outrage of 1934 but also hints at what will become his mature perspective on modernism. After declaring that he "embrace[s] most of the tenets Eliot holds in peculiar abhorrence," Frye suggests that in moving from the United States to England and declaring himself "Classical in literature, royalist in politics, and Anglo-Catholic in religion,"

> Eliot has merely exchanged one form of humanism for another and has not yet escaped from the overemphasis on social and moral criteria of religious experience . . . . This I mention because I feel that his close association of religion and morality has had an unfortunate effect on his work: there must be many others besides myself who find the preaching in *The Rock* irritating and such essays as *Thoughts After Lambeth* and *After Strange Gods* unreadable. (*SE*, 428)

At the same time, Frye measures his critique at the conclusion of this paper, conceding that "those who call [Eliot] a reactionary can point to no D.H. Lawrence type of reaction: no *Plumed Serpent* with its schoolboyish Naziism," and states that "nothing that Eliot may do will injure the quality of what he has already done" (*SE*, 429): indications that he appreciated the difficulty of, and would likely return to, the task of sorting out the ideological implications from the obviously impressive poetic work of modernism's definitive voice.

His other early engagements with modern literature and thought were more uniformly positive. Within a few months of its publication in 1939, Frye discovered James Joyce's *Finnegans Wake*, "for ninety-eight cents on a remainder counter in Toronto" (see no. 50, p. 335 and n. 14), and was so fascinated by its fusion of modernist poetics and Romantic breadth that he would go on to produce two essays on it. By 1941, he had encountered and begun to digest the work of Sigmund Freud and C.G. Jung and, as he was now in a teaching position at Victoria College, his students helped to kindle other enthusiasms: his unusual friendship with Peter Fisher, who had a strong interest in mysticism and the occult, stoked Frye's own interests in this area and set him thinking about the work of W.B. Yeats. Frye had arguably been on a collision course with Yeats's Spenglerian rhapsody *A Vision* since the publication of its second edition in 1937, and while he ultimately arrived at a very qualified position on it, it would require three essays for him to come to terms with what he called the "haunting ghost" of Yeats (*SM*, xi). Similarly, the enrolment in Frye's graduate course on Blake of Hugh Kenner, who would go on to a career in modernist criticism to rival his teacher's, kept him thinking not only about Joyce but another of Kenner's favourites, Ezra Pound, a writer almost as problematic as Eliot from Frye's perspective. By underlining Pound's importance, not least by producing a book on him which Frye would review, Kenner would provoke Frye to confront another modernist of troubling ideological complicities.

The results of Frye's thinking about modernism began to appear in the early 1940s in reviews, chiefly for the *Canadian Forum* and the *Hudson Review*. Many of these were responses to social or cultural events and developments (and thus may be found along with his later and more significant writings of this type in volume 11, *Northrop Frye on Modern Culture*). But most were literary reviews, and in many of these he experimented with and honed characterizations of the aesthetics and ideological relations of modern literature. His first major effort to relate modernism to Romanticism, however, was his initial paper on Yeats, which was published in 1947 after the appearance of *Fearful Symmetry* and made use of similar methodologies. Interestingly, just as he was beginning this reconciliatory task, Frye would, either by design, coincidence, or a consequence of his own emergent importance as a critic, seek out Wallace Stevens. As Imre Salusinszky has noted, Frye attended the English Institute conference of 1948 at Columbia University during which Stevens gave his address "Imagination as Value,"[16] a paper which defended the Romantic imagination as the ability to "project the idea of God into the idea of Man."[17] A somewhat anticlimactic personal meeting followed,[18] but Frye's intuitions about Stevens as a mainstay of Romantic thought in modern literature had nevertheless been confirmed, such that Frye would go on to clarify the poet's importance in two substantial essays on his work. Significantly, just months after meeting Stevens, Frye recorded in his diary a conversation in which he fielded a query from his graduate student David Hoeniger as to whether he would consider writing a book on T.S. Eliot:

> I said no: I could write only about people who were open at the top, & he was sealed off at the top. I had no idea what I meant, but he understood. People who enter into religious systems as [Eliot] has done deny the integrity of the verbal universe: the open top has something to do with the *als obs* [as if] basis of poetic truth. (*D*, 141).

This foreswearing was either premature or provisional, of course, as Frye would eventually return to the task implied in his student paper on Eliot and write a book on him. His modesty notwithstanding, what is significant about this entry is that it indicates, along with his experience with Stevens the previous year, that Frye had developed by this point a precise understanding of the ways in which the two poets differed and thus, insofar as they typified for him the modernist and Romantic perspectives in modern literature, of the relation between these. Most of Frye's writings on modern literature after 1947 proceed from or develop this understanding, and situate other major modern writers (such as Henry James, Robert Graves, George Orwell, Aldous Huxley, Samuel Beckett, Giorgio Bassani, Franz Kafka, and René Char) within it.

III

This understanding turns on the existence and function of the creative imagination, and its prominence in Romanticism as an indication of what Frye calls "the recovery of projection" (*ENC*, 100). Latent in *Fearful Symmetry* and central to works like *A Study of English Romanticism*, this was Frye's term for the great achievement of Romanticism, the reattribution or relocation to the human imagination of what had previously been understood as the work of a transcendent God, particularly the act of creation. Through Romanticism, this latter in particular came to be understood rather as the "spatial projection of reality" (*ENC*, 78) through human acts of perception and expression, a transformation which involved increased estimations of the power of symbolic and metaphorical language and of the rights and liberties of man: ideas which became central to Romanticism's general reassessment of humanity as (co)creator rather than merely creature. As Frye consistently points out, William Blake was the first English writer to mythologize this new order, manifesting it not only in the theme of heroic revolution but in his wholesale inversion of the cosmology of literary symbolism and representation. In Romanticism, the four-tiered cosmology of medieval and Renaissance literature—a structure of ascent to a heaven of perfect being and a human paradise from a fallen nature and a fiery, punitive hell—underwent an ethical reversal. Now symbolizing progressive imaginative states, these four levels appeared as a structure of descent to (and potentially a re-ascent from) a recreative furnace and an irrepressible nature from the corrupt civilization of a compulsive humanity and the alienating void of a tyrannical God. In the prefaces to *Fables of Identity* and *Spiritus Mundi*, in which his Stevens, Joyce, and two of his three Yeats papers were reprinted, Frye makes it clear that he can only approach modern literature by way of this vast imaginative revolution:

> The hinge of the total argument, I suppose, is my conception of Romanticism. The Romantic movement in English literature seems to me now to be a small part of one of the most decisive changes in the history of culture, so decisive as to make everything that has been written since post-Romantic, including, of course, everything that is regarded by its producers as anti-Romantic. One feature of this change that particularly interests me is the way in which the forms of human civilization come to be regarded as man-made rather than God-made. . . . Blake raises most insistently the question of the reality of the poetic vision, a reality which is neither subjective nor objective, but is brought into being through creation itself. (*FI*, 3)

Of modern writers, Frye suggests, Stevens perpetuates "the Blakean preoccupation with the reality of what is created," while Joyce and Yeats reflect upon "the tragic situation of the artist that results when he moves into the centre of civilization" (*FI*, 3). For Yeats, too, "there is nothing creative except what the human imagination produces," but it is Stevens who most consistently

> polarizes the imagination against a "reality" which is otherness, what the imagination is not and has to struggle with. Such reality cannot ultimately be the reality of physical nature or of constituted human society, which produce only the "realism" that for Stevens is something quite different. It is rather a spiritual reality, an otherness of a creative power not ourselves; and sooner or later all theories of creative imagination have to take account of it. (*SM*, xiii)

By contrast, one theory that does *not* take account of it is the modernism of T.S. Eliot. The anti-Romantic orientation of Eliot's theories openly spurns the imagination, rejecting the notion of human creation and thereby committing what Frye refers to as "the fallacy of the substantial idea" (*WTC*, 37/*EICT*, 349): the metaphysical assumption of a reality that transcends human creation in language and art and which therefore reasserts the pre-Romantic cosmology. In one of his essays on Blake, Frye therefore explains how:

> Since the Romantic movement, there has been a more conservative tendency to deprecate the central place it gave to the creative imagination and to return, or attempt to return, to the older hierarchy. T.S. Eliot is both a familiar and a coherent exponent of this tendency . . . . According to Eliot, it is the function of art, by imposing an order on life, to give us the sense of an order in life, and so to lead us into a state of serenity and reconciliation preparatory to another and superior kind of experience, where "that guide" can lead us no further. The implication is that there is a spiritually existential world above that of art, a world of action and behaviour, of which the most direct imitation in this world is not art but the sacramental act. This latter is a form of uncritical or precritical participation that leads to a genuinely religious contemplation, which for Eliot is a state of heightened consciousness with strong affinities to mysticism. Mysticism is a word that has been applied both to Blake and St. John of the Cross: in other words it has been rather loosely applied, because the two poets have little in common. It is clear that Eliot's mystical affinities are of the St. John of the Cross type. The function of art, for Eliot, is again of the subordinate or allegorical kind. Its order represents a higher existential order, hence its greatest ambition should be to get beyond itself, pointing to its superior reality with such urgency and clarity that it disappears in that reality. (*M&B*, 328)

The problem with this theory from the perspective of Romanticism, however, is that without a point or principle of human contact and involvement like the creative imagination, no such participation and signification is truly possible, and therefore this higher existential order is either unattainable or nonexistent altogether: Eliot's theory of literature, from Frye's perspective, is thus "sealed off at the top."

There is a means of redeeming literature which proceeds from such a metaphysical assumption, which is to treat it as though it was nevertheless composed by and for the creative imagination, just one which happens to prefer and project the pre-Romantic cosmology. As Frye remarks in an interview,

> You can put all the good things "up there" coming down to man in a shower of blessings. Or you can use the inverted framework. Metaphorically, it doesn't matter which you do. And you can have people using traditional Dantean cosmologies, as Eliot does, and make convincing poetry out of them. In a sense, that is what Yeats did too. I think that the answer is Jacob's ladder: there are angels ascending and there are angels descending. (*NFC*, 106/*INF*, 961)

The risk of insisting on the traditional cosmology, however, is that with its metaphors comes the suggestion of all the social ideologies which that cosmology was assumed to endorse or reflect. Frye thus hastens to add: "Mythically and metaphorically, as I say, it doesn't matter, but ideologically it's very apt to take on the colouring of the old authority structures" (*NFC*, 107/*INF*, 962). Here, in essence, is the source of the disturbing ideological implications of the literary modernism of poets like T.S. Eliot, who insist upon the pre-Romantic cosmology and its poetics: potentially reactionary positions naturally follow from such conceptions because of their traditional association with ideologies of compulsory belief and behaviour. The significance of Romanticism, according to Frye, is that it brought forth what he calls a "new" or "open mythology," whereas

> The Christian mythology of the Middle Ages and later was a closed mythology, that is, a structure of belief, imposed by compulsion on everyone. As a structure of belief, the primary means of understanding it was rational and conceptual, and no poet, outside of the Bible, was accorded the kind of authority that was given to the theologian. Romanticism, besides being a new mythology, also marks the beginning of an "open" attitude to mythology on the part of society, making mythology a structure of imagination, out of which beliefs come, rather than directly one of compulsory belief. . . . [T]he new mythology caused old things to be believed in a new way, and thus eventually transformed the spirit of their belief. It also made new types of belief possible, by creating a new mythical language that permitted their formulation. (*ENC*, 102)

The dangers of reaffirming a "closed mythology" in the twentieth century is the subject of Frye's *The Modern Century* (*NFMC*, 3–70), his penetrating study of the cultural (as opposed to the specifically literary) products of modernism. There he concludes, predictably, that an "open mythology" is, as Jan Gorak puts it, an indispensible means of responding "to modernity's collective desires and fears without transforming them into structures of domination" (*NFMC*, xxxviii). The goal of his literary criticism seems to have been to substantiate and bolster this view by uncovering and distinguishing the two structures of belief, their metaphorical cosmoi and ideological effects, in the major works, authors, and historical development of modern literature.

It should be quite apparent by now how Northrop Frye regarded modern literature. For Frye modernism represented a rotation of the Spenglerian cycle of culture that turned back the revolutionary premises and achievements of Romanticism and restored the metaphorical cosmology and ideological world view that had previously dominated Western thought and civilization. The preponderance of ironic (or what Frye often calls "demonic") symbolism in modern literature was obviously a consequence of its suspicion if not dismissal of the imagination, the demotion of the human capacity for verbal creation and identification required by its commitment to an older humanism and its native cosmology and ideology. Almost forty years before the observation of Albert Gelpi quoted earlier, Frye had deduced that what ultimately distinguished Romanticism from modernism was the latter's scepticism toward the possibility of the subject–object union that made imaginative creation or spiritual revelation, what Frye would later call *kerygma*, possible (and following Blake's notion of the imagination as "mental fight," he would obviate Gelpi's suggestion that such moments could not be "invoked," only "awaited"). Nor did he fail, as we have noted, to underline the ideological implications of this scepticism for literature. Indeed, it could be said that the second half of Frye's career, which saw him increasingly theorizing the spiritual significance of literature, was an effort to hasten another turn of the Spenglerian wheel, ideally creating such a consciousness of its cyclicality that it would on its next turn acquire a third dimension and become the spiral ascent that was his later apprehension of real cultural process (the clearest expression of this is the second half of *Words with Power*; cf. *WP*, 144–313/127–265). But long before this, Frye considered the possibility of an in-depth study of the cyclical descent of Romanticism into modernism: as Michael Dolzani reports, one of the eight great works of literary criticism that Frye planned to write, his so-called *ogdoad*, was one called *Rencontre*, which was to be a history of literature detailing "the great crisis that began with Romanticism and culminates in the crises of modernism."[19] Interestingly, in the work of literary history that he eventually did write that was thus later called *Rencontre* by its editor (*LS*, 3–130), an introduction to an anthology that was eventually abandoned, Frye breaks off his substantial account just as he begins discussing writers like Eliot, Pound, and Yeats in relation to modernism's imaginative conservatism (*LS*, 126–7). What Frye would have written, there or in the earlier, hypothetical *Rencontre*, may well have been a distillation or condensation of what he elucidates at length in the collected pieces in this volume.

IV

With all this in mind, an overview of this volume will observe that its contents fall into six general categories, reflecting the development and articulation of the perspective outlined above. The first category consists of Frye's short reviews for the *Canadian Forum*, the *Hudson Review*, and other periodicals, which comprise most of the first thirty-five pieces (nos. 1–22, 24–28, and 35). Here a young Frye welcomes modernism's ironizing and conventionalizing efforts even as he recognizes the Romantic concerns many of its practitioners neglect. In a review of several now-obscure poets, for instance, he notes that the "romantic search for loveliness" is being "ruthlessly outgrown" and that "in place of the melancholy of nostalgia has come a new kind of melancholy based on observation rather than temperament, which only revolution will cure" (7). In another review of 1940, he insightfully connects modernism's objectivity to the outbreak of war, and, previewing the phenomenological argument of *Fearful Symmetry*[20] (then in progress), remarks: "Perhaps the lurking fear which causes wars also prevents us from seeing nature as real rather than phenomenal, and if we could conquer that fear our present way of looking at the world might blow up in an apocalypse of matter and apotheosis of man" (12). Even at this point, Frye seems to be looking past the immediate aims of modernism to the larger good that could be advanced by its clarification of literary conventions: among the "interesting developments" he observes in modernism, for instance, is the "desire for a communicable set of symbols, which in turn leads to an exploration of mythology and religion as the most promising sources for them" (23). Acknowledging the difficulties of this process in another review, he makes a remark that is painfully relevant for our own "post-literate" era:

> It seems to me that the writers of today who are still working with the traditional means of expression . . . have a more important job than ever to do, of a completely highbrow kind. It is their task to stimulate as far as possible a public respect for good writing, to show that the real values of literature and the standards of beauty, wisdom, and intelligence are now exactly what they were in Homer's time, and to demonstrate that there are laws of culture just as there are laws of nature, and that a society which willfully ignores either set of laws is going to get into plenty of trouble. (37–8)

Reviewing the work of poet Kenneth Rexroth, Frye thus maintains that "however inevitable the trend away from the Classics may be, it remains true that an English literature which is not solidly established on Classical (and Biblical) education will never get far above high-class journalism" (41–2). He concludes that piece with a prescient declaration which forecasts his own emerging interpretation of the significance of literary modernism:

> Poets today are reaching out for some integration of twentieth-century ideas, among which the Spenglerian view of history, the theories of unconscious symbolism in psychology and anthropology, and the Nietzsche-Lawrence conception of the limitations of reason, are especially prominent. (42)

It is this very sensibility that Frye sees as aptly represented in the work of C.G. Jung and W. Pauli, which he reviews in "Nature and the Psyche" (no. 35). Though not a literary review *per se* (and included here irregularly: see preface), the piece shows how Frye understood ideas like Jung's infamous "synchronicity principle," his theory of meaningful coincidence and the review's main subject, as having an essentially aesthetic and critical relevance; thus he notes approvingly Jung's gloss of synchronicity as a manifestation of "a creative power working in time" and observes that the use of the word "creative" opens "an interesting line of approach for critics of the arts, as in all the arts patterns of coincidence are a formal principle." While he ultimately finds Jung's exploration of the phenomenon to be "disappointingly inconclusive," he nevertheless applauds the psychologist for having "put his finger on a central intellectual preoccupation of our time" (122).

Other reviews in this category, of the work of modernists of less significance to Frye such as H.G. Wells (no. 17), Virginia Woolf (no. 27), Mark Van Doren (no. 8), John Berryman (no. 8), and John Betjeman (no. 24), focus on more pragmatic and specifically literary qualities; but in doing so they exhibit Frye's increasingly effortless ability to move between—and, indeed, relate—speculative philosophy, psychology, theology, and developments in literary history.

The second category consists of Frye's theoretical essays and commentaries on the period in general—three papers clustered in the middle of his career which concisely lay out his mature perspective on modern literature. Of these, the most significant is surely "Religion and Modern Poetry" (no. 38), arguably his major statement on literary modernism insofar as it articulates his perspective in contrast to the "problems of poetry and belief" posed by the fallacies of Eliot's position (including what Frye calls the "scapegoat fallacy" of moral criticism). Predictably, Frye begins this paper by defending the critical fact and necessity of literature being understood as an imaginative creation: "our first reaction to a poem, whether religious or not, should not be, 'Does what is said here correspond to my beliefs or experiences?' but, 'Is what is said here an imaginatively coherent expression of any belief or experience?'" (147–8). He substantiates this through a review and extension of Aristotle's concepts of imitation and literary hypothesis:

> Just as art is connected with nature by mimesis, so it is connected with total human culture by a principle that we may call revelation, using that term in a purely humanistic context as the revelation by the human mind, through human art, of the vision of a human world. . . . There is no reason why a poet's revelation of the human world should have any kind of connection with a divine world or with any specifically religious doctrine: there is equally no reason why it should not. (150)

"By showing us how many intellectually possible and emotionally convincing types of revelation there are," Frye suggests, "poetry helps to protect our religion from the idolatry of arrogance" (153). The centrepiece of this essay, however, is Frye's categorization of modern poets according to whether they recognize the imaginative condition of literature and thus sponsor an "open mythology," or whether their poetry participates in a "closed mythology" of predetermined belief or religious outlook. At the head of the latter group, whose writing "is more or less conventionally religious in content, though good enough as poetry for the associative fallacy not to operate" is obviously Eliot who, along with Robert Lowell, Dylan Thomas, and W.H. Auden, proceeds in the ecclesiastical tradition of Dante, Milton, Donne, and Hopkins. At the head of the former group, who have "not been satisfied to remain with nature and with man as we find him, but [have] pushed on into the eternal and infinite worlds . . . but speculatively, and without sustained dependence on specific religious doctrines" (153) are Yeats and Stevens: these two, along with Robert Frost, e.e. cummings, and Hart Crane, proceed in the tradition of the great Romantics. While the first group is identifiably Catholic in affiliation, Frye suggests in the latter the less obvious but more pervasive influence of Protestantism:

> Protestantism has had practically no direct influence on modern poetry. In the Romantics, however, for whom the artist is a creator, participating in the creative energy of God, there is a natural analogy with Protestant religious experience. We see this clearly in Blake and Coleridge, and even Shelley and Keats, if not exactly Protestant poets, were poets that only a Protestant tradition could have produced. Much the same may be said of Yeats, whose symbolic language was drawn mainly from Irish myth and from Rosicrucianism, which was itself a broken-down form of Biblical typology. (157)

"One wonders," Frye therefore concludes, "whether poetry may not be doing its greatest service to religion by following its own bent for uninhibited imaginative speculation," since, unlike "the more precise language of the sacramental poets," it reminds us "that Scripture is poetic and not doctrinal, that Jesus taught in parables and not in syllogisms, and that our spiritual vision is in a riddle" (158).

Frye's identification of competing impulses in modern literature recurs in his "Comment" on a paper by Walter Ong at a conference on twentieth-century literature (no. 40), but here the distinction drawn is between critical understandings of literary history, and, indeed, of time itself. The overemphasis on Classicism, "studying the great literature of a perfected and completed culture," may "degenerate into pedantry, and when it does it pulls us into the past," Frye writes, obviously thinking of Eliot. But approaching contemporary literature as purely contemporary is no better as it may "degenerate into hysteria, pulling us into the flux of the pure present" (172). What is required to balance the pedantry of the perfected past and the hysteria of the pure present is a "historical imagination" that will allow "the study of twentieth-century literature" to be "not the reinforcing of the past by the present, but the reinforcing of the sense of the authority of tradition by a sense of participation in it" (171). What accomplishes this, Frye says, in a fine summary of his own perspective and methodology, is "a more unified critical approach," a view of literature as

> an order of words, in which certain structural principles, devices of plot, recurring imagery, and verbal rhythms can be seen in both completed and continuing literature, both in the greatest masterpieces and in works which are nothing by nobody, so that no gap is possible between scholarship and criticism, between the pastness and the presence of the same work. (172–3)

The importance of the imagination is also emphasized in the third piece in this category, which, like Frye's *Rencontre* essay, is a draft introduction for an anthology that was never published (no. 46). Here Frye confirms that it is indeed the "antagonism between the creative imagination and the social conditions in which it operate[s]" that creates the dominant symbolism of modernism: "This sense of antagonism expresses itself in irony, and the pervading tone of nearly all serious twentieth-century literature is ironic" (306). Such antagonisms typically prompt "a great development in mythopoeic literature," Frye says, and while he lines up modernism with the Elizabethan age of Spenser, Shakespeare, and Donne, and the advent of Romanticism as examples of this, the draft, again like *Rencontre*, breaks off before he can discuss it in detail. This is unfortunate, but, as we surmised earlier, we may look to Frye's practical criticism of the major modern writers for that discussion and detail.

V

This practical criticism constitutes the remaining four categories of writings in this volume, and insofar as Frye consistently characterizes the work of the great modern writers in relation to the principle of creative imagination, we may associate these four categories with the four imaginative levels of the Romantic cosmology. Such associations, predictably, also serve to suggest where each writer is located in the cyclical progression from Romanticism to modernism.

In a category corresponding to the celestial void of the top of the Romantic cosmology and therefore so-called "high" modernism, we find, predictably, Frye's writings on T.S. Eliot and Ezra Pound, who in Frye's critical imagination probably took on some of the qualities of the tyrannical sky-god who occupies this mythical space. This perhaps explains why *T.S. Eliot* (no. 41), in particular, would turn out to have the most tortured editorial history of any book in Frye's canon and become an object of personal dispute between the critic and his subject. When Frye initially submitted his original 216-page manuscript of the book to the publishers Oliver and Boyd, he was told it was too long; he then cut it to a mere 85 pages and resubmitted it, at which time he was told it was now too short and needed to be expanded to a predetermined length of 192 pages. Frye then expanded his manuscript to this length, employing his publisher's suggestion of opening the book with a biographical sketch of Eliot, although his critical approach considered biography largely immaterial and he later felt that it "rather spoiled the book in some respects" (*NFC*, 108/*INF*, 963). When the book was finally published in 1963, it was answered by a series of letters from Eliot's publishers Faber and Faber, pointing out a series of interpretatively irrelevant errors in dating in Frye's biographical sketch; objections that both Frye and Oliver and Boyd editor Robin Lorimer suspected were actually reactions to the unexalting tone of the biography and "Frye's excoriation of Eliot's ultra-conservative political and religious beliefs" (Ayre, 290). Remarkably, Oliver and Boyd's offer to publish a corrigendum was answered by a two-page memo from Eliot himself containing still more nitpickings of Frye's short account of his life, pointing out such monumental blunders as Frye's calling Baudelaire a *symboliste* rather than a forerunner of French *symbolisme* and that one cannot "join" Anglo-Catholicism *per se*, since Anglo Catholicism is merely an orientation within the Church of England. Oliver and Boyd weathered these pointless criticisms and Frye largely ignored them, except to digest copies of these exchanges that were forwarded to him.[21] After Eliot's death in 1965, however, Frye agreed to revise the book out of concern for accuracy and currency, and so a second edition appeared from Oliver and Boyd in 1968, followed by an updated second edition from the University of Chicago Press in 1981. The editorial challenges of presenting such a storied manuscript in a Collected Works context were made simpler, albeit regrettably, by the fact that efforts to turn up Frye's original 216-page draft were unsuccessful. Presented here is the book's second edition, with revised or omitted material of significance from the first edition restored in notes.

As Frye indicates, *T.S. Eliot* is intended merely as an introduction to the poet's work, an "elementary handbook" (183), which makes its depth of insight all the more striking. One of the reasons Frye was able to achieve this is that his basic strategy is to isolate the ideologically driven qualities of Eliot's work as the distant rumblings of an angry thunder-god and focus on its purely literary aspects, or as Frye put it, to "take all the reactionary element in Eliot and just snip it off with a pair of scissors and leave him intact as a man of letters" (*NFC*, 108/*INF*, 963): "it is possible to approach him deductively," Frye writes, "treating the structure of his thought and imagery as a consistent unit" (183). The first thing to go is the conception of history that stands behind so many of Eliot's views, a myth of steady decline that Frye jokingly calls the "butterslide" or, "in an image of *The Waste Land*, the bobsled or 'down we went' theory" of history (184)—a view which sharply contrasts with both the liberal-progressive theory of history and Frye's own cyclical view. Many of Eliot's polemical opinions, Frye suggests, from his opinions on race and class, to his sympathy for monarchy and social hierarchy, to his preference for Latin writers like Virgil and Dante over English writers like Shakespeare and Blake, can be understood as cultural derivations of his view of history. Momentarily revisiting the terms of Eliot's own moral judgments on him, Frye suggests that such opinions are a "heresy" of which the "orthodoxy" would be the "much larger 'truth' about our very complex cultural situation than the mythology of decline affords" (196). Standing even behind Eliot's view of history, of course, and driving it and all the rest of his views, is his resistance to the conception of the imagination, the increased prominence of which in literary and cultural history the poet sees as a gradual descent of human life into illusion. "Man is man because he can recognize supernatural realities, not because he can invent them,"[22] Frye quotes Eliot as saying, which prompts him to explain why such a distinction is itself illusory:

> A curious, and to me regrettable, feature of Eliot's critical theory is his avoidance of the term "imagination" . . . . The poet has an image-forming power, and his "philosophy" or body of "ideas" is arrived at by studying the conceptual implications of the structure of his images. Thus Yeats writes an essay called "The Philosophy of Shelley's Poetry," which is actually an essay on Shelley's imagery. This seems to me a much more valid critical procedure than talking about the poetry and the ideas of a poet as though they were separable things, separable enough even for a poet to "borrow" his philosophy from somebody else. Eliot's myth of decline contrasts Dante, who "had behind him the system of St. Thomas, to which his poem corresponds point to point," with Blake and Goethe and Shelley, who mistakenly invented their own philosophies. Blake's genius required, we are told, "a framework of accepted and traditional ideas which would have prevented him from indulging in a philosophy of his own." But when we read *Four Quartets*, whatever influences there may be from Bradley or Patanjali or St. John of the Cross or Heraclitus, we darkly suspect Eliot too of indulging in a philosophy of his own. (212)

Some aspects of Eliot's critical observations therefore meet with Frye's qualified approval, while he questions his interpretation of their significance. He consents to Eliot's defence of the ironizing poetic device of the objective correlative (see no. 37, n. 2), for instance, but he does not accept that its absence connotes a tragic "dissociation of sensibility." Similarly, he approves of Eliot's conception of a consistent, imitable, eminently quotable literary tradition (an idea, as we noted, which profoundly influenced him), but laments that Eliot cannot or will not say where the conventions, genres, and myths that constitute this tradition originate. Always standing between them, in other words, is their theoretical difference on the centrality of the imagination: literature, Frye insists, is "an imaginative world, and must be approached through . . . imagery" (213).

When Frye approaches the imagery of Eliot's work, he finds it, of course, to be thoroughly committed to ascent within a pre-Romantic cosmology. The cyclical imagery of *The Waste Land*, which Frye unpacks in a far-reaching archetypal reading, belongs to the poet's "infernal vision" or phase, his articulation of an interminable "nightmare life in death" witnessed or narrated by hollow men and women like Prufrock, Gerontion, Tiresias, and the Sibyl of Cumae. Eliot's real goal is revealed in his "purgatorial phase," which begins with *Ash-Wednesday* and culminates in *Four Quartets*, and also encompasses his plays. Frye's reading of *Ash-Wednesday* through biblical typology, Dante, and the liturgical calendar, shows it to involve an ascent through four increasingly fulfilling states, which Frye describes as *ascesis* or the vacuity of illusion, ordinary experience of memory and desire, nostalgic vision of intense experience, and spiritual vision of identity with divinity. Likewise, his interpretation of *Four Quartets*, which he condenses by inviting readers to produce a conceptual diagram that Eliot must have found painfully demystifying of his thought, sees its constituent poems as paralleling each other in a similar form (233): a reflective withdrawal from the axis of linear time and a descent to a vacant "dark night of the soul," followed by an ascent through the world of ordinary experience to an incarnational moment that restores innocence and invites one still higher into a concluding vision of divine plenitude. Through such ascents, Frye writes, Eliot strives to depict the "human tragedy . . . consumed in the divine comedy" (242). His criticism of Eliot's drama (which astute readers will suspect was likely an area where his original manuscript was substantially abbreviated) is in keeping with this, but more broadly: it sees each play as a comedy which "contains a tragedy instead of avoiding one" (243). Generally, "a central figure . . . goes through a spiritual purgation and attains a vision of the four worlds, being isolated from the other characters and most of the audience in the process" (245). In the end they form "a hierarchy of enlightenment, from the hero or heroine at the top to a bewildered chorus below, a kind of epiphany of a spiritual elite" (250).

By comparison, Frye's writings on Ezra Pound are obviously not as thoroughgoing, consisting only of a review of his work in relation to the Bollingen controversy of 1949 (no. 29) and a review of Hugh Kenner's *The Poetry of Ezra Pound* (no. 32): but clearly Frye regarded Pound as trying to hold the same high modernist ground as Eliot. What Pound seems to illustrate for Frye are the tragic dangers of extending Eliotic views inflexibly and socially. In the earlier piece, Frye wonders whether Pound is not "something of a charlatan" (84) and finds the *Cantos* to be "brittle and factitious, moments of rapturous contact with beauty constantly interrupted by a peevish resentment against the world of the present that keeps butting in" (85). Reviewing Kenner's impressive promotion of Pound's ideas, Frye finds, as he did with Eliot, much to appreciate in his critical theory, including the poet's emphasis on concrete particulars of imagery as a "repudiation of the Cartesian-Lockean view that knowledge is primarily of clear and distinct ideas" (100), but he is disappointed to see these positions used to advance "the anti-Romantic clichés of thirty years ago" (101). Ultimately, he finds Pound to be, like Eliot, a post-Romantic aborted by his acceptance of the "butterslide" view of history in which

> everything seemed to be going all right in the Middle Ages, but something awful happened with the Renaissance, and things have got steadily worse until a new light has dawned with the present generation, which is every generation from the Gothicists of the eighteenth century to us. Mr. Kenner takes Pound at his own valuation as the true neo-medieval Messiah, and so does not see that Pound the critic is a late pre-Raphaelite sniffing eagerly along the trail of the English Romantics, of Blake's minute particular, Coleridge's esemplastic power, and Keats's life of sensations. Pound the propagandist, on the other hand, was caught in the rubble of the Fascist terminal moraine that Continental Romanticism helped to push into our time. (102)

As a result, Frye sees Pound as lacking what Eliot managed to maintain in spite of himself, "the faculty of mythopoeia," and so he reasserts his original sense of the *Cantos* as "myth broken down into a pastiche of harangue and exempla" (104).

In another category, corresponding to the corrupt civilization at the second level of the Romantic cosmology, we find Frye's essays on the works of James Joyce and W.B. Yeats, which depict the compulsions of society locking it into a cyclical pattern that parodies the restoring cycle of nature (and which thus give them a form distinct from the transcendent aims of Eliot and Pound). Both of Frye's essays on Joyce's *Finnegans Wake* turn on his contrasting of Blake's universal man Albion with Joyce's Finnegan, who like Albion has fallen asleep into the cycles of historical time and material space, but who can only fragmentedly dream, rather than experience, an apocalyptic reawakening into spiritual and eternal being. "Quest and Cycle in *Finnegans Wake*" (no. 33) suggests that Finnegan asleep becomes the mysterious HCE who "gradually sinks under a mounting body of forgetfulness, rumour, and calumny" (107); efforts to awake him, represented by the characters Shem and Shaun, fail in the face of the female ALP, who represents the "vicious circles" of nature and history, and thus the dialectical process of the quest is overwhelmed by cyclical repetition. "Cycle and Apocalypse in *Finnegans Wake*" (no. 50) expands this reading through an intellectual genealogy that shows Joyce's conceptions of cyclical time and material space as being informed by Spengler's precursor Giambattista Vico and the Neoplatonic philosopher Giordano Bruno, and his understanding of our means of coping with these as being informed by Freud and Jung. Along the way, Frye makes the interesting assertion, now commonplace in Joycean criticism, that the obscure, composite style of *Finnegans Wake* (particularly the rhetorical units Frye calls charms and riddles) anticipates the self-referential and self-effacing dilemmas of language theorized in postmodern and poststructuralist literary theory. Both essays, however, come to the same conclusion: *Finnegans Wake* in itself depicts or conceives of no escape from the cyclical condition. There is no figure or element in Joyce's novel corresponding to Blake's Los, the creator-God-within and architect of the imagination. But since the imaginative quest-hero, the interpretative agent implied by Joyce's apocalyptic archetypes and references, must be somewhere, the only logical answer is that it is assumed to exist in the reader himself. Joyce possesses a conception of the imagination, in other words, but for him it is operative (and prophetically so, he hopes) outside the text, in the reader who alone stands between the unfinished final line of the book and the first line which completes it.

Similar but more complex is Frye's criticism of the work of W.B. Yeats, which shows it to be less "high" modernist than Joyce's if not covertly

Romantic. Frye was fascinated by Yeats for many reasons, not least of which is because in being poised historically between the two centuries Yeats had to test the two cosmologies. "Yeats and the Language of Symbolism" (no. 23) notes with approval Yeats's reliance on a Romantic, generally Kantian, theory and grammar of poetic symbolism, and celebrates his effort to systematize and harmonize it with occult, Celtic, eastern, and theosophical mythologies in order to "hint . . . at a universal language of symbolism" (57).[23] But Yeats's *A Vision*, a book which Frye sees as enticingly similar to Spengler's but troublingly metaphysical in its claims, is particularly problematic in relation to Yeats's efforts to do this. While Frye is intrigued at the prospect of using its array of personality types as a typology of literary characters, and finds its alternating "primary" and "antithetical" cycles of history to be a fascinating explanation for various archetypal oppositions, he ultimately finds such patterns deterministic: like *Finnegans Wake*, *A Vision* is "founded on a conception of cyclic fatality" (67). Boldly taking Yeats at his word about the book being a product of automatic writing, Frye regards its theory of spiritual ascent through the gyres of history as being obviated by its lack of a theory of creative power, which, like Eliot's metaphysics or lingering in Blake's Beulah (cf. *FS*, 232–3/231–2), closes it off at the top:

> The thing that seals off the upper limit of Yeats's *Vision*, again from Blake's point of view, is the uncreative mental condition in which Yeats attained his vision. He stands at his own phase 1, in a state of passivity so abject that he cannot even write his own book, and sees his aloof and aristocratic ideal above him, impossibly remote and lost in the turning stars. An active mind would, on the contrary, be the circumference of such a vision, which would then be lifted up into the spiritual or mental world and so become a created or dramatic form . . . (70)

Like *Finnegans Wake*, Yeats's *A Vision* has no conception of the imagination as operative in or behind the text, with predictable results. Approaching the book more directly in "The Rising of the Moon: A Study of *A Vision*" (no. 43), Frye shows how opposed archetypes and impulses of the fatalistic primary and antithetical cycles, of unity versus individuality, Christ versus Oedipus or Cuchulain, the Virgin and Dove versus Leda and the Swan, aristocracy versus democracy, lose much of their symbolic power without the ethical dialectic of the imagination. Noting Yeats's "preference for cyclical and rebirth symbolism" over "the kind of symbolism that separates reality into an apocalyptic and a demonic world" (259), Frye writes

> Visions of horror and violence certainly haunt his poetry, but in *A Vision* and elsewhere in his later essays, even in much of the poetry itself, they are all rationalized and explained away as part of the necessary bloodbath accompanying the birth of his new and repulsive Messiah. The absence of any sense of a demonic world, a world of evil and tyranny and meanness and torment, such as human desire utterly repudiates and bends every effort to get away from, is connected with, and is perhaps the cause of, the absence in *A Vision* of . . . dialectical imagery . . . (273)

But what Yeats "the sky-god worshipper" (62) neglects, Yeats the poet recognizes, and so it is poems like *Sailing to Byzantium* and *The Shadowy Waters* that depict "an eternal world which contains all the concrete imagery and physical reality associated elsewhere with the cycle of rebirth, which is not a mere plunge into nothingness and darkness by an infatuated soul" (274). Such poems are "apocalyptic . . . vision[s] of plenitude which [are] still not bound to time" (274), and

> For a theoretical construct to match this apocalyptic imagery we have to set aside the main body of *A Vision*, with its conception of unity and individuality as opposed and impossible ideals which only superhuman beings can reach, and look for another construct in which they are at the same point, and that point accessible to human life. (274)

This point, which Yeats is admittedly aiming for in the ascent through the "thirteenth cone" of *A Vision*, leads ultimately to "the One," Yeats's equivalent of the awakened Albion of Blake or, secondarily, the dreaming Finnegan of Joyce (276); but to reach it requires a descent through lower, human powers and then up "into a world in which subject and object become the human imagination and the human image, each being archetypes that recur in every individual man and poem" (275). This ascent occurs not through the theory of *A Vision* but through the process at work in such poems as *News for the Delphic Oracle* and *Byzantium*, which depict "the direct passage across from ordinary life to archetype" (277). Approached in this fashion, Frye writes

> the whole cycle of nature, of life and death and rebirth which man has

> dreamed, becomes a single gigantic image, and the process of redemption is to be finally understood as an identification with Man and a detachment from the cyclical image he has created. (277)

Having recognized this, Frye turns his hand to producing a survey of Yeats's entire poetic world in "The Top of the Tower: A Study of the Imagery of Yeats" (no. 45), which, he finds, articulates a traditional pre-Romantic cosmology of ascent, the levels of which he calls Logos, Eros, Adonis, and Thanatos visions, respectively (terms important to the uncompleted "Third Book" project that he was working on at the time, and which inform his last book *Words with Power*); but within that cosmology, Frye suggests, Yeats favours a Romantic descent in search of the powers of the creative imagination:

> Yeats . . . consistently rejects for himself, though not necessarily for anyone else, the sublimated goals of the Eros vision that lead on to the Logos vision, and prefers the sexual goal which leads inevitably to going back down into the cycle again. . . . This is not simply a temperamental choice: there is a major complication in Yeats's winding-stair imagery that did not exist for, say, Dante. In Christianity, and in Neoplatonism more speculatively, the sublimation of the sexual instinct is the preferred program, because the man inspired by love is ultimately not seeking a sexual partner, but is a creature returning to his creator. But for Yeats there is no creator in the picture except man himself. The sources of creation are not in a divine mind beyond the stars: they are in the "foul rag-and-bone shop of the heart" at the *bottom* of the ladder. (297)

Once this descent is completed, a "reversal of perspective from descent to the corrupt source of creation back up again through the process of creation" (302) becomes possible: a genuinely imaginative ascent. From his unique historical position on the cusp of the nineteenth and twentieth centuries, Yeats managed to accommodate the humanist concerns of the one era within the cosmology of the other, and this is probably the real source of Frye's fascination with his work.

In still another category, corresponding to the irrepressible nature at the third level of the Romantic cosmology, we find Frye's writings on Wallace Stevens and René Char: two unequivocal advocates of imaginative re-ascent who thus rejected Eliot's Classical, royalist, and Anglo-Catholic model and instead continued the "Romantic, revolutionary, and Protestant" tendencies of nineteenth-century poetry into the twentieth century (*FI*, 1). Frye's championing of Stevens above all other modern poets was driven by the fact that he saw Stevens as having "a sense of man assigned to recreate the universe, just as Blake had" (*NFC*, 110/*INF*, 964), a view rooted, as we have suggested, in his belief in the importance of the creative imagination. Thus in "The Realistic Oriole: A Study of Wallace Stevens" (no. 37), Frye begins by distilling from his work a detailed phenomenology of the imagination that is very much an updating of Romantic poetics to a modern context:

> The revolution of consciousness against routine is the starting point of all mental activity, and the centre of mental activity is imagination, the power of transforming "reality" into awareness of reality. Man can have no freedom except what begins in his own awareness of his condition. Naturally historical periods differ greatly in the amount of pressure put on free consciousness by the compulsions of ordinary life. In our own day this pressure has reached an almost intolerable degree that threatens to destroy freedom altogether and reduce human life to a level of totally preoccupied compulsion, like the life of an animal. One symptom of this is the popular demand that the artist should express in his work a sense of social obligation. The artist's primary obedience however is not to reality but to the "violence from within"[24] of the imagination that resists and arrests it. The minimum basis of the imagination, so to speak, is ironic realism, the act of simply becoming aware of the surrounding pressures of "things as they are." This develops the sense of alienation which is the immediate result of the imposing of consciousness on reality .... The "act of the mind" in which imagination begins, then, is an arresting of a flow of perceptions without and of impressions within. In that arrest there is born the principle of form or order: the inner violence of the imagination is a "rage for order." (130–1)

Through such a theory, art is understood as being "nature realized, a unity of being and knowing, existence and consciousness, achieved out of the flow of time and the fixity of space" (132); it is therefore "practical, not speculative; imaginative, not fantastic; it transforms experience, and does not merely interrupt it" (133). Reflecting on the very range of views on the imagination that we have been delineating, Frye muses about how

> In some ages, or with some poets, the emphasis is on the imaginative height-

> ening of reality . . . . At other times the emphasis is ironic, thrown on the minimum role of the imagination as the simple and subjective observer of reality, not withdrawn from it, but detached enough to feel that the power of transforming it has passed by. (133)

These two perspectives, he says, are represented in Stevens's poetry by states he calls the summer vision and the autumn vision, respectively, which are flanked by two others, the winter vision and the spring vision, representing the disappearance and rebirth of the imagination itself: the sequence is, as we have been assuming, both a cycle drawn analogically from nature and a cosmology of progressive imaginative states. Stevens foregrounds this in his famous characterizations of poetry as the "strange rhetoric" of "the analogy between nature and imagination,"[25] on the one hand, and "a transcendent analogue composed of the particulars of reality,"[26] on the other. Using these phases/states, Frye surveys the recurrent images and characters of Stevens's poetry, showing how "residual egos" like Peter Quince and Crispin give way to the emergence of the "central" or "major man," a modern *macroanthropos* like Joyce's Finnegan but more akin to Blake's Albion for its being imaginatively galvanized from the human realities below, and how this constitutes an ascent, from "things as they are," up the "the axis of everything" to the "Palaz of Hoon."[27] Thus Stevens's poetry itself articulates in microcosm the cyclical and cosmological structure that Frye seemed to intuit in the development of modern literature as a whole: a development in which Stevens would obviously represent the spring vision, opposing T.S. Eliot's autumn vision as Blake's hero Orc opposes his tyrannical Urizen. Frye therefore cannot resist opening and closing the paper by pointing out that Stevens's theory of the imagination enables a conception of metaphor that stands in sharp contrast to the "dualistic fallacy" of Eliot, a conception which allows Stevens's poetry to depict "a world of total metaphor, where the poet's vision may be identified with anything it visualizes," and thus to be "a poetry of 'revelation' in which all objects and experiences are united with a total mind" (142).

Having found most of these critical intuitions about Stevens's work and his relation to mainstream modernism (including his opposition to Eliot) confirmed by the publication of the poet's letters in 1967, Frye produced "Wallace Stevens and the Variation Form" (no. 47) in an effort to deepen and ramify his interpretations. Proceeding from his earlier paper's main idea of Stevens's work as "the result of a struggle, or balance, or compromise, or tension, between the two forces that he calls imagination and reality," Frye overlays an ekphrastic and musical metaphor on Stevens's cyclical and cosmic commitments and presents his poetry as "the variations that imagination makes on the theme of reality" (310). For Stevens, Frye notes, the imagination is "the principle of the unreal" which "breaks up and breaks down the tyranny of what is there by unifying itself with what is not there, and so suggesting the principle of variety in its existence" (314). The hypothetical sum of these imaginative variations is what Stevens famously calls the "Supreme Fiction," a conception which exceeds Eliot's idea of literary tradition (but which resembles Frye's own concept of "the order of words" [*AC*, 121/112]) insofar as:

> The supreme fiction is not a thing, something to be pointed to or contemplated or thought of as achieved. In its totality, the supreme fiction is poetry or the work of the imagination as a whole, but this totality never separates from the perceiving subject or becomes external. (318)

As a process, however, it does create "different levels or degrees of reality, arranged in a ladder or mountain or winding stair in which the poet has to undertake what he calls an 'ascent through illusion'" (313). In the last part of the essay, Frye draws some striking analogies between this ascent through imaginative variation and transformation and the natural processes of variation and transformation studied by evolutionary theory, not least through their relocation and reconceptualization of the creative process and, by implication at least, of God. Frye thus observes that, as in Blake, "God for Stevens, whatever he may be in himself, must be for man an unreality of the imagination, not a reality, and his creative power can manifest itself only in the creations of man" (318), or as the poet puts it in his *Final Soliloquy of the Interior Paramour*, "God and the imagination are one." This line of thinking, in particular, allows Frye to conclude the essay by specifically characterizing and positioning Stevens in relation to the other major modern poets:

> Stevens has nothing of Eliot's sense of the phenomenal world as a riddle, to be solved by some kind of conscious experience that annihilates it. . . . [A]t the top of Eliot's staircase is a total unification and an absorption of reality into the infinite being of God. . . . Eliot wants his pilgrimage to pass beyond the categories of time and space and the cycle of nature that revolves within these categories. . . . Stevens does not resemble Yeats any more closely than he resembles Eliot, but . . . as for Yeats, the top of the mountain or staircase or whatever has to be climbed is the top of the natural cycle, and the fulfil-

> ment of climbing it is in coming down again. In Stevens, the imagination is life, and the only way to kill it is to take it outside nature, into a world where it has swallowed nature and become a total periphery or circumference, instead of remaining "central." So for Stevens, as in a very different way for Joyce in *Finnegans Wake*, the cycle of nature is the only possible image of whatever is beyond the cycle. (323–4)

As Frye sees Ezra Pound as illustrating the dangers of applying high modernist views, he sees the virtues of applying Romantic principles in the work and life of René Char. In "Poetry of the Tout Ensemble" (no. 36), Frye reviews *Hypnos Waking*, a collection of poetry by and criticism on Char, and finds the title to be allusive of the Romantic idea of a "'real' world of waking consciousness and a submerged world of dream and desire," the latter of which is "the source of poetry and of all creative effort" (126). But the highly aphoristic poetry that Char produces by accessing this source, which Frye memorably suggests must be digested by what he calls the "Bloody Mary" principle ("it has to be swallowed at a gulp and allowed to explode from inside"), reveals it to be "not another world from ours but another way of dealing with it." Its verbal construction is not an attempt to render it transcendent or metaphysical; rather, "Char thinks of it existentially, as 'engaged' in a redemptive death-struggle with the kind of world that produces such things as the Nazi occupation" (126): this is one of several suggestions Frye makes that he sees the poet's commitment to the imaginative process as the reason for his heroic involvement in the French Resistance. "The 'real' world that produced the war is always here," Frye glosses, "and only poetry can do anything effective about it," the most effective thing being to transform it into something better. Thus, for Char, "poetry is a total gesture of revolution," quotes Frye (128). In contrast to the "mainly negative" gestures of other modern writers—the defiance of Pound, the "silence, exile, and cunning"[28] of Joyce, and the shifting allegiances of Eliot—Frye finds that it is "surprisingly reassuring to discover a poet, who, like René Char, is a man with a heroic personal record, and not less a poet for having it; who is both 'engaged' in his life and yet exact and difficult in his art" (124). All of these virtues, however, make him nothing other than "an old-fashioned Romantic liberal" (128), an understatement obviously intended to emphasize the relative scarcity of such figures in the literary world at the time that Frye was writing.

In a final category, corresponding to the recreative furnace at the bottom of the Romantic cosmology, we find Frye's writings on a group of modern writers whom he saw as advancing poetics that underwrite or enable many of the developments we have been discussing to this point: writers such Henry James, Robert Graves, George Orwell, Aldous Huxley, Franz Kafka, Samuel Beckett, and Giorgio Bassani, whose decimating mobilization of irony resembles but can be distinguished from that of Eliot for being transformative rather than transcendent. For Frye, Henry James typifies this process, the nuances of which he lays out in "Henry James and the Comedy of the Occult" (no. 51). Frye suggests that James's penchant for writing "occult fantasy," a genre he says involves such stock Jamesian themes as the obsession with time travel, parallel worlds, and ghosts, represents an exploration of the paradoxical coincidence of nothing and something, and the human ability to transform absence into presence and vice versa. Such themes, Frye says, "[challenge] us with the existence of a reality beyond realism which still may not be identifiable as real" (363). James's study of the *ex nihilo* miracle can be observed in such basic elements as the author's notoriously indirect writing style and plots to grandiose projects like reprinting his novels serially with discarded notes as a so-called "Collected Edition," which Frye calls an effort to "transform his entire *oeuvre* into one colossal logocentric monument to himself" (357)—a remark which raises the question of what Frye would have thought about the series of which the present volume is a part. It is essential to such themes that they turn tragic and ironic, as in *The Turn of the Screw*, and depict "a retreat from a genuine human life into the pseudo-logic of obsession" (358), something that might seem to be a negation of the creative imagination. This is because, Frye suggests, it is intended to call our attention to what might otherwise have been possible through the same power. Referring to James's remark that every tragic and ironic story should have a comic or "beautiful counterpart," he writes:

> The positive drive of a traditional comic story is towards a happy ending . . . . The story we read [in James] usually tells us of some failure to achieve this, whether a moral failure within an individual character or the result of a sinister or stupid social conspiracy. But we as readers can see something of what might have been achieved, and our wider vision is perhaps the beautiful counterpart James mentions. (368)

This is not the principle at work in *Finnegans Wake*, as here the imagination is present and operating, but operating in a parodic and arguably a more provocative form.

Frye's interpretation of the other writers in this group (which he was unfortunately able to deal with only in long reviews) shows their works to be concerned with similar themes and to unfold through essentially the same principle. His review of the work of Robert Graves (no. 34), whose mythographic study *The White Goddess* he had some admiration for, naturally focuses on Graves's poetic reiterations of that ironic myth, which Frye irreverently suggests is symptomatic of the human effort to "screw the inscrutable" (116). According to Frye, Graves belongs not to the "solemn" tradition of mythopoeia, which might be said to include Eliot, but to "the tradition of the writers who have turned mythical erudition into satire, to Rabelais and Apuleius, or to the exuberantly hyperbolic Celtic mythical poets": "The myths in his poetry, like the ghosts, seem to be not part of an objective system but a kaleidoscopic chaos of human fragments" (118). Such satirical myths, Frye writes, are "constructs so obviously hypothetical that they suggest an indefinite number of other possible constructs, each as ingenious and plausible as the author's" (119). Graves's achievement is thus not in creating a "systematic mythology," but in depicting "mythical use of poetic language, where we invent our own myths and apply them to an indefinite number of human themes" (118). Similarly, Frye's review and introduction of George Orwell (nos. 30 and 44), and his remarks on Aldous Huxley (no. 48) and Franz Kafka (no. 20, but more p. 160) indicate that he sees dystopias and parody utopias like *1984*, *Brave New World*, and *The Trial* as holding up a mirror to humanity, showing us a fully debased society that is "the logical form of what a great many of us have already shown that we want" (281), and thereby imploring us to turn to the imaginative work of creating something better, or anything at all. Each is, as Frye says of Orwell's novel, a modern *Inferno* (87, 279), the purpose of which is, as in Dante's original, to provoke us to right ourselves and start imagining an ascent. Frye's reviews of the poetry of Giorgio Bassani (no. 49) and Samuel Beckett's "Trilogy" (no. 39) suggest that these works take us to a place still lower, if that is conceivable, into the isolated ego which is complicit in the kind of totalitarian systems that inspired these works and which they address. Beckett's intent, in particular, Frye suggests, is to show "a mind half-freed from its own automatism . . . detached enough to feel imprisoned and enslaved, and to have no confidence in any of its assertions, but immediately to deny or contradict or qualify or put forward another hypothesis to whatever it says." The result is characters that produce "endless, querulous, compulsive, impersonal babble." This makes for "tedious book[s]," Frye suggests, but such "use of tedium is exuberant" (165–6), for its aim is for the tedium to shatter under its own weight: "Only when one is sufficiently detached from this compulsive babble to realize that one is uttering it can one achieve any genuine serenity, or the silence which is its habitat." What such works ultimately reveal is the "paradox" of the imaginative process, that "in a world given over to obsessive utterance, a world of television and radio and shouting dictators and tape recorders and beeping space ships, to restore silence is the role of serious writing" (167). That is to say, such works take us ultimately to what Frye in *Anatomy of Criticism* referred to as the "point of demonic epiphany" (*AC*, 238/223), an absolute void at the bottom of the cosmos at which anything that occurs is a created something that is better than the nothing that was there before, and thus initiates a new journey of ascent and, potentially, another cycle of literary history.

It is hardly compulsory, of course, to read the contents of this volume through this schema of categories and associations. Each item in this collection is first and foremost an independent unit of criticism with its own specific purpose and purview, and there are considerable rewards that come with approaching them individually. Nothing should obscure what Frye once said was the basic intent of all his criticism, which is to provide not a system but simply a critical "lumber-room" for "future generations" to "explore and get ideas from" (cf. *NFC*, 157–8/*INF*, 995). But such an arrangement does accord with Frye's larger critical project and perspective, including his sense of the ideological implications of literary metaphors and cosmologies, and perhaps gives us some sense of the account he might have provided of the development of literary modernism from Romanticism in the hypothetical, unwritten *Rencontre* and its unfinished brethren. The essence of Frye's critical legacy, as intimated at the outset, may in fact be his unique ability to attend to both kinds of tasks simultaneously, to apprehend both fundamental qualities and total structures, to root in the datum of practical criticism the far-reaching, speculative aims of literary theorization and systemization. In *Northrop Frye on Twentieth-Century Literature* we can see this rare quality in action, allowing a critic to accomplish what few, if any, others can claim:

to have produced a body of criticism which shows equal regard for the particular characteristics of modern literature, for the way in which these coalesce into an identifiable period of literary history, and for the significance of that period in relation to those preceding and succeeding it.

Northrop Frye on Twentieth-Century Literature

Photograph by F. Roy Kemp, 1975
(courtesy of Victoria University Library, Toronto)

1

Press Cuttings

April 1933

Comments on the Victoria College production of George Bernard Shaw's play Press Cuttings. *From the "Monocle" section of the college magazine,* Acta Victoriana, *57 (April 1933): 35–6. Frye had been one of the "Monocle" editors in the previous academic year, and was editor of* Acta *during 1932–33.*

Late one afternoon, having had the idea of work knocked out of me by an importunate scandal hunter for the Rag-em-offen, I strolled over to Hart House and happened in on a performance of Shaw's one-act comedy *Press Cuttings*. The play was by all odds the most enjoyable that I have ever witnessed in connection with the Dramatic Society. It was quite competently done; a little raw in spots, not as finished acting as some parts of the *Tragedy of Nan* or *The Silver Box*,[1] but never as bad as the larger works got at times. The performers showed all of the genius for correct casting that exists in this college, both for the Music Club and for the present society. With a little more rudeness and profanity in the direction, and with the players just a little more excited and frightened, the result could easily have outclassed anything of its kind on the campus. As it was, it was a startling revelation of what this college is capable of doing, and I went home looking for a moral.

I had not long to look. I have always urged the performance of Shaw as the big play for the Society ever since I could make myself at all heard. The reasons for which I reiterate.

The success of the ticket-selling campaign depends far more upon the organization than upon the play. Consequently, while the Society will assuredly go bankrupt if it does not get behind its big play and sell tickets for it, God help the Society if it once falls into the hands of an executive who deliberately picks the play itself from the box-office point of view! For this view is antagonistic to the drama, the finest and purest form of literary expression, and it never, in spite of its eternal repetition of the phrase, gives the public what it wants. It invents an imaginary abstract imbecility which it calls "the public" and proceeds to act on the assumption that this public hates drama as much as the box office does, by deliberately giving it the worst whenever possible. The truth is that "the public" wants only to be entertained; it will take anything that is given it, and will swallow champagne just as avidly as it will molasses. Now university students are supposed to like the drama, not to hate it as the theatre managers do. It is not expected that university organizations will spend their time in learning by heart a dreary, cheap, and silly farce by some unknown idiot under the pretext that it is "something light," or "snappy."

On the other hand, the box offices have succeeded in doing a great deal of harm. I have been told that the word "Tragedy" in the title of Masefield's moving and beautiful play was responsible in some degree for a shortage in ticket selling. Shaw is easily the greatest comedian of our time, and comedy is probably harder to act and affords better training in every way than tragedy. Besides, *ceteris paribus*, a name with a definite public appeal might help a great deal to facilitate the ticket campaign, and Shaw's certainly outshines any others. He is probably not only the most popular, but actually the greatest, of contemporary dramatists. He is worth doing, the logical man to do, both from an artistic and economic point of view, and, though Shaw himself would probably not admit it, this Society can do him and do him thoroughly and well. His outrageous royalty fee[2] is perhaps the only reason he has not gone on the boards before. We can only hope that the Dramatic Society will soon be in a position to take a chance.

2

Delicate Rhythms

December 1939

Review of Lloyd Frankenberg, The Red Kite *(New York: Farrar & Rinehart, 1939). From* Canadian Forum, *19 (December 1939): 295–6.*

This is the first volume of poems by a young American poet who shows a good deal of versatility in his range of subjects and metres. In the earlier poems the rhythm is fluent and assured, with a gentle syncopated lilt and effortless variations in speed. There is an expert use of onomatopoeia and echoing vowels which give a distinctive haunting and evocative quality to the writing:

> The surface bulks and bulges, breaks and sprays
> Lipping and lapping, clambering and is repulsed,
> Is lifted again, claps, lapses and drifts away
> And word of this goes every baffled where.
>
> [*The Water Wants All Sea,* ll. 7–10]

The delicate swaying rhythm and the pleasant gurgling sound make these little lyrics appealing even when the imagery is vague and perfunctory, as occasionally it is. These effects are carefully manufactured, it is true, but there is a very real charm of artifice.

The later poems are less lyrical and more elegiac, but do not gain much in depth of tone or expressive precision. Mr. Frankenberg is uneasily aware that a twentieth-century poet is challenged to be didactic, but he has not quite mastered the difficult art of making the explicit statement poetically suggestive, and an unsatisfactory muzziness envelopes both rhythm and imagery. His ideas seem to revolve around a pantheistic feeling of the personality of nature and a kind of Whitmanic-depressive sense of death as the reconciler of life, uniting scattered souls in its nirvana. Death provides what meaning there is to war, and an imaginative sympathy with this complete relaxation with all the tensions of life is the secret of wisdom: this is the central idea behind his remarkable long poem on Lazarus, who says:

> I am my own man knowing I am earth's,
> and she will have her way when all is done. [*I Lazarus*, sec. 24, ll. 424–5]

As is usual with first volumes, there are more echoes than unique sounds, but Mr. Frankenberg is a readable and interesting poet, a commendation which would be thought damning with faint praise[1] only in an unpoetic and over-advertising age.

3

Experiment

April 1940

Review of Poets of Tomorrow: First Selection *(London: Hogarth, 1939). From* Canadian Forum, *20 (April 1940): 26–7. The book under review is a short anthology of the work of poets Peter Hewett, H.B. Mallalieu, Ruthven Todd, and Robert Waller (only the first of which is named in the review).*

The Hogarth Press feels that some attempt should be made to win back the market for serious poetry that existed ten years ago, and is planning a series of books presenting the work of four or five younger poets at a time. The attempt deserves support: notice the price.[1]

These four poets are all about twenty-five, and all write, very well, the sort of poetry fashionable during the last decade. They are haunted by the miserable cruelty of the time, the murder of Spain,[2] the growing stampede of bourgeois imbecility, the politely useless sympathy of intellectuals. They are in full revolt against the popular and readable school of poets who flourished up to 1929 and specialized in individual reactions to beauty.[3] The romantic search for loveliness, and the melancholy of mere nostalgia, are equated by these writers with an adolescence which has been sweet, but must now be ruthlessly outgrown. Loveliness, the attractive part of beauty, is concealed from adult poets living in these newly darkened ages: ugliness, the repellent and challenging side, is now the external source of poetry. In place of the melancholy of nostalgia has come a new kind of melancholy based on observation rather than temperament, which only revolution will cure.

The intense desire for revolution adds to this new melancholy a new sense of decorum, that is, the belief in the special importance of a certain kind of subject matter. Their poetry is therefore mainly the expression of a single mood. They offer passionate criticisms of life: they are as didactic as a monk working through the seven sins: their tone is prophetic and denunciatory. Their distrust of loveliness at times expands into a distrust of poetry itself as an impotent political weapon. They feel that an age of social crisis makes the holiday emotions, those of love, for instance, more intense because more transient, their insistence on this being rather pathetic. They believe in the comparative imminence of revolution, but they hardly look for it in their own time, and as their avoidance of the more consoling formulas of religion amounts to a phobia, they seem to be still in the unrelieved pessimism of the Victorian Buddhists.[4] It is curious that poetry so contemporary and nourished on fashionable contemporary models (Hewett names Hopkins [9]) should sound so exactly like a sepulchral echo of Matthew Arnold, but so it is. At times their ignoring of religion seems almost like a deliberate and desperate privation: one wonders if Moloch himself ever demanded more from his child-murdering, self-castrating worshippers than the great god *Zeitgeist*.

The resemblances between the four are perhaps more significant, so far, than their differences, but they all build on a basis of solid technical competence, and often rise above it to an impressive height. Anyone who is interested, not only in modern poetry as such, but in studying its development during the past two decades and predicting its immediate future, would be well advised to acquire this book.

4

Poetry (I)

April 1940

Review of May Rooker-Clark, Late Blossoms *(London: A.H. Stockwell, 1940); Fisher Davidson,* Two Sonnets for a Centenary *(n.p.: 1939); John A.B. McLeish,* Ode in a Winter Evening, and Other Poems *(Montreal: J. Lovell, 1938); and William Thow,* Poet and Salesman *(Toronto: Ryerson Press, 1939). From* Canadian Forum, *20 (April 1940): 29–30.*

Late Blossoms, by May Rooker-Clark, is a collection of very gentle little verses by a pleasant-looking lady whose picture forms the frontispiece. Some are descriptive, with a great deal of snow in them; some are moralizing ones of the keepsake variety. Needless to say, the former are better, and one called *Summers of Song* has its points.

Two Sonnets for a Centenary, by Fisher Davidson, are on William Lyon Mackenzie[1] and Durham.[2] They are on the schoolroom level, but with practice he may do something with the sonnet form, as he seems to have some idea of it: "voyage" and "rage" will never do for rhymes, though.

Ode in a Winter Evening, by John A.B. McLeish, is the work of a romantic poet with considerable metrical fluency. When this fluency is supported by sufficient care in the choice of ideas and images, the poetry attains some dignity and solidity. The title poem and another called *The Search* have good things in them: the rest have had less work put on them and relapse too often into jingle. The poet tries didactic and religious themes occasionally, but has nothing very new or distinctive to say about them, which means that these poems hardly rise above commonplaces.

William Thow's *Poet and Salesman* shows a good deal of slipshod versifying and some unsuccessful facetiousness, but it also shows an energetic and active mind: even at his worst he is bad only because he is not satisfied with mediocrity. *Neurasthenia,* the last poem in his collection, is a remarkable performance: if he can write that he can write better things, and if he writes better things he will be well worth reading.

5

Poetry (II)

July 1940

Review of Oscar Williams, The Man Coming toward You *(New York: Oxford University Press, 1940); and Paul Potts,* A Poet's Testament *(London: Whitman Press, 1940). From* Canadian Forum, *20 (July 1940): 125–6.*

The poems in Mr. Williams's book are very homogeneous: none are bad, not many stand out particularly, and nearly all sound more or less alike. Mr. Williams is not fond of free verse; he prefers regular beats, resonant rhymes, and in general a simple quatrain stanza. His imagery and diction are based on a complicated private symbolism, with a good many animals in it, in which certain words such as "skyline" and "quicksilver" have hieroglyphic meanings.[1] A string of declarative sentences containing an interlocking system of mixed metaphors is therefore the general appearance the poetry presents. Like this:

> A canyonful of bells shivers to bits in a fit of innocence:
> The railway station bends its head around the napes of silence:
> Everywhere the shadows are budding on the tree of substance,
> Flowering into large leopards grounded swiftly on the pylons.
>
> [*Railway Station*, ll. 17–20.]

This is called "metaphysical" in the jargon of literary criticism: it is an association of images deliberately made far-fetched in order to suggest the strain between the synthetic view of the world sought by poetry and the analytic approach to it offered by sense experience. Mr. Williams's technique, which seems to owe something to Hart Crane, is always expert, but is not very versatile in mood: he is generally too heavy for fantasy and too pedantic for satire. I like him best when he is most oracular and visionary.

The past, according to Mr. Williams, is a nightmare of cruelty and injustice: man has founded one civilization after another which has perished in a welter of blood, and only a faint trickle of art survives. The present is equally a nightmare haunted by the enormous industrial monster science has created, and it too is meeting the same fate. The reason for this is that science is not abstract, but the product of a human mind, and that mind is still in the grip of a life force fundamentally blind and unconscious. Try as it may, humanity cannot get beyond myth and hallucination, and science has not solved, it rather expresses, the riddle of the hostility of the world to man and of man to himself. Perhaps the lurking fear which causes wars also prevents us from seeing nature as real rather than phenomenal, and if we could conquer that fear our present way of looking at the world might blow up in an apocalypse of matter and apotheosis of man. But, though Mr. Williams seems to hint darkly at such a possibility, he loses his nerve, and the poems in the section called "Tomorrow" bear a depressing resemblance to those called "Today."

One rather annoying mannerism is common enough in modern poetry to be worth a digression. Some nineteenth-century American poets developed a disastrous kenning-type consisting of an abstract noun in the genitive followed by an adjective and a concrete noun. I pick "life's best oil," "Fortune's fickle moon," "Death's idle gulf," and about a dozen more out of a poem by James Russell Lowell [*Ode Recited at the Harvard Commemoration*]. This is obsolescent, but a turned-around form of it persists. I open Mr. Williams at random and find "the royal warhorses of music," "the secret spit of conscience," "the headlined arms of tomorrow," and four others in one short poem [*New Year's, 1940, U.S.A.*]. Otherwise, Mr. Williams is skilful, subtle, and often profound, though his consistently oblique diction and monotonous rhythms make a rather crustacean cover for his sensibility.

Paul Potts is a Canadian Communist living in England, and has appeared in the *Forum*. His verses have the castration complex frequent in left-wing poetry: the worker is simple and virile and the bourgeois soft and complicated, and if poetry has punch and guts and *cojones*, it doesn't need any other poetic qualities to be taken to the great heart of the masses. They follow this stereotype so closely that they sometimes read almost like parody: slapdash rhythmless *vers libre*, crude caricatures of the ruling class, raucous abuse of The System, prophecies of

The Day—everything an unsympathetic reactionary would expect to find and nothing to surprise him. Mr. Potts does his best to convince us that he is an authentic folk poet and a Canadian Mayakovsky,[2] but his work smacks of the party committee rooms rather than the park bench or the breadline, and it is not surprising to find that, as is usual with self-conscious poetry written around a theory, the critical preface is by far the best thing in the book. The English may like it better, as it is harder for them to distinguish sincerity from affectation in the use of colloquial American speech. Hugh MacDiarmid contributes a somewhat absent-minded second preface.

6

Henry Wells

October 1940

Untitled review of Henry W. Wells, New Poets from Old *(New York: Columbia University Press, 1940). From* Canadian Forum, *20 (October 1940): 221–2.*

This book is a study of the influence of older poets on contemporaries, with special attention, of course, to deliberate borrowings, avowed indebtedness, and conscious or unconscious echoes. It is full of genuine and fascinating erudition, and for the first time (so far as I know) we find gathered into one volume examples of the influence of Anglo-Saxon poetry on Hopkins and MacLeish, of Langland on Day Lewis, of Skelton on Auden, of the murkier Elizabethans on Cummings, of Herrick on Davies, of Donne on Yeats and Elinor Wylie, of Pope on the Sitwells, and many others.

The Americans are far better handled than the Europeans. Mr. Wells has very interesting things to say about Robinson, cummings, Wallace Stevens, Conrad Aiken, and Vachel Lindsay: his notes on the last two expand from his subject into excellent critical essays. I have never seen anything better on Lindsay. In fact, I wish the book had been a series of essays on Mr. Wells's favourite poets.

The treatment of Yeats is perfunctory and that of Eliot impatient; the book is not too shapely and at times thrashes around in its huge subject; there are barren stretches of historical commonplace in the section on form, and much vague criticism of the no-they-go-*there* type:

> The golden age died with Shakespeare; the Augustan age is now seen to have commenced considerably earlier than was once assumed. Donne

> stood in every way closer to the generation of the great Elizabethans, to which he belonged by birth, than to that of the Cavaliers; while most of the Cavaliers stand nearer to the Augustans of the Restoration period than to the Elizabethans. [231]

But for all its faults it will be very useful to anyone interested in the subject, and for students beginning the moderns I should think it would be essential.

One important point implied by the book could have been made clearer. The revaluation of the metaphysicals and the Elizabethan tragedians is done;[1] there is no point in gloating over it any more. There poets and scholars worked together. Now poets are forging ahead of the critics: they find something peculiarly modern and useful in the work of older poets of the darker and more awkward ages. Critics, on the other hand, are still wandering in a pseudo-Darwinian haze of periods of transition and florescence. The hieratic and Byzantine poems of the Anglo-Saxons are really part of the protozoic slime from which Shakespeare and Milton emerged. The genius of English literature got so exhausted fighting the Wars of the Roses that it had to spend a century clearing its throat in order to voice the poetry of Spenser, Shakespeare, and Donne. Any eighteenth-century poet who made a sniffy remark about Pope "prepared the way" for Wordsworth. And so on. If poets today are finding more to use (without raising the question of "greatness") in Skelton than in Spenser, in *Beowulf* than in *Paradise Lost*, in Churchill than in Dryden, modern criticism will just have to catch up.

7

Irene Moody

October 1940

Untitled review of Irene H. Moody, Lava *(Toronto: Macmillan, 1940). From* Canadian Forum, *20 (October 1940): 222.*

Mrs. Moody is a practised imagist,[1] specializing in the short *vers libre* impression and the evocative descriptive phrase. In the longer poems this last sometimes alternates with more prosaic rhythms and produces an uneven texture. As in so many imagist poems, particularly Canadian ones, the vocabulary is in more than one sense too precious. There is enough amber and crystal and ivory to stock a museum, enough gold and precious stones to build a Byzantine palace. I suppose poetry written by women is apt to absorb some of the sense of elaborate decorative design that would otherwise have gone into lace or needlepoint (this is not a sneer) but it's far too facile to call waves "lucent walls of jade" [*The Choice*, l. 3], and however valuable amethysts or sapphires may be in economics, their lovely names make only a specious glitter in poetry.

The poems which are didactic and directly concerned with 1940[2] are almost entirely unsuccessful, and some of the most sincerely felt can only be called doggerel. Propaganda today is a military weapon dropping bombs on culture: these bombs are bound to do a great deal of damage, and at least one of poetry's guns, indignant and passionate denunciation, has been completely spiked. That is no doubt the chief reason for the failure of such poems as *Is It True?* and *The Veterans Offer*. Her chief religious idea seems to be the Shavian creative evolution one of God as the glacier and us as the terminal moraine, which, though dead as a religion, survives as a haunting and hideous myth.

There remains a small but attractive group of epigrams, mainly concerned with the revealing of personal emotion. Here the poet not only feels but expresses herself sincerely, and I think enough of them ring the bell to make the book worth recommending.

8

Poetry (III)

October 1942

Review of Mark van Doren, Our Lady Peace and Other War Poems *(Norfolk, Conn.: New Directions, 1942); and John Berryman,* Poems *(Norfolk: New Directions, 1942). From* Canadian Forum, *22 (October 1942): 220.*

A poet today is usually a cultured liberal intellectual: that's his union card, the caste mark in his forehead. He usually writes lyrical poetry about war and Fascism, and he usually deprecates them. I happen to have the same caste mark, and by virtue of it I have patiently read, and occasionally reviewed, at least several hundred, if not thousand, lyrics by which members of this caste communicate to one another in subtly cadenced murmurings the fact that they deprecate war and Fascism. The similarity of all these lyrics in tone, mood, subject, and form is so oppressive that the strain of trying to find something new to say about two more contributions is getting me down.

All the average poet knows about war and Fascism is what he sees in the papers. Yet he feels that he should be much subtler and more profound, that it is his duty to be prophetic, to have a deeper insight into imaginative values than the reporter or civil servant. But what is this deeper prophetic insight based on? Thus saith who, or what? For the average poet has no God and no coherent ideas behind his symbols, and he writes on social themes as a set task. He is anxious for the good of humanity, but is too keenly aware of its actual or latent menaces to be confident or loyal to it. His symbolism and imagery are therefore disjointed and shot out at random into the blue, and his diction becomes an indirect and oblique way of concealing the fact that he has really very little to say.

Trees continue to grow and seasons to revolve while men die. So they do. We disagree about the nature of the spiritual world but in wartime most of us feel that there is Something There. Yes, I know. In this world the well-intentioned are often the most confused, and the least confused often have evil and sinister intentions. God, that's true. Once I felt sweet love but now I feel stern necessity and challenge. I'm sure you must. The tone is unvarying, queasily apocalyptic, owlishly oracular, and plaintively querulous.

I am not saying that these two books are bad: I am saying that they are not bad. Where there is no exuberance, there can be no lapses in taste, but only a consistently skilful knack of turning out melodious and readable verses. A glance over the titles—*Crisis, Epidemic, Total War, Defeatist, New York Unbombed, River Rouge, 1932, 1 September 1939, Communist, The Dangerous Year*—will show us what to expect, and we are not disappointed. Mr. van Doren is subtle, scholarly, a faultless technician, and many of his poems have a lovely and delicate fragrance. Mr. Berryman, slightly the more interesting, builds up longer poems of considerable passion and power, and *The Statue* and *At Chinese Checkers* deserve a place in any anthological angelic choir.

What worries me is the assumption implied in the name of the publisher, that all modern poets are pioneers, experimenters, and poetic revolutionaries. These two books are not "New Directions": they are contributions, and very typical ones, to the rigorous convention which has dominated poetry for some years now, the convention of the elegiac lament over contemporary social evils. This convention, from a purely literary point of view, is the most portentous bore since the eighteenth-century pastoral, and we have had enough of it. We don't want posterity to think of us as Britons who prepared for war by painting themselves blue with woe. It isn't technically a good convention: its solemn and resonant tone is apt to become soggy and indigestible with so heavily accented a language as ours. One feels that our poets are being handed the what's-the-use-in-times-like-these line so much that they are beginning to sell out poetry to it.

I don't know why I think of Shelley at this point, but I do. Shelley also deprecated war and Fascism, or what meant Fascism in his time.[1] He yelled and screamed and got hysterical about it; he blithered and spluttered his way through huge sloppy poems with enough bad lines to torpedo through an epic; he hawked absurd pamphlets around the streets of Dublin; he made up gross and obscene libels against England's king and government; he fought for pacifism, atheism, revolution, free love, vegetarianism—anything rather than hopeless complaint and constipated elegance. I should like to go and read some Shelley now, if it's all right with everyone.

9

New Directions (I)

December 1942

Review of New Directions in Prose and Poetry, 1942, *ed. James Laughlin (New York: New Directions, 1942). From* Canadian Forum, *22 (December 1942): 282–4, where the review was headed "A Mixed Bag." Reprinted in* RW, *149–52.*

This is a very mixed bag, ranging from tripe to a few quite decent things, each of which deserves a careful review in itself. A book so uneven in interest starts at once an inquiry into the principles on which its material was collected, and for those we must look at the editor's preface. "You need only study literary history," he says, "to see that writing goes stale and soft in periods when the innovators and the nonconformists are stifled. Tradition and experiment, working against each other, produce a lively literature; neither one can be dispensed with" [xi].

Now I think that the assumption behind those four words "working against each other" is baloney. Pendulum theories of art don't work. Poems and pictures are real things; "tradition" and "experiment" are abstract nouns. To judge a concrete thing in terms of one abstract quality is to study it in one of many possible aspects. Which may well be worth doing. But to look at all art as split down the middle into an antithesis of abstract qualities hamstrings all criticism and insults all masterpieces; for the better the work of art, the more rewarding it will be to study it from opposing points of view. Thus, one could write an interesting essay on *Ulysses* as an experimental novel, and an equally interesting one on *Ulysses* as a traditional novel. But *Ulysses* is not "essentially" either; it is not "essentially" anything but a novel. A poet who starts in to write poems may get somewhere: a poet who starts in to write traditional poetry or experimental poetry will certainly get nowhere; just as a painter who gets seduced into producing examples of an "ism" in modern painting will soon forget how to paint pictures. All critical epithets of this kind are based on a *fait accompli*: if they get involved with the creative process itself they are certain to make it miscarry. When John Stuart Mill talked about an antithesis between the conservative work of a Coleridge or a de Vigny and the radical work of a Bentham or a Shelley,[1] he was, in relation to his time, talking a reasonable amount of sense, though treading on dangerous ground. But even this went out with crinolines, and for a conception of "tradition" which identifies it with the derivative or imitative, and of "experiment" which identifies it with a negative deviation from some undefined "traditional" standard, there is nothing whatever to be said. No art of any importance can fit such a dialectic. The original writer always starts something new, and because he does so always returns to origins. The radical writer always starts something new, and because he does so always returns to radices or roots. There cannot be the distinction between form and content that such a critical standard assumes: an artist with a fine mind cannot produce a traditional (if that means a conventional) work of art however hard he tries: an artist with a commonplace mind cannot experiment, however diligently he may imitate the latest fad.

The editor admits that in a collection of "experiments" there will be some tret: "The final value of many of the things we have published is not so much in what they are in themselves as in what they will lead to in the work of other writers who may develop what is here begun" [xii]. This also is a fallacy, this time a false analogy with science. Science does evolve and improve: it has an experimental avant-garde engaged in exploring and opening up new fields; it demands a specialization in which each man must "treat his chosen segment with technical precision" [xiii], to quote the editor again. But none of this is relevant to art, which never evolves or improves. The American post office represents, as compared with a Palaeolithic cave, a great progress of science, but a WPA mural[2] cannot be better than Magdalenian drawings of bisons and reindeers.

It is primarily this experimental fallacy which accounts for the distressing and puzzling contrast between the creative and the critical writing produced by the New Directions press. This annual is full of what looks like the work of clever undergraduates. There is the same condescending use of fantasy for purposes of pedantic allegory, the same earnest, moral, heavy-handed satire, that one finds in good undergraduate work.

Yet New Directions is turning out some of the best criticism in the business, and it is making a heroic effort to translate and criticize many of the best European writers, including Rimbaud, Rilke, Kafka, and a long list in preparation which I sincerely hope will do well. It is doing what the Modern Library did before it discovered that reprinting permanent best sellers and the Hundred Greatest Classics was a faster way to make money. This annual, too, is invariably better in criticism and translation. The symposium on Ford Madox Ford at the end is admirable. There are some poems by a Frenchman named Jouve,[3] translated by David Gascoyne, which, though they require a pretty technical knowledge of the Apocalypse, are more subtle and assured than any of the other poetry. And a little fable by Kafka ["Jackals and Arabs"], translated by Mimi Bartel, is certainly the most masterly specimen of the prose.

Now of course Kafka is the big shot in experimental circles today, and most of the contributors have dropped the left-wing "social realism" of which earlier annuals were full and are rushing to imitate his technique of delicate and disturbing allegory, his ability to suggest religious patterns within common experience, and his nightmarish power of making the psychopathic seem normal. His influence is accompanied by that of his French predecessors and analogues, from the Flaubert of the *Tentation* to late surrealists like the so-called Comte de Lautréamont.[4] Some of the results of this, as we should expect, are merely second-hand Poe, but there are more interesting developments. Surrealism, in the sense (or nonsense) of private libido symbolism, is less evident here than a desire for a communicable set of symbols, which in turn leads to an exploration of mythology and religion as the most promising sources for them. There are two remarkable "essays" by Paul Goodman[5] which are at least as much stories as essays, based on a curious linking of abstract arguments (some of them attempt to express semi-conscious intuitions), contemporary vignettes, and an archetypal myth, in one case the Alcestis legend, in the other a story concerning Tiberius. There is a real idea here, and one worth following up. Kafka-like, too, is a scene by Louis Second called "Apollinaris," which is quite deeply felt in spite of its affected style. There is a touch of parody in the treatment of a religious theme here which recurs in "Star in the West," by Robert Clairmont, a rather silly satire on the founding of a cult, and in "Blackout in the Cathedral," by Georg Mann, the story of a pro-Franco Thomist scholar and fake saint. This latter is a bit wearying and heavy-laden, but its general structure is quite sound.

Those who are mature enough to write because they feel like it and not because they are curious to see what happens when they do are naturally the easiest to read. The veteran pioneer, William Carlos Williams, contributes a play [*Trial Horse No. 1: Many Loves*] which is amusing enough to offset the fact that the hero is a misunderstood experimenting genius. A series of *Poems in Construction* by Richard Eberhart also deserves careful and sympathetic reading. There are lapses and splutters, and, like most contemporary poets, he loses all delicacy of taste and his ear freezes like a Polish asset whenever he touches on the war. But there is also sincerity, eloquence, and a passionate desire to hammer out some kind of personal synthesis. A newcomer, Marcia Nardi, also brings some beautiful though I should think quite "traditional" lyrics [*A Group of Poems*] to the experimental altar. As usual, the New Directions annual is a floundering and exasperating book: as usual, there is enough good stuff to make it worth your while.

10

Review of *New Writing and Daylight* (I)

April 1943

Untitled review of New Writing and Daylight, Winter, 1942–43 *(London: Hogarth, 1943). From the "Books of the Month" section of* Canadian Forum, *23 (April 1943): 21–2.*

This is the second issue of the combined groups mentioned in the title, the first having appeared last summer. A reviewer who did not see the summer issue is therefore at an initial disadvantage, as many of the articles are marked "Part Two."

The book contains poems, stories, sketches, and critical essays by young writers who are nearly all in the armed forces. The general level of competence is high, somewhere between the amateur conception of writing as a means of personal expression and the professional conception of it as a skilled labour. The poetry has a firmness of touch and accuracy of effect that is encouraging, and indicates that the cult of politically inspired romantic melancholy, which was getting so sterile and impotent, is on its way out. Day Lewis, who contributes three poems,[1] seems, after many false starts, to be attaining the stature of something very like a major poet. A less well-known writer, Terence Tiller, is also producing remarkable work.[2]

The stories, mostly war sketches, are more uneven, and cling more closely to prewar conventions: in fact, the war stories read almost exactly like the war stories of the last war, as far as the human emotions in them are concerned. A study of an IRA murder by Patrick Boyle [*The Lake*], and of a model girls' school by Julia Strachey [*Pioneer City*], have a good deal of intensity and sharpness, in spite of a lack of integration in the style.

The critical articles are more immediately interesting, and, as is usually the case in such collections, contain most of the best writing. Here we can see more clearly what the present literary problems in England are and how writers are dealing with them. What to do with war itself is, of course, the main thing. Thus Stephen Spender feels that the Sassoon–Owen approach to the last war was too negative, and depended on a false antithesis between the soldier who was idealized because he was at the front and the politician who was cursed because he stayed home [82]. Spender feels that writers should do better with a presumably better war, but is obviously not too happy about it [80–1]. Sewell Stokes, on the drama, points out that the American social conscience is more sharply pointed in its plays than the English, which makes Rice and Odets and Hellman more interesting than English dramatists [93–4]. G.W. Stonier regards *Mrs. Miniver* and its like as products of a kind of nostalgic snobbery which mental resistance to a war is apt to engender,[3] but which is not the less dangerous [97]. And several contributors, notably John Hampson, who writes a very interesting if nonconclusive essay on it [*The "Tough" Timers*], are fascinated by the cult of toughness and violence in American literature. They seem to feel, if they do not say so, that the English inability to appreciate this quality also made them underestimate the dynamic revolutionary power of Nazism.

A brilliant young Greek, Demetrios Capetanakis, contributes an essay on Stefan George, the German poet of the divine führer who didn't like what the Nazis offered him as an incarnation. This essay is worth the price of admission in itself. Reading it, one can see how tragically complicated the whole problem of Nazism is, and how obvious it is that when the Germans talk about the Jews they mean themselves. For their relation to our time is exactly that of the Jews to the Roman world: the same superstitions of racial purity, the same alternation of scholarship and fanatical rebellion, the same legalizing of culture, the same longing for a conquering Messiah, the same tendency to believe that every crackpot who comes along may be one. Czech and Polish contributions[4] also help to give this volume a less inbred appearance than most of its kind.

11

Review of *Voices* and *Genesis*

June 1943

A review of Voices: A Quarterly of Poetry, *Canadian issue, ed. Ralph Gustafson (Spring 1943), and* Genesis, Book One, *by Delmore Schwartz (New York: J. Laughlin, 1943). From* Canadian Forum, *23 (June 1943): 68–70. Reprinted as "A Lovely Evening" in* RW, *152–7.*

The critic's lot, like the policeman's, is not a happy one. He is perhaps the only person who feels the disadvantages of universal free education and a low rate of illiteracy. For those who can read and write, will, and there is perhaps no adult north of the Rio Grande who has not attempted some form of creative writing. Much of this is, of course, a mere response to middle-class competitive snobbery, which gives to proficiency in the arts a good deal of prestige. Cinderella mythology, besides, always dies hard, and the notion that successful writers can live on the Riviera and keep mistresses has been responsible for filling many waste baskets. Poetry written by anyone so ignorant will of course be doggerel; but, allowing for that, allowing for the semi-literates who have never got past the identification of poetry with *Excelsior*, allowing for the saps who think that poetry is a spontaneous excretion of maudlin sexual, religious, and patriotic emotions, allowing for the maternal pressure of "you could get good money for that" on a daughter's harmless metrical doodles, allowing for every variety of vulgarity, blatancy, self-conceit, bewilderment, and ignorance, the fact remains that the number of people capable of producing a steady stream of good readable verse is little short of appalling. The public—for this is not a public of readers, but of writers, for nearly everyone who habitually reads poetry also writes it, or intends to—has a professional interest in seeing how the trick is turned.

The critic's job is to operate the turbines by which this Niagara of creative energy can be brought into people's homes, to pick the one or two seeds out of the millions which are predestined by nature to live. He has a mathematical intuition that practically all of it is ephemeral; but he must not be asleep when the exception is thrust under his nose, or rather his quivering antennae. The metallic glitter of a needle is easy to distinguish from any given wisp of hay in a stack: but is it so easy to distinguish the gloss of accomplished mediocrity from the polish of perfected simplicity? There is no use being tough; it is a critic's job to be sensitive. Confronted by a mother with a newborn baby, no one will say that with its heredity it is certain to be a fool, or make ribald references to the manner in which it was conceived. And the process of poetic reproduction is equally hedged with taboos. It may be that the sacredness of inspiration is a superstition and that the importance of good art is overestimated, but the critic cannot take that into account. Had he lived a century earlier, he would perhaps not have infected Keats with tuberculosis; but could he have discerned major genius in the volume of 1817?[1] If he is a sympathetic critic, sooner or later he will find himself asserting that *Moods and Memories*, by Matilda Meataxe (New York, 1942), has a languorous and effulgent charm that is worthy of comparison with Keats. That is the first bite out of the apple of his forbidden tree, the tree of no knowledge of good or bad. If he feels that he is now stuck with Matilda, *facilis descensus Averno*;[2] the next step is to become a professional barker for the newspapers and lay in a stock of ginger-beer adjectives. If he renounces Matilda and all her works, including *Arcadian Rambles* (1943), *Full Fathoms* (1944), and *A Damsel with a Dulcimer* (1945), then where is he? The publisher will refuse to send his magazine any more free review copies; the public will picture him as a Heydrich[3] of fluttering genius, transfixing it with epigrammatic pins and a smug leer; and the poet will feel that there is no use going on writing in a world full of iron-skulled clodhoppers who don't even read the stuff, let alone savour the tender and fragrant synthesis he has made of his unspoken love for Dora, the smell of frying eggs, and the resemblance of moss to a sponge. But if the world is indifferent to the poet's nostalgia, it is still more unimpressed by the critic's adherence to his standards, however dogged. The poet can always write another book to console himself; the critic can only, like Alice, weep himself a pool of self-pitying tears and run the risk of being deflated and drowned in it afterwards.

Is there no middle way, then, between the flunkey critic who thinks everything he reads is just wonderful and leaves the impression that we are living in a heaven in which anyone who has passed his entrance can pick up a harp and burst into acceptable song, and the querulous critic who ignores everything a poem is and confines himself to complaints of what it isn't? Yes, I think so. The root of the difficulty with Matilda is that the reference to Keats is premature. T.S. Eliot says somewhere, in connection I think with Marianne Moore, that in dealing with a contemporary poet one should not worry about whether he is great or inspired or immortal and avoid all comparisons with dead poets who admittedly are. One should, he says, look rather for some such quality as "genuineness."[4] This means that the critic will have to take both himself and the poetry much less seriously, and realize that a Last Judgment and final separation of sheep from goats is a job for omniscience. His claim to be a critic rests simply on the fact that he likes reading poetry, that he finds it pleasant and not a duty, that reading poetry is one of the best ways of entertaining himself in leisure moments. All real critics have said, and will continue to say to the end of time, that the function of poetry is to delight and to instruct,[5] to amuse and to interest. Poetry which is not instructive is insipid; poetry which is not delightful is a bore. Tons of poetry can, up to a point, satisfy these two demands. If the critic finds that the poetry has got stuck in his mind, that he finds himself going back again and again to it, it is probably pretty good stuff. If not, the fact that he may like it very much does not necessarily mean that the poet is immortal, any more than a girl's "Thanks for a lovely evening" necessarily means lifelong marriage.

The picking of one or two fertile seeds, therefore, is not a matter of snap judgments, but of leisured experience. And if the critic is unable to relax and enjoy minor poetry, it is largely due to the barbaric public for whom he is writing. People who like mystery stories will buy them even if they are villainously written and would be intolerable to read again; why should not people who like poetry buy something that a sincere and intelligent poet, who has no hope of making money and very little of acquiring fame, has done the best he can with, even if his best is a long way short of titanic? But they don't, and so the critic, if he cares about poetry, will fall into the stupid Hollywoodish most-supercolossal-masterpiece-of-all-time jingle. If he hates poetry, and many critics do, he will grouch.

Thus in the small anthology of current Canadian poems, many of the best of which first appeared in the *Forum*, there is much that is both delightful and instructive. Pungent and often brilliant wit is the most delightful feature: we find this in E.J. Pratt's *The Truant*, easily the most important poem in the collection,[6] in some exquisite lyrics of Robert Finch,[7] in the little quatrains on the poets contributed by Leo Kennedy,[8] in Patrick Anderson's agreeably loquacious chatter.[9] There is instruction, too, to be found in P.K. Page's clairvoyant vision of underpaid stenographers [*The Stenographers*], in the editor's *Epithalamium*, and in F.R. Scott's *Flux*. These honourable mentions, if they amount to that, are somewhat random: very few of the thirty-five pages of poems contain dull or incompetent work, and its most objectionable feature is its omissions. Incidentally, what this country needs is a few bilingual collections.

Mr. Schwartz's *Genesis* is a more ambitious effort, and when one reads in his introduction that he is trying to emulate the morbid pedestrianism of Donne, Hardy, Webster, and Wordsworth [ix], one instinctively relapses into either the querulous or the flunkeyish jargon. The latter would begin: "Mr. Schwartz has succeeded in capturing the fulgurous wit and stringent paradox of Donne, the Luciferial theodicy of Hardy, the (fill in later) of Webster, the (fill in later) of Wordsworth." To change this to the querulous, add the word "not." Forgetting the introduction, one finds that Hershey Green, a young man with insomnia, is telling the story of his childhood in prose, or rather in a sprawling loosely cadenced verse somewhat like that of Robinson Jeffers. His narrative is concerned with the bullying he suffered from being sensitive and Jewish, the torment that the mystery of sex brings to that age, the misery of a child who has to live with quarrelling parents, and the nostalgic immediacy of certain imaginative experiences, notably those connected with snow and Christmas, which form associative patterns later on. Each episode of the narrative is commented on in blank verse by a group of ghosts around the bed, who make moral judgments and ironic reflections, interpret the events in terms of Freudian mythology or of their social context and relation to "Capitalismus," relate them to the great literary conceptions, Hamlet, Orestes, Quixote, which are based on just such universally average situations, and point out the significance of movies and baseball and comic strips from the stratospheric point of view. The whole scheme is worked out with considerable intelligence and power, the writing is competent, and much of what the chorus says is strikingly acute and profound. The trouble is that the story is commonplace, even squalid, and while this was the poet's deliberate intention, there is no distinction in the telling of it to make up for the fact that it has been told hundreds of times before. The whole Wordsworthian notion that the duller the subject, the more universal the poetic archetype it represents, is a very dubious one anyway.[10] The choruses are infinitely better than the narrative, but could do with more wit and bounce. When Blake said that "Exuberance is Beauty," he had something [*The Marriage of Heaven and Hell*, pl. 10, l. 64; E38]. Thanks for a lovely evening.

12

Review of *New Writing and Daylight* (II)

October 1944

A review of New Writing and Daylight, Winter 1943–44, *ed. John Lehmann (London: Hogarth, 1944). From* Canadian Forum, *24 (October 1944): 163–5.*

This is the fourth collection of poems, stories, and essays by young writers in England, many if not most of whom are in uniform, to be issued under this title. The special feature of *New Writing and Daylight* is that it attempts to give as full representation as possible to the work of foreign and colonial writers now stationed in England; and this issue contains Czech, Greek, and Brazilian names. Spender and Edith Sitwell are the best-known contributors. As in most such collections, the poetry is better than the stories, and the critical essays better than the poetry. The essays include one on Dostoevsky and one on the Greek influence in Russian art, both excellent. These essays give the impression, and occasionally even say, that there can be no new writing in England until there is some daylight, which implies among other things the end of the war. In the meantime, England is full of intelligent and cultured writers who know how writing is done, appreciate whatever has been done well, but whose own chariots of genius simply have to be laid up until the inspiration necessary to run them is less drastically rationed. One essay says wistfully, "There is no serious living English novelist who might not suddenly break new ground" [45], but even that remark contributes to the general feeling of suspension, not exactly of activity, but of the real exuberance of creative energy.

This last is not of course a product of "self-expression"; it is the result of making one's personality a medium or prism in order that a created form greater than that personality, with its own laws of existence, may be revealed without distortion or interference. This is beautifully recorded in this volume by Peter Yates, in a poem called *The Prophet's Elegy*. But all that the writer can be a medium for just now is the grinning monster of the war. Prose fiction is the form which deals most directly with the chaos of wartime experience, and the stories in this book, ranging from a ponderous anti-Fascist satire to slight nostalgic reminiscences, are no exception to the general rule that contemporary fiction is as becalmed as the Ancient Mariner. The poetry, on the other hand, seems to be gathering together much larger powers of synthesis. Poetry can make symbols of images, whereas the attempt to work out symbolic relationships in prose is apt to result in laboriously elaborate epigrams. Poetry can use erudition and critical intelligence, which in fiction is just stuck in, and sticks out: as somebody in one of these stories says, "I've read all Tolstoy, Dostoevsky, Hardy, and most of Balzac since this war began—and nothing ever seems to happen" [13]. I should think that when creative energies are set free again it will be poetry that will be the first to pick up. A revived poetry may of course impart some warmth to fiction, like the virgin in King David's bed,[1] but the most promising type of fiction is precisely that which makes the freest use of symbolism: Kafka, for instance, and perhaps some of those curious tortured Nazi allegories like the *Auf Den Marmor Klippen*[2] referred to by John Lehmann in the last essay of the book.

13
Joseph Schull

October 1944

Review of Joseph Schull, I, Jones, Soldier *(Toronto: Macmillan, 1944). From* Canadian Forum, *24 (October 1944): 166.*

This is a narrative poem describing the thoughts in the mind of an officer just before zero hour. Jones is a sensitive soldier, and is not content to go into action with a merely physical integration; he wants a spiritual one, too, and some insight into the fundamental faiths which are the laws of his own being and consequently the causes of his being there. He reviews his military career up to that point with a good deal of detachment and humour, and rejects the ready-made formulas—patriotism, justice of one's cause, product of a Depression generation, and the rest—with a sharp insight. When he gets down to his mental bedrock, he finds "one earth, one Man, one Truth" [48]: perhaps in answer, though the poet does not say so, to the "Ein Reich, ein Volk, ein Führer"[1] with which he is challenged by his enemy. These are of course inarticulate ideas, and he talks very vaguely about them, but fundamental ideas usually are inarticulate, and the poem does not lose its narrative logic.

The writing is rather facile, though there are fewer clichés than one might expect; there is the usual sandwiching of nostalgia and narrative; there is a good deal of the spineless and flaccid rhythm of too easily written free verse, and a certain amount of blather. But there is a very real sincerity, and much of the readability and continuity which sincerity on such a theme is likely to give. A great deal of what the soldier has to say about this war must be expressed in verse, and verse of this straightforward narrative kind, which avoids doggerel only by avoiding rhyme.

The same theme expressed in prose would become intolerably gaseous, but it makes an interesting and readable poem, and one can only hope that the market for this type of poetry will grow larger as the flood of I-saw-it-with-my-own-eyes books grows smaller.

14

New Directions (II)

November 1944

Review of New Directions in Prose and Poetry, 1944, *ed. James Laughlin (Norfolk, Conn.: New Directions, 1944). From* Canadian Forum, *24 (November 1944): 189–90. Reprinted as "Experimental Writing" in* RW, *157–9.*

When I reviewed the seventh annual *New Directions* a year ago [no. 9], I attacked the theory of "experiment" which underlies it: a theory which is partly an application of the two-party system of politics to literature, and partly a conception of expanding development in the use of literary techniques which is based on a fallacious analogy with science. I notice that Mr. Laughlin is still talking the same nonsense on such matters ("a technique which fails with the writer who developed it may become a potent tool in the hands of a succeeding writer able to realize it more effectively" [xv]), and that his collection has about the same proportion of tripe to interesting reading. He admits that much of it may not be very good, but insists that a place is needed for writers who have resisted all forms of commercialism in order to write as they please. No one can deny this; and anyway, New Directions, which has the most consistently interesting booklist in the country, and has done more that any other publishing house for the up-to-date intelligent reader, is entitled to a sympathetic consideration of anything it chooses to send out.

I am getting tired of making the same remark about contemporary collections of writing—that the critical essays are always much the best, and the fiction nearly always the worst, the poetry coming between. The best part of this book is the section of little-known writings by Lorca and a remarkable collection of Latin Americans. The poetry varies from good to bad and the greater part of the fiction is lousy. Kafka remains an important influence; there is a good deal of very heavy-handed fantasy, in which Marx and Freud and other worthies come to life or appear at a Last Judgment; and *Finnegans Wake* is beginning to affect "experimental" technique increasingly. This last is true of the one Canadian who appears in the book, A.M. Klein. Some of the poems he contributes are among his best, particularly *Love*. (I may note parenthetically that his suggestion that *Finnegans Wake* is an illustration of Poe's "Poetic Principle" is one hundred per cent wrong.) As usual, there is always something in the ragbag which is worth the price of admission. The veteran experimenters, Paul Goodman, Meyer Liben, Kenneth Patchen, W. Carlos Williams, are back again; though one misses the continuation, promised in the last annual, of Georg Mann's vitriolic satires. But there are some good things by newcomers, notably a fine long poem by Kenneth Rexroth [*The Phoenix and the Tortoise*], a brilliant *tour de force* called *Definition and Destruction of the Personage*, by Eduardo Anguita, and some eloquent poetry by Pablo Neruda.[1] One may read much in *New Directions* annuals that bores and irritates, but one never feels that anyone interested in contemporary writing can afford to pass them up.

It seems to me that the real "new direction" in modern literature is a gigantic revolution in literary techniques brought about by the movie, the radio, the magazine, the newspaper, and their subsidiaries, which latter include the comic strips, the journalist's book, the popular fiction designed to begin as a magazine serial and end as a movie, and so on. The revolution is greater than anything in literature since the invention of the printing press, and the parallel there is instructive. The printing press provided a medium for journalism and pamphleteering; it provided accurate editions of classics (compare the developments in gramophone recordings, microfilm, and photostats today); and it increased the output of popular literature. The thing it did not do was instantly to stimulate a new growth of highbrow writing. Many of the highbrows, the lyric poets at least, continued to pass their work around in manuscript and to pretend not to care much for printing. It seems to me that the writers of today who are still working with the traditional means of expression and are not interested in Hollywood or soap-opera contracts, have a more important job than ever to do, of a completely highbrow kind. It is their task to stimulate as far as possible a public respect for good writing, to show that the real values of literature and the standards of beauty, wisdom, and intelligence are now exactly what they were in Homer's time, and to demonstrate that there are laws of culture just as there are laws of nature, and that a society which willfully ignores either set of laws is going to get into plenty of trouble.

The writer with something really important to say will probably be highly educated, even erudite, and well acquainted with the profounder aspects of whatever social phenomena come within his range. His next problem is to digest this erudition and insight into an artistic form, which means absorbing it completely into whatever genre, novel, lyric, short story, or drama, he chooses. This is where most of the contributors to this volume have stopped. They have both erudition and insight, but have not succeeded in digesting it; hence much of what they say is a critical essay in the nominal form of a lyric, short story, drama, or what not. The result of this is to suggest the breaking down of these genres, and it is this sense of breaking down that gives the collection its "experimental" character. That is, the outstanding weakness in their writing is interpreted as its primary virtue. That, at any rate, is how I feel about the *New Directions Annual*, no. 8; and if my discussion of it is rather general, it is because the literary aim of the volume itself, as distinct from the individual contributions to it, is equally so.

15

Karl Shapiro

December 1944

Review of Karl Shapiro, V-Letter and Other Poems *(New York: Reynal & Hitchcock, 1944). From* Canadian Forum, *24 (December 1944): 213–14.*

This is the second volume of one of the best contemporary poets, now on active service in the South Pacific, where most of the poems in it were written. Probably few of those who have followed his work will consider it the equal of the earlier book, *Person, Place and Thing*; but the poems are attractive, if seldom deeply moving, and, though some are trivial, the book as a whole is a pleasure to read. As he says, he is not a "war" poet: he is simply a poet who happens to be in the army, and because he is a poet patterns go on forming and metres go on clicking in his mind, regardless of what else is happening [vi]. Sometimes, of course, the war enters the poetry—most poignantly, perhaps, in the poem on the amputation [*The Leg*]—but on the whole Mr. Shapiro makes no attempt to "interpret" the war to us by composing metrical editorials.

Mr. Shapiro has a rhythmic smoothness of a kind that needs regular metre and rhyme: he seems especially partial to sonnets. His poetry is the expression of an alert, agile, and intelligent mind, tolerant and in the best sense of the word refined. He has no verbal magic, no volcanic reserves of emotional power, and no gnarled intellectualism. A hostile critic could call him superficial, but it would be fairer to say that he gives one the surface attractiveness of poetry: the ripples, the flecks of sunlight, and the spray. If, as he says, he tries to write like a Christian one day and like a Jew the next [vi], it is clear that there are depths in both Christianity and Judaism that he will not express. But that is not his business: his business is with a precision of statement and an accurately modulating wit which can give to an image a clear and sharp poetic outline:

> He talks to overhear, she to withdraw
> To some interior feminine fireside
> Where the back arches, beauty puts forth a paw
> Like a black puma stretching in velvet pride,
>
> Making him think of cats, a stray of which
> Some days sets up a howling in his brain,
> Pure interference such as this neat bitch
> Seems to create from listening disdain. [*The Intellectual*, ll. 8–16]

16

Kenneth Rexroth

December 1944

Review of Kenneth Rexroth, The Phoenix and the Tortoise *(Norfolk, Conn.: New Directions, 1944). From* Canadian Forum, *24 (December 1944): 214–15.*

This collection consists of the long title poem, a group of shorter poems, and another group of imitations and paraphrases, chiefly of late Classical epigram-writers. Mr. Rexroth prefers a short accentual free verse line, and in his vocabulary makes constant and at times excessive use of technical and abstract terms. The writing, in spite of occasional Eliot and Lawrence cadences, is admirably clear and intelligent, sounding perhaps a good deal more like *The Testament of Beauty*[1] than the poet intended it to do. He is seldom obscure and even more seldom without something interesting to say, and his poetry makes, on its surface level, thoroughly enjoyable reading. His competence and assurance suggest that he has already found a style which he will not be likely to transcend in future; but all that that means is that his present volume shows achievement rather than promise.

The fact that Mr. Rexroth is much better than average, whatever the average may be, is partly due to his Classical scholarship. An educational system that attempts to promote the writing and study of English and at the same time minimizes, when it does not actually discourage, the learning of Latin and Greek, is, for all serious literary purposes, about as efficient as a dentist who extracts a molar and leaves both roots still sticking in the jaw; and, however inevitable the trend away from the Classics may be, it remains true that an English literature which is not solidly established on Classical (and Biblical) education will never get far above high-class journalism. The reason for this is that literature, in contrast to science, is dependent on a personal authority; on the fact that a great writer is a model of good writing to be imitated by all beginners yesterday, today, and forever; and that it takes centuries for any writer to establish so unqualified an ascendancy. A new writer can get no authority into his own writing until he is sufficiently steeped in this personal tradition; and writing that has no authority has no unity, because it lacks the assured technique, the emotional balance, and the accuracy of vision which unified art must have. America today is full of excellent writers bursting with a creative energy which could become genius if it were disciplined: lacking discipline, it becomes a spluttering burble. Mr. Rexroth is perhaps not a genius, whatever that is, but he is a cultivated writer with a sense of authority, which nowadays is often a much better thing to be than a genius.

Mr. Rexroth has studied especially the Hellenistic and Byzantine periods: he has evidently been influenced by Spengler's cyclic conception of history, and is primarily interested in the historical parallels between late Roman times and our own. The title poem is based on the same idea. The escape from this wheel of time, according to the poet, is up a kind of Platonic ladder of love; in a sexuality which is disciplined by the sacramental unity of marriage and develops into a sense of kinship with humanity. As a vision of human life is a fundamentally tragic one, this sense of kinship implies a contrasting divine comedy. Mr. Rexroth is, it is clear, a deeply religious poet, hampered by a curious prudery from saying exactly what he means and feels about religion. His work also shows that poets today are reaching out for some integration of twentieth-century ideas, among which the Spenglerian view of history, the theories of unconscious symbolism in psychology and anthropology, and the Nietzsche-Lawrence conception of the limitations of reason, are especially prominent. Mr. Rexroth's development will probably be along the lines of clarifying and digesting this integration. I say digesting, because at present he is still capable of emitting hunks of raw erudition like "Scotus—Luther—Kierkegaard—Barth—" [*The Phoenix and the Tortoise,* l. 259], or again:

> Marx. Kropotkin. Adams. Acton.
> Spengler. Toynbee. [ll. 549–50]

But nevertheless he shows that contemporary poets are working out a unification of twentieth-century thought which will have profound effects on postwar life when it begins to filter from the arts into the sciences, and from the sciences into, for example, the front pages of the *Canadian Forum*.

17

Idols of the Marketplace

September 1946

From Canadian Forum, *26 (September 1946): 124–5.*

English literature had two obituaries on its hands last month.[1] Bernard Shaw, it is true, continues to turn up to all his funerals as lively as Finnegan, though without his taste in whisky. But the incredible writing energy of H.G. Wells, which in the last few years, with a succession of querulous valedictories, seemed to be sinking into a nervous tic, has stopped at last. Both writers are now in the trough of appreciation into which all great artists must fall between their later years, when young men are looking for younger masters or asserting themselves, and their final embalming as harmless classics. But even now no one can seriously deny that one is a dramatist and the other a novelist of major importance, apart from all their other achievements.

Both men reached maturity at a time when "artist" tended to mean a lover of sheltered beauty who was unwilling to recognize his social responsibilities. Both reacted violently against such a conception of art, and insisted that if that sort of thing was art then they were journalists, propagandists, tub-thumpers, professional scribblers, charlatans, or anything at all rather than artists. Both were great popularizers of modern ideas, and both preached a gospel of a sane and balanced rationalism, sufficiently free from prejudice, superstition, and ignorance to be "normal," not in the sense that most people have it, but in the sense that enough people must acquire it for civilization to survive. Wells did not look beyond such a rational position; Shaw did, but regarded it as the necessary minimum.

Wells's range was therefore narrower but more intense: he was never fooled into thinking, as Shaw was during the Boer War, that imperialism could be a transitional phase of socialism, and therefore he understood the meaning of Fascism, as Shaw never did.[2] There is nothing in Shaw corresponding to Wells's horrifying fantasies of a Robot world or his vicious anti-Fascist satires, like *The Autocracy of Mr. Parham,* which prophesied Hitler's rise to power long before it occurred. As for Shaw, Chesterton's conception of him as a descendant of the Puritans is not likely to last:[3] he is as pure a pagan as anyone can now be, far more so than Anatole France, for instance, because less self-conscious about it. Like the hero of *Major Barbara,* he is the incarnation of Greek culture in the modern world: his humorous, quizzical philosophy and his diet of weeds and water are of the age of Diogenes and Socrates; his disturbing problem plays and brilliant satires reek with the spirit of Euripides and Aristophanes; his morals are Aristotelian and his visions of a world disappearing into a whirlpool of pure thought are Platonic. One hopes that he will follow the example of the people in *Back to Methusaleh* and be found still chortling on his three-hundredth birthday at the "short-livers" who kill themselves by lethal habits.

18

A.E. Coppard and T.F. Powys

November 1946

Review of A.E. Coppard, Selected Tales *(London: J. Cape, 1946) and T.F. Powys,* Bottle's Path and Other Stories *(London: Chatto & Windus, 1946). From* Canadian Forum, *26 (November 1946): 187.*

It was an excellent idea to make a one-volume selection from Coppard's twelve books of short stories, probably all out of print by now, and put back into circulation an interesting writer, who, except for anthologies, has rather dropped out of sight. He is still very readable, though his mannered style ("the ruckle of partridges, or the nifty gallop of a hare" [107]) has lost the smartness of novelty, and the straightforward stories stand up better than the more widely known fantasies. And remember T.F. Powys, not to be confused (though he always was) with John Cowper Powys or Llewelyn Powys: T.F. Powys of *Mr. Weston's Good Wine,* with its Celtic whimsy, its pawky humour, and its allegorical religiosity? Here he is in what is practically a new collection of tales, and all the characters have names like Tiddy, Twiddy, Nutty, Dally, and Polley. Peace, it's wonderful. How these writers bring back the 1920s, when James Branch Cabell[1] was a great prose stylist and Norman Douglas[2] required reading! They should be read in a room full of Russian-ballet decor and orange dragons on black curtains, beside a drink served by a breastless maid in bangs.

19

George Orwell, *Animal Farm*

December 1946

A review of George Orwell, Animal Farm *(New York: Harcourt Brace, 1946). From the "Turning New Leaves" section of* Canadian Forum, *26 (December 1946): 211–12. Reprinted as "Orwell and Marxism" in NFCL, 204–6; and in* George Orwell: The Critical Heritage, *ed. Jeffrey Meyers (London: Routledge & Kegan Paul, 1975), 206–8. First published in Britain in 1945.*

George Orwell's satire on Russian Communism, *Animal Farm,* has just appeared in America, but its fame has preceded it, and surely by now everyone has heard of the fable of the animals who revolted and set up a republic on a farm, how the pigs seized control and how, led by a dictatorial boar named Napoleon, they finally became human beings walking on two legs and carrying whips just as the old Farmer Jones had done. At each stage of this receding revolution one of the seven principles of the original rebellion becomes corrupted, so that "no animal shall kill any other animal" has added to it the words "without cause" when there is a great slaughter of the so-called sympathizers of an exiled pig named Snowball [76], and "no animal shall sleep in a bed" takes on "with sheets" when the pigs move into the human farmhouse and monopolize its luxuries [57]. Eventually there is only one principle left, modified to "all animals are equal, but some are more equal than others" [112], as Animal Farm, changed back to Manor Farm, is welcomed into the community of human farms again after its neighbours have realized that it makes its "lower" animals work harder on less food than any other farm, so that the model workers' republic becomes a model of exploited labour.

The story is very well written, especially the Snowball episode, which suggests that the Communist "Trotskyite" is a conception on much the same mental plane as the Nazi "Jew," and the vicious irony of the end of Boxer the work horse is perhaps really great satire. On the other hand, the satire of the episode corresponding to the German invasion seems to be both silly and heartless, and the final metamorphosis of pigs into humans at the end is a fantastic disruption of the sober logic of the tale. The reason for the change in method was to conclude the story by showing the end of Communism under Stalin as a replica of its beginning under the tsar. Such an alignment is, of course, complete nonsense, and as Mr. Orwell must know it to be nonsense, his motive for adopting it was presumably that he did not know how otherwise to get his allegory rounded off with a neat epigrammatic finish.

Animal Farm adopts one of the classical formulas of satire, the corruption of principle by expediency, of which Swift's *A Tale of a Tub* is the greatest example. It is an account of the bogging down of Utopian aspirations in the quicksand of human nature which could have been written by a contemporary of Artemus Ward about one of the cooperative communities attempted in America during the last century. But for the same reason it completely misses the point as a satire on the Russian development of Marxism, and as expressing the disillusionment which many men of good will feel about Russia. The reason for that disillusionment would be much better expressed as the corruption of expediency by principle. For the whole point about Marxism was surely that it was the first revolutionary movement in history which attempted to start with a concrete historical situation instead of vast *a priori* generalizations of the "all men are equal" type, and which aimed at scientific rather than Utopian objectives. Marx and Engels worked out a revolutionary technique based on an analysis of history known as dialectical materialism, which appeared in the nineteenth century at a time when metaphysical materialism was a fashionable creed, but which Marx and Engels always insisted was a quite different thing from metaphysical materialism.

Today, in the Western democracies, the Marxist approach to historical and economic problems is, whether he realizes it or not, an inseparable part of the modern educated man's consciousness, no less than electrons or dinosaurs, while metaphysical materialism is as dead as the dodo, or would be if it were not for one thing. For a number of reasons, chief among them the comprehensiveness of the demands made on a revolutionary by a revolutionary philosophy, the distinction just made failed utterly to establish itself in practice as it did in theory. Official Marxism today announces on page 1 that dialectical materialism is to be carefully distinguished from metaphysical materialism, and then insists from page 2 to the end that Marxism is nevertheless a complete materialist metaphysic of experience, with materialist answers to such questions as the existence of God, the origin of knowledge, and the meaning of culture. Thus instead of including itself in the body of modern thought and giving a revolutionary dynamic to that body, Marxism has become a self-contained dogmatic system, and one so exclusive in its approach to the remainder of modern thought as to appear increasingly antiquated and sectarian. Yet this metaphysical materialism has no other basis than that of its original dialectic, its program of revolutionary action. The result is an absolutizing of expediency which makes expediency a principle in itself. From this springs the reckless intellectual dishonesty which it is so hard not to find in modern Communism, and which is naturally capable of rationalizing any form of action, however ruthless.

A really searching satire on Russian Communism, then, would be more deeply concerned with the underlying reasons for its transformation from a proletarian dictatorship into a kind of parody of the Catholic Church. Mr. Orwell does not bother with motivation: he makes his Napoleon inscrutably ambitious, and lets it go at that, and as far as he is concerned some old reactionary bromide like "you can't change human nature" is as good a moral as any other for his fable. But he, like Koestler, is an example of a large number of writers in the Western democracies who during the last fifteen years have done their level best to adopt the Russian interpretation of Marxism as their own world outlook and have failed. The last fifteen years have witnessed a startling decline in the prestige of Communist ideology in the arts, and some of the contemporary changes in taste which have resulted will be examined in future contributions to this column.

20

Review of *New Writing and Daylight* (III)

February 1947

Review of New Writing and Daylight, *1946, ed. John Lehmann (London: John Lehmann, 1946); and* Poems from New Writing: 1936–46 *(London: John Lehmann, 1946). From* Canadian Forum, *26 (February 1947): 261.*

This anthology of stories, poems, criticism, and sketches has been appearing in bound volumes about twice a year since 1942. It is edited and published by John Lehmann, and has contained much of the best writing produced in English during that time. It has always taken particular pains to include work, in translation or otherwise, by Continental writers, many of whom were with the British army during the war. The latest issue seems to feature Greek and Czech names especially. This issue also contains a symposium on the future of fiction to which Rose Macaulay, V.S. Pritchett, Arthur Koestler, and Osbert Sitwell contribute, poems by Louis MacNeice [*Autolycus*] and George Barker [*The Five Faces of Pity*], and critical essays on Valéry, Picasso, and Klee,[1] the Picasso article being a well-written and well-informed hostile criticism, which is probably pretty rare.

The selection of poetry contributed to this periodical of course does not pretend to be an adequate anthology of contemporary British poetry, but it provides a fair proportion of it. The better-known contributors are Auden, MacNeice, Spender, Edith Sitwell, Day Lewis, Gascoyne, Lorca, Pierre Jean Jouve, William Plomer, and one Canadian, Earle Birney.[2] One gets the impression that Britain has gone through a profound spiritual experience like that of France after 1870, and that such collections as this are the foothills of an approaching British Renaissance. In contemporary British poetry there is passion, sincerity, sanity, high technical competence, infinite variety of style and mood, and a highly educated public to be addressed—in short, there is everything, but the total effect is one of promise rather than achievement, as though Britain's Rimbauds and Verlaines were coming with a new generation.

21

Review of *The Kafka Problem*

February 1947

Review of The Kafka Problem, *ed. Angel Flores (New York: New Directions, 1947). From* Canadian Forum, *26 (February 1947): 262.*

A symposium of essays and critical studies on the great German writer, now one of the major influences on modern literature. How deeply he has penetrated into our culture is indicated by the names of the contributors, which include W.H. Auden, Albert Camus ["Hope and Absurdity"], Max Lerner ["The Human Voyage"], Franz Werfel ["Recollections"], and Denis Saurat ["A Note on *The Castle*"], to mention only the best-known ones, and which appear to represent at least a dozen literatures. The book is an essential supplement to the translations of Kafka's works which are now appearing, many of them also published by New Directions. The designer of the book thinks it's cute to list an essay on "Kafka's Quest" by W.H. Auden as "k.'s quest—w.h. auden," but don't let that put you off.

22

Henry James, *Roderick Hudson*

August 1947

Untitled review of Henry James, Roderick Hudson *(London: John Lehmann, 1947). From* Canadian Forum, *27 (August 1947): 118–19.*

The revival of Henry James and the reissue of his works proceed apace, and we may confidently look forward to a time when it will be possible to buy a copy of *The Golden Bowl* or *The Wings of a Dove*. *Roderick Hudson* is James's first important novel, and is pure James for all its indebtedness in theme to Hawthorne's *Marble Faun* (a novel which must have haunted James all his life, as he refers to it in *The Sense of the Past*),[1] and in style to Howells. The reader unacquainted with James could not do better than start in with this witty and incisive story, which offers a sheer reading pleasure that is hard to beat. It has none of the features that so often put the common reader off the later books: the haywire syntax, the pansyish mannerisms ("she wonderfully observed," and the like), the smothering of definite periods under stuttering parentheses, and the almost cubist analytical perspective which obliterates all the usual distinctions between the significant and the trivial. As in the later *Portrait of a Lady*, the setting is Europe and the characters American expatriates in varying degrees of disguise, and the subject is a kind of overture to James's work, with most of his later motifs formulated in it.

23

Yeats and the Language of Symbolism

October 1947

From FI, *218–37. Originally published in* University of Toronto Quarterly (UTQ), *17 (October 1947): 1–17. For the reprint in* FI, *Frye revised four sentences (the* UTQ *variants of which are here given in notes) and added one note.*

I

In reading any poem we have to know at least two languages: the language the poet is writing and the language of poetry itself. The former exists in the words the poet uses, the latter in the images and ideas which those words express. And just as the words of a language are a set of verbal conventions, so the imagery of poetry is a set of symbolic conventions. This set of symbolic conventions differs from a symbolic system, such as a religion or a metaphysic, in being concerned, not with a content, but with a mode of apprehension. Religions, philosophies, and other symbolic systems are as a rule presented as doctrines; poetic symbolism is a language. Sometimes a symbolic system, such as Classical mythology, may lose its doctrinal content and so become purely linguistic, but this does not affect the distinction. So while poetry can be made of any account of spiritual reality because it is itself the language of spiritual reality, it does not follow that poetry represents something truer, because broader, than religion or philosophy. The French language is a much broader thing than the philosophy of Montaigne or Pascal, and we can learn French without being converted to any Frenchman's views; but the French language itself represents no truth.

Just as the teacher of a language is a grammarian, so one of the functions of the literary critic is to be a grammarian of imagery, interpreting the symbolic systems of religion and philosophy in terms of poetic language. Yeats provides a fine example of such criticism in his essay on the philosophy of Shelley's poetry,[1] though the use of the word "philosophy" here is, as just said, misleading. I imagine that the greatest creative periods in art are also those in which criticism is most aware of the importance of this particular task. In Elizabethan criticism, for instance, the importance attached to symbolic grammar comes out in the mythological handbooks, the elaborate allegorical commentaries on Virgil and Ovid, and the textbooks of rhetoric, in which every conceivable mode of utterance is studied and classified with what seems to us now the mere exuberance of pedantry. It may be true that, as Samuel Butler said:

> . . . all a rhetorician's rules
> Teach nothing but to name his tools. [*Hudibras*, pt. 1, canto 1, ll. 89–90]

But if a critic, or for that matter a poet, cannot name his tools, the world is not likely to concede much authority to his craft. We should not entrust our cars to a mechanic who lived entirely in a world of gadgets and doohickeys. In any case the Elizabethan critical tradition, which, whatever one thinks of it, is certainly essential to the age of Spenserian allegory and court masque, eventually broke down. Augustan criticism had a grammatical interest in form, but its scope was far narrower, and by the Romantic period, in spite of the gigantic efforts of Coleridge, criticism was rapidly heading for a limbo of "appreciation," reflective *belles lettres*, and cogent comments.

The axioms and postulates of criticism cannot be taken over ready-made from theology, philosophy, or science. They have to grow out of the art which the criticism is dealing with. Hence each art has its own criticism, and whether aesthetics is a legitimate branch of philosophy or not, I do not see that a theory of beauty in general can have a direct application to any branch of criticism. When Lessing in the *Laokoön* protested against confusing the canons of the different arts,[2] this was really the question he was raising. The importance of the question is not overthrown by historical criticism, which is a different subject altogether, and which deals with such conceptions as Baroque, Renaissance, Rococo, Gothic, Romantic, where all cultural products of a period are seen as symbols of that period. Beauty, the icon of aesthetics, is as big a stumbling block to criticism as happiness is to morals, and it is significant that in our ordinary language about art the word is practically obsolete, having been long replaced simply by "good." For one thing, it has become sentimentalized in meaning until it is now synonymous with the particular quality of beauty more exactly described as loveliness. The reason for this is that ideas of beauty tend insensibly to become ideas of propriety and decorum. When we speak of the human body as beautiful we mean a body of someone in good physical condition between about eighteen and thirty, and when Degas expresses interest in thick-bottomed matrons squatting in hip-baths, we confuse the shock to our sense of propriety with a shock to our sense of beauty.[3] The same thing happens when Ibsen claims venereal disease as a subject for tragedy.[4] The cult of beauty, then, is reactionary: it is continually setting up barriers to the conquest of experience by art, and limits the variety of expression in art wherever it can.

But with the breakdown of a tradition of grammatical criticism, ideas of general beauty become the critic's chief subject matter; hence the nineteenth century was the golden age of aesthetic criticism. Criticism reacted on art, and when critics forgot how to teach the language of poetic imagery the poets forgot how to use it, the creative counterpart of aesthetic criticism being, of course, aestheticism. This fact affected both the content and the form of late Romantic poetry. The content illustrates what may be called a Berlitz[5] approach to symbolic language, apprehending it by means of evocation and sympathetic intuition, in which the first rule of criticism is never to push the meaning of an image too far, which means never giving it a grammatical or systematic meaning. The form similarly illustrates a deliberate fragmentation of poetic experience, in which the lack of explicit grammatical pattern is less noticeable. In the larger picture the different arts, having lost their particular critiques, tend to become one another's metaphors, as music becomes a metaphor for poetry in Mallarmé. In the age we are dealing with, Ruskin alone had any real sense of a critical workshop, and yet, as he was deeply involved with an aesthetic which continually relapses into propriety, and moral propriety at that, most of his direct influence on art was pernicious.

We shall never fully understand the nineteenth century until we realize how hampered its poets were by the lack of a coherent tradition of criticism which would have organized the language of poetic symbolism for them. This lack compelled many of them to turn to the symbolic systems available in their time to develop a poetic language out of them as best they might. Many conversions of poets to the Roman Catholic Church were obviously connected with the possibility of finding their language in the iconography of that church. Other poets turned like

Swinburne to a pagan mythology, still others, like Wagner and the early Yeats, to a national one; some worked out mythologies or metaphysics of their own, Poe's *Eureka* being an example only slightly less bizarre than Yeats's *Vision*.[6] Connected with the same situation was the growing influence of occult systems in poetic thought, especially in France and Germany. The occult tradition, stemming as it did partly from Swedenborg and St. Martin in the West and partly from an increasing flow of information about Hindu and Buddhist philosophies, was especially attractive because it seemed to hint more clearly at a universal language of symbolism. This tradition comes to its climax near the end of the century with Madame Blavatsky's huge *The Secret Doctrine*, after which the growth of the scientific study of comparative religion and psychoanalysis took the whole question out of the palsied hands of literary critics. Madame Blavatsky may well have been, like Paracelsus, a good deal of a charlatan. Henley said of her, "Of course she gets up fraudulent miracles, but a person of genius has to do something."[7] Yet *The Secret Doctrine*, whatever else it is, is a very remarkable essay on the morphology of symbols, and the charlatanism of its author is less a reflection on her than on the age that compelled her to express herself in such devious ways.

Most of the minor poets, however, followed the Romantic and aesthetic path, and this was true of the "Cheshire Cheese" group with whom Yeats was first associated. This group included Lionel Johnson and Ernest Dowson, with Wilde and Francis Thompson on the fringes, and their technique of relentless beautifying appears in much of Yeats's early work, notably *The Secret Rose* and the first version of *Oisin*. He is following the same models also in those poems of escape, like *The Land of Heart's Desire*, which are aesthetic anti-Victorian melodramas with beauty as hero and duty as villain. And in his transformation of a tough, humorous, and extravagant Irish mythology into nostalgic romance and worn-out Court of Love situations, as in *Deirdre*, we can see the poet to whom William Morris said, "You write my sort of poetry."[8] Many features of the aesthetic attitude, too, remained with Yeats all his life. He never lost a sense of the beautiful which was closely allied to a sense of propriety. He never became reconciled to the realistic explorers of art, never understood what Degas and Ibsen were driving at, and even in his *Last Poems*, when his practice is increasingly contradicting his theory, he is still talking about art in terms of conventional idealized forms, in which the intellectual symmetry of Pythagoras or St. Thomas grows into the organic symmetry of Phidias and Michelangelo.

And yet the deliberate pull of Yeats's genius away from the Cheshire Cheese is unmistakable. Everyone who has studied the early poems has barked his shins over the later revisions of them, and pondered the curiously tasteless blunders which Yeats occasionally makes in these revisions. Cheshire Cheese poetry, like Romantic poetry in general, only more so, depends on an evocative and intuitive approach to the significance of poetic imagery; hence it depends, not on things, but on qualifications of things, not on a pattern of images, but on a background of attributes. The emphasis in such poetry therefore falls on carefully composed epithets and radioactive adjectives. Now when Yeats, in *The Sorrow of Love*, changes "curd-pale moon" to "climbing moon,"[9] the change from the noisy to the quiet epithet throws a much greater weight on the noun, and indicates that "moon" has acquired a systematic and grammatical meaning in Yeats's poetry. Other changes are motivated by a desire to tighten up the syntax, which in a euphuistic poetry of epithets tends to become flaccid, because the connective tissues of sentences emphasize continuity of meaning rather than radiating suggestiveness. The reasons for Yeats's wanting to rewrite his early poems instead of merely writing them off are not clear, but one guess may be hazarded. Yeats is one of the growing poets: his technique, his ideas, his attitude to life, are in a constant state of revolution and metamorphosis. He belongs with Goethe and Beethoven, not with the artists who simply unfold, like Blake and Mozart. This phenomenon of metamorphic growth, which must surely have reached its limit in Picasso, seems to be comparatively new in the arts, and so a somewhat unwelcome characteristic to Yeats himself, who preferred the more traditional unfolding rhythm. Perhaps it too is a by-product of the breakdown of criticism. Dante unfolds into the *Divine Comedy* because the grammar of its symbolism is present in the culture of his time; Goethe grows into the second part of *Faust* because he has to rediscover the conventions of symbolism for himself. Yeats, then, may have been compelled to "grow" by a personal search for symbols, and if so, his revisions may signify a desire to force the developing body of his work into a single unfolding unit.

II

Yeats looked for a language of symbols in two obvious places: in the traditional mythology of Ireland, including both its heroic saga and its popular folklore, and in the occultism of his own day which had a doctrine in theosophy[10] and a discipline in spiritualism. The association between the occult and the native Irish is of long standing,[11] and Yeats's determination to have Blavatsky, Swedenborg, and F.W.H. Myers rubbing shoulders with Fionn and Cuchulain[12] is not due to a merely personal crochet. He looked in this mixture for a mythological pattern which, though not that of traditional Christianity, would be reconcilable with it, in the sense of being another illustration of the same total imaginative apprehension of reality. We are not surprised, then, to find Yeats forming counterparts to Christian ideas out of his own myths. His first important play was *The Countess Cathleen*, produced amid vociferous boos at the turn of the century. The story concerns a character who is really a female and Irish Jesus, redeeming the world by selling her soul to the devil and then cheating the devil by the purity of her nature, very much as in the pre-Anselm theory of the Atonement.[13] As Yeats calmly remarks in a note, the story illustrates "one of the supreme parables of the world,"[14] and it is perhaps not astonishing that some of his more orthodox contemporaries, however foolishly they may have expressed their objections, felt that all was not well. The dying king of the theatre has often proved a formidable rival of the dying god of the Church, and the audience may have realized more clearly than Yeats himself that something anti-Christian was taking shape, the traditional cult of Dionysus and Oedipus revived to overthrow that of Christ. We shall return to this in a moment.

The cult of the legend is apt to lead to archaism, to sentimentalizing a certain period in the past. If we believe with Swinburne that the world has grown gray with the breath of Christ [*Hymn to Proserpine*, l. 35], we are making a historical fall out of Christianity and a historical golden age out of the Classical era. Consequently we shall tend to think of the creative imagination as concerned with reviving the faded splendours of Classical culture, which will lead to a good deal of faking and antiquing when we come to deal directly with that culture. The same is true of the Romantic medievalism of Morris and Chesterton, where the fall is placed in the Renaissance or Reformation, as it is by Ruskin, who actually calls the Renaissance a fall in *The Stones of Venice*.[15] The late Romantic milieu of the early Yeats was full of historical myths of this kind and Yeats inherited a view of history which stems from a writer whom he consistently despised—Carlyle. The age of heroic action and imaginative splendour, according to this dialectic, died with the age of faith, and since then self-consciousness, Puritanism, rationalism, mercantilism, and all the spectral ghosts of abstraction have destroyed the individual and the supernatural at once, and left a thin, bloodless, envious, sedentary, sceptical, materialistic, *bourgeois* sissy as the typical man of our own age. In his early essay on Spenser, for instance, Yeats is so preoccupied with this myth that he hardly succeeds in getting anything intelligent said about Spenser; and he never outgrew it.[16] Ireland thus comes to mean for him among other things a region sheltered from the worst fury of abstraction and metropolitan materialism, where culture still has roots, where communal art forms like the drama are still possible, and where the brave man and the beautiful woman still command respect.

When Spengler's *Decline of the West* appeared after the First World War it owed its popularity to the fact that it gave both complete expression to a myth which had been widely accepted for a century and an intelligible account of that myth. Cultures were, Spengler said, organisms, subject to the organic rhythms of growth, maturation, and decay, and our present metropolitan civilization is a "Western" culture in the same stage of decline that Classical culture was in at the time of the Punic Wars. From 1917 on, Yeats was absorbed by his *Vision*, a complicated occult system based on a twenty-eight–phase lunar cycle and a system of double cones, which was dictated to him by spirits who worked through his wife's gift for automatic writing, and Spengler's was evidently one of the books these spirits read, or possibly wrote. Spengler does not postulate a *general* cyclic movement in history, but his tables of cultures use the names of the four seasons, and if our time is the "winter" of Western culture a returning spring is at any rate suggested. The *Vision* has an interesting passage on the influence of Frobenius on Spengler [258–60] which suggests, I think correctly, that a general cyclic theory was actually in Spengler's mind. In any case the general cycle is in Vico, one of Spengler's predecessors, who had also a more direct influence on Yeats through Croce, as he had on Joyce.

The *Vision* presents an astrological theory of history, according to which history moves alternately through "antithetical" and "primary" cycles, the former being subjective, aristocratic, violent, and antinomian, the latter objective, democratic, self-sacrificing, and theistic. Each cycle embraces two millennia. The Classical period from 2000 B.C. to the Christian era was an "antithetical" cycle, and our own Christian cycle is a "primary" one. A cycle is at its height halfway through, at the fifteenth phase, when it is also nearest the opposite pole. Thus the Christian era was at its most antithetical in a Byzantine period, in Yeats a quasi-historical fairyland reminding us of Lawrence's Etruscan myth. When

Byzantium fell its culture took root in the West, producing the antithetical Renaissance civilization which had always made so strong an appeal to Yeats. Castiglione's *Courtier*, the great textbook of antithetical discipline, was one of his favourite books, and he felt that his pantheon of Irish heroes, Burke being an obvious member, had a deep spiritual affinity with the proud and aristocratic ideals of the age of chivalry, of the noble horseman who casts a cold eye on the squalor of life and death alike, and leaves his servants to do his "living" for him, to quote the famous tag from *Axël* that Yeats kept repeating all his life.[17]

We are now in the last century of the Christian era, at the very nadir of primary abstraction, and are approaching the return of an antithetical age. Like Nietzsche, Yeats prophesies the time when Christianity will give place to an opposing culture of proud beauty and invincible violence, the reign of the Antichrist now slouching toward Bethlehem to be born, of the centaur whose humanity is inseparable from the brute, of Shelley's Demogorgon who awakens from the earth as the "mummy wheat" of the preceding Classical culture begins to sprout again [*On a Picture of a Black Centaur by Edmund Dulac*, l. 7; *Conjunctions*, l. 2]. The dove and the virgin are to go and Leda and the swan are to come back, in the form of the watchful and ironic heron of the Irish marshes and his fanatical priestess. The new birth is to be however a welter of blood and pain, full of the screams of the new birds of prey who replace the dove of peace, like the leaderless falcon turning in the widening gyre, and full of the hound voices of furies in pursuit of blood. Like Spengler, though for slightly different reasons, Yeats sees in the fascist cult of brutal violence something profoundly characteristic of our own time and of the immediate future.

He had to talk himself into this, for he saw fascism first as it really is, when Ireland was occupied by the Black and Tans.[18] Later, when Wyndham Lewis was publicizing Hitler and Pound Mussolini, and Eliot was issuing encyclicals to the faithful informing them that the people who think are now reading Charles Maurras, Yeats had a passing dalliance with the Irish Blue Shirts.[19] But there are other features of this new civilization more genuinely attractive to him. As in Lawrence, the Christ of the new era is to be a sexual rather than a virginal god, and in many of Yeats's last poems the sex act, again as in Lawrence, practically becomes the basis of a new fertility ritual. Yeats's preference of the heroic virtues to the Christian ones comes out, too, in his plays *Calvary* and *Resurrection*, where the historical Jesus appears as a rather stupefied and bemused figure, turning the wheel of time towards the surrender of human powers to a dehumanized God.

Yet his celebrations of a new birth are enforced, to use a technical term from the *Vision*, and all through his work runs the melancholy of the *Götterdämmerung*. It is a bitter Kilkenny cat-fight that Yeats makes out of history, the hero and the god, the young man and the old man, destroying one another as the gyres of history grind together on a common axis. Oedipus kills his father and Cuchulain his son, and the hero of *Purgatory* kills both as a sacrifice to his mother, his feelings for whom are a remarkably repulsive mixture of incest and necrophilia. In *On Baile's Strand*, Cuchulain after killing his son wanders mad into a world of chaos, like Lear on the heath. But unlike Lear he does not recover his humanity, and only a fool and a blind man are on the stage when the curtain falls. The fool is the last phase of the lunar cycle in the *Vision*, and the blind man I take to represent the dark moonless night that follows it, the phase 1 that ends and begins the cycle.[20]

In searching for a new language of symbols, then, Yeats was to a great extent simply fulfilling the Romantic tradition from which he had started, his final position being simply a more systematic expression of the Romanticism of Nietzsche and Lawrence. Even his Byzantium, the spiritual source of the fifteenth-century culture that was the model of the pre-Raphaelites, betrays its Romantic origin. His conception of the great man also falls well within the Romantic orbit. One of the fundamental conceptions of early Romantic mythology is that the revolutionary political situation of its time is a recreation of the rebellion of Prometheus, the Titanic ally of man, against an abstract tyranny represented by a sky-god. The sky-god is a metropolitan imperialist as his opponent is an earth-bound anarchist; hence the eruption of Promethean heroes in Romantic poetry, the Kossuths and Kościuszkos and Bolívars and Garibaldis who fight for the freedom of all humanity in a decentralized or nationalist form. This national aspect of the Romantic Messiah myth is especially congenial to countries like Ireland, or like Mexico as Lawrence saw it, where national and radical ideas are closely linked.

In Yeats the sky-god worshipper belongs to a rabble, a pack of curs snarling at the heels of an aloof and aristocratic hero representing the antithetical values of Irish culture, Parnell, for example, or Wilde, or Synge (though Synge is actually a primary type), or perhaps himself. In an aloof and aristocratic civilization such heroes would be leaders, but in a primary one like our own the noble animal is pulled down by the cur, and his heroism fulfils itself, like the setting sun, in the waning glamour of the lost cause. In the rewritten ending[21] of *The King's Threshold* the heroic poet dies having maintained his defiance both of the tyrant king and of the leprous sky-god, Blake's Jehovah, whom he incarnates, but with no other resolution of the conflict than his own death. And in Yeats's last play, *The Death of Cuchulain*, the ignoble and helpless collapse of his favourite hero will give some idea of the imaginative nihilism that the poet's mind finally reached. In Yeats as in most great Romantics the cult of the hero turns out to be a cult of the death of the hero, an Eroica symphony with a funeral march at its heart.

III

The language of early Romantic symbolism is a Kantian language, by which I do not mean that it is founded on Kant, but that it implies a popularized metaphysic with predominantly Kantian features. The Romantic poet splits reality into a world of experience and a world of perception, the former world, Kant's noumenon, being interpreted by poetry and the latter or phenomenal world being the only object of rational knowledge. The gap between rational and poetic knowledge accounts for the importance of suggestion and evocation in Romantic art, and for the distrust of didactic qualities. For the poet as well as the reasoner, however, nature is the vehicle of interpretation, hence nature to the poet is, as in Baudelaire's *Correspondances*, a shrine of mysterious oracles; and in the darkness of the noumenal world, where there must yet be direct contact with nature, we depend less on the expanded pupils of vision than on the twitching whiskers of feeling.

But as Romantic art develops, popularized Kant becomes popularized Schopenhauer, and as the phenomenal world is the object of consciousness, the noumenal world tends to become associated with the subconscious, a world of will underlying the world of idea. Such a world of will, being submoral and subintellectual, may from the point of view of consciousness be described as evil and brutal, hence Romantic art becomes infused with all the symbols of the "Romantic agony": sadism, Satanism, pessimism, the cults of the beauty of pain, the religion of blasphemy, the curse of genius, and, above all, the malignant grinning female, the Medusa, the Sphinx, La Gioconda, La Belle Dame sans Merci, or whatever her name may be, who presides over so many Romantic love affairs, and has affected Yeats's relations with the beautiful Maud Gonne. The world as will is, of course, an essential part of the order of nature, hence it is really a hyperphysical world, and in no sense a spiritual one.

The Romantic conception of the hyperphysical world appears in Freud's psychological myth of a subconscious libido and a censoring consciousness. Freud himself has noted the resemblance of his metaphysic to Schopenhauer's,[22] though not the significance of that resemblance. The influence of Freud on Yeats was indirect, but there was more of it than Yeats realized, some of it coming again through Lawrence. It is reflected in his choice of Oedipus as the symbol of the antithetical Christ about to be reborn. More immediate were the Darwinian developments of the same idea: a glance at Hardy is enough to show how easily Darwin and Schopenhauer fit together. The evolutionary dialectic destroyed the separateness of created forms, and reduced all life to a single interlocking family: even, one may say, and Samuel Butler did say,[23] a single superorganism, a known God who is also the world of will and life force. Thus in this conception of a hyperphysical world the old seventeenth-century doctrine of the *anima mundi*[24] is reabsorbed into literary symbolism, though of course with a very different context, and ideas of race memory and telepathy appear as by-products of it.

In Irish mythology there is a world of gods, the Tuatha Dé Danaan, who were driven underground by man long ago and now inhabit a world antipodal to our own, whose "Beltane" (May 1) is our "Samhain" (November 1); a world of fairies or Sidhe living in the Tir-na-n-Og, the country of eternal youth, where personality has much more of that aloof and aristocratic spirit that marks the antithetical, the Classical and Nietzschean, idea of the mingling of the divine and human, as opposed to the primary or Christian view of it. This myth of gods buried under the tyranny of consciousness, nature, and reason, in Joyce the Finnegan concealed under the blanket of HCE, corresponds to the Greek myth of the Titans, of whom Prometheus was one, and neatly fits the metaphysical myth we have been tracing. A remark of Blavatsky's that our world has another attached to it at the North Pole, forming a dumbbell-shaped cosmos, is quoted in *The Trembling of the Veil*.[25] And as, according to all Romantic presuppositions, the source of the mythopoeic faculty is the subconscious, Yeats endeavours, he tells us in *Per Amica Silentia Lunae*,[26] to sink his mind below consciousness into the stream of the *anima mundi*, in order to become a medium of a creative power which has its basis in the organically traditional, the genus or race, rather than the individual, and which will bring the ancestral gods and myths of that race out of a stream of racial memory.

In a rather silly play, *The Hour-Glass*, an exponent of sceptical materialism is told by an angel that he has to accept this antipodal fairy-world or else. He is given an hour to produce a believer in it, and an hourglass, from which the play takes its name, appears on the stage. This hourglass, the simplest possible emblem of time, is, though Yeats apparently has tried not to notice the fact, the fundamental symbol of his own *Vision*, the double gyre with time passing from one cone to the other, and reversing its position when the progress is complete. In this play, however, it represents the relation of the fairy-world to our own. This relation obviously cannot be historical, like the Classical–Christian double gyre; yet the fairies to some extent share a common time and space with us, for they live, like the spirits in Dante's Purgatory, on the other side of our own world, however we interpret the word "side."

We can understand where this world is if we think of spiritualism, which, in spite of its name, investigates on scientific principles a world not of spirits but of nature, a world where the conceptions of time, space, substance, and form appear still to operate, and which seems to be an essential part of the *anima mundi*. Thus the hourglass really represents the gyre of organic life which goes from birth to death, and then, invisible to the organic world but still within nature, from death to rebirth. The idea of rebirth is essential if the conception is to retain its hourglass figure. In the *Vision* two double gyres, the four faculties, make up the Spenglerian movement of visible time or history, and two others at right angles to them, the four principles, make up this other cycle of life, death, and rebirth. Yeats gives a detailed account of the half-dozen stages that the dead man goes through on his way to rebirth. One of them consists in reliving, sometimes for centuries, the passionate moments of one's life [226], as Swift lives through the loves of Stella and Vanessa in *The Words upon the Window Pane*. The chief function of this world however is expiatory or purgatorial, reminding us again of Dante's Purgatory, on top of which is the Garden of Eden from whence all seeds of life fall back into our world, though of course in Dante this cyclic movement does not affect human souls.

The idea of reincarnation came to Yeats from Oriental sources through theosophy. A much better account than he gives of the progress from death to rebirth is in *The Tibetan Book of the Dead*, as it is called in the

English translation, where the world inhabited is called Bardo.[27] In the Japanese Noh plays, too, which so deeply affected Yeats's dramatic technique, the Bardo-world is the normal setting. The contrast between the gentleness of the Japanese plays and the ferocity of Yeats is curious. In one of them, *Nishikigi*, two dead lovers are reunited by a priest; in Yeats's *Dreaming of the Bones* two Irish lovers must be forever separated because of their treachery to Ireland. *The Hour-Glass* is said to have frightened a man into attending mass for some weeks, and in *The Dreaming of the Bones* the evangelist again appears with a knuckle-duster, evidently prepared to adapt the old threats to a new priestcraft. In another Noh play, *Hagoromo*, a fairy, in order to get back a headdress a priest has stolen from her, teaches him the dance of the phases of the moon. She is a harmless and pretty creature, a Sally Rand[28] who has lost her fan, and it is hardly likely that her lessons had anything of the Procrustean pedantry of Yeats's garrulous and opinionated spooks. In a third, *Kamusaka*, a dead brigand is reconciled to the young man who kills him; in Yeats's *Purgatory* (an ironic title if ever there was one, though it is true that a similar irony is found in *Hamlet*), the double murder already mentioned is combined with the idea of an ancestral curse operating with irresistible power in both this life and the next.

Of course Yeats had read too much mysticism not to postulate a final deliverance from these gyres, a "thirteenth cone" or sphere of the pure present where time and space are transcended. But in spite of this theoretical escape, the *Vision* is a depressing book. Perhaps Yeats is right in believing that he had developed special faculties for communicating with some unknown but objective type of intelligence. But if his "spiritual instructors" have an objective existence, all one can say is that Yeats reminds us of those unfortunate wretches who turn themselves into walking crystal sets by getting manganese dust on their silver fillings, and are thus exposed to a cataract of ethereal drivel that most of us can, up to a point, shut out. Everything that is interesting and valuable in the *Vision* is directly connected with its subjective aspect. For one thing, it suggests what seems to me on other grounds highly probable: that a good deal of our thinking is elaborated from subconscious diagrams. This comes out not only in the geometrical figures we use, "a point of view," "a sphere of influence," "a line of action," and so on, but also in the spatial implications of the most ordinary particles: "beside," "between," "on the other hand," and the like. The *Vision* begins by dividing all human types among twenty-eight phases [105–84], and even this, for all its arbitrary straitjacketing, might have become the subconscious foundation of an art form like the one represented in Chaucer's company of twenty-nine pilgrims, who evidently seem to be something of a perfect circle of planetary and humorous temperament. It is a pity that the qualities which enabled Chaucer to transform his perfect circle into great art were qualities that Yeats felt he ought to distrust—characterization and comedy.

I have laid such stress on the *Vision* because it does give an account, for better or worse, of the symbolic structure which underlies Yeats's poetry from at least 1917 onward. And from what we have said about the Romantic nature of that poetry, it is clear that the *Vision* is among other things one of the grammars of Romantic symbolism. It presents a physical or phenomenal world apprehended by the consciousness and a hyperphysical world apprehended by the subconscious, and in so doing it preserves the original Romantic cult of nature which led to identifying spiritual and hyperphysical reality. It does not get, except in theory, to any order above that of nature or to any mode of consciousness in which the gap between subject and object is bridged. The poles of the *Vision*, phases 1 and 15, are a purely objective condition of self-abnegation and a purely subjective one of complete beauty respectively, both of which are superhuman incarnations. And as the fundamental process in nature as we ordinarily perceive it is the cycle, the *Vision* reflects a Romantic pessimism founded on a conception of cyclic fatality, such as we find in Lawrence, in Spengler, in Nietzsche, who also tried to formulate a doctrine of recurrence, and in many others.

It remains finally to compare Yeats's symbolism with that of some earlier poet who knew a greater tradition than the Romantic one, a comparison which may involve some rather technical points of symbolic grammar.

IV

Of pre-Romantic English poets, the two who had the most formative influence on Yeats were also the two greatest linguists of symbolism in English literature—Blake and Spenser. Yeats and his friend Ellis undertook an edition of Blake in 1889, which appeared in three volumes in 1893. They approached Blake however from the wrong side of Blavatsky: that is, they had already acquired a smattering of occultism, and they expected to find in Blake an occult system or secret doctrine instead of a poetic language. But what Blake needed most in 1889 was a clean, complete, and accurate text, and neither of his editors knew much about editing, nor could they read Blake's handwriting with consistent accuracy.[29] Again, Blake, though a very systematic thinker, sharply warns his reader against what he calls "mathematic form" [*On Virgil*, ll. 12, 14], and this includes all the Euclidean paraphernalia of diagrams, figures, tables of symbols, and the like, which inevitably appear when symbolism is treated as a dead language. The result is an overschematized commentary full of false symmetries, which, itself more difficult to understand than Blake, is still further confused by centrifugal expositions of Boehme and Swedenborg. As Yeats very truly remarks in the course of this work, "Any student of occultism . . . should especially notice Blake's association of black with darkness."[30] But Yeats tells us in his essay on Spenser that Spenser's symbols kept welling up again in his mind long after he had forgotten having met them in Spenser,[31] and it is not possible that the Blake whom he had studied so exhaustively can have failed to influence him in the same way.

Complex as Blake's symbolism is, it is at least uncluttered by all the chain-of-being apparatus of eons, emanations, world souls, and demiurges which Yeats inherited from the occult tradition. In Blake the world as mental reality, which is inside the human mind, and the world as physical appearance, which is outside it, present a contrast in which the latter is a shadow or reflection of the former, and thus a sort of parody or inversion of it. In the physical world man is an isolated individual centre of perception; in the spiritual world he is identical with a universal circumference of perception, a titanic man whom Blake calls Albion. In the physical world man is aware of an antithesis of divine Creator and human creature; in the spiritual world both of these disappear into the unity of God and Man which is Jesus. In the physical world man seems to be in the centre of a chain of being halfway between matter and God; in the spiritual world Man has pulled this chain into his own body, as Zeus threatens to do in the *Iliad* [bk. 8, ll. 22–32]. The real form of the mineral world is that of a city; that of the vegetable world a tree of life; that of the animal world a single body; and that of the human world the real presence of the God-Man Jesus: and all these forms are one form.

Hence in Blake's symbolism we find a series of antitheses expressing the contrast of the two worlds. There is a tree of life and a tree of mystery, a city of God and a city of destruction, and so on. This antithetical pattern is found in Yeats too. The two trees appear in the poem of that name, and hints of the two cities in the Byzantium poems, though in the famous

Sailing to Byzantium it is actually Shelley who takes the lead as Yeats stands in the tomb of Galla Placidia in Ravenna, a cavern of the type that Spengler calls the "prime symbol" of Byzantine culture,[32] and sees in the dome of many-coloured glass above him a reflection of something very like the New Testament city of living stones.

In order to pass from the physical world to the spiritual world in Blake, man's mind has to blow up and turn inside out: in more sober language, man has to use his imagination and train himself, with the help of works of art, to reverse the natural perspective. Blake's symbol for this turning inside out is the vortex, an image rather similar to Yeats's gyre, though the difference is more significant than the resemblance. In Yeats the spiritual life in this world is, again like Dante's Purgatory, a gigantic cone, a mountain or tower encircled by a winding stair spiralling upward through one life after another until it reaches an apex. The source of the idea is not Dante, but a childhood memory of smoke rising from the whirling spools of a "pern mill" so that it looked as though it were coming out of a burning mountain.[33] This cone image supplies the titles of two of Yeats's later books, *The Tower* and *The Winding Stair*.

But if we turn to the early work we find that the chief symbol there is not that of Dante's Purgatory, but that of his Paradise, the multifoliate rose, the flaming tree of life or transfigured cross which is the permanent spiritual form of eternity, the spiral which has lost its progressive or temporal shape. Evidently, then, the thought of passing from the apex of the purgatorial cone into eternity predominated in Yeats's mind up to about 1917, after which the idea of rebirth from the apex, which, as we have seen, is also hinted at in Dante, begins to displace it, though never completely.

Dante puts the Garden of Eden at the apex of his Purgatory, and both Blake and Spenser also have a lower Paradise in their symbolism, associated with the moon and with the Bardo world of the dead and unborn, which is yet a hyperphysical world and a part of the cyclic order of nature. Blake calls it Beulah and Spenser the Gardens of Adonis. As both poets are Protestants, neither gives it a purgatorial function, but in both it is a place of rebirth to some extent. Blake's Beulah, the more sharply realized conception, has two gates, a lower gate of rebirth and an upper gate of escape, and in Blake's symbolism the crisis or vortex of vision comes at the upper gate; Spenser's *Faerie Queene* ends with a similar crisis at the corresponding place, the sphere of the moon, in the *Cantos of Mutabilitie*.

Yeats's *Vision* is, from Blake's point of view, a vision of the physical world, which Blake calls Generation, and of a hyperphysical world or Beulah with the upper limit sealed off. His account of this cyclic world, as such, has much in common with Blake. Blake too has a historical cycle in which the young man and the old man, whom he calls Orc and Urizen, kill each other off, and a still larger cycle of death and rebirth which he presents in *The Mental Traveller*. Yeats's claim that his *Vision* explains *The Mental Traveller*, or more accurately expounds the same aspect of symbolism, is correct enough [213]. The two poets also make a very similar use of the moon and a lunar cycle of twenty-eight phases. Blake's lower and upper gates correspond to Yeats's phases 1 and 15, the phase of total surrender and the phase of complete beauty, both poets being indebted to Homer's cave of the nymphs [*Odyssey*, bk. 13, ll. 102–12], and Porphyry's commentary on it [*De Antro nympharum*], for the conception.

Now the thing that seals off the upper limit of Yeats's *Vision*, again from Blake's point of view, is the uncreative mental condition in which Yeats attained his vision. He stands at his own phase 1, in a state of passivity so abject that he cannot even write his own book, and sees his aloof and aristocratic ideal above him, impossibly remote and lost in the turning stars. An active mind would, on the contrary, be the circumference of such a vision, which would then be lifted up into the spiritual or mental world and so become a created or dramatic form, as Chaucer's circle of pilgrims does. The upper limit of the present *Vision*, phase 15, the perfect antithetical self, would in that case become the lower limit, the aspect in which the vision appears to the physical world. We should then have what Yeats calls the creative mind and the mask, the mental or imaginative reality of the vision itself and the external form in which it appears to others. And just as Blake, when he spoke of his poems as dictated, was talking about a state of the most active concentration, so Yeats never entrusted anything except the *Vision* to his spirits; everywhere else he is the active circumference and not the passive centre of what he is doing. We should expect, therefore, to find all the rest of his work turning on this conception of creative mind and mask, the opposition of mental reality and physical appearance, the latter, the mask, having all of that proud and aristocratic aloofness which Yeats so valued in the world of appearance.

This is certainly what we get in the essay *Per Amica Silentia Lunae*, the bottle out of which the smoky genie of the *Vision* emerged. There, Yeats sees the artist, as an ordinary or natural man in the physical world, using his creative genius to visualize a mode of existence as different as possible from the one forced on him by his own shortcomings. Thus Morris, a blundering and tactless man, creates an imaginative world of precise and exquisite taste, and the ferociously irascible Landor expresses himself in an art of languid gentleness. The artist searches for a mask, originally to conceal his natural self, but ultimately to reveal his imaginative self, the body of his art. The conception comes of course from drama, perhaps partly from Synge's subtle analysis of such a personal mask in *The Playboy of the Western World*, and it underlies Yeats's own dramatic theory. In his ideal play the audience is select, the actors masked, and the theme traditional and symbolic, so that the outward form of the drama preserves, like the Japanese play from which it is derived, the mask of the heroic and aristocratic virtues. But in this theory of drama the poet must find a common ground with his audience in conventional themes and symbols which emerge from traditions embedded in racial and subconscious memories. The true initiates in the audience, when they pierce the mask, find themselves within a mental form which is at once the dramatist's mind and the *anima mundi* of their common subconsciousness. It is clear, then, that the mask does not relate only to the poet's own life, to his quarrel with himself as Yeats says:[34] if the mask is to reveal anything effective, it must also be to some extent the mask of the age. Hence the great poets of every generation will be those who can identify a personal mask with a historical one.

Thus Romanticism, on Yeats's theory, would arise as a mask or countervision, an imaginative protest, against the industrial revolution, and end by being a form in which the culture of the industrial revolution expresses itself. Similarly with the general conspectus of Yeats's thought: modern Italian philosophy with the stress laid on its fascist elements, the Japanese *samurai* code, Spengler's theory of history,[35] Nietzsche's cult of the heroic superman, Irish nationalism, the personal influence of Ezra Pound, and the attempt to reach through the viscera deeper truths than reason knows. This also forms a mask or opposed vision for what to Yeats and the others seemed the essential shortcomings of our age: a cult of mediocre vulgarity and a lack of nobility and heroism. The Yeatsian drama is a curious example of this imaginative opposition. We remember its characteristics: an intimate impersonality, directly addressed to a small audience by the dramatist, full of traditional symbolism, stripped to the barest essentials of costume, scenery, and lighting, tragic or at least melancholy in tone, reflecting aristocratic ideals, and with all individuality of character subordinated to a unity of theme. This dramatic form is, point for point, the exact opposite of the chief dramatic form of our age, the movie, with its vast unselected audience and its comic or sentimental realistic spectacle-form which has no dramatist and in which the private lives of the actors are on the whole more interesting than the play they are in.

But there is one point that Yeats never gets clear in his mind, except in one play called *The Unicorn from the Stars*, and for that very reason we must get it clear. Once a poet finds his mask, and it becomes the outward form of his *creative* life, it loses all real connection with his natural life. Art is not autotherapy: Morris did not cure his tactlessness by writing romances about people with plenty of tact. The poet, by presenting us with a vision of nobility and heroism, detaches that vision from our ordinary lives. He thus works in a direction exactly opposite to that of the political leader who insists on trying to attach it, and so perverts its nature, as Fascism perverted the Nietzschean gospel of heroic virtue into the most monstrous negation of it that the world has ever seen. Siegfried may be a genuine enough heroic ideal in Wagner; but whenever anyone attempts to act like Siegfried, he instantly becomes an Alberich. The artist, of course, is always, like Narcissus, apt to become enamoured with the reflecting illusion of his own mask. Yeats himself did not possess every kind of high intelligence, and some affectations resulting from a pedantic streak in his make-up led him into a certain amount of social and political dithering. But for all that we should not be too quick to plaster a fascist label on Yeats's myth merely because a conspiracy of thugs happened to debase that myth instead of some other one. We come back here to our original point that poetic symbolism is language and not truth, a means of expression and not a body of doctrine, not something to look at but something to look and speak through, a dramatic mask. "The poet," said Sir Philip Sidney, "never affirmeth":[36] when he does affirm he not only ceases to be a poet, but is as likely to be wrong as anyone else.

Yeats began his career with a set of Romantic values and an intuition, recorded on the first page of his *Collected Poems*, that "words alone are certain good" (*The Song of the Happy Shepherd*, l. 10). As he went on, his Romantic values consolidated into a tragic mask, through which we hear voices full of terror, cruelty, and a dreadful beauty, voices of the malignant ghosts of the dead repeating their passionate crimes. No one can deny that a tragic and terrible mask is the obvious reflection of our age; nor is it an easy mask to wear, since it is not for those who take refuge either in moral outrage or in facile bravado. But as it begins to settle on the creator of lovely and fragile Victorian poetry a new exuberance comes into the voice. In Yeats's early poems we find neither youth nor age, but an after-dinner dream of both; in the *Last Poems* the lusts of youth break out beside the "old man's eagle mind" flying far above the conflicts of illusion [*An Acre of Grass*, l. 24]. For while illusion enslaves, vision emancipates, and even the thought of death in a dying world seems a buoyant thought, a defiant upstream leap of the elderly salmon returning to the place of seed.

In the early play *The King's Threshold* a poet goes on a hunger strike at a king's court because he is excluded from the high table where the bishops and councillors sit. But the issue is not fairly presented: the poet does not want mere equality with others; he wants to be recognized as himself the true king, the creator of social values whose praise of gold inspires others to strut about under gold crowns. Like Milton's Samson, or the Jesus of whom Samson was a prototype, he is a tragic hero to his followers and the buffoon of a Philistine carnival; yet the tragedy ends in triumph and the carnival in confusion. In one version the king admits that he has usurped the poet's title and surrenders; in another the poet starves;[37] but in both versions what the poet says is:

> And I would have all know that when all falls
> In ruin, poetry calls out in joy,
> Being the scattering hand, the bursting pod,
> The victim's joy among the holy flame,
> God's laughter at the shattering of the world. [ll. 185–9]

24
The Betjeman Brand

December 1947

A review of John Betjeman, Slick But Not Streamlined: Poems and Short Pieces, *selected and with an introduction by W.H. Auden (Garden City, N.Y.: Doubleday, 1947). From* Poetry: A Magazine of Verse, *71 (December 1947): 162–5. Reprinted in* Poetry: A Magazine of Verse, *121 (October 1972): 48–50.*

This book introduces to American readers the light verse of John Betjeman, now something of a cult in England, along with a few prose pieces. Though its origins go back to the Middle Ages, when practically all secular verse was light, light verse did not clearly emerge as a separate type until the beginning of the nineteenth century. Since then, it has been handicapped by a persistent association with parody, and by some absurd fashions, notably the extensive corseting into ballades and sestinas which followed Austin Dobson. Mr. Auden, who introduces the book, has already performed a major service to criticism by isolating and identifying the type and its traditions in his *The Oxford Book of Light Verse*, and this anthology has given a new significance to many aspects of poetry and a new importance to several poets, Skelton, for example.

Mr. Betjeman is straight in the middle of the nineteenth-century light verse tradition. One can see the influence of Praed and Clough, of *The Ingoldsby Legends* and the *Corn-Law Rhymes*, and sometimes (as in the poem on Oscar Wilde [*The Arrest of Oscar Wilde at the Cadogan Hotel*]) of the vast corpus of naive verse which sporadically gets into provincial newspapers. His prose pieces show him to be the type of writer from whom one would expect light verse. He is a lover of Oxford and of Oxford's intensely localized brand of humour; he has a minute knowledge of English building, especially churches, which is both historical and antiquarian, and of a remarkably catholic range; and he seems to be, like so many Oxonians, a lover of tradition in religion and society who struggles hard to keep his Toryism urbane and yet becomes occasionally querulous when vulgarity pushes him too hard. In short, a less sectarian Belloc,[1] a less pedantic C.S. Lewis. His fondness for place names and his sympathy with all aspects of English life, including bank-holiday crowds and the industrial cities of the Midlands, help to document a concrete and witty observation of his country.

Light verse offers many advantages: one can experiment with triple rhythms and double rhymes that would wreck a "serious" poem; one can relapse into doggerel and get away with it; and one can make an incongruous image an asset instead of a liability. One can also digest even the most vulgar details of life without worrying about literary tact. On the other hand, one has to preserve a very delicate balance of tone, for light verse has its special kind of bathos. The smallest error of taste will make satire sound cheap and humour glib, and if one leans back too far to avoid this, there is the opposite danger of sentimentality. In this meditation of a lady in Westminster Abbey—

Gracious Lord, oh bomb the Germans.
  Spare their women for Thy Sake,
And if that is not too easy
  We will pardon Thy Mistake.
But, gracious Lord, whate'er shall be,
Don't let anyone bomb me. [*In Westminster Abbey*, ll. 7–12]

—the balance of tone is perfect, and the reader is at once detached from and identified with this vision of a frightened and selfish humanity. Mr. Betjeman cannot keep this up indefinitely: perhaps no one could. But he comes near to sustaining it in a few poems: *Senex*, *Margate*, *Calvinistic Evensong*, and an extraordinary *tour de force* called *Group Life: Letchworth* are among them. It is interesting to notice, too, that, like many other writers of light verse, Mr. Betjeman's most striking effects are in the grotesque and macabre, where the contrast of tone and subject gives the latter the eeriness it requires. Take this from an elegy on a deaf man:

And when he could not hear me speak
  He smiled and looked so wise

That now I do not like to think
  Of maggots in his eyes. [*On a Portrait of a Deaf Man*, ll. 13–16]

Or this allegorical description of the lusts of the flesh:

Get down from me! I thunder there
  You spaniels! Shut your jaws!
Your teeth are stuffed with underwear,
Suspenders torn asunder there
  And buttocks in your paws! [*Senex*, ll. 21–5]

And if his total achievement is rather slight in spite of all his skill, perhaps that is because his academic delight in the passing show somehow lacks dynamic: the pleasure in recording experience seems part of an unwillingness to attempt to transform it.

25

Edith Sitwell, *The Shadow of Cain*

January 1948

Review of Edith Sitwell, The Shadow of Cain *(London: John Lehmann, 1947). From* Canadian Forum, *27 (January 1948): 238.*

When the war began one of the many things that no one could have predicted to happen at the end of it was Edith Sitwell's latest poetry. By 1940 every critic had more or less buried the playgirl of roller-coaster rhythms and snap-the-whip imagery as a curious example of what they did in the 1920s. One unlucky critic said so publicly, and the outraged Edith sued for libel, and won.[1] Silly as that libel suit was, she was right. She is now a major poet, a necessary part of one's literary education and current reading alike,[2] and this poem is a beautiful and erudite proof of the fact.

26

For Tory and Leftist

March 1948

A review of a translation of Virgil's Georgics, *by Cecil Day Lewis (New York: Oxford University Press, 1947). From* Poetry: A Magazine of Verse, *71 (March 1948): 337–8.*

One thinks of Max Beerbohm's famous portrait of the "statesman of olden time, making without wish for emolument a flat but faithful translation of the *Georgics*, in English hexameters."[1] And it is not perhaps hard to see why the honourable gentleman should be doing this. He looks like a simple-minded eighteenth-century Tory, and, if he has not exactly a poetic ear, great poetry has made something of the direct impact on him that it often does make on simple people, especially when they can attach its subject to their own experience. The attachment here is clear enough: as a landowner, he would naturally think of the tranquillity, the leisure (for him), and the paternal social organization of rural life as the mainstay of all the civilized values of his age. So Virgil's "O fortunatos nimium sua si bona norint agricolas"[2] would seem to him in the words of the elegant Mr. Pope, what oft was thought, but ne'er so well expressed.

Mr. Day Lewis is a professional writer, and one hopes that he would never write anything without at least a wish for emolument. His version is not flat, and it is not too faithful to be unidiomatic. It is based on a hexameter line, but an English hexameter of six accented beats, with a musical variability of syllables. For the rest, he is a twentieth-century intellectual and his political background is left-wing. If it were not for a remark in the preface about his hope for a more decentralized economy springing up around smaller centres [xi], one would wonder what the point of contact with Max Beerbohm's statesman is. An English poet who turns in disgust from the industry, commerce, and war that have insulted and befouled his countryside for a century finds himself facing the pre-industrial Tory, who would also have hated these things, though in apprehension rather than retrospect. And both of them find their way thereby back to Virgil, who saw in the small farm and an imaginative devotion to the land and its gods a principle of moral virtue and economic stability that might yet do something to arrest the luxurious decline of Rome.

Nothing is easier than to compare a translation to its disadvantage with the original, and about all that need be said on this point is that Mr. Lewis is accurate and unpretentious, and makes no effort to translate the untranslatable. Virgil writes so easily that there is something of a *tour de force* in the way that he raises a technical discussion of farming into magnificent and complex Latinity. Mr. Lewis has very sensibly followed the subject rather than the treatment, and as an English poem his translation has much in common with the best of the English bucolic school: with Shanks, Blunden,[3] Edward Thomas, and Victoria Sackville-West's *The Land*.

27
Virginia Woolf

March 1948

Review of Virginia Woolf, The Moment and Other Essays *(London: Hogarth Press, 1948). From* Canadian Forum, *27 (March 1948): 284–5.*

This book (an attractive little book, with its jacket design by the author's sister Vanessa Bell) is a collection of miscellaneous literary essays, including a number of reviews, consisting of both published and unpublished material gathered together after the author's death. It forms a pendant, along with a previous collection called *The Death of the Moth*, to the two well-known volumes *The Common Reader*.[1] Like its predecessors, it makes very agreeable reading, but indicates that Virginia Woolf was as minor a figure in criticism as she was a major one in the novel. She was a great novelist, with a conscience about form and structure more Continental than English. For the English novel, as she occasionally complains, has usually been rather like one of the county houses it so often describes [103–4]: rambling in structure, provincial in setting, showing a good deal of improvising in the building, full of drafts caused by loose ends of plot and loopholes in motivation, and with the less mentionable aspects of existence difficult of access yet marked by a pervasive smell. Virginia Woolf's novels looked "experimental," not because she was trying stunts but because she went all out for whatever novel she was writing, determined not to let it go until every detail had been hammered into the right shape and place. So although words like "subtlety" and "delicacy" spring to mind first in connection with her, these qualities are, as they should be, the results of a great imaginative energy and vigorous craftsmanship.

But in these essays the subtlety and delicacy exist by themselves, and so, one is rather disconcerted to note, they often have exactly the qualities that a reader who disliked her novels would expect to find. Like her one bad novel, *Orlando*, they suffer from a self-conscious delicacy of perception. There is an arch female cuteness and an irritating female trick of avoiding the straight abstract line of argument in order to dither with a metaphor. "That fiction is a lady, and a lady who has somehow got herself into trouble, is a thought that must often have struck her admirers. Many gallant gentlemen have ridden to her rescue, chief among them Sir Walter Raleigh and Mr. Percy Lubbock" [89]. And so on. Her nostalgia for tradition often seems to develop a lurking assumption that reactionary social views are somehow the most elegant ones. Her intelligence expresses itself in a languorous rhythm, like a shy but highly cultivated woman at tea who fills the air with bright chatter while wishing she could be doing something else.

Yet it is very pleasant to read her affectionate tribute to Roger Fry and her tolerant sketch of the dismal Edmund Gosse, to hear her speak with quiet authority about the novel and make such sensitive and pointed comments about Scott, Congreve, Dickens, and Lawrence, and to follow her through her reviews of the gossipy memoirs and diaries she loved so much, the books that bring the sounds and smells and human passions of a dead age back to life. Being a novelist herself, she is not a wholly trustworthy critic of other novelists, but she makes up for this by some exceptional insights—she has, for example, a curious ability to put her finger on any sense of personal insecurity on the novelist's part. As she herself remarks in another connection, "Here we have intuitions rather than facts—the lights and shades that come after books are read, the general shifting surface of a large expanse of print" [108].

28

Four Short Reviews

July 1949

Brief reviews of Percy Coates, The World is Wide Enough *(London: John Lehmann, 1949); Tanya Matthews,* Russian Child and Russian Wife *(London: Victor Gallancz, 1949); Holland M. Smith,* Coral and Brass *(New York: Scribner's, 1949); and Raymond F. Mikesell and Hollis B. Chenery,* Arabian Oil *(Chapel Hill: University of North Carolina Press, 1949). From* Canadian Forum, *29 (July 1949): 96.*

Russian Child and Russian Wife

Memoirs of a girl born about the time of the Revolution, who lived in Russia until recently, when a marriage to an English correspondent enabled her to get out of the country. The book is nonpolitical, and concentrates on the standard nostalgic material of memoirs. But in the background is a lumbering and fumbling bureaucracy which gradually changes as the book proceeds from well-meaning Marxist pedantry to an intolerable opportunistic tyranny.

The World is Wide Enough

An excellently written, and consequently very readable, story of two Yorkshire waifs who live the life of what in America would be called hoboes, until their ability to box gets them into the professional ring. The narrative is well paced and the bitter Midland town scenes very vivid and concrete. Recommended.

Arabian Oil

The blurb says: "This factual and technical study not only provides useful information regarding the technical, legal, and economic problems of oil recovery in the Middle East, but it also presents a significant case study of a foreign investment and its relation to U.S. foreign economic policy."[1] It is hardly possible for a short notice to improve on the comprehensiveness and accuracy of that statement.

Coral and Brass

The "brass" of the title refers to the General of Marines who writes his memoirs of the Pacific campaign with the aid of a ghost writer.[2] The main emphasis is on the contribution made by the Marines, and there are occasional criticisms of other services and of the administration for lack of support. The story is told with vigour and what the General has to say should interest anyone interested in the tactical aspect of the Pacific War.

29

Ezra Pound

September 1949

From Canadian Forum, *29 (September 1949): 125, where it was published under the heading "To Define True Madness."*

A lively controversy has been going on in the press over an award for poetry made recently to a volume of Ezra Pound's *Cantos*. Pound is American by birth, supported the Mussolini regime actively until his capture by American troops, and was brought back to face a charge of treason, escaping through a plea of insanity.[1] Both the charge and the plea are technically correct, but as a traitor Pound was never in the class of Lord Haw-Haw or Axis Sally,[2] and it would be rather inconsistent to execute him at the same time that such grotesquely indulgent sentences are being given to the gorillas in the Nazi concentration camps.

Up to about 1930 Pound was one of the freshest and most original of contemporary poets. His earlier poetry can be found in a New Directions volume called *Personae*, and, though as a poetic achievement it hardly ranks with the work of Eliot or Yeats or Auden or Edith Sitwell, it is still impressive enough. He was doubtless always something of a charlatan, but his personal influence on and encouragement of his contemporaries was very considerable, and both Yeats and Eliot have gone out of their way to express their appreciation of it.[3] His scholarly and cultural interests, however cranky and erratic, brought some exotic Provençal and Chinese flavours not only into his own poetry but into the culture of his time. Then, at what should have been the height of his powers, he undertook a vast, erudite, encyclopedic epic project, a poetic vision of all history in a hundred cantos which would do for his own time what Dante had done for the Middle Ages. The project was no doubt far beyond his powers even when he began it, but the earlier *Cantos* are full of great beauty and charm.

But the real world, to Pound, was always a museum of antiquities, and writing a great epic demands a far more direct contact with contemporary life than he was willing to make. Even at their best the *Cantos* are brittle and factitious, moments of rapturous contact with beauty constantly interrupted by a peevish resentment against the world of the present that keeps butting in. In the later *Cantos* the resentment becomes shrill and hysterical, the poet screaming abuse at everything he hates, or thinks he hates, apparently convinced that vigorous language is the same thing as violent language. The attitude is almost a parody of the American expatriate fleeing the intolerable vulgarity of democracy and ready to support any European government that seems likely to make the trains run on time or encourage servants and tradesmen to be more civil and obedient. At their worst, the *Cantos* are really mad, the mutterings of free association followed by the shouting of obscenities. It is difficult to see why anyone would want to pin a blue ribbon on the last set. But the tragedy of Pound—for it is a real tragedy—throws a sharp and hard light on the cultural malaise of our time. The war against fascism is not over, but one phase of it is over—the phase in which dangerous enemies are those who explicitly call themselves Fascists. Democracy is surely strong enough to consider such a case as Pound's, neither with fear and anger nor with perverse admiration, but simply with a desire to know what drove him mad. The true diagnosis lies far below either a complacent or a sentimental verdict.

30
George Orwell

March 1950

Unsigned editorial from Canadian Forum, *29 (March 1950): 265–6. Reprinted in* RW, *399–401.*

George Orwell, whose real name was Eric Blair, died recently of tuberculosis while still in his forties. His background was public-school upper-middle-class society—or, at any rate, a career in that class was certainly open to him. He saw service with the Imperial army in Burma, and was not encouraged by what he saw of imperialism. In politics he drifted far to the left of Communism, and took part in the Spanish war in an anarchist brigade. He was thus an anti-Stalinist revolutionary, but there was never anything in him of the "god that failed"[1] bluster of the Communist converts who despise those who have never been taken in by Communism almost as much as they do the Communists.

His earlier books, which have been recently republished, are notable for a certain candid simplicity rather than for any more distinctive qualities. A savage story with a Burmese setting is one of them, and a straightforward account of what it feels like to be a hobo in London and Paris is another. He began to become well known with a brilliant collection of critical essays, *Dickens, Dali and Others,* where he showed ability as a kind of literary sociologist. He saw clearly how art and literature grow out of human life; he saw the importance of both popular and highbrow art, and he understood how a split between popularity and good taste is unhealthy for both. Then came his brilliant satire on Russia, *Animal Farm,* with its wonderful touches of wit like the slogan, "All men are equal, but some are more equal than others."[2] This satire gave him fame, but his essential point, that the Stalinist tyranny is a mere continuation of the tsarist one, is made a little too neatly, and one feels that what he really has to say cannot be contained within pure satire.

His last book, *1984*, was written under the shadow of death. There was on the one hand a compulsion to finish it; on the other, perhaps, a feeling that after flinging a book like this into the public face anything further would be an anticlimax. For *1984* is a very wonderful novel, one of the greatest the twentieth century has yet produced, and, again, great by reason of its utter simplicity. He wrote the novel that so many of us have wanted to write or see written, simply because he had the courage to look the present world straight in the face and the ability to set down what he saw there without panic or any desire to moralize. He had written the *Inferno* of the twentieth century, and however inferior he may be to Dante in all literary respects, he excels him in one point: his hell is a real hell, a dreadful state of torment that could last forever and yet is potentially here now.

It is a great mistake to read the book as entirely, or even primarily, a satire on Russian Communism. Communist features fill the foreground of the book, and Communism takes its rightful place in the world's contemporary evil, which is well up front. But what Orwell had the courage to see is that, as Communism is simply the entrenched tyranny of a small ruling class, its interests are identical with those forces within the democracies which make for oligarchic dictatorship. To agree with Russia not to use atomic bombs could under certain circumstances be worse than blowing the world to pieces, and for good. That would only be death, and Orwell is talking about hell. The terrible vision he gives of the world divided into three great powers, none able or willing to conquer one another, engaged in a form of permanent war just bad enough to cause misery and yet not bad enough ever to end that misery—that is the threat we have to look in the face first, as Dante had to sound the depths of evil and treachery before he could reach the mountain of improvement.

31

Novels on Several Occasions

Winter 1950–51

Review of Ernest Hemingway, Across the River and Into the Trees *(New York: Scribner's, 1950); Budd Schulberg,* The Disenchanted *(New York: Random House, 1950); William Goyen,* The House of Breath *(New York: Random House, 1950); Alberto Moravia,* Two Adolescents *(New York: Farrar, Straus, 1950); Charles Williams,* Shadows of Ecstasy *(New York: Pellegrini & Cudahy, 1950); Marcel Aymé,* The Barkeep of Blémont *(New York: Harper, 1950?); and C. Virgil Gheorghiu,* The Twenty-Fifth Hour *(New York: Harper, 1950). From* Hudson Review, *3 (Winter 1950–51): 611–19. Reprinted in* NFCL, *207–18; partially reprinted in* Twentieth-Century Literary Criticism, *ed. Dennis Poupard (Detroit: Gale Research, 1983), 488. Paragraphs on Hemingway reprinted in* Ernest Hemingway: The Critical Reception, *ed. Robert O. Stephens (np: Burt Franklin, 1977), 333; and in* Hemingway: The Critical Heritage *(London: Routledge & Kegan Paul, 1982), 393–5.*

The theme of *Across the River and Into the Trees* is death in Venice, with Colonel Cantwell, a reduced brigadier and a "beat-up old bastard" [180], as a military counterpart to Mann's beat-up old novelist. The colonel is a lonely man. Around him is an impersonal hatred directed, like a salute, at his uniform; behind him is the wreck of a marriage and of the career of a good professional soldier; in front of him is his next and last heart attack. He meets all this with a compelling dignity, and there is pathos in his struggles to control his temper, to be "kind," and to avoid boring other people with his bitterness. It is not that he wants to be liked, but that he senses the rejection of humanity which is involved in every real breakdown of human contact. He has reached the rank in the army at which his superior officers give their orders in terms of a hideous "big picture" [237] in which strategy is based on politics and publicity stunts instead of on fighting. He cannot cope with this because he cannot relate it to his job of leading men into battle; and when the war is over, he feels his kinship with those who have been maimed and victimized by war, as he knows that no one has profited from it except profiteers. But he has gone far past the stage at which the word "failure" means anything to him. His approaching death gives a bitter intensity to the ordinary events of his life: to the food and drink of his last meals, to his last look at the violated beauty of Italy, and, above all, to his love for a nineteen-year-old Contessa who comes to him, a dream girl out of a dream city, to offer him an unconditional devotion. Everything that remains for him in life he accepts, simply and without question. The girl loves him, we are told, because he is never "sad": there is no self-pity which rejects life by clinging to the ego. On the contrary, he has some tenderness for braggarts and charlatans who respond to the exuberance in life, and if there is a desire that still holds him, it is for children to continue his own life, which may be one reason why he calls the Contessa "daughter." It is a great theme, and in the hands of someone competent to deal with it—say Ernest Hemingway—it might have been a long short story of overwhelming power.

It is pleasant to dwell on the idea and postpone the fact. In the opening scene and in the curt description of the colonel's death, there is something of the old Hemingway grip. In between, however, the story lies around in bits and pieces, with no serious effort to articulate it. The colonel is entitled to rancorous prejudice—the reader doesn't expect him to be a Buddhist sage, and in his political and military reflections one wouldn't mind the clichés of a commonplace grouch if they built up to something bigger, but they don't. We expect to find the love scenes stripped of eloquence, but not to encounter a cloying singsong of "I love you truly" and a repetitiousness that looks like padding. The role of the Contessa is that of a more attractive version of a deferential yes-man. The colonel wanders in an empty limbo between a dead and an unborn world, at no point related to other human beings in a way that would give his story any representative importance. As far as anyone can be, he is an island entire of itself.

This last, of course, is part of Hemingway's point. His story is intended to be a study in isolation, of how the standards of a decent soldier are betrayed by modern war. The colonel is not a writer, and the things that are happening to him he assumes to be incommunicable, because he has found them so. And he dominates the book so much that something of his distrust of communication seems to have leaked into the author and paralysed his will to write. In this kind of story the hero's loneliness must be compensated for by the author's desire to tell the story and, to adopt one of his own cadences, tell it truly. But this involves the total detachment of author from character which comes when sympathy and insight are informed by professional skill. This detachment has not been reached, and the book remains technically on the amateurish level in which the most articulate character sounds like a mouthpiece for the author. Hence all the self-pity and egotism which have been thrown out the door reappear in the windows between the lines. The reader is practically compelled to read the story the wrong way, and the result is a continuous sense of embarrassment.

Budd Schulberg's *The Disenchanted* adopts a scheme not unlike Hemingway's. The story is the final macabre souse of an American novelist, Manley Halliday, fabulously rich and successful in the 1920s, now (the book is dated around 1938, so that the bender decade is recollected, not in tranquility, but during the hangover) ridden by debts, compulsive memories, a wrecked wife, diabetes, alcoholism, neglect, and self-neglect. The role of Hemingway's heroine is played by a younger writer, Shed Stearns, who is of the Depression generation, and whose harassed solicitude is less uncritical than hers and more touching. Instead of the big picture of strategy we have the big pictures of Hollywood, where a producer named Victor Milgrim is giving the ex-genius his last chance.

That the prototype of Halliday is Scott Fitzgerald is not, to put it mildly, much of a secret, but the author has begun with a quotation from Henry James asking us not to make too much of this. I myself forgot it entirely as soon as I recognized in Schulberg's wistful, genteel bum the outlines of a more familiar figure. All the well-loved conventions follow in his wake. The same dapper-seedy, timid-jaunty appearance; the same juxtaposition of luscious dreams (here presented as memories of a wonderful past that we can't quite believe in) and a miserable reality; the same crazy plot that lurches from one nightmare to another until it explodes in a crescendo of slapstick and tragedy. The only time Halliday reveals a mind superior to that of any other educated drunk is when he makes some acute remarks on Chaplin films. No, the book is far closer to *City Lights* than to *The Great Gatsby*.

Halliday rose to success by brilliant satire on the phony society he saw around him. It was not important, as Stearns at first thought, that he should understand the real significance of his satire. It was important that he should detach himself from the society he described, that in his success he should consistently bite the hands that fed him, which seems to be the only personal rule imposed by art on the artist. Failing in this, he became, as Blake says, what he beheld,[1] and was swept into a noisy and vulgar inferno where he got a hot glare of publicity but never any privacy. The society happened to be the America of the 1920s, but there is nothing peculiar to that age about the situation itself, as the author comes near to suggesting—the second postwar era's attitude to the first occasionally gets a shade prissy. Henry James long before had shown how society sits like a fumbling, witless sea anemone waiting for someone with genius, beauty, freshness, or whatever else permits free movement to come within reach of its tentacles. It caught Halliday, and here the Chaplin parallel breaks down. Halliday retains his dignity because he makes society look as ridiculous as himself. But not, as in Chaplin, far more so—he has lost his innocence, as the Chaplin hero never does, and the best he gets with society is a split decision.[2]

The story is well written in spite of its unvarying *martellato* style, and the dialogue—a soft gilding of wit over a paste of wisecracks—is admirable. Yet, to make it more than a *Lost Weekend* with cultural overtones, Halliday needs to be tragic rather than pathetic, and he has to be heroic to be tragic. The heroic dimension in him could come only from his genius: we should see not only the destruction of the man, but the blinding of the vision that was presumably in the man. The discovery that his final bit of writing is a masterpiece sounds like a contribution to the plot by Victor Milgrim—again, I am taking the story as it stands and not as fictional biography. Halliday's wife is forever trying to translate the *Saison en enfer*, and somewhere in his flashbacks (called "Old Business," which I dislike) we should have caught a glimpse of the demon whispering into his ear those fatal, lying words that end "dérèglement de tous les sens."[3]

William Goyen's *The House of Breath*, a first novel, begins with a rather dismaying rush of words and some self-conscious mannerisms, notably a kind of nudging parenthesis, but it soon settles down and becomes a style of some power as well as readability. The title refers to a house in an East Texas village, the past life of which is evoked, partly through a narrator who spent his boyhood there, and partly through the reflective monologues of the people who have lived in it. The pervading tone of the book is thus one of nostalgic reminiscence. This would normally be discouraging, because the emotional urgency of nostalgia is so often mistaken for inspiration, and yet it is one of the hardest moods to communicate. But here is one author who has boldly faced material that dozens of writers have failed with and made something of it. There is some fine and sensitive description of the woods and the river and the farm animals and the changing seasons, and an intricate but clearly developed pattern of themes and symbols is built up somewhat after the manner of Virginia Woolf. The house is thought of as haunted by its memories, and the monologues are extracted from it as though Yeats were right, and it was possible to sink into an *anima mundi* where one could tune in on a psychic ether of memory and points of brooding return. It sounds ectoplasmic, but it has been skilfully done, and when we finish this remarkable book we have a panorama of a dozen interconnected and brilliantly summarized lives.

The author has an acute ear for the slurred elisions, agglutinative syntax, and somnolent rhythms of vernacular speech, and he is particularly successful with females and the female mood of querulous patience. He has also discovered that when East Texas lifts up its voice in complaint the result is very suggestive of a banshee wail, which adds point to his scheme. He appears to be a little afraid that his characters will not get enough sympathy from the reader unless he insists on their claims to it. At any rate his genuine humour seems a bit furtive and some of his symbolism is over-italicized—the village the house is in is called Charity, for instance, which evidently means something, and there are other traces of portentousness. But these are trifles in a book that gets an extraordinary amount said in its 180 pages, a book which, if it remains something of a stunt, is an outstandingly clever and successful one.

Each of Moravia's stories of Italian schoolboys deserves the higher compliment of being called a story that you can put down. One pursues a clumsy and faked narrative as one gets through a crowd on a sidewalk, in haste to be rid of it—a point often overlooked by those who sit up all night over mystery stories. Moravia fits normal life: one can drop his Agostino or Luca anywhere with a coherent structure already in one's mind, secure in the writer's ability to continue it properly. Nothing happens to Agostino except that boredom, bad company, and ambiguous feelings toward his widowed mother fill him with a typically adolescent misery. Nothing happens to Luca except that he gets sick and recovers, his nurse climbing into his bed during his convalescence. The virtuosity of the born storyteller then goes to work. The story of Luca takes us deep into the death wish that caused his illness, and shows how acts that outwardly seem only perverse or petulant really belong to an inner sacrificial drama. And as Luca recovers, the archetypal significance of what he has done takes shape. His story is a humble but genuine example of what the great religions are talking about: of losing one's life to find it, of gaining charity through renunciation, of becoming free by cutting oneself loose from everything that attaches and motivates. Symbols, ordinarily as hard to make convincing in fiction as jokes, drop into the right places, from the very adroit use of the *Purgatorio* to the final sentence about a train coming out of a tunnel into daylight. It is characteristic of such a story that a quiet word like "nausea" or "absurdity" (neither likely to be the invention of the unobtrusive translator), simply because it is the right word for its context, can bring more of what Sartre and Camus respectively are trying to say into focus than a good many pages of Sartre's metaphysics.

In the background of Moravia's stories is a solid sense of bourgeois Italian society, its values, its folklore, and its class conflicts. There is something oddly old-fashioned about this solidity: it is like finding good carpentry and seasoned lumber in a flossy new bungalow, and one feels that the swaying Venetian backdrops of Hemingway or the dissolving pan shots of Schulberg are unfortunately more up to date. Moravia still clings in technique to the old traditions of novel writing in which those who had a sense of established society, like Austen and Dickens and Trollope, wrote with authority in the centre of the tradition, while those who lacked it, like Scott and Lytton and Wilkie Collins, had to depend on plot formulas for support. This kind of novel is disappearing with the society that produced it, and a new approach has become necessary. Society is not a containing unit for characters any more: it is too nomadic and too much an open arena of clashing personalities and ideologies. Even in *The House of Breath* the emphasis is thrown on the centrifugal movement away from the community. One can see the new plot formulas of the successors of Lytton and Collins shaping up in modern middlebrow thrillers, and the question naturally arises of what central vision has replaced the social vision of Austen and Trollope.

My guess is that it is a vision based on the sense of moral autonomy. The plot formulas of today's thrillers are solutions to problems. Why did A murder B? Because of narcissist conflicts resulting from a mother fixation—psychological thriller. Because the romanticism of a privileged class led him to make a scapegoat of a personal enemy—class-conscious thriller. Because the act of sin breaks out of the intolerable suspense of moral indifference—theological thriller. All these use dialectics and treat a condition as a determining cause. I call them thrillers because the characters are propelled by the movement of the extraneous dialectic, instead of simply acting out what they are. I think that the central tradition sees man as conditioned at every point, but self-determined, so that all these dialectics are contained, so to speak, with none of them allowed to dominate the novel or dictate its resolution. Thus Schulberg's first novel, *What Makes Sammy Run*? would have been a dialectic formula with some Marxist or Freudian solution if the author had concentrated on trying to answer the question instead of on the irreducible fact of Sammy's running. If I am right, then the existentialist doctrine of moral freedom has a good deal of historical and literary point, though so far it seems to me to have produced only a fourth thriller formula.

Charles Williams's *Shadows of Ecstasy* is an intellectual thriller, and its ancestors are Lytton and Rider Haggard—it is by *Zanoni* out of *She*, if my grammar is right. The hero, or villain, Nigel Considine, has, by a super-yogi discipline, enabled himself to live indefinitely (two hundred years and going strong), and has begun an attempt at a "second evolution of man" [46], politically the resurgence of Africa, and psychologically the calling up of the unawakened powers of passion and will, which has for its ultimate goal the return from death. Because this program is the result of a human will to power, Considine is a kind of Antichrist, and we are supposed to pick up a great variety of allusions to different aspects of Antichrist as we go on. If we get them all—they include the Bible, Caesar, Constantine (whose name the hero echoes), Yeats's Byzantium, Dante's Emperor, Milton's Satan, and the superman of Nietzsche and Shaw—we get quite a liberal education.

It is a good thriller, written with humour and relaxation, with more respect for the art of fiction, more tolerance of irony, and less didactic hectoring than are usual with Williams. The fantasy has its own logic, and the characters and setting are studied carefully enough to give us the comfortable sense of a familiar world taking a holiday from routine. It is not giving anything away to say that the Galilean conquers, but though the author's Christian dialectic determines the solution, it does not try to force the reader's assent, and so avoids the disadvantages of melodrama. The losing side gets our sympathy and a chance to put on a good show: we do not feel pushed around nor do we get claustrophobia from a closed system of thought. In all these respects *Shadows of Ecstasy* offers a remarkable contrast to a better known but far cruder version of the same story, *All Hallows Eve*, where the Aunt-Sally epithet "morbid" seems to me for once appropriate.

On the other hand, Marcel Aymé's very able satire, *The Barkeep of Blémont*, is what I mean by fiction in the central tradition. Blémont is a small provincial town, and the kind of intrigue that goes on there is the same old intrigue, love affairs, political jockeying, graft, and the screening of self-interest by humbug. But the time is 1945: the humbug is the exposure of "collaboration," the graft is profiteering, the jockeying is in terms of Communist tactics which have the police terrorized and the middle class almost resigned to defeat, and the love affairs are engaged in by people who have, or are trying to get, political influence. The individual who tries to mind his own business in such an environment merely creates a power vacuum. The attaching of individuals to pressure groups is as though the children of a tough and badly run school had been supplied with rubber truncheons. There is a brutal lynching, watched and approved by the whole town; there is a vicious beating in public ignored by the police; a hunted Nazi gives himself up to certain death; the police lock up people without influence at the bidding of people who have it, and the barkeep, an amiable gorilla who loves Racine and is trying to sweat out hexameters himself, is shot, quite unnecessarily, while resisting the arrest of his muse. One pole of the book is represented by a Vichyite collaborator and war profiteer named Monglant, who is adroit enough to keep his money and become equally influential in the new regime, besides being in cahoots with the Communists. But a fear of public opinion makes him as unable to enjoy his possessions as any other miser, and he finally discovers that his only pleasure is in watching and causing pain. This, of course, is the cancer of Nazism, still uncured after its defeat.

In spite of all this, the tonality of *The Barkeep of Blémont* is one of balanced and unstampeded maturity. When the characters have political ideologies, they patter glibly through the gramophone records that we expect to hear; but we are shown with great clarity how the ultimate use of such apparatus is always to rationalize essential human activities, like bearing false witness or coveting one's neighbour's wife. The psychological drives coincide with the political ones: brutalities not only demonstrate political strength but give sexual pleasure, and a Nazi can get that way because he needs love. But the author sees no logical determining force in social behaviour. Society may at any time be caught in the bondage of fear and hypocrisy, and the freedom of the individuals in that society suffers accordingly. But man himself, society as a whole, is self-imprisoned, and the easy fatalism that externalizes the imprisoning power is making an evil god out of the dark shadow of humanity.

This at any rate is the doctrine of a character named Watrin, who polarizes Monglant, and who seems to mean something rather special to the author, as he gets the last word. Watrin, for reasons too complicated to go into here, has gained an innocent vision of life: the world is newly created for him each morning; he feels that not only nature but man can be loved, if not admired, and he not only enjoys the present but is hopeful of the future. It is reassuring to have him as a spokesman, if he is that, for what is on the whole, apart from some rather nagging irony, a wise and witty book. It is also somewhat disconcerting to notice that the characters who are better than "all too human," Watrin and the barkeep, are touched with slightly sentimental fantasy, and are not quite believable.

We have now to hear from Virgil Gheorghiu, who wrote *The Twenty-Fifth Hour* to prove that man has lost his moral autonomy for good. The two chief characters of this book are Romanians, one a peasant named Johann Moritz and the other an intellectual named Traian Koruga, and the story begins in the Nazified Europe of 1938. The peasant's wife is coveted by a sergeant who gets rid of his rival by accusing him of being a Jew, and the peasant starts on a picaresque journey like those of Candide and Schweik, except that Gheorghiu's satiric touch is not light and his skill in character-drawing is not up to giving us a real picture of innocent simplicity. Johann is imprisoned, tortured, sold as slave labour to Germany, declared to be one of the world's purest Aryans by a Nazi race pundit, dragooned into the S.S., and imprisoned again as a Nazi by the Americans. The intellectual is, in the now somewhat hackneyed *Faux-monnayeurs* formula, writing a novel called *The Twenty-Fifth Hour,* and is persecuted by the Nazis for his Jewish wife and by the Americans, under whom he eventually dies, as an enemy alien. The novel ends with Johann conscripted again to fight for the Americans in the third world war with Russia, which has just begun.

The thesis both of Koruga's book and of the one that encircles it is that all humane and individual values have been wiped out by a technological civilization which can deal only with quantitative units. Men have become the "apes of robots" [46]: their admiration for the efficiency of machines has led to the deification of mechanical values. Eliot, Auden, Northrop, Keyserling, and others are quoted in support, sometimes strangely out of context. It makes no difference what any modern power calls its ideology: its end product will be the same, a bureaucracy of officials who have authority but no freedom. The official can only act mechanically and function on a subhuman generalizing level; he wants the people in front of him to be filed and forgotten, and he gets angry and flustered whenever he is reminded that they are unique human beings. The title means that the human race has already had it: not even a Messiah can save us now. For though Gheorghiu sees much the same facts as Aymé, he is not sustained by the latter's belief in the permanence of society: he sees only the individual and the mass, and his outlook has all the hopelessness of his very common type of naive and introverted anarchism. Koruga, though called a saint, is not really even a martyr, for a martyr is a witness to another community: he is only a victim, and whatever he represents dies with him.

There is probably very little in this book which has not happened, and doubtless nothing which could not happen. It is difficult to know what to say for art when it is outstared by truth, or some kinds of truth. In the face of torture and humiliation it seems almost pedantic to say that the fiction-writing is perfunctory and the social theories slapdash. The book is humourless and preachy, but its subject is not amusing, and maybe we could do with a sermon. The "apes of robots" doctrine is as oversimplified as a dictator's oratory, but the facts it tries to explain are as grim as ever. The irony is contrived and overdone, but so is the irony of a refugee's life. As for the "too late" thesis, one may feel that the very existence of so earnest a book tends to contradict, if not the thesis itself, at any rate the author's belief in it. But one sympathizes with the shrillness of tone, with his anger at our easy boredom and short memories, at the Erewhonian in us who feels that nobody's suffering is undeserved if he makes us uncomfortable to hear about him. In any case Gheorghiu's conviction that American democracy can bring nothing to Europe but a third invasion of stupid and brutal officials makes *The Twenty-Fifth Hour* a document of great importance: it reflects an attitude too frequent among non-Communist Europeans to be shrugged off, and whatever reasons and evidence it presents need to be carefully examined. The hatred of occupied countries for an alien uniform, which Hemingway's colonel discovers but fails to understand, is expressed here from its own point of view.

32

Phalanx of Particulars

Winter 1952

Review of Hugh Kenner, The Poetry of Ezra Pound *(Norfolk, Calif.: New Directions, 1951). From* Hudson Review, *4 (Winter 1952): 627–31. Reprinted in* NFCL, *197–203.*

Ezra Pound is not exactly unread or even neglected, but he is, so to speak, unidentified. Criticism has not fitted him into his cultural milieu as it has fitted Joyce, Eliot, and Yeats; and our perspective on our culture is bound to be astigmatic until he comes into focus. The delay is due to certain prejudices against Pound, which fall into three main groups. Some feel that Pound's reputation ought to wait until a time when a man with his political record can be more calmly appraised. Others feel that, while Pound has obviously been an enthusiastic, generous, and often discerning man, he has not obviously been a wise man, and a glance at his work seems to confirm the impression of an exuberant crank. Still others are willing to concede his importance, but are simply not enough attracted to his idiom to grapple with all that Provençal and social credit and Chinese. All three groups do not so much reject Pound as postpone him, and are waiting for someone to begin the critical organization of his work.

It is fortunate for everyone concerned, including Pound, that the first full-length critical study of Pound should be written by Mr. Kenner and not by the sort of punk who is more usually first in a new field. Mr. Kenner has accomplished his primary task of making it impossible for any serious reader of poetry to dismiss Pound out of mere petulance or suspicion. He has had the vision and the ability not only to argue for Pound on the proper grounds, but to present him in something like his proper context. He shows how clearly Pound grasped the essential fact about poetry, that it is a structure of images and that its structural principle is the juxtaposition of images. This is linked with Pound's interest in imagism, with Aristotle's conception of metaphor, and with the Chinese development of the ideogram or image cluster as the basis of language. Next comes the repudiation of the Cartesian-Lockean view that knowledge is primarily of clear and distinct ideas, a view which reduces poetry to rhetoric, or rather to false rhetoric, which is the figuration of ideas, an attempt at teaching or self-expression by means of loading ideas with the emotional charges of analogy and illustration. This develops in literature the central principle of false rhetoric, which is "style," the art of making all parts of a verbal structure sound alike, and like the author. Pound's attitude to language replaces the false rhetoric of style with the true rhetoric of decorum, of making every part of a verbal structure sound like what it is.

The implications of this go far beyond literature. To base a technique of poetry on the conviction that there is no such thing as a clear and distinct idea is to restore to philosophy a theory of knowledge founded on the perception of particulars. This in turn reacts on literature, and gives poetry, which is the definition of images, its true place as the central act of creative vision and knowledge. Poetry thus becomes, for the reader, revelation, and, for the poet, discovery. The essential technical innovations in the ability of poetry to express emotions and unite images can, Pound says, be identified by a sufficiently astute critic.

To distinguish the poet from the compulsive babbler is an act of fateful social and political importance. It is the central form of the distinction between the free act which proceeds from self-knowledge, and the act which proceeds from mysterious compulsion. Those who are slaves to the latter are so because they have never articulated their emotions, but have allowed them to remain passions, or secret masters of the soul. The free society, of which the pattern is in Confucius, springs from the activity of free men, who, like Jefferson and John Adams, are self-disciplined and articulate men. The form of compulsive action is cupidity, and in a slave state the great men are parasites or usurers, whose function it is to adulterate the currency, whether of words or of coins. The connection between accuracy in poetry and freedom in life Pound calls *ching ming*, the ideogram of which appears to mean something like "rule by the word."[1] In the West *ching ming* was at its height throughout the tradition of courtesy (the only word I know in English that unites the disciplines of speech and social act) which runs from the Provençal poets through the great Italian writers and painters to the Neoplatonics and Castiglione in Medicean Florence. After that, an advancing wave of cupidity debased all currencies alike, muddied the lines of art, and forced words into the slough of jargon (which, as Orwell has shown more incisively than Pound, is the result of a passion for lying).

All this and much more is in Mr. Kenner's book. If I have made it clear that the reader cannot afford to pass it up, I can be frank about my opinion of its faults. The superficial faults, which do not affect the book's virtues, may be summed up in the remark that Mr. Kenner is not very good at polemic. There is too much laboured irony directed at a number of hollow men, some of them straw. "Consideration of these facts may engender some *a priori* suspicion that the man who devotes a lifetime to the amelioration of poetry does not necessarily incur the limiting connotations of 'aestheticism'" [40]. That sentence is not an example of *ching ming*. The author runs to ellipsis and allusion, and, like a bad lecturer, dribbles quasi-facetious asides out of the corner of his mouth which are only audible to a front row, and interfere with the exposition. One doesn't mind his having crotchets, and saying that Freud "remains hopelessly old-fashioned, a model-T Mephisto smelling of *Trilby*" [145], even if one finds the remark rather silly, but it is confusing to meet it in a discussion of Pound's use of Propertius. Nor should he deprecate source-hunting, nor talk about schematic commentary on a difficult and complex poem as though it were a regrettable necessity like excretion, to be pushed into the backhouse of a third appendix. Criticism, like poetry, is either precise statement or blather. There is no need to distrust any kind of precise statement.

Above all, I am sorry to see the anti-Milton and anti-Romantic clichés of thirty years ago carried on into this book. "Pound is a far more important figure than Browning or Landor, Eliot than Tennyson or Shelley" [19]. "Milton's blank verse, punctuated almost entirely by enjambed or caesural thumps, is largely remarkable for what it excludes; communications from Jonson, Marvell, Chaucer, do not pass beyond that 'Chinese wall'" [156]. Time has deprived such value judgments of the only meaning they ever had, which was a specific tactical meaning, a regrouping of critical forces between 1915 and 1930 designed to get new kinds of poetry accepted and obscurantist conventions thrown out. Thus Pound, working out his conception of technical discovery in poetry, depreciates Milton's achievement on the ground that something that sounds like Milton can be detected in Jacobean drama a few years earlier. This should not be taken today as a serious critical dictum, as Mr. Kenner urges, but as a quite funny parody of the sort of pedantic nonsense that historicism unchecked by taste will fall into. Nemesis follows such hybris. It is clear that Mr. Kenner is a little resentful of the way in which the sensibilities of contemporary readers of poetry have been monopolized by Eliot's rhythms and cadences. It looks as though Eliot's "Chinese wall" remark were coming home to roost.[2]

There is far more than a difference of opinion involved here. When Mr. Kenner comes to fit Pound into his tradition, he writes—very helpfully—about the way that the technical discoveries of French prose, notably in Flaubert, ran through Laforgue and Corbière into the English cultural milieu out of which imagism and the prose of Ford Madox Ford and Wyndham Lewis emerged. He does not say that the structure of Pound's thought, especially the way he unites art and economics, is thoroughly Ruskinian. It was Ruskin too who popularized the Romantic, or butterslide, view of history: everything seemed to be going all right in the Middle Ages, but something awful happened with the Renaissance, and things have got steadily worse until a new light has dawned with the present generation, which is every generation from the Gothicists of the eighteenth century to us. Mr. Kenner takes Pound at his own valuation as the true neo-medieval Messiah, and so does not see that Pound the critic is a late pre-Raphaelite sniffing eagerly along the trail of the English Romantics, of Blake's minute particular, Coleridge's esemplastic power, and Keats's life of sensations. Pound the propagandist, on the other hand, was caught in the rubble of the Fascist terminal moraine that Continental Romanticism helped to push into our time. For Ruskin derives from Carlyle, and Carlyle has his roots in Fichte.

I can see why Mr. Kenner refuses as far as possible to discuss the personal tragedy of Pound,[3] but I am not sure that he is right in doing so. Mauberley is warned by the vulgarian Nixon against repeating the lost cause of the "Nineties,"[4] and there is much in Pound's career that reminds us of Oscar Wilde. There are not many genuine examples of the "Hero as Poet," but Wilde was certainly one of them, and his trial and imprison ent was the climax of a life which was one long act of disciplined but desperate courage, a super-quixotic courage that hurled itself straight into the flailing arms of the windmill of Philistinism, knowing quite well that it was nothing but a damned old windmill. And the dream of Ezra Pound is a heroic dream, whatever else it is. To rescue the revolutionary energy of America from the cant of avarice, and the cultural tradition of Europe from the cant of pedantry, and then to unite the real humanity of the one with the real liberality of the other—this may be a grandiloquent ambition, but it is not cheap. When we think of this, and then think of the road that led to the cage in Pisa and to further cages beyond, it is clear that some response, beyond pity as well as beyond Mr. Hillyer's terror,[5] is demanded from us.

I am left still wondering whether Pound, like Wilde, is not more significant as a martyr or witness to the poetic vision than as a shaper of it. If the units of poetry are particular images, it follows that the substance of poetry, the thing that we look for, is not anything relayed from the area of ideas, but the total image which the particulars compose. This total image is the myth or archetype which informs the poetry, and the presentation of myth gives a poet the only impersonality he can have. Poets who have nothing to construct are the ones who have everything to *say*, inspiring messages, great thoughts, rich experiences, and so on. Such poets address their readers directly: no separate poetic form evolves that the reader can contemplate instead. The existence of this separate form is what gives a great poet serenity, urbanity, stabilizing balance, and the ability to forget and to respect his audience at the same time.

What Pound seems to me to lack is the thing that Milton and the Romantics preeminently had—the faculty of mythopoeia. He has plenty of what he calls logopoeia, verbal cleverness and subtle rhythm, wit and craftsmanship, deftness at building up a theme out of a mass of disparate materials. One may dislike the texture of his work—I find it, all too often, as harsh and gritty as a pile of dirty spinach—and still be continually fascinated by the "particulars" in it. But as one reads, the sense of an enveloping body of vision does not come, and one continues to slither along the surface, never out of reach of the excited, hectoring voice of direct address. In the *Cantos*, the structural and recurrent themes, the organizing images, the "ground bass" or controlling rhythms [282], seem to lead, not towards a great epic image of life, but towards clear and distinct ideas in Pound's mind. This being the contrary of Pound's own views, the *Cantos*, at their best, give the impression of brilliant rhetoric trying to persuade us of the desirability of being the opposite of what it is. When Mr. Kenner says, "Pound's impersonality is Flaubertian: an effacement of the personal accidents of the perceiving medium in the interests of accurate registration of *moeurs contemporaines*" [166], he is saying what

I suppose a sympathetic critic of Pound ought to say; yet it seems to me fantastically untrue. I see in the *Cantos* a structural myth broken down into a pastiche of harangue and exempla. When Pound says,

> Go, song, surely thou mayest
> Whither it please thee
> For so art thou ornate that thy reasons
> Shall be praised from thy understanders,
> With others hast thou no will to make company. . . . [*Canto* 36, ll. 80–4]

he seems to me to be telling the whole truth about himself as a poet.

I sincerely hope that all of this is quite wrong: it is, after all, the kind of thing that used to be said, and can no longer be said, about Joyce. Mr. Kenner will doubtless convince others that it is wrong, and in any case much more work on Pound has yet to be done. And whatever is done will look back with gratitude and admiration to Mr. Kenner's study, and will follow the broad lines of the course he has charted.

33

Quest and Cycle in *Finnegans Wake*

December 1955

From FI, *256–64. The same text, originally delivered at the December 1955 Modern Language Association convention in Chicago (Ayre, 254), was first published in the* James Joyce Review, *1, no. 1 (2 February 1957): 39–42.*

Finnegans Wake[1] belongs to the epic tradition, and epic writers have always been unusually conscious of tradition. Joyce's immediate predecessors in his type of epic were the mythological poets of the Romantic period, and among these Blake is clearly the most important for the study of Joyce. Blake's work is middle-class, nineteenth-century, moral, romantic, sentimental, and fervently rhetorical, and these were the cultural qualities that Joyce, to the dismay of many of his critics, most deeply loved and appreciated. I propose first to set out the major parallels between Blake's myth of Albion and Joyce's myth of Finnegan.

Blake's myth is derived chiefly from the Bible, and the Bible for Blake was a kind of definitive myth extending from the beginning to the end of time (creation to apocalypse) and from the centre to the circumference of space (individual to universal man). The chief principle of Blake's symbolism is the concrete universal, the identity of the individual and the class, which he expresses in the metaphor of distance: "When distant they appear as One Man but as you approach they appear Multitudes of Nations" [*A Vision of the Last Judgment*, p. 76; E556–7]. The two poles of Blake's myth are man awake, or Jesus, and man asleep, or Albion. Man awake is God; man asleep is historical and biological man. The Bible is revelation, a message from Jesus to Albion, but an imaginative or poetic revelation, for Jesus employed parables, not syllogisms. Churches, being social, are founded on rational and legal versions of revelation, and hence are subordinate in authority to the agents of the creative Word itself, the prophets and prophetic artists. What the latter communicate is a completely catholic Christianity or "everlasting gospel," in which "all religions are one" [cf. E518–25, 1–2].

In Joyce there is also the doctrine of the priority of the imaginative over the doctrinal Word. In the *Portrait* the artist and the priest, who are both aspects of Stephen, struggle for the possession of this Word, and the artist wins out. In Joyce's personal life his break with the Catholic Church meant, not that he wanted to believe in something else, but that he wanted to transfer the mythical structure of the Church from faith and doctrine to creative imagination, thereby exchanging dogmatic Catholicism for imaginative catholicity. The usual cliché that art is no substitute for religion does not begin to apply to either Blake or Joyce. Blake thought of his Prophecies, especially *The Four Zoas*, which is subtitled "A Dream of Nine Nights," as addressed by the artist to the ear of the sleeping Albion, and the same point is expressed in Joyce's symbol of the earwig. In Joyce too the concrete universal, the identity of individual and total man, is the organizing principle of the symbolism.

Albion has the same connections with England and London that Finnegan has with Ireland and Dublin. Both are what Blake calls "Giant forms" [*Jerusalem*, pl. 3; E145], embracing both the subjective and the objective worlds, the landscape of England and Ireland respectively being formed out of their bodies. In Blake, the fact that Albion is asleep means that he has "fallen" asleep, and his fall was into the dream world of external nature. This world moves in circles, or perhaps rather ellipses, revolving around two foci that Blake calls Orc and Urizen. Orc is youth, energy, rebelliousness, and sexual vitality; Urizen is age, prudence, law, and worldly wisdom. Orc is the dying god or John Barleycorn who is killed at the height of his powers; Urizen is the Olympian sky-god or "President of the Immortals."[2] In his later works Blake tends to employ the single term "Luvah" for the whole Orc–Urizen cycle.

Luvah in Joyce is HCE, who in his earlier phases is the immanent dying god of the cyclical fertility of nature, and is said to be submerged under Lough Neagh in north Ireland, just as the sleeping Albion in Blake is the true Atlantis, submerged under the Atlantic Ocean. In Blake the sleeping Albion *is* Luvah, just as the fully awakened Albion would be identified with Jesus. The analogy suggests the solution of a vexing problem in Joyce. As in *Alice through the Looking Glass*, to which it owes so much, the final question left with the reader of *Finnegans Wake* is, "Which dreamed it?"[3] If the dreamer is HCE, the place of Finnegan, who is also the husband of ALP, seems difficult to account for, and the simplest answer is that the dreamer is Finnegan, the communal human unconscious of Dublin, who while he is asleep is identical with HCE, and to a lesser extent with the other speaking characters. In the course of the book HCE gradually sinks under a mounting body of forgetfulness, rumour, and calumny until he becomes Urizenic, associated with the Scandinavian, Roman, and English invaders who have imposed structures of external authority on Ireland. In Blake the opposition of Orc and Urizen is accompanied by certain paired symbols, such as the spear and the shield, which correspond to the tree and stone in Joyce.

In both Blake and Joyce the cyclical movement of nature extends to human history. Joyce derives from Vico, probably with some help from Spengler, a conception of a historical cycle in four stages, an age of myth, an age of metaphysics, an age of positivism, and a final age of dissolution bringing us back to the beginning again. Blake's cycle has four parallel stages, symbolized by the birth of Orc, a moment of terror corresponding to Joyce's "thunderclap";[4] the imprisoning of Orc, corresponding to the shift in power from the Word to the Church recorded in *The Mookse and the Gripes*;[5] Urizen "exploring his dens" [e.g., *The Book of Urizen*, chaps. 7–8, pl. 20; E80–1], which is eighteenth-century positivism and corresponds to British imperialism in Joyce; and a final age of chaos. In Blake there is the possibility of choosing, in the final stage, between an apocalypse or awakening of Man and a return to another cycle: Blake stresses the apocalyptic alternative and Joyce the cyclical one. In Blake the ninth night of *The Four Zoas* and the fourth part of *Jerusalem* are given over to the apocalypse; at the end of the eighth night of *The Four Zoas* and the third part of *Jerusalem* we have a vision of pure cycle, the end of the age of Luther, or Blake's own time, going back to the beginning of history "in Eternal Circle" [*Jerusalem*, chap. 3, pl. 75; E231]. This corresponds to the end of Joyce's sixteenth chapter, just before the *ricorso* or last chapter begins: "Tiers, tiers and tiers. Rounds" [590:30]. The last page of *Finnegans Wake* describes the sinking of ALP into her "old feary father,"[6] as the Liffey river finally reaches the sea. As *Finnegans Wake* goes around in a circle, this event immediately precedes the fall of Finnegan on the first page, and corresponds exactly to the first event of *The Four Zoas*, the sinking of Enitharmon into the sea-god Tharmas, an event immediately followed by the fall of Albion.

Human history according to Blake occupies seven great ages, which are subdivided into a series of twenty-eight "Churches," or historical versions of the creative Word. In each age an imaginative polarity shapes up between the artist and the priest, the prophet and the worldly wise man. In *The Marriage of Heaven and Hell* Blake calls the artist-prophets "Devils" and their opponents "Angels"—both, he says, are essential to human life, for "without Contraries is no Progression" [pl. 3; E34], but it is also inevitable that each group should regard the other as demonic. In Joyce too there are seven periods of HCE's sleep, symbolized by the seven colours of the spectrum and by female figures who represent a dim but constant infidelity to HCE. A similar role is played by the twenty-eight "Maggies," who in the literal allegory are the schoolmates of HCE's daughter Isabel. Constantly throughout history, too, there is a "collideorscape" [143:28], or conflict of what Blake would call "Mental Fight" [*Preface* to *Milton*, l. 13; E95] and worldly prudence in which one contender is Shem, the outcast artist-prophet, and the other Shaun, the worldly priest. From the reader's point of view Shaun is merely a derivative and distorted version of Shem, but from the world's point of view the struggle of the brothers is a "mime of Mick and Nick" [cf. 219:18–19], a contest of Michael and Satan in which Shaun is Michael and Shem the conquered power of darkness, and it is to this latter point of view that the "Maggies" adhere. Blake's poem *Milton* is also based on a conflict of Michael and Satan, in which Michael represents the artist and Satan worldly wisdom, and here too Satan is the hero to the female characters who in Blake's myth correspond to the "Maggies."

In Blake the struggle between good and evil conceals a genuine dialectic of eternal life and eternal death, the separation of which is achieved only in the apocalypse. Satan in Blake is the death principle, including not only physical death but all the workings of the death impulse in human life, the discouraging or prohibiting of free activity which Blake calls the "accusation of Sin" [*Jerusalem*, pl. 64, l. 22; E215], and which he associates with the three accusers of Socrates and the three comforters of Job. In Joyce the dream of HCE is unable to escape from a neurotic circling around some accusation of guilt which seems to emanate from a mysterious "cad," who is associated with the serpent in Paradise and with three male figures, generally soldiers, sometimes the sons of Noah or the human race in general. These in turn melt into the lampooners of HCE, and are closely associated with twelve "Morphios" [142:29], the patrons of HCE's pub, whose function it is to encourage and continue the sleeping state. Similarly in Blake the sleep of Albion is encouraged and prolonged by twelve "Sons of Albion" who, like their counterparts in Joyce, are associated both with the zodiac and with jury trials.

In Blake what man, in any context, creates is his "emanation," which exists in a feminine relation to him. God the Creator is male, and everything he creates is at once his wife and daughter. Just as "companies of nations" appear as one man at a distance, so a multitude of created things appears as "a City yet a Woman," called Jerusalem in Blake [*The Four Zoas: Night the Ninth*, p. 122, l. 18; E391]. In the fall Albion abandoned his creative power for the contemplation of his creation, which then separated from him and became external to him, the teasing, tantalizing female nature which Blake calls Vala. In Joyce there are several Vala figures, apart from the "Maggies" already mentioned. The original fall of HCE is connected somehow with two elusive but not quite hidden girls, whom Joyce, for etymological reasons, calls "minxes," and whose many names seem to revolve around "Rose" and "Lily"—the symbolism of red and white has affinities with the fact that Vala in Blake is called indifferently a virgin and a harlot, the two aspects in which Vala is named Tirzah and Rahab respectively. Then there is the mirror or leap-year girl, the twenty-ninth Maggie and the narcist reflection of Isabel, who is associated with Isoult, as Blake associates Vala with the convention of courtly love, and also with Swift's Stella and Vanessa: one is reminded of the way that Tirzah and Rahab are associated with Milton's wives and daughters in Blake's poem on Milton.

These are the major parallels between the two myths: the parallel sometimes suggested between Blake's four Zoas and Joyce's four old men[7] is not a genuine one. The Zoas in Blake are his major figures Los, Orc, Urizen, and Tharmas, and are fully individualized: the four old men in Joyce are always a chorus, and seem unintegrated to the rest of the symbolism. These four men are inorganic tradition, or, more accurately, the conscious memory: they are linked to the four evangelists, to the four historians of Ireland,[8] and to the psychoanalytic technique of trying to clear the mind of guilt by awakening the memory. In Joyce, as in Blake, the memory and the creative imagination are distinct or even opposed principles. The nearest equivalent in Blake to the four old men would be the four chief sons of Los in their "abstract" form.

We pass now to the major point of contrast between the two. The hero of Blake's Prophecies, who is at once artist, prophet, blacksmith, and the spirit of time, is called Los. The "emanation" of Los is Enitharmon, who represents space, and is consequently the presiding spirit of the false daylight world of common sense. In the fallen world her natural affinities are with Urizen or worldly reason, and Los has the task of subduing her to himself. In Joyce a similar connection of time with imagination and of space with rationalism appears in the relation of Shem and Shaun. In both Blake and Joyce, of course, this creative time, which is something like Bergson's *durée*,[9] is quite distinct from clock time, which is an element in the fall. In Blake clock time is represented by the Spectre of Urthona, another principle that Los has to subdue; in Joyce it appears in the "cad's" original demand for the time which produced a stuttering or repetitive response from HCE. But there is no Los figure in *Finnegans Wake*; the spirit of time and the source of Shem's creative power is the female figure of ALP, Blake's Enitharmon.

The *Portrait of the Artist* ends with Stephen's appeal to the "old father, old artificer." This father, the spiritual or imaginative Dedalus who built the labyrinth and then flew out of it, is a figure very close to Blake's Los, the prophetic blacksmith who builds the "Mundane Shell" [*Milton*, pl. 34, l. 31; E134]. An association is implied between Stephen and Icarus, and in some respects *Ulysses* is a version of the fall of Icarus. Stephen, an intellectual of the type usually described as in the clouds or up in the air, comes back to Dublin and in his contact with Bloom meets a new kind of father, neither his spiritual nor his physical father but Everyman, the man of earth and common humanity, who is yet isolated enough from his society to be individual too, an Israel as well as an Adam. Stephen approaches this communion with a certain amount of shuddering and distaste, but the descent to the earth is clearly necessary for him. Traditionally, however, the earth is Mother Earth, and what we are left with is a female monologue of a being at once maternal, marital, and meretricious, who enfolds a vast number of lovers, including Bloom and possibly Stephen, and yet is narcist too, in a state of self-absorption which absorbs the lover. Marion Bloom is a Penelope who embraces all her suitors as well as her husband, and whose sexual versatility seems much the same thing as the weaving of her never-finished web—the web being also one of Blake's symbols for female sexuality. The drowsy spinning of the earth, absorbed in its own cyclical movement, constantly affirming but never forming, is what Marion sinks into, taking the whole book with her. Blake, if he had read *Ulysses*, would probably have recoiled in horror from its celebration of the triumph of what he calls the "Female Will" [*Jerusalem*, pl. 30, ll. 31, 39; E176–7], the persistence of the sleep of externality.

In most epic fictions there are two main elements: the quest of the hero and the shape of the hero's world. The quest is dialectic: when the dragon dies or the enemy falls there is an upward movement from bondage to liberty, from the powers of darkness to renewed life. The hero's world however is the order of nature, which moves in what Joyce calls "vicious cicles."[10] The relation of the dialectic quest to the cycle of nature depends on the dimensions of the hero. At one extreme we have the divine quest, or myth of the hero as god, where all the symbols of the turning year are swallowed up in the quest. The myth of Christ subordinates all the cyclical symbolism of Christmas and Easter to the separation of death and hell from the Resurrection. At the opposite extreme is the ironic vision, where the quest is seen inside an inevitably and perpetually recurring cycle, where everything that is done, however heroic, has sooner or later to be done over again. In between we have, first, the romantic quest, or myth of the hero in a marvellous or miraculous world, where the laws of nature are slightly suspended in the hero's favour. At its most concentrated the romantic quest takes the form of a sacramental ascent out of the order of nature, as it does in Dante and the Grail romances. Next comes the heroic quest proper, the theme of the traditional Classical epic, where the action begins *in medias res*, and then works forward to the end and back to the beginning of a cyclical total action. In the *Odyssey*, for example, the total action moves from Ithaca back to Ithaca; in the *Aeneid* from Troy to New Troy, and in *Paradise Lost*, where Christ is the hero, from the presence of God back to his presence again. In each epic the finishing point is the starting point renewed and transformed by the hero's quest.

In the mythological poems of Blake's day, such as *Prometheus Unbound*, *Faust*, or Blake's own *Jerusalem*, the epic action is normally an intellectual quest, and the mythical events are symbols of psychological ones. Hence there is a strong tendency to revert, in a more subjective way, to the sacramental quest of romance. Here again the quest takes precedence over the cycle: in Shelley, man is redeemed, and nature follows obediently with an enormous springtime rebirth. Yet in the minor poems of this period there are more ironic patterns. Blake's *Mental Traveller*, for example, presents a cycle in which two characters, one male and one female, act on one another in what Yeats would call a double gyre, the man growing old as the woman grows young and vice versa. There are four main phases of the relationship: a mother–son phase, a husband–wife phase, a father–daughter phase, and a fourth phase that Blake calls spectre and emanation, terms corresponding roughly to Shelley's alastor and epipsyche. None of these relations is quite true: the "mother" is a nurse, the "wife" is merely "bound down" for the male's delight, the "daughter" is a changeling, and the "emanation" does not emanate, but remains elusive and external. The male figure represents humanity, and therefore includes women; the female figure is external nature, which humanity partially subdues in a series of cyclical movements known as cultures or civilizations. The controlling symbolism, as the four phases and the continual failure of contact suggest, is lunar.

Most of the epics and epic actions of the twentieth century are ironic, and it is *The Mental Traveller*, not *Prometheus Unbound* or *Jerusalem*, that is nearest in form to them. In Proust, as in Blake and Joyce, creative time is the hero, but it is subordinate to clock time, and the only paradise it can reach is a lost paradise. In Yeats we find again a lunar symbolism and a double gyre, the cycle of Leda and the swan giving place to the cycle of the dove and the virgin and then returning, a vision which Yeats was quite correct in associating with *The Mental Traveller*.[11] In Eliot's *Waste Land* there is a fire sermon and a thunder sermon, both with apocalyptic contexts, but again the natural cycle of the river flowing out to sea and returning through death by water in the spring rains is the containing form of the poem. The latest recruit to the ironic vision is Robert Graves, in whom, as in Blake and in Yeats, the presiding genius of the natural cycle is an ambivalent female figure, a white goddess associated with the moon, partly a virgin and partly a harlot.

In Blake, then, the central figure is male because the containing form of Blake's epic is apocalyptic and dialectic, giving priority to a spiritual and imaginative quest which ends by breaking clear of the natural cycle altogether. In Joyce the central figure is female because the containing form is ironic and cyclical. ALP, like Blake's Vala, grows younger as HCE grows older; she is introduced as a grandmother but by the end of *Haveth Childers Everywhere* she has become filial. Yet we notice two things about ALP: she has very little of the religious quality of the Beatrice and Virgin Mary figures who loom so large in Eliot, yet she has even less of the malignant grinning female, the *femme fatale* of the Romantic agony and of Yeats and Graves in our day. She is an endlessly faithful and solicitous wife and mother, patiently collecting, like Isis, the fragments of her disorderly husband, patiently waiting, like Solveig,[12] for him to finish his wanderings and come back to her. She runs through her natural cycle and achieves no quest herself, but she is clearly the kind of being who makes a quest possible.

Who then is the hero who achieves the quest? It is not Shem, for here as in *Ulysses* the artist is part of the cycle, and Joyce's view of him is detached and ironic. It is not HCE, nor Shaun, nor even Finnegan, who never does wake up even if HCE does. Eventually it dawns on us that it is the *reader* who achieves the quest, the reader who, to the extent that he masters the book of "Doublends Jined,"[13] is in a position to look down on its rotation, and see its total form as something more than rotation. The dreamer, after establishing contact with the vast empire of unconscious knowledge, wakes up forgetting his dream, like Nebuchadnezzar, leaving it to the "ideal reader suffering from an ideal insomnia" [120:13–14], as Joyce calls him, to reforge the broken links between myth and consciousness. In Blake the quest contains the cycle and in Joyce the cycle contains the quest, but there is the same challenge to the reader, and the same rewards for him, in Joyce's "mamafesta" [104:4] that there is in Blake's "Allegory addressed to the Intellectual powers" [Letter to Thomas Butts, 6 July 1803; E730].

34

Graves, Gods, and Scholars

Summer 1956

Review of Robert Graves, Collected Poems *(New York: Doubleday, 1955). From* Hudson Review, *9 (Summer 1956): 298–302. Reprinted in* NFCL, *230–6.*

The trouble with being a literary critic is that one gets filing cards in the memory, and one is continually having to fish them out and wonder if the clichés typed on them are really so very bright. I imagine a good many people roughly familiar with modern poetry have some sort of card in their memories reading in effect: "Graves, Robert. Does tight, epigrammatic lyrics in the Hardy-Housman tradition; closer in technique to Blunden and de la Mare than to Eliot, Pound, or Yeats; a minor poet but one of the best of the post-Georgians." There is some factual basis for such a note, but in terms of "covering" its subject it would hardly make an honest woman of Lady Godiva. Whatever one thinks of Mr. Graves as a poet, novelist, critic, translator, mythographer, editor, anthologist, collaborator, surveyor of modernist poetry, or restorer of the Nazarene gospel, there can be no reasonable doubt that Mr. Graves is big, and bigness is certainly one important attribute of greatness. He is not a minor poet; he is not a minor anything.

Of all evidences of bigness, one of the most impressive is a sense of the expendable. The present volume is as much selected as collected poems: Mr. Graves has written many fine poems that are not here, which indicates, not only that he is highly self-critical, but that he believes that the poet always knows what his essential poems are. I have some reservations about this latter view, but on the other hand every poet has the right to his own canon, and it is as an author's canon that the present collection should be read.

Lyrical poetry normally begins in an associative process in which sound is as important as sense, a process much of which is submerged below consciousness. Such a process may go in either of two directions. It may become oracular, ambiguous in sense and echoic in sound, in which case it is addressed in part to an uncritical faculty, concerned with casting a spell and demanding emotional surrender. Or it may become witty, addressing itself to the critical intelligence and the detached consciousness. The ingredients of paronomasia and assonance are common to both, and it depends on the context whether, for instance, Poe's line "The viol, the violet and the vine" [*The City in the Sea*, l. 23] or Pope's "Great Cibber's brazen, brainless brothers stand" [*The Dunciad*, bk. 1, l. 32] is oracular or witty.

Mr. Graves is an epigrammatic writer who remains in full intellectual control of his work. The meaning of his poem never gets away from him, never dissolves in a drowsy charm of sound. He is a poet to whom theme means a good deal: every poem is aimed directly at a definite human or mythical situation, and usually hits it squarely in its central paradox. The technique corresponds. In the earlier pages one watches him practising forms with a sharp rhythmical bite: Mother Goose rhythms, ballads and eight-six quatrains, and, in the fine *In Procession*, Skeltonics reminding us how much Mr. Graves has done to rehabilitate Skelton. The deep incision produced by exact metre and clear thought makes some unforgettably sharp outlines:

> Courtesies of good-morning and good-evening
> From rustic lips fail as the town encroaches:
> Soon nothing passes but the cold quick stare
> Of eyes that see ghosts, yet too many for fear. [*On Dwelling*, ll. 1–4]

Later in the book we get more unrhymed poems, where the metrical and mental discipline have to stand alone, and finally, in the poems that come from or are contemporary with *The White Goddess*, incantation itself. But as the poet has approached incantation from the opposite end, his enchanters speak in a curiously reasonable and expository voice. Thus the Sirens urge Chronos:

> Compared with this, what are the plains
> Of Elis, where you ruled as king?
> A wilderness indeed. [*The Sirens' Welcome to Chronos*, ll. 22–4)

The poetic personality revealed in the book is one of sturdy independence, pragmatic common sense, and a consistently quizzical attitude to systematized forms of experience, especially the religious. From this point of view Mr. Graves's collected poems could hardly have come at a better time. We have had a good deal of ecclesiasticized poetry, full of the dilemma of modern man, Kierkegaardian *Angst*, and the facile resonance of the penitential mood. Mr. Graves is strongly in revolt against all this, and he is old enough to have the authority of a contemporary classic, carrying on a tradition that goes back to the nineteenth century through Henley and Housman; a tradition that has more in common with Clough than with Arnold. He writes not humbly but defiantly of "Self-Praise," and says:

> Confess, creatures, how sulkily ourselves
>   We hiss with doom, fuel of a sodden age—
> Not rapt up roaring to the chimney stack
>   On incandescent clouds of spirit or rage. [*Under the Pot*, ll. 5–8]

He is occasionally betrayed into cliché on this point, as in *Ogres and Pygmies*, but the sense of candour and freshness remains the primary one.

Mr. Graves is becoming an influence on contemporary British poetry in such a way as to suggest that we may be ready to repeat, on a very small scale of decades rather than millennia, Yeats's pattern of progress from Christian humility to the tragic pride of Oedipus the riddle-guesser.[1] Certainly no one can doubt that Mr. Graves is by far the greatest riddle-guesser of our time: all the Gordian knots of antiquity, from the song of the sirens to the number of Antichrist, fall to pieces at the swing of his sword. Readers who are still bemused by the oracular, still accustomed to think of poetry as Lenten reading and of the poet as a psychopomp, may put their hands confidingly into Mr. Graves's with the hope of being led, like Prufrock, to some overwhelming question, perhaps even an answer. And as they proceed, whether through this book or through the formidable series of mythological works, a central myth begins to take shape. This, of course, is the myth of the white goddess, the mother-harlot, virgin-slut, "Sister of the mirage and echo" [*The White Goddess*, l. 6], whose elusive and treacherous beauty has inspired poets from prehistoric times to the last whimpers of courtly love in Baudelaire. "It is a poet's privilege and fate" [*Darien*, l. 1] to fall in hopeless love with her: condemned by his genius to go on trying to screw the inscrutable, he must stumble groaningly around the four seasons of her adoration, from the rapture of spring to the reviling of winter:

> But we are gifted, even in November
> Rawest of seasons, with so huge a sense
> Of her nakedly worn magnificence
> We forget cruelty and past betrayal,
> Heedless of where the next bright bolt may fall.
>
> [*The White Goddess*, ll. 18–22]

That's it, then: "There is one story and one story only" [*To Juan at the Summer Solstice*, l. 1]. The key to all myths, the answer to all riddles, the source of all great poems, is the story of Attis and Cybele, where a feminine principle remains enthroned and a masculine one follows the cycle of nature, a Lord of the May who is soon "dethroned," and turned into a doomed victim like Actaeon, while the poet urges:

> Run, though you hope for nothing: to stay your foot
> Would be ingratitude, a sour denial
> That the life she bestowed was sweet. [*Dethronement*, ll. 16–18]

The Attis–Cybele story is very important in mythology; it underlies a vast number of poems; its ramifications are nearly as widespread as those of poetry itself. All this no one would wish to deny. One feels nevertheless that there is something dismally corny about isolating the myth in this way and in this form; something of rotten-ripe late Romanticism; something that suggests the masochism of Swinburne or some of the worst effects of Maud Gonne on Yeats rather than anything typical of Mr. Graves. So we go back and run through his book again.

We notice that the central theme of a relatively early poem, *Warning to Children*, is that of the boxes of Silenus, the image with which Rabelais begins.[2] In the next poem, a most important poem called *Alice*, we read:

> Nor did Victoria's golden rule extend
> Beyond the glass: it came to the dead end
> Where empty hearses turn about; thereafter
> Begins that lubberland of dream and laughter,
> The red-and-white-flower-spangled hedge, the grass
> Where Apuleius pastured his Gold Ass,
> Where young Gargantua made whole holiday . . . [ll. 31–7]

We begin to wonder if perhaps Mr. Graves does not after all belong, not to the solemnly systematic mythographers, not to the tradition of Apollodorus and Natalis Comes and George Eliot's Casaubon, but to the tradition of the writers who have turned mythical erudition into satire, to Rabelais and Apuleius, or to the exuberantly hyperbolic Celtic mythical poets. The combination of erudite satire and lyrical gifts is not uncommon: we find it in Petronius, in Heine, in Joyce, and (counting his lethal scholarly essays as erudite satire) in Housman. Perhaps Mr. Graves's oracle too is the oracle of the Holy Bottle:[3] certainly the myths in his poetry, like the ghosts, seem to be not part of an objective system but a kaleidoscopic chaos of human fragments. As he says:

> Now I know the mermaid kin
> I find them bound by natural laws:
> They have neither tail nor fin,
> But are deadlier for that cause. [*Mermaid, Dragon, Fiend,* ll. 13–16]

He does not lead us towards an objective or systematic mythology: he leads us towards the mythical use of poetic language, where we invent our own myths and apply them to an indefinite number of human themes. He has several *doppelgänger* poems, in which he develops the theme of the looking-glass world as this world looked at mythically: as, in short, the world constructed by love and imagination. This is the theme of *The Climate of Thought*, of *The Terraced Valley*, and several other poems.

Perhaps, then, his attraction to the white-goddess myth is simply that it is an ironic myth, ambiguous in its moral values, and providing in its human incarnations what is essentially a heap of broken images. In contrast, the masculine protest myths of father-gods, introduced to our culture by the prophet Ezekiel, according to *The White Goddess*, stand for order, system, and the limiting of poetic themes by artificial standards of truth and morality. In such poems as the early *Reproach*, where Christ appears as an accusing father, in *The Eremites*, in *The Bards*, and elsewhere, we see the perversion of life that results from enthroning a male god in the sky in place of a mother. Perhaps we may understand from these poems how we are to read such a book as *Wife to Mr. Milton*: less as biography or literary criticism than as a blow struck in defence of the white goddess, and one in the eye for the prophet Ezekiel. The ambivalence of Mr. Graves's attitude to myth reminds one of Samuel Butler, whom he curiously resembles in many ways. Butler was so subtle and poker-faced an ironist that some of his parodies, such as the Book of the Machines in *Erewhon*, take in the casual reader, who is apt to assume that it's a straight Frankenstein fantasy. Others, such as *The Fair Haven*, took in nearly the whole reading public in their day. And there are still others so *very* subtle that they seem to have taken in Samuel Butler himself. His account of the Resurrection,[4] for instance, reads like a deadly parody of Victorian pseudo-rationalism going to work on the Gospel narratives, but Butler appears to have taken it seriously, as he did his notions about the *Odyssey* (some of them shared by Mr. Graves) and about Shakespeare's Sonnets. Similarly, *King Jesus* and *The Nazarene Gospel Restored* impress one primarily as mythical satire: i.e., as constructs so obviously hypothetical that they suggest an indefinite number of other possible constructs, each as ingenious and plausible as the author's—or as the orthodox version. But Mr. Graves appears to take them "seriously," as in some way definitive or exclusive. But fortunately we can dodge that issue in reading the poetry, and find the central path to his mind through something like this:

> He is quick, thinking in clear images;
> I am slow, thinking in broken images.
>
> He becomes dull, trusting to his clear images;
> I become sharp, mistrusting my broken images . . .
>
> He in a new confusion of his understanding;
> I in a new understanding of my confusion.

[*In Broken Images*, ll. 1–4, 13–14]

35

Nature and the Psyche

January 1957

From the American Journal of Psychiatry, *113, no. 7 (January 1957): 669–70. Copyright 1957. Review of C.G. Jung and W. Pauli,* The Interpretation of Nature and the Psyche, *translated by R.F.C. Hull and Priscilla Silz (New York: Pantheon Books for the Bollingen Foundation, 1955). Appeared in German in 1952.*

This book consists of two essays. The first, by C.G. Jung, on "Synchronicity: An Acausal Connecting Principle," has for its theme the phenomenon generally known as "sheer coincidence." A novelist, let us say, has just decided to call a character in his book Mr. Tackhammer, when there is a knock at the door and a Mr. Tackhammer is announced. Coincidences as unlikely as this have happened to a great many people, perhaps nearly everyone. They make a strong impact on the mind: they have, Jung says, a quality of the numinous, but their general effect is to paralyse one's mental processes. A primitive mind has no difficulty with coincidence, because, though strange, it is thoroughly in accord with the primitive view of the world as arbitrary events produced by mysterious powers. But a modern educated person immediately asks himself, "Well, so what?" and if there appears to be no answer, he can only dismiss the matter. Explanations, when forthcoming, are usually based on an unconvincing theory of causation: some agent, whether Providence or a secret power of the mind, is assumed to have brought the coincidence about through a transmission of energy.

The essay argues that coincidences are in fact uncaused, and are phenomena relating to the unconscious, specifically to that deeper level of it which Jung calls the collective unconscious. Occasionally there are exceptions to the general operations of causality: things "just happen" in a way which excludes both chance and causation. This is what Jung means by synchronicity. A hypothesis of synchronicity underlies all modes of divination, including astrology; it is found in all cases of premonition, and the same hypothesis is necessary to account for the Rhine experiments in extrasensory perception.[1] For telepathic and extrasensory knowledge cannot be explained causally by any theory of transmission: it is uncaused knowledge springing from the unconscious. The unconscious, unlike the conscious, does not operate in a world of causality, or of space and time, nor, on the collective level, does it operate in a world divided into subjects and objects. Its world is a totality of correspondence. The idea of correspondence, with its philosophical by-products of the microcosm and the monad, is then briefly traced from Plato and the Chinese Tao down to Leibniz. Jung's somewhat manic tendency to see the whole of philosophy as an allegory of Jungianism comes out in such remarks as, "Expressed in modern language, the microcosm which contains 'the images of all creation' would be the collective unconscious" (107). The argument grinds uncertainly to a stop in a footnote (142), full of quotations from the Church Fathers about the independence of God's creative power from temporal succession.

Is coincidence, then, merely to be regarded as an opportunity for meditating on the essential oneness of all being? Jung insists that synchronicity is "meaningful" and that the conception of explanation does apply to it. But if it can be explained it can hardly be distinguished from *all* forms of causation. The word "cause" is employed throughout in its narrow empirical sense of an efficient cause which always precedes its effect and transmits energy to it. Forms of causation which do not precede the effect, such as Aristotle's final cause, or even his less controversial formal cause, have many affinities with synchronicity, as Jung himself observes.

Further, it could be almost a definition of coincidence that it is a bit of design or pattern which we are unable to see any use for. Whatever philosophical criticisms have been directed against time, space, and causality, they have been extremely useful conceptions, and if synchronicity is to be recognized as a fourth principle equal in importance to these other three (134), one naturally wonders what its use is. It seems to me that the only way to make it a real power in modern thought is to do what Jung explicitly refuses to do (144) and associate synchronicity with other forms of synchronization. This would give us the principle that nature, like the human mind, works by *Gestalten* or patterns of configuration,[2] a principle which we badly need for such problems as, say, the evolution of a warm-blooded animal. Jung speaks of synchronistic phenomena as manifestations of a creative power working in time [143]. The word "creative" could open up an interesting line of approach for critics of the arts, as in all the arts patterns of coincidence are a formal principle. But it is clear from the context that Jung is thinking of a total creative process in which God, nature, and the human mind are all identical. And as an explanation of coincidence, this is only a dressed-up restatement of the primitive view that coincidences are caused by the agency of a supernatural being. Causation has not been excluded: it has merely been transferred from the origin of the coincidence to its *telos*. Jung is a seminal thinker, and here as elsewhere he put his finger on a central intellectual preoccupation of our time, but his treatment of it is disappointingly inconclusive.

The second essay, "The Influence of Archetypal Ideas on the Scientific Theories of Kepler," by W. Pauli, examines an instance of a general principle which is something like this: in all sciences there are two elements: the facts observed and the mental structure which interrelates them. The formal principles of that structure are usually diagrams or images. Some philosophers, such as Plato with his divided line and his cave [*Republic*, bks. 6, 7], know this and make it obvious; others are unconscious of their formal principles, and so project them into the world itself. In an occultist we have an extreme example of a thinker who works deductively with patterns and diagrams and tries to fit observations into them. In most modern scientists we see the opposite extreme, a mental process so focused on observation that it is quite unconscious of the way in which inner patterns or formal principles of thought are selecting, guiding, and relating the facts observed. These patterns or formal principles of thought are called "archetypes" by followers of Jung. From this point of view a study of a thinker who stands on the boundary line of occultism and modern science, revealing both the scientific respect for observation and the occult fascination with symmetrical patterns of thought, would be of particular value.

Kepler is such a thinker: he has a hierarchical view of the universe which starts with the Trinity and works down through a series of correspondences to the earth, which he thinks of as a single living organism. He regards the sphere as the most beautiful and complete of all forms, the symbol of Godhead, and because of this preference he is led to champion the new heliocentric view of the planetary orbits. The author remarks that "in Kepler the symbolical picture precedes the conscious formulation of a natural law" [171]. In spite of this aesthetic and speculative apparatus (it would be psychologically more accurate to say because of it) he discovered some of the essential laws of planetary motion and became an indispensable predecessor of Newton. The quotations from Kepler show a vigorous candid mind, and such remarks of his as "the mind itself, if it had never possessed an eye, would *demand* an eye in order to comprehend things outside itself" are typical of a great age of discovery and intellectual excitement [165]. His controversy with Robert Fludd is also touched on, to show the contrast in attitude between the victorious new science, concerned with quantitative measurement and observation, and the older occult view which denied that the human soul was a part of nature because it was of the essence of God who has no parts, and which regarded all division and measurement as reprehensible.

The author closes with some very elliptical remarks, summarized from another article, which fit his essay to its predecessor.[3] He suggests that the old picture of a subjective observer contemplating an objective world, the psychological processes of the one having no real relation to the physical processes of the other, is breaking down. Automatic observation by instruments brings the objective principle into subjective perception; modern psychology makes the psyche itself an object of study. Further, the act of selection in experiment is an interference with an objective causal sequence; it brings the elements of creation into it, and as creation is always contingent, we return to that sense of the significant exception to causality which we see in coincidence. Thus the argument of the two essays taken together is apparently that the sense of uncaused total significance is the psychological origin of knowledge.

36

Poetry of the Tout Ensemble

Spring 1957

Review of René Char, Hypnos Waking: Poems and Prose, *selected and translated by Jackson Mathews, with the collaboration of William Carlos Williams, Richard Wilbur, William J. Smith, Barbara Howes, W.S. Merwin, and James Wright (New York: Random House, 1956); and* René Char's Poetry: Studies, *by Maurice Blanchot, Gabriel Bounoure, Albert Camus, Georges Mounin, Gaëtan Picon, René Ménard, James Wright (Rome, Italy: Éditions De Luca, 1956). From* Hudson Review, *10 (Spring 1957): 122–5. Reprinted in* NFCL, *237–42.*

One of the most fashionable poets in English literature, Charles Doughty, made the unfashionable remark, "The poet's task is not to meditate on human vanity, but to serve his country." Most of us would perhaps feel that such an observation was, first, quixotic (what country cares whether its poets want to serve it or not?), and, second, a recommending of what would in practice be a dismal bureaucratic flunkeyism, like the pseudo-arts of totalitarian states. In any case the gestures of twentieth-century writers are mainly negative ones: gestures of defiance (Pound), of detachment (Valéry), of silence, exile, and cunning (Joyce),[1] of suicide, of transferred allegiance (Eliot), of religious conversion (usually to Catholicism in countries where Protestantism is popular), and so on. It is chiefly in such contexts as the French Resistance, where the negative gesture is appropriate, that we feel how much real truth there is in Doughty's statement. Certainly it seems surprisingly reassuring to discover a poet, who, like René Char, is a man with a heroic personal record,[2] and not less a poet for having it; who is both "engaged" in his life and yet exact and difficult in his art.

A new poet usually impresses his immediate contemporaries as "experimental," or some similar term meaning relatively unintelligible. By the time criticism has made an experimental poet intelligible it has also made him traditional. If he resists this process he drops out of sight, not because he was experimental, but because he was superficially traditional, a member of a school who went along for the ride. The criticism of Char, as revealed by a recent little volume, is still in the first stages. What it says about Char is largely a series of amiable and enthusiastic gargles: we read sentence after sentence with no actual content, beyond a general emotional aim of deprecating analysis in favour of applause. Such writing results from an effort to convey the direct experience of reading the poet, an experience for which there are, of course, no words. One understands and sympathizes with it; but a glance at Char is enough to show that for him, as for Wallace Stevens, "poetry is the subject of the poem" [*The Man with the Blue Guitar*, sec. 22]: he is intensely preoccupied with the theory and function of poetry. Besides, even in straight evaluation one is still left with the question: is Char's present reputation based solely on his merits, or is it in some measure due to the fact that he corresponds so closely to what an educated Frenchman, brought up in the tradition of Rimbaud and aware of the tremendous spiritual potential of the Resistance, would expect the next great poet to be like?

Char's most obvious affinities are with the surrealists: like them he emphasizes the contrast between logical thought, which operates discursively and descriptively, and poetic thought, which operates by the immediate metaphorical identification of images. The latter is a direct and primitive form of thought which impresses the logical thinker as illogical to the verge of lunacy, or, if he is forced to take it seriously, as incredibly difficult and esoteric. Ordinary prose, or poetry approximating the idiom of prose like Wordsworth's, comes to terms with the logical thinker, which is what John Stuart Mill meant by calling Wordsworth the poet of unpoetical natures.[3] Ordinary metre also comes to terms with him, as usually it is easy to see what concessions have been made from reason to rhyme. Char writes a good deal of his best poetry in the form of aphorisms, sentences which have the rhythm of prose but the imagery and concentration of poetry. These sentences are oracular, like the aphorisms of Heraclitus, a philosopher who has deeply impressed Char. Linear reading, of the kind we apply both to ordinary prose and to metre, will not do for them. The aphorism works on the principle of the Bloody Mary: it has to be swallowed at a gulp and allowed to explode from inside. It makes possible a kind of concentration that puts a considerable strain on Char's translators, who nonetheless do a both accurate and eloquent job. "What I have to do is hell" [125], for instance, renders what in Char is simply "Devoirs infernaux." *Le Poème pulvérisé* shows in its title how constantly Char works in the tradition of "fragmentation," deliberately breaking down everything that is continuous into a series of epiphanies or *illuminations*.

Char's imagery is based on the principle of opposites, another Heraclitean conception. The centre of this principle is expressed in the title of the English collection, *Hypnos Waking*. In ordinary life we have a "real" world of waking consciousness and a submerged world of dream and desire. The latter is the source of poetry and of all creative effort: it struggles "against the real" [53] to create a world that makes more sense in terms of desire. "The poet must keep an equal balance between the physical world of waking and the dreadful ease of sleep; these are the lines of knowledge between which he lays the subtle body of the poem" [51]. Poetry finds its fulfilment in a universe of its own, a universe symbolized by the term "Word" (*le Verbe*, as distinct from *le mot* or *la parole*), which is of course not another world from ours but another way of dealing with it. This verbal universe, a world of poetry rather than of poems or individuals, is also a human universe, a world of realized freedom, desire, and intelligence. "Man be my metaphor," says Dylan Thomas [*If I Were Tickled by the Rub of Love*, l. 49], and Char says, "The being we do not know is an infinite being; he may arrive, and turn our anguish and our burden to dawn in our arteries" [61]. Like Rilke, he calls this being an "angel" to keep it "free of religious compromise" [95]. Thus, again as in Rilke, the poetic vision is from the circumference, not the centre. "Do not seek the limits of the sea. You contain them" [255]. For just as the poem finds its ultimate meaning in a total poetic universe, so man finds his own being in the corresponding human totality. "Imagination consists in expelling from reality several incomplete persons, and then using the magic and subversive powers of desire to bring them back in the form of one entirely satisfying presence" [49]. "Later," says the poet, "you will be identified as some disintegrated giant, lord of the impossible" [187].

The conception of a verbal universe comes of course from Mallarmé: it is also in Valéry, but whereas Valéry tends to think of the poet's world in Platonic and contemplative terms, Char thinks of it existentially, as "engaged" in a redemptive death-struggle with the kind of world that produces such things as the Nazi occupation. "In poetry, only when there is communication and a free ordering of the totality of things among themselves, through us, are we ourselves engaged and defined" [55]. Hence he is obliged to struggle against the world of the "Hitlerian shadows,"[4] where there can be no such thing as a "dialogue between two human beings" [151]. Hence too fighters in the Resistance discover that "the language in use here comes from the sense of wonder communicated by the beings and things we live with in continual intimacy" [109]. The sense that there is no otherness, that the moment of time encloses the whole of experience, breeds the kind of desperation that allows tyranny to flourish. "Have nothing to do with those in whose eyes man is merely a passing shade of the color on earth's tormented back" [205].

Thus the conventional religious conception of a world of eternal life, from which the "real" world has fallen and to which it will some day return, becomes in Char, as it does in most poets whether religious in temperament or not, an allegory of the poetic universe. There is a fall: "When the dam of man broke . . . words were heard in the distance . . . struggling to resist the enormous pressure" [189]. Char's poems are "poems of the illuminated absolute, of the madly impossible resurrection" [215]. This latter pole is usually placed in the future: poetry is "life's future held in requalified man" [207], and he asks whether the quest for a great being is "merely the finger of the chained present touching the future still at liberty" [257]. All through *Leaves of Hypnos*, a poetic diary of his fighting in the Resistance, we read of a new world dawning. Yet this feeling is not the usual donkey's carrot of people at war who hypnotize themselves into believing that the war is worthwhile because of all the wonderful things that will happen after it. Many of Char's associates in the Resistance entered the Maquis[5] simply to be flattered by their own conscience: he will have nothing to do with this, and nothing to do with the future of the illusions to which it gives rise. The "real" world that produced the war is always here, and only poetry can do anything effective about it.

The total impression one gets of Char is of a powerful and somewhat humourless poet grinding and churning his way like a bulldozer through the jungles of emotional confusion in contemporary life. Reading him, we see chiefly a chaos of uprooted trees, flying rocks, and "pulverized" soil; retrospectively, we see an impressive sense of direction and a good deal of courage and perseverance in following it. We have mentioned Dylan Thomas: the contrast between them indicates how much difference in national temperament there still is even in this shrinking world. Char has nothing of Thomas's very British and Dickensian zest for absurdity: like Sartre and Camus, he can deal with the absurd only when he has got it established as a metaphysical principle, and can see at a distance that man's "head trails a wake through the galaxy of the absurd" [169]. Nevertheless, there is a more important issue which is common to both traditions. We have heard a good deal about the "dissociation of sensibility"[6] in nineteenth-century poetry; we have naturally heard much less about a parallel dissociation in our own time, between poets of genuine warmth of feeling easily carried away by rhetoric (Jeffers, Lawrence), and poets of great technical skill who set up ironic barriers against feeling (Auden, Stevens).

Turning again to Char's critics, we notice how much they seem to think of Char as a kind of antidote to such a dissociation. We learn that Char is "a giant—a real physical giant" [117], who gives a sense of personal authority because he "is a poet who believes what he says, and whose word we can trust" [79]. His "poetry is a total gesture of revolution" [78], looking for a bigger transformation of society than, say, Marxism could achieve: he "is not a Christian" but "Salvation is always on his mind" [103]. He sounds in short like an old-fashioned Romantic liberal, and there are certainly many worse things to be than that. His references to Heraclitus and Georges de la Tour are in the height of intellectual fashion, yet his critics keep coming back to the same point: something which has long been neglected is being reasserted in Char. Rimbaud, Valéry, even Mallarmé: each seems to represent a dead end of some kind: they are all in different ways voices of silence, and Char, his admirers say, restores one's faith in both the present and the future of French poetry. None of them would mention Victor Hugo, yet one wonders whether in the welcome given Char there is not some sense of relief that there should finally be someone in France who knows all the tricks of twentieth-century style and still is not ashamed to echo the hoarse, uninhibited rhetoric of the great exile of Jersey who, both in literature and life, would, as Char says today of himself, "write no poem of acquiescence" [127].

37

The Realistic Oriole: A Study of Wallace Stevens

Autumn 1957

From FI, *238–55. The same text appeared first in* Hudson Review, *10 (Autumn 1957): 353–70. Reprinted in* Wallace Stevens: A Collection of Critical Essays, *ed. Marie Boroff (Englewood Cliffs, N.J.: Prentice-Hall, 1963), 161–76, and in* Modern Poetry: Essays in Criticism, *ed. John Hollander (New York: Oxford University Press, 1968), 267–84. Partially reprinted in* Twentieth-Century Literary Criticism, *ed. Sharon K. Hall (Detroit: Gale Research, 1980), 3:452–3. Frye's original parenthetical citations of Stevens's poetry in this essay, which are by page number in* The Collected Poems of Wallace Stevens (CP) *(New York: Knopf, 1954), have been moved to endnotes and now include poem titles and line numbers. His parenthetical citations of Stevens's essays, which are by page number in* The Necessary Angel *(New York: Knopf, 1951), preceded by the letters* NA, *have been retained.*

Wallace Stevens was a poet for whom the theory and the practice of poetry were inseparable. His poetic vision is informed by a metaphysic; his metaphysic is informed by a theory of knowledge; his theory of knowledge is informed by a poetic vision. He says of one of his long meditative poems that it displays "the theory of poetry / As the life of poetry,"[1] and in the introduction to his critical essays that by the theory of poetry he means "poetry itself, the naked poem" (*NA*, viii). He thus stands in contrast to the dualistic approach of Eliot, who so often speaks of poetry as though it were an emotional and sensational soul looking for a "correlative"[2] skeleton of thought to be provided by a philosopher, a Cartesian ghost trying to find a machine that will fit. No poet of any status—certainly not Eliot himself—has ever "taken over" someone else's structure of thought, and the dualistic fallacy can only beget more fallacies. Stevens is of particular interest and value to the critical theorist because he sees so clearly that the only ideas the poet can deal with are those directly involved with, and implied by, his own writing: that, in short, "Poetry is the subject of the poem."[3]

It has been established in criticism ever since Aristotle that histories are direct verbal imitations of action, and that anything in literature with a story in it is a secondary imitation of an action [*Poetics*, chaps. 1, 2]. This means, not that the story is at two removes from reality, but that its actions are representative and typical rather than specific. For some reason it has not been nearly so well understood that discursive writing is not thinking, but a direct verbal imitation of thought; that any poem with an idea in it is a secondary imitation of thought, and hence deals with representative or typical thought: that is, with forms of thought rather than specific propositions. Poetry is concerned with the ambiguities, the unconscious diagrams, the metaphors and the images out of which actual ideas grow. Poet and painter alike operate in "the flux / Between the thing as idea and / The idea as thing."[4] Stevens is an admirable poet in whom to study the processes of poetic thought at work, and such processes are part of what he means by the phrase "supreme fiction" which enters the title of his longest poem. The poet, he says, "gives to life the supreme fictions without which we are unable to conceive of it" (*NA*, 31), and fictions imitate ideas as well as events.

Any discussion of poetry has to begin with the field or area that it works in, the field described by Aristotle as nature. Stevens calls it "reality," by which he means, not simply the external physical world, but "things as they are" [*NA*, 25], the existential process that includes ordinary human life on the level of absorption in routine activity. Human intelligence can resist routine by arresting it in an act of consciousness, but the normal tendency of routine is to work against consciousness. The revolution of consciousness against routine is the starting point of all mental activity, and the centre of mental activity is imagination, the power of transforming "reality" into awareness of reality. Man can have no freedom except what begins in his own awareness of his condition. Naturally historical periods differ greatly in the amount of pressure put on free consciousness by the compulsions of ordinary life. In our own day this pressure has reached an almost intolerable degree that threatens to destroy freedom altogether and reduce human life to a level of totally preoccupied compulsion, like the life of an animal. One symptom of this is the popular demand that the artist should express in his work a sense of social obligation. The artist's primary obedience however is not to reality but to the "violence from within" (*NA*, 36) of the imagination that resists and arrests it. The minimum basis of the imagination, so to speak, is ironic realism, the act of simply becoming aware of the surrounding pressures of "things as they are." This develops the sense of alienation which is the immediate result of the imposing of consciousness on reality:

> From this the poem springs: that we live in a place
> That is not our own and, much more, not ourselves.[5]

The "act of the mind"[6] in which imagination begins, then, is an arresting of a flow of perceptions without and of impressions within. In that arrest there is born the principle of form or order: the inner violence of the imagination is a "rage for order."[7] It produces the "jar in Tennessee,"[8] the object which not only is form in itself, but creates form out of all its surroundings. Stevens follows Coleridge in distinguishing the transforming of experience by the imagination from the rearranging of it by the "fancy," and ranks the former higher[9] (ignoring, if he knew it, T.E. Hulme's clever pseudocritical reversal of the two).[10] The imagination contains reason and emotion, but the imagination keeps form concrete and particular, whereas emotion and reason are more apt to seek the vague and the general respectively.

There are two forms of mental activity that Stevens regards as unpoetic. One is the breaking down of a world of discrete objects into an amorphous and invisible substratum, a search for a "pediment of appearance,"[11] a slate-coloured world of substance[12] which destroys all form and particularity, symbolized by the bodiless serpent introduced in *The Auroras of Autumn*, "form gulping after formlessness."[13] This error is typically an error of reason. The other error is the breaking down of the individual mind in an attempt to make it a medium for some kind of universal or pantheistic mind. This is typically an error of emotion, and one that Stevens in his essays calls "romantic," which is a little confusing when his own poetry is so centrally in the Romantic tradition. What he means by it is the preference of the invisible to the visible which impels a poet to develop a false rhetoric intended to be the voice, not of himself, but of some invisible superbard within him (*NA*, 61).[14] In *Jumbo*, Stevens points out that such false rhetoric comes, not from the annihilation of the ego, but from the ego itself, from "Narcissus, prince / Of the secondary men."[15] Such an attitude produces the "nigger mystic,"[16] a phrase which naturally has nothing to do with Negroes, but refers to the kind of intellectual absolute that has been compared to a night in which all cows are black, a world clearly no improvement on "reality," which is also one colour (*NA*, 26).[17]

A third mode of mental activity, which is poetic but not Stevens's kind of poetry, is the attempt to suggest or evoke universals of mind or substance, to work at the threshold of consciousness and produce what Stevens calls "marginal" poetry and associates with Valéry (*NA*, 115). Whatever its merit, such poetry for him is in contrast with "central" poetry based on the concrete and particular act of mental experience. Stevens speaks of the imagination as moving from the hieratic to the credible (*NA*, 58), and marginal poetry, like the structures of reason and the surrenderings of emotion, seeks a "hierophant Omega"[18] or ultimate mystery. There is a strong tendency, a kind of intellectual death-wish, to conceive of order in terms of finality, as something that keeps receding from experience until experience stops, when it becomes the mirage of an "after-life" on which all hierophants, whether poets or priests, depend. But for the imagination "Reality is the beginning not the end,"[19] "The imperfect is our paradise,"[20] and the only order worth having is the "violent order" produced by the explosion of imaginative energy, which is also a "great disorder."[21]

This central view of poetry is for Stevens based on the straight Aristotelian principle that if art is not quite nature, at least it grows naturally out of nature (*Poetics*, 4). He dislikes the term "imitation," but only because he thinks it means the naive copying of an external world: in its proper Aristotelian sense of creating a form of which nature is the content, Stevens's poetry is as imitative as Pope's. Art then is not so much nature methodized as nature realized, a unity of being and knowing, existence and consciousness, achieved out of the flow of time and the fixity of space. In content it is reality and we are "Participants of its being";[22] in form it is an art which "[speaks] the feeling" for "things as they are."[23] All through Stevens's poetry we find the symbol of the alphabet or syllable, the imaginative key to reality which, by bringing reality into consciousness, heightens the sense of both, "A nature that is created in what it says."[24]

However, the imagination does bring something to reality which is not there in the first place, hence the imagination contains an element of the "unreal" which the imaginative form incorporates. This unreal is connected with the fact that conscious experience is liberated experience.

The unreal, "The fabulous and its intrinsic verse,"[25] is the sense of exhilaration and splendour in art, the "radiant and productive" atmosphere which it both creates and breathes, the sense of the virile and the heroic implied by the term "creative" itself, "the way of thinking by which we project the idea of God into the idea of man" (*NA*, 150). All art has this essential elegance or nobility, including ironic realism, but the nobility is an attribute of art, not its goal: one attains it by not trying for it, as though it were definable or extrinsic. Although art is in one sense an escape from reality (i.e., in the sense in which it is an escape *of* reality), and although art is a heightening of consciousness, it is not enough for art simply to give one a vision of a better world. Art is practical, not speculative; imaginative, not fantastic; it transforms experience, and does not merely interrupt it. The unreal in imaginative perception is most simply described as the sense that if something is not there it at least ought to be there. But this feeling in art is anything but wistful: it has created the tone of all the civilizations of history. Thus the "central" poet, by working outwards from a beginning instead of onwards toward an end, helps to achieve the only genuine kind of progress. As Stevens says, in a passage which explains the ambivalence of the term "mystic" in his work: "The adherents of the central are also mystics to begin with. But all their desire and all their ambition is to press away from mysticism toward that ultimate good sense which we term civilization" (*NA*, 116).

Such ultimate good sense depends on preserving a balance between objective reality and the subjective unreal element in the imagination. Exaggerating the latter gives us the false heroics that produce the aggressive symbols of warfare and the cult of "men suited to public ferns."[26] Exaggerating the former gives us the weariness of mind that bores the "fretful concubine"[27] in her splendid surroundings. Within art itself there has been a corresponding alternation of emphasis. In some ages, or with some poets, the emphasis is on the imaginative heightening of reality by visions of a Yeatsian "noble rider"[28]

> On his gold horse striding, like a conjured beast,
> Miraculous in its panache and swish.[29]

At other times the emphasis is ironic, thrown on the minimum role of the imagination as the simple and subjective observer of reality, not withdrawn from it, but detached enough to feel that the power of transforming it has passed by. These two emphases, the green and the red as Stevens calls them,[30] appear in Stevens's own poetry as the summer vision and the autumn vision respectively.

The summer vision of life is the *gaya scienza*,[31] the *Lebensweisheit-spielerei*, in which things are perceived in their essential radiance, when "The World is Larger."[32] This summer vision extends all over the *Harmonium* poems, with their glowing still lifes and gorgeous landscapes of Florida and the Caribbean coasts. Its dominating image is the sun, "that brave man,"[33] the hero of nature who lives in heaven but transforms the earth from his mountain-top,[34] "the strong man vaguely seen."[35] As "we are men of sun,"[36] our creative life is his, hence the feeling of alienation from nature in which consciousness begins is really inspired by exactly the opposite feeling. "I am what is around me,"[37] the poet says; the jar in Tennessee expresses the form in Tennessee as well as in itself, and one feels increasingly that "The soul . . . is composed / Of the external world"[38] in the sense that in the imagination we have "The inhuman making choice of a human self" (*NA*, 89), a subhuman world coming to a point of imaginative light in a focus of individuality and consciousness. Such a point of imaginative light is a human counterpart of the sun. The poet absorbs the reality he contemplates "as the Angevine / Absorbs Anjou"[39] just as the sun's light, by giving itself and taking nothing, absorbs the world in itself. The echo to the great trumpet call of "Let there be light" is "All things in the sun are sun."[40]

There are two aspects of the summer vision, which might be called, in Marvellian language, the visions of the golden lamp and of the green night. The latter is the more contemplative vision of the student in the tradition of Milton's penseroso poet, Shelley's Athanase, and Yeats's old man in the tower. In this vision the sun is replaced by the moon,[41] or, more frequently, "the evening star,"[42] the human counterpart of which is the student's candle.[43] Its personified form, corresponding to the sun, is often female, an "archaic"[44] or "green queen,"[45] the "desired"[46] one who eventually becomes an "interior paramour"[47] or Jungian anima,[48] the motionless spinning Penelope[49] to whom every voyager returns, the eternal Eve or naked bride[50] of the relaxed imagination. Here we are, of course, in danger of the death-wish vision, of reading a blank book. Some of the irony of this is in *Phosphor Reading by his Own Light*, as well as in *The Reader*. The bride of such a narcist vision is the sinister *Madame La Fleurie*. But in its genuine form such contemplation is the source of major imagination,[51] and hence Stevens, like Yeats, has his tower-mountain of vision or "Palaz of Hoon,"[52] where sun and poet come into alignment:

It is the natural tower of all the world,
The point of survey, green's green apogee,
But a tower more precious than the view beyond,
A point of survey squatting like a throne,
Axis of everything.[53]

From this point of survey we are lifted above the "cat," symbol of life absorbed in being without consciousness, and the "rabbit" who is "king of the ghosts" and is absorbed in consciousness without being.[54]

The autumnal vision begins in the poet's own situation. To perceive "reality" as dingy or unattractive is itself an imaginative act (*The Plain Sense of Things*), but an ironic act, an irony deepened by the fact that other modes of perception are equally possible, the oriole being as realistic as the crow,[55] and there can be no question of accepting only one as true. It is a curious tendency in human nature to believe in disillusionment: that is, to think we are nearest the truth when we have established as much falsehood as possible. This is the vision of *Mrs. Alfred Uruguay*, who approaches her mountain of contemplation the wrong way round, starting at the bottom instead of the top. (Her name is apparently based on an association with "Montevideo.") The root of the reductive tendency, at least in poetry, is perhaps the transience of the emotional mood which is the framework of the lyric. In *Harmonium* the various elaborations of vision are seen as projected from a residual ego, a comedian or clown (Peter Quince is the leader of a group of clowns),[56] who by himself has only the vision of the "*esprit bâtard*," the juggler in motley who is also a magician and whose efforts are "conjurations."[57] When we add the clown's conjurations to the clown we get "man the abstraction, the comic sum":[58] the term "abstraction" will meet us again.

This *esprit bâtard* or dimmed vision of greater maturity, *un monocle d'un oncle*, so to speak, comes into the foreground after the *Credences of Summer* and the *Things of August* have passed by. In September the web of the imagination's pupa is woven;[59] in November the moon lights up only the death of the god;[60] at the onset of winter the auroras of a vanished heroism flicker over the sky, while in the foreground stand the scarecrows or hollow men of the present.[61]

To this vision belong the bitter *Man on the Dump*, the ironic *Esthétique du Mal*, with its urbane treatment of the religio-literary clichés, such as "The death of Satan was a tragedy / For the imagination,"[62] which are the stock in trade of lesser poets, and the difficult and painfully written war poems. It is more typical of Stevens, of course, to emphasize the reality which is present in the imaginative heightening of misery, the drudge's dream of *The Ordinary Women* which nonetheless reminds us that "Imagination is the will of things."[63] The true form of the autumnal vision is not the irony which robs man of his dignity, but the tragedy which confers it (*In a Bad Time*).

At the end of autumn come the terrors of winter, the sense of a world disintegrating into chaos which we feel socially when we see the annihilation wars of our time, and individually when we face the fact of death in others or for ourselves. We have spoken of Stevens's dislike of projecting the religious imagination into a world remote in space and time. The woman in *Sunday Morning* stays home from church and meditates on religion surrounded by the brilliant oranges and greens of the summer vision, and in *A High-Toned Old Christian Woman* it is suggested that the poet, seeking an increase rather than a diminishing of life, gets closer to a genuinely religious sense than morality with its taboos and denials. For Stevens all real religion is concerned with a renewal of earth rather than with a surrender to heaven. He even says "the great poems of heaven and hell have been written and the great poem of the earth remains to be written" (*NA*, 142). It is part of his own ambition to compose hymns "Happy rather than holy but happy-high"[64] which will "take the place / Of empty heaven,"[65] and he looks forward to a world in which "all men are priests."[66] As this last phrase shows, he has no interest in turning to some cellophane-wrapped version of neo-paganism. He sees, like Yeats, that the poet is a *Connoisseur of Chaos* aware that *Poetry is a Destructive Force*, and Stevens's imagery, for all its luxuriance and good humour, is full of menace. From the "firecat" of the opening page of the *Collected Poems*,[67] through the screaming peacocks of *Domination of Black*, the buzzard of *The Jack-Rabbit*,[68] the butcher of *A Weak Mind in the Mountains*, the bodiless serpent of *The Auroras of Autumn*, and the bloody lion of *Puella Parvula*, we are aware that a simple song of *carpe diem* is not enough.

In the later poems there is a growing preoccupation with death, as, not the end of life or an introduction to something unconnected with life, but itself a part of life and giving to life itself an extra dimension. This view is very close to Rilke, especially the Rilke of the Orpheus sonnets, which are, like Stevens's poetry in general, "a constant sacrament of praise."[69] "What a ghastly situation it would be," Stevens remarks, "if the world of the dead was actually different from the world of the living" (*NA*, 76), and in several poems, especially the remarkable *Owl in the Sarcophagus*, there are references to carrying on the memories or "souvenirs" of the past into a world which is not so much future as timeless, a world of recognition or "rendezvous,"[70] and which lies in the opposite direction from the world of dreams:

> There is a monotonous babbling in our dreams
> That makes them our dependent heirs, the heirs
> Of dreamers buried in our sleep, and not
> The oncoming fantasies of better birth.[71]

In the poems of the winter vision the solar hero and the green queen become increasingly identified with the father and mother of a Freudian imago.[72] The father and mother in turn expand into a continuous life throughout time of which we form our unitary realizations. The father, "the bearded peer,"[73] extends back to the primordial sea,[74] the mother to the original maternity of nature, the "Lady Lowzen" of *Oak Leaves Are Hands*. In *The Owl in the Sarcophagus* these figures are personified as sleep and memory. The ambivalence of the female figure is expressed by the contrast between the "regina of the clouds" in *Le Monocle de Mon Oncle* and the "sister and mother and diviner love" of *To the One of Fictive Music*. The poet determined to show that "being / Includes death and the imagination"[75] must go through the same world as the "nigger mystic," for a "nigger cemetery"[76] lies in front of him too, just as the sunrise of the early play, *Three Travellers Watch a Sunrise*, is heralded by a hanged man.[77] The search for death through life which is a part of such recreation leads to a final confronting of the self and the rock (*NA*, viii),[78] the identification of consciousness and reality in which the living soul is identified with its tombstone which is equally its body.[79] In this final triumph of vision over death the death symbols are turned into symbols of life. The author of the Apocalypse prophesies to his "back-ache" (which is partly the *Weltschmerz* of the past) that the venom of the bodiless serpent will be one with its wisdom.[80] The "black river" of death, Swatara,[81] becomes *The River of Rivers in Connecticut*, a river *this* side of the Styx which "flows nowhere, like a sea" because it is in a world in which there is no more sea.[82]

If we listen carefully to the voice of "the auroral creature musing in the mind,"[83] the auroras of autumn will become, not the after-images of remembrance, but the *Morgenrot* of a new recognition. As the cycle turns through death to a new life, we meet images of spring, the central one being some modification of Venus rising from the sea: the "paltry nude" of the poem of that name; *Infanta Marina;* Susanna lying in "A wave, interminably flowing";[84] *Celle qui fût Héaulmiette* reborn from the mother and father of the winter vision, the mother having the "vague severed arms" of the maternal Venus of Milo. This reborn girl is the Jungian anima or interior paramour spoken of before, the *Golden Woman in a Silver Mirror*. She is also associated with the bird of Venus, *The Dove in the Belly* (cf. *Thinking of a Relation between the Images of Metaphors* and *Song of Fixed Accord*). It is also a bird's cry, but one outside the poet, which heralds "A new knowledge of reality" in the last line of the *Collected Poems*.[85] The spring vision often has its origin in the commonplace, or in the kind of innocent gaudiness that marks exuberant life. Of the spring images in *Celle qui fût Héaulmiette* the author remarks affectionately, "Another American vulgarity";[86] the "paltry nude" is a gilded ship's prow, and the "emperor of ice-cream" presides over funeral obsequies in a shabby household. "It is the invasion of humanity / That counts," remarks a character in *Three Travellers Watch a Sunrise*.[87] "Only the rich remember the past,"[88] the poet says, and even in *Final Soliloquy of the Interior Paramour* there is still a parenthetical association of new vision with a poverty which has nothing to lose.

In *Peter Quince at the Clavier* beauty is called "The fitful tracing of a portal."[89] Portal to what? The word itself seems to mean something to Stevens (*NA*, 60, 155), and in the obviously very personal conclusion of *The Rock* it is replaced by "gate."[90] Perhaps Stevens, like Blake, has so far only given us the end of a golden string,[91] and after traversing the circle of natural images we have still to seek the centre.

The normal unit of poetic expression is the metaphor, and Stevens was well aware of the importance of metaphor, as is evident from the many poems which use the word in title or text. His conception of metaphor is regrettably unclear, though clearer in the poetry than in the essays. He speaks of the creative process as beginning in the perception of "resemblance," adding that metamorphosis might be a better word (*NA*, 72). By resemblance he does not mean naive or associative resemblance, of the type that calls a flower a bleeding heart, but the repetitions of colour and pattern in nature which become the elements of formal design in art. He goes on to develop this conception of resemblance into a conception of "analogy" which, beginning in straight allegory, ends in the perception that "poetry becomes and is a transcendent analogue composed of the particulars of reality" (*NA*, 130). But nowhere in his essays does he suggest that metaphor is anything more than likeness or parallelism. "There is always an analogy between nature and the imagination, and possibly poetry is merely the strange rhetoric of that parallel" (*NA*, 118).

Clearly, if poetry is "merely" this, the use of metaphor could only accentuate what Stevens's poetry tries to annihilate, the sense of a contrast or great gulf fixed between subject and object, consciousness and existence. And in fact we often find metaphor used pejoratively in the poems as a form of avoiding direct contact with reality. *The Motive for Metaphor*, we are told, is the shrinking from immediate experience. Stevens appears to mean by such metaphor, however, simile or comparison, "the intricate evasions of as"[92] (cf. *Add This to Rhetoric*). And metaphor is actually nothing of the kind. In its literal grammatical form metaphor is a statement of identity: this is that, A is B. And Stevens has a very strong sense of the crucial importance of poetic identification, where "as and is are one," as it is only there that one finds "The poem of pure reality, untouched / By trope or deviation."[93] Occasionally it occurs to him that metaphor might be used in a less pejorative sense. He speaks of "The metaphor that murders metaphor" (*NA*, 84), implying that a better kind of metaphor can get murdered, and *Metaphor as Degeneration* ends in a query how metaphor can really be degeneration when it is part of the process of seeing death as a part of life.

When metaphor says that one thing "is" another thing, or that a man, a woman and a blackbird are one,[94] things are being identified *with* other things. In logical identity there is only identification *as*. If I say that the Queen of England "is" Elizabeth II, I have not identified one person with another, but one person as herself. Poetry also has this type of identification, for in poetic metaphor things are identified with each other, yet each is identified as itself, and retains that identity. When a man, a woman, and a blackbird are said to be one, each remains what it is, and the identification heightens the distinctive form of each. Such a metaphor is necessarily illogical (or anti-logical, as in "A violent disorder is an order") and hence poetic metaphors are opposed to likeness or similarity. A perception that a man, a woman, and a blackbird were in some respects alike would be logical, but would not make much of a poem. Unfortunately in prose speech we often use the word "identical" to mean very similar, as in the phrase "identical twins," and this use makes it difficult to express the idea of poetic identity in a prose essay. But if twins were really identical they would be the same person, and hence could be different in form, like a man and the same man as a boy of seven. A world of total simile, where everything was like everything else, would be a world of total monotony; a world of total metaphor, where everything is identified as itself and with everything else, would be a world where subject and object, reality and mental organization of reality, are one. Such a world of total metaphor is the formal cause of poetry. Stevens makes it clear that the poet seeks the particular and discrete image: many of the poems in *Parts of a World*, such as *On the Road Home*, express what the title of the book expresses, the uniqueness of every act of vision. Yet it is through the particular and discrete that we reach the unity of the imagination, which respects individuality, in contrast to the logical unity of the generalizing reason, which destroys it. The false unity of the dominating mind is what Stevens condemns in *The Bagatelles the Madrigals*, and in the third part of *The Pure Good of Theory*, where we find again a pejorative use of the term "metaphor."

When a thing is identified as itself, it becomes an individual of a class or total form: when we identify a brown and green mass as a tree we provide a class name for it. This is the relating of species to genera which Aristotle spoke of as one of the central aspects of metaphor. The distinctively poetic use of such metaphor is the identifying of an individual with its class, where a tree becomes Wordsworth's "tree, of many, one" [*Ode: Intimations of Immortality*, l. 51], or a man becomes mankind. Poets ordinarily do not, like some philosophers, replace individual objects with their total forms; they do not, like allegorists, represent total forms by individuals. They see individual and class as metaphorically identical: in other words they work with *myths*, many of whom are human figures in whom the individual has been identified with its universal or total form.

Such myths, "archaic forms, giants / Of sense, evoking one thing in many men,"[95] play a large role in Stevens's imagery. For some reason he speaks of the myth as "abstract." *The Ultimate Poem Is Abstract*,[96] and the first requirement of the "supreme fiction" is that it must be abstract,[97] though as far as dictionary meanings are concerned one would expect rather to hear that it must be concrete. By abstract Stevens apparently means artificial in its proper sense, something constructed rather than generalized. In such a passage as this we can see the myth forming out of "repetitions" as the individual soldier becomes the unknown soldier, and the unknown soldier the Adonis or continuously martyred god:

How red the rose that is the soldier's wound,
The wounds of many soldiers, the wounds of all

The soldiers that have fallen, red in blood,
The soldier of time grown deathless in great size.[98]

Just as there is false metaphor, so there is false myth. There is in particular the perverted myth of the average or "root-man,"[99] described more expressively as "the total man of glubbal glub."[100] Whenever we have the root-man we have, by compensation, "The super-man friseured, possessing and possessed,"[101] which is the perversion of the idea of *Übermenschlichkeit*[102] into the Carlylean great man or military hero. Wars are in their imaginative aspect a *gigantomachia* of competing aggressive myths. The war myth or hero of death is the great enemy of the imagination: he cannot be directly fought except by another war myth; he can only be contained in a greater and more genuine form of the same myth.[103] The genuine form of the war hero is the "major man"[104] who, in *The Owl in the Sarcophagus*, is personified as peace, the direct opposite of the war hero, and the third of the figures in "the mythology of modern death" which, along with sleep and memory, conquer death for life.

We thus arrive at the conception of a universal or "central man,"[105] who may be identified with any man, such as a fisherman listening to wood-doves:

The fisherman might be the single man
In whose breast, the dove, alighting, would grow still.

This passage, which combines the myth of the central man with the anima myth of the "dove in the belly," is from a poem with the painfully exact title, *Thinking of a Relation between the Images of Metaphors*.[106] The central man is often symbolized by glass or transparency, as in *Asides on the Oboe* and in *Prologues to What is Possible*. If there is a central man, there is also a "central mind"[107] of which the poet feels peculiarly a part. Similarly there is a "central poem"[108] identical with the world, and finally a "general being or human universe,"[109] of which all imaginative work forms part:

That's it. The lover writes, the believer hears,
The poet mumbles and the painter sees,
Each one, his fated eccentricity,
As a part, but part, but tenacious particle,
Of the skeleton of the ether, the total

Of letters, prophecies, perceptions, clods
Of color, the giant of nothingness, each one
And the giant ever changing, living in change.[110]

In *Sketch of the Ultimate Politician* we get a glimpse of this human universe as an infinite City of Man.

To sum up: the imaginative act breaks down the separation between subject and object, the perceiver shut up in "the enclosures of hypotheses"[111] like an embryo in a "naked egg"[112] or glass shell,[113] and a perceived world similarly imprisoned in the remoteness of its "irreducible X" (*NA*, 83), which is also an egg.[114] Separation is then replaced by the direct, primitive identification which Stevens ought to have called metaphor and which, not having a word for it, he calls "description" in one of his definitive poems [*Description without Place*], a term to which he elsewhere adds "apotheosis"[115] and "transformation,"[116] which come nearer to what he really means. The maxim that art should conceal art is based on the sense that in the greatest art we have no sense of manipulating, posing, or dominating over nature, but rather of emancipating it. "One confides in what has no / Concealed creator,"[117] the poet says, and again:

There might be, too, a change immenser than
A poet's metaphors in which being would

Come true, a point in the fire of music where
Dazzle yields to a clarity and we observe,

And observing is completing and we are content,
In a world that shrinks to an immediate whole,

That we do not need to understand, complete
Without secret arrangements of it in the mind.[118]

The theoretical postulate of Stevens's poetry is a world of total metaphor, where the poet's vision may be identified with anything it visualizes. For such poetry the most accurate word is "apocalyptic," a poetry of "revelation"[119] in which all objects and experiences are united with a total mind. Such poetry gives us:

. . . the book of reconciliation,
Book of a concept only possible

In description, canon central in itself,
The thesis of the plentifullest John.[120]

Apocalypse, however, is one of the two great narrative myths that expand "reality," with its categories of time and space, into an infinite and eternal world. A myth of a total man recovering a total world is hardly possible without a corresponding myth of a fall, or some account of what is wrong with our present perspective. Stevens's version of the fall is similar to that of the "Orphic poet" at the end of Emerson's *Nature*:

Why, then, inquire
Who has divided the world, what entrepreneur?
No man. The self, the chrysalis of all men

Became divided in the leisure of blue day
And more, in branchings after day. One part
Held fast tenaciously in common earth

And one from central earth to central sky
And in moonlit extensions of them in the mind
Searched out such majesty as it could find.[121]

Such poetry sounds religious, and in fact does have the infinite perspective of religion, for the limits of the imagination are the conceivable, not the real, and it extends over death as well as life. In the imagination the categories of "reality," space and time, are reversed into form and creation respectively, for art is *Description without Place* standing at the centre of "ideal time" (*NA*, 88), and its poetry is "even older than the ancient world" (*NA*, 145). Religion seems to have a monopoly of talking about infinite and eternal worlds, and poetry that uses such conceptions seems to be inspired by a specifically religious interest. But the more we study poetry, the more we realize that the dogmatic limiting of the poet's imagination to human and subhuman nature that we find, for instance, in Hardy and Housman, is not normal to poetry but a technical *tour de force*. It is the normal language of poetic imagination itself that is heard when Yeats says that man has invented death;[122] when Eliot reaches the still point of the turning world [*Burnt Norton*, l. 64]; when Rilke speaks of the poet's perspective as that of an angel containing all time and space, blind and looking into himself;[123] when Stevens finds his home in "The place of meta-men and para-things."[124] Such language may or may not go with a religious commitment: in itself it is simply poetry speaking as poetry must when it gets to a certain pitch of metaphorical concentration. Stevens says that his motive is neither "to console / Nor sanctify, but plainly to propound."[125]

In *Harmonium*, published in the Scott Fitzgerald decade, Stevens moves in a highly sensuous atmosphere of fine pictures, good food, exquisite taste, and luxury cruises. In the later poems, though the writing is as studiously oblique as ever, the sensuousness has largely disappeared, and the reader accustomed only to *Harmonium* may feel that Stevens's inspiration has failed him, or that he is attracted by themes outside his capacity, or that the impact of war and other ironies of the autumnal vision has shut him up in an uncommunicative didacticism. Such a view of Stevens is of course superficial, but the critical issue it raises is a genuine one.

In the criticism of drama there is a phase in which the term "theatrical" becomes pejorative, when one tries to distinguish genuine dramatic imagination from the conventional clichés of dramatic rhetoric. Of course eventually this pejorative use has to disappear, because Shakespeare and Aeschylus are quite as theatrical as Cecil de Mille. Similarly, one also goes through a stage, though a shorter one, in which the term "poetic" may acquire a slightly pejorative cast, as when one may decide, several hundred pages deep in Swinburne, that Swinburne can sometimes be a poetic bore. Eventually one realizes that the "poetic" quality comes from allusiveness, the incorporating into the texture of echoes, cadences, names, and thoughts derived from the author's previous literary experience. Swinburne is poetic in a poor sense when he is being a parasite on the literary tradition; Eliot is poetic in a better sense when, in his own phrase, he steals rather than imitates.[126] The "poetic" normally expresses itself as what one might loosely call word magic or incantation, charm in its original sense of spell, as it reinforces the "act of the mind" in poetry with the dream-like reverberations, echoes, and enlarged significances of the memory and the unconscious. We suggested at the beginning that Eliot lacks what Stevens has, the sense of an autonomous poetic theory as an inseparable part of poetic practice. On the other hand Eliot has preeminently the sense of a creative tradition, and this sense is partly what makes his poetry so uniquely penetrating, so easy to memorize unconsciously.

In Stevens there is a good deal of incantation and imitative harmony;

but the deliberately "magical" poems, such as *The Idea of Order at Key West, To the One of Fictive Music*, and the later *Song of Fixed Accord* have the special function of expressing a stasis or harmony between imagination and reality, and hence have something of a conscious rhetorical exercise about them. In *The Idea of Order at Key West* the sense of carefully controlled artifice enters the theme as well. In other poems where the texture is dryer and harder, the schemata on which "word magic" depends are reduced to a minimum. The rhymes, for instance, when they occur, are usually sharp barking assonances, parody rhymes (e.g., "The Swedish cart to be part of the heart"),[127] and the metres, like the curious blank *terza rima* used so often, are almost parody metres. A quality that is not far from being anti-"poetic" seems to emerge.

Just as the "poetic" is derived mainly from the reverberations of tradition, so it is clear that the anti-"poetic" quality in Stevens is the result of his determination to make it new, in Pound's phrase,[128] to achieve in each poem a unique expression and force his reader to make a correspondingly unique act of apprehension. This is a part of what he means by "abstract" as a quality of the "supreme fiction." It was Whitman who urged American writers to lay less emphasis on tradition,[129] thereby starting another tradition of his own, and it is significant that Whitman is one of the very few traditional poets Stevens refers to, though he has little in common with him technically. It is partly his sense of a poem as belonging to experiment rather than tradition, separated from the stream of time with its conventional echoes, that gives Stevens's poetry its marked affinity with pictures, an affinity shown also in the curiously formalized symmetry of the longer poems. *Notes toward a Supreme Fiction*, for instance, has three parts of ten sections each, each section with seven tercets, and similarly rectangular distributions of material are found in other poems.

When we meet a poet who has so much rhetorical skill, and yet lays so much emphasis on novelty and freshness of approach, the skill acquires a quality of courage: a courage that is without compromise in a world full of cheap rhetoric, yet uses none of the ready-made mixes of rhetoric in a world full of compromise. Stevens was one of the most courageous poets of our time, and his conception of the poem as "the heroic effort to live expressed / As victory"[130] was unyielding from the beginning. Courage implies persistence, and persistence in a distinctive strain often develops its complementary opposite as well, as with Blake's fool who by persisting in his folly became wise [*The Marriage of Heaven and Hell*, pl.

7; E36]. It was persistence that transformed the tropical lushness of *Harmonium* into the austere clairvoyance of *The Rock,* the luxurious demon into the necessary angel, and so rounded out a vision of major scope and intensity. As a result Stevens became, unlike many others who may have started off with equal abilities, not one of our expendable rhetoricians, but one of our small handful of essential poets.

38

Religion and Modern Poetry

1958–59

From Challenge and Response: Modern Ideas and Religion, *ed. Randolph C. Chalmers and John A. Irving (Toronto: Ryerson Press, 1959), 23–36. Reprinted in* RW, *228–41.*

I

I apologize in advance for a somewhat abstract introduction, but the problems of poetry and belief are still too complex and too little understood for us to dispense with some preliminary explanation.

Poetry has from the earliest times been confused with oratory. The structure of both is rhetorical; they both have a strong emotional appeal, and there are other factors in common. Yet there is a crucial difference: the poet, *qua* poet, never addresses a reader directly. If he did, he ought to be judged, as we judge everything that is said to us directly, by the standards of truth and falsehood. But "the poet never affirmeth," as Sidney says:[1] his statements are not statements of fact, and he is not conveying ideas or messages to us; he is putting words into patterns. Direct speech is signal language, which tends to disappear when its function is accomplished: even a long book, if written purely as direct statement, survives only tentatively, as a convenience of reference. The poet proceeds hypothetically; he does not say "this is so," but "let this be," and in consequence, the poem tends not to disappear, but to repeat itself in the same form. Hence our first reaction to a poem, whether religious or not, should not be, "Does what is said here correspond to my beliefs or experiences?" but, "Is what is said here an imaginatively coherent expression of any belief or experience?" The former question distorts the poem into a direct statement; the latter does not.

Most of the major fallacies that untrained readers fall into arise from the confusion of poetry with direct statement. One is the so-called "intentional fallacy,"[2] the transfer of the legitimate question of fact, "What does this poem say here?" to the hazy pseudo-problem of "What did the poet mean by this?" Another is the muddle over the conception of "inspiration." It is the reader, not the poet, who is, or should be, inspired by great poetry. The metaphor of inspiration was originally devised by the poets to account for their own feeling that they were not speaking directly to a reader; that they were not shaping their poems so much as releasing them; that their minds were places where things happened to words, often independently of their conscious wills. Hence the conventional appeal to a Muse who speaks through the poet. But this metaphor becomes very misleading if it suggests that a poem is directly addressed by a Muse, or whatever it is, through the poet to the reader. This would make a poet simply a medium, and would put his craftsmanship on the level of a medium's ability to go into a trance and speak with the voice of a defunct eight-year-old named Susie.

A still more deeply rooted fallacy is the notion that good and bad inhere in works of art as moral qualities. If we are directly addressed by a saint or a sinner, the content of what they say may be morally good or bad because it comes directly from people who are habitually good or bad. A poem not being a direct statement, it can be good or bad only in its own categories: an evil or wicked poem is a contradiction in terms, no matter how sinful we may think the poet was after consulting his biography. In literature this fallacy results in a demand for censorship, which is a form of the scapegoat fallacy, of projecting our own sins on something else and then removing it from our sight. When Milton remarked in *Areopagitica* that a wise man will make a better use of an idle pamphlet than a fool will of Holy Scripture,[3] he blew the bottom out of the superstition of censorship. It is the reader who is primarily responsible for the moral quality of what he reads, and it is the desire to evade this responsibility, either for oneself or, more commonly, on behalf of others assumed to be less intelligent, that produces the censor.

We meet poetry, of course, in a state of engagement: we are already involved in a great variety of beliefs, opinions, prejudices, situations, with emotional currents running toward or away from everything we encounter, poetry included. We have a very strong impulse to make an associative response to poetry: to react to its content according to our stock responses, instead of judging its form in a specific aesthetic response. The tendency to stock response is rationalized in many ways, and the feeling that there is something morally irresponsible about an aesthetic judgment is not confined to "puritans," as anyone who has taught undergraduates is well aware. But poetry is a specific thing, and has to be met specifically, with the aesthetic response appropriate to it, and with all our religious, moral, social, and personal anxieties kept, for the moment, quiet. Aristotle's principle of catharsis, though applied by him only to tragedy, is actually the principle of aesthetic response [*Poetics*, 6]: pity and fear (i.e., the attracting and repelling emotions making for moral judgment) are relevant to art, but are not, finally, to be attached to it. Once we have learned to make this type of judgment, poetry begins to become our own imaginative possession, and the impression that its great utterances make on us becomes intensified from pleasurable reaction to something more like meditation. At that stage, our particular religious, moral, and social commitments come again into play, and we find that, among the best poets, some mean more to us than others for personal reasons. But the number who reach that stage is small.

The minor fallacies of the associative response may be briefly dealt with. Personal sincerity is of no importance in poetry (because personal sincerity as such is inarticulate); it is only literary sincerity that matters: the ability to persuade the reader that one is being sincere by the skill with which one can move words around. A poet may be consumed with a desire to write some kind of verse and be capable only of writing quite different kinds. A deeply religious person writing poetry may produce doggerel (the verb should be stronger than "may," as a glance at our hymn books will show); a poet quite indifferent to any kind of religious belief may write imperishable religious verse. In fact his absence of commitment may be an advantage to him as a poet.

II

Literature, and more especially poetry, has for centuries been regarded as the central discipline of the "humanities," which in their turn were thought of as the studies concerned with human life, as distinct from science, the study of nature, and divinity, the study of God. The link between poetry and nature was established in the theory of criticism by Aristotle [*Poetics*, chaps. 1, 2]. In Aristotle's conception of mimesis, art imitates nature in the sense that art is a form that has nature for its content. In a picture of flowers, the only form that painted flowers have is a pictorial form. Nature remains outside the work of art as its environment, but not as its model. Painted flowers are not simply second-hand copies or ghosts of real flowers: the painter would be a fool if he tried to compete with nature on nature's own ground. But the painter is not providing us with a substitute for our actual experience of flowers; he is providing us with a human idea or form of which flowers are the content. The "nature" which literary critics and readers deal with, therefore, is inside the art, or "contained" by it, not outside it. Further, poems are imaginative, not rational or descriptive, and the limit of the imagination is not the credible or the reasonable, but the conceivable. The most fantastic and impossible things are still conceivable, and may be so without being unnatural.

Science studies nature directly: it is concerned with the world as it is. The arts are the skills that man has evolved out of nature for the purpose of turning the physical world into a world with a human form and a physical content, the human form that we usually call civilization or culture. One pole of art, then, is the material it works with, and this material is derived from nature. The other pole of art is the total form it works toward, the vision of a human world, culture or civilization or whatever we call it, which the individual work of art participates in. And just as art is connected with nature by mimesis, so it is connected with total human culture by a principle that we may call revelation, using that term in a purely humanistic context as the revelation by the human mind, through human art, of the vision of a human world. Such a vision may be called, in Aristotelian terms, the *telos* or formal cause of human life: whatever sense the poet may have of the context, the meaning, the possibilities in, or the ultimate destiny of the human situation. This is the world that the poet reveals, as distinct from the world of nature that he imitates.

There is no reason why a poet's revelation of the human world should have any kind of connection with a divine world or with any specifically religious doctrine: there is equally no reason why it should not. The most one can say is that as the limit of the imagination is the conceivable and not the possible, there is a kind of innate expanding impetus in poetry towards the conceivable limits of imagination, which are the infinite and the eternal. There is thus a natural alliance between the language of the imagination and the teachings of most of the higher religions. The poet may follow closely the canons of divine revelation as they are accepted in whatever religion is contemporary with him, or he may ignore these canons and concentrate on some other aspect of human experience, real or imagined. In either case, whatever he reveals, he reveals in human terms.

We must take the same precautions in interpreting what a poet reveals that we take in interpreting what he imitates. In poetic imitation, the fantastic is not necessarily unnatural; in poetic revelation, the heretical is not necessarily unauthentic. In imitation, it would be silly to think of a flower picture as merely a two-dimensional and oily substitute for real flowers; it would be equally silly to think of religious poetry as a metrical substitute for actual religious experience. In imitation, we do not ask that the poet confine himself to experiences like those that we have had; in revelation, we do not ask that he confine himself to beliefs that we hold. In approaching modern poetry with a religious interest, our motto must be William Blake's "Every thing possible to be believ'd is an image of truth" [*The Marriage of Heaven and Hell*, pl. 8, l. 38; E37].

Some poets feel that the source of revelation is the same as the source of imitation: in other words, that nature should be our teacher. Wordsworth, with reservations, was such a poet, and his revelation tends to focus on moments of intense awareness of identity with nature, where the human and physical orders are fused into a single "motion and a spirit" [*Tintern Abbey*, l. 100], when "we feel that we are greater than we know" [*The River Duddon*, Sonnet 34, *Afterthought*, l. 14]. Such a revelation is emotionally precise and intellectually vague: if a poet is very good at this kind of revelation, he is unlikely to be equally good at other kinds where intellectual precision is called for. If we compare the great moments of *The Prelude* with the *Ecclesiastical Sonnets*, we can see that this is true of Wordsworth.

Other poets feel that what man and nature have in common is not so much creation as chaos: that from nature comes the murmuring of mysterious oracles, hints, symbols, and compelling moods, which find echoes in the more dimly lit areas of the mind. Thus Baudelaire:

> Comme de longs échos qui de loin se confondent,
> Dans une ténébreuse et profonde unité,
> Vaste comme la nuit et comme la clarté,
> Les parfums, les couleurs et les sons se répondent.
>
> [*Correspondances*, ll. 5–8]

Such a feeling recurs throughout the poetry of Robert Frost, in *Stopping by Woods on a Snowy Evening*, and elsewhere. Again, we see when we turn to Frost's *Masque of Reason*, a variation on the theme of Job, that Frost is less successful at this more specific type of revelation. Similar moods are evoked, in a different way by a different kind of poet—Walter de la Mare—in connection with the sense that other forms of life are locked up in inscrutable prisons of consciousness. This is the feeling that inspires most of the beliefs in or imaginative conceptions of fairies and elemental spirits, and accounts for the prominence of such themes in de la Mare.

Still other poets respond most strongly to the sense of the cleavage between human consciousness and the subhuman, submoral, indifferent nature from which it has evolved. Thomas Hardy, who, considered as a religious poet, might be described as about two-thirds of a Presbyterian, is concerned less with any actual God than with the idol that man creates when he tries to worship the mindless mechanism of the sky. This idol, considered as a god, can only be an abysmally stupid and muddled god, yet there is always the disturbing possibility that this "Vast Imbecility" is the only god we have [*Nature's Questioning*, l. 13]. Some poets however take the opposite view and see in the antagonism between man's intellect and the rest of his nature the root of his cruelty and malice. D.H. Lawrence is deeply stirred by the sense that man is the prodigal son of nature; that the loving deity to whom he should be reconciled is Eros, not Agape, a god whose gifts are those of rebirth rather than immortality. Robert Graves feels that all the genuine inspiration of poetry by religion is derived from the ancient Mediterranean cult of a mother-goddess to whom a male lover was annually sacrificed, and that the introduction of a Father-God was a disaster to poetry and religion alike.

Some poets feel that man is walled off from a higher destiny by superconscious powers that he can never reach and that are indifferent to him. This feeling, which is as old as the *Iliad*—or the Gilgamesh epic—is evoked by the austere angels of Rilke's *Duino Elegies*. On a simpler level it recurs in the farmers of A.E. Housman cursing "whatever brute and blackguard made the world" [*The Chestnut Casts His Flambeaux*, l. 12]. Others, such as Robinson Jeffers, see nothing in front of man except his gradual disappearance as a natural species. Ezra Pound finds the source of his vision of the human world in Confucius and the "unwobbling pivot"[4] of the Word—the human word, not a divine word made flesh.

We could go on for a long time. In his younger days Yeats proposed to found a new religion on what the greatest poets have revealed.[5] It is already clear that any such religion would have a versatile but remarkably confused apostolic creed. No, there is no religion of poetry, but poetry may have a valuable religious service to perform nonetheless. The stronger our faith in a religion, the sharper our doubts become of our adequacy to practise or even understand its precepts. By showing us how many intellectually possible and emotionally convincing types of revelation there are, poetry helps to protect our religion from the idolatry of arrogance. Our experience of religion begins in faith and bears fruit in charity. Our experience of poetry begins, in Coleridge's phrase, in a willing suspension of disbelief, and bears fruit in a willing suspension of intolerance.

There are two main types of poetry in which the reader concerned with both religion and poetry may be primarily interested. One type is poetry that is more or less conventionally religious in content, though good enough as poetry for the associative fallacy not to operate. The other is poetry that has not been satisfied to remain with nature and with man as we find him, but has pushed on into the eternal and infinite worlds, into the realms of death and afterlife, but speculatively, and without sustained dependence on specific religious doctrines. In twentieth-century English poetry, the best-known poet of the former type is T.S. Eliot, of the latter type W.B. Yeats.

III

At the turn of the century the dominant conventions in English poetry were Romantic ones, as Victorian poetry had made no essential break with Romanticism. So far as it dealt with revelation, Romantic poetry tended to be an individual recreation of experience. The poet might find the essential meaning of experience inside or outside the Christian tradition; he might even, as Shelley did, abandon his last major poem with the question, "Then what is life?" [*The Triumph of Life*, l. 544]. But the favourite metaphor for writing poetry was that of "creation," and the poet tended to think of himself as participating in a wider creative process, whether divine, natural, or demiurgical. Hence an emphasis on the individual discovery and recreation of even the most traditionally accepted values; hence too an incorporation of a great deal of argument, meditation, rumination, as the poet shaped and worked his way toward his vision of the world. In Browning, for instance, we have a poet within the Protestant tradition for whom the central fact of that vision was the Incarnation. But in Browning the Incarnation is usually reached by some form of argument, whether connected with Old Testament prophecy (*Saul*), New Testament history (*A Death in the Desert*), accidental discovery by a contemporary (*Epistle to Karshish*), repudiation from the sceptics (*Cleon*), or the poet's own experience (*Christmas Eve and Easter Day*). However much we may admire these poems, the amount of sheer *talk* in them reminds us of Erasmus's translation of the opening of the Fourth Gospel: *in principio erat sermo*.[6]

The Romantic values went out of fashion during the First World War, partly because the German tradition had been closely associated with them. In a clever and very influential piece of pseudo-criticism, T.E. Hulme attacked Romanticism as "spilt religion,"[7] and advocated a return to Classical values, which for him included intellectual clarity, emotional discipline, emphasis on the craftsmanship of writing, and a sense of the limitations of human effort which in religion is expressed by the doctrine of original sin. In imitating nature, the poet may be fanciful or he may be realistic, accepting and studying nature as it is. What Hulme was advocating was a movement in revelation corresponding to realism in the imitation of nature. The traditional Christian values are there, to be accepted and studied, and the poet is set free to do his own work properly only when he is not wasting his energy pretending to invent or rediscover his ideas. Such an attitude throws its influence on the side of the Catholic acceptance of divine revelation through the historical and traditional church.

Hulme is only one of a great many indications of a change of taste, but he is a simple and useful one for explaining certain attitudes in T.S. Eliot. In Eliot, as in Browning, the central religious conception is the Incarnation, but in Eliot the Incarnation is a spiritual presence immediately confronting the physical presence of a squalid and sterile world. The two presences run contrapuntally against one another, sometimes using the same natural imagery, but more frequently in a relation of mutual parody. Thus in an early *Prelude* we have

> The conscience of a blackened street
> Impatient to assume the world. [*Preludes*, ll. 46–7]

set over against

> The notion of some infinitely gentle
> Infinitely suffering thing. [*Preludes*, ll. 50–1]

In *Gerontion* "Christ the tiger" is set over against the dying old man, whose spiritual exhaustion not only makes him see Christ as a devouring wrath, but makes him feel that Christ's death was less of a humiliation than his continued presence in the church:

> To be eaten, to be divided, to be drunk
> Among whispers; by Mr. Silvero
> With caressing hands . . . [ll. 22–4]

In *The Waste Land* the irony is more complex: here Christ is associated with all the imagery of Frazer's dying god, and he rises appropriately in the spring; but he is only an invisible figure: in the foreground of the poem is the aged and impotent "fisher king," identified with the first Adam, and with the waste land of twentieth-century civilization, who sits helplessly on the bank of the Thames waiting for the fisher of men.

The language of the Quartets is still more elaborately sacramental. In these poems the physical world is a temporal flux, the river of Heraclitus into which no one steps twice, pulled from the past into the future, like the trains in the London tube, "In appetency, on its metalled ways" [*Burnt Norton*, l. 28]. In the Incarnation the spiritual world crosses the physical one at right angles, forming an axis that is "the still point of the turning world" [l. 64], neither temporal nor timeless, but holding them both in an "impossible union" [*The Dry Salvages*, l. 220]. The moment of the Incarnation, repeated daily in the Mass, is repeated also, potentially, in every moment of experience, though most of us never realize anything of this except a vague sense of spiritual significance that is gone before we are aware of it:

> These are only hints and guesses,
> Hints followed by guesses; and the rest
> Is prayer, observance, discipline, thought and action.
> The hint half guessed, the gift half understood, is Incarnation.
> [*The Dry Salvages*, ll. 216–19]

The technical result of Eliot's treatment of the Incarnation is that the symbolic and typological language of the Bible and the church, which had almost dropped out of English poetry after Milton, is now being used again as a poetic language. In *Ash-Wednesday*, for instance, the central theme has at least four symbolic voices, to use a musical metaphor: the climb up the purgatorial mountain towards the Garden of Eden, taken from Dante; the wandering through the wilderness to the Promised Land; the exile of Adam and his return to Eden at the Last Judgment; and the Lent and Easter of the liturgical year. Such language was being revived in the '20s of this century through many other influences. The increased popularity of Donne and the other metaphysicals was one such influence; the belated publication of the poems of Gerard Manley Hopkins, the Victorian Catholic convert and Jesuit priest, was another. The title of one of Hopkins's sonnets, *That Nature Is a Heraclitean Fire and of the Comfort of the Resurrection*, indicates some affinity with Eliot in poetic thinking, if not in technique. But it was Eliot who did most to popularize this religious language and make it available for other poets.

A good deal of the alleged obscurity of modern poetry disappears for readers who understand a modicum of the symbolism of Christianity. Such a stanza as this from Robert Lowell's *The Drunken Fisherman* should be clear enough to anyone who can understand the pun on the word "peter":

> The Fisher's sons must cast about
> When shallow waters peter out.
> I will catch Christ with a greased worm,
> And when the Prince of Darkness stalks
> My bloodstream to its Stygian term . . .
> On water the Man-Fisher walks. [ll. 35–40]

For Dylan Thomas, who gets most of his symbolic language straight from his evangelical Welsh background, the city and garden of the Bible are the framework of human experience, from the memories of his own childhood, when "it was all Adam and maiden"[8] to the moment of death when

> . . . I must enter again the round
> Zion of the water bead
> And the synagogue of the ear of corn . . .
> Or sow my salt seed
> In the least valley of sackcloth to mourn . . .
> [*The Refusal to Mourn the Death, by Fire, of a Child in London*, ll. 7–9, 11–12]

And in W.H. Auden, whose religious position is close to Eliot's, the birth and death of Christ are, at each moment, simultaneous with the events of our own lives, as in *Nones* the Crucifixion throws its shadow across all future history:

> This mutilated flesh, our victim,
> Explains too nakedly, too well,
> The spell of the asparagus garden,
> The aim of our chalk-pit game: stamps,
> Bird's eggs are not the same . . .
> . . . Wherever
> The sun shines, brooks run, books are written,
> There will also be this death. [ll. 49–53, 62–4]

In most of these poets (though not in Thomas) the religious feeling is intensely Catholic in the sense that the sacramental life initiated by the Church is the informing power of ordinary life. Protestantism has had practically no direct influence on modern poetry. In the Romantics, however, for whom the artist is a creator, participating in the creative energy of God, there is a natural analogy with Protestant religious experience. We see this clearly in Blake and Coleridge, and even Shelley and Keats, if not exactly Protestant poets, were poets that only a Protestant tradition could have produced. Much the same may be said of Yeats, whose symbolic language was drawn mainly from Irish myth and from Rosicrucianism, which was itself a broken-down form of Biblical typology. Yeats prophesies the imminent end of the Christian era, with an Antichrist slouching "towards Bethlehem to be born" [*The Second Coming*, l. 22], with a new Leda and swan replacing the Virgin and the dove, with an aristocratic, violent, and tragic civilization coming to replace the milder virtues of Christianity. Yet he recurs over and over to a fundamental conviction that, somehow or other, man, through his imagination or creative power, must have an infinite and eternal dimension. In *Sailing to Byzantium* the heavenly city which the poet wishes to reach at death is also a human palace of art, and in *The Tower* he is still more explicit that death is one of the illusions of the fall of man, and that man's real humanity is eternal:

> And I declare my faith:
> I mock Plotinus' thought

And cry in Plato's teeth,
Death and life were not
Till man made up the whole,
Made lock, stock and barrel
Out of his bitter soul,
Aye, sun and moon and star, all,
And further add to that
That, being dead, we rise,
Dream and so create
Translunar Paradise. [pt. 3, ll. 25–36]

The sense of the divinity of the imagination is not extinct among poets, nor is it likely to become so. There are glints of it in Frost, in e.e. cummings, even in Hart Crane. Wallace Stevens, also, moves from the amused detachment of such early poems as *Sunday Morning*, an elaborate rationalization of a woman's reluctance to go to church, toward the curious wistfulness of his last poems:

Here, now, we forget each other and ourselves.
We feel the obscurity of an order, a whole,
A knowledge, that which arranged the rendezvous

Within its vital boundary, in the mind.
We say God and the imagination are one . . .
How high that highest candle lights the dark.

Out of this same light, out of the central mind,
We make a dwelling in the evening air,
In which being there together is enough.
[*Final Soliloquy of the Interior Paramour*, ll. 10–18]

One wonders whether poetry may not be doing its greatest service to religion by following its own bent for uninhibited imaginative speculation. Perhaps it is this vague and hopeful illusion, rather than the more precise language of the sacramental poets, that reminds us most clearly that Scripture is poetic and not doctrinal, that Jesus taught in parables and not in syllogisms, and that our spiritual vision is in a riddle.

39

The Nightmare Life in Death

August 1960

Review of Samuel Beckett, "Molloy," "Malone Dies," and "The Unnamable": Three Novels *(New York: Grove Press, 1959). From* Hudson Review, *13 (August 1960): 442–9. Reprinted in* Twentieth-Century Interpretations of "Molloy," "Malone Dies," "The Unnamable," *ed. J.D. O'Hara (Englewood Cliffs, N.J.: Prentice-Hall, 1970), 26–45; in* Samuel Beckett: The Critical Heritage, *ed. Laurence Graver and Raymond Federman (London: Routledge & Kegan Paul, 1979), 206–14; and in* NFCL, *219–29.*

In every age the theory of society and the theory of personality have closely approached each other. In Plato the wise man's mind is a dictatorship of reason over appetite, with the will acting as a thought police hunting down and exterminating all lawless impulses [*Republic*, chaps. 7, 9]. The ideal state, with its philosopher-king, guards, and artisans, has the corresponding social form. Michael explains to Adam in *Paradise Lost* that tyranny must exist in society as long as passion dominates reason in individuals, as they are called [bk. 12, ll. 79–101]. In our day Marxism finds its psychological counterpart in the behaviourism and conditioned reflexes of Pavlov, and the Freudian picture of man is also the picture of western Europe and America, hoping that its blocks and tensions and hysterical explosions will settle into some kind of precarious working agreement. In this alignment religion has regularly formed a third, its gods and their enemies deriving their characteristics from whatever is highest and lowest in the personal–social picture. A good deal of the best fiction of our time has employed a kind of myth that might be read as a psychological, a social, or a religious allegory, except that it cannot be reduced to an allegory, but remains a myth, moving in all three areas of life at once, and thereby interconnecting them as well. The powerful appeal of Kafka for our age is largely due to the way in which such stories as *The Trial* or *The Castle* manage to suggest at once the atmosphere of an anxiety dream, the theology of the Book of Job, and the police terrorism and bureaucratic anonymity of the society that inspired Freud's term "censor." It was the same appeal in the myth of *Waiting for Godot* that, so to speak, identified Samuel Beckett as a contemporary writer.

As a fiction writer Samuel Beckett derives from Proust and Joyce, and his essay on Proust[1] is a good place to start from in examining his own work. This essay puts Proust in a context that is curiously Oriental in its view of personality. "Normal" people, we learn, are driven along through time on a current of habit energy, an energy which, because habitual, is mostly automatic. This energy relates itself to the present by the will, to the past by voluntary or selective memory, to the future by desire and expectation. It is a subjective energy, although it has no consistent or permanent subject, for the ego that desires now can at best only possess later, by which time it is a different ego and wants something else. But an illusion of continuity is kept up by the speed, like a motion picture, and it generates a corresponding objective illusion, where things run along in the expected and habitual form of causality. Some people try to get off this time machine, either because they have more sensitivity or, perhaps, some kind of physical weakness that makes it not an exhilarating joyride but a nightmare of frustration and despair. Among these are artists like Proust, who look behind the surface of the ego, behind voluntary to involuntary memory, behind will and desire to conscious perception. As soon as the subjective motion picture disappears, the objective one disappears too, and we have recurring contacts between a particular moment and a particular object, as in the epiphanies of the madeleine and the phrase in Vinteuil's music.[2] Here the object, stripped of the habitual and expected response, appears in all the enchanted glow of uniqueness, and the relation of the moment to such an object is a relation of identity. Such a relation, achieved between two human beings, would be love, in contrast to the ego's pursuit of the object of desire, like Odette or Albertine, which tantalizes precisely because it is never loved. In the relation of identity consciousness has triumphed over time, and destroys the prison of habit with its double illusion stretching forever into past and future. At that moment we may enter what Proust and Beckett agree is the only possible type of paradise, that which has been lost. For the ego only two forms of failure are possible, the failure to possess, which may be tragic, and the failure to communicate, which is normally comic.

In the early story *Murphy*, the hero is an Irishman with an Irish interest in the occult—several of Beckett's characters are readers of Æ—and a profound disinclination to work. We first meet him naked, strapped to a chair, and practising trance.[3] He has however no interest in any genuine mental discipline, and feels an affinity with the easygoing Belacqua of Dante's *Purgatorio*,[4] also mentioned in *Molloy* [8], who was in no hurry to begin his climb up the mountain. What he is really looking for is a self-contained egocentric consciousness, "windowless, like a monad,"[5] that no outward events can injure or distort. He is prodded by the heroine Celia into looking for a job, and eventually finds one as a male nurse in a lunatic asylum. In the asylum he discovers a kinship with the psychotic patients, who are trying to find the same thing in their own way, and his sympathy with them not only gives him a job he can do but makes him something rather better than a "seedy solipsist."[6] To take this job he turns his back on Celia and other people who are said to need him, but in the airless microcosm of his mental retreat there is the one weak spot that makes him human and not completely selfish, a need for communication. He looks for this in the eye of Endon, his best friend among the patients, but sees no recognition in the eye, only his own image reflected in the pupil. "The last Mr. Murphy saw of Mr. Endon was Mr. Murphy unseen by Mr. Endon."[7] He then commits suicide. The same image of the unrecognizing eye occurs in the one-act play *Embers* and in *Krapp's Last Tape*, where Krapp, more completely bound to memory and desire than Murphy, and so a figure of less dignity if also of less absurdity, looks into his mistress's eyes and says "Let me in."[8] Another echo in this phrase will meet us in a moment.

The figure of the pure ego in a closed auto-erotic circle meets us many times in Beckett's masturbating, carrot-chewing, stone-sucking characters. A more traditional image of the consciousness goaded by desire or memory (an actual goad appears in one of Beckett's pantomimes), is that of master and servant. Already in *Murphy* we have, in the characters Neary and Cooper, an adumbration of the Hamm and Clov of *Endgame*, a servant who cannot sit and a master who cannot stand, bound together in some way and yet longing to be rid of each other. *Watt* tells the story of a servant who drifts into a house owned by a Mr. Knott, one of a long procession of servants absorbed and expelled from it by some unseen force. Technically the book is a contrast to *Murphy*, which is written in an epigrammatic wisecracking style. In *Watt* there is a shaggy-dog type of deliberately misleading humour, expressing itself in a maddeningly prolix pseudo-logic. One notes the use of a device more recently popularized by Lawrence Durrell, of putting some of the debris of the material collected into an appendix. "Only fatigue and disgust prevented its incorporation,"[9] the author demurely informs us. The most trivial actions of Watt, most of which are very similar to those we perform ourselves every day, are exhaustively catalogued in an elaborate pretence of obsessive realism, and we can see how such "realism" in fiction, pushed to so logical a conclusion, soon gives the effect of living in a kind of casual and unpunishing hell. Watt finally decides that "if one of these things was worth doing, all were worth doing, but that none was worth doing, no, not one, but that all were unadvisable, without exception."[10]

In *Waiting for Godot*, as everyone knows, two dreary men in bowler hats stand around waiting for the mysterious Godot, who never appears but only sends a messenger to say he will not come. It is a favourite device of ironic fiction, from Kafka to Menotti's opera *The Consul*, to make the central character someone who not only fails to manifest himself but whose very existence is called in question. The two men wonder whether in some way they are "tied" to Godot, but decide that they probably are not, though they are afraid he might punish them if they desert their post. They also feel tied to one another, though each feels he would do better on his own. They resemble criminals in that they feel that they have no rights: "we got rid of them,"[11] one says, and is exhorted by a stage direction to say it distinctly. They stand in front of a dead tree, speculating, like many of Beckett's characters, about hanging themselves from it, and one of them feels an uneasy kinship with the thieves crucified with Christ. Instead of Godot, there appears a diabolical figure named Pozzo (pool: the overtones extend from Satan to Narcissus), driving an animal in human shape named Lucky, with a whip and a rope. Lucky, we are told, thinks he is entangled in a net: the image of being fished for by some omnipotent and malignant angler recurs in *The Unnamable*. In the second act the two turn up again, but this time Pozzo is blind and helpless, like Hamm in *Endgame*.

When the double illusion of a continuous ego and a continuous causality is abolished, what appears in its place? First of all, the ego is stripped of all individuality and is seen merely as representative of all of its kind. When asked for their names, one of the two men waiting for Godot answers "Adam,"[12] and the other one says: "At this place, at this moment of time, all mankind is us."[13] Similar echoes are awakened by the Biblical title of the play *All That Fall*, with its discussion of the falling sparrow in the Gospels and its final image of the child falling from the train, its death unheeded by the only character who was on the train. Other characters have such names as Watt, Knott, and Krapp, suggestive of infantile jokes and of what in *Molloy* are called "decaying circus clowns" [43]. The dramatic convention parodied in *Waiting for Godot* is clearly the act that killed vaudeville, the weary dialogue of two faceless figures who will say anything to put off leaving the stage. In the "gallery of moribunds" [137] we are about to examine there is a series of speakers whose names begin with M, one of whom, Macmann, has the most obvious everyman associations. In this trilogy, however, there is a more thoroughgoing examination of the unreality of the ego, and one which seems to owe something to the sequence of three chapters in *Finnegans Wake* in which Shaun is studied under the names Shaun, Jaun, and Yawn, until he disappears into the larger form of HCE.[14] It is the "Yawn" chapter that Beckett most frequently refers to.[15] In reading the trilogy we should keep in mind the remark in the essay on Proust that "the heart of the cauliflower or the ideal core of the onion would represent a more appropriate tribute to the labours of poetical excavation than the crown of bay."[16]

Molloy is divided into two parts: the first is Molloy's own narrative; the second is the narrative of Jacques Moran, who receives a message through one Gaber from an undefined Youdi to go and find Molloy. The echoes of Gabriel and Yahweh make it obvious by analogy that the name "Godot" is intended to sound like "God." Youdi, or someone similar to him, is once referred to as "the Obidil" [46], which is an anagram of libido. The associations of Molloy are Irish, pagan, and a Caliban-like intelligence rooted in a disillusioned sensitivity. Moran is French, nominally Christian, and a harsher and more aggressive type of sterility. Molloy, like many of Beckett's characters, is so crippled as to resemble the experiments on mutilated and beheaded animals that try to establish how much life is consistent with death. He is also under a wandering curse, like the Wandering Jew, and is trying to find his mother. There are echoes of the wandering figure in Chaucer's *Pardoner's Tale*, who keeps knocking on the ground with his staff and begging his mother to let him in. But Molloy does not exactly long for death, because for him the universe is also a vast auto-erotic ring, a serpent with its tail in its mouth, and it knows no real difference between life and death. Overtones of *Ulysses* appear in his sojourn with Lousse (Circe), and the mention of "moly" suggests an association with his name [69]. He is also, more Biblically, "in an Egypt without bounds, without infant, without mother"

[86], and a dim memory of Faust appears in his account of various sciences studied and abandoned, of which magic alone remained [48–9]. Like the contemporary beats (in *Murphy*, incidentally, the padded cells are called "pads"),[17] he finds around him a world of confident and adjusted squares, who sometimes take the form of police and bully him. "They wake up, hale and hearty, their tongues hanging out for order, beauty and justice, baying for their due" [87]. The landscape around him, described in terms similar to Dante's *Inferno*, changes, but he is unable to go out of his "region," and realizes that he is not moving at all. The only real change is a progressive physical deterioration and a growing loss of such social contact as he has. The landscape finally changes to a forest and Molloy, too exhausted to walk and unable, like Beckett's other servants, to sit, crawls on his belly like a serpent until he finally stops. He arrives at his mother's house, but characteristically we learn this not from the last sentence but from the first one, as the narrative goes around in a Viconian circle.

Just before the end of his account, Molloy, who hears voices of "prompters" in his mind, is told that help is coming. Moran sets off to find Molloy, aware that his real quest is to find Molloy inside himself, as a kind of Hyde to his Jekyll. He starts out with his son, whom he is trying to nag into becoming a faithful replica of himself, and he ties his son to him with a rope, as Pozzo does Lucky. The son breaks away, Moran sees Molloy but does not realize who he is, and gets another order to go back home. He confesses: "I was not made for the great light that devours, a dim lamp was all I had been given, and patience without end, to shine it on the empty shadows" [144]. This ignominious quest for self-knowledge does not find Molloy as a separate entity, but it does turn Moran into a double of Molloy, in ironic contrast to his attitude to his son. Various details in the imagery, the bicycle that they both start with, the stiffening leg, and others, emphasize the growing identity. Moran's narrative, which starts out in clear prose, soon breaks down into the same associative paragraphless monologue that Molloy uses. The quest is a dismal failure as far as Moran and Molloy are concerned, but how far are they concerned? Moran can still say: "What I was doing I was doing neither for Molloy, who mattered nothing to me, nor for myself, of whom I despaired, but on behalf of a cause which, while having need of us to be accomplished, was in its essence anonymous, and would subsist, haunting the minds of men, when its miserable artisans should be no more" [154].

The forest vanishes and we find ourselves in an asylum cell with a figure named Malone, who is waiting to die. Here there is a more definite expectation of the event of death, and an awareness of a specific quantity of time before it occurs. Malone decides to fill in the interval by telling himself stories, and the stories gradually converge on a figure named Macmann, to whom Malone seems related somewhat as Proust is to the "Marcel" of his book, or Joyce to Stephen and Shem. Here an ego is projecting himself into a more typical figure (I suppose Malone and Macmann have echoes of "man alone" and "son of man," respectively, as most of the echoes in Beckett's names appear to be English), and Macmann gradually moves into the cell and takes over the identity of Malone. Malone dreams of his own death, which is simultaneously occurring, in a vision of a group of madmen going for a picnic in a boat on the Saturday morning between Good Friday and Easter, a ghastly parody of the beginning of the *Purgatorio*. Dante's angelic pilot is replaced by a brutal attendant named Lemuel, a destroying angel who murders most of the passengers.

In *The Unnamable* we come as near to the core of the onion as it is possible to come, and discover of course that there is no core, no undividable unit of continuous personality. It is difficult to say just where or what the Unnamable is, because, as in the brothel scene of *Ulysses*, his fluctuating moods create their own surroundings. One hypothesis is that he is sitting in a crouched posture with tears pouring out of his eyes, like some of the damned in Dante, or like the Heraclitus who became the weeping philosopher by contemplating the flowing of all things. Another is that he is in a jar outside a Paris restaurant opposite a horsemeat shop, suspended between life and death like the sibyl in Petronius who presides over *The Waste Land*.

Ordinarily we are aware of a duality between mind and body, of the necessity of keeping the body still to let the mind work. If we sit quietly we become aware of bodily processes, notably the heartbeat and pulse, carrying on automatically and involuntarily. Some religious disciplines, such as yoga, go another stage, and try to keep the mind still to set some higher principle free. When this happens, the mind can be seen from the outside as a rushing current of thoughts and associations and memories and worries and images suggested by desire, pulsating automatically and with all the habit energy of the ego behind it. Each monologue in the trilogy suggests a mind half-freed from its own automatism. It is detached enough to feel imprisoned and enslaved, and to have no confidence in any of its assertions, but immediately to deny or contradict or qualify or put forward another hypothesis to whatever it says. But it is particularly the monologue of *The Unnamable*, an endless, querulous, compulsive, impersonal babble, much the same in effect whether read in French or in English, and with no purpose except to keep going, that most clearly suggests a "stream of consciousness" from which real consciousness is somehow absent. *The Unnamable* could readily be called a tedious book, but its use of tedium is exuberant, and in this respect it resembles *Watt*.

The Unnamable, who vaguely remembers having been Malone and Molloy, decides that he will be someone called Mahood, then that he will be something called Worm, then wonders whether all his meditations really are put into his mind by "them," that is, by Youdi and the rest, for his sense of compulsion easily externalizes itself. If he knows anything, it is that he is not necessarily himself, and that it was nonsense for Descartes to infer that he was himself because he was doubting it. All Beckett's speakers are like the parrot in *Malone Dies*, who could be taught to say *"Nihil in intellectu,"* but refused to learn the rest of the sentence [298].[18] All of them, again, especially Malone, are oppressed by the pervasive lying of the imagination, by the way in which one unconsciously falsifies the facts to make a fiction more symmetrical. But even Malone begins to realize that there is no escape from fiction. There are no facts to be accurately described, only hypotheses to be set up: no choice of words will express the truth, for one has only a choice of rhetorical masks. Malone says of his own continuum: "I slip into him, I suppose in the hope of learning something. But it is a stratum, strata, without debris or vestiges. But before I am done I shall find traces of what was" [310].

In *The Unnamable*, as we make our way through "this sound that will never stop, monotonous beyond words and yet not altogether devoid of a certain variety" [484], the Unnamable's own desire to escape, to the extent that he ever formulates it as such, communicates itself to us. The tired, tireless, hypnotic voice, muttering like a disembodied spirit at a seance, or like our own subconscious if we acquire the trick of listening to it, makes us feel that we would be ready to try anything to get away from it, even if we are also its prisoner. There is little use going to "them," to Youdi or Godot, because they are illusions of personality too. Conventional religion promises only resurrection, which both in *Murphy* and in the Proust essay is described as an impertinence. But "beyond them is that other who will not give me quittance until they have abandoned me as inutilizable and restored me to myself" [458]. That other must exist, if only because it is not here. And so, in the interminable last sentence, we reach the core of the onion, the resolve to find in art the secret of identity, the paradise that has been lost, the one genuine act of consciousness in the interlocking gyres (the Dante-Yeats image is explicitly referred to) of automatism:

> . . . the attempt must be made, in the old stories incomprehensibly mine, to find his, it must be there somewhere, it must have been mine, before being his, I'll recognize it, in the end I'll recognize it, the story of the silence that he never left, that I should never have left, that I may never find again, that I may find again, then it will be he, it will be I, it will be the place, the silence, the end, the beginning, the beginning again . . . [575–6]

Many curiously significant remarks are made about silence in the trilogy. Molloy, for example, says: "about me all goes really silent, from time to time, whereas for the righteous the tumult of the world never stops" [34]. The Unnamable says: "This voice that speaks, knowing that it lies, indifferent to what it says, too old perhaps and too abased ever to succeed in saying the words that would be its last, knowing itself useless and its uselessness in vain, not listening to itself but to the silence that it breaks" [424]. Only when one is sufficiently detached from this compulsive babble to realize that one is uttering it can one achieve any genuine serenity, or the silence which is its habitat. "To restore silence is the role of objects," says Molloy [12], but this is not Beckett's final paradox. His final paradox is the conception of the imaginative process which underlies and informs his remarkable achievement. In a world given over to obsessive utterance, a world of television and radio and shouting dictators and tape recorders and beeping space ships, to restore silence is the role of serious writing.

40

Comment

May 1961

Response to Walter J. Ong's paper, "Synchronic Present: The Academic Future of Modern Literature in America," given at a conference on twentieth-century literature at Michigan State University. From Approaches to the Study of Twentieth-Century Literature, *Proceedings of the Conference in the Study of Twentieth-Century Literature, 2–4 May 1961 (East Lansing: Michigan State University, 1961), 79–83. The parenthetical page citations in this piece refer to this volume.*

This conference is fortunate in having a paper so broad in its range and striking in its formulations as Father Ong's to consider in its opening sessions. It would be hard to imagine a better kind of basis for the serious discussion of twentieth-century criticism. What follows is intended only as a variation on some of Father Ong's highly original themes.

Of all the ways of conceiving time, two are particularly relevant to Father Ong's "Synchronic Present." One is linear time, with its three categories of past, present, and future, the conception of time we need to live in a world of clocks and calendars and of conferences held at nine-thirty in the morning. It is a peculiarity of linear time that none of its three categories exists: the past is no longer, the future is not yet, the present is never quite. Still, it is the father of all necessary fictions, and it is only the creators of unnecessary fictions, or poets, who seem to feel restive about it. Poets may hate and fear it, like Shakespeare, or dream of regaining it, like Proust, but they seldom use it directly, except for rhetorical questions about the snows of yesteryear.

Poets tend rather toward the more primitive view of time set out in the tense system of the Hebrew language, the categories of Presocratic philosophy, and the imagery of the Eliot Quartets. Here the linear view of time forms part of an antithesis between the perfect and the imperfect, the complete and the continuous, being and becoming. The time in which everything dissolves and disappears is related to or contrasted with another perspective on time in which effects move toward their cause instead of running away from it. Continuous time, or chronos, is an entropy clock, an irreversible movement in the direction of the increasingly predictable. But another kind of time is at hand, a *kairos* in which something not wholly temporal becomes manifest in time, and so is always potentially here and now. From the beginning of the Book of Genesis, where things take their temporal being from spoken words, to Norbert Wiener's dictum that communication overcomes entropy,[1] this view of time has been particularly congenial to the verbal arts.

For the arts, including the verbal arts, do not, like the sciences, improve: they revolve around certain classics, or models, which will remain models as long as the art endures. The attitude to culture known as humanism, which means specifically the attitude of Western Europe to Classical culture between the sixteenth and eighteenth centuries, is the only attitude possible for what we call the humanities. The arts begin with their traditional classics as their primary data: all education in those arts is founded on them. But these classics are not, when properly studied, thought of as the heritage of the past. They are not in the past tense at all, but in the perfect tense. They are that portion of the art which has been completed, is now manifest, and is being extended by contemporary efforts. If *Paradise Lost* got on academic curricula before the rest of English literature, as Father Ong tells us, it was not only because it resembled the Classical epic in form, but because it demonstrated so well the vitality of that form [61]. Shakespeare had not, as Father Ong says, studied the plot structure of Kyd and Marlowe or psychoanalysed the audience of the beargarden [73]. But he had studied the plot structure of Plautus and Terence, and he knew enough psychology to know that devices which would work in Republican Rome would also work in Tudor London.

After the eighteenth century, the sense of Classical literature as immediately confronting the present age became a somewhat less self-evident fact. It required more historical imagination; its imitation became more indirect; and hence a tension developed between its pastness and its presence, between what the scholar knew about its meaning for its own time and what the reader felt about its meaning for himself. The rise of philology, too, with its quasi-scientific laws, encouraged certain scholars to feel that there were sterile safe periods in the humanities, areas of pure research where a present reference would not be called for. So when the academic study of the vernacular languages developed, the tendency to think in the past rather than in the perfect tense was already well under way. It was right and inevitable that such scholarship should provoke a reaction, that contemporary writers should be studied, and that erudite and allusive writers should be particularly valued because of the way in which their reading and influences could suggest a contemporary guide into the labyrinth of the past. This tendency, which crystallized around Eliot in the 1920s, was not academic in origin: I should trace it back to such phenomena as the Browning societies of the late nineteenth century.

It is clear that every great work of art has two poles of significance: its meaning for its own time and its meaning for us. There must always be some tensions between these two points: we cannot recapture the immediacy of Renaissance humanism, its confidence that the *Aeneid* was an allegory of the Renaissance prince and that *De Oratore* was a guide to success in the Renaissance court. But in proportion as historical scholarship and critical response separate, they become pedantic. The pedantry which tells the eager student that he is kidnapping Donne if he feels that Donne is speaking directly to him, and the pedantry which brings nothing to Donne but a modern dictionary and a ready-made set of twentieth-century associations, are equally pointless. I have my personal pair of markers, buoys indicating shallow waters on each side. One is a graduate student I met at a party who was writing a thesis on Yeats, and told me that he found such poems as *Ego Dominus Tuus* and *Phases of the Moon* very difficult. I agreed, but suggested that *A Vision* might throw some light on them. He informed me that *A Vision* was a work he had determined never to read, as it represented the kind of background apparatus which he considered irrelevant to criticism. The other is a Middle English scholar who was asked for his opinion of John Livingston Lowes's book on Chaucer,[2] and said: "Well, I don't know: it's a—a—a—an inspirational sort of thing, isn't it?"

If the study of perfected literature ought never to become wholly a study of the past, so the study of contemporary literature ought never to become wholly a study of the present. Of course criticism of contemporaries has to follow the production of their work: not until Theodore Roethke has produced some poems can an article be written on "The Vegetal Radicalism of Theodore Roethke."[3] But it would be wrong to think of twentieth-century criticism as a kind of unending cops-and-robbers race. Or, to use an image more suitable to the dignity of this gathering, the critic need not be only an Atalanta scrambling after the Hesperidean golden fruits tossed at him by the poets who have all they can do to keep just ahead of him. What the study of twentieth-century literature means is not the reinforcing of the past by the present, but the reinforcing of the sense of the authority of tradition by a sense of participation in it. To study the literature of our own time is to conceive of literature as a continuing process of which poet and critic are equally a part. To do this effectively, we need, I think, some axioms of procedure, all but one of which I can extract from Father Ong's paper.

The relation of writing and criticism is the relation of the practice to the theory of literature. Wherever theory and practice are separated, everything goes wrong. It is superstitious to think of the producers of poetry and fiction as a separate group of "creative" people: to do so implies that the creativity is inherent in the genres they are using, not in them. I have often read periodicals in which the criticism was not only better written but seemed to me much less of an academic exercise than the poetry and fiction. I am not sure about Father Ong's suggestion that the era of the printed book is drawing to a close with the rise of mass media. It seems to me that the printed book, with its established text and its mechanically accurate reproduction, is the inevitable form of the verbal classic or model, in whatever age it is produced. But of course a great fluidity of literary form, especially in popular literature, has been made possible by the mass media. A story which starts as a serial in a women's magazine and goes through a chrysalis stage as a novel before finally becoming a movie is an example. Professor Lord's book on the Yugoslav oral epic,[4] to which Father Ong refers, and parallel studies of folk tales, indicate that the more fluid the form becomes, the more invariable become the motifs out of which it is composed, and popular literature, like popular architecture, is in large measure constructed out of prefabricated units.

Father Ong refers to my colleague Professor Marshall McLuhan [64], who is one of the few contemporary critics to realize another axiom: at no point can the criticism of contemporary literature be separated from the study of the whole verbal culture of our time, which includes, of course, the whole verbal anarchy of our time. The milieu of William Faulkner and Wallace Stevens cannot be confined to impressive generalizations about the decay of the old South after the Civil War, or about the decline in New England self-reliance caused by the rise of the Hartford

Insurance Company. It includes—I speak only of the verbal milieu—the *Reader's Digest* with its articles on how to love your leukemia or religion is later than you think; it includes the Gertrude Stein–style readers studied in grade 1; it includes advertisements of softerized toilet tissues and of the only dentifrice that contains cyanide; it includes teachers'-college theses on the placing of shots in basketball and the correlation of bad temper with loss of sleep. The sense of the relevance of trivia is the penalty we pay for the heightened sense of a universal present which the mass media have created, and to which Father Ong refers [72–3]. But the study of trivia is not itself necessarily trivial. I should have much more respect for twentieth-century criticism if it produced fewer articles on the conception of tradition in Eliot and gave more attention to the ways in which the literary imagination of contemporary man is actually being formed and nourished. It is particularly in verbal education that such criticism is important, for the critic is above all a teacher, not of the writers he studies, but of the younger writers who study him. The effective criticism of the age of Spenser was not in Webbe or Puttenham, or even in Sidney or Ben Jonson. It was in the area that Father Ong, in his other capacity as a Renaissance scholar, has done much to illuminate: in rhetorical and mythological handbooks, textbooks in grammar and logic, annotated translations, encyclopedic treatises and cosmologies, collections of adagia, and all that went to form the cultivated mind of that time.

The study of perfect and completed literature is a liberal education, liberal because it gives us a standard of comparison by which to evaluate our own time. In its purest form it is a Classical education, studying the great literature of a perfected and completed culture. Such a study may degenerate into pedantry, and when it does it pulls us into the past. The study of contemporary literature is an engaged and involved education, and we have to beware of allowing it to degenerate into hysteria, pulling us into the flux of the pure present. I do not think I am contradicting myself when I say this and at the same time point to the relevance of the context of contemporary verbal culture, much of which is trash. One can only study verbal trash in a spirit of profound detachment, seeing it not as the latest thing in literary fashion but as part of a continuing process.

The sense of antagonism between historical and "new" criticism is now, Father Ong says, out of date. I am not sure whether he implies that their methods have combined or have merely mixed. I feel myself that a more unified critical approach is necessary, a view of literature as an order of words, in which certain structural principles, devices of plot, recurring imagery, and verbal rhythms can be seen in both completed and continuing literature, both in the greatest masterpieces and in works which are nothing by nobody, so that no gap is possible between scholarship and criticism, between the pastness and the presence of the same work. And with this resounding plug for my own critical methods I am content to leave Father Ong's paper—the starting point, I should hope, of an intensified critical activity which will guide future generations in their researches into plot structure in *Little Orphan Annie*, or the development of the oratorical style of Fidel Castro, or whatever else seems to them of central significance in the verbal culture of our age.

General Session II: "Synchronic Present"

General Discussion

Here Frye responds to Mr. Jaffe's comments that both the writer and the teacher/critic of literature should not be viewed as reflecting an irreconcilable split of artist and academic, but as sharing a mutual project of reacting to and reflecting "the whole mode and complexity of society." He also responds to Mr. Peters's reply that this notion of a shared project between "teacher and producer" implies (and requires) a more objective, "anthropological" approach both in creative and critical writing, an approach which always works with the "larger cultural context" in mind.

Well, I made a long speech yesterday to the Canadian Conference of the Arts Meeting in Toronto, and with great presence of mind I did not bring the paper with me.[5] But the point of my remarks was that with the enormous increase in the sense of the past in all the arts, enormous expansion of possible techniques has opened to the contemporary artist because he is now a citizen of all time and space, and isn't just pushed along at the end of a Greek or Roman or Western European movement. And because of this the arts have got into an academic and scholarly role in which they are experimenting with their new techniques, and that this is the real sociological reason why the wealthy foundations have subsidized the artists and why university administrators employ them in summer sessions; because the arts are becoming absorbed into the educational process, so that the creative and the academic in our particular age seem to me almost to have become the same thing.

Mr. Baldanza asks if anyone on the panel more familiar with André Malraux's works could comment on a possible parallel between the sense of synchronic time in his work and in Father Ong's paper.

Well, the particular relevance of Malraux's thesis to Father Ong's argument is, I take it, his demonstration of the fact, not only of the enormous extension of the knowledge of the past, and the technical knowledge that has given to the artist, but also his sense that the forms of art are autonomous, that you learn your techniques as artists from your craftsmanship, and you learn your craftsmanship (but what is really your scholarship)—that is, the impulse to express yourself pictorially comes primarily from your familiarity with forms of painting in your earlier experience, so that the conventions, the pictorial conventions of painting, organize the way in which the picture is painted—that is, the artist does not confront nature directly, he works within the prison of the conventions of his time.

Mr. Adams asks Frye to comment on time as a structural principle of literature, and to elaborate on his ideas about cyclical symbolism as the form the structure takes (in contrast to the diachronic or synchronic views of time proposed by Father Ong).

Yes. I should like to put in a plug for the cyclical view of time, in opposition to what Father Ong has said. I don't think it is a view of time which extends itself necessarily to any feeling of unending recurrence such as we have, distorted, in Nietzsche and elsewhere. The perception of nature as moving in cyclical rhythm is merely one of the central devices which poetry, like the other arts, has used to give some sense of shape to a world of pure flux, and of pure becoming; and in the Renaissance writers, no less than in the modern writers, you find the same use of nature as manifesting a principle of *being* in the flux of *becoming*. That is what happens in Spenser's *Mutabilitie Cantos*, for example, where the cycle of days and hours and seasons is brought forward by Mutability as a part of her argument, as a demonstration of the fact that mutability extends over the whole chain of being. But the evidence is ambivalent—that is, turns against her because the cycle actually manifests the principle of order in a cosmos, and so Jove is confirmed in his imperial see. And there you have a poetic image dealt with from the general tone of metaphysical comedy—but it seem to me that poetry is utterly helpless without some use of the natural cycle, simply as an element of poetic grammar.

Father Ong responds to Frye by suggesting that the infinitely expanded understanding of the physical universe provided by modern science negates the possibility of any true repetition: the seasons are the same only superficially; everything when observed closely will have some kind of variability. The cyclical sense of time is then an outmoded notion leaving modern poets with only the fiction of cyclicalism to rely on. Frye continues:

The sciences have to deal with prediction, because they deal with the only kinds of things that can be predicted. The poet lives in an atavistic, primitive, archaic universe; the sun rises in the east and sets in the west; and whatever he can see from his own house, as William Blake says, such space is his universe, and the world is flat [*Milton*, pl. 29, ll. 5–9; E127]. And that is one reason why the arts are unable to absorb the sciences, and why they turn to people like Blavatsky and Swedenborg rather than to the reputable scientist.

Mr. Smith comments that the poets Frye describes are only one kind of poet, such as Blake. Frye cuts him off:

Are there other kinds?

Discussion Group II: "Contemporary Literary Criticism"

General Discussion

There's an excellent little book called *Anatomy of Criticism*. (*Laughter*.) It solves all these problems, mostly on the opening pages. (*Laughter*.) It makes a particular distinction between direct experience and criticism. Direct experience is contact with a work of literature, which is essentially wordless. That is what Mr. Shattuck had in mind when he spoke of an instructor reading something, and somebody else understanding what he means without any words passing; and then there is also a conceptual structure known as criticism, which is something quite different and which does have to be made of some kind of framework of ideas. And on a point of personal privilege, Mr. Krieger—may I thank you not only for you excessive generosity in your references to me, but also for pointing out that I am concerned with rather more that the fertility rites of the bongo bongo.

Discussion Group III: "Historical Study and Comparative Literature"

General Discussion

Frye contributes to a discussion of the use of translations in comparative literature courses, and of the dangers of the importation of a contemporary perspective by translators of ancient texts:

It seems to me, Mr. Weisinger, that there is one major problem inherent in the study of contemporary literature in relation to its time. If you are studying what a seventeenth-century poet meant to his own time, that is to some extent an isolatable problem—when you balance that against what he means to us. Surely the danger of misunderstanding a contemporary writer is very much greater, simply because he is a contemporary. If I am studying Milton, I know I will have to take certain precautions about what Milton meant in *Paradise Lost*—just what a seventeenth-century poet would mean, not what I would have him mean. But when I'm dealing with somebody writing in the twentieth century, someone from a very different cultural, ethical background from myself, I no longer have that separate isolatable narrowing of scholarship. It seems to me that does create an additional difficulty for the twentieth-century scholar.

Here Frye responds directly to Mr. Scott's question, "Why do most of us in a contemporary literature course spend weeks on T.S. Eliot and hours on Robert Frost?" He then comments on the issues brought up regarding the literary critic's role: is it one of scholarship or value judgments; can these even be separated—particularly when studying texts from the past?

I would say that it is simply a pedagogical problem; that is, students need more help with certain types of modern poets than with others. I should think on the question of value judgment—it's in literature rather as it is in religion, there are two ways of arriving at faith. You can make a statement of what you believe—a very impressive statement like the Athanasian Creed—and you can repeat that on Sunday morning, but by Monday evening your actions may have shown that you actually believe in something quite different. And similarly, I think that the statements of what critics say they believe about literature, whether extremists or not, which may be impressive and reassuring, seem to be much less important than the kind of assumed value judgment which Father Ong referred to; the fact is that Faulkner is taught in a literature course and *Gone with the Wind* isn't.

I would only carry that another stage further, and that is to say that I think that scholarship is the thing that has the power of veto over value judgment; that is, the things that make value judgments inadequate are usually a lack of knowledge of the range and variety of scope of literature, and most of the great blunders of criticism (like Rymer in calling *Othello* a bloody farce)[6] are the result of consistent taste applied on too narrow a basis of scholarship.

General Session III: Discussion of "Some Remarks on Programs for Graduate Students in the Field of Recent Literature" (Professor Clarence Gohdes, Duke University)

General Discussion

Concern is expressed about the potentially damaging effects of the trend of studying modern literature to the exclusion of a thorough knowledge of the literature of the past. Father Ong counters this concern with support for the exclusive study of modern literature on the graduate level. Frye continues the discussion:

I would suggest a view that might erase any worry about too large a number of students concentrating on Faulkner or modern literature generally. Let them become visitors. It seems to me that the problem is not so much that we are being inundated, as that we are not selective enough on the basis of getting people who are generally interested in literature. And I am not worried about being overflooded. I should think it would be the other way around.

One other thing bothers me with your remarks. It is the assumption that the field corrupts the man, and not the man the field. It is as though in the Eden of scholarship, that old devil, contemporary literature, betrays the young, innocent graduate student. And by implication, therefore, only in the traditional fields do we have heroic Adams. But having, myself, in the course of a somewhat sad career read many articles of the nature of the progeny of Eos, I am sure that the same could be said of all fields. I do not think the field corrupts the man; it is a question of what the man is like before he gets to the field.

Frye's discourse follows several comments on the proximity of and/or antagonism between "creative" writers and the academic world.

My own experience in Canada is one that might, perhaps, interest this group. I have been on committees for awarding fellowships or scholarships in creative writing in which half the committee was English Canadian and the other half French Canadian. And I was rather struck by the fact that all the French Canadian writers seemed to be working either for the National Film Board or for the Canadian Broadcasting Corporation, and that we have almost never awarded a scholarship in the creative arts to a French Canadian who was academic. But on the English side, the academics are closed shop. They practically never give a scholarship to a man who is not a university employee of some kind. And it seems to me a peculiarity of the Anglo-Saxon world, at any rate, that in our time the creative and the academic should have gotten so close together.

I suspect, too, that the uneasy relationship to which both Mr. Young and Father Ong refer is partly a literary convention; that is, the writers who are subsidized by benevolent foundations are also expected to produce the kind of highly conventionalized writing that gives the public the impression of a writer writing like a writer. And this, of course, does not disturb the academic world because it is a cliché, growing out of nineteenth-century Romanticism I suppose, that the creative person is supposed to bite the hand that feeds him.

41

T.S. Eliot

1963

Text taken from the revised (paperback) edition (Edinburgh: Oliver & Boyd, 1968), reprinted New York: Capricorn Books, 1972, and, with an updated bibliography, as T.S. Eliot: An Introduction *(Chicago: University of Chicago Press, 1981). The first edition was a paperback published in Edinburgh by Oliver & Boyd and in New York by Grove in 1963, and reprinted by Barnes & Noble in New York in 1966. Later printings of the first edition had corrected errors noted on an errata slip. The major revisions made by Frye for the 1968 edition (though not those of date or appropriate changes of tense) are given in notes to the text below. For explanation of these changes and the interesting editorial history of this book, see the editor's introduction (xlii–xliii) and the correspondence with Oliver & Boyd in NFF, 1988, box 61, file 5. The editor acknowledges and thanks Dr. Jean O'Grady for her assistance in detailing the editorial history of these revisions.*

All editions include a bibliography (not reproduced here) compiled with the help of Donald Gallup's T.S. Eliot: A Bibliography *(London: Faber; New York: Harcourt, 1952); in his Acknowledgments Frye writes, "I am greatly indebted to my colleague Miss Jay Macpherson for preparing the Bibliography and for much helpful advice on the text." The book has been translated into Spanish, Korean, Japanese, and Portuguese. There are some notes for the introduction and biography in Notebook 13 (NFF, 1991, box 24), and a draft of the introduction is in NFF, 1988, box 1, file t.*

I Introduction

Thomas Stearns Eliot was born in St. Louis, Missouri, on 26 September 1888. His father was in business there, and his grandfather was a Unitarian minister who had much to do with the establishing of Washington University in St. Louis. His mother was also a writer, and her dramatic poem on Savonarola, edited by her son, indicates an early source of Eliot's interest in poetic drama. The Eliot family had come in the seventeenth century to New England,[1] and for many reasons it was natural that Eliot should go to New England for his university education. He entered Harvard in 1906, when Charles William Eliot was president, a distant relative but, as some glancing references make clear,[2] not intellectually a very congenial figure to his namesake. Eliot wrote poetry at Harvard, but was not especially precocious as a poet. He developed an interest in philosophy that might have made him a distinguished philosopher if he had chosen an academic career.[3] He was caught up in the widespread interest in Oriental philosophy at Harvard, and tells us that he was stopped from going further into it by a fear of losing his sense of participation in the Western tradition.[4] William James was a great name at Harvard, but psychology and pragmatism have had little appeal for Eliot, including the psychological criticism in the tradition of Sainte-Beuve. It may be significant that Eliot's doctoral thesis (accepted, but not presented for the degree, and recently published) was on F.H. Bradley, who represented a very different tradition of philosophical thought.[5]

A travelling fellowship took Eliot to Germany in 1914, and it was eighteen years before he returned to America. In the fall he entered Merton College, Oxford, to read philosophy. He had earlier discovered the French *symboliste* poets, more particularly Laforgue,[6] and had learned from them how to apply the language of poetry to contemporary life. "The kind of poetry that I needed," he says, "to teach me the use of my own voice, did not exist in English at all; it was only to be found in French."[7] He learned much from the chief English study of these poets, Arthur Symons's *The Symbolist Movement in Literature.* His first major poem, *The Love Song of J. Alfred Prufrock,* completed in 1911, appeared in 1915 in *Poetry,* a magazine recently founded in Chicago, and a main outlet for the stream of new American poetry of which Eliot's work formed part. In the same year (1915) he married and settled in England. He had met Ezra Pound in 1914, and later met Wyndham Lewis and James Joyce, contributing also to the magazines and anthologies that Pound's driving energy was establishing. His first prose work was an essay on Pound published anonymously in America in 1917.[8] *Prufrock and Other Observations* was also published in 1917, showing the influence of Laforgue most markedly in the lunar symbolism and the use of ironic dialogue. In 1919 a second group of poems appeared, and in the same year a collection of the two books, called at first *Ara Vos Prec* and then simply *Poems* (1920). With this volume Eliot's early poetry was virtually complete.

A collection of early essays called *The Sacred Wood,* and including "Tradition and the Individual Talent," which outlined his "impersonal" theory of the poetic process, appeared also in 1920. Although Eliot's general position, "Classical in literature, royalist in politics, anglo-catholic in religion," was not announced until the preface to *For Lancelot Andrewes* in 1928, it was clear that their opposites, Romanticism, "Whiggery," and secularism, were already in the intellectual doghouse. There followed three influential essays on Marvell, Dryden, and the metaphysical poets (*Homage to John Dryden,* 1924).[9] In 1922 Eliot began his own periodical, *Criterion,* which he edited until 1939, the purpose of which was, he tells us, to create a place for the new attitudes to literature and criticism, and to make English letters a part of the European cultural community.[10]

The first issue of *Criterion* carried *The Waste Land,* a long poem that Eliot had been working on for some time. In its original form it is said to have run to over eight hundred lines, then in consultation with Ezra Pound, who was accustomed to editing other poets with the greatest confidence, it was cut to its present length. No doubt most readers of Eliot would prefer to have the original version,[11] but it is possible that Pound's editing improved the poem, and very probable that it made it more enigmatic. The poem is dedicated to Pound as *il miglior fabbro,* a phrase from Dante used as a chapter heading in Pound's *Spirit of Romance.* With this poem and its successor *The Hollow Men* (1925), Eliot found himself, somewhat to his chagrin, the spokesman of a postwar attitude which found in his waste-land imagery an "objective correlative" (of which more later) for its disillusionment, or what Eliot calls its illusion of being disillusioned.[12]

For such readers it was a shock when Eliot, after becoming a naturalized British subject and joining the Church of England in 1927,[13] announced the position already quoted in *For Lancelot Andrewes,* but, on the whole, the new attitude was consistent enough with the earlier one, only the content being changed. Still, the change of content did turn Eliot from a satiric to a devotional poet, a practising Anglo-Catholic layman ready to write a verse play for a campaign to build new churches (*The Rock,* 1934), or to charge a heavy brigade of irony at the religiously light-minded:

And on Easter Day, we couldn't get to the country,
So we took young Cyril to church. [*Coriolan*, pt. 1, *Triumphal March*, l. 44]

Eliot joined the publishing house of Faber and Gwyer, later Faber and Faber, in 1925, and shortly became a director.[14] He returned to the United States in 1932 as Professor of Poetry at Harvard, in which office he delivered the lectures called *The Use of Poetry and the Use of Criticism*. These were followed by a more doctrinaire series given at Virginia in 1933 and published as *After Strange Gods*, ominously subtitled "A Primer of Modern Heresy." During the 1930s Eliot's critical writing became increasingly concerned with what he calls "the struggle against Liberalism."[15] His later social criticism is represented by two essays, *The Idea of a Christian Society* (1940) and *Notes towards the Definition of Culture* (1948), the former especially[16] reflecting much of the spirit of that miserable time between Munich and Dunkirk.

It was mainly during the 1930s that Eliot completed *Four Quartets*, the culmination of his nondramatic poetry. The last Quartet, *Little Gidding*, takes us up to the time when the Nazi bombs were falling in London.[17] Meanwhile his interest in drama, which began with *Sweeney Agonistes* (1927) and continued in *The Rock*, had led to the writing of *Murder in the Cathedral* (1935), a tragedy on the murder of Becket, and *The Family Reunion* (1939), with a country-house setting in which the Furies of Aeschylus make a disconcerting and, according to Eliot, unstageable appearance.[18]

After the war Eliot continued to live in England, with occasional visits to America.[19] He wrote relatively little nondramatic poetry in his later years, apart from a collection of children's verse, reminiscent of Edward Lear, *Old Possum's Book of Practical Cats* (1939). "Possum" is a nickname for Eliot, occurring in Pound's *Cantos*.[20] He returned to drama with the tragicomedy *The Cocktail Party* (1949), perhaps the most commercially successful of all his plays. This was followed by two other comedies, *The Confidential Clerk* (1953) and *The Elder Statesman* (1958). Both were produced at the Edinburgh Festival and have had good runs, but have never equalled the popularity of their predecessors. There was also a steady series of critical essays, most of them, as one would expect with an established writer, lectures given on special occasions. Many of these were collected in a volume called *On Poetry and Poets* (1956). In 1948 Eliot received two of the greatest honours a contemporary writer can obtain, the Order of Merit and the Nobel Prize for Literature, and a few years later the Hanseatic Goethe Prize. In 1947 his wife, who had been ill for some time, died and in 1957 he married Valerie Fletcher, to whom *On Poetry and Poets* and *The Elder Statesman* are dedicated. He died in early January of 1965.[21]

Eliot's poems and plays have each been collected in a single volume, and the reader of Eliot will also find essential *Selected Essays* and a posthumous collection, *To Criticize the Critic*, besides the other critical works referred to above. Even these do not contain everything that a student of Eliot would want, as there are still many uncollected and fugitive pieces, and many prefaces to books.[22] The present book, by policy, avoids referring to any writing of Eliot not readily accessible to the ordinary reader.

A thorough knowledge of Eliot is compulsory for anyone interested in contemporary literature. Whether he is liked or disliked is of no importance, but he must be read. So much is assumed by the present book: further value judgments and estimates of comparative greatness are the concern of the reader. The literature on Eliot is enormous, and the present addition to it is an elementary handbook, claiming no originality beyond that of arrangement.[23] Blake remarks that an intellectually honest man changes his opinions but not his principles [Annotations to *An Apology for the Bible*, p. 3: E613], and this is so true of Eliot that it is possible to approach him deductively, treating the structure of his thought and imagery as a consistent unit. Such an approach saves a good deal of space without being misleading. In dealing with the poetry I have tried to emphasize the structure and to avoid getting lost in the allusions.

Almost every major poet has expressed certain social and intellectual attitudes which may be essential to the understanding of his poetry but are often unacceptable to many of his readers. This is no less true of Eliot than it is of Yeats or Pound or Whitman or Hopkins. It is, or should be, a central principle of criticism than no major poet stands or falls by his views, however closely they may be identified with his creative work. If I begin with what seem the clichés of hostility to Eliot, passages from *After Strange Gods* and the like, it is for the purpose of defining, as quickly as possible, what must be considered but can also be clearly separated from Eliot's permanent achievement, leaving that achievement intact.[24]

II Antique Drum

An American moving to Europe to live is likely to become more sharply aware of the "Western" context and origin of his cultural tradition, and hence to be attracted to some theory about the shape and development of that tradition. Such theories fall into two main groups, the going-up and the going-down. The going-up one started as the humanistic view, predominant from the sixteenth to the eighteenth century and implied in the title of Gibbon's *Decline and Fall*. This is a U-shaped parabola reaching its bottom with the "triumph of barbarism and religion"[25] in the Dark Ages, and moving upward with the revival of learning. Not only Gibbon but the deeply conservative Johnson assumed a steady improvement of life and manners up to his time, an assumption which Eliot regards as a major source of Johnson's strength and security as a critic.[26] The complementary or Romantic view is an inverted U rising to its height in medieval "Gothic" and falling off with the Renaissance, and is most articulate in Ruskin.[27]

In the late nineteenth century the going-up parabola lost its opening curve and developed into a theory of progress, which Darwin's theory of evolution was supposed to confirm scientifically. The key to progress was the growing respect for individual freedom, making for democracy in politics, and liberalism, with a strong affinity to Protestantism, in thought. The descendant of the Ruskinian view we may call, in an image of *The Waste Land*, the bobsled or "down we went" theory. According to this, the height of civilization was reached in the Middle Ages, when society, religion, and the arts expressed a common set of standards and values. This does not mean that living conditions were better then—a point which could hardly matter less—but that the cultural synthesis of the Middle Ages symbolizes an ideal of European community. All history since represents a degeneration of this ideal. Christendom breaks down into nations, the church into heresies and sects, knowledge into specializations, and the end of the process is what the writer is sorrowfully contemplating in his own time: "the disintegration of Christendom, the decay of a common belief and a common culture."[28]

This view, though held as far on the left as William Morris, is more congenial to such Catholic apologists as Chesterton, and to such literary critics as Ezra Pound, whose conception of "usura"[29] sums up a good deal of its demonology. Eliot's social criticism, and much of his literary criticism, falls within this framework. He is uniformly opposed to theories of progress that invoke the authority of evolution, and contemptuous of writers who attempt to popularize a progressive view, like H.G. Wells. The "disintegration" of Europe began soon after Dante's time; a "diminution" of all aspects of culture has afflicted England since Queen

Anne; the nineteenth century was an age of progressive "degradation"; in the last fifty years evidences of "decline" are visible in every department of human activity. Eliot adopts, too, the rhetorical device, found in Newman and others, of asserting that "There are two and only two finally tenable hypotheses about life: the Catholic and the materialistic."[30] Everything which is neither, including Protestantism, "Whiggery," liberalism, and humanism, is in between, and consequently forms a series of queasy transitional hesitations, each worse than the one before it.

We are reminded of Spengler's *Decline of the West*, a best seller in Germany when Eliot was writing *The Waste Land*, which sees history as a series of cultures that behave like organisms, so that their decline is an inevitable aging process. Eliot could doubtless take only the lowest view of Spengler's book, but Spengler's is the most coherent statement of the theory of Western decline, and any writer who adopts a version of that theory gets involved in Spenglerian metaphors. Thus Eliot falls into such phrases as "an age of immaturity or an age of senility,"[31] utters prophecies about "the dark ages before us"[32]and "the barbarian nomads of the future,"[33] and incorporates references to blood and soil in his otherwise very un-Teutonic vocabulary.

Eliot belonged to one of the great dynastic New England families who have supplied so much cultural and political leadership in American life, and, like other American writers with such names as Adams and Lowell, reflects the preoccupations of an unacknowledged aristocracy, preoccupations with tradition, with breeding, with the loss of common social assumptions. "The mind resorts to reason for want of training," said Henry Adams, and Adams felt that man could worship only "silent and infinite force," either in the spiritual form of the Virgin of Chartres or in the material form of the dynamo[34]—a close parallel to Eliot's dialectic. Eliot feels that man's natural society is not classless, but one in which "an aristocracy should have a peculiar and essential function."[35] A functional aristocracy implies a functional peasantry. The small regional community, homogeneous in race and preferably in language, is the proper cultural unit. We are even told that "it would appear to be for the best that the great majority of human beings should go on living in the place in which they were born."[36] In the essays on culture and Christian society much attention is paid to Welsh and Scottish cultural nationalism as a "safeguard" against the tendency "to lose their racial character."[37] In *After Strange Gods* Eliot, addressing a Virginian audience, expresses sympathy with the conservative neo-agrarian movement of Southern intellectuals, and remarks: "I think that the chances for the re-establishment of a native culture are perhaps better here than in New England. You are farther away from New York; you have been less industrialized and less invaded by foreign races; and you have a more opulent soil."[38]

In the poetry the mingling of races and the sense of lost pedigree symbolize a disintegration of culture, like the ethnical miscellany in *Gerontion* and the woman in *The Waste Land* who claims to be *echt deutsch* because she comes from Lithuania [*The Waste Land*, l. 12]. A more squalid mongrelism may be represented by Sam Wauchope in *Sweeney Agonistes*, whom his American friends boast to be "a real live Britisher," but who appears to be nothing more than a Canadian [*Sweeney Agonistes: Fragment of a Prologue*, l. 187]. In *Gerontion* and elsewhere the Jew embodies the rootlessness of the modern metropolis, and Virginia, with a different problem on its hands, is informed that "reasons of race and religion combine to make any large number of free-thinking Jews undesirable."[39] Behind this is a belief that "blood kinship" and attachment to the soil are features of a "harmony with nature" which a genuine society has, "unintelligible to the industrialized mind."[40]

These features of Eliot's thought are well known, widely criticized, and for most readers fantastic or repellent. It is therefore important to realize that the historical myth behind them is not essential to his real argument. The real decline is from an ideal which may be symbolized by medieval culture, but remains in the present to condemn and challenge the contemporary world. Thus the historical myth is projected from a conception of two levels of human life which are always simultaneously present.

All views of life that Eliot would call serious or mature distinguish between two selves in man: the selfish and the self-respecting. These are not only distinguishable but opposed, and in Christianity the opposition is total, as for it the selfish self is to be annihilated, and the other is the immortal soul one is trying to save. Theories of conduct exalting the freedom of the personality or character without making this distinction are disastrous. They lead to a breakdown of community, for the ordinary or selfish self is locked in its private jail cell, "each in his prison" [*The Waste Land*, l. 414], its only relation to society being an aggressive or acquisitive one. The argument of *After Strange Gods* leads up to and concludes with an attack on the undiscriminating theory of personality. What is admired in modern culture "tends naturally to be the *unregenerate* personality."[41] We thus have a lower level of ordinary or mere personality, or what we shall loosely call the ego, and the higher level of the genuine self. The ordinary personality is Rousseau's noble savage: it regards the community as a limitation of its freedom, and judges the community according to the amount of inconvenience to the ego that it causes. Eliot starts from Burke's view that society is prior to the individual. As Burke says, art is man's nature:[42] the human world is a civilized one, an order of nature distinct from the physical world. Laws for the will, beliefs for the reason, and great classics of culture for the imagination, are there from the beginning. If a man is a twentieth-century Englishman, he cannot claim that he is a timeless and spaceless "I": his context cannot be separated from his real personality, which it completes and fulfils.

The particular continuum into which an individual is born, Eliot calls his culture or tradition. By culture Eliot means "that which makes life worth living":[43] one's total way of life, including art and education, but also cooking and sports. By tradition, also, Eliot means both a conscious and an unconscious life in a social continuum. "What I mean by tradition involves all those habitual actions, habits, and customs . . . which represent the blood kinship of 'the same people living in the same place.'"[44] The significance of the phrase "blood kinship" we have already commented on. Political life may become worldwide and depersonalized, but culture, in poetry and painting as in fine wines, demands locality, a realized environment. Eliot stresses the feeling for soil and local community in his essays on Virgil and Kipling, two poets who have little in common except a popular reputation for being imperialists.

In Matthew Arnold's conception of culture, religion is a cultural product, a part of which culture is the whole; hence the human value of a religion lies mainly in the quality of its worldliness. In Eliot religion forms a third level above human society. Its presence there guarantees Burke's distinction between a higher order of human and a lower order of physical nature. "If this 'supernatural' is suppressed . . . the *dualism* of man and nature collapses at once. Man is man because he can recognize supernatural realities, not because he can invent them."[45] Hence human culture is aligned with a spiritual reality which is superior to it and yet within it, the kind of relationship represented in Christianity by the Incarnation. Eliot stresses the importance of this conception when he speaks of culture metaphorically as the "incarnation" of a religion, the human manifestation of a superhuman reality. A culture's religion "should mean for the individual and for the group something toward which they strive, not merely something which they possess,"[46] and it demonstrates that "the natural life and the supernatural life have a conformity to each other which neither has with the mechanistic life."[47] In *After Strange Gods* Eliot uses "orthodoxy" to mean a conscious and voluntary commitment to the religious aspect of tradition. No culture which repudiates religion and deifies itself, like Marxist Communism, can get man out of the squirrel cage of the ego, though it may "on its own level" give "an apparent meaning to life."[48]

The genuine personality, then, is concrete man, man in the context of certain social institutions, whether nation, church, culture, or social class. The ego or ordinary personality is an abstraction, and a parasitic by-product of the genuine personality; it is anti-cultural and anti-traditional. But as the ego is not the genuine self, it is really subhuman.

> The lengthened shadow of a man
> Is history, said Emerson,
> Who had not seen the silhouette
> Of Sweeney straddled in the sun. [*Sweeney Erect*, ll. 25–8]

What Emerson said was: "An institution is the lengthened shadow of a man."[49] In Eliot the reverse is true: the natural man or ego is the shadow of an institution, or man in genuine society. Swift's Yahoo is pure natural man, what man would be without institutions. Eliot's Sweeney is not a Yahoo, but his "silhouette" reminds us of one. At the end of his essay on Baudelaire, Eliot quotes T.E. Hulme as saying that institutions are necessary because man is essentially bad.

An authoritarian inference from original sin is not very logical, for those entrusted with imposing social discipline on others cannot by hypothesis be any better themselves. Eliot does not say that he approves of what Hulme says, but only that Baudelaire would have done so. But still Eliot thinks of democracy as permeated by the natural man's admiration for himself. What the natural man wants is only generic: food, houses, sexual intercourse, and possessions, and a society which accepts these wants as genuine social ends becomes totalitarian. Fascism and Communism are the products of strong tendencies within democracy itself, and our horror at these products springs from the ego's dislike of inconvenience rather than love of freedom. Eliot makes much of the virtue of humility, which he says in *East Coker* provides "The only wisdom we can hope to acquire" [l. 98]. Humility is the opposite of pride, traditionally the essence of sin, and pride is life centred in the ego. The "proud" attitude to social evils is to regard them as wholly external to oneself, for oneself, in a state of pride, is not to be examined, much less condemned. It ascribes everything it dislikes to an economic system or political party, expects miraculous results from a transfer of power, and is always in a revolutionary attitude.

Tradition for Eliot is far from being a cult of doing what has been done before. "Humility" is also a prerequisite of originality. The self-expression that springs from pride is more egocentric, but less individual, for the only self that can get expressed in this way is one just like everyone else. "Cousin Nancy" smokes and dances and impresses her aunts as modern, and fulfils "Waldo" Emerson's doctrine of self-reliance and "Matthew" Arnold's individualized culture, but what she does is still only fashionable conformity. The last line of this poem is quoted from Meredith's sonnet on the hopeless rebellion of Lucifer [*Lucifer in Starlight*, l. 14], and aligns Nancy with the same futility.

For most people acceptance of culture and tradition is unconscious, expressed in assumption and prejudice. A man is hardly a human being at all until he has entered a tradition, or what some call a social contract. But "What is important is a structure of society in which there will be, from 'top' to 'bottom,' a continuous gradation of cultural levels . . . we should not consider the upper levels as possessing *more* culture than the lower, but as representing a more conscious culture and a greater specialization of culture."[50] There should be, therefore, an "elite" of those for whom culture and tradition have become conscious. They include poets for at least two reasons. First, "poetry differs from every other art in having a value for the people of the poet's race and language, which it can have for no other." Second, "unless we have those few men who combine an exceptional sensibility with an exceptional power over words, our own ability, not merely to express, but even to feel any but the crudest emotions, will degenerate."[51] They also include critics, who depend on "a settled society" "in which the differences of religious and political views are not extreme."[52] This last implies that the elite should have a close connection with the culture's religion.

Religion sees human life in relation to superhuman life, as a kind of continuous imitation of it. This is expressed in certain acts, or sacraments, and in certain forms of thought, or dogmas, derived from revelation. Religion cannot be identical with culture, except in the City of God or in a very primitive society;[53] but if religion and culture draw apart, society loses its sense of direction, and the elite and the unreflecting masses become unintelligible to each other. Eliot's conception of religion is thus a sacramental and Catholic one: the Church is the definitive form of ritual and faith, and the essence of religion is participation in the Church. Protestant conceptions of the church would doubtless not be admissible to Eliot if we could suppose he knew what they were. When he says "the life of Protestantism depends upon the survival of that against which it protests,"[54] we are apparently to take this lugubrious pun as representing his understanding of the faith that the head of his church defends.

Eliot's "elite" are interpreters of their society, and show that what is most deliberately and consciously cultured in any society is also central to it, and guides its main current. Eliot, like Arnold, feels that "the dissentients must remain marginal,"[55] even when they form the majority. For Eliot admits, even stresses, that we can have an *Athanasius contra mundum* situation in which "the man who is 'representative' of his time may be in opposition to the most widely accepted beliefs of his time."[56] If Athanasius is right, he is in the "centre" of his society; if he is wrong or partly right, he is "marginal." Neither Eliot nor Arnold has explored the difficulties in this metaphor very far. Eliot's elite is similar, as he recognizes, to Coleridge's "clerisy,"[57] but Eliot's argument is more pro-Catholic, stressing the importance of contemplative orders in the church. Coleridge's differences from him on these points "now sound merely quaint."[58] In Eliot, as again in Arnold, the Establishment is society's recognition both of the centrality of the church and of the distinction between the church and the marginal sects. Of disestablishment Eliot says, "the risks are so great that such an act can be nothing but a desperate measure,"[59] a strong statement for a poet brought up in the United States.

It follows that education should have the socially engaged personality as its goal. One type of education, distinguished by Eliot as instruction or information, is designed to provide the ego with extended powers. This type usually depends on a socially subversive theory aiming at transforming society by equality of opportunity. The fable of the belly and members is replaced in Eliot by an analogy of the head and trunk of the body politic. We feel that we are members of one body when the culture of a minority is the conscious form of the culture of the majority. Education should aim at a social ideal like Newman's gentleman, whose leisure and good taste are produced by an awareness of social context rather than by class privilege or private enterprise.[60] Arnold's conception of culture is evaluative, the *best* that has been thought and said, and as such plays a revolutionary role in society. "Culture seeks to do away with classes,"[61] and the permeation of society by culture tends toward equality. In Eliot the conception of culture is descriptive, hence it plays no revolutionary role. The classes of the past may give place to the elites of the future, but culture itself does nothing to disturb the class structure.

Eliot's literary criticism falls into two parts, a literary polemic derived from the myth of decline and a critical theory derived from the study and practice of literature. The former is what concerns us here.

The progressive view of history produced the post-Romantic conception of English literature which Eliot challenged. According to this, originality in poetry is an aspect of individual freedom in life; hence Shakespeare, who drew individuals so well, and Milton, a Protestant revolutionary, express the real genius of English literature. The era from Dryden to Johnson was an inferior and prosier age, but the Romantic movement re-established the main tradition, which continued in Britain through Tennyson and Swinburne, and in America through Whitman's conception of poetry as self-expression.

Eliot's historical view of English literature is a point-for-point reversal of the progressive one. The post-Romantic conception of "personality," failing to distinguish the craftsman from the ordinary personality, assumes that the former is the medium or vehicle of the latter, instead of the other way round. In "Tradition and the Individual Talent" Eliot speaks of the poetic process as "impersonal," not an expression of personality but an "escape" from it.[62] The poet's mind is a place where something happens to words, like a catalyser which accompanies but does not manipulate a chemical action. In other early essays, though Eliot agrees with Arnold about the immaturity of the Romantic poets, he means by "Romanticism" chiefly the popular post-Romantic residue of their influence which is contemporary with himself. This Romanticism, he says, "leads its disciples only back upon themselves."[63] Romanticism, then, as a creative process emanating from and returning to the ego, occupies the foreground of Eliot's historical dialectic, the contemporary world at the bottom of the Western mountain, as far as we can get from the "anti-romantic" "practical sense of realities" in Dante's *Vita nuova*.[64]

The First World War discredited the view that the northern, liberal, largely Protestant cultures of England and Germany were, with America, the architects of a new world. Latin and Catholic Europe began to look like a cultural as well as a political ally. The essay on Blake in *The Sacred Wood* is full of anti-Nordic mythology: Blake's Prophecies "illustrate the crankiness, the eccentricity, which frequently affects writers outside of the Latin tradition."[65] So although Eliot's view of literature is "classical," his Classicism regards Latin medieval culture, and Dante in particular, as the culmination of the Classical achievement. Dante's greatness is partly a product of a time when Europe "was mentally more united than we can now conceive." At such a time literature achieves its greatest power and clarity: "there is an opacity, or inspissation of poetic style throughout Europe after the Renaissance."[66] So Eliot explicitly prefers the culture which produced Dante to that which produced Shakespeare.[67]

Eliot reiterates that Shakespeare is as great a poet as Dante, but, reflecting an age nearer ours, the materials out of which his poetry is made are shoddier. "Dante made great poetry out of a great philosophy of life; and Shakespeare made equally great poetry out of an inferior and muddled philosophy of life."[68] Eliot, like Shaw, finds Shakespeare's philosophy of life a mass of platitudes with a pessimistic slant, and agrees with Archer that Elizabethan drama is an "impure art," though his moral is the opposite of Archer's belief in "progress . . . and in the superiority and efficiency of the present age."[69] He also agrees with Arnold that Shakespeare is too clever to have a good effect on tradition. "If you try to imitate Shakespeare you will certainly produce a series of stilted, forced, and violent distortions of language."[70] The conclusion is that we should admire Shakespeare, but not for liberal or Romantic reasons. Shakespeare does not always take a maturely dim view of human nature: his rhetoric may yield to his hero's desire to "see himself in a dramatic light,"[71] as Othello does in his Aleppo speech [5.2.338–56], where he shows a lack of humility. We are told that *Hamlet,* the Bible of the Romantics, is "most certainly an artistic failure,"[72] and (in two grinning footnotes) that Rymer, the seventeenth-century critic who called *Othello* a bloody farce, "makes out a very good case."[73]

The reader may be confused by the suggestion that Shakespeare made his poetry "out of" a philosophy, whether profound or what Eliot calls "rag-bag."[74] Eliot establishes three main philosophical connections with Shakespeare, the Cerberus of the modern world raising its heads. The ancestor of modern sceptical liberalism is Montaigne, to whom Shakespeare owed much (here Eliot may have been over-influenced by J.M. Robertson, as he was in his *Hamlet* essay by Robertson's disintegrating fantasies). The ancestor of Romantic egoism is Seneca the Stoic, whose conception of the hero seems like a cult of spiritual pride. The ancestry of the secularism that ends in expediency is in the cynical political views ascribed by the Elizabethans to Machiavelli. Machiavelli himself said that unscrupulousness in politics is necessary because men are "ungrateful, fickle, false, cowards, covetous," which sounds like a belief in original sin, hence "In Machiavelli there is no cynicism whatever."[75]

Eliot's political attitude is said in the preface to *For Lancelot Andrewes* to be "royalist." Royalism for Eliot, as for Burke, could well mean the maintaining of a symbol of continuity in society clear of party politics or class struggle. But though Eliot announced an *Outline of Royalism*[76] and speaks of the divine right of kings as a "noble faith,"[77] the conception has little importance in his work except as an indication that he was taking a side in the seventeenth-century Civil War. Much of Eliot's criticism revolves around the first part of the seventeenth century, a period he approaches as one which contains in embryo all the disintegrating tendencies of our time. Shakespeare, Tourneur, and Jonson can still control them while reflecting them, but Massinger and Ford are beginning to yield to them. Then came the Civil War, the Puritan emigrations, including the Eliots from East Coker, the closing of the theatres, the overthrow of everything catholic in the Church of England from the Little Gidding community to Archbishop Laud, and the poetry of Milton. With all this the tradition of English culture fell to pieces, and the modern world was born. For anyone concerned to oppose the tendencies of that world, "the Civil War is not ended,"[78] as Eliot was still insisting as late as 1947.

Milton was a poet of the devil's party and at least the devil probably knew it. He subjected the language to a deterioration which meant that on later writing his influence could only be for the worse. He built a "Chinese wall" across poetry, the work of a man imaginatively as well as physically blind, showing a vague visual sense and leading nowhere "outside of the mazes of sound."[79] His rhetoric is that of "the greatest of all eccentrics,"[80] valid only for Milton himself, an apotheosis of the ego. It is full of tricks like "the facile use of resonant names"[81] which Marlowe outgrew, and Marlowe's Mephistopheles "renders Milton's Satan superfluous."[82] Johnson was right in finding *Lycidas* full of "absurdities";[83] *L'Allegro* and *Il Penseroso* are on a level with "the lighter and less successful poems of Keats";[84] Swinburne is praised for abusing *Comus*, which is also called "the death of the masque."[85]

With Dryden the real tradition was to some degree re-established, for it is "easier to get back to healthy language from Dryden."[86] Though Eliot admires Pope and does what he can to rehabilitate Dryden and Johnson as poets and critics, he does not maintain that the Augustan age produced a poet of the stature of, say, Racine in France. Of the Romantics, those who best illustrate the egocentric quality of Romanticism are Byron and Shelley. The fact that Shelley, as a man, was "self-centred, and sometimes almost a blackguard"[87] is relevant, because although "Wordsworth does not present a very pleasing personality either," Shelley's "abuse of poetry"[88] is greater. Byron's egoism is connected with the "defective sensibility"[89] which made him write English like a dead language. Blake's work is egocentric because it contains a philosophy which Blake thought out himself instead of borrowing from his tradition. In reputation the biggest figure in this period is Goethe, and Goethe "dabbled in both philosophy and poetry and made no great success of either."[90]

Contemporary literature is of course full of the detritus of Romanticism. "Religion and Literature," an essay unlikely ever to rank with *Areopagitica* as a ringing manifesto of intellectual freedom, says that "while individual modern writers of eminence can be improving, contemporary literature as a whole tends to be degrading."[91] Hardy is "a powerful personality uncurbed by any institutional attachment," who expressed that personality without having anything "particularly wholesome or edifying" to express.[92] D.H. Lawrence's "vision is spiritual, but spiritually sick."[93] Yeats, with his little-Ireland folklore and his occultism, has a minor and peripheral mythology. (So did the Hebrew prophets and Christian apostles, but, as explained above, they were really central, because right.) Elsewhere we find slighting references to Bernard Shaw, H.G. Wells, and Bertrand Russell. These are prose writers, and "good prose cannot be written by a people without convictions."[94] What convictions they are also seems to be important. Our attention is called "to the great excellence of Bishop Hensley Henson's prose," but we are told that Russell, in his quasi-Stoical *A Free Man's Worship*, wrote "bad prose."[95]

"We all agree about the 'cultural breakdown,'"[96] says Eliot, but myths of decline usually have a codicil: the writer has something contemporary to recommend which promises to arrest the decline of civilization. Eliot himself points out that his historical dialectic, on its literary side, is attached to a tactical campaign to get new types of writing recognized.[97] Of the writers he defends, Ezra Pound and James Joyce are the most prominent. Romantic, Protestant, and liberal tendencies in the English tradition make it more culturally schismatic than the French tradition, where Racine and Baudelaire "are in some ways more like each other than they are like anyone else,"[98] and which is closer to the Latin centre of European culture. It is significant that Pound and Joyce reflect the influence of Latin and Catholic civilization, and significant too that their cultural conservatism seems to go with originality of expression. The discovery, with the belated publication of the poetry of Hopkins, that the most disturbingly original Victorian poet was a Jesuit priest looked like confirmation of the same principle, but in *After Strange Gods* Eliot refuses to play this ace and finesses with Joyce, the "most ethically orthodox writer"[99] of our time.

Eliot's skill in quotation and in setting passages of unequal merit beside each other put his handling of his critical polemic on an unusually high level of objectivity. Only occasionally can we see the rhetorical shading of the arguments. In the final canto of the *Inferno* we come upon Dante's Satan, with three heads, one of which is meditatively chewing Judas Iscariot. The uninstructed reader might find the scene a trifle barbaric, and feel that what Milton did with Satan was more civilized. Eliot, recognizing the danger, says: "The vision of Satan may seem grotesque, especially if we have fixed in our minds the curly-haired Byronic hero of Milton."[100] This remark is too remote from Milton to be even misleading: it is sheer polemic and nothing more. In his essay on Sir John Davies, Eliot sets a passage from *Orchestra* beside one from *The Ancient Mariner* containing the line "His great bright eye most silently," and says parenthetically that "most" is a blemish.[101] Considering that *The Ancient Mariner* is a deliberate imitation of ballad idiom, with its bits of metrical putty, it is perhaps not a blemish. But a sense of the superiority of pre-Romantic craftsmanship has been quietly implanted in the reader's mind.

With the Second World War and the completion of *Little Gidding*, the Civil War reached an armistice on its last battlefield. Eliot, Pound, and Joyce were by that time established writers. In later essays the polemical tone is abandoned, the Romantics are referred to without much animus, and the terms "classic" and "romantic" are now said to belong to "literary politics."[102] A second essay on Milton holds a cautious Geiger counter up to that poet and decides that "at last" it is safe for poets to read him.[103] In pointing out that Milton can hardly have been a worse influence on later epic than Shakespeare on later verse drama, Eliot comes close to saying that every major poet builds a "Chinese wall"—a principle that will in due course be applied to Eliot himself. "That every great work of poetry tends to make impossible the production of equally great works of the same kind is indisputable."[104] The greater urbanity sometimes goes with a loss of incisiveness. "I should myself rate Campion as a more important poet than Herrick, though very much below Herbert" sounds amateurish compared to an earlier statement that the critic's task is to isolate quality, not to determine rank.[105]

The best comment on Eliot's polemic is that of his mentor in *Little Gidding*: "These things have served their purpose; let them be" [l. 116]. We may consider applying to Eliot his own early comment that Arnold "went for game outside of the literary preserve altogether," which "we must regret," because it "might perhaps have been carried on as effectively, if not quite so neatly, by some disciple (had there been one) in an editorial position on a newspaper."[106] Certainly when we read in *The Idea of a Christian Society*, "It is a matter of concern not only in this country, but has been mentioned with concern by the late Supreme Pontiff . . . that the masses of the people have become increasingly alienated from Christianity,"[107] we may wonder if it really needed a writer of Eliot's abilities to produce that sentence. A poet's specific task has something to do with visualizing the Promised Land: on the historical level, he may often be a lost leader, a Moses floundering in a legal desert.[108] As Eliot says, it is the Word in the desert that is most likely to hear "The loud lament of the disconsolate chimera" [*Burnt Norton*, l. 161]. It is difficult to feel that Eliot's view of Western culture is anything more than a heresy in his own sense of the word, a partial insight with "a seductive simplicity" which is "altogether more plausible than the truth."[109] The orthodoxy of which it is a heresy would be, or include, a much larger "truth" about our very complex situation than the mythology of decline affords. Nevertheless, the construct from which Eliot's social criticism is projected is also that of his poetry, hence it illuminates our understanding of his poetry and its relation to his own time.

III Dialect of the Tribe

We now come to Eliot's criticism properly speaking. So many critical theories claim to derive from Eliot that he seems rather in the position of the country squire in Smollett to whom young women in the neighbourhood ascribed their fatherless offspring, confident of his good-natured support. Such late essays as "The Frontiers of Criticism" record some bewilderment at this impossibly fertile paternity. His criticism, like his social polemic, is based on the two levels of "personality," the egocentric and the cultivated. Anyone who thinks of writing poetry as a self-expressive activity may imagine that he is creating something out of nothing, like God: but nothing like this happens. The impulse to write can only come from previous literary experience, and is conditioned by poetic conventions throughout. The new poem, like the new baby, is born into a verbal society, an order of words already there. Hence the view that "originality" consists in making a fresh start in literature is a half-truth. An essential part of creative power is in past literature. Every poet inherits a literary continuum which has come down from Homer to our own day, and feels that this continuum "has a simultaneous existence and composes a simultaneous order."[110] His relation to literary tradition may be implicit or explicit: the quotation and allusion so abundant in Eliot belong to the explicit relation. Education in the humanities ought to put us in possession of the common cultural tradition on which new poetry is based. Otherwise poetry will fail to communicate, and it is no good blaming the poet if it does.

Imitativeness is usually, and rightly, taken as a sign of immaturity in a poet. But when a poet achieves his own style, his relation to former poets becomes much more specific. "One of the surest of tests is the way in which a poet borrows. Immature poets imitate; mature poets steal."[111] Eliot is one of the poets who make a possessive use of sources. It is fascinating to compare a passage in A.C. Benson's *Life of Fitzgerald* with the opening lines of *Gerontion*, or a passage in Charles Maurras with *Triumphal March*, and see how Eliot divined the poetic possibilities inherent in these passages. There are also many altered or adapted lines: thus Chapman's "Under the chariot of the snowy Bear" [*Bussy D'Ambois*, 5.3.153], itself an echo from Seneca,[112] becomes "Beyond the circuit of the shuddering Bear" in *Gerontion* [l. 69]. A very minor poem, the third of the *Five-Finger Exercises*, is said to contain echoes from five poets in its fourteen lines.[113] Sometimes the echo is not verbal but structural, like the echo of Donne's "*Per fretum febris*, by these straits to die" [*Hymn to God, My God, in my Sickness*, l. 10], at the end of *Gerontion*. The faint aroma of Kipling's *They* around the rose-garden episode of *Burnt Norton* is more elusive, as is the "shadow" of Dowson's *Cynara* which is said to have influenced the shadow in *The Hollow Men*, a poem it could hardly resemble less. Of course we should not invariably assume that such allusions throw light on the meaning of the poem that echoes them, still less that the emotional effect of the original can simply be added to Eliot's poem by such an echo.

Eliot has also spoken of the importance of studying other languages than one's own. The poet should be a Burbank with a Baedeker, cross-breeding English with Continental and Classical traditions, as Eliot's study of Dante and of French *symbolisme* did for modern English poetry. The majority of Eliot's adaptations, however, are from English literature, and in any case the cross-breeding rule applies to phraseology rather than rhythm. The use of Dante's idiom in the second section of *Little Gidding* is a *tour de force* unparalleled in English poetry, but it does not use the *terza rima* form. And in *Murder in the Cathedral* the reader must decide for himself whether the hymn "Still the horror"[114] is closer in rhythm to *Dies irae*, which is its model, or to *Hiawatha*.

We notice that allusive and echoic poetry often has a curiously penetrating quality about it. For Eliot the capacity of poetry to be unconsciously memorized is a criterion of genuineness, and the capacity of Eliot's own poetry for this is extraordinary. It is one thing to dislike his poetry or decry its reputation; it is another thing to forget it, once carefully read. His prodigious influence may even exaggerate his merits, for, as he says, "when we come to the point of making a statement about poetry, it is the poetry that sticks in our minds that weights that statement,"[115] and Eliot does stick in our minds. Perhaps the echoic aspect of his poetry gives us a minor clue to its mnemonic adhesiveness.

A certain amount of borrowing must be voluntary: but the main creative process is involuntary, or at least applied to something that does not depend on the will, like landing a fish. The poet has no idea of what he wants to say until he has found the words of his poem, and "When you have the words for it, the 'thing' for which the words had to be found has disappeared, replaced by a poem."[116] What the poet has at first is a kind of rhythm or movement, which becomes manifest in words and "may bring to birth the idea and the image."[117] The poet has experiences of no discernible pattern which may range from the smell of cooking to the reading of Spinoza; but in him they sink to the bottom of the mind, to "suffer a sea change" there—for Ariel's song seems to have some association in Eliot's mind with the process.[118] They then return as an amorphous something demanding verbal form. The poet may not know what is coming up, but whatever it is, his whole being is directed to realizing it. One can see here another reason why humility is a major virtue to Eliot. The self-important ego has no place here: the poet, as Rémy de Gourmont says, has to transmute his own personality drop by drop into the creative personality.[119] The language of the poets who succeed in doing this shows a peculiar transparency. "Language in a healthy state presents the object, is so close to the object that the two are identified."[120]

When the amorphous thing appears clearly, it needs a name. Eliot calls it "emotion," a word which is not consistently distinguished from "feeling." It is not what we usually mean by emotion, however: it is a presentation, as immediate experience, of a complex of images and ideas. As Ezra Pound says, poetry provides equations, like mathematics, but equations for emotions.[121] The capacity of the poet to produce such equations and of the reader to respond to them Eliot calls "sensibility." This is one of Eliot's favourite words, partly a translation of the French *sensibilité*, and it implies subtlety, delicacy, and refinement. In practice, if not in theory, it seems to stop short of the quality that Eliot speaks of, in connection with Shakespeare, as a "terrifying clairvoyance."[122] The human clairvoyance of Shakespeare, the physical clairvoyance of Homer, the spiritual clairvoyance of Blake, seem to elude Eliot's sensibility, which turns rather to Dante, to Virgil, and to Baudelaire.

When the right words are there, the images and ideas of which they are now the transparent medium form what Eliot calls the "objective correlatives"[123] of the emotion. They make the emotion communicable to the reader, and are evidence that the poet's sensibility has been clarified. In great poetry we are aware of the variety of experiences that can be fused together, and great poetry differs from lesser poetry not by any ethical quality like "sublimity," but by an intensity of combination. Such poetry "fuses the old and obliterated and the trite, the current, and the new and surprising, the most ancient and the most civilised mentality."[124] In such unity of varieties there is "a recognition, implicit in the expression of every experience, of other kinds of experience which are possible."[125] Eliot has his "touchstone" passages: one is a speech in the third act of Tourneur's *Revenger's Tragedy*, and another is the final canto of the *Paradiso*. Of a passage in this canto Eliot says: "It is the real right thing, the power of establishing relations between beauty of the most diverse sorts; it is the utmost power of the poet."[126]

Poets on the highest level possess, Eliot says, "a mechanism of sensibility which could devour any kind of experience."[127] The two aspects of this mechanism, subjective and objective, are often described by Eliot in terms of music and the visual arts respectively. Poetry begins in a rhythm too far down in the unconscious to be reached by the ego, and probably released by a relaxing of the normal inhibitions of consciousness. The awareness of this rhythm is an "auditory imagination," beautifully described by Eliot as "the feeling for syllable and rhythm, penetrating far below the conscious levels of thought and feeling, invigorating every word; sinking to the most primitive and forgotten, returning to the origin and bringing something back, seeking the beginning and the end."[128]

The poet is concerned not to *say* anything, but to articulate this rhythm, and in this he resembles the composer; for the poetic "structure will first appear in terms of something analogous to musical form."[129] But the articulation itself takes the form of "clear visual images," which form the golden mean between "the extremes of incantation and meaning."[130] Images include concepts, for to the poet the concept is "a direct sensuous apprehension of thought, or a recreation of thought into feeling."[131]

In the age of Donne what Eliot calls sensibility was called wit, and what he calls an objective correlative was called a conceit, or something conceived. "Wit" has a more intellectual sound than "sensibility" or "emotion," and indicates why poetry of Donne's school is called "metaphysical." Its "metaphysical" quality is actually a technique of fusing images and ideas which is deliberately strained and forced. Hence there is a latent irony in its conceits, a suggestion of the grotesque which seems conscious, and so intellectual. The metaphysical poets had a unified sensibility, but their strained ingenuity shows the difficulty of retaining it at that time, with Milton and Puritanism around the corner. There is a similar feeling of explicit tension about unified sensibility when it revives in modern times with Laforgue and other *symbolistes*. The inference is that "it appears likely that poets in our civilization, as it exists at present, must be *difficult*."[132]

Inferior poetry also has a subjective and an objective aspect, but of a different kind. Even the greatest poet may fail to perfect his work if the emotion gets wrapped around something in his personal life, and produces a spilled-over intensity not properly expressed in the poem. Eliot believes this to have happened with *Hamlet*. But inferior poetry falls into two types: poetry which is not objectively clarified, and remains emotionally murky, and poetry not conceived at the deepest level, and so written consciously and voluntarily. Eliot says these types constitute a "dissociation of sensibility,"[133] going to one or the other extreme of incantation and meaning.

We may meet a passage like this in Eliot's plays:

> He has a heart of gold. But, not to beat about the bush,
> He's rather a rough diamond.[134]

The question whether this is "good poetry" or not depends simply on its appropriateness to the character of the person who speaks it. Such appropriateness is dramatic rhetoric in its proper sense of decorum. But a more egocentric craftsman might be unwilling to put a character into one of his plays who would naturally express himself in amiable clichés, as Eliot's Eggerson does here. If we read Seneca's plays, we notice a quality in them that we call rhetorical in a different sense, meaning that each speaker in turn is impressing us with his, or rather the author's, eloquence. The poetry has become verbal, in the sense that it is now an art of words, not an art of which words are the transparent medium. Seneca was a Stoic, and perhaps the rhetoric in his plays has something to do with Stoic spiritual pride. Such pride corresponded to strong tendencies in Elizabethan drama, reflected, if transcended, even by Shakespeare. Eliot's essay on Massinger[135] is a particularly subtle analysis of this kind of rhetorical haze settling into a later writer.

Milton, for Eliot, is a more extreme example of an impressive rhetoric setting up a half-translucent curtain of sound in front of the visions. With the Romantics we find a cult of the oracular, a sense of the strangeness in reality which is perverted into "a short cut to the strangeness without the reality."[136] Here vagueness is felt to be a virtue. In Swinburne's soft-focus technique we feel that it is "the word that gives him the thrill, not the object."[137] Such poetry tends to create a self-sufficient world of words, which does not even "depend upon some world which it simulates."[138] Mallarmé among the *symbolistes*, and still more Maeterlinck, were affected by similar influences.

A simpler form of dissociation occurs when a poet is trying to evoke a mood by verbal magic. Such poetry seeks, not unity, but uniformity: it aims at its mood and excludes everything that might "disturb" it or break its spell. If the poem is intended to be serious, it is uniformly serious, that is, solemn. In Gray's *Elegy*, a poem for which Eliot has an unusually strong dislike, we settle into a country churchyard at night and have the appropriate feelings and reflections, but there are no suggestions of other moods mixing with them, as there would be in Marvell; hence the feeling is cruder than in Marvell. This kind of dissociation seeks the sentimental, the ready-made associative path, and eventually collapses into an insipid sense of propriety. It is outraged when it finds such a line as "I shall wear the bottoms of my trousers rolled" in a poem that also mentions mermaids [*The Love Song of J. Alfred Prufrock*, l. 121].

We can also have intellectual dissociation, where poetry does not transform its ideas into immediate emotional experience. Allegory in Dante is a method that "makes for simplicity and intelligibility," because "for a competent poet, allegory means *clear visual images*."[139] A poet who fails to transmute concepts into direct apprehension is not so much intellectual as reflective or ruminating, as Eliot says of the later work of Tennyson and Browning, achieving the facile continuity of pursuing a train of thought. Actually meaning is subordinate to structure, and poets may "find it expedient to occupy their conscious mind with the craftsman's problems, leaving the deeper meaning to emerge from a lower level."[140] A poem may make its impact on a reader before the reader has started to think about what it means: the impact can be so disturbing that the meaning may even have a reassuring and sedative effect, keeping the reader's mind diverted and quiet, like a bit of meat thrown to a watchdog by a burglar.[141]

The conception of "clear visual images" as the mean between the extremes of incantation and meaning belongs, we should note, to the polemic of the 1920s rather than to literary criticism. Here as everywhere the road of excess leads to the palace of wisdom [*The Marriage of Heaven and Hell*, pl. 7, l. 3; E35]. Eliot has achieved his hold on the modern reader's imagination not by clear visual images, but by uniting the extremes of incantation and meaning:

Dawn points, and another day
Prepares for heat and silence. Out at sea the dawn wind
Wrinkles and slides. I am here
Or there, or elsewhere. In my beginning. [*East Coker*, ll. 48–51]

There is no doubt about the power of incantation in this passage, nor about the fact that, as Browning's Lippo says of the world, it means intensely, and means good [*Fra Lippo Lippi*, l. 314]. But it is not a poetry of clear visual images, the only word that even looks like one, "wrinkles," being an echo from Tennyson [*Palace of Art*, l. 138].

The poet's experiences are shaped into a unity which takes its place in a literary tradition. One would suppose that the shaping process has something to do with the literary tradition itself. How otherwise could the process be called, even as a figure of speech, impersonal? But I can find no proof-text in Eliot that clearly suggests how the literary tradition is embodied in conventions, genres, and mythical structures, and how those in turn exert a defining power on the poet's mind. He says that there are two levels of impersonality, one the craftsman's level of convention, such as we have in an anthology piece of Lovelace or Campion, and a higher one "achieved by the maturing artist."[142] But convention does not conceal personality: it detaches and releases the poetic personality from the ordinary one. At the same time the word "impersonal," though perhaps deliberately paradoxical, does express part of our response to the greatest art, the feeling Eliot describes as "this realizes the genius of the language," as distinct from the feeling "this is a man of genius using the language."[143]

Eliot says that there are four ways of thinking: talking to others, to one other, to oneself, and to God—the identity of thinking and talking here is interesting—also that there are three voices of poetry: the poet talking to himself, to others, and through a character.[144] We may reduce these to two kinds of writing. Sometimes the poet is writing out what takes shape in his mind, and cannot think of an audience until he has finished. There are other genres which are inherently rhetorical, where the poet is conditioned by an audience during the act of writing. Of these, the one relevant to Eliot is poetic drama.

During the 1920s and 1930s Eliot's popular reputation was that of an erudite highbrow of whom it was only to be expected that he should conclude his longest poem with a barrage of Sanskrit. But such a reputation would be contradictory to Eliot's view of the "elite" as responsible for articulating the unconscious culture of their societies. Eliot would like, he says, an audience that could neither read nor write[145]—though one fears that this remark is based only on the cliché about the superiority of the uneducated to the half-educated. His criticism has always shown a preoccupation with the possibility of verse drama, which, he says, no fatalistic philosophy of history should prevent us from trying to get.[146] The central problems of poetic drama, for him, have always been connected with versification and diction.

In self-expressive writing, something voluntary has buried itself into the act of writing. What results is often "free" verse in the sense of verse allowing an uninhibited flow from the expressing ego. No verse is free, Eliot says, for the man who wants to do a good job.[147] When bad free verse rhymes and scans, we call it doggerel. Eliot does not speak of doggerel, but he does employ a distinction between "poetry" and "verse," leaving it, as here, in inverted commas. By "verse" is meant a kind of poetry which directly faces an audience, and is conditioned in expression by that audience. Eliot is fascinated by the problem of "verse," and recognizes that some important poets, notably Kipling, are primarily writers of "verse."

The broadest form of "verse" is deliberate doggerel, which is used in *Sweeney Agonistes*, and closely related is "light verse," as we have it in *Old Possum's Book of Practical Cats*. One feels that the poems in strict quatrains, such as *The Hippopotamus*, are closer to "verse" than *Gerontion* because more predictable in metre and more explicitly satiric in tone. The arranging of words in formal patterns gives an effect of conscious wit, and the use of long words like "Polyphiloprogenitive" is broadly comic [*Mr. Eliot's Sunday Morning Service*, l. 1]. Yet even in *Prufrock* the tumbling down of wistful reverie into preoccupation is represented by an artful sinking from "poetry" into "verse":

> Should I, after tea and cakes and ices,
> Have the strength to force the moment to its crisis? [ll. 79–80]

Finally, there is the continuous poem addressed to a listening audience, which, whether epic or narrative or drama, needs a predictable metre and consequently some basis in "verse."

The effect of "verse" is normally continuous, and once a regular rhythm is set up, a habitual or expected quality enters the writing. The effect of "poetry" is rather to arrest the movement and force the reader's mind to intensify instead of going forward. "Poetry" thus seems to be essentially discontinuous. One of the most obvious features of *The Waste Land* and *Four Quartets* is the fact that they are written in a discontinuous sequence of movements: the continuity of the poems as a whole has been, so to speak, handed over to the reader. But in verse drama the problem of continuity can no longer be avoided or solved in this way. "No poet can write a poem of amplitude," Eliot says, "unless he is a master of the prosaic,"[148] and again, "the poet who could not write 'verse' when verse was needed, would be without that sense of structure which is required to make a poem of any length readable."[149] In Shakespeare the moments of greatest poetic intensity, such as Macbeth's "Tomorrow" speech [5.5.21–30], are also the moments of greatest dramatic intensity. In drama, then, two principles are involved: a structural principle, concerned with the total design, of which the basis is "verse," and a textural principle, which moves from "verse" into "poetry" in moments of intensity, and back into "verse" in moments of relaxation, where continuity of structure is the important thing.

What holds these together is a "common style," which is produced by a "collaboration between a great many people talking a living language and a very few people writing it."[150] This style is conversational, not the grand style of rhetoric, where there is a standard to be met, and so a sense of "sinking" whenever the rhetoric relaxes. Dante is the greatest master of such common style, and hence the best model for imitation. Shakespeare, with his dazzling verbal cleverness, departs more from common style, and Milton abandons it. But to get out of touch with common style is literary decadence, and the balance must right itself. There have been three main revolutions of diction in English literature attempting to rescue the common style. The first was that of Waller and Denham, completed by Dryden, against Miltonic Baroque; the second was that of Wordsworth; the third was that of Eliot and Pound against the dissociated Georgians.[151]

"Verse" normally has, first, a metrical pattern, such as the iambic pentameter of Shakespeare. Second, it has a prose or semantic rhythm which is simultaneously present and syncopates against it. There is, third, in English verse, an accentual stress pattern, which in iambic pentameter usually has four beats. This four-stress line is the bedrock of English versification: it is the rhythm of alliterative verse, of nursery rhymes and of ballads, all rhythms close to Eliot. It differs from a metre in being a musical rhythm, in which the number of syllables between stresses is variable. In Eliot this rhythm is heard most clearly in *Sweeney Agonistes*, where the variable number of syllables syncopates against a heavy beat, producing a verbal parallel to jazz. Such a stress pattern is useful only for parody. In the plays we have an accentual line, close to prose in effect, which Eliot describes as a line of three main beats with a caesura.[152] Naturally he must know, but this is my book, and what I hear is four beats:

> *Well*, not di*rect*ly. *Ju*lia had a *tel*egram
> *Ask*ing her to *come*, and to *bring* me *with* her.
> *Ju*lia was del*ayed*, and *sent* me on a*head*.[153]

Such lines are quite different in effect from the opening lines of *Prufrock*, where the pattern of three beats and a caesura is much easier to see, and even more different from the short lines in which the Quartets (except *East Coker*) end, and which are three-beat lines without caesura.

In the early poetry we often find a rhythm very like that of Jacobean drama, except that the accentual pattern has come to dominate the metrical one. In the last part of *Gerontion* the long final words ("adulterated," "deliberations," "inquisition" [ll. 59, 62, 57]) fit into a four-stress conception of the line much more neatly than into pentameter. Elsewhere the accentual rhythm is varied in a great number of ways. Let us look at the famous opening lines of *The Waste Land*:

> April is the cruelest month, breeding
> Lilacs out of the dead land, mixing
> Memory and desire, stirring
> Dull roots with spring rain.

The first line, which establishes the tonality, is a normal four-stress line. In the second the second stress hovers over unaccented beats and comes down on a syncopated one. In the third line the third stress is a "rest," occurring in the pause between "desire" and "stirring." The fourth line is really a two-stress line in which each stress has been split in two by falling on a spondee, and so assimilated to the four-stress pattern. We can sometimes see a connection with some of the earlier four-stress patterns in English prosody, such as medieval alliterative verse: compare the rhythm of

> Ganga was sunken, and the limp leaves
> Waited for rain, while the black clouds . . . [ll. 396–7]

with this from *Sir Gawain and the Green Knight*:

> The brygge was brayde doun, and the brode gates
> Unbarred and born open upon bothe halve. . . . [2069–70]

Each of the short sections of the longer poems has as a rule its own rhythmical pattern. The third section of *East Coker* begins with a rhythm based on a six-stress line, heard very clearly in "Dis*tin*guished *ci*vil *serv*ants, *chair*men of *ma*ny com*mit*tees" [l. 106]. The line "And *cold* the *sense* and *lost* the *mo*tive of *ac*tion" [l. 101] has five stresses, but we feel that the first two occupy the time of three. *Murder in the Cathedral* has passages of five-stress lines, which, being longer than pentameters, can accommodate more easily the polysyllabic clatter of modern educated speech:

> I see nothing quite conclusive in the art of temporal government,
> But violence, duplicity and frequent malversation.[154]

Such a line is cumbersome for ordinary dialogue, though it fits the specialized hieratic context it was designed for well enough.

In the early poems no reader can miss the rhetorical contrast between the sharp realism, full of dingy words and calculated bathos, and the dreamy romanticism, full of "dying falls," which distinguish the world of crumpets from the world of trumpets, in the words of *A Cooking Egg* [ll. 29, 31]. In his essay on Dante Eliot distinguishes the "low dream," the wish-fulfilment of the ego, from the "high dream" or vision which is Dante's proper subject.[155] In the devotional poetry we have again two contrasting styles, that of the "high dream," and deliberately prosaic passages indicating a return to ordinary consciousness. The rhetoric of the "high dream" does not differ greatly from that of the "low dream" in the early poems except in being free from parody and in a few special features. One of these is a technique of repetition of sound representing a concentration on a single idea. The opening of the fifth section of *Ash-Wednesday*, with such lines as "Against the Word the unstilled world still whirled" [l. 156], is an example. A practice of inter-rhyming ("Words, after speech, reach;" "It tosses up our losses," etc. [*Burnt Norton*, l. 142; *The Dry Salvages*, l. 22]) has something of the same rhetorical function.

The transition from "poetry" to "verse" in the dramas may be measured by the role of the chorus in them. Rymer, the denigrator of *Othello*, once remarked: "What Reformation may not we expect, now that in France they see the necessity of a Chorus to their Tragedies?"[156] and Eliot also begins full of enthusiasm for the chorus. *Sweeney Agonistes* is really a continuous chorus, and the choruses in *The Rock* are the only valuable part of the play, or pageant. In *Murder in the Cathedral* the chorus has its traditional role of providing an emotional tension alternating with that of the action. In *The Family Reunion* the minor characters occasionally form a chorus, and the more articulate ones sometimes withdraw from dialogue into monologue. Eliot has criticized these passages as too much like operatic arias, but surely every speech that does not directly advance the action *is* an operatic aria. In any case the chorus in *The Cocktail Party* is cut down to one scene, and in the next two plays it disappears altogether.

Thus the plays show a gradual retreat from "poetry" into "verse" which tightens up the structure, perhaps at the cost of other qualities. Eliot is well aware of the importance of structure in drama as being what Aristotle called its "soul" [*Poetics*, 6], the integrity whereby a "reality of moral synthesis"[157] is conveyed. Many readers of Eliot feel that no character in the plays matches in vividness the characterization of Prufrock or Gerontion or Sweeney. Eliot speaks of the way in which "the creation of a character in a drama consists in the process of transfusion of the personality, or, in a deeper sense, the life, of the author into the character."[158] But for Eliot himself "poetry" is clearly essential to this full transmutation, and there seems to be something in the plays and their "verse" which tends to inhibit its fullness.

The two *genres* of Eliot's work, drama, and the kind of nondramatic poem which is, as he says, a form of "meditative verse"[159] and not a lyric, sum up between them the public and the private aspects of literature. The basis of the former is "verse," of the latter, "poetry." When Eliot speaks of poetic drama, he seems to think of it as an ideal combination of public and private utterance. He describes this ideal genre eloquently, in language anticipating *Four Quartets,* when he says that at a play we may "perceive a pattern behind the pattern into which the characters deliberately involve themselves; the kind of pattern which we perceive in our own lives only at rare moments of inattention and detachment, drowsing in sunlight."[160] We may feel that no drama of Eliot quite reaches this ideal. But then Eliot assumes that poetic drama is always and necessarily a stage play. This assumption is consistent with his view of the stratification of culture, but even so it may be questioned. Perhaps *The Waste Land,* where loveliness peeps fitfully through squalor and an invisible divine presence haunts the misery of Europe, is closer to what Eliot really means by poetic drama than any of his plays.

Drama, an ensemble performance for an audience, is the most striking example of the fact that the arts belong to the continuum of tradition and culture, and form part of its civilizing influence. In great drama there is something for all levels of society at once.[161] But although the life of civilized man is superior to the barbarian, there is still the third level of which culture is a continuous imitation, the level of religion.

Acceptance of a specific tradition is not uncritical relativism, doing in Rome as the Romans do merely because they do it. There are wider laws of reason and beauty that make all human culture intelligible to every culture. This is so obvious that many feel that we should obliterate our local cultures and merge them into a global uniformity. Eliot does not share this view, but he recognizes, in changing his mind about Goethe, the link between catholicity of taste and universality of outlook—in this case "the problem of reconciliation and the definition of the Great European."[162] In the same essay he remarks that "wisdom is *logos koinos* (κοινός), the same for all men everywhere."[163] This phrase ("common *logos*") comes from an aphorism of Heraclitus, for whom *logos* meant much more than simply word or reason, because "to the Greek there was something inexplicable about *logos* so that it was a participation of man in the divine."[164] This aphorism is one of the two mottoes of *Four Quartets*.

We need, to begin with, some sense of reality which absorbs the ego into society. This means a set of specific loyalties, to a family, to a local culture, to a church, at most to a nation. In these loyalties our sense of individuality is not lost but fulfilled. Still, we cannot find ultimate reality in them: we are driven towards something universal, the same for all men everywhere. If we try to expand our loyalties, replacing a people with Mankind, a church with Truth or Goodness, something goes wrong. We lose our original sense of individuality as our loyalties get broader and fuzzier. Speaking of Stoical and other philosophies, Eliot says: "A man does not join himself with the Universe so long as he has anything else to join himself with."[165] The universal we reach ought to include within it the individuality with which we started: it should be a supreme Self which gives each self its identity.

The ego lives in a world of illusion in which the primary categories are those of time and space. Time as we ordinarily experience it has three dimensions, past, present, and future. None of these dimensions exists: the past is no longer, the future not yet, the present never quite. The centre of time is now, but there is no such time as now. Similarly, the centre of space is "here," but there is no such place as here. All places are "there": the best we can do is to draw a circle around ourselves and say that here is inside it. The result of the egocentric view is loneliness, a sense of alienation from a world that keeps running away from it.

For man in his social context, time and space have more meaning. Tradition gives meaning to time, and a localized culture surrounds a part of nature and makes it "here." But the historical perspective can breed new fallacies, such as the genetic fallacy, the tendency to disown the past by assuming that religion and culture are essentially what they have developed from, instead of "accustoming ourselves to find meaning in *final causes* rather than in origins."[166] No structure of reason or science founded on the illusions of ordinary perception can remove its own foundations: what is needed is a transformation of ordinary perception itself, some kind of direct experience that is individual but not egocentric, in contact with reality and not with appearance.

This line of thought naturally leads to an interest in the mystics. For the mystic, ordinary experience is attained by ordinary consciousness: if we feel that such experience is not real enough, we must turn to real consciousness, ordinary experience on a higher plane. Such a consciousness, curiously enough, brings us to more primitive and archaic modes of thought, especially in conceiving time and space. The appearance of time, the past–present–future continuum, belongs to a world of becoming, where there is no identity because everything changes into something else. Over against it is a world which is not timeless, but a world where "all is always now" [*Burnt Norton*, l. 152]. Similarly the illusion of space, the length–breadth–thickness continuum of "there," becomes "here," the area covered by a focus of consciousness. The mystic finds, at the heart of the illusion of time, a real present, and, at the heart of the illusion of space, a real presence.

Eliot's first philosophical interest was in F.H. Bradley. In Bradley's *Appearance and Reality*, "appearance" is a mass of logically impossible and self-contradictory impressions of time, space, change, causation, and the like, where there is a huge fission between subject and object, "mine" and "this." We have to go on to a reality which is an "Absolute," where all contradictions of appearance are reconciled. The Absolute can only be reached by an "immediate experience" in which reason, will, and feeling all fulfil themselves. Thus what started as a nineteenth-century idealist's problem about how far we can "know reality" ends as a kind of mystical primer. In the Indian philosophy which Eliot next studied, the ego is a product of an automatic natural energy, called *karma*, which expresses itself as desire, and involves one in suffering. Over against this is a consciousness of a self beyond mind and body, a self which is not a separate ego but identical with a total self (*Atman*). The end of the process, summed up in the phrase "Thou art That,"[167] is an objectivity which achieves self-identification, a paradoxical union very like that of the poetic process in Eliot.

In Christianity, *logos* means, not word, reason, or universal wisdom, but the Person of Christ. This *Logos* enters the continuum of history at a point in time and stays there, and ever since each moment is a potential moment of real as well as of ordinary consciousness. Our progress toward real consciousness may take us in either of two opposite directions, which reach the same point. "The way up and the way down are one and the same," Heraclitus says,[168] in an aphorism which is the second motto of the Quartets. We may call these ways the way of plenitude and the way of vacancy, to use terms found in *Burnt Norton*. The former is exemplified by the encyclopedic symbolism of Dante's *Commedia*; the other is described by St. John of the Cross as a "dark night of the soul," where by an ascesis of everything that attaches us outwardly, we reach the same divine presence.

Poetry is also a direct and total experience, "the experience both of a moment and of a lifetime."[169] It carries us beyond ordinary consciousness because it is "a function of all art to give us some perception of an order in life, by imposing an order upon it."[170] We listen to a symphony in ordinary time, but its beginning implies an end; we look at a picture in ordinary space, but its tense energy is arrested movement, as a Chinese jar gives us a sense that it "Moves perpetually in its stillness" [*Burnt Norton*, l. 146]. Thus art is a technique of meditation, using that word in its technical sense as a means of learning to experience reality. The complete absorption in the object demanded of the poet recurs in the religious life: in comparing Donne's sermons with Andrewes's, for example, Eliot says that Donne "is constantly finding an object which shall be adequate to his feelings; Andrewes is wholly absorbed in the object and therefore responds with the adequate emotion."[171] Art is a psychopomp only, however, or, as Eliot says in a passage clearly intended to be a central statement of his belief: "It is ultimately the function of art, in imposing a credible order upon reality, and thereby eliciting some perception of an order *in* reality, to bring us to a condition of serenity, stillness, and reconciliation; and then leave us, as Virgil left Dante, to proceed toward a region where that guide can avail us no farther."[172] The serenity and stillness at the end of the *Purgatorio* or Shakespeare's romances is itself an experience, and a very profound one: but it is also a condition of a further kind of experience of which poetry is the shadow and not the substance.

It is obvious that the quality of poetry is not affected by the poet's beliefs; nor does the poet *qua* poet believe at all: it is what he produces, not what he believes, that is his poetry, even if he could not have produced it without belief. There are many discussions of this point in Eliot, some of them very inconclusive. In general, however, what he finds in Christianity does not give him a formula for value judgments on poetry, but a conception of the function and context of poetry. We start with what he calls, quoting Andrewes, "The word within the word, unable to speak a word" [*Gerontion*, l. 118], at the hidden centre of reality. And, for Eliot as for Coleridge before him, we end with the Word as the circumference of reality, containing within itself time, space, and poetry viewed in the light of "the conception of poetry as a living whole of all the poetry that has ever been written."[173] This last is an experience of poetry as the Song of Man which is also, like the poem which inspired St. John of the Cross, the Song of Songs, and also, like the *Bhagavadgita*, to Eliot the greatest poem in the world next to Dante, the Song of God.

IV Unreal City

Eliot's earlier poetry is mainly satiric, and presents a world that may be summed up as a world without laughter, love, or children. The laughter is of the sinister and terrible kind that psychologists say the laughter in dreams is: we have the laughing woman in *Hysteria*, Sweeney "Letting his arms hang down to laugh" [*Sweeney among the Nightingales*, l. 2], and Mr. Apollinax laughing "like an irresponsible foetus" [*Mr. Apollinax*, l. 7]. The few children are shadowy, sinister, or pathetic, like the blank-faced urchin in *Rhapsody on a Windy Night* and the ragged girl who watches the pompous Directeur "Et crève d'amour" [*Le Directeur*, l. 22]—this being the only use of the word "love," I think, in Eliot's poetry before *Ash-Wednesday*. After *The Hollow Men* the poetry becomes increasingly devotional in tone, but there is no real change of attitude, only a back and a front view from the same poetic edifice. In the later poetry the "I," the speaker of the poem, is a *persona* of the poet himself; in the earlier work the narrators are created characters, speaking with the poet's voice but not for him.

A curious, and to me regrettable, feature of Eliot's critical theory is his avoidance of the term "imagination," except in the phrase "auditory imagination" at the furthest remove from the poetic product. The poet has an image-forming power, and his "philosophy" or body of "ideas" is arrived at by studying the conceptual implications of the structure of his images. Thus Yeats writes an essay called "The Philosophy of Shelley's Poetry," which is actually an essay on Shelley's imagery. This seems to me a much more valid critical procedure than talking about the poetry and the ideas of a poet as though they were separable things, separable enough even for a poet to "borrow" his philosophy from somebody else. Eliot's myth of decline contrasts Dante, who "had behind him the system of St. Thomas, to which his poem corresponds point to point,"[174] with Blake and Goethe and Shelley, who mistakenly invented their own philosophies. Blake's genius required, we are told, "a framework of accepted and traditional ideas which would have prevented him from indulging in a philosophy of his own."[175] But when we read *Four Quartets*, whatever influences there may be from Bradley or Patanjali or St. John of the Cross or Heraclitus, we darkly suspect Eliot too of indulging in a philosophy of his own.

Eliot speaks of the "major" poet as one whose entire work has a unity which is greater than the sum of its parts.[176] Elsewhere he speaks of the "world" that a poet creates, and remarks that all Shakespeare's work is one poem.[177] Eliot is clearly a major poet in this sense: he cannot be sampled in anthologies, and we understand each poem of his better for having read the others. But, if we are right, his total work is an imaginative world, and must be approached through his imagery, as Yeats approached Shelley. Yeats says, "I only made my pleasure in {Shelley} contented pleasure by massing in my imagination his recurring images . . . till his world had grown solid underfoot and consistent enough for the soul's habitation."[178] Let us see if we can domesticate ourselves in Eliot's world in the same way.

Poets tend to identify, by metaphor, the different aspects of cyclical movement in nature. Winter, death or old age, night, ruins, and the sea have ready-made associations with each other, and so have spring, youth or birth, dawn, the city, and rain or fountains. Eliot's fondness for cyclical imagery meets us at every turn. The December setting of *Murder in the Cathedral*, the cold March of *The Family Reunion*, the "midwinter spring" of *Little Gidding*, are deeply wrought into the texture of the imagery. In *The Dry Salvages* he says of the cycle of water:

> His rhythm was present in the nursery bedroom,
> In the rank ailanthus of the April dooryard,
> In the smell of grapes on the autumn table,
> And the evening circle in the winter gaslight. [ll. 11–14]

In *Portrait of a Lady* there is a sequence of four encounters carefully dated December, April, August, and October. The opening page of *The Waste Land* starts with April and goes through the coming of summer to the word "winter." The five little lyrics called *Landscapes* are arranged in the order of the seasons, and the seagull in the last poem has a special association with the end of the cycle, reappearing in *Gerontion* and the fourth section of *The Waste Land*. These groups of images make up not only a cycle but an opposition. Youth and age, spring and winter, dawn and darkness, rain and sea, form two contrasting states. Blake calls these states innocence and experience, and his terms are useful even for Eliot. For poets with a religious imagination, there are also heaven and hell, the paradisal and demonic realities underlying the mixture of good and evil in human life. Heaven and hell can be represented in poetry only by images of existence, hence images of innocence—the garden, perpetual spring, eternal youth—are closely associated with heaven or paradise, and images of repugnant experience—the desert, the sea, the prison, the tomb—are associated with hell. But for any poet who follows this structure of symbolism, including Eliot, there are four worlds, and heaven and innocence, hell and experience, are distinguished as well as associated.

In Dante's *Commedia* we have a *Paradiso* and an *Inferno*, and two intermediate worlds on the surface of this earth. One is the world of experience, the Europe of 1300, which permeates the whole poem by allusion and illustration. The other is the mountain of the *Purgatorio*, where Dante journeys upward in quest of innocence and reaches the garden of Eden. For Eliot, there would be two places in Dante's world charged with a peculiar intensity: the place where the vision of experience begins to be a vision of hell, and the place where the vision of innocence begins to be a vision of paradise.

The former place is described in canto 3 of the *Inferno*, where Dante, guided by Virgil, passes through the gates of hell into a crowd of people who lived "without blame or praise" [l. 35]. They are not strictly in hell, because they "never were alive" [l. 60], and can neither live nor die. "Let us not speak of them, but look and pass on," says Virgil [l. 49], so Dante goes on to the brink of the river Acheron, on the opposite shore of which is hell proper, the frontier that Eliot sometimes speaks of as crossed by a soul when it commits a mortal sin.

This scene is closely associated in Eliot's mind with the vision of modern life in Baudelaire's *Fleurs du mal*, especially in *Au Lecteur* and the opening of *Les Septs Vieillards*. In Baudelaire modern life in the "fourmillante cité" [*Les Septs Vieillards*, l. 1] is characterized by boredom or ennui. Ennui is not so much sin as the state of sin: it is kept from positive vice, not by virtue, but by the negative vices of indolence and fear. For real vice "Notre âme, hélas! n'est pas assez hardie," Baudelaire says [*Au Lecteur*, l. 28]; one lives in a world that Ecclesiastes calls "vanity," or mist [1:2]. The dedication of Eliot's *Prufrock* volume quotes a passage from the *Purgatorio* ending "Treating shadows as a solid thing" [canto 21, l. 137], and the feeling that what the world calls substance is really shadow runs all through Eliot's poetry.

There are three ways of reacting to this world. One is to live in it without realizing that one is really dead, a realization that may take many years, as Mary says in *The Family Reunion*.[179] Another is to recognize its unreality and scramble up into daylight, in other words to live an honest life that is at least not futile. A third is the full understanding that such a world is not only the entrance to hell, but that all hell is implicit in it.

Eliot speaks of "the boredom, and the horror, and the glory,"[180] which describe three of his four worlds. His vision of evil, however, is seldom a vision of horror or violence, except offstage, as in the crucifixion of Celia Coplestone in *The Cocktail Party*. There seem to be sinister goings-on in the background of *Sweeney among the Nightingales*, but all that we see clearly is a dull brothel with yawning whores and gaping pimps. The misery of war-torn Europe is in the background of *The Waste Land*, but all we hear are voices asking querulously, "Are you alive, or not?" [l. 126]. We have to see in such incidents as the seduction of the typist, who lets her body be used like a public urinal because "she is bored and tired" [l. 236], the full horror of the denial of humanity.

The motto of *Prufrock* comes from later in the *Inferno*, but it echoes Virgil's remark in canto 3 that "The world does not allow the report of (such people) to exist" [l. 47]. Prufrock himself would like to be Lazarus, come back from the dead, but is out of touch with the power that could perform such a miracle. In *The Waste Land* the poet, watching the crowds on London Bridge, repeats another line from the same canto 3: "I had not thought death had undone so many" [l. 53; *The Waste Land*, l. 63]. Most of the people are coming out of tube stations, and the subway is a good image for this waste-land world because, like Dante's scene, it is just below the surface of the ground. The third section of *Burnt Norton* takes us further into this "place of disaffection" [l. 93], a world neither of daylight nor darkness, inhabited by "unhealthy souls" [l. 111] who seem less souls than the bloodless shades of a Homeric Hades.

In *The Hollow Men* we are "Gathered on the beach of this tumid river" [l. 60], the Acheron-Thames, separated from the "lost / violent" souls in the real hell [ll. 15–16], who apparently include the Kurtz of Conrad's *Heart of Darkness*. Kurtz had a sense not of the boredom but of "the horror," and he is really "dead," whereas the hollow men are merely not alive, and cannot make the act of surrender involved in actual death. Like others later in the *Inferno*, the hollow men respond passively to winds, "behaving as the wind behaves" [l. 35], a parody of the Holy Spirit blowing where it pleases [cf. John 3:8]. The wind suggests also Gerontion driven by the Trades, the crowds in *Burnt Norton* driven by wind or expelled from the tube stations like an eructation, and the statement in *The Rock* that "Man without God is a seed upon the wind, driven this way and that" [pt. 7, l. 3]. Images of blown seeds, of scarecrows or "old guys," of bubbles and vapours, of shadowy and fitful appearances like Hadrian's "animula, vagula, blandula," represent a conception of the soul far removed from the Christian spiritual body. In the plays, too, the action usually turns on the growing realization of the emptiness of the dead–alive world by the central character, flanking whom are subordinate characters who get back into ordinary life.

The opposite pole, at which the vision of innocence becomes paradisal, meets us at the end of canto 26 of the *Purgatorio,* where Dante purges himself of his last sin, lechery, and is about to enter the ring of fire that separates him from Eden. The closing lines of this canto, beginning with "Ara vos prec," the original title of Eliot's 1920 book of poems, are frequently alluded to in Eliot. The image of refining fire, especially as a cure for lechery, is the organizing image of "The Fire Sermon" in *The Waste Land,* and similar imagery dominates *Little Gidding*. In Eden, where Dante renews the innocence of childhood, or rather of the childhood of man, the state of Adam before his fall, he meets a young girl, Matilda, who is gathering flowers and is compared to Proserpine [canto 28].

All through Eliot's work runs the image of a "secret garden" (a phrase in *The Confidential Clerk*),[181] associated with childhood, with spring flowers and rains, with a young girl, and with innocence—or at least leaving it is associated with guilt. In *La Figlia Che Piange,* the narrator's memory revolves around a girl with "her arms full of flowers" [l. 20], deserted by a man "As the soul leaves the body torn and bruised" [l. 11]. A similar Matilda figure appears in *The Waste Land* as the "hyacinth girl," where the narrator speaks of "Looking into the heart of light, the silence" [l. 41]. The phrase "heart of light" recurs in the rose-garden episode at the beginning of *Burnt Norton* [l. 39]. In *The Family Reunion* Harry tells Agatha of his childhood at Wishwood and of a "rose-garden" which one enters, like Alice in Wonderland, through a "little door."[182]

This situation is parodied in other poems. In *Portrait of a Lady* the narrator, a most unheroic character preoccupied with "self-possession," goes through a series of interviews with an aging spinster surrounded with the atmosphere of blighted romance ("Juliet's tomb"). He finally drifts off leaving her "Slowly twisting the lilac stalks" [l. 46] and staring bleakly into the loneliness of what is left of her life. In *Dans le Restaurant* an old waiter is reminded by spring rains of a sexual experience he had in childhood with a little girl. The narrator is disgusted by the teller of the story, but his attitude to the story itself is more ambivalent: "De quel droit payes-tu des expériences comme moi?" he says [l. 23].

Prufrock and Gerontion are talking to themselves, and the "you" addressed in both poems is "a familiar compound ghost" [*Little Gidding,* l.

98], made up chiefly of memories. But Prufrock's meditation is called a love song, and sometimes the "you" takes on a female aspect; in *Gerontion* the only connection of the "you" with anything feminine is the fact that the main subject of the last paragraph is passion and the stimulation of the senses. But a vestigial Matilda figure is still there in both poems, and the fact that she is so shadowy is part of Prufrock's frustration and Gerontion's cynicism. In *A Cooking Egg*, the narrator, taking off from Villon's complaint of having lived an inglorious life for thirty years, contrasts his earlier life with Pipit, a "penny world" [l. 25] that was still a world of eagles and trumpets, with his desiccated adult life. The curious title means, apparently, a not-so-fresh egg: the egg as a symbol of a self-enclosed existence meets us again in *Sweeney Agonistes*. For a woman, a similar childhood memory would be of a boy, like that of Marie in *The Waste Land*, who remembers her quasi-sexual excitement in sledding with her cousin, and associates mountains with freedom thereafter. In Dante Matilda gives place to Beatrice, and Beatrice is the "high dream" inspired by a childhood memory—Dante says at the age of nine, which according to Eliot is probably too late.[183] Most of the above parodies are childhood memories on the egocentric level of the "low dream."

The most concentrated of all visions of a lost or transitory state of innocence is the rose-garden episode in *Burnt Norton*, where we enter "our first world" [ll. 23–4], a world full of invisible presences, and where the water of life and the two traditional paradisal flowers, the lotus of the East and the rose of the West, appear briefly before the vision fades [l. 38]. The phrase "the leaves were full of children" [l. 42] suggests that the children are the tree they are in, the tree of life. Parental or guardian figures, "dignified, invisible" [l. 25], are also present; perhaps even a divine presence inhabits the garden, as was said of the original Eden. In ordinary life the rose-garden is usually some kind of private or hidden retreat: but all such retreats are screen memories of man's lost innocence. Since the fall, Eden has been closed up, guarded by angels. In *Mr. Eliot's Sunday Morning Service* we have a glimpse of a paradise "Sustained by staring Seraphim" [l. 22], but in the foreground we see only "sable presbyters" [l. 17] darkening the window pane, merging into the "epicene" bees "Along the garden-wall" [ll. 28, 25]. In *Triumphal March* the hero is still in contact with a paradisal vision, but the "hedge" that the soldiers of his preposterous retinue make around him indicates that he is unlikely to remain so.

We notice the prominence of the word "light" at the end of this poem.

Eden now lies at the centre of human consciousness, too deep for even dreams to reach, as the "heart of light" shining in an uncomprehending darkness. Its threatening angels are usually replaced in Eliot by birds or animals. In *Gerontion* the tiger, a traditional symbol of Antichrist, is the symbol of wrath, the eternal spiritual opposition of the worlds of Christ and Gerontion. In *Burnt Norton* a thrush first leads us into and then drives us out of the rose-garden, and a raven appears in the corresponding section of *The Family Reunion*. The childish discovery of forbidden knowledge in *Dans le Restaurant* is interrupted by a "gros chien" [l. 17], and a dog in *The Waste Land* is introduced as a "friend to men" [l. 74], who scratches up corpses and is consequently a nuisance to those who want to stay buried. The point of view of the latter is represented by a much less enterprising dog, the Yorkshire terrier of *Five-Finger Exercises*, who remains "safe and warm" in the midst of a brown waste land with a dry tree [II, l. 6].

The worlds of experience and innocence, the subway and the rose-garden, may be called respectively, using terms from *The Hollow Men*, "death's dream kingdom" [ll. 20, 30] and "death's other kingdom" [ll. 14, 46]. The reader may have begun to suspect that they are the "objective correlatives" of the two levels of personality dealt with in the previous chapters. Death's dream kingdom is the world of Prufrock and Gerontion, the "cracked and brown" waste land [*Mr. Eliot's Sunday Morning Service*, l. 12], the stubble field of the hollow men. As it is a world without identity, it is a world of "deliberate disguises" [*The Hollow Men*, l. 32], usually symbolized in Eliot, following another hint from Baudelaire's *Au Lecteur*, as animals—a different use of the animal from the one just mentioned, though related. The narrator in *Portrait of a Lady* says,

> And I must borrow every changing shape
> To find expression . . . dance, dance
> Like a dancing bear,
> Cry like a parrot, chatter like an ape, [ll. 109–12]

and the narrator in *Mélange adultère de tout* proposes a series of camouflages, the climax a birthday in Africa when he will be "Vêtu d'une peau de girafe" [l. 18].

Human consciousness cannot identify permanently with innocence or with experience. If it could, they would become the eternal realities of heaven or hell. Those who accept experience voluntarily can only do so through detachment, not through identification, still less through the dead–alive indifference which in the third section of *Little Gidding* is carefully distinguished from detachment. The chorus in *Murder in the Cathedral* achieves a momentary identification with experience in the "death-bringers" chorus, which thereby becomes an epiphany of hell; hence its imagery is full of animals, leading to "the horror of the ape."[184] In the rose-garden episode of *Burnt Norton* innocence becomes, for an instant, an epiphany of paradise. We notice that Becket's comment on the chorus and the thrush's comment on the rose-garden vision are the same: "Human kind cannot bear very much reality."[185]

Death's other kingdom is, besides the vision of lost innocence, the heaven of religion, appearing in this form in *The Hollow Men* as the "multifoliate rose" of Dante's *Paradiso* [l. 64; *Paradiso*, canto 30, l. 116]. Many do not believe in a future or eternal life, but another aspect of death's other kingdom is irrefutable—the past. The great cultural achievements of the past remain in the present to represent another world which is both here and out of reach. Thus the wretched couple in *Lune de miel*, unable to sleep for bugs and stench, are mocked by the Byzantine "forme précise" of St. Apollinaire [l. 18], who, being stone, has no impulse to scratch. We are always in a later phase of our cycle, individual or historical, than our past, and thus a sense of losing energy or innocence is practically inseparable from consciousness itself.

The two kingdoms are also contrasted in the minds of Prufrock and Gerontion, who exemplify a theme, running through all of Eliot's work, of assuming a double part. In addressing a "you" who is also themselves, they follow a dialectic which separates the world they are in, and have committed themselves to, from a paradisal world set over against it, which they contemplate until they feel finally separated from it. In *Prufrock* this latter world is a wish-fulfilment world symbolized by the sea. It is the sea of the mermaids, as opposed to the sea of ordinary experience in which Prufrock awakens and "drowns," the latter being the sea in which he is a pair of ragged claws, and which in the apocalypse, according to the Bible, will disappear [Revelation 21:1], taking Prufrock with it. Gerontion, as his name indicates, is an old man at the point of death, his reverie a parody of Newman's *The Dream of Gerontius*. All the images surrounding him are of the end of the natural cycle: the decaying house which is a symbol of his dying body, the gull, the sea, and the winter. Gerontion's knowledge becomes exclusively the forbidden knowledge of good and evil, tears "shaken from the wrath-bearing tree" [l. 48], in contrast to Christ, who belongs to "the juvenescence of the year" [l. 19]. Both poems move towards a self-recognition scene, a scene which is parody because it is the ego, the illusory self capable only of death, that is recognized.

Sweeney, as an *homme moyen sensuel*—or perhaps a trifle more than *moyen*—is more adapted to his world than Prufrock or Gerontion, which may be one reason why he is associated with animals. He is called "Apeneck Sweeney" [l. 1], is compared to a zebra, a giraffe, and an orang-outang, and is clearly blood brother to *The Hippopotamus*. We have noted his connection with the Yahoo or pure natural man, and his role as the guardian of the "horned gate" [l. 8], of the true or high dream which comes from Eden into experience, also associates him with the original fall of man. But Sweeney has a more likeable side, especially in *Sweeney Agonistes*. In this poem the two extremes of existence, hell and heaven, are indicated by two epigraphs, one (repeated in *The Family Reunion*) a speech of Orestes in Aeschylus and the other a passage from St. John of the Cross. Between these limits Sweeney works out his own version of the two inner worlds. Innocence is the "crocodile isle" that he proposes taking Doris to, its embryonic withdrawal from life symbolized by an egg [*Sweeney Agonistes: Fragment of an Agon*, ll. 20, 78]. There follows a macabre story of a man keeping a girl's corpse in a bathtub full of lysol, the story being told not as a newspaper sensation but as a parable of the kind of ordinary life that is indistinguishable from death. Sweeney is not haunted by furies like Orestes or Harry Monchensey, and he is unlikely to get far with St. John of the Cross, but he is no fool, and his troubled vision is something much more than a song for simians.

The two Coriolan poems, *Triumphal March* and *Difficulties of a Statesman*, are concerned with the theme of heroism, in its traditional form—all Eliot's other heroes are martyrs. Heroism, being a form of energy in which no shadow falls between idea and reality, belongs to innocence, but it can seek expression only in experience, and its relation to experience is normally tragic in consequence. Coriolanus, as the hero of what Eliot calls Shakespeare's most successful play,[186] is a person of great integrity, but his inability to operate the social machinery of tact and compromise keeps him imprisoned in that integrity. Thus he appears on two levels of isolation, the isolation of the hero and the isolation of the ego. We all know the latter kind, and occasionally it catches an echo of the former, the "broken Coriolanus" of *The Waste Land* [l. 417]. In *Triumphal March* Eliot's hero is still genuinely detached, and a closer model for him than Shakespeare's Coriolanus would be perhaps the Arjuna of the *Bhagavadgita*, who is mentioned in *The Dry Salvages* [l. 169]. In this work, an episode from the Indian epic *Mahabharata*, Arjuna finds himself on a battlefield fighting kinsmen, and has the kind of doubts about the value of what he is doing that Western heroes, including Coriolanus, are seldom afflicted with. His charioteer, the god Krishna in disguise, explains that as life is a battlefield, there is nowhere else to go, and eventually he reveals himself in a theophany, manifesting to Arjuna what Eliot calls in *Triumphal March* "the still point of the turning world" [l. 34], of which more later. But in *Difficulties of a Statesman*, the inner paradise is breaking up and fading, the mother, so dominating and sinister a figure in Shakespeare, is beginning to replace it, the tone of parody deepens, and Coriolan is becoming less of a tragic hero and more of a victim.

There are several of these victim figures in Eliot. The drowned Phoenician sailor Phlebas, who appears in *Dans le Restaurant* and *The Waste Land*, has a strong feeling of Adonis about him, as his nationality suggests. In *Animula*, which takes its name from the poem of Hadrian's already mentioned, the poet traces the life cycle of unheroic man from birth to death, with echoes from Dante and Baudelaire, as a continuous distraction, no moment in it focused in a state of real consciousness. This life is then contrasted with figures of energy, heroism, or beauty cut down in fullness of life, who include another Adonis figure: "Floret, by the boarhound slain between the yew trees" [l. 36]. With this line the mournful family of yews enters Eliot's poetry, to return in *Ash-Wednesday* and *Four Quartets*. In *Burbank with a Baedeker* Eliot adopts the common Henry James situation of a fresh American innocence betrayed by a wily and venal Europe. Nothing very terrible happens to Burbank, but the overtones of Princess Volupine, besides her Jonsonian and Venetian name, are those of a macabre corpse-like Venus rising from the sea in the city of Venus, of Cleopatra sitting on her barge, and perhaps of the blue-eyed hag Sycorax. Possibly even Sweeney, for all his broad bottom, may have enough exuberance and vitality to be a victim of the same type. At any rate some kind of sacrificial ritual seems to be building up around him in *Sweeney among the Nightingales*, although some readers feel that the atmosphere of this poem is that of a sexual dream, a sleeping contrast, or parallel, to *Sweeney Erect*.

The only way to adjust perfectly to the dead–alive world is to be either a body without a mind, like the pneumatic Grishkin in *Whispers of Immortality*, or a mind without a body, like the abstract entities that circumambulate her. In *Mr. Eliot's Sunday Morning Service* the opposition of Sweeney and the polymaths is less radical, but similar, and so is the opposition of the hippopotamus and the Laodicean church. Eliot's early imagery revolves around two figures: the youth or girl, killed or betrayed or deserted in fullness of life, and the weary old or middle-aged man who dreams of life in an after-dinner sleep—the phrase from *Measure for Measure* which forms the motto of *Gerontion*. The latter group includes, besides Gerontion, Prufrock (not old, but, as Shaw says of one of his characters, one whom age cannot wither because he has never bloomed),[187] Tiresias in *The Waste Land*, Simeon, glad to slip quietly out of the world before the sword of the Word enters it, and the bewildered Magi who would be "glad of another death" [*Journey of the Magi*, l. 43]. The speaker in *Lines for an Old Man*, under whose sardonic and malevolent eye "The dullard knows that he is mad" [l. 13], is a considerably more vigorous type, said to have some connection with Mallarmé. The former group (Phlebas, Burbank, Floret, La Figlia Che Piange) belong to the world of innocence, and the image chiefly associated with them is that of water.

Experience is largely an accumulating of grime and corruption, and water is its cleansing agent. In *Dans le Restaurant*, as the waiter shuffles off to what the narrator hopes is a bath, we encounter Phlebas lying in the sea, and the effect is an appreciation of what Keats calls the sea's task of pure ablution. In *The Waste Land* the Thames carries the filth of London into the sea, where we meet Phlebas again, and the healing waters return as rain at the end, reminding us of the symbolism of baptism in Christianity. In *Mr. Eliot's Sunday Morning Service* the contrast of the "baptized God" [l. 11] and Sweeney shifting hams in his bath is parallel to the contrast in *Dans le Restaurant* between the slobbering waiter and the rainy weather outside which is called "the beggars' washday" [l. 5]. The theme of "death by water" contains by implication a theme of rebirth by water, hence the theme of parodied self-recognition in Prufrock and Gerontion may have its opposite too, and we should expect this opposite recognition also to be associated with water.

In Dante's encounter with Matilda it is the brilliance of Matilda's eyes (and later those of Beatrice) that particularly impresses Dante. By contrast, the hollow men feel the reproachful eyes of those who are in death's other kingdom, and dare not meet those eyes even in dreams, for they belong to a vision deeper than the "low dream" they have. Closely related to *The Hollow Men* are two poems which, with one of its sections, originally formed a group called "Doris's Dream Songs." One, *Eyes that last I saw in tears*, speaks of a "division" [l. 2] from eyes that in this world are seen only without tears, and hence as mocking or derisive. In the other, *The wind sprang up at four o'clock*, the dreamer seems to be entering death's other kingdom, seen as a river which takes on the form of "a face that sweats with tears" [l. 8]. These are strange dreams for Sweeney's practical and not over-visionary paramour. The second one especially seems to suggest that death may be the point at which one enters a spiritual community, as birth is the point at which one enters the ordinary human one.

One of the places where the "shadow" of *The Hollow Men* is said to fall is between the essence and the descent [ll. 88–9], and perhaps in ascent the shadow of life in experience rejoins its substance. When Dante meets Matilda in Eden, he recovers his original state, as he would have been without the fall, hence the meeting with Matilda has in it the recognition of his original nature, as though he were ending his life where he began it, as though Matilda were a part of himself that he is rejoining. The rose-garden world is the world of the might-have-been, and our lives run in counterpoint to another life we might have lived if man had not fallen out of Eden. A passage from Shelley's *Prometheus Unbound* which suggests that man is simultaneously a substance and a shadow in different worlds, the two uniting at death, in language as well as imagery very close to Eliot, is quoted at a crucial point of *The Cocktail Party*.[188]

The ironic parody of this theme has its literary ancestry too. In a ghost story of Henry James, *The Jolly Corner*, a man meets himself as he might have been, and this story is referred to in *The Family Reunion*.[189] A rather similar ghost story by May Sinclair, *Where Their Fire Is Not Quenched*, is alluded to in *The Elder Statesman*.[190] But the archetype of all such ironic recognition scenes is the encounter of Aeneas and Dido in Virgil's hell, where Aeneas receives what Eliot calls "the most telling snub in all poetry."[191] This scene in the Aeneid is a contrast to Aeneas's earlier meeting with his mother Venus, a line from which forms the epigraph to *La Figlia Che Piange*.

La Figlia Che Piange represents the "beginning" of Eliot's symbolism; the "end," which is the same point, is represented by *Marina*. Marina in Shakespeare was the daughter of a Phoenician sailor, whose reunion with her forms one of those long recognition scenes, usually involving a father, a daughter, and a sea, that are characteristic of Shakespeare's late comedies.[192] In Eliot the narrator is "crossing the bar," setting out into the sea of death in a leaky boat which, like Gerontion's house, symbolizes his own body. The evil creatures of the shadow-world he is leaving behind become "unsubstantial," the thrush, the bird of the *Burnt Norton* rose-garden, is calling him, and as the end of his life rejoins its beginning, "images return" [*Marina*, l. 4]. He begins to remember his past life, as Phlebas "passed the stages of his age and youth" [*The Waste Land*, l. 317] ("sa vie antérieure" in the French version, which establishes a more definite link with Baudelaire's *La Vie antérieure*, with its imagery of submarine reincarnation). Gradually, as the world "under sleep" [*Marina*, l. 21] begins to open up, with the whispering laughter of the children in the trees (for the sea is vanishing, as in the Biblical apocalypse, and the rose-garden is taking its place), a face takes shape, the bodily form of a new life.

The Waste Land is a vision of Europe, mainly of London, at the end of the First World War, and is the climax of Eliot's "infernal" vision. It appeared in 1922, just before the poet had reached thirty-five, the middle of life's journey, when Dante began the *Inferno*. The setting is civilization in the winter of its discontent, and the images are those of the end of the natural cycle: winter, the "brown land" [l. 175], ruins (including the nursery-rhyme collapse of London Bridge and, in the notes, the proposed demolition of nineteen city churches), and the Thames flowing to the sea. This world is physically above ground but spiritually subterranean, a world of shadows, corpses, and buried seeds. The inhabitants live the "buried life" (a phrase from *Portrait of a Lady* [l. 53]) of seeds in winter: they await the spring rains resentfully, for real life would be their death. Human beings who live like seeds, egocentrically, cannot form a community but only an aggregate, where "Each man fixed his eyes before his feet" [l. 65], imprisoned in a spiritual solitude that recalls the story of the death of Ugolino in Dante. Such lines as "And if it rains, a closed car at four" [l. 136] associate human life with its vegetative metaphors.

Dante's journey through hell begins on Good Friday evening, and he emerges on the other side of the earth on Easter Sunday morning. Thus his journey fits inside the three-day rhythm of the redemption, where Christ is buried on Friday evening, descends to hell on Saturday, and rises on Sunday morning. Similarly in the first section of *The Waste Land*, "The Burial of the Dead," we sink into the lower world of the "unreal city" [ll. 60, 207], crowds streaming into it like the damned in Dante. Here Christ appears as Isaiah's "shadow of a rock in a weary land" [32:2], before we descend to the shades below, or as the possible power of resurrection in Ezekiel's valley of dry bones. We remain in the underworld all through the next two sections, and then follows "Death by Water," evidently physical death, as burial in earth symbolizes the physical life which is spiritual death. Physical death is the final judgment between the seeds who can understand the commands of the thunder and die to a new life, and those who merely die and are rejected, as the sterile seed is rejected by nature. The last section repeats the image of a streaming crowd, "hooded hordes swarming" [l. 369], an apocalypse in which the invisible presence of the risen Christ accompanies scenes of terror and chaos as the valley of dry bones becomes "an exceeding great army," as Ezekiel says [37:10].

Easter represents the end of a long period of religious symbolism in which a "dying god," a spirit representing the fertility of nature, was thought to die and rise again, usually in a three-day festival. The information about the cults of Adonis, Attis, Osiris, and others collected in Frazer's *Golden Bough* is referred to by Eliot in the notes. In these rites a red or purple flower was associated with the god's blood: this appears in the hyacinths of *The Waste Land* and perhaps the "belladonna" [l. 49] or deadly nightshade (as well as in the dogwood and judas of *Gerontion*, the lilacs of *Ash-Wednesday*, and elsewhere). The death of Adonis was mourned by women representing the spirit of the earth, and the line "Murmur of maternal lamentation" [l. 368] associates this with the Biblical weeping of Rachel.

As later in *Four Quartets*, there is an elaborate imagery of the four elements. The cycle of water, from spring rains and the wet hair of the hyacinth girl to the Thames flowing out to sea, returning as the rains bringing new life to the parched land, is most prominent. According to Charles Lamb, Webster's *Call for the robin redbreast and the wren*, and Shakespeare's *Full fathom five* are the great elegies of death by earth and water respectively in the language,[193] and both are referred to in *The Waste Land*. In "The Fire Sermon" there is the implicit contrast between the St. Augustine and Buddha[194] who appear at the end, seeking "the fire that refines them" (the last line of canto 26 of the *Purgatorio*), and those who are burning in their own lusts with heat but without light. The air is hidden in the "brown fog" of a London winter [ll. 61, 208]; it blows freshly towards home but leaves Tristan as far away as the Ancient Mariner or Ulysses; it stirs up and confuses the perfumes of the woman in "A Game of Chess"; it is the element of the fearful apparitions and mirages of the closing scenes. The Ovidian theme of metamorphosis, associated chiefly with Philomela's transformation to a bird, runs through the poem, and modulates into the swallow of the *Pervigilium Veneris*. The dissolving and reforming of physical elements suggest that the reality of which they are an appearance is a spiritual substance, the risen Christ.

Apart from Easter, the idea of a descent into hell came to Dante from the sixth book of the *Aeneid*, where Aeneas enters the lower world with the aid of a "golden bough" and the Cumaean Sibyl. Another story about the Cumaean Sibyl hanging in a jar between heaven and earth and wanting only to die, a most vivid image of the "nightmare life in death" [*The Rime of the Ancient Mariner*, l. 193] which is Eliot's theme, is told by Petronius, and forms the motto of the poem. Another, or perhaps the same, Sibyl is said to have asked the gods for as many years to live as she held grains of sand in her hand, but forgot to ask for continuous youth, in other words real life. She may be behind the phrase "fear in a handful of dust" [l. 30]. The Sibyl is parodied in *The Waste Land* by Madame Sosostris, with her fake Egyptian name and her "wicked pack of cards" [l. 46]. Aeneas sees, besides Dido, the shades and a hell of torments, a further world of rebirth into new life.

Virgil in turn drew for his vision from the *Odyssey*, where Ulysses calls up the shades to consult Tiresias. *The Waste Land*, we are told in the notes, is a reverie of Tiresias, who has the same relation to it that Gerontion has to his poem, and whose hermaphroditic shadow-mind contains all the men and women who appear in it. Tiresias had been both a man and a woman, and was considered an authority on the pleasures of sexual intercourse from both points of view, but the production of children is beyond him, and all the sexual unions in the poem are as sterile as the waste land itself. Eliot leaves it to Pound, however, to elaborate the Odyssey scene in his first canto: *The Waste Land* is an intensely Latin poem, owing much more to Virgil and Ovid.

The contrasting figure to Tiresias is Phlebas, sailing (as we learn from *Dans le Restaurant*) to Britain in quest of tin, symbolizing a commerce which continues in "Mr. Eugenides, the Smyrna merchant," whose "pocket full of currants" [ll. 209–10] makes a startling pun on the "current" that picks the bones of Phlebas. Carthage was a Phoenician colony, the hereditary enemy of Rome (the naval battle of Mylae is referred to in passing [l. 70]), and from Carthage, a "cauldron of unholy loves" [l. 307n. citing *Confessions*, bk. 3], St. Augustine, repeating the journey of Aeneas, went to Italy to become a Christian. He later returned to become bishop of nearby Hippo, and a note left by Joyce, "Eliot: Bishop of Hippo," associates him neatly with the author of *The Hippopotamus*.[195]

In Virgil and Homer the motive for the underworld journey is to learn the future, the kind of knowledge ordinarily closed to mankind. Thus Ulysses in Homer wishes to know his personal fate, and is told that he will return home and eventually meet death from the sea, like Phlebas. A similar anxiety to know the future is gratified by Madame Sosostris, and *The Dry Salvages* later explains that a shoddy occultism pandering to man's desire to know his future is characteristic of sterile cultures [ll. 188–204]. In *The Waste Land* the coming of Christianity represents the turning of Classical culture from its winter into a new spring, for the natural cycle is also associated with the cycles of civilization. This may be one reason for the prominence of the poets, Virgil and Ovid, who were contemporary with Christ. Whatever future faces us today would, then, logically be connected with a second coming of Christ. The second coming, however, is not a future but a present event, a confronting of man with an immediate demand for self-surrender, sympathy, and control, virtues which are primarily social and moral, and are preliminary to the Christian faith, hope, and love. The London churches, St. Magnus Martyr, St. Mary Woolnoth, and others, stand like sentinels to testify to the presence of the risen Christ in the ruins of Europe.

Thus the underworld journey seems to be an initiation, a learning of mysteries. It is an old theory that the sixth book of the *Aeneid* is an allegory of initiation into Eleusinian mysteries, and a similar theory was applied to Shakespeare's *Tempest* by Colin Still in *Shakespeare's Mystery Play*, a book mentioned in Eliot's preface to Wilson Knight's *Wheel of Fire* and published the year before *The Waste Land*. The court party in *The Tempest* make, like Aeneas and Augustine, a journey to Italy from Tunis (identified with Carthage by Gonzalo); they are thrown on an island off the Italian coast and go through an experience there which brings them to self-knowledge and repentance. Ferdinand, the hero, mourns the drowning of his father, and finds him alive after all, while in wooing Miranda he has to appease and then be reconciled with Miranda's father. In Christianity, similarly, Christ as the second Adam succeeds but also redeems the first Adam, and appeases and is reconciled with his eternal Father. This similarity between the Christian myth and the structure of comedy will meet us in the plays. The recognition scene in *The Tempest* discovers Ferdinand playing chess with Miranda, a game which ends either in checkmate, the death of the king, or in stalemate, like the two unions in the second section of *The Waste Land* which is called "A Game of Chess." Here Miranda is replaced by two female wrecks, with bad nerves and bad teeth respectively, corresponding to the spiritual and physical narcoses symbolized by burial in earth and in water. The former is a "Lady of the Rocks" who has overtones of Dido, Cleopatra, Pope's Belinda, Keats's Lamia, the Great Whore of the Bible, and other stylish vixens; the latter has no literary splendours around her except a dim recall of the drowned Ophelia. Eliot's note on his title for this section refers to two plays of Middleton and does not mention *The Tempest*, but we cannot always trust Eliot's notes.[196]

The Tempest uses the romance theme of the prince who comes to a strange land and marries its king's daughter. In stories of the St. George and Perseus type the king is aged or suffering from a mysterious wound symbolizing sexual impotence; the land he rules is therefore waste, on the principles of sympathetic magic, and it is ravaged by a sea-monster for the same reason. The hero kills the monster and succeeds to the kingdom. In the background is a nature myth of winter turning to spring, sea and snow turning to spring rain, age turning to youth, a sleeping beauty awakened by her prince charming. But if the monster *is* winter, the hero must enter and emerge from it, like Jonah in the Bible, must die himself and be reborn. There is no monster in Eliot, but there are vestiges of his open mouth in the references to "Dead mountain mouth of carious teeth" [l. 339] and "This decayed hole among the mountains" [l. 386]. With the theme of death and revival the dragon-killer story merges with the dying-god story.

In some medieval versions of the same myth studied by Jessie Weston in *From Ritual to Romance*, cited by Eliot as a source for *The Waste Land*, the youthful knight comes to a waste land ruled by an aged and wounded "fisher king." Two mystical signs, a lance and a cup, are exhibited to him: had he asked their meaning the king would have been healed. Here the theme of descent and temporary death is represented by a "Chapel Perilous," an empty lighted chapel where the hero must pass a night while the lights are extinguished one by one. In the final section of *The Waste Land* the Chapel Perilous represents the underworld of death and burial, the tomb from which Christ rises. The lance and cup, originally fertility and sexual symbols, became associated with the lance of Longinus and the Holy Grail in the Passion of Christ. They are to be connected also with the two red suits of the modern pack of cards, the diamond being a lancehead and the heart a chalice. Our cards are derived from a much more elaborate set, the Tarots, consulted by Madame Sosostris, which have twenty-two additional "trumps" with such names as the hanged man, the falling tower, death, the last judgment, and so on. Some of these, and others invented by Eliot, are mentioned in *The Waste Land*.

Another monster is slain by Jesus in his Easter victory over death and hell: the leviathan of the Old Testament, a sea-monster who *is* the sea, as he is death and hell, and also the devil, the serpent of Paradise, described in *The Rock* as "the great snake at the bottom of the pit of the world" [X, l. 7]. In the Bible he or a similar monster is also identified with the kingdoms of tyranny—Egypt, Babylon, and the Phoenician city of Tyre. Thus the world that needs redemption is to be conceived as imprisoned in the monster's belly, whence the Messiah, following Jonah, descends to deliver it. In Christian iconography hell is often represented as an open-mouthed monster, from which Jesus emerges with the procession of the redeemed behind him, these forming a ghostly background to the final section of *The Waste Land*. The world to be redeemed is symbolically under water as well as under the earth, which gives point to the symbolism of fishing in the Gospels, and establishes a link with the "fisher king" of romance. Eliot's fisher king, sitting gloomily on the shore at the end of the poem with his "arid plain" behind him [l. 425], thus corresponds to Adam, or human nature that cannot redeem itself. The progression of *bateaux ivres*, from Tristan's faraway ship to the "narrow canoe" of a girl's seduction [l. 295], ending with the shipwrecked Phlebas, has the same relation to Adam that the responding boat [l. 419], the symbol of the virtue of "control," has to the fisher of men who had the power to command the sea.

V From Fire by Fire

Eliot's later poems and the five plays, all of which are comedies or triumphant tragedies, belong to his "purgatorial" vision. *Ash-Wednesday* (in six parts, numbered here for convenience) presents us with a desert, a garden, and a stairway between them. The stairway is the *escalina* or winding mountain of Dante's purgatory. In St. John of the Cross the "dark night of the soul" is described as a spiritual dryness like that of a desert, and here again is a "ladder," equated with the "figure of the ten stairs" of St. Benedict referred to in *Burnt Norton* [l. 163]. St. John also calls his purgation an "ascent of Mount Carmel," adding that it could also be called a descent, a remark bringing us toward Heraclitus's "the way up and the way down are the same" [fragment 60]. The stairway appears in the "infernal" vision in many ironic contexts, usually connected with failure in love. La Figlia Che Piange stands "on the highest pavement of the stair" [l. 1]; the narrator in *Portrait of a Lady* nearly loses his precious "self-possession" at the top of his lady's stair [l. 101]; Prufrock wonders if there is time to turn back and descend the stair; the "young man carbuncular" climbs a staircase to the typist's flat [*The Waste Land*, l. 231]; the narrators of *Rhapsody on a Windy Night* and *The "Boston Evening Transcript"* make their assignations with time and life at the top of steps; Princess Volupine climbs the water-stair to desert Burbank for Klein.

Desert and garden are central symbols in our literary and religious tradition, and a number of complexes of this symbolism have become so closely associated as to be readily identified. Seven of these, five from the Bible, one from Dante, and one from the church calendar, are identified in *Ash-Wednesday*.

First, Adam, the "ruined millionaire" [*East Coker*, l. 160] is condemned to earn his living in the wilderness, but is ultimately to be led back to Eden and have the tree and river of life restored to him. Second, Israel wanders in the desert forty years trying to enter its Promised Land, the Canaan they finally conquered being more of a desert than a garden, as is indicated by the desert setting of the line: "This is the land. We have our inheritance" (II [l. 95]). Third, there is Israel in its later exile, urged by the prophets to return and rebuild its temple. Jeremiah, finding no one to listen to him, was forced to cry: "O earth, earth, earth, hear the Word of the Lord" [22:29]. In *Ash-Wednesday* "earth" is altered to "wind" (II), partly because the listening wind is associated with the Spirit inspiring the prophet. Isaiah speaks of the desert blossoming as the rose; Ezekiel in Babylon saw the valley of dry bones taking on the bodies of resurrection (II); Micah speaks the reproaches of the Word to a disobedient people (V). A later rebuilder of the temple, Nehemiah, figures in *The Rock*, but not here, where building imagery is not wanted. Fourth, there is the contrast, in two books ascribed to Solomon, between the world of vanity with "the burden of the grasshopper" in Ecclesiastes (II [l. 65]), and the garden of the Bride and her sister in the Song of Songs. St. John of the Cross wrote his treatise on the dark night as a commentary on a poem based on the Song of Songs. In Eliot's garden there is a "Lady" (II [l. 42]), later a "veiled sister" (VI [l. 168]), who corresponds to Beatrice in Dante, besides the presence of the Virgin herself.

Fifth, the life of Christ is polarized between his temptation, where he wanders forty days in the desert, and his Passion, which extends from the agony in the garden to his Resurrection in another garden. In the Gospels, his ministry comes between these events, but in Biblical typology the temptation corresponds to the forty-year wandering of Israel in the desert under Moses, and the Resurrection to the conquest of the Promised Land by Joshua, who has the same name as Jesus. Hence (sixth) the commemorating of the temptation by the church in the forty days of Lent, which begins on Ash Wednesday, is immediately followed by the celebration of the Resurrection in Easter. Finally, and seventh, Dante's *Purgatorio* takes us up a rocky mountain of penance into "our first world" of Eden [*Burnt Norton*, ll. 23, 24].

The desert of *Ash-Wednesday* is the "brown land" of the earlier poems, but, except for the references to "noise" in part 5, it is conceived not as a sterile society but as a shrivelled individual spiritual life, a chapel perilous or house of the dead. Its main features parallel and contrast with those of the garden world above it. It is "The place of solitude where three dreams cross" (VI [l. 205]), apparently the dreams of waking consciousness, memory, and dream proper, all of them animated by desire, all of them having no end but death. It is a place of thirst, in contrast to the fountains and springs of the garden, where water can only be miraculously provided, as it was to Moses and to Samson (the story of Samson's thirst may be glanced at in the line "The broken jaw of our lost kingdoms" in *The Hollow Men* [l. 56]).[197] Above the desert, the inhabitants of the garden have abandoned the "low dream" for the "higher dream," and memory for a life "In ignorance and in knowledge of eternal dolour" (IV [l. 125]). In Dante the river Lethe, which obliterates the memory of sin, and the river Eunoe, which restores unfallen knowledge, are in Eden. In Eliot's garden there can still be talk of "trivial" things (IV [l. 124]), the word being an erudite pun on the three-way crossing of ordinary life.

The three dreams appear in the second section as three leopards eating the body and leaving only the dry bones. We are reminded of the three beasts encountered by Dante at the beginning of the *Inferno* and of the world, flesh, and devil, symbolized as three beasts, in St. John of the Cross. The contrasting image is that of the unicorns, emblems of chastity and of Christ, drawing the "gilded hearse" of the body about to be glorified (IV [l. 140]). The limit of the desert is marked by two "blue rocks" (V [l. 181, 206]), suggesting the clashing Symplegades of the Argonautic voyage, and that in turn suggesting the open-mouthed monster of hell, mentioned earlier. The limit of the garden is marked by two yew trees (IV, VI), apparently representing the spiritual death of the first two sections and the physical death which follows it. At the same time the scene of the poem is "The desert in the garden and the garden in the desert" (V [l. 182]); the two worlds occupy the same time and space.

The narrator is in middle life, beginning to realize that life is a parabola. He is not content however with the chagrin of ordinary experience: he wants to kill the ego, reduce it to scattered bones in a desert, pulverize it on Ash Wednesday into the dust from which it came. He descends from despair founded on disillusionment to despair founded on reality, the despair of finding anything in the past worth clinging to. The experiences worth clinging to are discontinuous, and pull one off the track of memory and desire. It is only when the narrator's very bones have stopped clinging together that he can become aware of any other reality, and his separating bones are in contrast to the prayer at the end: "Suffer me not to be separated" (VI [l. 218]). The leopards, however terrifying, are really agents of redemption, an ambiguity which meets us often in the plays.

The poet, in climbing his stairway, looks down to see that he has been detached from his temporal self. The Jacob who dreamed of the ladder to heaven also wrestled with the angel, and the poet sees himself, "the same shape" (III [l. 98]), in a lower world fighting the demon of hope and despair. He then sees more clearly that he is escaping from "the toothed gullet of an agèd shark" (III [l. 106]), like Jonah, or Dante from hell. The glances below are followed by a vision on his own level, where the world of memory and desire suddenly reappears in the form of a dancing Pan figure, and where the memories of "Lilac and brown hair" (III [l. 113]) suggest that we are in the world of the hyacinth girl and La Figlia Che Piange. Finally we reach the garden, where Pan is reduced to a statue with a "breathless" flute (IV [l. 143]), and where we meet the greater recognition scene hinted at in *Marina*:

> One who moves in the time between sleep and waking, wearing
> White light folded, sheathed about her, folded. [ll. 133–4]

Ordinary consciousness reasserts itself, and we are back (V) in the desert, like Elijah, who sat down under a "juniper tree" (II [l. 42, 89]) and prayed to die. The juniper tree is also associated with a resurrection from bones in a fairy tale of Grimm.[198] Elijah, after earthquakes and thunder, heard the still small voice of the Word [1 Kings 19:12], but the poet is in a world of constant noise and distraction which is determined not to listen. So although the poem begins with renunciation, "Because I do not hope to turn again" (I [l. 1]), it ends with the world of memory and desire stronger than ever: "Although I do not hope to turn again" (VI [l. 185]). The "unbroken wings" (VI [l. 194]) of sailing ships mock the "agèd eagle" (I [l. 6]) who cannot renew his youth, and "the empty forms between the ivory gates" (VI [l. 202]) of illusory dreams come to him with the unbearable beauty of a lost paradise.

The experiences in *Ash-Wednesday* take place on four levels: the level of spiritual vision or high dream in III and IV; the level of nostalgic vision in VI; the level of ordinary experience, of disillusionment and distraction, in I and V, and the level of ascesis or self-denial in II. The first level is a world of identity, where the individual is identified with his community, a member of one body, without losing his individuality:

> The single Rose
> Is now the Garden
> Where all loves end (II [ll. 73–5]).

The second level is a world where experiences of peculiar intensity are linked by memory and impose a pattern of greater significance and sadness on ordinary life—very like the *temps retrouvé* of Proust. The third level is ordinary experience, where the ego tries to achieve identity through "memory and desire" [*The Waste Land*, l. 3], and the fourth level is the concentrating of consciousness designed to break up the illusions of the ego. These four levels recur in the Quartets.

A book this size has no space for full commentary on *Four Quartets*, and some "audio-visual aids" will have to do instead. Draw a horizontal line on a page, then a vertical line of the same length cutting it in two and forming a cross, then a circle of which these lines are diameters, then a smaller circle inside with the same centre. The horizontal line is clock time, the Heraclitean flux, the river into which no one steps twice. The vertical line is the presence of God descending into time, and crossing it at the Incarnation, forming the "still point of the turning world" [*Burnt Norton*, ll. 64, 139]. The top and bottom of the vertical line represent the goals of the way up and the way down, though we cannot show that they are the same point in two dimensions. The top and bottom halves of the larger circle are the visions of plenitude and of vacancy respectively;

the top and bottom halves of the smaller circle are the world of the rose-garden and (not unnaturally for an inner circle) of the subway, innocence and experience. (Subway is, to me at any rate, "The common word exact without vulgarity" [*Little Gidding*, l. 224], though if one had the freedom of *Finnegans Wake* one could describe Eliot's inner circle as a "tuberose.") What lies below experience is ascesis or dark night. There is thus no hell in *Four Quartets*, which belong entirely to the purgatorial vision.

In each Quartet there are five sections, all except the fourth divided into two parts by theme, and usually by metre as well, making nine parts in all. Two parts, IV and IIa, are lyrical; the rest is in a meditative style, which sometimes, especially in III, becomes deliberately prosaic. Subject to a principle of context to be explained in a moment, all four poems have much the same structure and narrative movement. We begin (Ia) on the horizontal line of time, in a mood and with imagery that set the tonality for that poem. Then we go on to a vision of plenitude (Ib) which in three of the Quartets is reached through a "loop in time" (a phrase from *The Family Reunion*),[199] and is associated with the past. There follows (IIa) a lyric which brings the emotional impact of this vision into focus. Then we come to the awareness of the present moment (IIb), the centre of our diagram, thence to ordinary experience (IIIa), thence to a withdrawal from ordinary experience (IIIb), which takes us into a lyrical "dark night" vision (IV). Then comes a passage dealing with or alluding to the relation of art to human experience (Va), and a final resolution in the tonality with which we began (Vb).

Burnt Norton, the first Quartet, is an apocalyptic poem, and gives us a bird's-eye view of the whole range of experience covered in its successors. In *The Waste Land* there were two descents, one into earth, symbolizing ordinary experience, and one into water, then an upward turn anticipated by a "fire sermon." Similarly, after *Burnt Norton*, we descend into the muddy and practical world of *East Coker*, then into the water of *The Dry Salvages*. There we realize that, like Dante after he passed the centre of the world at the end of the *Inferno*, we are travelling, emotionally speaking, in the opposite direction. In the last two Quartets what corresponds to the earlier visions of the "way up" (Ib and IIa) are visions of loss and despair: it is the "dark night" lyric (IV) that is the focus of hope. *Burnt Norton* trails off rather plaintively at the end, but *Little Gidding* begins in a mood of penance and takes us back to the rose-garden with which *Burnt Norton* began. Thus the four Quartets form a single cycle that begins and ends at the same point.

The archetype of this cycle is the Bible, which begins with the story of man in a garden. Man then falls into a wilderness or waste land, and into a still deeper chaos symbolized by a flood. At the end of time he is restored to his garden, and to the tree and water of life that he lost with it. But by that time the garden has become a city as well, a fiery city glowing with gold and precious stones, so that the tree of life (symbolized in Dante by a rose) is a tree in which "the fire and the rose are one" [*Little Gidding*, l. 262].

On the horizontal line of time, where we are dragged backwards into an unknown future facing the past, the primary emotion is anxiety. Efforts to find clues in the past that will make the future more predictable range from a "popular" (i.e., progressive) belief in evolution to tea-cup reading, but in any case:

> Men's curiosity searches past and future
> And clings to that dimension. [*The Dry Salvages*, ll. 203–4]

The past is no more reassuring than the future: the mouth of hell, we could almost say, is the previous moment, when what was up to then possible passes forever into an unchangeable past. Or, if not the mouth of hell, it is certainly the mouth of death, nibbling off our lives like the leopards in *Ash-Wednesday*, and we feel (though in the opposite sense from the one intended in the context) that "the time of death is every moment" [*The Dry Salvages*, l. 161]. The egocentric life breeds panic, and panic breeds attachment, the clutch of the drowning man. In thought, attachment eventually leads to superstition, and every man becomes superstitious when he is sufficiently frightened.

Most of us take a less conscious view of time, because we are impelled by a natural force which Eliot calls desire, and which keeps us going like a train moving "In appetency, on its metalled ways" [*Burnt Norton*, l. 128]. We get used to riding backwards; there is a constant change of scene, and consequently a possibility of unbroken distraction. As we get older and our powers fail, we enter the world of boredom, and move from the anxieties of Prufrock to the indifference of Gerontion. Here we lose our sense of attachment, but not the egocentric core of it, and gain nothing except perhaps a "deliberate hebetude" [*East Coker*, l. 79]. One has to be sure of being kept firmly under sedation at all times if such a life is to be tolerable.

The fact which presses in on consciousness is the necessity for a detachment that is not merely indifference. There seems to be a constant cycle turning in time and nature, but nothing exactly repeats itself. We learn little if anything from past experience, because every situation is a new one. We get hurt in experience, and change so rapidly that we have the illusion of being healed by time, but the hurt remains if we do not. Our dreams and ambitions are continually being wrecked on some sunken rocks hidden in our past lives. It is easier to see this with others than with ourselves, and diagnosing the limitations of others is one of our favourite amusements.

A curious paradox is involved here. In the first place, it is true that "time is no healer: the patient is no longer here" [*The Dry Salvages*, l. 133]. But at the same time there is a healing factor in the very change of patient. We find a continuous vitality in ourselves which "Sings below inveterate scars" [*Burnt Norton*, l. 52], and prevents those of us who are not hopeless neurotics from revolving around the same point. The same paradox applies to the future. It is not hard to see why we are told in the Gospels not to take thought for the morrow. It is obvious that nothing we do will have the results we intend it to have. Our intentions drift off into the land of the might have been, and posterity sees them as nostalgic memories, vicarious rose-gardens. Yet without some commitment, some feeling that something will be here when we are not, it would be hard to find a standard that would make one line of conduct better than another.

The resolution of the paradox begins in a detachment which rejects the continuity of time. The moments of our life are discontinuous, and relate to another dimension of life altogether. Nothing remains of our past lives, yet we are convinced that we are the same person we were earlier, and this continuum of identity is the solid bottom of experience, the foundation we can build on. Our building materials are the continuous institutions, more particularly the church, which make up our human home. The structure we find ourselves inhabiting is an identity that is in time but somehow not of it, a present moment which, unlike most present moments, is not chained by desire and anxiety to past and future:

> This is the use of memory:
> For liberation—not less of love but expanding
> Of love beyond desire, and so liberation
> From the future as well as the past. [*Little Gidding*, ll. 159–62]

It is easy to imagine a God above time who can see the whole continuum at once, as a man in an aeroplane can see a bend in the road concealed to the pedestrian. But a timeless God is of no use to us, and a temporal God would be as much in the flux as we are. Christianity presents us with the conception of a timeless God substantially entering time, a paradoxical and "impossible union" [*The Dry Salvages*, l. 220] which was achieved once for all by the Incarnation, and is repeated every day in the church's sacrament. But the entry into time was also an entry into each one of us, making it possible for us to live in this impossible union of two existences, if only for brief instants. This is a conception which gives a different meaning, not simply to life, but to every moment in the experience of life. Every moment is potentially the "still point of the turning world," the apprehension of a real present and a real presence in time and space, which is ourselves and yet annihilates everything that we habitually call ourselves.

Nobody but a saint could make such moments of apprehension continuous, or even frequent. Most of us have moments of a greater than ordinary awareness, but do not know what to do with them, or what their real significance is. In a world where the "shadow" of *The Hollow Men* falls "between the emotion / and the response" [ll. 80–1], we usually have the awareness first and the consciousness of having had it follows later. But whether an instant later or many years later, the consciousness comes to a different person. The reality of all such moments, "The hint half guessed, the gift half understood, is Incarnation" [*The Dry Salvages*, l. 219]. In an early "Prelude," the poet, surveying a "blackened street," is "moved by fancies" [*Preludes*, ll. 46, 48] which take the form of

> The notion of some infinitely gentle
> Infinitely suffering thing. [ll. 50–1]

In that context, of course, this could be nothing more than a "notion," but even so it is described in terms which make it clear what its reality would be if that reality were grasped. The recognition of the presence of God in the world is the central spiritual act: the self-recognition glanced at in the previous chapter depends on it. Its product is sanctity, or life with a sacramental shape, conformed to the pattern of what is above human life. Such sanctity is the only form of wisdom that is not based ultimately on illusion.

In *Burnt Norton* we begin (Ia) with the horizontal line of time. The most natural intellectual way of unifying time is through complete fatalism.

A foreordained future has in a sense already happened, so the present moment is real in the sense that it is the same as every other moment. The opening of *Burnt Norton*, in a heavy rhythm like soldiers marching through mud, tells us that "perhaps" all time is *chronos* or clock-tick, in which everything will disappear and be "unredeemable" [ll. 2, 5]. In this grim philosophy there is no place for a "might have been," for nothing could have happened except what did happen. But nobody's life is like this: we all have doors to little secret gardens in which, as Harry says in *The Family Reunion*, "what did not happen is as true as what did happen."[200] After the transient rose-garden vision (Ib), there follows (IIa) a lyric which brings its vision into focus as a larger vision of plenitude in the form of correspondence, all the levels of the chain of being from stars to mud revolving around a "bedded axle-tree" [*Burnt Norton*, l. 50], the last word being a common Elizabethan term for the mechanism on which the universe turns. The stars, the seasons, the organic rhythms of the body, form interlocking patterns in a cosmic dance like that of the *Paradiso* or Davies' *Orchestra*. The image of hunter and hunted on earth being "reconciled" among the stars [*Burnt Norton*, l. 63], as so frequently at the end of Ovid's tales of metamorphosis, is met earlier in an ironic form in *Sweeney among the Nightingales*, where the hunting of Sweeney is preceded by the veiling of "Gloomy Orion and the Dog" [l. 9].

We now start on our way down, first to the crossing point or the present moment (IIb). This, in *Burnt Norton*, is time in the sense of the Biblical *kairos*, as distinct from *chronos*; the present and presence of a *Logos* neither timeless nor temporal, but now and forever. One is aware of assuming a double part here, of being neither in nor out of time, but in a state of *Erhebung*, an exaltation which is not clear of its origin but is rather a hovering or brooding state like that of the Spirit on chaos, or the poet "seeking the beginning and the end" of his poem.

The awareness of the present moment carries us through ordinary experience (IIIa), symbolized by the London tube, in detachment. But for the "way down" we must go deeper (IIIb), into the dark night of the chapel perilous, the state of ascesis symbolized by death in the grave (IV) with the yew tree bending over us, too far away from the sun for the sunflower to turn to us. Here we realize, not simply that the *Logos* is in death as well as life, but that "the moment of the rose and the moment of the yew-tree / Are of equal duration" [*Little Gidding*, ll. 235–6], that the top of the way up, the bottom of the way down, and the still point in the middle, are all in the same place.

In the final section (Va) art takes its place, in the way explained earlier, as a technique of meditation, showing by its form how the beginning and the end can be in the same time. *Burnt Norton* puts a considerable stress on the "formal pattern" [l. 33], the dance of life which is both movement and form, a state of becoming which is not merely liquid and a state of being which is not merely solid. This combination of movement and form is equally present in all the arts, whether they present themselves in time like music or in space like pottery. But the conception of life as a dance or formal pattern manifested by art can easily become glib and facile unless we realize that the foundations of the palace of art are built on the shifting sands of the waste land. The conception itself, though easy to formulate, cannot be realized except at rare moments. For practically the whole of life we are standing in a "ridiculous" waste desert (Vb) when the voices of the children in the rose-garden are as mocking and more elusive than the "shrieking voices" of the desert itself [*Burnt Norton*, ll. 177, 156].

In *Burnt Norton* we are not confused by the incongruity of "Garlic and sapphires in the mud" [l. 49] because we are watching the cosmic patterns that form on the turning wheel. In *East Coker* we get into the mud, the ordinary world of confusion, and the tone is more sombre and realistic. The discussion of the arts (Va) is concerned not with their formal perfection but with the poet's struggles with words. The present moment (IIb) is here only a moment at which one realizes that nothing can be expected from past or future. The sense of ordinary experience (IIIa) is correspondingly more gloomy: here the recall of the undergound train is in the middle of an *ubi sunt* elegy on the disappearance of all things in time. The close of this part of the poem (IIIb) is a passage based on St. John of the Cross, but recalling some of the contradictions associated with the world of appearance by Bradley.

What corresponds in *East Coker* to the rose-garden and yew tree of *Burnt Norton* (Ib and IV) are two visions of marking time by the repetition of ritual. In the former we have a midsummer-night dance of country peasants, which the poet again stumbles on through a loop in time, an instinctive response to the cycles of the seasons and human life, with the innocence of a community unawakened to self-consciousness. The dark night vision is that of the sacraments of the church, where the bleak hospital imagery, the pedantic allegory, the concentration on Good Friday, and the harsh whether-you-like-it-or-not dogmatism are in sharp and consistent contrast. The *East Coker* counterpart to the vision of correspondence (IIa) is a natural apocalypse, the sense of time stretching out from winter to the returning ice age. In the *East Coker* context of humility and concern with the present moment this kind of vision is out of key: there is a pretentious "I accept the universe"[201] feeling about it that the poet turns his back on (IIb).

East Coker is, by virtue of its theme and context, a more personal poem than *Burnt Norton*. *Burnt Norton* is, we are told, the name of a country house in Gloucester which was burned in the eighteenth century. Its connection with the poem does not, to put it mildly, leap to the eye, beyond a very vague suggestion of the home of a "ruined millionaire." But East Coker was the place from which the Eliots left for Massachusetts in the seventeenth century, and the return of the poet, as an Anglo-Catholic and naturalized British subject, to his own historical embryo, so to speak, provides the reversible motto, said to have been that of Mary Queen of Scots, "In my end is my beginning," for the poem [l. 211]. An earlier Thomas Elyot, author of the sixteenth-century treatise *The Gouvernour*, is quoted in the country dance section [ll. 24–47]. Thus the poem moves toward the kind of self-recognition that we have met already in other contexts in Eliot. The poet's natural life follows the cycle of nature around to its end in the sea in the final lines of the poem, and its focusing points are the moments of frustration and impotence behind which is:

> . . . echoed ecstasy
> Not lost, but requiring, pointing to the agony
> Of death and birth. [ll. 132–4]

The Dry Salvages is the most explicit of the Quartets, and its surface meaning should cause little difficulty if the main ideas of the four poems have been grasped. Although the railway train, above ground this time, reappears (IIIb), horizontal time is conceived rather as a driving power that shakes and pounds us with its rhythm, filling our lives with desire and our minds with distraction. This power is symbolized by the cycle of water, which begins with old man river, the flooding Mississippi that flows past Eliot's birthplace, of which the plenitude or fulfilment is the ocean. The beauty of the great reverie on the sea (Ib) does not conceal the sense of terror and waste, manifest in the grotesque junkpile of "dry salvage" (the pun is implicit in the title) it spews up on shore. We are back to the fisher king of *The Waste Land*. In the following lyric (IIa), an adapted sestina, the sense of *de profundis*, of human life crying like Jonah from the belly of hell, deepens and intensifies. The dialectical symbols for the poem suggest Henry Adams. At one extreme we have the "worshippers of the machine" [l. 10], building bridges across the Mississippi and forgetting its potential dangers until it floods. The sinister warning sounds that keep the time of the ocean, the clang of the foghorn and the "groaner" that echo the terrors of fishermen's wives, modulate into the "angelus" in a prayer to the Virgin [ll. 34, 187]. This leads the theme of sinking into the sea into images of absorption, and those in turn lead to the apprehension of a real presence (the Incarnation is explicitly named in this poem). The arts appear (Va) only in a reference to hearing music so deeply that absorption becomes identification.

Little Gidding was a seventeenth-century community of Anglican contemplatives, and symbolizes, like East Coker in a different way, the poet's return to the point in history at which, for him, the modern world began. In *East Coker* an Eliot who is now an Anglo-Catholic and British subject returns to the point of his beginning and end; in *Little Gidding* he visits the place that Charles I, the "broken king" [l. 27], also visited during his defeat by Parliament. The Nazi air raids have begun, and it is clearly time to end the Civil War; hence allusions to the seventeenth century form part of a general amnesty in which Cavalier and Roundhead are "folded in a single party" [l. 194]. The water imagery of *The Dry Salvages* is horizontal; in *Little Gidding* the dominant image is fire, which moves vertically. The presence of the *Logos* is symbolized by a fire descending from heaven, the fire of divine love which kindles a human love springing up in response. The divine fire is the "pentecostal fire" (Ia) [l. 10], the tongues of flame which were the Holy Spirit, the "Dove descending" (IV) [l. 203] on the apostles. The human fire is represented by Hercules (IV) [l. 213], who in the agony of his poisoned shirt kindled a funeral pyre and ascended to heaven on it, one of the few human beings accepted by the Classical gods. Here the dialectic of communion and moments of agony, emergent in *The Dry Salvages*, is completed. The imagery is parodied by the Nazi bombing plane (called, in a figure more symmetrical than fortunate, the "dark dove" [l. 84]), and the answering fires breaking out of the "disfigured street" in London [l. 150].

Many seventeenth-century writers were fascinated by a curious experiment of burning a flower, usually a rose, to ashes and seeing the ghost of the flower hovering over the ashes, which apparently afforded a dubious argument for immortality, or, at least, the permanence of things in time. Yeats says he tried this experiment without results.[202] In *Little Gidding* the "spectre of the Rose" cannot be summoned by any return to the past, and the "burnt roses" leave nothing but "Ash on an old man's sleeve" [ll. 56–7]. Yet at the end the rose-garden of *Burnt Norton* (the title of this poem is becoming more significant) reappears, not only unharmed by the fire like the three men in Daniel [3:25], but itself on fire, a burning bush never consumed. We move from the endless destruction of physical substance (IIa)—Heraclitus speaks of the elements dying each other's lives, living each other's deaths[203]—to the eternity of spiritual substance, "A condition of complete simplicity" [l. 256], attained only by the holocaust of everything in time, the reborn phoenix.

The "loop in time" here (Ib) is the poet's visit to Little Gidding and his feeling of communication with the dead, a communication "tongued with fire" [l. 53], a tradition recreated in individual experience. This communication materializes in the present moment (IIb) of a London air raid, where the poet meets "a familiar compound ghost" [l. 98], the body of his poetic teachers in one form, from Dante to Ezra Pound, like Dante himself meeting his master Brunetto Latini in hell, which the burning London street resembles. The poet "assumed a double part" [l. 100] so that he was both talking to the master and watching himself being talked to. The talker, who is wholly involved in the state of experience, gets little encouragement beyond a prophecy of failing powers and growing disillusionment. There is a suggestion of Palinurus about the ghost, and we recall Eliot's remark about Aeneas: "*His* reward was hardly more than a narrow beachhead and a political marriage in a weary middle age."[204] But the watcher has achieved the detachment in ordinary experience (IIIa) that is not to be compared with mere disillusionment. We are travelling in the opposite direction from *Burnt Norton*, and the poet's self-detachment leads (IIIb), not to the "world of perpetual solitude" [*Burnt Norton*, l. 118], but to acceptance and reconciliation, a "lifetime burning in every moment" [*East Coker*, l. 196]. Sin itself is "Behovely" [*Little Gidding*, l. 169]—meaning, roughly, that it is a kind of negative tribute to human dignity—and sooner or later the human tragedy is consumed in the divine comedy. History, like the lives that make it up, becomes "a pattern / Of timeless moments" [*Little Gidding*, ll. 237–8], and the significant acts of history, such as martyrdoms, merge into the significant words of poetry (Va), both of which are, as Dante says, "Legato con amor in un volume,"[205] bound up by Love into the Book of the Word.

The word "comedy" applies to stories with a happy ending. A young man and woman are in love, their love is thwarted, and some twist in the plot brings them together, reconciles parents or exposes villains, and creates a happier society assumed to begin as soon as the play ends. In a comedy's end is its beginning. The end restores what the audience has seen all along to be the desirable state of affairs, hence in a comedy's beginning is its end.

This kind of comedy is cyclical, confined to Eliot's two inner worlds. A younger generation normally outwits an older one, and we feel a sense of rebirth and a new state of innocence growing out of the play's experience. There is another kind of comedy where the complications in front of the happy ending become tragic, so that the comedy contains a tragedy instead of avoiding one. The Christian myth, where Christ appeases the wrath of his Father and becomes the Bridegroom of his redeemed church, who is both a Bride and a new society, is a "divine comedy" in which the two greatest tragedies, the fall of man and the Crucifixion, are episodes. Some profound comedies, such as the late plays of Shakespeare, also contain tragic actions instead of avoiding them, and throw the emphasis on reconciliation and forgiveness rather than on a happy ending. Some Greek tragedies put the tragic action within a larger action that concludes in a tone of serenity or even happiness. There are four such tragedies in Greek drama, Aeschylus's *Eumenides*, Sophocles' *Oedipus at Colonus*, Euripides' *Alcestis*, and Euripides' *Ion*, and each has been an important influence on one of Eliot's plays.

In *Murder in the Cathedral* the dialectical and purgatorial aspect of the Christian "comic" action is at its clearest. The foreground action is a tragedy in which the hero knows that

> . . . all things
> Proceed to a joyful consummation.[206]

Of the four worlds, there is no place for the rose-garden: we begin in experience, represented by the chorus. The chorus becomes increasingly aware that experience is the doorway of hell, and as the murderers move closer the women of Canterbury are haunted by images of beasts of prey, filth, and corruption, ending in the cry: "The Lords of Hell are here."[207] Meanwhile Becket is immediately involved in a sequence of temptations. The chorus describes him as "unaffrayed among the shades,"[208] and he says himself, in language recalling the *Purgatorio* line "Treating shadows as a solid thing":

> . . . the substance of our first act
> Will be shadows, and the strife with shadows.[209]

The first tempter, "Leave-well-alone," presents a temptation that Becket has gone too far to yield to even if he were capable of it. Its object however is not to persuade him to desert, but merely to remain in his mind as a source of distraction, confusing him in crucial moments:

> Voices under sleep, waking a dead world,
> So that the mind may not be whole in the present.[210]

Temptations of compromise and of intrigue follow, but the dangerous temptation is an unexpected fourth one to "do the right deed for the wrong reason":[211] to persevere in integrity and die a glorious martyr's death. This temptation is really an act of grace, something that Becket would never even have encountered by himself, much less overcome. The fact that the fourth tempter, as he leaves, repeats, word for word, Becket's opening speech in the play, indicates that Becket at this point has "assumed a double part," separating his real immortal self from the unpurified part of himself. Both this theme and the theme of something apparently demonic turning out to be an agent of grace are frequent in the other plays.

Murder in the Cathedral falls into two parts, each leading up to a prose speech addressed to the audience, a little like the parabasis in Aristophanes. The first speech is Becket's sermon after he has overcome the conflict in his mind and is awaiting martyrdom; the second is an apology for his murder made by the murderers. One is the voice of reason accommodating revelation to human ears; the other is the voice of rationalization accommodating a criminal act to public opinion. The first part, the conflict of Becket with temptation, is the dramatic action properly speaking, and the action of the second part, the external conflict between Becket and his murderers, is the completing of it.

In *The Family Reunion*, Harry, Lord Monchensey, returns to his mother's house, significantly named Wishwood, to meet her and an assemblage of relatives on her birthday. Harry is, like the women of Canterbury, haunted by a sense of latent evil hiding behind his life. His wife was drowned at sea, and he says he pushed her overboard, but nobody believes him. He says that for the feeling he has "the particular has no language":[212] he can express it only in symbols of guilt, but in itself it is closer to the "origin of wretchedness,"[213] or original sin. If nothing changed in time, one might repeat an earlier experience, and Harry might find his other self in boyhood at home, his counterpart in the rose-garden. But, as his aunt Agatha foresees, his self-recognition is of the ironic kind, as in Henry James's story *The Jolly Corner*, to which she refers.[214] What happens is the opposite: Harry's haunting sense of evil is objectified at Wishwood in the form of the Furies. These are the beings he has fled from as he comes back to his rose-garden world, only to find that they are directly in front of him there, threatening cherubim over his Eden. He now sees that he must pursue them, that he cannot escape the guilt they symbolize but must accept it as the basis of a wider understanding. He must think, not "there they are," but "here they are." Thus the Furies, like Becket's last temptation, are really a gift of grace: they are hounds of heaven or agents of the dark night. They turn into "bright angels,"[215] and he goes off to an unknown destiny.

Harry is not an attractive character, and he may be, as Eliot says later, something of a prig.[216] He goes from absorption in one kind of self to absorption in another kind, and from the outside it is hard to know whether he is saintly or selfish. In particular, it is not clear why his enlightenment should force him to leave Wishwood: the word "missionary"[217] is dropped, anticipating a theme of *The Cocktail Party*, but not developed. Then again, in any play which recalls the *Oresteia*, the dramatist is in duty bound to introduce the theme of a family "curse": the theme is introduced, but does not give the concluding action much sharpness of outline. Still, Harry's action makes his Wishwood another Chapel Perilous in which one must die to be reborn. In the original Chapel Perilous the lights of the chapel are gradually extinguished during the knight's vigil: this rite is performed on the candles of his mother Amy's birthday cake, while Amy, all her hopes for Wishwood annihilated by Harry's refusal to stay there, is dying offstage.

The main themes of all Eliot's plays are present in this one. There is a central figure who goes through a spiritual purgation and attains a vision of the four worlds, being isolated from the other characters and most of the audience in the process. There is something of this theme even in *Sweeney Agonistes*, and Eliot elsewhere speaks of it as a central interest of his in drama. In three of the five plays this enlightenment cuts the central figure off from marriage, and in the other two there is no question of marriage. There is also a subordinate group of those who, without full enlightenment, manage to achieve enough detachment to live a real life, and this is the level for which marriage, or a renewed understanding in an old marriage, seems to be appropriate. It is represented by the Chamberlaynes in *The Cocktail Party*, by the Mulhammers and their progeny in *The Confidential Clerk*, by Monica and Charles Hemington in *The Elder Statesman*. In *The Family Reunion* we have only Mary on this level, and Mary, left without matrimonial prospects when Harry fixes his eyes on the horizon, is forced to be content (though she seems so) with a fellowship in a women's college. The theme of a son imitating his father's career point for point is in three of the plays, and the somewhat oracular role of Agatha as a spiritual guardian recurs in the blessing ritual in *The Cocktail Party* and, more farcically, in the Mrs. Guzzard of *The Confidential Clerk*. The Chapel Perilous is represented by a "sanatorium" in *The Cocktail Party* and *The Elder Statesman*.

In *The Cocktail Party* there are some references to Euripides' *Alcestis*, which explain both the allegorical meaning of the "sanatorium" as a house of death and the fact that Harcourt-Reilly, the psychiatrist whose role corresponds to Euripides' Heracles, sings like a drunk in the first act and talks like a priest with the keys of death and hell in the second one. At the beginning, Edward Chamberlayne, deserted by his wife Lavinia, is giving a cocktail party unwillingly, to the guests he could not put off. He has the selfishness of Euripides' Admetus, but Lavinia is no Alcestis. Reilly, who has crashed the party, convinces Edward that he must have Lavinia back by the simple manoeuvre of telling him how lucky he is without her. Some fairly ruthless play therapy completes the cure, and in the final scene they are giving another cocktail party together, as an act of free choice. Thus the cocktail party symbolizes Eliot's lesser initiation, the emergence from the world of Dante's canto 3 into ordinary daylight.

Celia, the heroine, gets a profounder sense of original sin, and of the spiritual isolation that accompanies it. Looked at from this point of view, there is no human community at all: each individual is alone by himself, and alienated from God. The sense of sin, which is equally personal and impersonal, is too oppressive for Celia to reconcile herself to the human condition like the Chamberlaynes, and she starts on a spiritual journey which takes her into an austere nursing order, thence to martyrdom by crucifixion in Africa. The journey is described in terms recalling the Lady in *Comus*: Celia's humility and innocence make her spiritually invulnerable, for all the physical horror of her death. Harcourt-Reilly tells us that he realized, in a premonition, that Celia would die a violent death, and the important question was which self she would be committed to at the moment of her death. Martyrdom, especially a hideous one, carries with it an unanswerable (and perhaps unfair) authority, and when the news of Celia's crucifixion is communicated to the others Edward says:

> —If this was right for Celia—
> There must be something else that is terribly wrong,
> And the rest of us are somehow involved in the wrong.[218]

The answer, that "every moment is a fresh beginning,"[219] echoes the Quartets.

The Confidential Clerk turns on the ancient device of the recognition scene, where hero or heroine discover their long-lost parents. There are seven characters, four in an older generation, Sir Claude Mulhammer, his wife Lady Elizabeth, his "confidential clerk" Eggerson, the pivot of the dramatic action, and Mrs. Guzzard, who has a role like that of Buttercup in *Pinafore*. These four sit around a table and identify their offspring among the other three: Colby Simpkins, the hero and Eggerson's successor as confidential clerk, Lucasta Angel, the heroine, and B. Kaghan, who marries her. Mrs. Guzzard, the dealer in this curious poker game, assigns Simpkins to herself, though both Sir Claude and Lady Elizabeth are convinced that he is a son of theirs by a previous liaison, and he finally goes off in a foster-son relationship to Eggerson. Thus everybody of the older generation in the play claims him as a son, though his real father, the late Mr. Guzzard, does not appear. Lady Elizabeth's son is Kaghan and Lucasta is Sir Claude's daughter.

The atmosphere of demure farce is sustained throughout, and, as the hero remarks rather dazedly, everybody seems to have a heart of gold. The plot complications are closer to Menandrine New Comedy than to *Ion* (to which however New Comedy owed a good deal), and still closer to Wilde's *Importance of Being Ernest*, though it lacks the exuberance of Wilde ("marry into a waiting-room, and contract an alliance with a parcel?").[220] The word "farce" reminds us of the high respect for farce that Eliot shows in his dramatic essays, where he speaks of it as the creation of a distorted but self-consistent world, found in Rabelais, Dickens, and even Marlowe.[221] *Sweeney Agonistes*, with its pounding jazz rhythms and its weird expressionistic staging, is farce in this sense. *The Confidential Clerk* is a different kind of farce, a comedy in which the structure has been deliberately overcomplicated, and so turned up one notch from the conventional well-made play into a parody of such a play.

The imagery of this comedy is confined to the inner worlds, here symbolized by the suburban garden and the "City," and the upper world is entered by marriage. Sir Claude has for his "secret garden" a frustrated desire to be a potter. Simpkins falls into the same pattern as long as he believes himself to be Sir Claude's son, though his ambition is to be an organist. Unlike Marvell, Simpkins is not satisfied to be in his garden alone:

> If I were religious, God would walk in my garden
> And that would make the world outside it real
> And acceptable, I think.[222]

This remark indicates a possibility of further growth in him. He resents the fact that he will never be a first-rate organist, but when he learns that his real father was a frustrated organist too, humility comes to his aid and he becomes an organist on his own level. Like Harry, he transfers allegiance from one self to another, hence Lucasta can say:

> . . . You're either an egotist
> Or something so different from the rest of us
> That we can't judge you.[223]

The Elder Statesman, which could be performed by the same seven actors needed for its predecessor, returns us, in a domestic and familiar setting, to the pattern of *Murder in the Cathedral*. The elder statesman, Lord Claverton, retired and at the point of death, has given his life to a social role, and is a hypocrite in the original sense, a masked actor whose real life is in his *persona*. A weak spot in his self-sufficiency is indicated by his possessive attitude toward his daughter Monica and his son Michael. Two people out of his past, an Oxford chum now named Gomez, a low type who takes ice in his whisky, and a former mistress, Mrs. Carghill, turn up in the role of accusing spirits, reminding him of previous misdeeds. The woman tells him, quoting a friend, that he has been kept from real vice, like Baudelaire's *lecteur*, not by virtue, but by the counter-vices of laziness and cowardice:

> "That man is hollow." That's what she said.
> Or did she say "yellow"? I'm not quite sure.[224]

Their vampire-like professions of friendship ("I need you, Dick, to give me reality," Gomez says)[225] suggest something almost demonic about them, as though the action were occurring in some waterless place after death—a suggestion intensified when another "sanatorium" opens up in the second act, run by a female who would be even more at home in hell than Harcourt-Reilly, as she keeps a television set in the "Silence Room." But Claverton's accusers are not demons, only self-justifying human beings, and they are, like Harry's Furies, instruments of grace. The elder statesman's *persona* breaks up and he confesses his misdeeds to Monica. They are not very black, probably because, as he says:

> It's harder to confess the sin that no one believes in
> Than the crime that everyone can appreciate.[226]

This also reminds us of Harry, though the careful cleaning up of his past gives rather the impression of substituting a sentimental reality for a moral reality, to use terms from Eliot's essay on Heywood. There is also a good deal of talk about the relief following confession which sounds less like moral reality than like moral rearmament. Perhaps in his reaction the elder statesman underestimates the importance of the *persona*.

The dénouement occurs when Michael goes off with the two accusers to start a new career. Michael symbolizes a part of his personality that Claverton, assuming a double part, is ready to hand over to his tormentors: "For the *me* he rejected, I reject also."[227] But he is not repudiating Michael: the fact that he is willing to see him begin a new life under Gomez's auspices, however unwillingly, is part of the annihilation of his ego. The rest is represented by Monica's marriage, a reminiscence perhaps of the conclusion of *Oedipus at Colonus*, where Antigone's desire to sacrifice herself for her father is gently thwarted. The elder statesman dies by himself, in the garden outside the sanatorium under a beech tree.

The dramatic monologues of Prufrock and Gerontion are studies of self-romanticizing egos who are intermittently conscious of something more in their lives. Thoughts of the risen Lazarus and the martyred John the Baptist, witnesses to the power of Christ, float vaguely around Prufrock's brain. Gerontion, a more intelligent man, is more clearly aware of the "word within the word"[228] and of the divine presence concealed in the bodies of his friends. These monologues are in a form of dramatic meditative verse in which a romantic illusion strangles a visionary conscience. In the comedies this form is turned inside out. Here we have a meditative drama in which we meet first a group of amiable but self-deceiving egos. They then form a hierarchy of enlightenment, from the hero or heroine at the top to a bewildered chorus below, a kind of epiphany of a spiritual elite.

Since the 1920s, critics have become increasingly aware of the continuity of the English Romantic tradition and of Eliot's place in it. The plays show the tension between Romantic and evangelical values that we should expect if we thought of Eliot as a poet in the main current of the English literary tradition, which runs through Milton and the Romantics. *Murder in the Cathedral*, with its sequence of temptations, is closer in conception to *Samson Agonistes* than to anything in Greek tragedy. Harry, prig or not, is as Byronic a figure as contemporary drama affords, and when another character in the same play says,

> And now I don't feel safe. As if the earth should open
> Right to the centre, as I was about to cross Pall Mall,[229]

we are closer to Bunyan's interpreter's house than we are to the House of Atreus. The later comedies, with their alternately urbane and earnest texture, Sheridan crossed with John Wesley, reflect the same tension. One cannot both accept a tradition and decide what it is to be. For appreciating the real place of Eliot's drama, and perhaps his poetry too, in English literature, the amnesty proposed in *Little Gidding* does not go far enough. The greatness of his achievement will finally be understood, not in the context of the tradition he chose, but in the context of the tradition that chose him.

42

Tribute to John Crowe Ransom

1964

From John Crowe Ransom: A Tribute from the Community of Letters, *ed. D. David Long and Michael R. Burr. Supplement to* Kenyon Collegian, *90, no. 7 (1964): 5.*

I am very pleased to have an opportunity of extending congratulations and tribute to Mr. John Crowe Ransom. There can hardly be many living Americans who have done more for American life and letters, in making life lively and letters literary. He is a most original and distinguished poet—something of a victim of anthologies, it is true, which keep reprinting the same three or four poems and do not give their readers much sense of the variety of his work, but a poet whose best work is unforgettable. As a critic, he has added a whole new dimension to the appreciation of literature and to the techniques of reading it with understanding. It is possible to be a fine poet and still be a perverse crank, but Mr. Ransom's teaching and personal influence have always been completely healthy, an influence which makes the subject primary and the personality secondary. A character in Bernard Shaw remarks how disastrous it is when a man of genius is not also a man of honour;[1] a student of Mr. Ransom's, in any capacity, is impelled to reflect how fortunate it is when a man of genius is also a man of dedication.

43

The Rising of the Moon: A Study of *A Vision*

1965

From SM, *245–74. Originally published in* An Honoured Guest: New Essays on W.B. Yeats, *ed. Denis Donoghue and J.R. Mulrye (London: Edward Arnold, 1965), 8–33, without the two notes included in* SM, *296, and with a few minor variants here given in notes. Typescripts are in NFF, 1988, box 1, files v and w, and 1991, box 36, file 4. Frye provides references in the text to Yeats's* Collected Poems *(London: Macmillan, 1950), and to his* A Vision, *remarking in a prefatory note on the latter that "As I am dealing only with* A Vision *in its totality, having abandoned the project of tracing its development from its sketchy first edition, I am using the latest (1962) edition of it, subtitled 'A Reissue with the Author's Final Revisions,' and my page references are to that edition."*

I

Literature is one of the products of the constructive or imaginative power in the mind, and is the verbal part of the process of transforming the nonhuman world into something with a human shape and meaning, the process that we call culture or civilization. In literature, particularly in poetry, the nonhuman or natural world is symbolically associated with the human world. The two great principles of association are analogy and identity, which are repeated in the grammatical forms of the simile and metaphor respectively: "A is like B," and "A is B." Identity is found in mythology, which is concerned with gods, that is, beings in human shape identified with various aspects of physical nature. Hence mythology is a congenial language for poets, and even the more conceptual language of theology has to deal with some doctrines, such as the identity of Christ with God and Man, which can be expressed grammatically only in the form of metaphor. Another religious language, typology, is founded on analogy, and appears in Swedenborg's conception of "correspondence," which he applies to his interpretation of the Bible.[1] Analogy and identity are prominent in the associative cosmology of the Ptolemaic universe, where the seven planets are associated with the seven metals, the four elements with the four humours, and so on. As the sense of the objective validity of these associations waned, they became increasingly confined to occultism, in its various branches. Occult constructs, or constructs that unite occult and mythological or typological concepts, such as we find in Boehme, Swedenborg, and later Blavatsky, have played an important part in the mythopoeic poetry of the last two centuries. It is unnecessary to labour the point that Yeats had absorbed an immense amount of associative apparatus, much of it traditional, from his Rosicrucian and Golden Dawn studies.

These associative constructs, considered apart from whatever assertions they may make about the structure of the external world, become a framework of associations of imagery, in other words, "metaphors for poetry," which is what Yeats's instructors said they were bringing him [8]. In this context we can understand Valéry's remark that cosmology is one of the oldest of the *literary* arts.[2] Nobody would attempt the serious study of Dante's *Commedia* or *Paradise Lost* without studying their cosmologies, and the fact that no objective validity is now attached to these cosmologies does not affect their importance as structural principles of the poems they are in. Further, every major poet has his own structure of imagery, and we soon become familiar with the way in which certain images are repeated in different contexts through his work. If we push this familiarity into a systematic study, we find ourselves creating out of the poet's total work a single and symmetrical world of images: in short, a cosmology. Yeats himself provides a brilliant and pioneering example of such criticism in his early essay on "The Philosophy of Shelley's Poetry." The word "philosophy" is misleading, as he is not looking for ideas that express meaning but for images that contain it: his reason for using the word is to emphasize the consistency of structure that he finds in Shelley's work.

A further step would lead us to the more schematic elements in poetic thought which are implicit in the whole process of association. Poetic thought is inherently schematic, though some poets, of course, are more obviously schematic than others. Blake is very obviously so: there are several diagrams in his engraved poems reminding us of similar diagrams in *A Vision*, and Crabb Robinson tells us of his enthusiasm for the diagrams that William Law provided for his translation of Boehme.[3] The study of the cosmology of the *Commedia* or *Paradise Lost*, just mentioned, would, if our commentaries provided no diagrams, soon bring us to pencil and paper, and this is even more true of Dante's *Convivio*, which, if closer to more widely accepted speculations in Dante's day, is a work not different in kind from *A Vision*. Yeats, in company with Edwin J. Ellis, made an early study of Blake, laying great stress on the schematic elements in Blake's imagery, and the second volume of their edition of Blake, whatever Ellis may have contributed to it (not much, one gathers from Yeats's letters),[4] represents a kind of trial run for *A Vision*. The influence of Dante is also very strong, though later, and *Ego Dominus Tuus*, one of the central poems of the *Vision* period, takes its title from the *Vita nuova*.

Analogy and identity produce, not only the two commonest figures of poetic speech, but the two major patterns of poetic imagery. One of these is the cyclical pattern, based on the assimilation of the death and rebirth of life in the human world to the natural cycles of sun, moon, water, and the seasons. The other we may call the dialectical rhythm, the movement towards a separation of happiness from misery, the hero from the villain, heaven from hell. The two halves of this separation correspond in imagery to the two phases of the cycle, the images of the desirable world being youth, spring, morning, and the like, and of the undesirable world their opposites.

In the traditional Christian pattern of symbolism, as we have it in Dante, there are, at the poles of reality, two eternally separated and opposed worlds, heaven and hell, beatitude and damnation. Heaven is symbolized by the starry spheres, now all that is left of the order of nature as God originally planned it. In between is the present order of nature, which exists on two levels. One is the level of physical nature and fallen humanity, the ordinary world of experience, Italy in 1300, which pervades the poem though it is not a setting for any part of it. The other is the level of human nature as it was before the fall, represented by the Garden of Eden, which Dante reaches by climbing the mountain of Purgatory. This mountain is a narrowing cone or gyre in shape, a winding stair (*escalina*), and as Dante proceeds up it, shedding a deadly sin at each stage, he recovers the freedom of will and the moral innocence that man had before his fall. When he reaches Eden he is told that it is among other things a place of seed, that all forms of life on earth, except human lives, proceed from and return to it.[5]

Dante's order of nature is, then, a cyclical movement. Christian doctrine prevents Dante from ascribing this cyclical movement to human life, but purgatory and rebirth are associated even in him. Yeats saw in the doctrine of purgatory, which in Dante is a second life on the surface of this earth, an accommodating of Eastern and Platonic conceptions of reincarnation to Christianity. Dante's mountain of purgatory, again, is directly underneath the moon, where the vision of *Paradiso* begins, and so it suggests the conception of nature as a cycle under the moon, the mountain forming a gyre narrowing to a point. An opposite gyre, though this is not explicit in Dante, would begin to broaden again for all forms of life that are reborn at that point. For Yeats the "pern mill" whose smoke made Ben Bulben look like a burning mountain was an early source of an associating of a mountain with fire and with the spinning of double gyres.[6]

In Spenser's *Faerie Queene*, though there are brief glimpses of a heaven and a hell, the main concern is with the two intermediate worlds: the England of Spenser's own day, which, like Dante's Italy, is present only by allegory, and the world of "Faerie," which is a world of moral realization, like Dante's purgatory, where the good is separated from the bad. In this world of faerie we find the Gardens of Adonis, a "Paradise" on a "Mount" which is also a place of death and rebirth, not said to affect only nonhuman lives. It is not said either to be directly under the moon, but in the *Mutabilitie Cantos* the "sublunary" principle of change and decay, Mutability herself, thrusts her way into the moon and demands to be recognized as the ruler of the world above as well. The debate of being and becoming that results confines Mutability to the lower world, and leaves the starry spheres in their place as symbols of heaven. The trial to hear her case is held on top of "Arlo Hill," like Ben Bulben an Irish mountain.

In Blake the main bent of symbolism is increasingly dialectical, towards the final separation of human redemption from human misery that he depicts in so many pictures of the Last Judgment. His treatment of the cycle is more complicated. Coming as he does after Newton, Blake rejects the traditional association of the starry spheres with the unfallen world. For him the starry heavens are also a projection of man's fallen state, and the unfallen world has to be sought within. The child, taking the world for granted as a place made chiefly for his benefit, lives in a state of innocence recalling the traditional unfallen life in the Garden of

Eden. Blake calls this state of innocence Beulah, and associates it with the moon. As the child grows into an adult he moves into the state of experience, and his childlike wish to see the world in a better shape is driven underground into the subconscious. Beulah thus becomes an explosive, volcanic world which breaks into experience periodically in revolution, and its presiding genius is the youthful rebel Orc, as the presiding genius of experience is Urizen, the old man in the sky.

In *The Marriage of Heaven and Hell* the principles of rebellion and of conservatism are associated with "Devils" and "Angels" respectively, the "Devils" being called that because they are regarded with such horror by their opponents. The two principles represent "Contraries," and without contraries, according to Blake, there is no progression [E34]. These contraries have a close relationship to Yeats's conceptions of antithetical and primary, presently to be considered. Human life, both individual and social, tends to run in a cycle from Orc's revolt to Urizen's conservatism and back. A similar cycle is traced in the poem called *The Mental Traveller*, a major and acknowledged influence on Yeats's *A Vision* [213]. In this poem the entire cycle is divided into four main phases, but another poem of Blake's, *My Spectre around Me*, which again deals with a cycle, assigns seven "loves" to four phases, making twenty-eight in all.

In his *Descriptive Catalogue*, written as a commentary on some of his paintings, Blake discusses the General Prologue to the *Canterbury Tales*. Considering Chaucer's constant use of astrology, including a tantalizing allusion to the twenty-eight phases of the moon in *The Franklin's Tale*, and assuming his interest in combinations of the seven planetary and the four humorous temperaments, one would expect his "Well nine and twenty in a company" [l. 24] to consist of twenty-eight characters plus Chaucer himself. In actual count there may be one or two more,[7] but more important than the number is Blake's suggestion that "The characters of Chaucer's Pilgrims are the characters which compose all ages and nations: as one age falls, another rises, different to mortal sight, but to immortals only the same; for we see the same characters repeated again and again" [*A Descriptive Catalogue*, p. 9; E532]. This sounds very like a statement of Yeats's own theory of personal archetypes, of which more later. There are echoes of the *Descriptive Catalogue* in *A Vision* and elsewhere in Yeats: compare, for example, the discussion of beauty, ugliness, and the Dancing Faun in the commentary on phase 2 (106–7) with Blake's commentary on his picture *The Ancient Britons*. In Blake's later Prophecies human history from Adam to Milton is divided into twenty-eight periods or "Churches," and the twenty-eight cathedral cities of England, or "Albion," the hero of *Jerusalem*, play a prominent role in that poem. In Blake's version of the apocalypse, Albion becomes absorbed into the body of Jesus, who is portrayed in the Book of Revelation as surrounded in heaven by twenty-eight beings, the twenty-four "elders" and the four "Zoas."

In Classical literature there are two visions of recurrence and rebirth that particularly impressed Yeats. One is the myth of Er (or "the man of Ur," as Yeats insists on calling him [203, 252]) in Plato's *Republic*; the other is the journey of Aeneas to the underworld, where it is foretold that "Another Troy shall rise and set," in Yeats's echo of Virgil's words.[8] Virgil's tendency to see the moon as the symbol of cyclical human life is recorded in his phrase *per amica silentia lunae* (*Aeneid*, bk. 2, l. 255), employed by Yeats as a title. The cave of the nymphs in Homer's *Odyssey*, which has a southern gate for gods and a northern one for mortals, is the subject of an allegorical commentary by Porphyry, *De Antro nympharum*, a source of *Among School Children*, and the same symbolism had previously found its way into Blake's *Book of Thel*. The two gates are reflected in the opposed phases 15 and 1 of Yeats's lunar cycle, the former being a beauty too great for human life and the latter the point of mortality. Many other suggestions came to Yeats from his reading which we have no space to deal with. His debt to the Catholic poets of the later nineteenth century has perhaps not been sufficiently studied: he quotes (250) from one very remarkable prototype of his Easter symbolism, an ode by Francis Thompson.

The well-known introduction to *A Vision* explains how it was dictated to Yeats by invisible spiritual instructors who worked through his wife's gift for automatic writing. Not having any explanation of my own to offer of this account, I propose to accept his at its face value. But it seems obvious that *A Vision* should be approached as a key to the structure of symbolism and imagery in Yeats's own poetry, as what Yeats calls in another connection "the emergence of the philosophy of my own poetry, the unconscious becoming conscious."[9] If we did not have *A Vision*, a critic could still do with Yeats what Yeats did with Shelley: extract a poetic cosmology or created world of images from his work. Such a cosmology would have, or at least begin with, the same general outline as *A Vision*. It would lack its detail, but the detail is seldom rewarding either for the light it throws on Yeats or in its own right as part of "a rule of thumb that somehow explained the world," in Yeats's phrase [81]. That is, no critic could discover from Yeats's poetry that Queen Victoria belongs to phase 24 of a lunar historical cycle [172], but then this does not tell us anything of much value about either Yeats or Queen Victoria. On the other hand, the cosmology that one could extract from Yeats's poetry would be more complete than *A Vision*, for the poet in Yeats knew much more about poetic symbolism than his instructors did.

To say this is to define an attitude to his instructors, so far as they may be thought of as instructing us. The great advantage of *A Vision* was that it increased Yeats's awareness of and power to control his own creative process, and so did much to provide the self-renewing vitality, the series of bursts of energy from within, like a jet engine, which is so extraordinary a feature of Yeats's development. It also emphasized certain forward intellectual developments for him, such as the sense of the poetic relevance of history and philosophy, and thus helped to make his later poetry more concrete and precise. One obvious modern parallel to *A Vision* is Poe's *Eureka*,[10] but *Eureka* is neurotic in a way that *A Vision* is not: it hints at vast significance but expresses itself with very little precision, whereas *A Vision* at least says what it has to say. The schematic elaboration of *A Vision* was not very congenial to Yeats's temperament, and would probably never have been undertaken had it not come to him in this involuntary form: one thinks of the condescension with which, in the poem *The Dawn*, he looks down upon

> the withered men that saw
> From their pedantic Babylon
> The careless planets in their courses,
> The stars fade out where the moon comes,
> And took their tablets and did sums. [ll. 5–9]

But there were also disadvantages in being "overwhelmed by miracle" [25]. The traditions about the kind of spirits that Yeats evoked seem to suggest that they are, when separated from the mind of the person who controls them, mischievous, irresponsible, even malignant. This is doubtless why Prospero in *The Tempest* nagged and bullied his spirits unmercifully. Yeats distinguishes such spirits as "Frustrators," but whether or not the warning "Remember we will deceive you if we can" came from them [12–13], he subjected himself passively to his instructors, in a way that made it impossible for him to detect frustration or irrelevance until pages of it had been written. *A Vision*, as a result, is a fragmentary and often misleading guide to the structure of imagery in Yeats. It is to the students of Yeats what *De Doctrina Christiana* is to the student of Milton: a nuisance that he can't pretend doesn't exist.

The analogy between human and natural worlds founded on the cycle is a central principle of symbolism, and we have seen that it is traditional to make the moon the focus of it. Structures of the same cyclical and lunar shape may be found in *Finnegans Wake*, with its twenty-eight "Maggies," in Robert Graves's white-goddess mythology, in Pound's *Pisan Cantos*. In Western cyclical symbolism the human emphasis falls on the social and historical rather than the individual. Reincarnation was never accepted in Christianity nor widely held in the West, and so it has been the cycle of nations and empires that for Western poetry is assimilated to the rotation of life and death and rebirth. Yeats's interest in reincarnation gives his cyclical symbolism an individual emphasis as well, but his instructors knew far less about this than they did about the more solidly established historical cycle. One fragment of this part of the construct survives in a letter to Ethel Mannin, and there Yeats says that he only half understands it himself.[11] There remains the dialectical structure of symbolism, the separation of reality into an apocalyptic and a demonic world where all images in each world are identified by metaphor. This symbolism is quite clear in Yeats's poetry, but *A Vision* is not an adequate guide to it. We proceed to deal with the three main aspects of Yeats's symbolism, the historical cycle, the individual cycle, and the apocalyptic imagery, using *A Vision*, for the reasons just given, in a progressively more fragmentary way.

II

There are two great rhythmical movements in all living beings: a movement towards unity and a movement towards individuality. These are opposed and contrasting movements, and are symbolized in Yeats by a double gyre, a movement in one direction which, as it grows more pervasive, develops the counteracting movement within itself, so that the apex of the next gyre appears in the middle of the base of the preceding one and moves back through it. The simplest way to represent the entire double-gyre rotation is by a circle. Because of its traditional association with the moon, this circle has twenty-eight phases, and the twenty-eight–phase cycle exists, Yeats says, in every completed movement, whether it takes a moment or thousands of years to complete itself.

But, of course, it is in the larger rhythms of history that the detail is easiest to see. Yeats sees history as forming a series of cycles, each lasting about two thousand years, with each cycle going through twenty-eight parallel phases. The conception is similar in many ways to that of Spengler's *Decline of the West*, and Yeats often remarks on the similarity of his views to Spengler's [11, 18, 259–61].

In Spengler, who is most rewarding when he is read as a Romantic and symbolic poet, each historical cycle or "culture" exhibits the rhythms of growth, maturation, and decline characteristic of an organism, though Spengler also uses the metaphor of the four seasons. There were, for instance, a Classical and a Western cycle, each having a "spring" of feudal economy and heroic aristocracy, a Renaissance "summer" of city-states, an "autumn" in Periclean Athens and the eighteenth century, when the cultural possibilities of the cycle were exhausted, and a "winter," ushered in by Alexander and Napoleon respectively, when a "culture" changes to a technological "civilization" of huge cities, dictatorships, and annihilation wars. In between comes a Near Eastern or "Magian" culture, with its spring at the birth of Christ and its later stages in the period of Mohammedanism, the religion of the crescent moon. In each cycle the period of highest development is the period of greatest individuality in both art and political life, and both the early and the late stages are marked by a strong sense of communal or mass-consciousness.

In Yeats this communal consciousness is part of the drive toward unity. It is the primitive mentality in which all historical cycles begin, and the decadent mentality in which they end, hence it is the "primary" rhythm of existence. Over against it is an "antithetical" development of individuality, which reaches its greatest height in the hero. In primitive society the communal consciousness is so strong that there hardly seems to be any real individuality, as we know it, at all. Those who show signs of individual consciousness often have simply a different kind of unity, with animals or with the fairies and other spirits of the invisible world, like the inspired fools who haunt romantic literature (phase 2). The types from phase 2 to about phase 6 are intellectually simple and self-contained: phase 6 is the phase of Walt Whitman, who never quite distinguished individual from communal well-being. Individuality begins in the unhappy and tormented souls who are aware of a double pull within them around phase 8. As we cross the quadrant of phase 8 we begin to move into the antithetical area, beginning with intense and withdrawn figures like Parnell (phase 10) or Nietzsche (phase 12). Individuality then advances to heroic proportions, and we have "sensualists" so complete that they represent a kind of antithesis to sanctity (phase 13), artists of tempestuous passion, women of fully ripened physical beauty, and heroes of arrogant pride like the heroes of Shakespeare's tragedies.

At the point of highest development represented by phase 15 the counter-movement back to communal consciousness begins. Artists become less embodiments of passion and more intellectualized (phase 21), or technicians (phase 23); heroes come to think of themselves as servants of impersonal force, like Napoleon (phase 20), or the money-obsessed characters in Balzac; women come to be guardians of a generally accepted morality like Queen Victoria (phase 24). The "personality," which is the fully developed individuality, becomes the "character," a subjective conception implying that something objective to it is greater. Yeats speaks of the antithetical types as subjective too, but their subjectivity creates its own world, whereas primary subjectivity first separates itself from the objective world, then is increasingly drawn to it as a unity destined to absorb all subjects. These two aspects of subjectivity are symbolized in Yeats by two expressions of the eye: the stare, which sees nothing but expresses an inner consciousness, and the glance, the subject looking *at* a reality set over against it. At later primary stages personality becomes more fragmented, this fragmentation being represented by the physical deformity of the hunchback (phase 26), and the mental deformity of the fool (phase 28). What Spengler calls the "second religiousness"[12] comes into society in the forms of spiritualism, theosophy, and various forms of revived occultism, seeking the same kind of kinship with the invisible world, at the other end of the social cycle, that primitive societies show in their myths and folk tales and so-called superstitions. Yeats often recurs to the similarity between the primitive and the sophisticated conceptions of unseen beings, the legendary rumour in remote cottages and the seances in suburban parlours. The entire cycle describes a progression through the four elements of earth, water, air, and fire, each quadrant having a particular relationship to each element.

The conception on which the whole of *A Vision* turns is the contrast of antithetical and primary natures, which is part of a dichotomy that runs through Yeats's writing and thinking. In an early letter he says: "I have always considered myself a voice of what I believe to be a greater renaissance—the revolt of the soul against the intellect—now beginning in the world,"[13] and this involves a preference of the swordsman to the saint, of the aristocratic to the democratic virtues, of the reality of beauty to the reality of truth, of (to use categories from Eliot's *Burnt Norton*) the way of plenitude to the way of vacancy. The contrast is so far-reaching that it may be simplest to set all its aspects out at once in a table, though many of them will not be intelligible until farther on in this essay.

ANTITHETICAL	PRIMARY
individuality	unity
Leda and Swan	Virgin and Dove
Oedipus	Christ
son kills father	son appeases father
incest with mother	redemption of mother and bride
drive toward nature	drive toward God
tragic	comic
master-morality	servant-morality
aristocratic	democratic
discord	concord
quality	quantity
freedom	necessity
fiction	truth
evil	good
art	science
ecstasy	wisdom
kindred	mechanism
particularity	abstraction
lunar	solar
natural	reasonable
war	peace
personality	character
Michael Robartes	Owen Aherne
Oisin	St. Patrick
(Eros)	(Agape)
(Chinese Yang)	(Chinese Yin)
(Nietzsche's Apollo)	(Nietzsche's Dionysus)
(Blake's Orc, "Devils," Rintrah, "Science of Wrath")	(Blake's Urizen, "Angels," Palamabron, "Science of Pity"

Many of these categories come from page 52 of *A Vision*, that of quality and quantity from page 130. The Apollonian and Dionysian categories seem curiously placed, but Yeats thinks of Apollo as a creative force and of Dionysus as a transcendent one.

The drive to individuality is a drive toward nature, Yeats says, and has for its goal a complete physical self-fulfilment or "Unity of Being," which may be attained in the phases close to phase 15, the phase of the full moon. Phase 15 itself realizes this so completely that it cannot be achieved in human life at all. We thus arrive at the difficult conception of a creature which is superhuman because it is completely natural. We are not told much about these phase 15 beings, beyond a mysterious passage in "The Phases of the Moon" [61], but, of course, a perfect human harmony could also be symbolized by perfect sexual intercourse, and we are told in that delightful poem *Solomon and the Witch* that a union of this kind would restore man to the unfallen world. Yeats strongly hints that Christ was a superhuman incarnation, a unique entry of phase 15 into human life, though an explicit statement on this point would doubtless have annoyed his instructors. He often refers, for instance, to an alleged belief that Christ was the only man exactly six feet high [273]. Why so arbitrary a measure as the foot should have been in the mind of the Trinity from all eternity is not clear, but the meaning is that Christ had the perfect "Unity of Being" which, Yeats tells us, Dante compares to a perfectly proportioned human body [82, 258, 291].

The opposite drive toward an objective unity is a drive toward "God," and has as its goal an absorption in God (phase 1) which is similarly a superhuman phase of pure "plasticity." Hence the real direction of the attempt in the primary phases to subordinate oneself to objective powers is revealed in the religious leader (phase 25) and most clearly of all in the saint (phase 27). As far as this twenty-eight-phase cycle of being is concerned, "God" for Yeats appears to be a character like the button-moulder in *Peer Gynt*, pounding everything to dust with the pestle of the moon, a cosmic spider or vampire who swallows the Many in the One. In short, God occupies the place of Death, which makes Yeats's remark that he tends to write coldly of God something of an understatement.[14]

We have spoken so far of a general social cycle from primitivism to decadence, but there are two more specific ones in Yeats, which correspond to the Classical and Western cycles in Spengler. Draw a circle on a page and mark its four cardinal points 1, 8, 15, and 22. These phases on Yeats's historical calendar (or at least the most important of several he uses) are a thousand years apart. Phase 1 is 2000 B.C.; phase 8 is 1000 B.C.; phase 15 is the time of Christ; phase 22 is A.D. 1000; phase 1 is therefore our own time as well as 2000 B.C., and phase 8 is also a thousand years from now. Classical civilization extends from phase 8 to 22, 1000 B.C. to A.D. 1000, and Christian civilization, which is our own, from A.D. 1000 to 3000, phases 22 to 8. We are half-way through the latter now, at the same point Classical civilization reached in the time of Christ. Phases 8 and 22 are represented by Troy and Byzantium, one an Asiatic city destroyed by Europeans and the other a European city captured by Asiatics, yet so close together that Byzantium, when it became a centre of Roman power, was thought of as a new Troy. Each civilization is the opposite or complement of its predecessor. Classical civilization was essentially antithetical, tragic, heroic, and strongly individualized; Christian civilization is therefore essentially primary, democratic, altruistic, and based on a subject–object attitude to reality. Byzantium was the main source of early Irish culture, and its place in Yeats's thought gives a special significance to his allusions to people roughly contemporary with its golden age, such as Charlemagne and Harun Al-Rashid.

Half-way through, a civilization generates the beginning of its counteracting movement, hence Christ, the presiding genius of the civilization that began a millennium later, appears in the middle of the Classical cycle. "The Incarnation," says Yeats, "invoked modern science and modern efficiency, and individualized emotion."[15] Thus a religious movement cuts the cycle of civilizations at right angles, and Christianity as a religion extends from the time of Christ to about our own day. It follows that a similar Messianic figure announcing Classical civilization must have appeared around 2000 B.C., and that another, announcing a second antithetical civilization of the future, is to appear somewhere around our own time. Yeats speaks of an antithetical influx setting in "a considerable time before" (208) the close of its predecessor, perhaps to rationalize his conception of his own function.[16] In 2000 B.C., in the middle of a pre-Classical culture associated vaguely by Yeats with "Babylonian starlight,"[17] the annunciation of the Greek culture pattern was made, in what way we do not know, but surviving in two myths. One is the myth of Leda and the swan, the divine bird impregnating the human woman, the fulfilment of their union being, eventually, the fall of Troy, which began Greek history, properly speaking. The other is the myth of Oedipus, whose parricide and mother incest set the tragic and heroic tone of an antithetical culture. The complementary myths appear with the birth of Christ, the myth of the dove and the Virgin and the myth of the son appeasing his father's wrath and redeeming his mother and bride. Our own day is the period of the annunciation of a new Oedipus and Leda mythology, heralding the tragic and warlike age of the future and ushering in a religion contrasting with Christianity. The Messiah of our day is an Antichrist, that is, an antithetical Christ, the terrible reborn Babe of Blake's *Mental Traveller*. As Christ's mother was a virgin, so the new Messiah's mother, in *The Adoration of the Magi*, is a harlot and a devotee of the Black Mass, resembling the Virgin only in being rejected by the society of her time. In *The Herne's Egg* the new Messiah is to be born in Ireland, the Judaea of the West, the offspring of a heron and his fanatical priestess. What this Messiah has to announce, of course, is the future age when "another Troy shall rise and set."

In Spengler each culture has a "prime symbol" expressing its inner essence, which is a Doric column for the Classical, a cavern for the Magian, a garden for the Chinese, and so on. For some reason he gives no primary symbol for Western culture, saying only that it is characterized by a drive into the infinite. Yeats, learning from Pound that Frobenius found two major symbols in Africa, a cavern and an altar with sixteen roads leading from it, suggests that Spengler took his Magian cavern from Frobenius, and should have provided us with the altar for the Western symbol. In Yeats the middle "Magian" cycle is replaced by the conception of a religious cycle cutting the historical one midway, but Yeats resembles Spengler in associating Christ, who was born in a manger and rose from a tomb, with the cavern. Hence "At or near the central point of our civilization must come *antithetical* revelation, the turbulent child of the Altar" [204]. Yeats, however, does not use the altar as a symbol for our own time in his poetry, though the cavern appears as an image of the passage from death to rebirth (phase 1, more or less) in *The Hour before Dawn*. The chief images he does use are those of birds and animals. The bird is often the swan, for obvious reasons, but with a whole parliament of fowls in addition. If we take three representative poems on this theme, *The Second Coming, Demon and Beast,* and *On a Picture of a Black Centaur by Edmund Dulac*, we find a gyring falcon in the first, a gyring gull and a green-headed duck in the second, and "horrible green birds" [l. 16] in the third, accompanying the age in which the "demon" (not daimon, which is a quite different conception) of late phases gives place to the "beast" of early ones, the "rough beast" of *The Second Coming* [l. 21] who modulates into the centaurs of the Dulac poem.

Everybody belongs fundamentally to one of the twenty-six human phases or types, but, of course, a man of any phase can be born at any time in history. If a social cycle has reached, say, phase 22 (more or less the Victorian period in European culture), those who belong to phases near 22 will be typical of their time, and those of early phases (George Borrow and Carlyle in phase 7, for example) have a more difficult adjustment to make. But a man may also be typical or atypical of his own phase, and Yeats begins many of his descriptions, very confusingly, by dealing with the "out of phase" variant of the type. Yeats further tells us that[18] he cannot point to historical examples of several of the phases, partly because many of the more primary ones do not produce types who make any impression on history.

For one reason or another, what Yeats calls in *The Gift of Harun Al-Rashid*

> Those terrible implacable straight lines
> Drawn through the wandering vegetative dream [ll. 142–3]

turn out in practice to be nearly as accommodating as Baconian ciphers in Shakespeare. For instance, Yeats says that each millennium of the two-thousand-year cycle can be considered as a complete twenty-eight-phase wheel in itself, so that we are also near the phase 1 end of the first millennium of our Christian civilization, which adds to its chaos. This millennium reached its antithetical height of phase 15 at the Quattrocento, when "men attained to personality in great numbers," and when Europe was infused by the spirit of the recently fallen Byzantium. This curtailed millennial version of the rhythm of Western culture, which incidentally is much closer to Spengler, lies behind most of Yeats's references to Michelangelo and to one of his seminal books, Castiglione's *Courtier* (see, for example, *The People*). In the Renaissance there was also a kind of minor annunciation of the opposite kind of civilization, and so Yeats has reasons (he tells us in a passage in "On the Boiler" inexplicably omitted from the recent volume *Explorations*) both to "adore" and to "detest" the Renaissance.[19]

Again, there are larger rhythms in history, obtained by adding a solar and zodiacal cycle to the lunar one. One of these is the "Great Year," traditionally formed by the precession of the equinoxes, and which lasts for twenty-six thousand years, a "year" of twelve "months" of two thousand odd years each. One of these Great Years ended and began with Christ, who rose from the dead at the "full moon in March" which marks that point [250]. Caesar was assassinated at another full moon in March a few decades earlier [196]. Yeats points out how contemporaries of Christ, such as Virgil in the *Fourth Eclogue* and Horace in the *Carmen saeculare*, felt a peculiar cyclical significance about that time which Christianity itself, anxious[20] to get away from cyclical theories, ignored. The birth of Christ took place at a (primary) conjunction of Mars and Venus, and our new Messiah will be born at the opposite conjunction of Jupiter and Saturn, when the "mummy wheat" of the buried Classical civilization will start to sprout [*On a Picture of a Black Centaur by Edmund Dulac*, l. 7; *Conjunctions*, l. 2].

The emotional focus of *A Vision* is also that of Yeats's life, the sense that his own time is a time of a trembling of the veil of the temple, eventually defined as a myth of a new religious dispensation announcing a new God to replace Christ and accompanied by the traditional signs of the end of the world. Yeats traces his sense of an imminent Armageddon back to such early poems as *The Hosting of the Sidhe* and *The Valley of the Black Pig*. A note to the former poem tells us that the sidhe or fairy folk of Ireland dance in gyres or whirlwinds which are called the dance of the daughters of Herodias:[21] the last section of *Nineteen Hundred and Nineteen* applies this imagery to Yeats's own time. Although our own time is phase 15 of the Christian era, it can be read in different ways on Yeats's various clocks, and Yeats tends to think of it primarily as a passing through phase 1, when a great age has finally reached the crescent of the "fool" and hears the irrational cry ("the scream of Juno's peacock" [268]) of a new birth.

Yeats's treatment of the theme of contemporary annunciation exhibits a complete emotional range, from the most raucous nonsense to the most serene wisdom. We may divide his personal reactions to it into a cycle of six phases. First comes the phase of the deplorable if harmless rabble-rouser of "On the Boiler," shouting for a "just war," hailing Fascism as the force that will restore all the traditional heroic dignities to society, and prophesying a new "science" compounded of spiritualism and selective breeding. Some of Yeats's instructors appear to have been incapable of distinguishing a lunar vision from a lunatic one, and this phase in Yeats seems to be part of the backwash from revising *A Vision* around 1937. In an early letter Yeats says: "Every influence has a shadow, as it were, an unbalanced—the unbalanced is the Kabalistic definition of evil—duplicate of itself."[22] Fortunately this phase is not allowed to spoil much of his poetry, though it is creeping around the fringes of *Under Ben Bulben*.

The second phase is that of the traditionalist who stresses the importance of convention and manners, "where all's accustomed, ceremonious," and sees the preservation of this as preliminary to developing a new aristocracy [*A Prayer for My Daughter*, l. 74]. Yeats's cabinet of great Irishmen—Swift, Burke, Berkeley, and others—are called upon to endorse this attitude, which is also heard in a simpler form in the contented reveries emanating from Coole Park and Stockholm on the values of hereditary privilege. The third phase is that of the neo-pagan, the poet who celebrates a rebirth of physical energy and sexual desire, who insists on the sacredness of bodily functions, who helps Crazy Jane to refute the Bishop on the primacy of the life of the soul, and who asks the unanswerable question:

> If soul may look and body touch,
> Which is the more blest? [*The Lady's Second Song*, ll. 19–20]

The fourth phase is that of the teacher, the author of the *Samhain* essays who stands out against a "primary" mob, assuming the role, in his own literary context, of

> A great man in his pride
> Confronting murderous men. [*Death*, ll. 7–8]

This is the critic who patiently points out to his Irish audience that no true patriotism can be built on the stock response and no true religion on the consecration of it; that the morality of art must always be liberal, and that the sectarian instinct, "a pretended hatred of vice and a real hatred of intellect,"[23] is always part of the mob, whether it expresses itself in politics, religion, or art. The fifth phase is the prophet, the troubled visionary of *The Second Coming* and elsewhere, who sees and records but does not try to rationalize the horror and violence of his own time, who can understand the ferocity of "The weasel's twist, the weasel's tooth" [*Nineteen Hundred and Nineteen*, l. 92] without confusing it with heroism. Finally, there is the phase of the sage, the poet of *Lapis Lazuli* who can speak of the "gaiety that leaps up before danger or difficulty,"[24] and who understands that even horror and violence can inspire a kind of exuberance. We notice that all these phases which are directly connected with literature are very precious attributes of Yeats, but that for the others the best we can do is to apply to Yeats what Yeats himself says of Shelley: "Great as Shelley is, those theories about the coming changes of the world, which he has built up with so much elaborate passion, hurry him from life continually."[25]

Or, as Yeats also says, "All art is the disengaging of a soul from place and history."[26] It has doubtless occurred to more than one reader of *A Vision* that Yeats might more easily have seen his cycle, not as the archetypal forms of human life, but of human imagination: in other words as a perfect circle of literary or mythical types, which is how Blake saw the pilgrims of Chaucer. Many of Yeats's examples are writers who, like Whitman at phase 6, have made their lives conform to literary patterns, or who, like Shakespeare at phase 20, are described by the kind of poetry they produced and not personally. The primitives of phases 2 to 7 are much easier to understand as archetypes of pastoral or Romantic conventions in literature; Dostoevsky's Idiot is the only example given of phase 8; and Nietzsche's Zarathustra fits better into the "Forerunner" position of phase 12 than Nietzsche himself. Phase 15 would then become intelligible as the phase of the poet's ideal or male Muse: the Eros of Dante and Chaucer, the "Ille" of *Ego Dominus Tuus*, the beautiful youth of Shakespeare's sonnets, and the like. The high antithetical phases would be much more clearly represented by characters in Shakespeare or Irish legend, and the high primary ones by characters in Balzac and Browning, than they are by Galsworthy or Lamarck or "a certain actress."[27]

Such a rearrangement would bring out the real relation of the *Vision* cycle of types to Yeats's own characters. The fool and the blind man who remain on the stage at the end of *On Baile's Strand* symbolize the disappearance of the Cuchulain cycle (which is symbolically the Christian cycle, too, as Cuchulain was contemporary with Christ), the blind man representing the dark moonless night of phase 1. The happy natural fool of *The Hour-Glass* is also a fool of phase 28, with a Creative Mind from the "Player on Pan's Pipes" of phase 2. In *Resurrection* a blind man and a lame man, the two together making up the physical deformity of the "hunchback," appear beside a saint, and in *The Player Queen* the opposition of Decima and the Queen she supplants is a burlesque illustration of the opposition of phases 13 and 27, antithetical and primary perfection. The Queen in any case is a much better example of what Yeats appears to mean by sanctity than the historical examples he gives, which are Socrates and Pascal [180].

III

In the cycle of *The Mental Traveller* Blake symbolizes the subjective and objective aspects of life as male and female. All human beings including women are symbolically male, part of the reborn "Boy," and nature, or the physical environment that is temporarily transformed into human shape by a culture, is what is symbolically female. Male and female cycles rotate in opposite directions, one growing older as the other grows younger. *A Vision* refers briefly to this symbolism (213, 262), but *A Vision* says little about the objective aspect of civilization. The conception of the individual is much more complicated. Here, as in Blake, there are subjective and objective factors, but there are two of each, making four "Faculties" in all. An individual may be thought of as acting man (Will) or as seeing, knowing, or thinking man (Creative Mind). Insofar as he thinks or knows or sees, man operates on a known or seen world, a set of *données* or given facts and truths and events that make up what Yeats calls the Body of Fate. Insofar as he acts, he acts in the light of a certain vision of action, which Yeats calls the Mask, and which includes both what he wants to make of himself and what he wants to make of the world around him. In "antithetical" phases action is motivated by an "image" springing from the self which complements the Will: in "primary" phases, where man is more apt to say, with Hic in *Ego Dominus Tuus*, "I would find myself and not an image" [l. 10], it is motivated by a desire to act on the world as a separated or impersonal thing, and eventually by a desire to be absorbed in that world. Each man is defined by the phase of his Will, and his Mask comes from the phase directly opposite, fourteen phases away. The Body of Fate is similarly opposite the Creative Mind, and Will and Creative Mind are related by the fact that, like male and female principles in Blake, they rotate in opposite directions. The details are too complicated to go into here, but a man of phase 23 is actually made up of a Will of phase 23, a Mask of phase 9, a Creative Mind of phase 7, and a Body of Fate of phase 21.

In the Platonic tradition the relation of Creative Mind and Will is differently conceived. There is a superior intelligible world and an inferior physical world. In the latter the body perceives and acts on the image; in the former the soul perceives the form or idea, not as an object, but as something ultimately identical with itself. The soul and the world of forms are imprisoned in the physical world and struggle to break out of it. For Yeats, too, there is another way of looking at the four Faculties we have just dealt with. If we think of man as actor and creator, we see his life as an interplay of action and thought; if we think of him as a creature, we see his life as a physical contact with objects out of which a higher kind of identity is trying to emerge. In this perspective the four "Faculties" become four "Principles." Will and Mask now become two lower Principles, Husk and Passionate Body, the physical subject and the physical object. Creative Mind and Body of Fate become Spirit and Celestial Body, the soul and the world of forms. This introduces a dialectical element into the cycle, a movement out of it into a world of changeless being.

From the beginning Yeats's poetic world comprised a state of experience and a state of innocence, the latter being associated with the Irish fairy world, a "land of heart's desire"[28] where there was an eternal youth of dancing and revelry. In *The Celtic Twilight* this world is once described as the paradise still buried under the fallen world,[29] but its associations are usually more specific. Yeats quotes legends indicating that the seasons of this world are the reverse of ours, like the southern hemisphere, and, in the *Autobiographies*, a remark of Madame Blavatsky that we live in a dumbbell-shaped cosmos, with an antipodal world at our North Pole.[30] This conception is most readily visualized as an hour-glass, the emblem of time and the basis of Yeats's "double gyre" diagrams, and in the play that is explicitly called *The Hour-Glass* we are told that "There are two living countries, the one visible and the other invisible; and when it is winter with us it is summer in that country."[31] The fairy world has occasionally, according to legend and folk tale, caught up human beings, who found, when they returned to their own world, that time moves much faster here than there, and that a few days in fairyland had been many years of human life. As Yeats began to try to fit together what he knew of Irish legend with what he read in Swedenborg or learned at seances, he also began to think of his fairy world as complementary to our own in time as well as climate, and as moving from age to youth. He often refers to Swedenborg as saying that the angels move towards their youth in time, as we move towards age.

Yeats's doctrine of reincarnation eventually annexed this world and transformed it into the world that we enter at death and leave again at birth, which is also a rebirth. It lost most of its cheerfulness in this process and acquired many of the characteristics of a penal regime. Book 3 of *A Vision*, called "The Soul in Judgment," is supposed to tell us what his instructors knew about the antipodal world, but Yeats speaks of this section with some disappointment as more fragmentary than he hoped it would be.[32] It uses a good deal of material from the earlier essay "Swedenborg, Mediums, and the Desolate Places." The discarnate soul is pulled in the ideal direction of Spirit and Celestial Body, and away from Husk and Passionate Body, by a series of spiritual or imaginative repetitions of the major emotional crises of its earthly life, which tend eventually to exhaust them, as the confessional techniques of psychology are supposed to do with neuroses. Yeats calls this the "dreaming back," the most important of several stages of the return to rebirth. A violent crime may be re-enacted for centuries in the same spot, a fact which accounts for many types of ghost story; brutal masters and submissive slaves may exchange roles in a tenebrous saturnalia. Yeats suggests that our dreams, though they use our own experiences and desires as material, are actually part of the psychic life of the dead moving backwards to rebirth through us. The more fully a life has been lived, the less expiation is needed and the more successful the next life. Another life is, in fact, part of the whole "dreaming back" operation, so that every life is a movement from birth to death and simultaneously part of a purgatorial movement from death to rebirth. When a Spirit is completely purified and ready for what in Christianity would be heaven, it may seek rebirth as an act of deliberate choice, like the Bodhisattva in Buddhism.

In the Eastern religions the cycle of life, death, and rebirth is regarded as an enslavement, from which all genuine spiritual effort tries to liberate itself by reducing the physical world to unreality. The attitude of the Christian saint, even without a belief in reincarnation, is similar. Such a course is, according to some moods of Yeats, opposed to that of the poet and artist, whose function it is to show the reality incarnate in the appearance of the physical world and in the physical emotional life of man. The poet accepts the plenitude of the phenomenal world, and in the cycle of Faculties the most strongly "antithetical" types, heroes and beautiful women who are driven by the passions of a titanic ego, are the poet's natural subjects. Long before *A Vision* Yeats had written: "If it be true that God is a circle whose centre is everywhere, the saint goes to the centre, the poet and artist to the ring where everything comes round again."[33] Hence his emotional preference of the "antithetical" to the "primary," of the way of the poet to the way of the saint, leads to a preference for cyclical and rebirth symbolism in contrast to the kind of symbolism that separates reality into an apocalyptic and a demonic world.

The conflict of the abstract vision of the saint and the concrete vision of the poet, one seeking deliverance from the wheel of life and the other ready to accept the return of it, is the theme of many of Yeats's best-known poems. The setting of such poems is some modification of the top of Dante's mountain of purgatory, a winding stair in a tower leading upwards to a point at which one may contemplate both an eternal world above and a cyclical world below. In *A Dialogue of Self and Soul* the Soul summons to an upward climb into the dark; the Self, preoccupied with the dying-god symbol of the Japanese ceremonial sword wrapped in embroidered silk with flowers of "heart's purple," looks downward into rebirth and maintains "I am content to live it all again" [ll. 27, 57]. In *Vacillation*, where there is a similar dialogue between Soul and Heart, the opening image is the tree of Attis which stands between eternity and rebirth, and the final contrast is between the saint whose body remains uncorrupted and the poet who deliberately seeks the cycle of corruption in generation symbolized by Samson's riddle of the lion and the honeycomb. In *Among School Children* there is a similar antithesis between the nun and the mother, the former symbolizing the direct ascent to eternity and the latter the cycle of generation. Here the tree, appearing at the end instead of at the beginning, seems a resolving or reconciling image rather than one of "vacillation," but the contrast remains in the poem's argument.

However much imaginative sympathy we may have with these poems as poems, they indicate a deficiency in *A Vision* as an expression of some of Yeats's more profound insights. Yeats speaks of Emerson and Whitman as "writers who have begun to seem superficial precisely because they lack the Vision of Evil,"[34] but his own lack of a sense of evil borders on the frivolous. Visions of horror and violence certainly haunt his poetry, but in *A Vision* and elsewhere in his later essays, even in much of the poetry itself, they are all rationalized and explained away as part of the necessary bloodbath accompanying the birth of his new and repulsive Messiah. The absence of any sense of a demonic world, a world of evil and tyranny and meanness and torment, such as human desire utterly repudiates and bends every effort to get away from, is connected with, and is perhaps the cause of, the absence in *A Vision* of the kind of dialectical imagery that appears in, say, *The Two Trees*, which in Blake would be the tree of life and the tree of mystery. Occasionally in earlier prose writings we get glimpses of a whole dimension of symbolism that seems to have got strangled in *A Vision*. Yeats says in an early essay: "To lunar influence belong all thoughts and emotions that were created by the community, by the common people, by nobody knows who, and to the sun all that came from the high disciplined or individual kingly mind."[35] This imagery is repeated in *A Dialogue of Self and Soul*, but in *A Vision* the sun is "primary," and has been absorbed into the lunar cycle: the solar and zodiacal symbolism in *A Vision*, already glanced at, only extends the lunar cycle, and adds nothing new in kind.

What we miss in *A Vision*, and in Yeats's speculative prose generally, is the kind of construct that would correspond to such a poem as *Sailing to Byzantium*. This poem presents an eternal world which contains all the concrete imagery and physical reality associated elsewhere with the cycle of rebirth, which is not a mere plunge into nothingness and darkness by an infatuated soul, and yet is clear of the suggestion that nothing really lasts except what Blake calls the "same dull round" [*There is No Natural Religion*]. Such a poem is apocalyptic, a vision of plenitude which is still not bound to time. *The Shadowy Waters*, also, differs from the later poems of the *Vacillation* group in that the chief characters go on to finish their quest and the subordinate characters (the sailors) return to the world. The goal of the quest is also described in apocalyptic terms:

> Where the world ends
> The mind is made unchanging, for it finds
> Miracle, ecstasy, the impossible hope,
> The flagstone under all, the fire of fires,
> The roots of the world. [*The Shadowy Waters*, ll. 101–5]

For a theoretical construct to match this apocalyptic imagery we have to set aside the main body of *A Vision*, with its conception of unity and individuality as opposed and impossible ideals which only superhuman beings can reach, and look for another construct in which they are at the same point, and that point accessible to human life.

There are two apocalyptic symbols in *A Vision*: one is the "Record" (193) or consolidated form of all the images of "ultimate reality," associated by Yeats, I think correctly, with Blake's Golgonooza. The other and more important one is the "Thirteenth Cone," which is not really a cone but a sphere, and which "is that cycle which may deliver us from the twelve cycles of time and space" [210]. We are further told, in what ought to be one of the key passages of *A Vision*, that this thirteenth cone confronts every cycle of life, large or small, as "the reflection or messenger of the final deliverance," and at the very end of the book it is said to exist in every man and to be what is called by man his freedom [210, 302]. There are also "teaching spirits" of this thirteenth cone who direct and inspire those who are in the cycle, and Yeats calls the thirteenth cone his substitute for God. He speaks of it as "like some great dancer," recalling the great last line of *Among School Children* which unites being and becoming, imagination and image (210, 240).

The temporary mixture of four Faculties that constitutes what is ordinarily thought of as an individual is not final human reality. A poet discovers this, for example, when he realizes that the images that great poetry uses are traditional, archetypal, conventional images, and that the emotions he employs to set these images forth are traditional and conventional emotions, representing states of being greater than himself. Thus the poet finds himself drawn out of his Husk into his Spirit, and thereby enters into much larger conceptions of what subject and object are. He is drawn up into a world in which subject and object become the human imagination and the human image, each being archetypes that recur in every individual man and poem. These great traditional states of being which the poet enters into and expresses are akin to the "Giant forms" [E145, 202] of Blake's Prophecies—Orc, Tharmas, Los, and the rest—and, more generally, to the "gods" of beauty and nature and war who inform so much of literature. Yeats sometimes calls them "moods," and speaks of them as divine beings whose dreams form our own waking lives. Thus in *The Shadowy Waters* the central characters discover that

> We have fallen in the dreams the Ever-living
> Breathe on the burnished mirror of the world. [131–2]

In *A Vision* the poetic imagination begins in the self of the individual, but moves in the direction of identifying with a greater self called the "daimon," and the process of purgation between lives has for its eventual goal a similar identification.

Apart from the contrast of self and soul, there is also an abstract vision associated, not with sanctity, but with art itself. This is the vision linked with the name of Pythagoras, whose mathematical genius "planned" the art of exquisite proportion embodied in Greek sculpture and architecture. The role of art in imposing mathematical proportion on reality is connected by Yeats also with the geometrical diagrams of his own *Vision*, which he compares to the forms of Brancusi sculpture. Here we see how art, no less than sanctity, moves in the direction of a greater identity. In the poem *To Dorothy Wellesley* it is not the soul that climbs the stair towards darkness, but the poetic power, which ascends in search of identity with the greater forms and figures of existence represented by the "Proud Furies." Such identity is no loss of individuality; it is merely a loss of what we might call the ego. In Yeats's terms, it loses character and gains personality. The saint attains a powerful personality by forgetting about his ego; but the poet, too, as Yeats says, "must die every day he lives, be reborn, as it is said in the Burial Service, an incorruptible self."[36] For the poet, Yeats also says, "is never the bundle of accident and incoherence that sits down to breakfast: he has been reborn as an idea."[37]

"I think," says Yeats, "that much of the confusion of modern philosophy . . . comes from our renouncing the ancient hierarchy of beings from man up to the One."[38] The process of entering into a life greater than our ordinary one, which every poet knows, is a process of entering into this hierarchy, and of beginning to ascend the stair of life. The Thirteenth Cone, therefore, is a symbol of the way in which man emancipates himself by becoming part of Man, through a series of greater human forms. Here we move toward an existence in which phases 1 and 15, unity and individuality, are the same point. It is therefore impossible that the "One" could be anything but Man, or something identical or identifiable with man. Yeats refers occasionally to the "One" as a sleeping giant like Blake's Albion or Joyce's Finnegan (*The Mountain Tomb*, *The Old Stone Cross*, etc.), but he is even nearer the centre of his own intuitions when he speaks of man as having created death, when he says that there is nothing but life and that nothing exists but a stream of souls, and that man has, out of his own mind, made up the whole story of life and death and still can

> Dream, and so create
> Translunar Paradise. [*The Tower*, ll. 155–6]

The Thirteenth Cone, then, represents the dialectical element in symbolism, where man is directly confronted by the greater form of himself which challenges him to identify himself with it. This confrontation is the real form of the double gyre. "The repose of man is the choice of the Daimon, and the repose of the Daimon the choice of man . . . I might have seen this, as it all follows from the words written by the beggar in *The Hour-Glass* upon the walls of Babylon."[39] He might also have seen that this conception of the double gyre reduces his twenty-eight-phase historical cycle to something largely useless as a commentary on his own poetry, except for the poems deliberately based on it.

Yeats often speaks of entering into these personal archetypes, daimons, or moods as a process of literal or symbolic death. "Wisdom is the property of the dead" [*Blood and the Moon*, l. 49], he says, and his fascination with the remark in *Axël*, "As for living, our servants will do that for us,"[40] is connected with the same conception. Yeats's own interpretation of the *Axël* passage is indicated in "The Tables of the Law": "certain others, and in always increasing numbers, were elected, not to live, but to reveal that hidden substance of God which is colour and music and softness and a sweet odour; and . . . these have no father but the Holy Spirit."[41] Two of his poems describe the direct passage across from ordinary life to archetype, *News for the Delphic Oracle* and *Byzantium*. The latter poem is mainly about images, which are, as often in Yeats, generated in water and borne across water by dolphins into the simplifying and purgatorial world of fire. The former poem applies the same movement to human souls, and makes it clear that nothing of the physical or concrete world is lost, or even sublimated, by the kind of redemption here described.

These two poems, then, deal with the consolidation of imaginations and images, the true subjects and the true objects, into a timeless unity. But, of course, the image is a product of the imagination: in the imaginative world the relation of subject and object is that of creator and creature. In this perspective the whole cycle of nature, of life and death and rebirth which man has dreamed, becomes a single gigantic image, and the process of redemption is to be finally understood as an identification with Man and a detachment from the cyclical image he has created. This ultimate insight in Yeats is the one expressed in his many references (one of which forms the last sentence of *A Vision*) to a passage in the *Odyssey* where Heracles, seen by Odysseus in hell, is said to be present in hell only in his shade, the real Heracles, the man in contrast to the image, being at the banquet of the immortal gods [bk. 11, ll. 690–4]. Here we come to the heart of what Yeats had to say as a poet. The vision of Heracles the man, eternally free from Heracles the shadowy image bound to an endless cycle, is nearer to being a "key" to Yeats's thought and imagination than anything else in *A Vision*. To use the phraseology of *Per Amica Silentia Lunae*, it is an insight he had acquired, not by eavesdropping on the babble of the *anima mundi*, but from his own fully conscious *anima hominis*, the repository of a deeper wisdom than the ghostly house of rumour ever knew.

44

Foreword to *1984*

1967

Foreword to 1984, *by George Orwell, Canadian Educational Edition, ed. Joseph Blakey (Don Mills, Ont.: Bellhaven House, 1967), vii–xii. A clean typescript is in NFF, 1988, box 1, file x.*

George Orwell, whose real name was Eric Blair, was born in 1903, of an Anglo-Indian family. He had a conventional public-school education, and then went back to India as a member of the Imperial Police. His experience of British imperialism in Burma is recorded in his book *Burmese Days*; it convinced him that imperialism was something he wanted no part of. It was one of his several encounters with the sources of tyranny in our time. Then he lived for a time as a vagrant or hobo, picking up jobs like washing dishes in Paris restaurants, and got a first-hand sense of what the Depression did to the human soul. He put that into his novels *A Clergyman's Daughter, Keep the Aspidistra Flying*, and several others. He was a socialist in politics, but he never idealized or vilified any class of people merely because they were a class, and he studied working-class English psychology with a straightforwardness that made these books the forerunners of later ones like *Room at the Top* and *Lucky Jim*. The Spanish war began; Orwell went to Spain to fight for the Loyalists and was wounded, and watched the Stalinist Communists systematically murdering and betraying their anarchist and Trotskyist allies. In his writings on Spain, particularly *Homage to Catalonia*, he shows how like in aim and motivation Russian Communism was to the Fascism it in theory opposed. In 1946 his first really popular book, *Animal Farm*, a satire directly aimed at Communist Russia, appeared, and in 1949 came his last book, *1984*. When he died the next year, he was called by one leading critic (V.S. Pritchett) the conscience of his generation.[1]

When *1984* first came out I reviewed it for the Canadian Broadcasting Corporation, and I said then what I would say now: that the book is a modern *Inferno*.[2] According to it, within a single generation, thirty-five years from the time of writing, the world will be divided into three totalitarian states, descended from the present democratic world, the Soviet Union, and China. Towards the end of the book we are given a history of the world from 1949 on which traces this development with the most hair-raising plausibility. The three world-states keep a constant war going on, not an all-out war, but just enough of one to keep hysteria simmering and consumer goods in short supply. Orwell shows that such a limited perpetual war would be a worse fate for humanity than its total extermination. There are three classes of people, the party bosses, the party workers, and the masses, called "proles." The bosses consist almost entirely of spies; the workers, the new middle class, are their main victims; and the masses are kept in a subhuman state with what is called "prolefeed"—popular songs and pornography run off computers. Through the "telescreen," a two-way television set, the spies can see and hear everything one does, all day and all night, and everything is focused on the dictator, an invisible figure, except for his photographs, who is called Big Brother.

All the stock consolations that we use to tell ourselves that such things couldn't happen here, or couldn't last if they did, are removed one after the other. The hero, Winston Smith (he was born in 1940 and is named, by a vicious irony, after Winston Churchill), tells himself that "if there is any hope it lies in the proles,"[3] but it is clear that the proles are too debased for any hope to be in them. It is an illusion of liberals that people don't do cruel things unless there is some motive behind them and some object in front of them, and that they'll stop when they've reached their objective. We are told in *1984* that cruelty is its own reward; the object of power is power, not something power can get. After Winston has been tortured to a certain point, he feels that he can gain at least a spiritual victory by being opposed in his mind to everything the tyrants stand for. But modern dictatorships know a great deal more about torture than they did, say, at the time of the Crucifixion of Christ. Winston is broken to the point at which he completely accepts everything being done to him; the last words of the book are, "He loved Big Brother." Further, there is no chance that people will become so stupefied that the tyrants will stop catching and torturing victims. There must be victims: tyranny demands sacrifice, and victims will always be provided. Except that individual men can die, life is, quite simply and literally, hell. And, like hell, it will last forever. There is no reason, in a state which controls both history and the news media, why Big brother should ever die.

1984 became very popular on its publication, because it was assumed that, like *Animal Farm*, it was simply an anti-Communist satire. Of course it is a satire on Communism, and a very powerful one. In the fifteen years that this book has been soaking into our minds it has become almost indispensable in expressing the way we feel about totalitarian methods. I have just read an article on the fall of Khrushchev, and the author, without any quotation marks or references, used the words "doublethink" and "unreason"—both words that came into the language with Orwell's book. The reason why it is so effective is that it strikes directly at the mental attitude that makes Communism possible. It is a commonplace of satires like *1984* that they present human beings as reduced to machines. And if we ask what is the difference between a human being and a machine, the answer is that the human being possesses its own will. An automobile can run faster and a computer think faster than a man, but the machine has no will of its own to do these things. In Communist propaganda the political necessity of saying something outweighs the truth of what is said; consequently truth, as a norm or standard, is subordinated to expediency. We all do this to some extent, but it's risky to lose the awareness that we are doing it. Orwell thinks of truth less as a virtue than as the sign of a healthily functioning mind. Lying weakens the will power, and it leaves one without the strength to resist the will of someone else, a mechanical instrument.

The book goes beyond the actual phenomena of Communism into the perversity of the human mind that has created it. The thing that gives dignity to man is consistency, the fact that he pursues a line of conduct and sticks to it. In society consistency takes the form of a continuity of tradition and history. The *1984* world has destroyed history and falsified all the records of the past, so there is no longer any basis for consistency or dignity. One of the models for Orwell's book is a story called *We*, written by a disillusioned Russian Bolshevist named Zamyatin and published in 1924. In this story the tyrants achieve their power by forcing all their subjects to undergo a lobotomy operation which removes the human personality by surgery. In the *1984* world there is no need to do this.

Yet even if history is destroyed, man still has language, and as long as he has language he will have the materials and concepts to think with. So the *1984* world destroys language as well, and replaces it with a purely automatic gabble called "Newspeak," which requires no conscious operation of the mind at all.

It would be a great mistake to assume that *1984* simply exhibits Communism to us like a monkey cage in a zoo, with the aim of making us feel more complacent about our superior liberties. The book shows us not a monkey cage but a mirror. Its society is the logical form of what a great many of us have already shown that we want. One of the things that most disgusted Orwell was the masochism of some of the intellectuals around him, who thought that any totalitarian government was better than democracy because it was more logical. Those who were pro-Communist ignored or explained away all the evidence that Stalin's government was brutal, corrupt, and treacherous. In other words they were willing to rewrite history in terms of their own prejudices. The history incorporated into *1984* remarks that most of the intellectuals in the democracies had become authoritarian by 1940, and there is far too much truth in that statement. Or, again, take McCarthyism, something that grew up after Orwell's book. I have read many letters in American papers defending McCarthy, and what most of them said in effect was: "Communism is such a danger that it doesn't matter if his accusations are true or not; how are we going to feel protected unless somebody is constantly being denounced?" That attitude was exactly the attitude that makes Big Brother possible. Nobody wants to have the tortures and spyings of that world applied to himself, but many of us would feel more comfortable if we knew that they were being applied to someone else who we could think of as dangerous. The fact that the world's most powerful democracy let McCarthy get away with pure bluff year after year did not indicate a fear of losing freedom to Communism; what it indicated was a fear of freedom itself.

So there was a real point in calling Orwell the conscience of his generation. We have covered about half the time between *1984* as a book and as a date. Winston Smith would now be a man of twenty-four. There is still enough to worry about in the world, heaven knows, but the feeling that we are actually a little further away from the *1984* world than we were fifteen years ago is very strong. We may be fooling ourselves; but even if we reach December 31, 1984, with our liberties relatively intact, Orwell's book will not be out of date. He has shown us too clearly what kind of a world our own folly and thoughtlessness can still produce. If we avoid tumbling into his hell, we shall have his honesty in facing the vision of that hell as one of the things we can thank for our escape. Orwell has shown us a society without love, without religion, without science, without art, without private life, without law, without any of the things that we today take as much for granted as air and water. We can take nothing for granted if we are to remain free, or even human.

45

The Top of the Tower: A Study of the Imagery of Yeats

12 August 1968

From StS, *257–77. This paper was originally delivered as a lecture at a conference on Yeats in Sligo, Ireland on 12 August 1968, and published in* Southern Review, *5, no. 3 (Summer, 1969): 850–71; reprinted in* William Butler Yeats: A Collection of Criticism, *ed. Patrick J. Keane (New York: McGraw-Hill, 1973), 119–38. For* StS *Frye made several small verbal changes and added three identifying notes. For a reissue of* StS *he suggested two minor corrections, here adopted and listed in the Emendations at the end of the volume (see letter of 31 October 1973, in NFF, 1988, box 61, file 4); however, they were not adopted in the 1974 paperback or 1980 hardcover reprint of* StS. *Typescripts are in NFF, 1988, box 2, files ll, mm, and nn.*

All poets speak the same symbolic language, but they have to learn it either by instinct or unconsciously from other poets. In the poetry of the Western world from medieval times to our own, there has been a framework for poetic symbolism with four main levels. On the top level is what I should call the Logos vision, which includes the conventional heaven of religion, the place of the presence of God. The central symbol of the Logos vision is the city, the Biblical New Jerusalem, but it is also often described in metaphors taken from mathematics or from music, the two areas being connected by the conception of "harmony." Central to Logos imagery, in all poetry before Newton's time at least, is the image of the orderly stars, moving in spheres which also give out a harmonious music, the archetype of the music we hear. The Logos vision is that of an order of existence designed by an intelligent Creator, and among its musical and mathematical images is that of the dance, which appears in Dante, in Sir John Davies' *Orchestra*, in the Eliot Quartets, and at the end of *Among School Children*. In the last poem the image of the chestnut tree, immediately preceding, recalls the traditional image of the earthly paradise, just below the circling stars, in which man was originally placed.

The stars in their courses are all that is now left of the order of nature as God originally designed it: the earthly paradise for man was lost with the fall of Adam. But everything that inspires and ennobles man helps him to ascend from the world of his fallen nature to something nearer his original home, traditionally the earthly paradise or the Garden of Eden. This ascent of the soul is another area of poetic symbolism that I shall call the Eros vision, because some form of human love almost invariably prompts it. Eros symbolism usually begins with the figure of the alienated poet, who is forced into writing poetry by being frustrated as a lover. The creative life thus appears as what students of animal behaviour call a displaced activity, a substituted outlet of a mainly erotic energy. In medieval times this led to the convention begun by the Provençal love poets and expanded by Dante and Petrarch. According to the more typical forms of this, an erotic relation is established between a poet and a lady which does not aim either at marriage or at any sexual "affair," but is intended from the beginning to pass through frustration to sublimation. The lady is too high in virtue or social rank to be sexually attainable: the poet is merely her servant and a servant of the God of Love, who has commanded him to love the lady. The lady then becomes the inspiration for everything good that the poet does, so that his dedication to her may also be an ascent of his soul toward virtue. In the chivalric romances this virtue is symbolized by the courage and strength of the knight-errant as he continues to rid the world of dragons and giants and tyrants. Such a convention is based on an erotic analogy to Christianity, and it was easy to fit it into the medieval Christian framework. In Christianity man has fallen from a higher state of being, and hence a love-inspired ascent of the soul may be thought of as a partial return to its original state, the state symbolized by Adam in Eden. I say a partial return, because for Christianity no one can complete the process in this life: for Catholic Christianity it is completed after death in purgatory.

There are two main varieties of Eros vision, the explicitly sexual and the sublimated. We may call them, following Milton, the allegro and the penseroso visions, though of course they are far older than Milton: Ovid, for example, writes an art of love which moves toward sexual intercourse, and then deals with the "remedies" of love which take the opposite road. Milton's allegro vision is one of "unreprovèd pleasures free" [*L'Allegro*, l. 4] which take the narrator to an earthly paradise, where Orpheus may hear an erotic (Lydian) music that might restore his Eurydice to him; the penseroso vision is a sublimated love for a nun (vestal virgin) which makes the narrator a philosopher studying Plato in a lonely tower, and leaves him a prophet and hermit. A similar duality in the Eros vision exists in medieval poetry. In *The Romaunt of the Rose* the poet is a lover whose quest ends with his physical possession of his mistress's body: in Dante's *Purgatorio* the poet is impelled by his love for Beatrice to climb the mountain of purgatory to the Garden of Eden on top of it. There is no sexual culmination: Dante first meets a young girl, Matilda, but he is separated from her by a river; then he meets Beatrice, but Beatrice does not go farther than unveiling her mouth, the visible sex organ, so to speak.

The world that man entered with the fall of Adam and is now born into is a tragic world, and its central image is that of the dying god Adonis or Dionysus, a role which Christ adopts in his Incarnation. The tragic hero often recapitulates the dying god's typical life from mysterious birth to premature death; we also have an episodic form of this theme in the poems that deal with birth in this world as a loss of innocence or fall from a paradisal world to a lower one. Examples include poems by Vaughan and Traherne, Wordsworth's *Intimations of Immortality* ode, Blake's *Book of Thel*, Dylan Thomas's *Fern Hill*, and a passage in Yeats's *Among School Children*. Below this world of tragic or ironic experience is the Thanatos vision, including the hell of Christianity and the ironic visions of our day which present experience as an unending life in death.

All four of these worlds are clearly marked in Yeats's symbolism. The Logos vision, the "Thirteenth Cone" where Chance and Choice are one, is not often referred to, but it is integral to his imagery nonetheless. It is most explicitly described, perhaps, in the fourth of the *Supernatural Songs*:

> There all the barrel-hoops are knit,
> There all the serpent-tails are bit,
> There all the gyres converge in one,
> There all the planets drop in the Sun. [*There*, ll. 1–4]

This world is regularly associated with the sun in Yeats, and it stands above the cycle of life and death represented by the ouroboros or tail-biting serpent of the second line. Yeats tells us that this world in Plato is a world of pure Idea or Form, but that Plotinus transformed it into a "timeless individuality or daimon," preferring Socrates to his thought, and seeing the Logos world existentially as a total person rather than a total idea, containing "archetypes of all possible existences whether of man or brute."[1] Plotinus was, Yeats says, the first to establish this individuality as the sole source of being, though Yeats's Christian and Jewish readers, at least, might feel that a few other people had got to the conception a little earlier than Plotinus. The traditional associations of harmony appear in a remarkable early evocation of this Logos world in the poem *Paudeen*:

> on the lonely height where all are in God's eye,
> There cannot be, confusion of our sound forgot,
> A single soul that lacks a sweet crystalline cry. [ll. 6–8]

It is, however, the imagery of Eros that I want to consider more particularly in this essay. The theme of the sexually inspired ascent of the soul underlies the "tower" and "winding stair" images in Yeats. The most obvious source for the images is, again, the spiral *escalina* or staircase going up and around the mountain of Purgatory in Dante. It is interesting that the only contemporary poet producing work of comparable value to that of Yeats, T.S. Eliot, was also fascinated by staircases, and his *Ash-Wednesday*, with its winding stair and its explicit debt to the *Purgatorio*, belongs to the same period as the appearance of the same imagery in Yeats. The spiral shape of Dante's mountain links the winding stair with Yeats's gyre image. The gyre for Yeats is one of the central images of the cycle of life because it can be an emblem either of fertility and life or of death. The former produces the cornucopia or horn of plenty, an image appearing in *A Prayer for My Daughter*, and the latter the Charybdis or maelstrom. The activity of the poet, moving from a broad receptivity to the concentrated effort of creation, may be thought of as a spiral or vortex of energy moving from base to apex. This activity recapitulates, in its turn, the whole movement of life, of plants from receptive root to climactic fruit or blossom, and of animals who pass through the vortex of birth from one world to another. Once entered into the world of birth, another vortex pulls them back through its apex into death, which is symbolically a return to the mother. The death gyre appears in Dante's hell, which, like his purgatory, is a cone narrowing from base to apex.

The gyre is, of course, also a sexual symbol, male on the outside and female on the inside, and sex is closely connected with rising flames and the spiralling of smoke, fire being a traditional purgatorial image also. We may compare the rites of kindling the "need-fire" described in *The Golden Bough*, where a naked boy and girl go into a room together and make fire by twirling a pointed stick in a hole,[2] or what Yeats calls perning in a gyre. Sexual intercourse and the birth resulting from it form a double gyre or reversing movement into and out of the mother's body. The seashell, which appears in the first poem in Yeats's *Collected Poems*,[3] is another helical emblem of life arising out of the sea, and the ear, described by Blake, in a more sinister context, as "a whirlpool fierce to draw creations in" [*The Book of Thel*, pl. 6, l. 17; E6] is the vortex through which the Word is born in the Virgin's body in Yeats's *Mother of God*. Dante's greatest predecessor as an Eros poet was Plato, whose ascent of the soul is usually associated with the ladder. But, if we can believe Aristophanes' *The Clouds*, where Socrates is represented as dethroning the gods and replacing them with a new deity called *dinos* or "whirl" [l. 379], perhaps the gyre underlies the Socratic tradition too.

In the Bible the ascent from earth to heaven is also first represented by a ladder, the image of Jacob's, that is, Israel's, dream. From the point of view of later Christian typology, this ladder would be identical spiritually with the later journey of Israel as a people through the labyrinth of the desert toward their original home or Promised Land. The gyre is a conventionalized labyrinth, the crooked path of the serpent as distinct from the straight path of the arrow. The Promised Land is symbolically identical with the original Garden of Eden, and is represented in the New Testament by the vision of the Virgin Mother and her divine Child, the epiphany of divine innocence. The connecting link between the Promised Land and the Virgin is the *hortus conclusus* or enclosed garden of the Song of Songs, identified with the body of the Virgin in Christian symbolism. All these Biblical archetypes are incorporated in Dante. Dante begins with the standard medieval Eros theme, the alienated lover who is inspired by his love in the form of a vision. He goes up the mountain of purgatory, shedding one of the seven deadly sins at each stage, the last sin to be purged being, appropriately enough, lechery or excessive physical love, where again the image of fire appears. After this Dante finds himself in Eden, so that he has really regained his own childhood, not his individual childhood but his generic childhood as a son of Adam.

Thus Dante's quest up the Mountain has in a sense gone backward in time, removing the sins which accumulated in his ordinary experience like, to use a Yeatsian image, the wrappings of a mummy cloth around a mummy, and thus proceeding from his situation as a poet in mid-career back to the ultimate source of his life. Similarly, Yeats says of the spirits in his equivalent of purgatory: "They examine their past if undisturbed by our importunity, tracing events to their source, and as they take the form their thought suggests, seem to live backward through time."[4] After Virgil has left Dante with a grave benediction, in possession of his free will, his own pope and emperor, Beatrice appears, scolding like an Italian mamma, and Dante is immediately reduced to a whimpering and tearful child. An erotic impulse drives Dante from the sexual into the presexual, and from there to his own original state of innocence. It looks as though, psychologically, one of the goals of the Eros ascent is connected with the mother and the mother's encircling body (one thinks of another modern treatment of the theme in Auden's and Isherwood's *Ascent of F6*).

As the lover or visionary proceeds on his quest toward his own eternal youth, the shadow of ordinary life appears beside him in the form of an old man, who guides and instructs him on the journey but cannot enter the final paradise. This figure is represented by Moses in the Exodus story and by Virgil in Dante. In the New Testament we have Joseph, who also cannot enter the *hortus conclusus*, as well as the Magi of Matthew and the Simeon of Luke. I have mentioned Milton's allegro and penseroso visions, where there is a modulation of this theme. The figure of the philosopher in the tower, studying the stars of the Logos vision, is linked by Yeats both with Il Penseroso and with Shelley's Prince Athanase. In Milton's *Comus* the usual associations of hero or heroine and guardian are reversed: the Lady's chastity puts her in tune with the Logos harmonies of the heavenly world, but her attendant spirit goes back to an earthly paradise, identified with Spenser's Gardens of Adonis, of which more later. Most comedy is written in the Eros mode, and we notice in Shakespeare the penseroso figures of Jaques and Prospero, who withdraw from the festivity and multiple marriages at the end into a meditative solitude.

In Yeats the theme of a journey backward in time is reinforced by the "ancestral stair" [*Blood and the Moon*, l. 17] in which the poet travels in the track of his great predecessors, and by the personal and cultural memories in *The Tower*. Long before Yeats had made what he calls "the connection, still vague in my imagination, between pilgrimage and vision, scenery and the pilgrim's salvation,"[5] he had picked up the conception of two levels of existence, one that of ordinary life and the other a land of eternal youth, from the Irish legends of the Tir na nOg and the Sidhe dancing in the gyres of the whirling wind. In many stories of fairyland, the mortals who enter it find that time is arrested there, and that when they return to ordinary life they have become incredibly aged, in the role of the old man excluded from the earthly paradise.

There has been, as already indicated, an old feud between the sexual and the sublimated or religious versions of the Eros quest, and even in the sublimated versions some ambiguity recurs. The Israelites were able to enter the Promised Land only through the help of the harlot Rahab, and Rahab in Dante marks the boundary of what is in effect the total area of the lower Paradise, which stretches from the Garden of Eden, at the top of Mount Purgatory, just below the moon, to the sphere of Venus, the limit of the earth's shadow in Dante's astronomy. Rahab, the last soul seen in Venus, balances the figure of Matilda, the first soul seen in Eden. Similarly, the story of the Virgin Birth in the Bible comes very close to being a story of a forgiven harlot, and the forgiven harlot appears in the Gospels and later legends in the form of another Mary. In most paintings of the Crucifixion, Christ is flanked by both Marys, the forgiven harlot in red and the Virgin in blue. There is a similar duality in Yeats's portrayals of two aspects of the personality, one seeking the sexual cycle and the other trying to escape from it: an early example presents it in its true colours:

> She opened her door and her window,
> And the heart and the soul came through,
> To her right hand came the red one,
> To her left hand came the blue.[6]

For a complete Eros vision, therefore, we need a virgin, a child, and a harlot. When we add to them the eagle which flies upward into the Logos unity of the sun, and the lion which wanders alone in the wilderness, we have the five elements "That make the Muses sing."[7]

In Dante, the Mountain of Purgatory stands on an island on the other side of the earth, and the souls of the dead reach it by crossing water on the ship of death. As Dante emerges from hell, an angel arrives with a boatload of souls, dumps them down at the foot of the mountain, and hurries back for more. Similarly the wandering of Israel in the desert begins with the crossing of the Red Sea (identical with the escape from

Egypt, which is symbolically under the Red Sea with Pharaoh's army). The ancient ship of death image enters Yeats's poem *His Dream*, in *The Green Helmet* volume, but in *Byzantium* and in *News for the Delphic Oracle* the vehicular form, as Blake would call it, is not a ship but a dolphin, an equally traditional image of salvation out of the sea. The ascent up the desert mountain culminates in the vision of unfallen nature, symbolized as a rule by an unspoiled or redeemed female. Sometimes this female figure is identified with the moon, the traditional boundary between temporal and eternal worlds, which stands directly above the mountain in Dante and elsewhere. Thus the quest for ideal beauty of Keats's hero Endymion is represented by Endymion's love for Phoebe the moon-goddess. In Spenser's *Mutabilitie Cantos* a great debate, anticipating some of the similar debates in Yeats, is held in the sphere of the moon, which is also just above the top of an Irish mountain, *Arlo Hill*. The debate is between Mutability, the ruler of everything below the moon, who claims that everything above the moon is also hers, and Jove, the representative of the higher order of nature. The judge is Nature herself, who decides in favour of Jove, though she admits that there are cycles, and therefore some principle of change, on both levels. In other words, it is essential for a Renaissance Christian poet to keep a higher Logos vision above an Eros one.

The sublimated version of the Eros quest has been more popular in the past, not only for religious reasons, but because of the underlying paradox in the sexual relation expressed by Sir Thomas Browne: "United souls are not satisfied with embraces, but desire to be truly each other."[8] Poets insist on the imagery of mutual identity anyway, though, as we see in Donne's *The Extasie* and Shakespeare's *The Phoenix and Turtle*, usually with some underlying humour and sense of the paradox involved. This tone of paradoxical humour recurs in Yeats's *Solomon and the Witch*, where it is suggested that perfect sexual intercourse would restore the fallen world to its paradisal form. But perfect intercourse would be, as Blake says, a complete union of bodies rather than "a pompous High Priest entering by a Secret Place" [*Jerusalem*, pl. 69, l. 44; E223]. The capacity for such complete union is ascribed to the angels by Swedenborg, in a passage frequently referred to by Yeats, and one which connects this theme with that of a world adjacent to but different from ours where time runs backward from age towards youth.[9]

In the course of history there are certain gigantic cycles which are started off by a supernatural sex act of this kind, of the type preserved in mythology by the legends of the intercourse of a male bird and a woman, Leda and the swan, the Dove and the Virgin, Attracta and the Irish heron. Such cycles are marked by certain "conjunctions"—an astrological term with an obvious sexual overtone—of planets. The word "consummation" also has a sexual meaning, though in Christian theology it refers primarily to the eventual burning up of the world by fire. But fire, we saw, is a sexual image too, appearing in Dante's ring of fire and Shakespeare's phoenix, and Blake says in *The Marriage of Heaven and Hell* that the apocalypse by fire will take place through "an improvement of sensual enjoyment" [pl. 14; E39]. This image of the flame of the apocalypse being lit by sex comes into the image at the end of the first *Winding Stair* poem where the poet strikes a match to set fire to "the great gazebo," which is now a structure of guilt [*In Memory of Eva Gore-Booth and Con Markievicz*, l. 30].

Yeats carries his preference for the sexual to the sublimated quest to the point of making several parodies of the latter. The early volume *Responsibilities* is polarized in its symbolism between the figures of the sleeper and the wanderer, the figure who, like the traditional Enoch and Elijah, remains quietly awaiting the final end of things, and the figure who, like Cain or the Wandering Jew, is condemned to wander in the cycle of time. The latter figure is closely connected with the old man who is prevented from entering the earthly paradise, and appears in *Last Poems* as the "pilgrim" and the "wild old wicked man," who gets randier as he gets older.[10] Then again, we said that in traditional Christian symbolism the higher Logos vision is described in mathematical imagery, which indicates the Christian sense of the superiority of the sublimated and conceptual vision over the sexual one. Yeats makes the point that the element of mathematical formality in Greek art does not transcend the sexual, but is itself a powerful expression of the sexual. The art that "Pythagoras planned" [*The Statues*, l. 1] turns out to be an apotheosis of physical and sexual beauty, and the same is true of Renaissance art:

> Michael Angelo left a proof
> On the Sistine Chapel roof,
> Where but half-awakened Adam
> Can disturb globe-trotting Madam
> Till her bowels are in heat. [*Under Ben Bulben*, ll. 45–9]

On the other hand, Ribh denounces Patrick for being obsessed by a mathematical notion of a divine Trinity and replacing the old sexual trinity of father, mother, and child with it. Plotinus, whose vision culminates in a flight of the solitary to the solitary, and who was said by his biographer to have been ashamed of being in the body,[11] makes some surprising discoveries about his spiritual goal when he finally reaches it.

In *The Shadowy Waters* the hero and heroine are led on by Aengus, the Irish Eros, towards a world of total love in which the frustrations of ordinary experience have ceased to exist. Consequently they are leaving the world for a paradise:

> . . . in some island where the life of the world
> Leaps upward, as if all the streams o' the world
> Had run into one fountain. [ll. 559–61]

We recall that in the Song of Songs the image of the enclosed garden is paired with that of a "fountain sealed" [4:12] and the Eros image of journeying upstream to the source or spring of a river appears later in *The Tower* and elsewhere. *The Shadowy Waters* quest reaches a point at the limit of the cyclical world of time, where it impinges on the eternal world. The cycle of time is often symbolized in literature by a dragon or serpent, particularly the ouroboros serpent with its tail in its mouth, referred to in the "Supernatural Song" quoted above. Whether or not the ouroboros is the precise image in Yeats's mind in *The Shadowy Waters*, at any rate Dectora says:

> O ancient worm,
> Dragon that loved the world and held us to it,
> You are broken, you are broken. [ll. 597–9]

The sailors, on the other hand, follow the cycle and return to the world of time, laden with the treasure that is the more conventional reward of killing the dragon. In *The Herne's Egg*, although there is the apocalyptic embrace of the heron with his priestess, the priestess also requires a sexual act with a human lover in the cycle of time, in order to provide a womb for the body of the dead Congal seeking reincarnation, a theme which Yeats adapts from a sardonic Tibetan folk tale.[12]

These examples suggest that there are in fact three possible conclusions for the Eros ascent: the sublimated, the sexual, and the return back down the mountain to ordinary existence. In Dante it is impossible to go back down: the sacramental cable car runs in only one direction. But that is because ordinary life, running from birth to death, has already taken place: purgatory is the reversing movement after death, and for the same reason only the sublimated goal is possible for Dante. Obviously the sexual goal and the return are closely connected, for the natural result of intercourse with the bride is birth, and birth begins the descending movement. One reason why Virgil in Dante cannot get past the top of purgatory is that his imagination reached its limit, from Dante's point of view, in his vision of a world renewed by the birth of a divine child in the *Fourth Eclogue*. Renewal in time merely turns the cycle of time.

Yet even in Dante there is a faint suggestion that from Eden on top of the mountain all forms of life except human ones fall back into the lower world, and in Spenser's description of the Gardens of Adonis, or sexual paradise, there is a "Time," who is continually forcing seeds and embryos out of this world into the lower one. We saw that the typical figure of the descending movement from birth to death is Adonis, who forsakes the love of Venus for war and hunting, and who is killed when still young. Adonis symbolism thus complements Eros symbolism. In Christianity the downward journey is pre-eminently the journey of Christ from Incarnation to Crucifixion, the Agape or descent of love from creator to creature, in which Christ takes on an Adonis or dying-god role, clothed in Luvah's robes of blood, as Blake says, Luvah or Orc being Blake's Eros-Adonis figure. This journey is made by Christ in his capacity as the second Adam, a conscious and voluntary descent repeating and redeeming the first Adam's passionate fall. Thus Spenser, after writing two Hymns on Love and Beauty in the regular Eros convention, follows them with a *Hymn of Heavenly Love* describing the Incarnation of Christ. The response of Christian faith to Christ's act forms one of the sublimated versions of the Eros ascent, the version symbolized by Eliot in *Little Gidding* as the ascending movement of fire. The conception of the Eros journey as a reversal of or response to a previous fall is Platonic also, though it is the Neoplatonists rather than Plato who lay stress on the original fall of the soul. Neoplatonic imagery merges with Christianity in the poems about the fall from innocence in childhood already mentioned.

Yeats was, as his *Autobiographies* tell us, fascinated by the notion of a double movement in life, and in the early play *The Hour-Glass* the conception of an antithetical world, whose summer is our winter, is presented in the symbol of the hourglass itself, the image of time as a double gyre, narrowing and broadening simultaneously. Thus the goal of the Eros ascent, the "land of heart's desire,"[13] was from the beginning linked to the tragedy and irony of the world of experience. The goal of the journey of love is usually beauty in some form or other, often an ideal beauty which combines the allegro figure of the imprisoned or sleeping maiden with the penseroso sense of harmony and order. A medieval symbol for such a goal of vision is the Holy Grail, which has female associations in its chalice shape and in its functions as a provider of food and as the container of the body or blood of Christ. The corresponding symbol in Yeats's early poetry is the rose, the symbol of sexual passion as the lily is of virginity, a symbol, as Yeats says, corresponding also to Shelley's intellectual beauty, except that he sees it "as suffering with man and not as something pursued and seen from afar."[14] The phrase implies, among other things, the interconnection of Eros and Adonis symbols. The rose is on the rood of time, just as, in *The Two Trees*, the tree of life is reflected in the tree of death. The colours of Eros are the red and white of St. Valentine, the patron of coupling birds like Shakespeare's red phoenix and white turtle; the colours of Adonis are the white and red of the dead body and spilled blood. These colours recur in an episode of the Parzival legend referred to by Yeats, where Parzival sees some blood drops on snow reminding him of his mistress so vividly that he falls into a trance. The poet-lover, inspired by Eros, moves upward toward a female figure who may be virgin mother or mistress; the hero, the incarnation of Adonis, is frequently born of a calumniated mother who may also be a virgin or mistress of a divine bird. Eros shoots arrows, and Adonis figures like St. Sebastian are stuck full of them; Eros seeks his mother Venus, and Adonis escapes Venus to go to his death. In some versions of the dying-god story, including the one Yeats prefers, Adonis is killed by Venus, or rather by the figure whom Robert Graves calls the white goddess, Blake Tirzah or the sinister mother, and Yeats the "staring virgin" [*Two Songs from a Play*, pt. 1, l. 1]. The complementary nature of Eros and Adonis imagery comes out vividly in *Parnell's Funeral*:

> A beautiful seated boy; a sacred bow;
> A woman, and an arrow on a string;
> A pierced boy, image of a star laid low.
> That woman, the Great Mother imaging,
> Cut out his heart. [ll. 10–14]

The torn-out heart and the severed head are the two most frequent images of the martyrdom of the hero: they have also some connection with the four suits of cards featured in the Hanrahan stories. Lance and chalice (the two red suits) are the emblems of the Passion of Christ; sword and dish symbolize the death of John the Baptist, who was born at the summer solstice, as Christ was at the winter solstice, decreasing as Christ increases in a double gyre relation to him. Except for one very significant passage in *A Vision* (212), there is not much about John the Baptist in Yeats, but there is a fair amount about Salome, one of the manifestations of the "staring virgin."

Yeats had grasped, even before Frazer's *Golden Bough* appeared, the identity in symbolism between the dying Christ and the Classical dying gods. The association he made all his life between Christ and Dionysus appears as early as *The Secret Rose*, where the rose may be sought either in the Holy Sepulchre or in the wine vat. The Adonis symbols in Yeats cluster around two central and traditional images. One is the image of hunting. The Celtic hounds of the other world, white with red ears, appear in the earlier poems with sexual associations, representing, according to Yeats, the frustrated and elusive pursuits of the sex war. Similar animals reappear in the *Hound Voice* of *Last Poems* and in the silenced dogs of *To Dorothy Wellesley*, and the theme of "violence of horses" [*Nineteen Hundred and Nineteen*, l. 113] incorporates the archetype of the Wild Hunt into the anarchy of Yeats's own time. The other is the image of the tangled and bloody wood, associated with the setting sun, where the hero lies dead or hung on a tree like Absalom, gored by a beast like Adonis, or torn to pieces by drunken Bacchantes like Orpheus. This wood forms the setting of *Her Vision in the Wood*, a poem in *A Woman Young and Old*.

We said that *The Shadowy Waters* portrays two lovers escaping to a paradisal Eros world, while the sailors return to the ordinary one. There had previously been threats of mutiny and conspiracy from the sailors, hence this poem is the earliest example in Yeats of the theme of debate at or near the limit of the Eros journey, which recurs in *A Dialogue of Self and Soul* and *Vacillation*. The point on the boundary of the cycle of this world and an immortal world above it, usually associated with the earthly paradise or the moon, or both, the symbolic top of the tower or mountain, is what I have elsewhere called the point of epiphany.[15] In *A Dialogue of Self and Soul* the soul is a disciple of Plotinus, and wants to go upward from the point of epiphany into the pure mystical identity of solitude of which Plotinus speaks. The self looks downward, fascinated by the Adonis symbols of the ceremonial sword and its silk covering embroidered with flowers of "heart's purple" [l. 28]. These things are "Emblematical of love and war," and the soul wants no part of them [l. 19]. The self speaks for the poet, who, unlike the mystic, is committed to images, to sense experience, and to the recurring wheel of life. It is clear that the Eros dialogue between the wise old guide and the impetuous lover is not always a matter of the guide's informing his charge. Perhaps, however, we should think of both speakers as aspects of the old man in the tower, as a development of the two figures of *Responsibilities* previously mentioned, the sleeper and the wanderer: those who await a final consummation either in repose or in restlessness.

We are left with a strong impression that, as in Eliot, the way up and the way down are the same (except that Eliot's directions are reversed, the "dark night" vision being the upward one in Yeats), and that if one succeeds in either, one gets both. It should be noticed, however, that the soul associates *guilt* with the double gyre of descent and return, speaking of "the *crime* of death and birth" [l. 24], and that the self does not finally accept guilt. In his resolve to "cast out remorse" [l. 68] the self's proposed descent is more like that of the bodhisattva in Eastern religions, and what he reaches by descent is the genuine earthly paradise, the total vision of innocence in which, going even beyond Blake's "Every thing that lives is holy" [e.g., E54], he can say "Everything we look upon is blest" [l. 72].

In *Among School Children* there is again a contrast between the nun, whose image retains "a marble or a bronze repose" [l. 52], and the mother, who is bound to the cycle of recurrence. Here the two ideals are seen more ironically as equally half-achievements, perfection being symbolized by the tree and the dancer, in whom spontaneity and discipline, vitality and harmony, have become the same thing, and where the body has not been broken by the soul, like the nun's, or by birth, like the mother's. *Vacillation* begins with one of the standard point-of-epiphany symbols, the tree of life or "labyrinth of the birds" [*Blood and the Moon*, l. 23], also represented by the chestnut tree in *Among School Children* and the living tree with its demonic reflection in *The Two Trees*. In *Vacillation*, as in *The Two Trees*, the tree has two aspects, one of which is the "Attis" tree on which the dying god, or his image, is hung. This tree thus again illustrates the interconnection of innocence and experience, Eros and Adonis. Here again the poet considers the sublimated goal of the perfection of life, whose symbol, a subtler one than the "marble and bronze" of *Among School Children*, is the incorruptible body of the dead saint. The poet again, however, chooses the cycle of death and rebirth out of corruption, the lion and honeycomb of Samson's riddle, though without challenging the traditional moral contrast between corruptible and incorruptible body.

Yeats, then, consistently rejects for himself, though not necessarily for anyone else, the sublimated goals of the Eros vision that lead on to the Logos vision, and prefers the sexual goal which leads inevitably to going back down into the cycle again. Because he is a poet, Yeats tells us, he must choose the path of the hero and the "swordsman" rather than the saint. This is not simply a temperamental choice: there is a major complication in Yeats's winding-stair imagery that did not exist for, say, Dante. In Christianity, and in Neoplatonism more speculatively, the sublimation of the sexual instinct is the preferred program, because the man inspired by love is ultimately not seeking a sexual partner, but is a creature returning to his creator. But for Yeats there is no creator in the picture except man himself. The sources of creation are not in a divine mind beyond the stars: they are in the "foul rag-and-bone shop of the heart" at the *bottom* of the ladder [*The Circus Animals' Desertion*, l. 40]. The alienation symbolized by the disdainful mistress of Eros poetry and by the "staring virgin" of Adonis poetry, who tear out the poet's or hero's heart, is the point to which all creation regularly recurs. To return to his creator, man has to come back down again, return on himself, seek the source of the creative powers which are close to the sexual instincts, and are therefore in "the place of excrement," as Crazy Jane says, partaking of the corruption out of which all life comes [*Crazy Jane Talks with the Bishop*, l. 16].

What is the consequence of such a choice? One consequence certainly is the incorporation into Yeats's imagery of a purely ironic view of human life and history, in which all things are ordered by a relentlessly turning cycle. The cycle is the form that the double gyre assumes when it becomes the controlling image of all life. It is a central doctrine of *A Vision* that reality can manifest itself only in a series of opposites, a doctrine Yeats associates with Nicholas Cusanus, as Joyce associates it with Bruno, and seeing a double gyre as a single cycle is the same principle in reverse. This cyclical and fatalistic view of history is the one that is set out in *A Vision*. The fatalism of *A Vision* is in part a reflection of the passivity of mind in which Yeats received it, but even so it is important to realize that *A Vision* is Yeats's *Inferno*, his demonic or Thanatos vision. We said that the Eros theme, which enters into the Petrarchan or Courtly Love convention, normally begins with frustration, in which the lover complains of and bewails the inflexible cruelty of his lady. Yeats's love for Maud Gonne provides the corresponding theme in his poetry, and Maud Gonne is repeatedly associated with Helen of Troy. Helen of Troy in turn, hatched from the egg of Leda, is the symbol of the eternal recurrence of history, the misery she caused inevitably repeating itself in future ages. We are not surprised to find *A Vision* astrological in symbolism: all hells contain parodies of heavens, and visions of harmony and fatality alike tend to be astrological in reference.

We are not surprised either to find the imagery of *A Vision* completely dominated by

> the circle of the moon
> That pitches common things about,
>
> [*Nineteen Hundred and Nineteen*, ll. 3–4]

for, in the traditional cosmology we have been dealing with, the world of the closed cycle of time is a sublunary world. Solar imagery never gets really integrated into *A Vision*, and references to solar symbolism elsewhere in Yeats suggest a pattern of far greater comprehensiveness than *A Vision* ever achieved. The same ironic sublunar perspective comes into *Blood and the Moon*, which turns on the melancholy adage *si la jeunesse savait, si la vieillesse pouvait.*[16] The Eros vision of youth is inseparable from the Adonis vision with its premature death and its "odour of blood," and the vision of wisdom pursued by age is an attempt to grasp the static order of something that must be dead before it can be understood [*Two Songs from a Play*, pt. 2, l. 6; *Blood and the Moon*, l. 40]. In this perspective every civilization leaves its structure unfinished, dying at the top, like Swift and his tree, and the rare individual who gets near the top finds only an empty lumber room full of dead butterflies. In this ironic perspective the "tower" built by human creative power is a structure of pride and arrogance, identical with the tower of Babel which stretched upwards towards the moon, only to be abandoned to ruin by dissensions in the mob. It is also the great "clock tower"[17] which marks but never escapes from the wheel of time. In the end it becomes the "black tower" of death, where "the dead upright" are watched by an immovable guard [*The Black Tower*, l. 7]. At the end of *Blood and the Moon* the moon appears, symbol, as it so often is, of a teasing and elusive perfection which is out of the reach of both the red blood of power and the white bones of wisdom. The moon stared at by the cat Minnaloushe is the image of a cycle that is always changing and yet never changing, as Oedipus kills his father and Cuchulain his son, age after age, through earth and purgatory alike. Behind it are the greater cycles symbolized by the "Full Moon in March,"[18] associated with the two great events of what may have been the one period of decisive change in history, the period between the death of Julius Caesar and the resurrection of Jesus Christ [196, 250].

In *A Vision*, human life struggles upward to the complete subjectivity of phase 15 and downward to the complete objectivity of phase 1 without ever attaining either. The struggle upward is said to be toward nature and the struggle downward toward God, but the completely natural phase 15 is supernatural, and at phase 1 "God" occupies the place of death. What is really at phase 1 is the mob, the undifferentiated mass of a late civilization, the mob to which "Church and State" have been reduced in Yeats's time, according to the poem of that name, and which every great man, or at least every great Irishman, has despised. The "primary" mob is Yeats's Satan, the accuser of mankind. It accuses by making the standard appeals of slave morality, the appeals to conscience, equality, and altruism. In short, it inspired the guilt-ridden political activism of Maud Gonne and the Gore-Booth sisters.[19] The dragon that kills the hero is, ultimately, the mob that drags him down, as the Irish mob slandered Parnell, attacked Synge, and murdered O'Higgins. One thinks of Spenser's Blatant Beast, the emblem of slander and envy. The opinionated female, according to one of Yeats's more tedious themes, expressed in *Michael Robartes and the Dancer* and elsewhere, fights for the dragon instead of the knight trying to rescue her, and thereby impersonates the "staring virgin" tearing out the hero's heart. A more serious aspect of this theme is the connection between Christianity and slave morality which made the sacrifice of Christ, according to *Calvary*, an outrage to Judas and Lazarus and meaningless to the heron and the swan, emblems of an "antithetical" cycle which complements and completes the "primary" half-achievement of Christ.

It is important to notice that the great wheel of *A Vision* turns in the opposite direction from the Eros-Adonis cycle. In the latter the comic rises and the tragic falls. All our language about comedy and tragedy, such as the metaphor in "catastrophe," and the word "fall" itself, shows how inevitable these associations are. But in *A Vision* Yeats is interested in the heroic rather than the tragic, and associates comedy with the kind of realism that he regarded as decadent. Hence in *A Vision* the tragic and heroic are the "antithetical" themes that rise out of the mass, and the comic is the "primary" mass that pulls everything down to itself. This introduces into the poetry certain tragic aspects of the Eros ascent, with the proud Furies climbing the stair of the bloody tower in *To Dorothy Wellesley*, and with the "odour of blood on the ancestral stair" in *Blood and the Moon*. Similarly, there is an innocent aspect of tragedy, which is the inward exuberance or gaiety of the heroic spirit, a gaiety much insisted on in the later poems, notably *Lapis Lazuli*. Such gaiety is unaffected by the tragic or ironic aspects of the world it is in, and which are seen only from the outside. It enables heroes like "the great lord of Chou" in *Vacillation* to say "Let all things pass away" in triumph or in disaster alike, the moment of experience having the reality that anything which dissolves in time misses [ll. 59, 61]. It is also this gay science, as it has been called, that encourages the poet to identify himself with the process of death and corruption and rebirth instead of attempting to escape from it like the saint or mystic.

We began by saying that traditionally there is a Logos vision in poetry, a vision of an intelligently ordered nature, and that this vision can also be found in Yeats. But the Logos vision is, again, traditionally attained only after an arduous upward striving of the soul, and Yeats, once he has attained this point, deliberately turns his back on the Logos vision and goes downward again. This in turn brings him into an infernal or ironic vision of an unending cyclical alternation of forces all through history. But, we said, the real reason for Yeats's turning away from the Logos vision was that for him the sources of creation were within man, in the corruption of the human heart. The language of symbolism usually begins with a creation myth, the story of how things came to be. In the history of mythology, it is the sexual creation myths that come first, stories of how the world was born, or revived like spring from winter. Such myths are centred on an earth-mother, and the more sophisticated myths of a sky-father who *makes* the world and imposes an intelligible pattern on it come later. Yeats speaks of

> the red-rose-bordered hem
> Of her, whose history began
> Before God made the angelic clan.[20]

It is the mother-centred sexual myth that Yeats appears to follow back to its source in the return to the mother which is at once birth and death, womb and tomb.

But having made this descent, Yeats finds that he has once again been sliding down half of a double gyre, this time the one given us by Heraclitus. Once he has made his journey to the heart of the corruptible, he finds that he can now go back again, up from the "fury and mire" of human veins [*Byzantium*, l. 8] toward a dry light, or genuine Logos vision (Heraclitus also uses the term "Logos" [cf. no. 41, p. 208]), in which the gleaming city of light is seen once more, but seen this time as a city whose maker and builder is man. The contrast between Yeats and Shelley on this point is instructive. Yeats speaks of Shelley as "constantly" using towers as poetic images,[21] and it is true that the word occurs very frequently in Shelley. But when it means a building, Shelley's tower tends to be a rather sinister image, like the "Tower of Famine" or the madhouse in *Julian and Maddalo*. Towers used apocalyptically, along with "domes" and "pyramids," are often not buildings, but mountains or clouds or other images of a regenerate nature. This is true even of the *Prometheus Unbound* passage misquoted by Yeats in *Blood and the Moon*, and even Prince Athanase only sits apart from men "*as* in a lonely tower" [*Prince Athanase*, pt. 1, l. 33]. Shelley is certainly a poet in the Eros tradition of Plato and Dante, but his contemplative counterpart of the earthly paradise (as presented in *The Sensitive Plant* and elsewhere) is rather the oracular cave, a much more obviously maternal symbol. The point is small but significant: Shelley, who died at thirty, revolves around an identification of man and a feminine nature; and Yeats's tower, building, and city imagery indicates a symbolism appropriate to an art that looks beyond nature into "the artifice of eternity" [*Sailing to Byzantium*, l. 24]. Like Blake, Yeats finds his real hero not in the Orc of the sexual and historical cycle, much less in the old man Urizen with his premature Logos vision, but in Los the blacksmith, the creative power that builds the eternal golden city out of time.

In *Sailing to Byzantium* the city is seen from afar, and the tower has expanded into an entire chain of being, ranging from the divine ("drowsy Emperor") through the spiritual (traditionally the angels and the stars, here the sages in the fire) and the human ("lords and ladies of Byzantium") down through the rest of creation with the bird and the tree transformed into gold. *Sailing to Byzantium* is very like a conventional Christian poem about the New Jerusalem awaiting the soul after death, except for the paradox in "the artifice of eternity." The builder of Byzantium is not a God conceived as independent of man, and when man is thought of as the only visible creator, nature is no longer a creation but a ruin, and man builds his palaces out of and in defiance of nature. In such a world the tree no longer has the "blind lush leaf" of the dying Attis, but is golden only; yet its gold is not the "staring fury" of *Vacillation* either [l. 17]. Just as the imagery both of the traditional Logos vision and of Yeats's ironic *Vision* is astrological, so the image of Byzantium arising out of the sea of death is alchemical, alchemy being the symbol of a creative *process* in which humanity and nature alike are burned up in the "consummation" of an immortal world of gold, the Golden Age come again.

This reversal of perspective from descent to the corrupt source of creation back up again through the process of creation is a reversal which affects the whole personality, not merely the technical skill of the poet. In *The Shadowy Waters* we are told that those who live ordinary passion-driven lives are helpless puppets of a dream dreamed by the gods. Their passions seem to operate on them as external forces, because, of course, the gods who are dreaming them are their own projected selves. In their view of things, this passive puppet-life is reality, and genuine desire, as expressed in dreams and in love, seems utterly impotent against it. The dreamer, the lover, and the poet are all engaged in reversing the current of reality: they are identifying themselves with the true gods, who are the powers of dream and love and creation themselves. These powers have become reality for them, and what the world calls reality has subsided into dream, the world of "living" that ought to be left to servants.[22] The true gods are the "fire-born moods" of an early poem [*The Moods*, l. 6], the "Presences" of *Among School Children*, and the "Daimons" of the later, profounder, and yet less well understood parts of *A Vision*.

In *Byzantium* the imagery is again Heraclitean and alchemical, the vision of *Sailing to Byzantium* seen from within as a process. We start out in the sea, the beginning and the end of life, and move from the "fury and mire" of human passion upward to the "changeless metal" [l. 22]. This is the movement of discarnation, opposite to the birth-to-death movement of incarnation, in which the spiral wrappings of the dead mummy are unwound, a movement that takes us beyond the world that is "by the moon embittered," and where the gong never ceases to strike [l. 21]. Perhaps, then, the intuition of so many poets, including Dante, that this journey of the soul is also connected with another life after ordinary death has something to be said for it. If man has invented death, as Yeats says, he can recover what he has projected, and find his home in the "translunar Paradise" which he himself can make, and has made [*The Tower*, l. 155].

The poet of the Byzantium poems has gone far beyond the mystery of the fifteenth phase of *A Vision*, presented there as something forever beyond human capacities. The fifteenth phase is guarded, we are told, by Christ and Buddha. Christ descended into the bottom of the cyclical world—made himself of no account, as Paul says—and then rose out of it, with a great company following. Buddha meditated on the deliverance of man from his own Narcissus image, "mirror on mirror mirrored" [*The Statues*, l. 22], the genuine Hercules in heaven liberated from his shadow in Hades. Just as in Eliot's *Burnt Norton* the summit of vision and the depth of annihilation are the same point, the still point of the turning world, so in Yeats the top of the tower is both the rag-and-bone shop of the heart and the translunar Paradise that the heart alone has created.

46

Draft Introduction to Twentieth-Century Literature

1972

From the typescript in NFF, 1988, box 4, file a. This was a draft introduction to the twentieth-century section of an anthology planned by Harcourt Brace Jovanovich, but never published.

The twentieth century has seen the entire world condensing into a single communication unit, and this process has naturally gone further in English than in any other language, as English is now the most dominant language in the world. Not only has there been an immense development of an "American Literature" written in English, but the question where a given author belongs to one side or other of the North Atlantic community is often difficult to decide. In order to save space, the editors have arbitrarily decided that Henry James and Ezra Pound are "American Literature," and that T.S. Eliot, born and educated in America, is "English Literature." Of the other authors, D.H. Lawrence, W.H. Auden, and many others have spent a large part of their lives in America. The same sense of an English literature extending beyond the orbit of Great Britain appears in many guises. Of the major English writers of the twentieth century, at least half a dozen are Anglo-Irish: one, Joseph Conrad, is Polish, and there are flourishing developments of English Literature in every continent of the world, with the possible exception of South America.

The content of much twentieth-century writing, especially fiction, reveals the same global context. Conrad and Somerset Maugham write of the penetration of Western capitalism, culture, and barbarism into Africa and the South Pacific. Henry James and the early Eliot write of a rootless, dispossessed class, neither American nor European, living indifferently in Chicago or Vienna, Virginia or Rome, without any imaginative relation to either. From the early George Moore in the nineteenth century, through Ernest Hemingway and Gertrude Stein in the 1920s, to Beckett in our day, Paris has been the centre of an expatriate literature written very largely in English, but again without reference to a specific English-speaking community.

When we look at the portrayal of this international population in modern poetry and fiction, one characteristic stands out immediately. Such people have no real neighbours; they fit into no social structure as the characters of Jane Austen or Trollope do; they are not essentially bound to a definite place, as most of Dickens's characters are to London. What holds them together is very largely a verbal structure of slogans, clichés, catchwords, the mass response to current events. The awareness of this kind of subintellectual life began with Flaubert's *Bouvard et Pécuchet*, whose minds moved entirely within what he drew off as a supplement to his book: *A Dictionary of Accepted Ideas*. Many of the characters of Hemingway and Beckett are most remarkable for their inarticulateness and their inability to communicate. The minds in the characters of Joyce are again sent swinging mechanically in response to advertisements or stock repeated phrases. In the novels of Galsworthy and Arnold Bennett the characters are not only formed by their social environment, but their minds are wholly conditioned at every point by the verbal stereotype of their class and age period.

The first stage in the imaginative portrayal of this aspect of modern man was an intensification of realism. It was Flaubert, again, who in *Madame Bovary* showed his heroine acting out her life within the stock responses suggested by her own sentimentality. The same thing happens with many characters in the plays of Ibsen. In *Arms and the Man* Bernard Shaw shows the connection between modern war and the shoddy romantic clichés about war which helped to popularize and support it. Many of Conrad's most carefully studied characters, including Lord Jim, never escape from the confused sense of ideology. The next stage is to show characters not only conditioned by their own myths, but driven by forces they do not understand and cannot control. The development of new psychological discoveries in the work of Freud and others was of immense benefit to novelists particularly, in showing the degree to which activity takes the form of unconscious symbolism, or the rationalizing of motives that are not understood. At this point it becomes clear that a great deal of human behaviour, to the extent that it is passive and lacking in self-awareness, is really the acting out of a complex mythology where the characters, corresponding to the gods of older myths, are social conditioning and psychological drives.

We begin to see here how powerful is the sense of antagonism between the creative imagination of the poet or novelist and the kind of life he sees around him. This sense of antagonism expresses itself in irony, and the pervading tone of nearly all serious twentieth-century literature is ironic. The antagonism begins in the nature of the creative imagination itself. Our communications have incredibly expanded in speed to the point at which news is almost instantaneous over the earth and even the longest journeys are now only a matter of hours. But there is always something slow and vegetable about the imagination: it can take in only a very restricted area in any one work. James Joyce lives in Paris with an international reputation, but his mind broods on the tiniest details of the layout of streets and buildings in Dublin. T.S. Eliot writes what appears to be an international poetry, yet *The Waste Land* is intensely rooted in London, even in the City of London. Elsewhere, Robert Frost is a poet of Northern New England, Wallace Stevens of Southern New England, Dylan Thomas of South Wales, Yeats of the Sligo country in Ireland. They may write of many other places, but when they do their writing seems to settle into its place in the same limited and concrete way. This is true even of D.H. Lawrence, whose work is so intensely of the English Midlands in feeling, and yet is quickly localized even when the setting is Mexico or Australia. We notice how many writers identify themselves with smaller and less populous communities, as Faulkner does with the state of Mississippi and Synge with the West of Ireland.

This sense of antagonism between the creative imagination and the social conditions in which it operated has occurred notably three times in English history, and each time has produced a great development of mythopoeic literature. The first was in the age of Elizabeth I and James I—the age of Spenser, Shakespeare, Donne, and the early Milton—when there was so strong a tension between the sense of national unity and the tremendous expanding force which produced the Puritan Revolution, the first settlement in America, the opening up of the Russian trade, and the beginnings of the East India Company. The second period was at the time of the French Revolution, the beginnings of the Industrial Revolution, and the growth of cities, the age which produced the poetry of Blake, Byron, Shelley, Keats, and the early Tennyson. The third great mythopoeic period of English literature was the period from 1920 to 1950, beginning with the First World War and ending roughly with the end of the Second. It remains to be seen why this period, like its predecessors, should be thought of as essentially a period of mythological creation.

47

Wallace Stevens and the Variation Form

1973

From SM, *275–94. First published in* Literary Theory and Structure: Essays in Honor of William K. Wimsatt, John Palmer, and Martin Price, *ed. Frank Brady (New Haven: Yale University Press, 1973), 395–414, and reprinted in abbreviated form in* English Studies Today, *5th ser., ed. Sencer Tonguç (Istanbul: Malbassi, 1973), 389–404. A typescript is in NFF, 1988, box 4, file i. As in no. 37, Frye's original citations of* The Collected Poems of Wallace Stevens (CP) *(New York: Knopf, 1954), which are by page, have been moved to endnotes and now include poem title and line number. However, Frye's method of parenthetically citing Stevens's other works has been retained, and uses the following abbreviations:* L *for* Letters of Wallace Stevens, *selected and ed. Holly Stevens (New York: Knopf, 1967);* NA *for* The Necessary Angel: Essays on Reality and the Imagination *(New York: Knopf, 1951); and* OP *for* Opus Posthumous *by Wallace Stevens, ed. Samuel French Morse (New York: Knopf, 1957).*

We cannot read far in Wallace Stevens's poetry without finding examples of a form that reminds us of the variation form in music, in which a theme is presented in a sequence of analogous but differing settings. Thus in *Sea Surface Full of Clouds* the same type of stanza is repeated five times, each with just enough variation to indicate that the same landscape is being seen through five different emotional moods. Another type of variation form appears in *Thirteen Ways of Looking at a Blackbird,* where a series of thirteen little imagist poems are related by the common theme of the blackbird, and which, to pursue the musical analogy perhaps further than it will go, gives more the effect of a chaconne or passacaglia. Sometimes the explicit theme is missing and only the variations appear, as in *Like Decorations in a Nigger Cemetery.*

We notice also that in the titles of Stevens's poems the image of variation frequently turns up, either literally, as in *Variations on a Summer Day*, or metaphorically, as in *Nuances of a Theme By Williams*, *Analysis of a Theme*, and, perhaps, *Repetitions of a Young Captain*. *The Man with the Blue Guitar* also gives us a strong sense of reading through a set of thirty-three variations, or related imaginative presentations, of a single theme. Then again, the long meditative theoretical poems written in a blank tercet form, *Notes toward a Supreme Fiction*, *The Auroras of Autumn*, *An Ordinary Evening in New Haven*, *The Pure Good of Theory*, are all divided into sections of the same length. *An Ordinary Evening* has thirty-one sections of six tercets each; the *Supreme Fiction*, three parts of ten sections each, thirty sections in all, each of seven tercets; and similarly with the others. This curious formal symmetry, which cannot be an accident, also reminds us of the classical variation form in which each variation has the same periodic structure and harmonic sequence. Even the numbers that often turn up remind us of the thirty Goldberg variations, the thirty-three Diabelli waltz variations, and so on.

The variation form in Stevens is a generic application of the principle that every image in a poem is a variation of the theme or subject of that poem. This principle is the first of three "effects of analogy" mentioned in Stevens's essay of that title. There are two other "effects." One is that "every image is a restatement of the subject of the image in the terms of an attitude" (*NA*, 128). This is practically the same thing as Eliot's objective correlative,[1] and is illustrated in *Sea Surface Full of Clouds*, where five different moods are unified by the fact that they all have the same correlative. Stevens also says, "In order to avoid abstractness, in writing, I search out instinctively things that express the abstract and yet are not in themselves abstractions" (*L*, 290). His example is the statue in *Owl's Clover*, which he also calls a "variable" symbol (*L*, 311). The implication is that such images are variations on the idea of the poem which is within the poem of words, the true as distinct from the nominal subject or theme (*OP*, 223). We note that the correlative in Stevens may pair with a concept as well as with an emotion, which helps to explain why his commentaries on his own poems in the letters are so often woodenly allegorical.

The third "effect of analogy" is that "every image is an intervention on the part of the image-maker" (*NA*, 128). This principle takes us deep into Stevens's central notion of poetry as the result of a struggle, or balance, or compromise, or tension, between the two forces that he calls imagination and reality. We notice that in the musical theme with variations, the theme is frequently a composition by someone else or comes from a different musical context. Similarly the poet works with imagination, which is what he has, and reality, which is given him. So, from Stevens's point of view, poems could be described as the variations that imagination makes on the theme of reality. In *Sea Surface Full of Clouds* a question is asked in each variation about who or what created the picture in front of us, and the answer, given each time in French, defines a distinctive mood of the imagination.

In a letter Stevens says, "Sometimes I believe most in the imagination for a long time, and then, without reasoning about it, turn to reality and believe in that and that alone. But both of these things project themselves endlessly and I want them to do just that" (*L*, 710). This somewhat helpless remark indicates the strength of the sense of polarity in his poetic world. Stevens often speaks of the intense pressure that the sense of external reality exerts on the modern mind. One of the *Adagia* says: "In the presence of extraordinary actuality, consciousness takes the place of imagination" (*OP*, 165). Consciousness, by itself, is simple awareness of the external world. It sees; it may even select what it sees, but it does not fight back. The consciousness fighting back, with a subjective violence corresponding to the objective violence of external pressure (cf. *NA*, 36),[2] is the consciousness rising to imagination.

The imagination confronts a reality which reflects itself but is not itself. If it is weak, it may either surrender to reality or run away from it. If it surrenders, we have what is usually called realism, which, as Stevens often makes clear, is almost the opposite of what he means by reality. He says, for instance, in connection with the painting of Jack Yeats, that "the purely realistic mind never experiences any passion for reality" (*L*, 597). This maxim would also apply to the "socialist realism" demanded in Marxist countries, for which Stevens never expresses anything but contempt. The imagination that runs away retreats from the genuinely imaginative world into a merely imaginary one, for, Stevens says, "If poetry is limited to the vaticinations of the imagination, it soon becomes worthless" (*L*, 500). Certain recurring symbols in Stevens represent the kind of pseudo-conquest of reality which the imagination pretends to make whenever reality is not there: one of them is the moon. Such imaginary triumphs take place in a self-contained world of words which is one of the things that Stevens means by false rhetoric, or "Rodomontade"[3] (*NA*, 61). The world of false rhetoric is a world where the imagination encounters no resistance from anything material, where the loneliness and alienation of the mind, about which Stevens speaks so eloquently, has consoled itself with pure solipsism.

Stevens says that it is a fundamental principle about the imagination that "it does not create except as it transforms" (*L*, 364). It is the function of reality to set free the imagination and not to inhibit it. Reality is at its most inhibiting when it is most externalized, as it is in our own time. In *Two or Three Ideas* Stevens speaks of the way in which the pressure of externality today has created a culture of what he calls "detached styles," and which he characterizes as "the unsuccessful, the ineffective, the arbitrary, the literary, the non-umbilical, that which in its highest degree would still be words" (*OP*, 212). In one prophetic flash, which sums up the essence of the world we have been living through for the past few years, he speaks of this world of false imagination as the product of "irrationality provoked by prayer, whisky, fasting, opium, or the hope of publicity" (*OP*, 218). It follows that Stevens does not accept the mystique of the unconscious and has nothing of Yeats's or Joyce's feeling for the dream world as having a peculiarly close relation to the creative process. He always associates creativity with cognition, with consciousness, even with calculation. "Writing poetry is a conscious activity. While poems may very well occur, they had very much better be caused" (*L*, 274).

Stevens associates his word "reality" with the phrase "things as they are" [*NA*, 25], which implies that for him reality has a close relation to the external physical world as we perceive it. The imagination contemplates "things as they are," seeing its own unreality mirrored in them, and its principle of contemplation Stevens calls resemblance or analogy. He also calls it, quite logically, "Narcissism" (*NA*, 80). This word points to the danger of uncontrolled imagination and the ease with which it can assume that there is another reality on the other side of things as they are. Traditional religious poetry, for instance, projects heavens and hells as objective and hidden realities, though it can construct them only out of the material of things as they are. Crispin, the hero of one of Stevens's most elaborate variation poems, soon comes to a point at which he can say, "Here was the veritable ding an sich, at last."[4] But this is a Kantian phrase, and Stevens is not Kantian: reality for him is always phenomenal, something that "seems" as well as is,[5] and there is no alternative version of it that the poet should be trying to reach. Hidden realities always turn out to be unreal, and therefore simply mirrors of the imagination itself. Similarly, "poetry will always be a phenomenal thing" (*L*, 300).

Stevens's arguments are poetic and not philosophical, and like many poetic arguments they turn on a verbal trick. The trick in this case consists in using the special-pleading term "reality" for the external physical world, which means that conceptions set over against this "reality" have to be called, or associated with, the unreal. Stevens is not unaware of this by any means, but his use of the word "reality," which becomes almost obsessive in the letters, indicates that, like his spiritual sister Emily Dickinson, he has a Puritanic distrust of all self-transcending mental efforts, especially mysticism. More particularly, he feels that, as the poet's language is the language of sense experience and concrete imagery, any poet who bypasses things as they are, however subtly, is dodging the central difficulty of poetry. Such poets, who look for some shortcut or secret passage through reality to something else, and regard poetry as a kind of verbal magic, have what Stevens calls a "marginal" imagination, and he associates this marginal imagination, which explores itself to find its own analogue in reality, with, among others, Valéry, Eliot, and Mallarmé [*NA*, 115].

Stevens goes even further in suggesting that the conquest of reality made by the reason is also somewhat facile compared to that of the imagination, because it is possible for reason, in some degree, to live in a self-contained world and shut its gates in the face of reality. One of the products of reason is the theological belief in reality as a creation, a product of the infinite imagination of God. Such a belief is repugnant to Stevens: this would mean that reality is analogous to the imagination. The poet is a Jacob who has to wrestle with the necessary angel of reality, and if reality is itself ultimately a "supreme fiction," or something made out of nothing, then all his agonized efforts and struggles are a put-up job, something fixed or rigged, as so many wrestling matches are. Stevens says:

> The arrangement contains the desire of
> The artist. But one confides in what has no
> Concealed creator. One walks easily
>
> The unpainted shore, accepts the world
> As anything but sculpture.[6]

So whatever the imagination may do to reality, reality continues to present something residually external, some donkey's carrot pulling us on, something sticking through everything we construct within it. Even in the moment of death (or what appears to be death, on the last page of the *Collected Poems*), we confront something "outside" giving us the sense of "a new knowledge of reality."[7] Or, as Stevens says in prose, "Poetry has to do with reality in that concrete and individual aspect of it which the mind can never tackle altogether on its own terms, with matter that is foreign and alien in a way in which abstract systems, ideas in which we detect an inherent pattern, a structure that belongs to the ideas themselves, can never be" (*OP*, 236). The imagination is driven by a "rage for order,"[8] but it works toward, not the complete ordering of existence, but rather a sense of equipoise or balance between itself and what is not itself.

We soon come to understand that for Stevens there are different levels or degrees of reality (*NA*, 7),[9] arranged in a ladder or mountain or winding stair in which the poet has to undertake what he calls an "ascent through illusion" (*NA*, 81). In his essay "A Collect of Philosophy" Stevens attempts to list a few philosophical conceptions which seem to him to be inherently poetic, meaning by that, presumably, conceptions that particularly appeal to him as a poet. Among these, the theme of *anabasis* or ascent, the theme of Dante, looms up prominently (*OP*, 193). At the bottom of the ladder is the sense of reality as an undifferentiated external world, or what Stevens calls a *Lumpenwelt* (*NA*, 174). Such a world, Stevens says, is "of one color" (*NA*, 26),[10] a "basic slate,"[11] a sinister or scowling "pediment of appearance."[12] As such, it forces the imagination to define itself as its opposite, or nothingness. At this point a construct emerges which is rather similar to the construct of being and nothingness in Sartre.[13] The *Lumpenwelt* is reality on the minimum imaginative basis; the imagination on the same basis is merely the unreal: reality is everything; the imagination is nothing. The imagination never brings anything into the world, Stevens says in an unconscious echo of the burial service (*NA*, 59), though it is not quite so true for him that it can take nothing out. This confrontation of being and nothingness, the starting point of imaginative energy, is the vision of the listener in *The Snow Man*, who,

> nothing himself, beholds
> Nothing that is not there and the nothing that is.[14]

Traditionally, the world of becoming has always been regarded as the product of being and nothingness. For Stevens there is no reality of being in the traditional sense of something that does not change. Whenever we try to imagine an unchanging ideal, we get involved in the hopeless paradox of Keats's Grecian urn, where the little town on the hidden side of the urn will never be inhabited to all eternity. The woman in *Sunday Morning* asks resentfully, "Why should she give her bounty to the dead?"[15] but soon comes to realize that she cannot have any alternative without change, and therefore death, at the heart of it. Reality is phenomenal and belongs to the world of becoming. In the very late poem *Of Mere Being* (*OP*, 117) the only unchanging thing about being is that it remains external, "at the end of the mind," "beyond the last thought."

Two of the requirements of the "supreme fiction" are that it must change and that it must give pleasure, and it is clear that for Stevens these two things are much the same thing, change being the only real source of pleasure. Over and over Stevens returns to what he calls "the motive for metaphor," the fact that what is change in reality is also pleasure in the imagination. The imagination, the principle of the unreal, breaks up and breaks down the tyranny of what is there by unifying itself with what is not there, and so suggesting the principle of variety in its existence. This is the point of identity on which all art is founded: in the imaginations of Cézanne and Klee, Stevens says, reality is transmuted from substance into subtlety (*NA*, 174). We get the idea of unchanging being from the thereness of the physical world, the fact that it doesn't go away. What does go away, and is to that extent unreal, is what the unreality of the imagination builds on. The imagination, in short, "skims the real for its unreal."[16]

This kind of activity gives us a relatively simple type of variation form, the kind represented by the *Blackbird* poem. Here the variations are what Stevens calls the "casual exfoliations" (*NA*, 86) of an imagination contemplating a real thing. The recipe for this type of variation form is given in the poem *Someone Puts a Pineapple Together*, one of "Three Academic Pieces" in *The Necessary Angel*:

Divest reality
Of its propriety. Admit the shaft
Of that third planet to the table and then . . . [*NA*, 86]

The third planet, he has explained, is the imagination, and there follow a series of twelve numbered variations on the pineapple. It is clear that such a conception of imagination and reality has much to do with the affinity to the pictorial in Stevens, with his fondness for subjects analogous to still life or landscape painting, where the real object and the imaginative variation of it are most dramatically exhibited. Such variation poems are fanciful in Coleridge's sense of the term: Stevens was familiar with Coleridge's distinction, which he acquired through his readings of I.A. Richards (*NA*, 10).[17] They are, so to speak, cyclical poems, where the variations simply surround the theme. As such, they are not the most serious kind of writing. Stevens speaks of the almost total exclusion of "thinking" from such a poem as *Variations on a Summer Day* (*L*, 346) and says also, "I have no doubt that supreme poetry can be produced only on the highest possible level of the cognitive" (*L*, 500). Again one thinks of the musical parallel. The greatest examples of the variation form, such as the last movement of Beethoven's Opus 111, do not merely diversify the theme: they are sequential and progressive forms as well, and we feel at the end that they have, so to speak, exhausted the theme, done what there is to be done with it. We have now to see if we can discover a sequential and progressive aspect to Stevens's variation form also.

We began with a confrontation between imagination and reality, in which the former is a negation, the opposite of reality. Then we found that the imagination can intensify reality by seizing on the "unreal" aspect of it, the aspect that changes and therefore gives pleasure. Stevens says, "A sense of reality keen enough to be in excess of the normal sense of reality creates a reality of its own" (*NA*, 79). As he goes on to say, this is a somewhat circular statement, and one would expect it to lead to some such principle as Blake's "As the Eye—Such the Object" [Annotations to *The Works of Sir Joshua Reynolds*, p. 34; E645], the principle that the degree of reality depends on the energy of the imagination. Stevens resists this implication, because of his constant fear that the imagination will simply replace reality and thereby deprive itself of its own material cause. For him the imagination is rather an informing principle of reality, transmuting its uniformity into variety, its "heavy scowl"[18] into lightness and pleasure. Still, it seems clear that we cannot go on indefinitely thinking of the imagination merely as a negation or nothingness.

The fact that the imagination seizes on the changing aspect of reality means that it lives in a continuous present. This means not only that "the imperfect is our paradise,"[19] but that the imagination is always beginning. The only reason for finishing anything is that we can then be rid of it and can come around to the point at which we can begin again. The shoddiness of being fixated on the past, of refusing to discard what he calls the "hieratic" (*NA*, 58), meets us everywhere in Stevens. The imagination in the sunlit world of reality is like food in hot weather: whatever is kept spoils. Hence "one of the motives in writing is renewal" (*OP*, 220). This emphasis on constant fresh beginnings is connected, naturally, with the steadfast resistance to anything resembling an echo or an influence from other poets in Stevens, in striking contrast to the absorption of echoes and influences that we find in, for instance, Eliot.

What is true of the past is also true of the future, the desire to use the imagination to make over reality that we find in so many romantics, revolutionaries, and spokesmen of the irrational. Stevens speaks of this desire with a good deal of sympathy and understanding, for instance, in his essay on the irrational in poetry (*OP*, 216), where he links the irrational, once again, with the pressure of external fact on the modern poet and his consequent sense of claustrophobia and desire for freedom. *Owl's Clover* is a carefully considered effort to come to terms with the revolutionary desire for freedom and equality on a vast social scale. But when the imagination is used as part of an attempt to make over reality, it imposes its own unreality on it. The result is that perversion of belief which we see in all religions, including the contemporary atheistic ones. Belief derives from the imaginative unreal: what we really believe in is a fiction, something we have made up ourselves. But all beliefs, when they become institutionalized, tend to ascribe some hidden reality to themselves, a projection of the imagination which can end only in disillusionment or self-hypnotism. The "romantic" of this type (Stevens uses the word "romantic" in several senses, but this one is pejorative: cf. *L*, 277) is "incapable of abstraction" (*NA*, 139), abstraction being among other things the ability to hold a belief as a "supreme fiction" without projecting it to the other side of reality.

At the same time Stevens holds to an intensely social conception of poetry and its function, though a deeply conservative one. The poet, he says, should try to reach the "centre," and by this he means first of all a social centre. The poet expresses among other things "that ultimate good sense which we term civilization" (*NA*, 116). For him reality includes human society as well. As such, the imagination defines the style of a culture or civilization: it is whatever it is that makes everything in Spain look Spanish, and makes every cultural product of Spain a variation on a Spanish theme. Stevens uses the phrase "variations on a theme" in connection with a closely related aspect of culture: the predominance and persistence of a convention, as in medieval or Chinese painting (*NA*, 73).

If we ask what the characteristics of such imaginative penetration of reality are in human life, the words "nobility" and "elegance" come fairly close, though Stevens admits that they are dangerous words. The quality in literature that we recognize as heroic, the power of the imagination to make things look more intensely real, is a quality of illusion in reality that is at the same time a growth in reality. The imagination is thus socially aristocratic, though not necessarily in a class sense. The more power it gains, the more freedom and privilege it enjoys, and the more confident society becomes about its culture. In a time like ours the imagination is more preoccupied in fighting its environment, which presses in on it much harder. In the poem *Mrs. Alfred Uruguay*, Mrs. Uruguay herself rides up a mountain in the state of the snow man, looking at her world honestly but reductively, as totally without illusion. She meets going down the mountain a "capable man" who recalls the noble rider of Stevens's earliest prose essay, whose imagination is of the same kind as her own, but is more emancipated, and hence to some extent its fulfilment. It is he who creates

> out of the martyrs' bones
> The ultimate of elegance: the imagined land.[20]

So our confrontation between a negative imagination and a positive reality has reached the point where this negation has informed human civilization and produced a style of living. This process, considered in an individual context, is the theme of the sequential variation form *The Comedian as the Letter C*. Crispin, the hero of the poem, begins with the principle: "Nota: Man is the intelligence of his soil," a strictly Cartesian principle in which man is the "sovereign ghost" [*CP*, 27]. This first variation is headed *The World without Imagination*. The fourth variation brings us to *The Idea of a Colony*, which begins:

> Nota: his soil is man's intelligence.
> That's better. That's worth crossing seas to find. [*CP*, 36]

Stevens calls Crispin a "profitless philosopher" [*CP*, 45–6], says that he never discovers the meaning of life (*L*, 293), that social contact would have been a catastrophe for him (*L*, 295), that he is an everyday man whose life has not the slightest adventure (*L*, 778), and symbolizes him by the one letter of the alphabet which has no distinctive sound of its own.

Nevertheless, Crispin works very hard to achieve his own kind of reality, and if he is not a poet he is at least a colonizer, someone who achieves a lifestyle out of a pilgrimage and a settlement in new surroundings. The poem as a whole goes around in an ironic circle, and Crispin ends much where he began, using his imagination as so many people do, to select and exclude rather than create, a realist who rejects reality. Hence the final line of the poem, "So may the relation of each man be clipped." Stevens may also have Crispin partly in mind when he says, "The man who has been brought up in an artificial school becomes intemperately real. The Mallarmiste becomes the proletarian novelist" (*OP*, 221). Still, Crispin represents something of the historical process that produced the culture and the tradition out of which Stevens himself developed, moving from Baroque Europe to realistic New England.

We have next to see how a negation can be an informing principle in reality. This brings us to Stevens's conception of the "supreme fiction." The imagination informs reality through fictions or myths (the word "fictive" in Stevens means mythical), which are the elements of a model world. This model world is not "reality," because it does not exist, it is not "there"; but it is an unborn or, perhaps, potential reality which becomes a growth out of reality itself. Stevens quotes Simone Weil, obviously with approval, on the subject of "decreation," a moving from the created to the uncreated, going in the opposite direction from destruction, which moves from the created to nothingness (*NA*, 174). The conception is Stevens's, though the terms are not. The first law of the supreme fiction is that it must be abstract. It is abstract for the same reason that a god is not reducible to his image. The supreme fiction is not a thing, something to be pointed to or contemplated or thought of as achieved. In its totality, the supreme fiction is poetry or the work of the imagination as a whole, but this totality never separates from the perceiving subject or becomes external. Stevens says, "The abstract does not exist, but . . . the fictive abstract is as immanent in the mind of the poet, as the idea of God is immanent in the mind of the theologian" (*L*, 434). This last indicates that God is one of the supreme fictions. God for Stevens, whatever he may be in himself, must be for man an unreality of the imagination, not a reality, and his creative power can manifest itself only in the creations of man. The explicit statement that God and the imagination are one is made by the "interior paramour," an anima-figure working under the direction of the imagination.[21]

According to Stevens, "The wonder and mystery of art, as indeed of religion in the last resort, is the revelation of something 'wholly other' by which the inexpressible loneliness of thinking is broken and enriched" (*OP*, 237).[22] The phrase "wholly other," which is in quotation marks, suggests the existential theology of Karl Barth, as relayed through a poet who calls himself a "dried-up Presbyterian" (*L*, 792). In Barth, of course, the otherness of God and the alienation of man are conditions of man's unregenerate state. God does not remain wholly other for two reasons: first, he has created and redeemed man; and second, he has revealed himself. Let us see what reality in Stevens can do along parallel lines.

When Crispin discovers that the Cartesian principle "Man is the intelligence of his soil" is less true than its reverse, that "his soil is man's intelligence," Stevens is saying that the antithesis of imagination and reality did not begin as such. Man grew out of "reality," and the consciousness which enables him also to draw away from it is a recent development. The human is "alien," but it is also "the inhuman making choice of a human self" (*NA*, 89). The imagination is a product of reality, its Adam, so to speak, or exiled son. Just as, in Dante's *Purgatorio*, the poet makes his way back to the Eden which is his own original home, so the imagination contemplates the "rock," the dead inert reality before it, and realizes that it is itself the rock come to life. "I am what is around me,"[23] the poet says, and he continually returns to the sense of the "wholly other" as not only the object but the origin of the sense of identity.

The rock is not dead, because it has never died; death is a process, not a condition. It represents rather the unconscious and undifferentiated external world at the bottom of the imaginative ladder, where the sense of thereness is overpowering and the imagination is simply its negation. In the course of time leaves cover the rock: life emerges from the inanimate, breaks up and diversifies the heavy *Lumpenwelt*. Life, then, if Stevens's general argument still applies, is the negation of the inanimate, the unreal at work in the real. The imagination does with "things as they are" what life does with the rock, and the poet's imagination is inseparably attached to the articulating of life in the rest of the world. The "howl" of the doves (*OP*, 97), the "cry" of the leaves (*OP*, 96), the sea in *The Idea of Order at Key West*, the *Bantams in Pine-Woods*, who are praising themselves and not a divine bantam in the rising sun, are all part of the symphony of life in which the poet has his own voice. We speak of a will to live, and similarly "imagination is the will of things."[24]

The poem *Oak Leaves Are Hands* describes a "Lady Lowzen," who is also the goddess Flora, and who continues to "skim the real for its unreal" in human imagination as formerly in the vegetable world. Lady Lowzen is "chromatic," and the delight of vegetable nature in colour supplies Stevens with his chief image for the imagination, which he thinks of as, so to speak, the colouring principle of reality. The basis of nature is metamorphosis, the basis of poetry is metaphor, and metaphor and metamorphosis are for Stevens interchangeable terms. Stevens completes the identification by saying "in metaphor the imagination is life" (*NA*, 73). In this context the variations which the imagination makes on reality join the Darwinian theme with variations in which every variety is a mutation thrown out toward the environment, the "reality" it has to struggle with, until a successful mutation blends and identifies with that reality.

The limit of poetry, as Stevens himself frequently remarks, has always been the imaginatively conceivable, not what is or "things as they are," and any poet deeply impressed by things as they are is apt to suffer from imaginative claustrophobia. Stevens has relegated God to the imaginative unreal, a fiction the human mind creates. He has made an uncompromising bourgeois rejection of all politically revolutionary values. He dismisses Nietzsche and his doctrine of the self-transcendence of man as being "as perfect a means of getting out of focus as a little bit too much to drink" (*L*, 432). What is left? How much further can a "harmonious skeptic"[25] carry his rage for order? Even things as they are present themes which the poet cannot avoid and yet can hardly deal with on their terms. For instance, a surprising number of Stevens's poems are about death, and death is one subject where the imagination, like Good Deeds in *Everyman*, may be prevailed on to accompany the poet as his guide, while "reality," in whatever form or disguise, will always mutter some excuse and slope off.[26] When Stevens gets to the point of saying that "Life and Nature are one" (*L*, 533), he has left very little room for any reality which he has not in some other context called unreal.

In Stevens's cultural situation about the only consistent "position" left is that of a secular humanism. But, he says, the more he sees of humanism the less he likes it, and, more briefly and explicitly, "humanism is not enough" (*L*, 489). He also says, "Between humanism and something else, it might be possible to create an acceptable fiction" (*L*, 449) and that "there are fictions that are extensions of reality" (*L*, 430). This last concession means that Stevens is capable, at least in his poetry, of sweeping "reality" out of the way as a superego symbol and of reducing it to its proper role as the material cause of poetry.

In reality, man is a social being, and society is partly an aggregate, a mass of men, often dominated by, and expressing their will through, some kind of hero or leader. The hero in this sense is a fiction which has been, like so many other fictions, misapplied and misunderstood by society. In two poems particularly, *Examination of the Hero in a Time of War* and *Life on a Battleship*, Stevens shows us how the dictatorial hero or charismatic leader is a false projection of the imagination, like the heavens and hells that are created by the imagination and are then asserted to be actual places in the world which is there. The genuine form of this fiction is the conception of all men as a single man, where the difference between the individual and the mass has ceased to exist. Or, as Stevens puts it, in commenting on a passage in *Notes toward a Supreme Fiction* which contains the phrase "leaner being,"[27] "The trouble with humanism is that man as God remains man, but there is an extension of man, the leaner being, in fiction, a possibly more than human human, a composite human. The act of recognizing him is the act of this leaner being moving in on us" (*L*, 434). This "leaner being" is the "central man" or "man of glass"[28] who is all men, and whom Stevens portrays as a titanic being striding the skies.[29] Even Crispin reaches an apotheosis of identity with this being (*OP*, 24).

In this conception of a "general being or human universe,"[30] we are still in the area of fictions, but by now we understand that the poet "gives to life the supreme fictions without which we are unable to conceive of it" (*NA*, 31). Whatever unreal grows out of reality becomes real, like the graft of art on nature which Polixenes urges on Perdita in *The Winter's Tale*.[31] The human universe is still a fiction and to that extent is not strictly true, but, as Abraham Cowley said of the philosophy of Thomas Hobbes, "'Tis so like Truth, 'twill serve our turn as well" [*To Mr. Hobs*, l. 11]. In any case, on this level of fiction we can understand how poetry can be called "a transcendent analogue composed of the particulars of reality" (*NA*, 130), the word "transcendent" here being used, I think, quite carefully in its philosophical sense as going beyond sense experience but not beyond the mental organization of that experience. Certain sentences in *The Necessary Angel* which Stevens mutters out of the corner of his mouth when he thinks his censor is not listening take on a new and illuminating significance. One such sentence is this one from "Imagination as Value": "The imagination that is satisfied by politics, whatever the nature of the politics, has not the same value as the imagination that seeks to satisfy, say, the universal mind, which, in the case of a poet, would be the imagination that tries to penetrate to basic images, basic emotions, and so to compose a fundamental poetry even older than the ancient world" (*NA*, 144–5). This universal mind is the mind that has produced "the essential poem at the centre of things,"[32] which is *the* supreme fiction as such. In this perspective, "reality" becomes the stabilizing principle which enables us, even as we outgrow our gods, to recognize, even in the act of coming around to the beginning again, that the creative faculties are always the same faculties and that "the things created are always the same things" (*OP*, 211). In all the variations of what might be we can still hear the theme of what is there.

The supreme fiction of the "central," which is the total form of both man and the human imagination, takes us into a very different context of variability, a context less Darwinian than Thomist. It would be easy, but simplistic, to say that ultimately what is real in Stevens is the universal, the universal being the theme of which the individual is the variation. Easy, because one could quote a good many passages from the later poems, at least, in support of it; but simplistic, because the traditional context of the real universal is a kind of essential world that Stevens never at any point accepts. "Logically," says Stevens, "I ought to believe in essential imagination, but that has its difficulties" (*L*, 370). In the early *Peter Quince at the Clavier* we have the line "The body dies; the body's beauty lives."[33] Considering the number of poets, in English literature and elsewhere, who would have drawn a Platonic inference from that statement, it comes as a deliberate and calculated shock for Stevens to say:

> Beauty is momentary in the mind—
> The fitful tracing of a portal,
> But in the flesh it is immortal.[34]

"A Collect of Philosophy" has nothing of medieval realism, though it reflects Stevens's fascination with Plato, but it does express a keen interest in such conceptions as Alexander's "compresence" of mind and existence, and, more particularly, in the great passage in Whitehead's *Science and the Modern World* in which Whitehead rejects the conception of "simple location" in space and announces the doctrine of interpenetration, the doctrine that everything is everywhere at once.[35] Stevens's comment on this passage is, "These words are pretty obviously words from a level where everything is poetic, as if the statement that every location involves an aspect of itself in every other location produced in the imagination a universal iridescence, a dithering of presences and, say, a complex of differences" (*OP*, 192). This last phrase shows that Stevens is still thinking within the metaphor of a theme and variations.

Stevens often refers to Eliot as a poet who represents the exact opposite of everything he stood for himself,[36] and perhaps we are now beginning to understand why. The fifth way of looking at a blackbird, for example, is a way that Eliot constantly refuses to look at it:

> I do not know which to prefer,
> The beauty of inflections
> Or the beauty of innuendoes,
> The blackbird whistling
> Or just after.[37]

"A Collect of Philosophy" assumes in passing that all knowledge is knowledge after the experience of the knowledge (*OP*, 190). For Eliot, the fact that there is a split second between an experience and the awareness of having had the experience is a memento of the fall of man. All three dimensions of time for Eliot are categories of unreality: the no longer, the not yet, and the never quite. Our ordinary existence in this time is the fallen shadow of the life we might have lived if there had been no fall, in which experience and consciousness would be the same thing, and in which the present moment would be a real moment, an eternal now. Eliot's imagination revolves around the figure of Percival in the Grail castle, who, in the words of *The Dry Salvages*, "had the experience but missed the meaning" [l. 95] because he was afraid to put the question that would have unified experience and meaning. In this sense we are all Prufrocks, vaguely aware that there is an "overwhelming question" [*The Love Song of J. Alfred Prufrock*, l. 10] to be asked, and wasting our lives in various devices for not asking it.

Stevens has nothing of Eliot's sense of the phenomenal world as a riddle, to be solved by some kind of conscious experience that annihilates it. When we start climbing the Ash-Wednesday staircase, we have to regard such things as "a slotted window bellied like the fig's fruit" [*Ash-Wednesday*, l. 108] as a distraction. This is because at the top of Eliot's staircase is a total unification and an absorption of reality into the infinite being of God. Like Dante whom he is following Eliot wants his pilgrimage to pass beyond the categories of time and space and the cycle of nature that revolves within these categories. The slotted window is an image of that cycle, the vegetable cycle of flower and fruit, the cycle of human life that begins with birth from a womb. Stevens does not resemble Yeats any more closely than he resembles Eliot, but, like Yeats, he sides with the "self" in the *Dialogue of Self and Soul*. For his Mrs. Uruguay, as for Yeats, the top of the mountain or staircase or whatever has to be climbed is the top of the natural cycle, and the fulfilment of climbing it is in coming down again. In Stevens, the imagination is life, and the only way to kill it is to take it outside nature, into a world where it has swallowed nature and become a total periphery or circumference, instead of remaining "central." So for Stevens, as in a very different way for Joyce in *Finnegans Wake*, the cycle of nature is the only possible image of whatever is beyond the cycle, "the same anew."[38]

There is an elaborate imagery of the seasons of the year in Stevens, where summer represents the expanded and fulfilled imagination, autumn the more restricted and realistic imagination, and winter the reduction to a black-and-white world where reality is "there" and the imagination set over against it is simply unreal. The emotional focus of this imagery comes at the moment in spring when the first blush of colour enters the world with "an access of color, a new and unobserved, slight dithering"[39] (the last word echoes the comment on Whitehead already quoted), or when a bird's cry "at the earliest ending of winter" signals "a new knowledge of reality,"[40] or at Easter. "On Easter," says Stevens, "the great ghost of what we call the next world invades and vivifies this present world, so that Easter seems like a day of two lights, one the sunlight of the bare and physical end of winter, the other the double light" (*OP*, 239). What Easter symbolizes to Stevens is that we are constantly trying to close up our world on the model of our own death, to become an "owl in the sarcophagus." As long as some reality is still outside us we are still alive, and what is still external in that reality is what has a renewing power for us. This vision is the point at which "Dazzle yields to a clarity and we observe,"[41] when we see the world as total process, extending over both death and life, always new, always just beginning, always full of hope, and possessed by the innocence of an uncreated world which is unreal only because it has never been fixed in death. This is also the point at which the paradox of reality and imagination comes into focus for the poet and he understands that

> We make, although inside an egg,
> Variations on the words spread sail.[42]

48
Aldous Huxley

4–5 December 1973

Comments on the CBC radio program "Ideas," during a series on "Aldous Huxley and Beyond." Transcribed from the CBC audiotape by Monika Lee. Regrettably, some of the interviewer's questions were not recoverable.

INTERVIEWER: This same intellectual isolation is one of the cornerstones of Huxley's fame, as Northrop Frye, professor emeritus, University of Toronto, points out.

FRYE: Well, Huxley is eminently worth reading, because of the quality of his intelligence, the far-ranging versatility of his intelligence, and his command in fiction of a form of satire which, I think, relatively few people have equalled. There is a kind of integration in Huxley, of intelligence and curiosity and vision, of interest in religion and society and science, which makes him a writer of the very highest quality of cultivation, if he doesn't have that kind of genius that speaks of the absolute authority of somebody who has reached the top level of literature. I think that in the twentieth century particularly, you have to deal with a kind of duality within some of the greatest writers. That is, you have, in the great poets of the twentieth century, an imagination which has made them great poets and, at the same time, a kind of ego which makes them rather repugnant to some people at any rate as personalities. That is, Eliot is a poet you've got to take account of in the twentieth century, but the quality of his mind and the quality of his social outlook puts a lot of people off. Then with Lawrence, you've got a great poet and you've got a hysteric and in Ezra Pound you've got a great poet and you've got a nut, and the critic particularly has to try to separate these two. Now in Huxley, I don't think that there is this kind of dichotomy of visionary and ego, because I think he was desperately anxious to overcome his ego, to try to absorb it in vision.

Interviewer: The author though, what about the blind author?
Frye: Major writers who have had trouble with their eyesight usually develop their ears to an extraordinary pitch of delicacy and perception. I'm thinking mainly of Milton and of Joyce. Those were blind or near blind writers and their ears took over at a certain point and produced this marvellous, oracular sound of *Paradise Lost* and of *Finnegans Wake*. In Huxley, I don't find that sensitivity to words as words. He seems always to think of words as a rather approximate way of conveying meanings, so that there isn't an oral sensitivity in his work that takes over.

Interviewer: How did he see his contemporaries?
Frye: I know that he was a great admirer of Lawrence and he presents that rather absurd figure of Rampion in *Point Counter Point* as a Lawrentian figure,[1] but I find Huxley easier to read in large quantities than I find Lawrence.

Frye: I think it's a great mistake to judge people in terms of literary genres that they didn't attempt. That is, Huxley's characters in a novel like *Point Counter Point* are not supposed to come to life. The characters are puppets. They are people who simply respond to stimulus and reflex. They are the people in the first level of Dante's *Inferno*, who, as Virgil says to Dante, are people who are not dead, because they never come to life. They'd never been alive. That's the kind of people that he's interested in drawing and so, as that kind of writer, he's a satirist, and I think a satirist in, say, the Peacock tradition, but not necessarily a novelist in the George Eliot or Trollope tradition. That's not what he's trying to do. I think that Huxley is writing a certain kind of comedy of manners, which requires his characters to be pretty automatic, doll-like figures.

Frye: Well, there have always been two kinds of works of fiction dealing with an imaginary society. There have been the utopias like Plato's *Republic* and More's *Utopia*. There are a great many of these in the nineteenth century as a kind of reaction to the anarchy of laissez-faire, like Edward Bellamy's *Looking Backward*, and then there is the satire, what is sometimes called the dystopia, which you have in *Gulliver's Travels* and in *Brave New World*, and Huxley is one of the people who seem to have written both genuine utopias and parody utopias, and I think that one of the things you notice is that the utopia, no matter how broad and humane the person may be who is composing it, is a rather anxiety-ridden book, I mean, a type of book, that is. In More's *Utopia*, there are laws preventing people from speaking too freely in public. You just get a glint of hysteria behind, and certainly, in Plato's *Republic*, you get a fanatical bunch of soldiers enforcing the law at the expense of the artisan class, the expulsion of poets and so on, so that really the parody utopia is simply the ideal state looked at with a slightly more quizzical eye. I think what's very interesting to me about *Brave New World* is that it is, of course, explicitly a parody utopia, but what it takes as its model is the happy, adjusted society and just looks at it from a different point of view, which shows that it's utterly horrible. So *Brave New World* is really the introduction, I think, to Huxley's Vedanta period,[2] because, in order to accept the kind of program of meditation that most of the great Oriental religions call for, you have to see ordinary life as a horror, as a kind of life in hell, and, of course, the superficial mind, happy and adjusted, can't see life in that way, and the importance of *Brave New World* is that it does show you just what happens to vulgar goals as adjustment and comfort and the immediate satisfaction of impulses, when they're really looked at from the human point of view.

INTERVIEWER: Francis Huxley or . . . Northrop Frye.
FRYE: I think his main interest as a writer for me is connected very closely with his interest in science. I don't think that anybody who didn't have a very specific interest in science could have made such fun of the technologically adjusted society, as Huxley does in *Brave New World*. I think that, again, the poet has a general interest rather than a specific one, and you do get passages in Huxley's works of fiction which are the result of a very specific scientific curiosity, which gives a certain precision to his vocabulary. I think that that is really a literary quality. That is, he transmutes his scientific interest into a kind of specific and concrete imagery.

49

Rolls Royce

1982

Introduction to Giorgio Bassani, Rolls Royce and Other Poems, *translated by Francesca Valente (Toronto: Aya Press, 1982), 7–9. A typescript is in NFF, 1988, box 48, file 1.*

The English reading public knows Giorgio Bassani chiefly as the author of two novels, *The Garden of the Finzi-Continis* and *Behind the Door,*[1] the former being also a successful television program. Both are quiet, gentle, melancholy stories about Jewish families in Ferrara during the Mussolini period. Mussolini's Fascism was bad enough in all conscience, but it was so much better than the slavering madness of Nazism that one feels almost nostalgic about it by comparison. The stories portray middle-class or aristocratic Jews, with some status in their society that they try hard to maintain, but forced gradually to realize what the reader sees with intolerable clarity from the beginning: the certainty of betrayal. A Jewish poet may speak of "my brother Jesus," as Irving Layton does,[2] but a Gentile reader of these books, especially *The Garden of the Finzi-Continis,* can only murmur "my brother Judas Iscariot."

Being an exile and an outcast is, of course, part of the human situation itself. At the beginning of *Behind the Door* the narrator, a lonely Jewish adolescent, picks out a line from Dante, "the exile that has been given me I cherish as an honor," and feels "this could be my device, I thought, my motto" [10]. Dante was exiled from Florence for being on the losing side in politics, and the racial laws (the title of one poem here) against Jews that the Fascists were cowed into making by the Nazis were an equally petty act of tyranny. But these are artificial forms of exile: everyone is exiled by time from his own past, and carries that loneliness around with him whatever his life has been like. This built-in loneliness is the subject of the theme poem *Rolls-Royce*, where the poet imagines himself carried through the streets of Ferrara by a symbol of luxury with no relation to any scale of civilized values.

The Rolls Royce is a dream car: an actual car, in the smaller and older towns of Italy, is even more of a symbol of alienation and intrusion, as it squawks and honks its way through the crowds of people who have been swarming over the streets for centuries. But even this purring vehicle, with its deferential chauffeur, emphasizes the distance in time from the poet's childhood the more closely it brings him to the same points in space. At other times the poet feels that his childhood, or his past generally, has survived in memory only to be entombed within his older body, as in *On the Telephone*, where a call to his mother recalls the childhood in him "alive and yet buried inside me like this for all these years" [ll. 12–13]. A similar vision in *I've Already Said It* shows us fresco painters, ruthlessly exploited by their employer so that they never see the world outside, having to produce what they do out of the darkness and loneliness within:

> inventing it for themselves,
> recalling it for themselves,
> and nothing more. [ll. 20–2]

The translations are uniformly close, reliable and eloquent, but here is one point where we need the Italian to convey the full weight of the desolation being expressed:

> inventandosela
> recordandosene e
> basta

And just as we are all exiled from our own past by time, so we are all betrayed by the aging and death in our finite lives. Soon after the Fascists passed the racial laws, the narrator's family (in *The Racial Laws*) defiantly planted a magnolia tree in their back yard, and, hemmed in as it was by four walls, it grew and grew. Mussolini and his Fascists are in the trash cans of history now, but even a tree planted in a spirit of courage and indomitable hope cannot live forever or grow indefinitely. Life is an insecure stability compared to death. Even when surrounded by well-meaning hosts on an American campus (at least it sounds American), there is still an unwillingness to accept the poet as alive, and still equipped with his indigestible uniqueness. They instinctively want to treat him as though he were already dead, and keep trying to weave him into some meaningless carpet of assimilations and trends and influences:

> And we agree on Lotto
> and Bellotto
> and even on Giotto
> but
> what about
> Zanzotto? [*On Campus*, ll. 19–24]

So even though, in *Saturnia*, the poet can feel a moment's complacency in looking at a weekend house and thinking that he is still alive and it looks very dead, in *Piazza Indipendenza* there is a reminder that houses are apt to survive living beings. In *Top Secretly* the poet thinks of his real identity as something that can slip away from any concentration of surroundings, whether of physical environment or personal relations. But even escape is dependent on the preserving of isolation.

If we try to recall our identity from conscious memories of the past, it retreats like a forgotten name, until we give up trying. But sometimes, when our minds are on something else, the movement is reversed: the memory comes out, as it did to Proust, touches the rememberer, and says, in several senses, "here you are." This happens in *You Ask Me How It Was and When*, where a sudden epiphany impels the poet with a desire to laugh, "along with its exact / opposite" [ll. 17–18]. Similarly, one's memory is full of acts of betrayal, some of them from without, an increasing number, as we get older, from within. Yet here too a moment may reach out with the reality of love and trust behind it, as in *I Really Couldn't Say, Friends*:

> I can only tell you that I let
> myself be led in darkness
> by someone who took
> me, silently, by the
> hand. [ll. 6–10]

In the last poem, *By Mail*, the poet suggests a deeper design in things, when, stranded in Detroit, his "heart" suddenly disappears down a filthy little alley and "succeeded at last / in finding you" [ll. 10–11]. The "mail" (*Lettera*) may not be a very convincing symbol of communication any more, but the few moments that break through to the centre of experience are as real now as they ever were, and a touch of their reality can still make our prisons of solitude and prejudice crumble into illusion.

50

Cycle and Apocalypse in *Finnegans Wake*

1987

From the typescript in NFF, 1988, box 49, file 3. First published in Vico and Joyce, *ed. Donald Phillip Verene (New York: State University of New York Press, 1987), 3–19, with numerous small editorial changes; the two Frye notes given here are reproduced from this publication. Reprinted from the typescript in* MM, *356–74. A very similar address was given as "Vico, Bruno, and the Wake" at three universities in California in February 1985, and published in the Italian* Mito Metafora Simbolo, *163–81.*

I

Since the fourteenth century, there has never been a time when English literature has not been influenced, often to the point of domination, by either French or Italian literary traditions, usually both at once. For Chaucer, the major foreign influence was Boccaccio, whose *Teseide* and *Filostrato* form the basis for *The Knight's Tale* and *Troilus and Criseyde* respectively. In Tudor times the Petrarchan sonnet was the central model, both in technique and theme, for lyric poetry, and Ariosto at least contributed very heavily to the major epic of the period, Spenser's *Faerie Queene*. After the Restoration, French influence, of the Neo-Classical type, rose to dominance, headed by the critical theories of Boileau, whose slighting reference to "le clinquant de Tasse"[1] marked the ascendancy of French satire over Italian romance. Romanticism, however, found Britain at war with France, when it was a patriotic duty to prove that French literature was second-rate, as we can see in Coleridge.[2] The second generation of Romantics brought back Italian as the dominant foreign influence: Byron translated a canto of Pulci;[3] Boiardo is a presence in Peacock's last story,

Gryll Grange; Shelley (and Keats in translation) owed much to Dante, who had previously had, for religious reasons, relatively little influence. Romantic Italianism reached its climax in Browning, although Browning reflects the pictorial and visual culture of Italy more than its literature.

In the generation of Joyce, Eliot, and Pound, which came to maturity around the First World War, Eliot's main debts are to the French: the Italian influences are, again, confined largely to Dante, whom he imitates with great skill in an episode in *Little Gidding*.[4] Ezra Pound's contacts with Italian literature, history, and art are of vast range and erudition, though they also include a good many red herrings. Joyce's Italianism is more centrally in the Romantic tradition. Stephen Dedalus in *Ulysses* complains, using the title of an Italian play, that he is the servant of two masters, one English and one Italian,[5] but there he is talking about the political ascendancy of Great Britain and the Roman Catholic domination in religion. As literary masters, the Italians predominate in Joyce over all other non-English influences. Joyce's great debt to Dante, at every stage of his career, has been fully documented in a book-length study,[6] and he owed much to other Italian writers, including Gabriele D'Annunzio, who cannot be considered here. But *Finnegans Wake* is dominated by two Italians not previously represented to any extent in English literature. One is Giambattista Vico, whom Joyce did much to make a major influence in our intellectual traditions ever since. The other is Giordano Bruno of Nola, in whom no previous writer in English except Coleridge seems to have been much interested, although he lived in England for a time and dedicated his two best-known books to Sir Philip Sidney.[7]

During the years when Joyce was working on *Finnegans Wake*, publishing fragments of it from time to time under the heading of *Work in Progress*, a group of his disciples brought out a volume of essays with the eminently off-putting title of *Our Exagmination Round His Factification for Incamination of Work in Progress*. The first of these essays, by the disciple whose name is by far the best known today, Samuel Beckett, was on Joyce's debt to Italian writers, more especially Vico.[8] Despite Beckett's expertise in Italian—all his major work reflects a masterly command of Dante—the essay is very inconclusive, mainly, I imagine, because the entire structure of *Finnegans Wake* was not yet visible, and the essays were designed to point to something about to emerge and not to expound on something already there. However, since then every commentary has been largely based on Joyce's use of Vico's cyclical conception of history.

Vico thinks of history as the repetition of a cycle that passes through four main phases: a mythical or poetic period, an age of the gods; then an aristocratic period dominated by heroes and heraldic crests; then a demotic period; and finally a *ricorso*, or return to chaos followed by the beginning of another cycle. Vico traces these four periods through the Classical age to the fall of the Roman Empire, and speaks of a new cycle beginning in the medieval period. In the twentieth century Spengler worked out a similar vision of history, although he uses the metaphor of organisms rather than cycles. Spengler influenced Yeats to some degree, but not Joyce. The first section of *Finnegans Wake*, covering the first eight chapters, deals with the mythical or poetic period of legend and myths of gods; the second section, in four chapters, with the aristocratic phase; the third, also in four chapters, with the demotic phase; and the final or seventeenth chapter with the *ricorso*. The book ends in the middle of a sentence which is completed by the opening words of the first page, thus dramatizing the cycle as vividly as words can well do.

In contrast, there seems relatively little concrete documentation for the influence of Bruno of Nola, and one of the most useful commentaries, which has Vico all over the place, does not even list Bruno in the index.[9] Yet Bruno was an early influence, coming to Joyce's attention before his growing trouble with his eyesight forced him to become increasingly dependent on the help of others for his reading. In his early pamphlet, "The Day of the Rabblement," he alludes to Bruno as "the Nolan," clearly with some pleasure in concealing the name of a dangerous heretic under a common Irish one. What the Nolan said, according to Joyce, was that no one can be a lover of the true and good without abhorring the multitude,[10] which suggests that the immature Joyce, looking for security in a world where his genius was not yet recognized, found some reassurance in Bruno's habitual arrogance of tone. Bruno's "heresy," evidently, seemed to Joyce less an attack on or repudiation of Catholic doctrines than the isolating of himself from the church through a justified spiritual pride—the same heresy he ascribes to Stephen in the *Portrait*. As far as Bruno's ideas were concerned, Joyce was less interested in the plurality of worlds, which so horrified Bruno's contemporaries, and concentrates on a principle largely derived by Bruno from Nicholas of Cusa, who was not only orthodox but a cardinal, the principle of polarity. Joyce tells Harriet Shaw Weaver in a letter that Bruno's philosophy "is a kind of dualism—every power in nature must evolve an opposite in order to realize itself and opposition brings reunion."[11] Most writers would be more likely to speak of Hegel in such a connection, but that is not the kind of source one looks for in Joyce. In the compulsory period of his education Joyce acquired some knowledge of the Aristotelian philosophical tradition, and learned very early the numbing effect of an allusion to St. Thomas Aquinas. But there is little evidence that the mature Joyce read technical philosophy with any patience or persistence—not even Heraclitus, who could have given him most of what he needed of the philosophy of polarity in a couple of aphorisms.

In a later letter to Harriet Weaver, Joyce says, referring to both Vico and Bruno: "I would not pay overmuch attention to these theories, beyond using them for all they are worth."[12] That is, cyclical theories of history and philosophies of polarity were not doctrines he wished to expound, the language of *Finnegans Wake* being clearly useless for expounding anything, but structural principles for the book. It is this question of structural principles that I should like to look into at the moment, rather than simple allusion. Many of Joyce's allusions, especially to run-of-the-mill fiction and poetry written in nineteenth-century Ireland, are there primarily because the setting is Irish; many of his structural principles derive from sources he seldom refers to. He owed a great deal more to Blake, for example, than one would realize from the number of references to him—more than he himself realized, probably. Again, if *Finnegans Wake* is a dream, the researches of Freud and Jung on dreams must be relevant to it, as both of these were prominent names in Joyce's milieu. Joyce's references to Freud and Jung are rare and usually in somewhat hostile contexts, but the hostility may be partly protective. When some of Freud was read to him he remarked that Vico had anticipated Freud,[13] but in view of his use of Freud's Oedipal and censorship conceptions, his theory of wit, and his analysis of the condensation and displacement of the dream work, the remark seems to be something of a *boutade*. Again, Joyce had personal reasons for not wanting to come too close to Jung, but Jung's "collective unconscious" may also be a structural principle in the book.

II

Finnegans Wake was published in the year that I began continuous teaching, and within a few months I bought the copy that I still have, for ninety-eight cents on a remainder counter in Toronto.[14] I was fascinated by the book, but was preoccupied at the time with the Blake Prophecies, and was in no position to go into orbit around it. When the Blake book was off my hands and I started working on the *Anatomy of Criticism,* I had to account, so to speak, for the existence of *Finnegans Wake.* True, there was a popular fallacy at the time, which I kept hearing for the next twenty years, that all works of literature were "unique," and that the critic should not try to detract from that uniqueness. The notion rested on a confusion between criticism as a body of knowledge about literature and the experience of reading, which is central to criticism but not part of it. Every experience is in some sense unique, but the unique as such cannot be an object of knowledge. So the task remained, as did, of course, the confusion.

It seemed to me that there was an epic form that tended to expand into a kind of imaginative encyclopedia, and that the limit of this encyclopedic form was the sacred book, the kind of scriptural myth that we find in the Bible, the *Prose Edda,* and in Hindu literature. The affinities of *Finnegans Wake,* for all its pervasive irony, appeared to be closest to that form, and I could see that the Bible (along with missals and prayer books, both Catholic and Anglican), the Koran, and the Egyptian *Book of the Dead* were much in Joyce's mind. Otherwise there seemed to be no critical theory that really illuminated what Joyce was doing. Joyce himself certainly did not provide one: his critical abilities were limited, and he seems to have been content to go along with the generally accepted statement that the language of *Finnegans Wake* is "dream language." But while it is true that the dream condenses and displaces and superimposes and puns and plays every kind of verbal trick, it hardly produces the linguistic Niagara that Joyce's seventeen years of work on *Finnegans Wake* accumulated. One cannot blame his contemporaries for insisting that he was wasting his genius on something that fell outside literature: one can only marvel at his persistence and inner confidence. But at his death, however extraordinary his achievement, it still seemed to be completely *sui generis,* and Eliot's remark that one *Finnegans Wake* was probably enough sounded like the most unassailable common sense.[15]

It was perhaps not until Jacques Derrida and his "deconstruction" techniques that the theory implied by *Finnegans Wake* really came into focus. The deconstructing critic tends to approach every text in the spirit in which Joyce approached the first drafts of his *Work in Progress* fragments. *Finnegans Wake* is a book in which practically every word provides, in addition to a surface meaning that may or may not be there, a great variety of "supplements" that lend a number of further aspects to the meaning. Deconstruction implies a concept not far removed from

Freud's concept of the censor, the process of achieving meaning by excluding unacceptable meanings; and Joyce's dream language, while the activity of censorship is certainly recorded in it, escapes, to a very unusual degree, from the kind of psychological gaps that mental censorship leaves in narrative-directed writing.

Then again, *Finnegans Wake* is a book of "traces." The central character, Finnegan himself, is effaced by his "death," or falling asleep—the two things seem to be much the same thing at the opening of the book—and what follows is a "differential" pursuit of echoes and reverberations into a world of words rather than a "logocentric" invoking of a presence. It is natural that commentators influenced by Derridean theories should be doubtful about the presence in the book of any continuous "story line" and regard the identity of the dreamer as an irrelevant question in a book where nothing has any consistent identity at all. I think however that Joyce, belonging to an older generation, was old-fashioned enough to prefer a set of narrative canons, however distinctively handled.

We begin with the figure of Finnegan, who is both Finn, the great legendary hero of Ireland, and the subject of a ballad about a hod-carrier who fell off a ladder, broke his neck, had a funeral wake in his honour, and woke up in the middle of it demanding a share of the whisky. In Joyce the twelve mourners at the wake persuade Finn to go back to sleep, and tell him that he is about to be superseded by another character, whose full name, we eventually learn, is Humphrey Chimpden Earwicker, but who is most commonly to be recognized by his initials HCE. Finn and HCE are frequently identified in the book, and both are married to the central female figure, whose full name is Anna Livia Plurabelle, with the initials ALP. Nevertheless we are told, as explicitly as we are told anything in the book, that Finn and HCE are distinguishable aspects of the same identity, like persons of the Trinity.

Finn seems to be Joyce's equivalent of the giant man out of whose body the world is made that we find in so many creation myths, although in *Finnegans Wake* his body seems to extend only from the Head of Howth on the northeast to Phoenix Park on the southwest. But this Dublin area is *a* world that mirrors and epitomizes *the* world, and in this sense Finn belongs to the family of the Indian Purusha, the Norse Ymir, the Kabbalistic Adam Kadmon or Qodmon, and Blake's Albion. HCE, then, is Finn-*again*, Finn asleep and dreaming, whose dream is the recurring cycle of history. A dream ends by waking up, but although there are various intimations of an awakening throughout the book, especially in the final chapter, the dream of human history is an unending dream in which all attempts to wake up continue to be baffled as Finn was at the beginning. Stephen Dedalus in *Ulysses* speaks of history as a nightmare from which he is trying to awake,[16] but it is clear that he never does wake up in that sense anywhere in the book. Similarly, the narrative of *Finnegans Wake* goes around in a circle to form the book of "Doublends Jined" (Dublin's Giant and double-ends joined),[17] and the *ricorso* at the end is not a resurrection but only a return. All the dreamers in *Finnegans Wake*, so far as they are individual people, may wake up and go about their business in the morning, but even so they are still contained within the larger dream of time.

HCE has two sons, Shem and Shaun, who represent the conflict that is the pervading characteristic of history, although they are both essentially aspects of HCE, according to the principle of polarity. Near the beginning of the book we enter a "museyroom" with mementoes of Napoleon and Wellington;[18] this episode was evidently suggested by an illustration in Freud's treatise on wit and the unconscious. Wellington is or could be considered an Irish hero: one thinks of Bernard Shaw's remark that the only match for a French army led by an Italian would be a British army led by an Irishman.[19] Apart from that, however, the result of the battle of Waterloo was not of great importance to Ireland, and in fact there are suggestions that Napoleon actually won the battle, as no doubt he did in his dreams on St. Helena. The essential point is that Napoleon and Wellington are both products of the same historical force of European imperialism, and in that context their opposition is illusory.

This is the simplest form of a conflict of polarities: in a slightly more complex one a defender of something in Ireland is fighting an invader who threatens it. Early in the book there is an encounter of two giants, Mutt and Jute: Jute seems to be connected with Danish invaders and Mutt with the Irish under Brian Boru who stopped them at the Battle of Clontarf. A century later there was the twelfth-century English conquest under Henry II, along with which came the absorption of the native Irish church by the Roman Catholic organization. The link between the two is afforded by the fact that the pope at the time of Henry II's invasion was Adrian IV, Nicholas Brakespear, the only pope of English origin. But even here the polarities merge. In the colloquy between Mutt and Jute, Mutt says of the tide coming in and going out of Dublin Bay:

> Hither, craching eastuards, they are in surgence; hence, cool at ebb, they requiesce. [17:25–6]

We note the prominence of the initial letters HCE at the beginning of each clause, indicating that invasion, resistance, withdrawal, and absorption, like the flow and ebb of the tide, are all aspects of the same force appearing as opposites.

In later historical periods the opposition can take a form like that of the "Devils" and "Angels" of Blake's *Marriage of Heaven and Hell*, where creative radicals struggle against established conservatives. As a rule the "Micks," the partisans of the "Angels" represented by St. Michael, are much more popular and highly regarded, especially by women, than the "Nicks," partisans of the opposite side, identified as that of "Old Nick" or the Devil by their opponents. In this aspect of the conflict "Shem," the writer and social misfit, becomes an exile and "Shaun" his brother assumes a great variety of social roles, including that of a highly indecorous priest. Joyce identifies himself to a great extent with Shem, and there is a good deal—many readers, including the present one, would say far too much—about Joyce's poverty and the neglect of his genius. Still, there is a good deal about Dante in Dante and even more about Bruno in Bruno. Vico also wrote an *Autobiography*,[20] and, as Hugh Kenner reminds us, tells us that he fell off a ladder in the library and was for a time thought to be dead.[21] There are other writer-heroes, notably Swift, and even a political one, Parnell.

The rivalry of brothers comes mainly from the Book of Genesis, where the chief archetypes are, first, Cain and Abel, and then Esau and Jacob. Often the two brothers expand into three. The line of succession runs through neither Cain nor Abel but through a third brother, Seth, and Noah also had three sons, of whom one was called Shem and another Ham, Ham being cursed and made subordinate to the others [Genesis 9:20–7]. Similarly the two "sons of thunder" (the significance of this word will meet us in a moment) among Jesus' disciples, James and John, whose names remind us of Shem and Shaun, are usually joined by a third, Peter. The theme of three brothers comes into such popular phrases as "Tom, Dick, and Harry," often echoed in the book, and into Swift's *Tale of a Tub*, where three brothers, Peter, Jack, and Martin, each think up their own way of perverting the teachings of the New Testament.

In any case the sons, or more generally the younger generation, whether two or three, may direct their rivalries not only against one another but against their father. This may take the regular Oedipus form of trying to replace him in the affections of the mother (ALP), or simply of cuckolding an older man, as notably in the Irish story of Tristram and

King Mark. This situation expands into the usual conflict of generations: the antagonism of Parnell to his predecessor Isaac Butt, of Joyce himself to Yeats, and above all of an interminable shaggy dog story (said to be originally a story in the repertoire of Joyce's father) of how a certain "Buckley" shot (or didn't shoot) a "Russian General" [338–55].

The female characters in *Finnegans Wake* reflect the ambiguity between the elusive, tantalizing siren whose indifference is deplored in so much poetry and the cherishing wife and mother whose constant care is the fostering of life. This is the usual relation of the daughter-figure Issy or Isabel, who is linked to Isolde, and who is eloquently described by the Joyce scholar Adeline Glasheen as "a triumph of female imbecility,"[22] to her mother ALP. Issy is usually portrayed as a narcissistic figure gazing into her own mirror reflection, recalling Alice before her adventures or the two women, Stella and her shadowy companion Rebecca Dingley, who were the recipients of Swift's Journal with its disguising "little language."[23] Here, naturally, the second or shadow girl readily turns into the younger woman in Swift's life, Vanessa. Like HCE and his sons, ALP and her daughter often merge into the same identity, but again they are polar opposites: we may call them, borrowing from both Robert Graves and the Song of Songs, the white goddess and the black bride. The former is what Blake would call the "Female Will" [*Jerusalem*, pl. 30, ll. 31, 39; E176–7], the retreating figure who fascinates, beckons, or betrays, but always eludes. The latter, who is consistently associated with the Liffey river flowing through Dublin, is the power of renewal that flows out into the sea on the last page of the book, just before returning to the headwaters of the "riverrun" [3:1] on the first page.

Most commentators believe that there is an individual dreamer at the core of the book, a tavern-keeper in Chapelizod, just up the Liffey river from Dublin. His name is generally assumed to be the filled-out form of HCE, but it is also possible that his name is Porter (there are other candidates), though his wife's name seems to be, in all of her contexts, consistently Anna Livia. This Earwicker, or Porter, seems to be of English, Protestant, and ultimately Scandinavian origin, his dream expressing some alienation about finding himself in Ireland (as he sinks into sleep we hear a voice saying "So This Is Dyoublong?" [13:4]). Thus there is a latent conflict with the other aspect of himself, Finn, though the reality masked by that opposition appears to lie outside the book. The individual dreamer, if he is there, has two sons, usually called Jerry and Kevin; a daughter Isabel; at least two servants, a pot-boy and a cleaning woman; twelve customers in his pub (the mourners at Finn's wake); and a number of shadowy neighbours, including a mysterious "Magrath" and the "Maggies," who are evidently schoolmates of Issy or Isabel.

We seem to have, then, three major concentric circles of dream. The innermost is the individual dream of the tavern-keeper, the outermost the dream of mankind which is history, while in between there is the constant metamorphosis of the relations of Shem to Shaun, the universalized forms of Jerry and Kevin. The individual story assimilates the intensely studied scenes of Dublin life in *Dubliners* into the book; the Shem–Shaun rivalries incorporate *Portrait of the Artist as a Young Man* and *Stephen Hero*, with their focus on the social and cultural situation of Joyce himself; the dream of the many-sided Everyman whose *periplus* voyage covers the whole of the known world incorporates *Ulysses*. In *Ulysses* Stephen is an ex-Catholic intellectual and the figure who eventually becomes a symbolic father is Jewish; in *Finnegans Wake*, which was completed during the rise of Nazism in Europe, these affinities are reversed, Shem being "Semitic" and Shaun mainly parody-Catholic. The activities of the tavern-keeper and his family during the previous day form the "manifest content" of the dream, the things on which the mind has not yet slept, as Freud says; the archetypal expansion of those activities to cover all human history forms the latent content. One would also expect the universal, autobiographical, and local imagery to predominate in turn through the three phases of Vico's cycle, and to some degree they do.

However expanded, the Dublin setting, or the Irish setting generally, remains constant throughout the book. One reason, not impossibly the decisive reason, why Vico and Bruno of Nola are so important in the dream is that there is a Vico Road just outside Dublin and a Dublin bookshop called Nowlan and Browne. It is clear that the *coincidentia oppositorum*, the real unity of apparent opposites, is only one small aspect of an epic quest in which the dragon to be slain, the enemy of the quest, is coincidence itself. A coincidence is a piece of design that one cannot find a use for, and in that sense there is no such thing as a coincidence in *Finnegans Wake*. If we ask who the hero is that is to achieve such a quest, the answer is, clearly, the reader of the book, "the ideal reader suffering from an ideal insomnia" [120:13–14], as Joyce says. This reader is not only the hero of *Finnegans Wake*; he is also the only character involved with it who is never allowed to sleep or dream.

The merging of the individual dream with the total dream of mankind appears to be the central postulate on which Joyce's book is based. In one extraordinary interview, Joyce spoke of himself as a kind of psychopomp summoning the spirits of the dead.[24] Naturally he would be most attracted to highly speculative thinkers who try to break out of the rigid Cartesian dualism in which so much of our intellectual attitude is still confined. One such thinker is Samuel Butler: Butler is not a major influence on *Finnegans Wake*, but there are several references to *Erewhon* and *The Way of All Flesh*. The latter is a *Bildungsroman* in which the author examines a younger version of himself in order to objectify the younger self and break something of its hold on him, as Joyce's *Portrait* does with Stephen Dedalus.

In his biological writings, Butler deals with the conception of personality in such a way as to show that the personality has no clear circumference or centre. All life interpenetrates with all other life, and all life constitutes a single being. In *The Way of All Flesh* (chapter 69) he draws the inference that eventually we shall have to abolish the distinction of subject and object, internal and external, and live and work within a purely metaphorical universe.[25] A few pages further on Butler quotes his hero as saying that no incontrovertible first premise for a philosophical system can ever be found, because "no one could get behind Bishop Berkeley."[26] Joyce's references to the story of Buckley and the Russian general, already mentioned, often refer to Buckley as "Berkeley," which would associate the "Russian General" with, perhaps, Lenin, who made Berkeley the cockshy for the bourgeois idealism he was out to destroy. In itself this is probably over-zealous commentary, but it is not inherently impossible that Berkeley should be for Joyce, as for Yeats, the Irish philosopher who had effectively removed the barriers between waking and dreaming life.

Butler and Berkeley lead us to an idealistic tradition from which Bruno also derived. In his book *God the Known and God the Unknown*, Butler equates his conception of the unity of all life with a "known" aspect of God.[27] Such a foray into natural theology may seem unusual for a post-Darwinian writer, but it brings us close to Bruno's doctrine *natura est deus in rebus*, that nature is an incarnation of God in whom "all is in all."[28] We referred earlier to Joyce's remark that Vico had anticipated Freud: perhaps, similarly, Bruno for him had anticipated something of Jung's "collective unconscious."

III

Like other scriptures, *Finnegans Wake* begins with the standard mythical themes of beginning: creation, fall (or some other myth about how man became mortal), and a universal deluge. In *Finnegans Wake* these are all essentially the same event: when man "fell" the world he fell into was this one, and this world is symbolically submarine as well as subterranean. The assimilation of the three events is identical with Blake's myth of the fall when, as he says in *Europe*:

> the five senses whelm'd
> In deluge o'er the earth-born man.
> [*Europe: A Prophecy*, pl. 10, ll. 10–11; E63]

In Blake's *Jerusalem* Albion lies asleep in Atlantis at the bottom of the "Sea of Time and Space"[29] for most of the poem, the archetypal leviathan or sea monster of the indefinite. Joyce's Finn is a land monster or "behemoth" whose "brontoichthyian form" (7:14, 20) can be dimly discerned in the landscape.

Freud's analysis of dreams gives us little sense of the real nature and importance of the anxiety dream, the deep uneasy guilt feelings that can hardly be explained as a mere blocking of desire. There is, however, an extraordinary flash of insight in De Quincey's "Mail Coach" essay, where De Quincey speaks of a sudden crisis in his own experience passing into his dreams and merging there with a sense of original sin, of the kind that no doubt prompted the fall myth itself, and which, he suggests, perhaps everybody dreams over again every night.[30] Nobody in *Finnegans Wake* seems to have heard of De Quincey except the least likely character, Isabel (285n. 6), but the individual dream of the tavern-keeper at least is constantly losing or finding its identity in some myth of the fall of man.

Mysterious things are hinted at about the dreamer's sons, who have expanded into three soldiers and remind us of the sons of Noah, of whom one saw his drunken father as he should not have been seen. The daughter has become two girls, whose bladders begin the running of water that flows through the book, where the voyeurism goes in the opposite direction. There is also an encounter in Phoenix Park, a place associated with death (the Phoenix Park murders) and treachery (the attempt to involve Parnell in them which was frustrated by one conspirator's misspelling of "hesitancy").[31] HCE is accosted by a "cad" (cadet or younger son) with a "pipe" (French slang for penis) and asked for the time [35:11]. He gives a stuttering answer and his "hesitancy" starts rumours spreading around the world. In a larger context the stutter marks the mechanical repetition of moments that is our experience of time, which according to St. Augustine began with the fall. The time when the question is asked appears to be 11:32, which is also twenty-eight to twelve, those being numbers prominent in human efforts to work out a calendar with the solar and lunar cycles. Both have associations in the book. Isabel's schoolmates, called the "Maggies," number twenty-eight, and the twelve mourners who persuade Finnegan to go back to sleep suggest a zodiacal cycle, just as, according to Blake, the twelve tribes of Israel in the desert were hypnotized by the zodiac ("sons of Albion") into giving up their revolution for a deified robot's legal code.

We are accustomed nowadays to hear that the unconscious, however defined, is linguistically structured as well as the consciousness.[32] Here again is something that Joyce might have absorbed from earlier writers: Butler, for example, tells us that all genuine and achieved knowledge is unconscious knowledge, the consciousness being concerned only with exploring the new and as yet unassimilated.[33] In the conscious world verbal exchange, though the chief means of communication, is also used quite as much to conceal or disguise communication. We build up ironic, self-enclosed verbal structures that others can penetrate only obliquely, or else we stylize what we say in dramatic attitudes conditioned by the characters of those we talk to. Meanwhile, the verbal currents boiling and swirling around in our unconscious keep up a constant jockeying for power, each trying to get to a place where it can dominate the ego. This gives a particular importance to the message from outside that bypasses the conscious mind and strikes directly into the unconscious. According to Vico, the cycle of history begins with the thunderclap, interpreted by men (then giants) as the voice of God. Later, we have oracles purporting to carry the voice of divine authority, and eventually (to move outside Vico), the sacred scripture develops a codified body of such messages.

In *Finnegans Wake* the inner babble of the individual mind expands into a vision of mankind as dreaming a communal dream of conflicting voices, with occasionally a voice of command or exceptional authority penetrating and for an instant silencing the tumult. The series of thunderclaps, of a hundred letters each, that mark the beginning of a new phase of history begins on the opening page, and HCE is associated with the "earwig" or *perce-oreille* ("Persse O'Reilly"), the insect that traditionally penetrates the ear of a sleeper. We may compare a line from the close of Blake's *Jerusalem*, just as the final apocalypse begins: "Her voice pierc'd Albions clay cold ear" [*Jerusalem*, pl. 95, l. 1; E254]. It is only the voice of the poet, the successor in society of the oracle and scripture, that carries this authority now, though the voice is constantly neglected. "Hear the voice of the Bard!" [*Songs of Experience: Introduction*, l. 1; E18], Blake pleaded, and went on to say that the Bard's message is outside time and descends directly from the voice of God in Eden. It was also Blake who applied to himself the motto of John the Baptist, "The Voice of one crying in the Wilderness."[34]

For a century after Blake's death poets were fascinated by the figure of John the Baptist, the herald and announcer of a new age, whose passion, unlike that of Jesus, involved their cherished theme of the *femme fatale*. Yeats, we remember, devoted much of his energy to proclaiming a new age and seeing signs of it in contemporary Ireland, even though, according to the most reliable of his clocks, the Christian era still has another thousand years to go. At the end of *Portrait of the Artist as a Young Man*, Stephen identifies his friend Cranly with John the Baptist,[35] clearly reserving a greater role for himself, which in *Ulysses* it seems obvious he is not going to attain. *Finnegans Wake* seems to me largely based on the theme of annunciation, with Vico and Bruno standing guard over it partly because their first names, Giambattista and Giordano, suggest John the Baptist at the Jordan.

The struggles of Shem and Shaun, with their metamorphoses, form the main action of the book. Shem is the "penman" or "punman" who carries on the poetic and oracular tradition, and two elements in his technique are important for understanding his oracular role. One is the incessant use of the thematic phrase. Such phrases as "the same anew,"[36] "up, guards, and at them," "Honi soit qui mal y pense," and dozens of others appear in astonishing variations throughout. This device is often linked to Wagner's leitmotif technique, although Joyce was not really a Wagnerian. In a preliterary age such thematic phrases would be magical formulas. The other technical element, which also harks back to preliterary magic, shows the poet as pre-eminently the knower of names, and, in the unconscious, calling a name can command an appearance. For all the distortion, there is a continuous orgy of naming in *Finnegans Wake*: books of the Bible, suras of the Koran, lyrics of Tom Moore, catalogues of rivers and cities, just for a start.

I have elsewhere spoken of two aspects of poetry deeply involved with the unconscious as charm and riddle.[37] Charm in particular is linked to the oracular, to the sense of magical compulsion in its tradition, to an appeal to the past that takes the form "as that was, so may this be." Riddle is rather a perplexing of the conscious intelligence that prompts one to "guess" or identify the object it presents without naming. The riddle is the home of the pun, the metaphor, the verbal clusters formed in the unconscious and rising to the conscious surface. The charm is the home of incantation, of the mystery hidden in sound. Charm and riddle are a psychological contrast, and if we stayed entirely within either area we should get a bad case of what Eliot calls dissociated sensibility.[38] If we stayed with the oracular world of charm, everything would seem solemn, awful, portentous, and the least breath of humour or irreverence would destroy the mood. If we stayed with the world of riddle, we should be subjected to an endless stream of irresponsible wisecracks. To walk the razor's edge between the two, to achieve an oracular charm that is witty and a wit that evokes profound and haunting depths of linguistic experience, is a considerable tour de force, not to speak of keeping it up for over six hundred pages.

In the first chapter we are told a strange tale of a certain Jarl van Hoother, the Earl of Howth in a Dutch or Scandinavian disguise, who is another context of HCE and who has two sons, named, in this tale, Tristopher and Hilary. A female figure known as a "prankquean" kidnaps first one son and then the other, keeping each in the wilderness for forty years and converting them to something else [22:13]. Tristopher is converted to being a "luderman" [21:30], presumably some form of playboy; Hilary is converted to a "tristian" [22:17], a sorrowful Christian or Tristram. As we read this we are reminded of Bruno's personal motto, used at the beginning of his play *Il Candelaio* and elsewhere: *in tristitia hilaris, in hilaritate tristis.*[39] The solemn and the gay are interchangeable aspects of the same thing, and this may well be the essence, for Joyce, of Bruno's theory of polarity.

Shem is the writer; Shaun is ultimately the product of what is written. Shaun is, first, the public that receives the poet's message, ridicules and belittles it when it cannot ignore it, and yet unconsciously keeps transforming and often perverting it into social institutions and codes of behaviour. Shem works directly in the stream of time that supplies the energy of history; Shaun spatializes what Shem does, though he himself does not really know this, and regards himself as the intermediary between authority, whatever its source, and the public. Shem fails to guess the most important riddle with which he is confronted, the "heliotrope" riddle in the mime chapter (9), but Shaun answers a great many riddles, his confidence undiminished by the number of answers that are either wrong or irrelevant. Finally, in the fifteenth chapter near the end, Shaun is subjected to a close and sustained inquiry which brings out the fact that he is really the sum total of the book itself, as one of its characters after another emerges from him. The last one to emerge is HCE, who speaks as the builder of cities and civilizations throughout history.

Yet even HCE is not the fundamental force of history, for the great cities of the past are ruins now, and the most impressive erections disappear in a world where "Gricks may rise and Troysirs fall" [11:35–6]. Below him is the river of time, the ALP who continually renews herself, and HCE along with herself. All through the book we keep hearing about a "letter" written by ALP, lost in a dungheap but representing a creative energy of communication that Shem is in much closer touch with than either Shaun or HCE. Shaun supplies us with a greatly distorted version of this letter, but a more authentic one emerges at the very end, just before the final farewell speech by ALP as she flows out and merges with the sea. ALP herself can only die and renew: as she sinks into her father the sea we catch a glimpse of the conjunction of bird and woman that marks the starting point of a new cycle of time, like those of Leda and the swan and the dove and the Virgin in Yeats:

> If I seen him bearing down on me now under whitespread wings like he'd come from Arkangels, I sink I'd die down over his feet, humbly dumbly, only to washup. (628:9–11)

But unlike the Magdalen whom she echoes, she is not present at a resurrection, only at a renewal. The book goes around in the circle of the *ricorso*. But there is another kind of vision hinted at in the very end of her letter:

> Hence we've lived in two worlds. He is another he what stays under the himp of holth. (619:11–12)

Of the two worlds, the higher one is the world of the turning cycle of life, death, and renewal; below it is the still sleeping Finn who is all mankind. When we are told at the beginning of the book that Finn is about to be superseded by HCE, we can see an analogy with the relation of Ireland to the constant stream of Irish invaders, Danish, Roman, British, and the rest. At the end we get a glimpse of an apocalypse opening up from below that will swallow the cycle: this does not happen, but the last line of *Finnegans Wake* contains the little noticed phrase "till thousends thee."[40] What looks like the primary meaning of this is "till thou sends thee" or thyself, a second coming or reunion of HCE and ALP with a permanently awakened Finn. We are left with the sense that the imagery of the cycle, with its death followed by renewal and return, is the only imagery that human language, conscious or unconscious, can draw on to express whatever is beyond the cycle. Also that there is one polarity in which the opposed forces can never unite: the apocalyptic separation of the states of life and death.

We are left, finally, with the ultimate categories of time and space. Time is the inner energy of life, flowing in a relatively undisturbed form during sleep; our waking consciousness constructs a spatialized world, HCE's world of buildings and mountains. Joyce, who identifies with Shem, was told during his lifetime by various Shaun figures, such as Wyndham Lewis, that he ought to pay more attention to the spatial and objective world. Of Joyce's two mentors, Vico was particularly the theorist of time and history; Bruno, with his doctrine of an infinite universe, explored a new conception of space, pointing out that Aristotle, for example, who was so constantly quoted against him, had no word for space.[41] Such words as *chora* and *topos* mean not space but place, space-*there*. And yet Vico's cyclical conception of historical process is really a vision of time within a spatial metaphor, and Bruno's conception of the identity of polarized opposites a vision of the spatial subject–object confrontation dissolving back into a temporal flux. All our experience collapses in on a deadlock of categories, and there is nothing in human language, even the expanded language of *Finnegans Wake*, to get us out. Nothing, that is, except its confrontation with an insomniac reader who is still outside the book, struggling to make a sense of it that cannot ultimately be limited even to Joyce's sense. Such a reader is the closest we can come to Lewis Carroll's Humpty Dumpty, HCE before he fell off his wall, who could explain all the poems that had ever been written, along with a number that hadn't been written yet.

When *Finnegans Wake* was published and the response confused and disappointing, Joyce stressed the wit of the book as its more obvious appeal, and asked why nobody could see that it was funny.[42] But we should not overlook its seriousness as well, or the fact that he apparently read, for instance, Blavatsky's *Isis Unveiled* with close attention,[43] was genuinely interested in Yeats's *Vision*,[44] except that he regretted, as do other readers of Yeats, its being imprisoned in a system disconnected from the poetry, and even spoke of minor and less seminal books on comparative mythology, such as Allen Upward's *Divine Mystery*,[45] as coming close to doing what he was trying to do in his way. The merits of these books are not significant: what they indicate is the existence of a motive in Joyce's compulsively careful organization very different from what the puns and so-called obscenities indicate by themselves. One can match the charm-and-riddle language of the book with much of the Old Testament and the Vedic Hymns, but one can also find a good deal of it in both Vico and Bruno. Vico's "new science" opened up a whole new field of scholarly endeavour, yet his central myth, which begins with giants terrified of a thunderclap, running into caves dragging their wives behind them, and so instituting private property, reads almost like parody. Bruno is a writer whose satire and scatology almost matches Joyce's own, who wrote a great deal of self-obsessed braggadocio, abuse of contemporaries, long meaningless catalogues, and heavy-handed humour, but who nonetheless died a martyr to his vision. Both writers are full of the contradictions of creative power itself, and both find their tradition continued in the epic of a drunken Irishman's mock-funeral wake that expands into the sleep of Eve and Adam under the circling stars.

51

Henry James and the Comedy of the Occult

19 October 1989

From Genre, Trope, Gender: Critical Essays, *ed. Barry Rutland (Ottawa: Carleton University Press, 1992), 13–31. Originally given as the Munro Beattie Lecture at Carleton University. Reprinted in* EAC, *109–29. There are notes for this paper in Notebook 6* (TBN, *104–26), and two typescripts in NFF, 1991, box 38, file 9.*

I

It is a genuine pleasure to be giving a lecture in honour of my old friend, Professor Munro Beattie. Our friendship goes back to undergraduate days at Victoria College, when we were fellow students of Pelham Edgar. Edgar's main scholarly interest was in Henry James, on whom he wrote a pioneering study published in 1927. *Henry James: Man and Author* is a badly organized book, but it is full of the candour and simplicity which was Edgar's great quality as a critic, and is an especially useful quality for such a subject. Munro Beattie shared this interest of Edgar's at once: I took much longer to be attracted to James, much as I respected and even envied my classmate's understanding of him. Whatever understanding of James I may have acquired since, I have at least read him, so I felt that a lecture devoted to him would be an appropriate personal tribute for this occasion.

It was logical enough, I suppose, for a Canadian critic of Edgar's generation, half British and half American in his own cultural background, to be fascinated by Henry James, with his North Atlantic preoccupations. James ignores Canada, but then, apart from Boston and New York, he largely ignores the United States as well, at least in his fiction. James thought of the European side of the Atlantic as providing tradition and cultural continuity, and of the American side as having a willingness to experiment and opportunity to expand. A complete human existence, then, would be located in some intermediate Atlantis that never quite comes up for air. One can find similar attitudes in Canadian or pre-Canadian writers from Haliburton to Grove and beyond, sometimes with the suggestion that in default of an Atlantis, Canada may have to do instead.

I first became really attracted to James when a student in Oxford, after I picked up, for a shilling apiece, the two novels James had left unfinished at his death, *The Ivory Tower* and *The Sense of the Past*, along with the notes for them that the author had left.[1] *The Ivory Tower*, which I shall return to later, confirmed all the things I felt I disliked about James at that time, but *The Sense of the Past* fascinated me: it was a story of time travel, about a twentieth-century American who walks into the English eighteenth century and exchanges places with an eighteenth-century English namesake equally attracted to the future. By chance a popular version of it, *Berkeley Square*, was running in the movie houses at the time. I could understand James's somewhat possessive interest, in his later years, in H.G. Wells as a writer who could carry on from where he stopped, as Wells seemed to have mastered representational and fantastic themes, including time travel, with equal fluency.

Time travel is one of the major themes developed since by the aspect of science fiction that is really occult fantasy. Another and closely related theme, that of identity in parallel worlds,[2] was also anticipated by James in "The Jolly Corner." These two stories, *The Sense of the Past* particularly, seemed to me central to everything that had preoccupied James from the beginning about the social and psychological culture shocks that the two sides of Atlantic civilization contained for one another. It puzzled me, however, not that *The Sense of the Past* was unfinished, as its theme became almost unmanageably complex even for James as it developed, but that so crucial a story should take the form of what was really a ghost story.

James wrote ghost stories at intervals all through his writing career, and sometimes we tend to ask whether a given story is or is not a ghost story, a question we should never think of asking with, say, Kafka's *Castle* or Beckett's *Molloy*. But the ghost story was a specific English Victorian genre, featured in the Christmas issues of family magazines, and James adhered to its conventions for most of his life: *The Turn of the Screw* is firmly embedded in them. In James's later fiction, in *The Sacred*

Fount, "The Beast in the Jungle," "The Altar of the Dead," we are well past the ghost story, and yet equally far beyond what is called "realism" too. And even in more representational fictions, such as *The Wings of the Dove* or *The Ambassadors*, we become increasingly aware of what Wallace Stevens calls "ghostlier demarcations, keener sounds" [*The Idea of Order at Key West*, l. 56], as objective and hidden worlds more and more interpenetrate. The reason for this is not that James came to "believe in" this or that, or that he was beginning to prefer one type of subject matter to another. The reason is purely technical: his work was getting more concentrated, and the imaginative possibilities covered increasingly larger areas than the surface story.

James's stories are mostly ironic versions, or inversions, of conventional comic patterns. In a simple comic action, such as a play of Molière, we have, over and over, the story of how a young couple want to get married, but find their way barred by a father with some obsession that makes him want to impose another pattern of life on his offspring. This obsession, called a "humour" by Ben Jonson, acts as a reversing movement, blocking the normal evolution of the action into a state of greater freedom, happiness, sexual fulfilment, and common sense, and dragging us backwards into the tyranny of the obsession. The miser in *L'Avare*, the snob in *Le Bourgeois Gentilhomme*, the hypochondriac in *Le Malade imaginaire*, the pedants in *Les Femmes savantes*, stand for a tyrannical past, as the normal action represented by the young people struggles towards a future. The "humours" also represent a partial or mutilated existence, in contrast to the wholeness of experience symbolized by the young lovers, who are, in theory, going to live happily ever after once the humour is won over or outwitted. A contrasting comic type is someone, usually a clever servant (*gracioso*), who is sympathetic to the young couple and helps to forward the comic action.

James occasionally approaches the traditional comic form, as in the brilliant *The Europeans*, where old-world people come to Boston, and where there are at the end three marriages, and a near-miss at a fourth, quite in the manner of a Shakespearean romantic comedy. But the ironic variants predominate, and in ironic actions there can be any degree of complication, from total frustration to a split decision. In James the positive goal of the comic action, which in an ironic story is so often missed or thwarted, is not the sexual fulfilment of young lovers, but an intensity of experience that sexual satisfaction only approximates. The vision of this intensity is what Strether, the central character of *The Ambassadors*, sees at the end of the story, and clings to in spite of his growing isolation from the other characters. Again, no scene in Henry James is more powerful than the scene in *The Wings of the Dove*, where Milly, realizing that she has a terminal illness and has only a short time to live, walks through London streets and parks, feeling the atmosphere around her as something so vibrant as to be almost tangible.[3] Characters in Henry James are going through this intensity all the time: the readers can see this, in the long dialogues and explanations in which the tiniest modulations of tone can have a portentous significance. But the characters themselves realize it only very seldom.

The story *What Maisie Knew*, being about a child, is, as the preface explains, the story of what Maisie knew but didn't altogether know she knew. That, incidentally, is the technical reason for an omniscient narrator, to tell us what his characters know but don't know they know, or feel but don't feel that they feel. In several of James's introductions to his works he mentions how the idea for it had originated in the smallest germ or seed of some anecdote, or even a passing reference, picked up perhaps at a dinner conversation. *What Maisie Knew* is one of these "seed" stories, and of his heroine James says after a few pages: "it was to be the fate of this patient little girl to see much more than she at first understood, but also even at first to understand much more than any little girl, however patient, had perhaps ever understood before."[4] Quite a statement when one looks at it. The phrase used about Milly Theale in *The Wings of the Dove*, "the potential heiress of all the ages,"[5] fits more quietly into its context, but is startling nonetheless. In *The Ambassadors* Strether sees young Chad open the door of a theatre box and the author says that his "perception of the young man's identity [. . .] had been quite one of the sensations that count in life."[6] In short, there is no such thing as a trivial incident: an immense amount of significance is always present potentially, and there are no limits to that amount.

In a story called "The Birthplace" a man gets a job, a tremendous windfall for him, of guide at Stratford to Shakespeare's house. As he goes on, he gradually loses his belief in the historical authenticity of what he's pointing to, and the quality of his sales talk is noticeably affected. A lot of tourist money is involved, so his bosses threaten him with dismissal, whereupon he pulls up his socks and goes into his spiel harder than ever. The implication is partly that the institution is more important than his views about it, his function being that of a guide, not a scholar. But the ramifications go much further. The story never uses the words Stratford or Shakespeare: the locale couldn't be more obvious, but their absence suggests another dimension. References to priests and temples are spattered all over the story, so much so that the reader is bound to ask: what kind of story would this be if this man were the guide to the Church of the Nativity at Bethlehem? Shakespeare is referred to throughout as "He" and "Him" with capitals; there's a comment about how the crowds kill him every day, and so on. So what seems on the surface a trivial story expands into, among other things, a vision showing us how every historical religion in the world has got started, by switching from history to mythology. This quasi-allegorical expansion is not typical of James, but it indicates his direction.

In another story, "The Real Thing," a painter who specializes in illustrations of fashionable life is confronted by a lady and a gentleman down on their luck, who propose to earn some money as his models, on the ground that they have practised being a lady and a gentleman all their lives, and are consequently "the real thing." The experiment is of course a failure, and the painter has to go back to his professional model, the lower-middle-class Miss Churm. For James, as for many writers since, realism and reality are very different principles. Realism aims at the "real thing," the objective world; reality, for a writer, is not objective but verbal. Realism gives us a surface that is "like" reality; reality itself is far more complex. Virginia Woolf's polemic, "Mr. Bennett and Mrs. Brown,"[7] is a simplified version of a thesis that James constantly expounds in his prefaces and other critical statements. William James once remarked that his brother's later novels were made out of "impalpable materials, air and the prismatic interferences of light, ingeniously focused by mirrors upon empty space."[8] One may reasonably read two things into this remark. First, William is saying that Henry's characters are treated as though they were ghosts, moving through ghostly incidents and settings in a transparent world. Second, that Henry James is doing with words what, say, Turner in his latest period was doing with paint: not representing objects so much as concentrating on the pictorial elements of colour and lighting.

The characters in James may be good or bad, but whatever they are they never let the verbal texture down. When they engage in dialogue, they "follow" like professional dancers; they "make out" incredible subtleties through the gaps in what is said; they "keep it up" if there is the slightest chance of their saying anything commonplace, their conversation never dangles a participle or bungles a subordinate clause. James understands very well that there are many areas of the psyche which are linguistically structured, and that everything actually said is a selection from many things that could have been said, and that would lead to quite different outcomes for the story if they had been said. In *The Golden Bowl* the heroine Maggie Verver spends hundreds of pages *not* saying to her stepmother: "keep your hands off my husband." What the characters cannot say the author says for them, weaving around them complex patterns of implication, explication, complication, and replication.

The leisure class, which devotes itself to visiting, dining out, seeing and being seen, which does not regard itself as withdrawn from society but feels that it *is* society, constitutes for James a novelist's laboratory, a place where the nuances of human relationship can be studied under controlled conditions. A leisure class means very complex and elaborate conventions, ritual dances around the two maypoles of sex and money which fill up its life. It forms a world in which, when Spectator A sees male B and female C together in a Paris suburb or the National Gallery, an emotional to-do can result that readers a century later have to make a considerable effort of historical imagination to understand. Sociologically, this may be all tinsel and puppet show, but sociological categories, however plausible, have to be handled with great care in literary criticism. For literary antics, what the novels of James give us, especially in the later period, is a shimmering texture of verbal brilliance. The function of a leisure class is to put on a show for the rest of society, and James sees to it that it does, at least verbally, whatever else it may do.

Next to intensity of experience comes intensity of observation, which is, of course, the quality that reproduces James's own work as a novelist. The observer is often a central character in a James story: Maria Gostrey, in *The Ambassadors*, understands so much of what goes on around her that she seems like a sibyl or prophetess, but she expressly says she's nothing of the kind: she simply "sees."[9] Observers may intervene in the action at crucial points, like Fanny Assingham in *The Golden Bowl*, who considers it "great fun"[10] to be an observer, but, like many other observers in James, also has guilt feelings about her responsibility for the action she watches. The unnamed heroine of *In the Cage* is a telegraph operator who decodes a love affair through the messages sent through her office, though she doesn't get it quite right. Such observant characters, who often affect the action in some way, correspond to the clever servants and similar forwarders of the action in traditional comedies. They intervene between the action and the reader, who observes everything but affects nothing.

Naturally this concentration is achieved at a considerable price. James's method is to proceed by indirections, oblique movements that keep avoiding the big dramatic scene which is the stock in trade of so many novelists. One feature of this is the retreat from what James calls "affairs" and E.M. Forster the world of telegrams and anger.[11] In his nearest approach to a detective story, *The Other House,* the theme is the callous murder of a four-year-old child. No police are brought in; the doctor is apparently squared and got to write a certificate for accidental death, and of the murderer it is said, in a phrase of numbing banality, "her doom will be to live."[12] "The Pupil" is a story of a tutor and a boy belonging to an utterly dishonest family who exploit the tutor's fondness for the boy by not paying him, and are absorbed in a social climbing that's too blatant to get them anywhere. At the end they're about to go to smash. It would be interesting to know how such a feckless lot does go to smash, but that would involve the author in "affairs," so he simply cuts off the story by killing the boy. In the notes to the unfinished *The Ivory Tower,* where the theme involves the world of business, James speaks of the work it will take to conceal not merely his lack of knowledge of the business world from the reader but his lack of interest in it.[13]

Sometimes there is a big dramatic scene at the beginning of a novel: two notable examples are *The Princess Casamassima* and *The Wings of the Dove.* The first is a powerful scene in which the hero, as a child, is brought by his adopted mother into the prison where his real mother is dying.[14] Nothing is communicated, because the mother speaks only French, a language no one else present can follow. *The Wings of the Dove* starts with a scene between Kate Croy and her no-good father,[15] who then disappears from the story. Such scenes are prologues only: they play no part in the story itself except as background to show us what a prominent character is trying to escape from. There is no mystery about why James should have failed as a dramatist, the drama being a form that can hardly get along without scenes of confrontation. The mystery is why he should have wanted to succeed in such a form. Like Browning, James was a dramatist in reverse: his genius was for considering situations from the point of view of individual characters. In *The Ring and the Book* Browning took a dramatic situation and worked it out through the points of view of all the major characters (and others) in turn. Henry James's corresponding experiment in reversed drama was *The Awkward Age,* and he was apparently trying to repeat the device in *The Ivory Tower.*[16]

Even the novelist, however, has an audience whose attention must be held from page to page. James's habit was to write (or, later, dictate) a long sketch of his novel in which he talked to himself about his plans for it. For unfinished novels, such as *The Ivory Tower* and *The Sense of the Past*, such notes are invaluable; for the finished books they were destroyed, but his attitude toward them is curiously ambivalent. In a story called "Death of a Lion," one of the most pungently written of all his stories, a shy, retiring writer is seized on by a socialite who makes him a victim of her parties. In its own eyes her society is utterly benevolent and appreciative, but the effect on him is more or less that of falling into a school of piranhas. He finally completes a manuscript on the verge of death; naturally someone wants to borrow it; naturally he loses it; naturally he makes a half-hearted search for it and can't find it (must have left it on a train). The writer dies after instructing his one real friend to rescue the notes and print them instead.

This suggestion that notes in which the author talks to himself about his book are the equivalent of the finished product connects in my mind with that extraordinary dinosaur, the Collected Edition, where James seems to be trying to transform his entire *oeuvre* into one colossal logocentric monument to himself. His unwillingness to let his earlier selves die produces a great number of editorial changes that are usually in the direction of altering direct statements to oblique ones. In the prefaces he sometimes expresses regret that he had not eliminated some lively and attractive character, like Henrietta Stackpole in *Portrait of a Lady*, as though he felt some distaste for getting a casual reader interested in his book. In general, the revisions seem to move in the direction of giving the reader the idiom of the author's notes for the novel instead of the novel itself. One disadvantage of James's approach is that the uniform articulateness of his characters tends to make them sound more or less alike when they speak, and the revising tendency not only increases this, but assimilates their speaking style to James's own. I say this because it seems to me connected with the fact that many of his best realized later stories are occult fantasies which could also be read as existing entirely within the central character's mind.

II

In the traditional comic action in Molière and others the "humour," or obsessed blocking character, is outwitted, usually by some unexpected twist in the plot that (as a rule) enables young love to emerge triumphant. In ironic actions the humour is more likely to retain some ascendancy throughout. But in Henry James we cannot have simple humours with simple obsessions, like Molière's miser. For James all obsessions have a miserly aspect, a clutching and clinging to some substitute for genuine human experience. A recurring theme in James is the fetishism that is absorbed by some substitute symbol of the intensity of experience. The obvious example is *The Spoils of Poynton*, where the central character of the story is a collection of furniture, which gets burned up at the end. An early story, "The Last of the Valerii," features an exhumed Classical statue; there is a wax mannequin in a story called "Rose Agathe," a portrait in "The Special Type," and so on. The symbolic objects of the last works, the golden bowl and the ivory tower, have similar connections. So do various morbid fascinations with the dead in the ghost stories, or with, for example, the *Nachlass* of a dead author. Closer to the traditional miser is the role of money in many of the international stories, where, usually, the Americans have it and the Europeans want it. In *The Golden Bowl* Adam Verver, who has made millions in America, retires from business and becomes a great collector for a museum of his own, and his son-in-law, the Italian Prince Amerigo, acquires the status of an expensive but uniquely desirable collector's item. This is only one element in his marriage, but it is the element symbolized by the crack or flaw in the golden bowl that gives the book its title.

Then again, the pedant is a familiar comic humour, but in James many characters who fail to achieve full experience have a pedantic or over-theoretical quality in them, a retreat from a genuine human life into the pseudo-logic of obsession. T.S. Eliot made a celebrated remark about James's having a mind so fine that no idea could violate it.[17] As a character in *The Europeans* says, "I don't entertain ideas; ideas entertain me."[18] This means among other things that the reader of Henry James gets nothing from the story except the whole story: there are no extractable things to be got out of it. James made this point in a spoof or parody story, "The Figure in the Carpet," which turns on a pun on the word "in." A novelist writes a story which is believed to contain some ineffable precious secret—the metaphor of a buried treasure, something to be removed from where it is, is employed. There is no secret, but the belief that there is one inspires a whole cult.

At the same time James's stories are full of characters who are victims of positive gang-rapes of ideas, and will go to any lengths to defend and elaborate them. In *The Bostonians*, for example, Olive Chancellor takes a younger woman under her protection to educate her in advanced feminist views, including the superior virtue of celibacy, with little if any awareness that she is rationalizing a considerably over-heated lesbian crush. Closer to our present theme is an early story, "Diary of a Man of Fifty," featuring a narrator who had walked out on an Italian countess because she received, and eventually married, the man who had killed her husband in a duel (she said her husband was a brute anyway). Twenty-five years later he goes back to Florence and finds her daughter there with a young Englishman whom he feels to be in exactly the same situation he was. He's so convinced that the situations are identical that he imposes on the reader, who's almost ready to believe that the story is a Kafkaesque nightmare. Gradually it dawns on the reader that the narrator is a nut, and fortunately it dawns on the young man too, who marries the daughter and is very happy with her. "I had a complete theory about her,"[19] the narrator says plaintively.

A story called "Lady Barberina," which is about as near to straight farce as James ever came, tells us of a pompous American doctor who marries a stupid English mooncalf, whose one accomplishment is to sit on a horse while it jumps fences. The American says he wants "race" in his marriage, with the result that his highly unadaptable partner regards him to the end as a "foreigner." This marriage, we learn, is suggested, in fact practically arranged, by an American woman with a theory: she's married very well in England and wants to build a "bridge" between the two countries.[20] In *The Wings of the Dove* Maud Lowder, a socialite, takes the brilliant but impoverished Kate Croy under her protection and refuses to allow her to marry anyone who is not a "great man": again a typical comic action with a blocking character acting out an obsessive theory. Mrs. Newsome in *The Ambassadors*, who never enters the action except by proxy, has a theory that her son Chad is living an immoral life in Paris, which he is from her point of view, and the whole action of the novel turns on this inflexible and provincial parental "humour." In *Portrait of a Lady* Ralph Touchett bestows a large fortune on the heroine Isabel Archer because of a theory that she will do something interesting with it. She does, too: she immediately constructs a theoretical air-castle of her own that leads her to refuse a most attractive proposal and throw herself away on a broken-down slob ("sterile dilettante,"[21] the text calls him).

These theoretical humours have a peculiarly close relation to the occult stories, because the occult by definition is unknown, and what we don't know we are impelled to concoct theories about. In a story called

"The Marriages" the central figure, a woman named Adela, is bitterly opposed to her father's remarrying because she's fixated on her dead mother's memory. She admits that her father seems happy, "and it's dreadful of him to want to be."[22] She breaks up the engagement by calling on the prospective stepmother and telling her a slanderous rigmarole about her father and mother. The stepmother-elect backs out, not because of what's told her, but because she can't stand the prospect of living with such a creature as Adela and Adela's father won't give her up. A relevant detail is that Adela believes that she's in spiritual communication with her mother, but considering what she does the connection seems morally dubious.

In another story, "The Friends of the Friends," which is explicitly a ghost story, a woman breaks off her engagement to her fiancé because she thinks he's more devoted to a dead woman than he is to her. He has seen the dead woman only once, and that was when she came to call on him, apparently after her death. It seems a somewhat strained reason for breaking off an engagement, but the living woman, who is also the narrator, has her theory to safeguard: "Everything in the facts was monstrous, and most of all my lucid perception of them: the only thing allied to nature and truth was my having to act on that perception . . . . When six years later, in solitude and silence, I heard of his death I hailed it as a direct contribution to my theory."[23] One step further takes us to a much more celebrated theoretician, the governess in *The Turn of the Screw*.

The setting of *The Turn of the Screw* is familiar: a governess is hired to supervise two beautiful children, a boy and a girl named Miles and Flora, in a country house. Her employer pays for the set-up but refuses to have anything else to do with it—a convention straight out of folk tale. The house is inhabited by a housekeeper and two dead servants, Peter Quint and Miss Jessel, who have, according to the housekeeper, exerted evil influences on the children. The governess sees the ghosts of the servants at various times, and is convinced that the children, for all their beauty and almost preternatural intelligence, are aware of these influences and continue to respond to them. This becomes obsessive with her, and her reaction to apparent evidence that this is true of Flora is merely an exultant: "thank God! It so justifies me!"[24]

It seems clear that the governess is a mass of sexual neuroses herself, and in general is as batty as a Kentucky cave. One episode will illustrate the point: she sees Miss Jessel looming behind Flora on one occasion; she tries to make the housekeeper see the ghost too; the child is frightened and says: "I don't know what you mean. I see nobody. I see nothing. I never *have*. I think you're cruel. I don't like you!"[25] This sounds like what any normal unhaunted child would say in the circumstances: the governess's reaction is to throw herself on the ground and go into hysterical convulsions. At the end of the story she is trying to get Miles to admit that he has been in connection with Peter Quint, whom she sees outside the window. Miles finally answers her question with "Peter Quint—you devil!"[26] where the devil is clearly the governess rather than the evil ghost. The shock of realizing his condition kills him, perhaps: anyway, the story ends with a fully justified governess and a dead child.

If we look at *The Turn of the Screw* from the standpoint of realism, the story can be seen only as the fantasy of a madwoman, bolstered by the gossip of an illiterate housekeeper. One has to think also of the Victorian governess's uncertain hold on the middle class, where servants are always vaguely menacing ghosts, threatening to pull her down to their social level. Much is said about Peter Quint as a "menial," and Flora's outburst is said to be that of "a vulgarly pert little girl in the street."[27] The reading of the story as a straight neurosis was more or less that of Edmund Wilson,[28] who never understood anything in literature except realism, but such a reduction is far too simplistic for James. The governess seems to be telling her own story as a first-person narrator, but her story is actually being read aloud by someone else who knew her, and gives the strongest guarantees of her sanity and responsibility. James himself seems to confirm this in the preface to *The Princess Casamassima*, where he includes her with Maisie and Fleda Vetch of *The Spoils of Poynton*, both impeccable heroines.

No, the governess is rather a Cassandra figure who does see what she thinks she sees, though she may be crazy, as Cassandra was. As Hamlet discovered, it is not always possible to preserve one's mental balance when confronted with ghosts. How far the children are aware of the evil influences around them is another question. Miles may be if Flora isn't: he was, we are told, expelled from his school without explanation, although he keeps teasing to be sent back there. In any case the governess's efforts to save the children are a violation of them as disastrous as anything the dead servants do. She is, in short, taken over by the evil she tries to fight.[29]

Of the many things *The Turn of the Screw* connects with, one is the total deadlock of conventional standards of "good" and "evil." There is a picture by Blake generally called *Good and Evil Angels Struggling for the Possession of a Child*. Judging from the various contexts in which this design appears in Blake, the child might be as badly off under the good as under the evil one. Similar deadlocks appear in various stories about writers and artists, though as a rule without ghosts. In "The Author of Beltraffio" the narrator visits a novelist who lives with a wife and small son. The wife has not read her husband's famous novel *Beltraffio*, but she "knows" it's a bad book, and she bends all her energies to keep control of the boy, to the point of sending away a doctor when he is dangerously ill. The boy dies—James is a prolific killer of children—and the mother repents sufficiently to put *Beltraffio* on her reading list. Conventional people's fears of literature or art that they think disturbs their moral values very quickly turn into a hatred of human intellect and imagination, and the conventional person is soon in the grip of an unseen evil force. James's father was interested in Swedenborg, and Swedenborg suggests that we are constantly surrounded by evil spirits, who are there but invisible, like the stars in daytime, but are unaware of us unless we do something to attract their attention. James himself owed something to Swedenborg—Lewis Lambert Strether, the hero of *The Ambassadors*, is named after a Swedenborgian novel by Balzac.[30]

Again, *The Turn of the Screw* is one of James's puzzle stories that admit of more than one reading, none of which we can say with confidence to be the right one. In a story called *The Sacred Fount*, a character at a weekend house party makes up fantasies about other people there, confides them to a woman, and is told they're nonsense. End of long and remarkably pointless story. Practically everybody reads the book on this level—the realistic level—and wonders why James wrote it. But there are various layers of ambiguity underneath. It is true that what the narrator is doing is a parody of an imaginative process rather than an example of it: no novelist goes to work by making up stories about the people around him. But still the narrator's construct has a reality of sorts: it is subjective reality confronted with objective reality, even if the two fail entirely to coincide. Beneath that is a still more elusive question. Why couldn't the narrator's fantasy be a real version of what is going on, told with a different perspective and emphasis? When the woman says impatiently about one of his figures, "there's really nothing in him at all,"[31] is she making a factual statement about any conceivable human being? But then we go back to the surface meaning, and realize that is doubtless truth also, if not *the* truth: James has many observers who get things wrong, and was bound to write a parody of the process sooner or later.

Such a story as *The Sacred Fount* brings the relation of reality and realism into sharp confrontation: either there is some hidden reality that the narrator's fantasies point to, however vaguely and inaccurately, or there is no discernible reason for setting them forth at all. This principle, which runs through all of James's work, gives the occult stories a particular significance. A ghostly world challenges us with the existence of a reality beyond realism which still may not be identifiable as real. *The Wings of the Dove*, for example, is not a ghost story, but it is a story of two attractive young lovers, Kate Croy and Morton Densher, who want to marry but are blocked by poverty and impotence. As in a Molière comedy, they outwit the blocking character Maud Lowder, but they do it by descending on a dying American heiress and extracting her money like vultures battening on a corpse. Morton Densher struggles for some sense of self-respect to the very end of the story, but is powerless in the grip of something quite as sinister as any Quint or Jessel. Nor can we identify this sinister force with Kate Croy: she is more resolute and ruthless than he is, but is quite as trapped in what seems to her an inescapable situation. Milly Theale, the heiress, dies in Venice, the city of Ben Jonson's play *Volpone*, where the theme of parasitism is set out brutally with nothing of James's ironic niceties or scruples.

It is also Venice that forms the setting of *The Aspern Papers*. Here Juliana, the ex-mistress of the young Romantic American poet, Jeffrey Aspern, dead for many years, lives with her niece Miss Tina in possession of all Aspern's papers. An American scholar, the narrator and one of a breed evidently as rapacious in James's day as now, comes to rent rooms in their palazzo. Juliana is a ferocious old harridan who is determined to extract as much American money from the scholar as she can, but has no intention of giving up a scrap of the papers, unless, perhaps, she can benefit her niece, the only human being now that she cares anything about. So Juliana and the narrator settle down to a watching and waiting game. The narrator remarks that the greatest vice is not knowing where to stop, and he is carried along to the point where he is mentally a thief and burglar and seducer of virgins, though he shrinks from the two physical acts of actually seizing the papers and actually marrying Miss Tina. His self-rationalizings get more desperate as the story proceeds. He is warned at the beginning that he may have to make love to Miss Tina: he says he would, recalls this later and calls it a "joke without consequences."[32] He breaks into Juliana's room and is caught by her, but maintains that he wasn't really about to steal the papers, just to "test a theory." Finally Juliana dies and Miss Tina destroys the papers, as she doesn't want anything to do with a man who in effect turned her down when she in effect proposed to him.

The Aspern Papers is not a ghost story, except to the degree that the dead poet may be watching the action sardonically from his portrait, as there are indications that he is. Several of James's stories deal with a dead author's reactions to the disposal of his papers. The fact that Aspern and his ex-mistress are Americans (the originals for the story were Byron and Jane Clairmont), and his period around 1820, brings the theme very close to *The Sense of the Past*. The story seems in any case as frightening as *The Turn of the Screw*, and more ambiguous in its moral categories. If Quint and Jessel do exist as ghosts, they are identifiably evil. But in *The Aspern Papers* there is once again a total deadlock which the categories of good and evil are quite useless to resolve. Modern morality would be solidly against Juliana and for the scholar, because this is an ironic age, which believes that a figure interesting to the public belongs totally to the public, and has no right to the smallest shred of privacy. But at the time of *The Aspern Papers*, privacy had its rights too: burning one's papers at death was a normal procedure, and for Juliana to keep her lover's letters safe from prying eyes carried its own justification.

I mentioned the Venetian setting of the story, and towards the end the narrator remarks about how "the Venetian figures, moving to and fro against the battered scenery of their little houses of comedy, strike you as members of an endless dramatic troupe."[33] There seems to be a reference to the bedrock of all European comedy, the *commedia dell'arte*, with its stock characters, its improvised plots, and its close relation to puppet theatre. One is reminded of the ballet-like plots of *What Maisie Knew* and *The Golden Bowl*, with their characters twining and intertwining in symmetrical patterns: a convention that runs all through fiction, especially comic fiction, though perhaps introduced in its modern form by Goethe's *Elective Affinities*, the title of which is a metaphor from chemical reactions. A James novel is "really" a story of forces of demonic evil and angelic innocence sweeping across fully articulate and intelligent beings who are largely unaware of them. It is just as "really" a story of chess pieces moving through an endgame that can result only in checkmate or stalemate. One has to read James by a stereo vision that brings the two realities into focus.

III

Apart from the various "humours," the fetishists and pedants, who fail to achieve any real intensity of experience, is there a general force that acts as a cause, apart from these effects? There are many answers, but one important one is certainly the narcosis of time. We eat and sleep, not when we are hungry or sleepy, but when it is time to eat or sleep, and the habit grows on us of committing experience to time, so that we drift along with its irreversible movement instead of withdrawing from it occasionally to become fully self-aware. The narcosis of time operates with peculiar power in the realm of expectation, where something is to happen in the future, as with the revolutionary programs, feminist in *The Bostonians* and social in *The Princess Casamassima*, that bemuse many of James's characters. There is also a struggle with time peculiar to the writer or artist, where the creator has to learn to relax his will and let things take their own time without drifting into laziness. This theme haunts James from *Roderick Hudson* on: a short story, "The Madonna of the Future," is a more conventional tale of an artist (American in Europe, of course) who keeps dreaming of a supreme masterpiece but never lifts a brush. The archetype for the story, referred to in the text, is Balzac's *Chef d'oeuvre inconnu*,[34] but the man in that story at least worked on his delusion. The theme means a good deal to James because he himself was no infant prodigy; he took a long time to develop, and the feeling of having to die before one has really begun to understand one's art comes into many stories, most poignantly "The Middle Years."

But the transfer of experience to expectation is at its clearest in the terrible story "The Beast in the Jungle," where John Marcher has been obsessed all his life by the notion that some tremendous experience, exhilarating or disastrous, awaits him at some time or other. Meanwhile he passes up every opportunity to achieve genuine experience, such as loving the sensitive and intelligent woman who loves him. Eventually the beast springs, along with Marcher's awareness that its name is Nothingness, and that he is now only a lost soul.

A gentler irony pervades a shorter tale called "The Bench of Desolation," where an elderly couple are sitting together on a bench beside the sea. The woman (I simplify slightly) has sued the man for breach of promise, and he has beggared himself for a lifetime in attempting to repay her—a theme slightly resembling de Maupassant's famous "Necklace" story. The woman tells him that she has carefully saved every penny he has paid her, because she knew more about money than he did, and she is paying it back with fivefold interest. What she forgot about was the passage of time, and that while she was saving his money he was spending his life. No other story in James has quite the eerie, otherworldly atmosphere of this one, in which, as in a Japanese Noh play, we seem to be in a world between death and birth, where all regrets have lost their relevance.

The next step takes us into the "international" theme so central in Henry James, where an American goes to Europe in search of deeper and richer experience. The movement is almost always eastward, and the protagonist is more frequently female than male. Again, the theme is a comic one, and the normal happy ending would be, as remarked earlier, not the right marriage necessarily, but the achievement of some kind of initiation into a fuller life. Ironic versions of this comic theme lead to frustrations of various kinds. One common story-type has the general pattern: naive innocent wealthy American girl goes to Europe, marries some very dubious Count de Spoons character, and wrecks her life.

The earliest major treatment of this theme, I think, is a story belonging to James's Paris period, "Madame de Mauves." Here a romantic American girl named Euphemia, her convent-educated head turned by historical romance, feels that marriage to a Frenchman of a very old aristocratic family would be marriage to a superman. The Baron she marries is not a superman and his eye soon wanders, and Euphemia's life becomes miserable. The Baron's sister gives her a severe lecture: the male de Mauves have been having it on the side since Merovingian times, and who does Euphemia think she is to object to such hoary whoring? The sister actually seems to think that if a vice has a long enough pedigree it becomes something admirable: an aspect of aristocracy and tradition that the romances had not discussed. An American named Longmore comes to console Euphemia; the Baron has just enough of a conscience to hope that Longmore will take his wife on, but the lady is not for that kind of burning, and talks Longmore into renouncing her. Longmore himself doesn't want renunciation: he wants experience, even if respectable. However, he goes back to America; the Baron then suddenly has a change of heart and falls madly in love with his wife again, but as she will now have nothing more to do with him either he shoots himself. An exasperating story, but significant in many ways.

The generic affinities of the story are interesting. Euphemia is a kind of Courtly Love mistress, covering the entire spectrum of sexual frustration from the ideal of sublimation who demands total renunciation of sex from her lovers, to the frigid ice statue whose cruelty kills or otherwise destroys the essential life of her lover, in this case including her repentant husband as well. A similar figure appears in the Aurora Coyne of *The Sense of the Past*, an American woman who has been to Europe, had some unknown bad experience there, and tries to extract a vow from the hero that he will never go to Europe, though she gives him no guarantees in return.

There are some remarkable episodes in this early story: Longmore has a dream in which he sees Euphemia across water, gets a boat to the other side, and finds she's back on the side he left. Boats and water are often associated with sexual experience in James, whether genuine, frustrated, or perverted: they appear prominently in *The Turn of the Screw* and *The Ambassadors*. Another episode features a pair of lovers, the woman socially a cut above the man, who is a fledgling artist, in a restaurant with the woman in charge of the restaurant making dire predictions. In later stories James would not feel the need of inserted episodes to show how the same archetypal situations recur in all ranks of society.

In *Portrait of a Lady*, already glanced at, we have an ironic parody of the type of magazine fiction that used to be addressed to a female reading public, and which usually featured a poor girl who eventually married a rich man, or else passed over the rich man and waited for Mr. Right. Isabel Archer, a rich girl, immediately passes over Mr. Right, Lord Warburton, and a group of American expatriates living in France pass her off on a Mr. All Wrong. In *Daisy Miller* there is no marriage, but Daisy is an attractive young woman who goes to Europe and is ostracized by the society around her for her free and unconventional American ways. She is not really "fast," much less loose: her trouble is that she refuses to think of herself, every moment of the day, as standing in a sexual trap as bait for some eligible young man, and posturing and displaying herself according to the rules of that game. Again the story is cut off by her death, but the essential point has been made. It was made again later by a reviewer who called the story an insult to American womanhood.

A minor and extremely unpleasant version of the same story-type is in a brief tale called "Four Meetings." Here an American woman who has always longed to see Europe finally gets to go there: as the ship docks at Havre a "cousin," a bum pretending to be an artist, descends on her and takes all her money; then she has to go back to America and the bum's whore, who calls herself a countess, settles in on her as a parasite. James says that every unpleasant story should have its beautiful counterpart:[35] I know of no beautiful counterpart to this one, but perhaps the principle he is referring to is different in shape. The positive drive of a traditional comic story is towards a happy ending, which in James's international stories, we said, means an initiation leading to a greater and fuller intensity of experience. The story we read usually tells us of some failure to achieve this, whether a moral failure within an individual character or the result of a sinister or stupid social conspiracy. But we as readers can see something of what might have been achieved, and our wider vision is perhaps the beautiful counterpart James mentions.

Certainly there is a great deal of beauty in the three great novels at the end of James's career, *The Wings of the Dove*, *The Ambassadors*, and *The Golden Bowl*, and there are many suggestions of positive as well as ironic resolutions. In *The Wings of the Dove* Milly Theale, with the hectic flush of death on her, nevertheless achieves a quality of life that carries her serenely over the heads of the lovers trying to get her money. In *The Ambassadors* four major characters all achieve something of the same quality, although their community disintegrates at the end. In *The Golden Bowl* Maggie Verver breaks out of her ironic dilemma by remaining in Europe with her Italian husband and outgrowing her emotional dependence on her father by sending him back to America with her stepmother. Such positive achievements represent an escape from what I have called the narcosis of time, the simple drifting from birth to death. I spoke at the beginning of the ideal fusion of American and European contributions to a full human life as perhaps attainable only in a submerged Atlantis. In Blake Atlantis is the kingdom of the imagination, and the ocean that rests on top of it he calls the "Sea of Time and Space."[36] At some point or other it seems to have occurred to James that the most concentrated possible treatment of his international theme would be one that cuts through our ordinary awareness of space and time.

It has been noted by James critics, Edgar among them, that in the traditional ghost story the dead haunt the living, whereas in James it is frequently the living who haunt the dead. One of the major reasons for well-to-do Americans going to Europe in the first place is to reinforce their sense of the past, to become more aware of their own cultural heritage. So Ralph Pendrell, the American hero of *The Sense of the Past*, having acquired a Regency house in London, becomes obsessed with the pastness of the house, and in particular with a curious portrait of a young man who has turned his back on the painter, evidently as a whim. We gradually learn that the subject of the portrait is another Ralph Pendrell of a century previous, who had come from an earlier America to marry the daughter of an English family and reconcile the two families. So the twentieth-century American vanishes into the Regency period, while his counterpart moves into the contemporary twentieth-century world.

The former finds himself in a dream world, where everything seems at first to go all right, as so often happens in dreams. Where certain things are not clear to him, he makes mistakes, and the mistakes produce some uneasiness in the people around him, as though they were subliminally aware of being haunted by a ghost from another age. Meanwhile he discovers that in addition to the daughter he is supposed to marry, there is another and considerably more attractive daughter, whom he is clearly going to fall in love with instead. His counterpart in the future, according to James's notes, is considerably displeased at this, and we realize that the arrangement is a rather unfair one: the hero of the story is imprisoned in the past, whereas his counterpart has all the freedom of the future.

However James would have worked the story out, it was a kind of abstract model of the type of story he had been telling all his life. The companion piece, "The Jolly Corner," is an even clearer example of the living haunting the dead, as the hero, an American named Spencer Brydon, who has spent his life in Europe, returns to New York to his ancestral house there, whence he proceeds to dig out a very reluctant ghost of the Spencer Brydon he would have been if he had stayed in America. Both stories leave it open to us to consider their central characters as simple lunatics, but somehow the willing suspension of disbelief does take hold; we accept the exchange of identities in time and space as imaginative realities, and can even see in them a structured form of some of the hidden entities that we get only fitful glimpses of in the more representational stories.

Another unfinished novel was *The Ivory Tower*. Here, for complex reasons we cannot go into, a man named Graham Fielder is left a large sum of money by an American millionaire, has no idea of what to do with it, gives it to a friend to look after for him; the friend promptly embezzles it, and the hero thinks up various reasons for not doing anything about it. He got the money in the first place through the influence of one of the two heroines, Rosanna Spearman, who is a warm-hearted and generous girl, but his affections are clearly moving in the direction of a much more tight-mouthed female who would be more likely to go off with the embezzler. Three books and part of a fourth, out of a projected ten, about someone who seems clearly to be, in post-Jamesian language, a wimp and a nerd. Soon after James started on it the 1914 war broke out, and the book was abandoned. All around him was an outbreak of hysterical fury that made the evil of Peter Quint and Miss Jessel, to say nothing of the evil of people who embezzle money when they are practically asked to do so, look like children in Hallowe'en masks. The well-dressed and articulate puppets were too wooden, too stiff and rattling, for James to have any more interest in manoeuvring them. He turned once again to his ghost story just before he died, because in its fantasy he saw the reality he had sought as an artist, whereas the realism in the social manners of his time had left him with a sense of total illusion.

Notes

Introduction

1 Appellations once applied to NF by Harold Bloom. See "Harold Bloom" in Imre Salusinszky, *Criticism in Society* (New York: Methuen, 1987), 58, 62.
2 See Marjorie Perloff's "Modernist Studies," in *Redrawing the Boundaries: The Transformation of English and American Literary Studies*, ed. Stephen Greenblatt and Giles Gunn (New York: Modern Language Association, 1992), 155, 154.
3 Ibid., 159.
4 See Robert Langbaum, *The Poetry of Experience: The Dramatic Monologue in Modern Literary Tradition* (London: Chatto & Windus, 1957).
5 See M.H. Abrams, "Structure and Style in the Greater Romantic Lyric," in *From Sensibility to Romanticism: Essays Presented to Frank A. Pottle*, ed. Frederick W. Hilles and Harold Bloom (New York: Oxford University Press, 1965).
6 Perloff, "Modernist Studies," 154.
7 See, for instance, Harold Bloom's *Yeats* (New York: Oxford University Press, 1970), *The Anxiety of Influence* (New York: Oxford University Press, 1973), and *A Map of Misreading* (New York: Oxford University Press, 1975).
8 Albert Gelpi, *A Coherent Splendor: The American Poetic Renaissance, 1910–1950* (New York: Cambridge, 1987), 4–5.
9 Perloff, "Modernist Studies," 161.
10 Ibid., 163.
11 Ibid., 163.
12 See Frank Kermode, *The Sense of an Ending* (London: Oxford University Press, 1967), 108.
13 See "Harold Bloom," in *Criticism in Society*, 62.
14 For an account of the epiphany in question, see Ayre, 44. Shaw's work, Ayre suggests, was for NF "a theater of his own irreconcilable tensions and . . . a model for his own early prose style." At this point, NF found Blake "impen-

etrable" and "had no idea that he would one day replace Shaw as a guide through the dark wood of [his] own evangelical protestantism" (Ayre, 48–9). Interestingly, he would substantially address Shaw only once afterward, in his radio talk "Writer as Prophet" (*LS*, 176–81), where he nevertheless puts him in the visionary company of Milton, Swift, and Blake.

15 See "Tradition and the Individual Talent," in T.S. Eliot's *Selected Essays* (London: Faber & Faber, 1951), 14.

16 See Imre Salusinszky's "Frye and Romanticism," in *Visionary Poetics: Essays on Northrop Frye's Criticism*, ed. Robert D. Denham and Thomas Willard (New York: Peter Lang, 1991), 65.

17 See Wallace Stevens, *The Necessary Angel: Essays on Reality and the Imagination* (New York: Knopf, 1951), 150.

18 Salusinszky relates that "after the talk, the young author of *Fearful Symmetry* was taken up to meet the distinguished speaker. Predictably, the encounter between these two unusually reserved men did not turn out to be one of the great literary meetings: Stevens spent the whole time asking Frye about various stockbrokers and insurance people he had met on his one visit to Toronto—nine years before Frye was born." See Salusinszky's "Frye and Romanticism," 65. In the telephone interview with Salusinszky in 1983 during which Frye had described this meeting, he had explained that "Stevens muttered [the paper] into his shirt collar, with the avenue traffic rolling outside. I was brought up to meet him afterwards, and I racked my brains for something to say about a paper of which I had not heard one complete sentence. Stevens saw that I was embarrassed, so he put me at ease by asking me about various stockbrokers and insurance people in Toronto, whom he had met the last time he had visited Toronto, which was in 1908" (*INF*, 692).

19 See Michael Dolzani, "The Book of the Dead: A Skeleton Key to Northrop Frye's Notebooks," in *Rereading Frye: The Published and Unpublished Works*, ed. David Boyd and Imre Salusinszky (Toronto: University of Toronto Press, 1999), 28.

20 For an extended discussion of this, see Glen Robert Gill, *Northrop Frye and the Phenomenology of Myth* (Toronto: University of Toronto Press, 2006), 101–77.

21 This correspondence is contained in NFF, 1988, box 61, file 5.

22 See "Second Thoughts about Humanism," in T.S. Eliot's *Selected Essays*, 485.

23 NF may later have perceived some limitations to this approach, as he stated in 1963 that, "though I repudiate nothing in [the paper], I should write it very differently now" (*FI*, 2).

24 See Wallace Stevens, *The Necessary Angel: Essays on Reality and the Imagination*, 36.

25 Ibid., 118.

26 Ibid., 130.
27 See *Large Red Man Reading*, l. 15, *Credences of Summer*, sec. 3, l. 5, and *Tea at the Palaz of Hoon*, in *The Collected Poems of Wallace Stevens* (New York: Knopf, 1954), 424, 373, 65, respectively.
28 The tactics proposed by Joyce's semi-autobiographical character Stephen Dedalus at the end of chap. 5 of *A Portrait of the Artist as a Young Man*, just before the diary entries that conclude the novel.

1. Press Cuttings

1 John Masefield's *Tragedy of Nan* had been performed by the Dramatic Society on 30 November and 1 and 2 December 1932; John Galsworthy's *The Silver Box* was its production in spring 1932, reviewed by NF (see *ENC*, 231–2).
2 George Bernard Shaw was known to charge high royalties for his plays, and scrupulously managed that income until he had accrued considerable wealth. NF may not have known when he wrote this that by this point in Shaw's life the playwright was putting most of his earnings into philanthropic causes, as when he donated the money from his 1925 Nobel Prize for Literature to subsidize an English edition of the work of the Swedish dramatist August Strindberg.

2. Delicate Rhythms

1 Frankenberg may indeed have felt that he was being damned with faint praise by NF in this review, as the poet published a somewhat unappreciative review of *FS* when it appeared seven years later. See "Forms of Freedom," *Saturday Review of Literature*, 30 (19 July 1947): 19.

3. Experiment

1 J. Howard Woolmer's *A Checklist of the Hogarth Press, 1917–1946* (Revere, Pa.: Woolmer/Brotherson, 1986) lists the original sale price of *Poets of Tomorrow: First Selection* as 6 shillings. This appears to have been quite a reasonable price at the time, approximately the cost of a pulp or "dime store" novel.
2 NF is obviously referring to the Fascist insurrection and civil war in Spain between 1936 and 1939. For further comments by NF on the poetic responses to this conflict, see no. 8.
3 NF is probably referring to the group of poets popularized by Laurence Binyon's anthology *The Golden Treasury of Modern Lyrics* (London: Macmillan, 1924), many of whom espoused the ethical and artistic authority of "the Beautiful." These included Binyon himself, Lascelles Abercrombie, Gordon Bottomley, and Walter de la Mare. Chief among these poets, arguably, was

Robert Bridges, whose most celebrated work *The Testament of Beauty* (Oxford: Clarendon, 1929) NF refers to in no. 16, p. 41.

4 The appellation "Victorian Buddhists" seems to be more idiosyncratic than conventional. NF is probably referring to Matthew Arnold, whose poetry registered an interest in Buddhism and whom NF names several lines later, but it is uncertain which other poets or thinkers he may have had in mind.

4. Poetry (I)

1 William Lyon Mackenzie was a Canadian journalist and political leader, and the grandfather of William Lyon Mackenzie King, Prime Minster of Canada, 1921–30 and 1935–48. William Lyon Mackenzie was elected the first mayor of Toronto in 1834, and in 1837, frustrated in his efforts at reform, he and a group of insurgents attempted to seize Toronto. The rebellion was quickly put down and Mackenzie and his group escaped to the United States. He was imprisoned for eighteen months by the U.S. authorities, and then worked as a journalist and writer until a proclamation of general amnesty allowed his return to Canada in 1849. Afterwards he served as a member of the Legislative Assembly of United Canada (Upper and Lower Canada), 1851–58.

2 John George Lambton, First Earl of Durham (usually referred to as Lord Durham), was appointed Governor General and High Commissioner of British North America and was sent to investigate the circumstances surrounding the Rebellion of Louis-Joseph Papineau and the Upper Canada Rebellion of 1837 (see n. 1, above). His *Report on the Affairs of British North America* of 1839, which recommended responsible government and a legislative union of the Canadas and the Maritime Provinces, is considered a founding document of Canadian nationhood. It is traditionally criticized, however, for its proposition of merging Upper and Lower Canada into one colony in order to bring about the extinction of the French language and culture in Canada through intermingling with the more numerous English.

5. Poetry (II)

1 NF appears to be using the term "hieroglyphic" in a literal sense here, as a sign with "sacred" (*hieros*) value and pictorial intent, in the context of the "complicated personal symbolism" he attributes to poet Oscar Williams. He is obviously not using the word in its conventional sense, in reference to ancient Egyptian pictographs, nor in the more theoretical context in which he uses it in *GC* (6/23). NF is correct in observing that the words "skyline" and "quicksilver" recur in this volume of poetry with unusual frequency: they appear five times in five different poems, respectively.

2 Vladimir Mayakovsky was a leading poet of the Russian Revolution of 1917 and the early Soviet period, and a founding figure in the socialist artistic movement called "Russian Futurism." His work was inspired by industrial and technological developments and borrowed techniques from painting and film. He was concerned with the problem of death throughout his life, and in 1930, haunted by criticism and disappointment in love, he shot himself.

6. Henry Wells

1 NF is referring to the promotion of the metaphysical poets and Renaissance dramatists (largely at the expense of Romantic writers) by critics of the early part of the twentieth century. The process was initiated in several essays by T.S. Eliot, most notably "The Metaphysical Poets" and "Andrew Marvell." See T.S. Eliot, *Selected Essays* (London: Faber & Faber, 1951). These essays profoundly influenced the direction of literary criticism in the first half of the twentieth century, until NF's own *FS*, along with the work of critics like Harold Bloom and Geoffrey Hartman, countered the trend and re-established the importance of Romanticism in literary and cultural studies. See also no. 37, n. 10.

7. Irene Moody

1 Imagism was a movement among early twentieth-century poets who were reacting against the traditions of Romantic idealism and Victorian moralism. In *Tendencies in Modern American Poetry* (Boston: Houghton Mifflin, 1917), Amy Lowell summarizes the aims of Imagism as being: 1) to use the exact word from common speech; 2) to avoid clichés; 3) to invent new rhythms; 4) to freely choose any subject; 5) to create concrete images, sharply outlined; 6) to achieve concentration and compression, the essence of poetry; and 7) to suggest rather than state.

2 Moody indicates in footnotes that two of her poems in this collection, *Radio-Sensitivity* and *To France*, were written in 1940, in response to various events in the early days of World War II (94, 96).

8. Poetry (III)

1 Percy Bysshe Shelley was notorious for vehemently speaking out and writing against various social and political orthodoxies and conservativisms in culture. Among his favourite topical causes were atheism, anarchism, free speech, class revolution, trade unionism, agricultural reform, Irish nationalism, Catholic emancipation, feminism, and the abolition of conventional

marriage. See, for instance, Michael Henry Scrivener, *Radical Shelley: The Philosophical Anarchism and Utopian Thought of Percy Bysshe Shelley* (Princeton: Princeton University Press, 1982).

9. New Directions (I)

1 NF is referring to a comparative discussion that takes place over three of J.S. Mill's essays, "Bentham," "The Writings of Alfred de Vigny," and "Coleridge." See the *Collected Works of John Stuart Mill*, vol. 1: *Autobiography and Literary Essays*, ed. John M. Robson and Jack Stillinger (Toronto: University of Toronto Press, 1981), 467, 497, and vol. 10: *Essays on Ethics, Religion and Society*, ed. John M. Robson (Toronto: University of Toronto Press, 1969), 78.

2 The WPA was a U.S. government agency created in 1935 by an executive order of President Franklin Delano Roosevelt as the Works Progress Administration. It was renamed the Work Projects Administration in 1939. It was designed to create jobs and income for the unemployed by putting them to work on projects of public benefit and beautification, including the creation of murals, paintings, and sculptures, the staging of musical and theatrical performances, and the writing of state and regional guidebooks. Though highly praised, the WPA's appropriation and payroll was drastically cut in 1939 and the agency officially went out of existence in 1943.

3 Pierre Jean Jouve was a French poet and novelist. His work found its primary inspiration and influences in the French Symbolist tradition, Christian mysticism, and psychoanalysis. See also no. 20.

4 Comte de Lautréamont was the pseudonym of the iconoclastic French surrealist Isidore Lucien Ducasse.

5 Paul Goodman's contribution to this volume actually consists of three pieces. In addition to the story-essays cited by NF, "Alcestis" and "Tiberius," there is a critical essay entitled "Literary Abstraction and Cubism."

10. Review of *New Writing and Daylight* (I)

1 The three poems by Day Lewis are *Word All Over*, *Reconciliation*, and *Departure in the Dark*.

2 Terence Tiller's work in this volume consists of his poems *The Blizzard in the Bottle*, *Being Oneself*, *Bathers*, and *Egyptian Dancer*.

3 The reference is to the Hollywood film of 1942.

4 The contributions referred to by NF are short stories by Jiri Mucha, a Czech writer, and Rosamond Oppersdorff (who according to a note is not a Pole but an American with a Polish husband) entitled "The Diary from Valmer" and "I Was Too Ignorant," respectively.

11. Review of *Voices* and *Genesis*

1 NF is referring to the popular myth that John Keats's death by tuberculosis in 1820 was brought on by criticism of him in *Blackwood's Magazine* for being a member of Leigh Hunt's "Cockney School" of poetry, and by a harsh review of *Endymion* in the *Quarterly Review*. The myth was popularized by Shelley's *Adonais: An Elegy on the Death of John Keats* and by Byron's *Don Juan*, which speaks of how Keats was "was killed off by one critique" and "snuffed out by an Article" (canto 11, ll. 473, 480). The "volume of 1817" is Keats's *Poems*.

2 "The way downward is easy from Avernus" (*Aeneid*, bk. 6, l. 187). A Latin proverb suggesting that the road to ruin is short and swift.

3 The reference, deliberately hyperbolic and ironic, is to Reinhard Heydrich (1904–42), a notorious officer in the Nazi SD (*Sicherheitsdienst*) and Gestapo and one of the architects of the "Final Solution."

4 T.S. Eliot writes in his introduction to Marianne Moore's *Selected Poems* (New York: Macmillan, 1935): "We know very little about the value of the work of our own contemporaries, almost as little as we know about our own. It may have merits which only exist for contemporary sensibility; it may have concealed virtues which only become apparent with time. How it will rank when we are all dead authors ourselves we cannot say with any precision. If one is to talk about one's contemporaries at all, therefore, it is important to make up our minds as to what we can affirm with confidence, and as to what must be a matter of doubting conjecture. The last thing, certainly, that we can or are likely to know about them is their 'greatness,' or their relative distinction or triviality in relation to the standard of 'greatness.' For in greatness are involved moral and social relations, relations which can only be perceived from a remoter perspective, and which may be said even to be created in the process of history: we cannot tell, in advance, what any poetry is going to do, how it will operate upon later generations. But the *genuineness* of poetry is something which we have some warrant for believing that a small number, but only a small number, of contemporary readers can recognize" (vii).

5 In his *Ars poetica*, Horace admonished that the purpose of poetry is *prodesse aut delectare*, "to delight and instruct," a sentiment famously echoed in Sir Phillip Sidney's *An Apology for Poetry*.

6 NF considered E.J. Pratt's *The Truant* not only the most important poem in this collection, as he states in this review, but "the greatest poem in Canadian literature" (*C*, 265). He took the compliment even further once when he suggested that it "is not only the greatest of Canadian poems, but one of the almost definitive poetic statements of our time" (*C*, 337). He also referred

to an occasion when Pratt read the poem to him as "a turning point in [his] life" (*C*, 337).

7 The lyrics in question are Finch's poems *Terminal, The Fire*, and *Rain Around a Library.*

8 NF refers to Kennedy's poems *Rake's Progress, Atheist's Tragedy, The Bride Wore Red, Salvationist, Fin de Siècle*, and *Sepulture d'un Poète Maudit.*

9 The reference is to Patrick Anderson's poems *Summer's Joe, Night Out*, and *Sacking.*

10 NF is referring to the rationale behind William Wordsworth's statement in "Preface to Lyrical Ballads" that his "principal object . . . was to choose incidents and situations from common life, and to relate or describe them, throughout, as far as was possible, in a selection of language really used by men." See "Preface to the Lyrical Ballads," *The Critical Tradition: Classic Texts and Contemporary Trends*, ed. David H. Richter (Boston: Bedford/St. Martin's, 1998), 303.

12. Review of *New Writing and Daylight* (II)

1 NF is referring to Abishag the Shunamite; see 1 Kings 1–4.

2 For NF's review of Ernst Jünger's novel *Auf Den Marmor Klippen* ("On the Marble Cliffs"), see *NFMC*, 211–14.

13. Joseph Schull

1 German for "One State, one People, one Leader": the primary slogan of the German Nazi party.

14. *New Directions* (II)

1 A total of fifteen poems by Pablo Neruda are included in this volume, all translated by Angel Flores: *Ars Poetica, Sonata and Destructions, Dead Gallop, Unity, Savor, Signifying Shadow, Ode with a Lament, Ode to Federico Garcia Lorca, Burial in the East, Explaining a Few Things, Song to the Mothers of Dead Loyalists, How Spain Used to Be, The Battle of the Jarama, Almaria*, and *Offended Lands.*

16. Kenneth Rexroth

1 See no. 3, n. 3.

17. Idols of the Marketplace

1 Wells died on 13 August 1946. Shaw, while having celebrated his ninetieth birthday on 26 July 1946, did not actually die until 2 November 1950.

2 See George Bernard Shaw, ed., "South Africa," in *Fabianism and the Empire* (London: Grant Richards, 1900), 22–38.
3 G.K. Chesterton, "The Puritan," in *George Bernard Shaw* (New York: John Lane, 1909), 34–52.

18. A.E. Coppard and T.F. Powys

1 James Branch Cabell was a prolific American writer of fantasy fiction who was immensely popular during the 1920s, but has fallen largely into obscurity. He is occasionally remembered for the unique achievement of writing an "octodecalogy" (an 18-volume work) called the *Biography of the Life of Manuel*, of which his controversial novel *Jurgen* (New York: Crown, 1919), once the subject of a failed obscenity suit against him, is a part. An annotated copy of Cabell's *Jurgen* is in the NFL.
2 Norman Douglas was a British novelist and travel writer who is remembered primarily for drawing upon his rich experiences in the Foreign Service for his novels, and for subtly interlacing his work with references to his homosexuality.

20. Review of *New Writing and Daylight* (III)

1 These essays are André Gide's "Paul Valery," Michael Ayrton's "A Master of Pastiche: A Personal Reaction to Picasso," and Keith Vaughan's "At the Klee Exhibition."
2 The contributions of these poets to this volume are: W.H. Auden, *Lay Your Sleeping Head, Palais des Beaux Arts, The Novelist, Refugee Blues, The Leaves of Life, In Memoriam Ernst Toller*; Louis MacNeice, *June Thunder, Poem, Meeting Point, Brother Five, Springboard, Schizophrene*; Stephen Spender, *The Sad Standards, Speech from a Play, No Orpheus No Eurydice, In Memoriam, Almond Blossom in Wartime*; Edith Sitwell, *One Day in Spring, Invocation, A Song of the Cold*; Cecil Day Lewis, *The Poet, The Fault, Word All Over, The Revenant*; David Gascoyne, *Snow in Europe, The Writer's Hand, The Gravel-Pit Field*; Federico Garcia Lorca, *The Dawn, Song*; Pierre Jean Jouve, *The Resurrection of the Dead, Insula Monti Majoris*; William Plomer, *French Lisette, The Widow's Plot, Pen Friends*; Earle Birney, *The Road to Nijmegen*.

22. Henry James, *Roderick Hudson*

1 At one point in the novel, the main character in Henry James's *The Sense of the Past* stops to ponder Nathaniel Hawthorne's *Marble Faun*: "He [Ralph Pendrel] recalled the chapter in Hawthorne's fine novel in which the young woman from New England kneels, for the lightening of her woe, to the old priest at St. Peter's, and felt that he sounded as never before the depth of

that passage." See *The Sense of the Past* (Fairfield, N.J.: Augustus M. Kelly, 1976), 89.

23. Yeats and the Language of Symbolism

1 W.B. Yeats, "The Philosophy of Shelley's Poetry" (1900).
2 See Gotthold Ephraim Lessing, *Laocoön,* chaps. 7 and 8.
3 If NF is referring to something other than Degas's obvious penchant for painting this subject, it may be to an oft-cited (but likely apocryphal) exchange between the artist and an annoyed hostess, who inquired, "Monsieur Degas, why do you make the women in your paintings so ugly?" Degas is said to have replied, "Because women *are* generally ugly, Madame." Assuming that his intention was other than to be insulting or misogynist, it was probably to emphasize that the purpose of art is to represent all aspects of reality, not merely the beautiful.
4 Ibsen's play *Ghosts* explores the impact of congenital venereal disease on a family.
5 The reference is to the Berlitz method, a technique of learning languages that uses practical experience and rote repetition rather than formal instruction of grammatical principles and vocabulary. It was developed in 1878 by Maximilian Berlitz, who founded Berlitz Inc., a company that provides language instruction services and products that utilize his approach.
6 NF used the second edition of Yeats's *A Vision* (London: Macmillan, 1937) in the preparation of this essay, and his parenthetical page references in this essay are keyed to this edition. It is sufficiently different from the first edition (London: T. Werner Laurie, 1925) that it can be and often is regarded as a wholly rewritten work. Annotated copies of a reissue of the second edition of *A Vision*, published in 1956, and the final edition, published in 1962, are in the NFL. NF used the latter for his two subsequent essays on Yeats (nos. 43 and 45), written in 1965 and 1969, respectively (see headnote to no. 43).
7 Quoted by Yeats in *The Trembling of the Veil*, bk. 1, sec. 19. See Yeats's *Autobiographies* (London: Macmillan, 1955), 174.
8 Quoted by Yeats in *The Trembling of the Veil*, bk. 1, sec. 13. See *Autobiographies*, 146.
9 This line (l. 10) from *The Sorrow of Love* actually went through three revisions. The line as originally written and published in 1891–92 referred to a "crumbling moon." In 1895, Yeats changed it to "curd-pale moon," and in 1925 to "climbing moon." The editor thanks Dr. Eleanor Cook for calling this to our attention. In the original publication of the essay and its reprint in *FI*, NF misquotes the changed line as "brilliant moon" (a phrase from the poem's second line), probably working from Yeats's inaccurate account of his editing of the poem in *Autobiographies* (435). See *The Variorum Edition of*

the Poems of W.B. Yeats, ed. Peter Allt and Russell K. Alspach (New York: Macmillan, 1957), 119–20.

10 As consolidated by Madame H.P. Blavatsky in her book *The Secret Doctrine* (1888), theosophy is a complex of esoteric ideas that presume the possibility of intercourse between God or other superior spirit(s) for the purpose of attaining superhuman knowledge or wisdom and advancing human spiritual evolution. It embraces a wide range of religious and philosophical principles, including many paranormal or occult practices. See Blavatsky's *The Secret Doctrine: The Synthesis of Science, Religion and Philosophy* (Pasadena, Calif.: Theosophical University Press, 1963). The NFL contains annotated copies of both the full and the abridged versions: *The Secret Doctrine: The Synthesis of Science, Religion and Philosophy*, unabridged verbatim ed., 2 vols. (Pasadena, Calif.: Theosophical University Press, 1970), annotated no. 1431; and *An Abridgement of "The Secret Doctrine"* (Wheaton, Ill.: Theosophical Publishing House, 1968, © 1966), annotated no. 1437.

11 Cf. Rosalind's reference to Pythagoras and Irish rats in *As You Like It* (3.2.165), and Samuel Butler's description of Ralph, the squire of Hudibras, as "A deep occult Philosopher, / As learn'd as the wild Irish are" [pt. 1, canto 1, ll. 537–8]. [NF]

12 F.W.H. Myers (1843–1901) was an English poet and essayist, an early researcher of psychic phenomena, and one of the founders of the Society for Psychical Research. Fionn refers to Fionn mac Cumhaill, central hero of the Fenian cycle in Irish mythology and father of the poet Oisín, whereas Cuchulain is the central hero of the earlier Ulster cycle.

13 NF seems to be referring here to the "ransom" theory of atonement developed by such early Christian thinkers as Irenaeus, Origen, Athanasius, and Augustine, which holds that the death of Christ was a ransom paid by God to Satan (who was presumed to hold dominion over the earth and human life). Anselm questioned this notion in his *Cur Deus Homo* (1098), arguing that Satan was under, not beyond, the power of God, and thus did not need to be paid a ransom. In that text Anselm instead puts forward what is called the "satisfaction" theory of atonement, the idea that the death of Christ satisfies the demands of divine justice.

14 *The Variorum Edition of the Plays of W.B. Yeats*, 170.

15 *The Stones of Venice*, vol. 1, chap. 1. Also, vol. 3 is subtitled "The Fall."

16 Yeats, "Edmund Spenser" (1906). *UTQ* adds after "outgrew," "partly because of what seems to me the very considerable influence of D.H. Lawrence on his later poetry."

17 In the play *Axël* (1890), by Jean Marie Mattias Philippe Auguste, Count de Villiers de L'Isle-Adam (1838–89), Count Axël Auersberg expresses an aristocratic distain for physical and temporal life by exclaiming "Live? Our servants will do that for us!" See *Axël* (London: Jarrolds, 1925), 284. Yeats

quotes the line in his preface to the singular English edition, and takes it as the epigraph of his *The Secret Rose.* NF is correct about Yeats's propensity for quoting the line. It turns up, either paraphrased or directly quoted, on at least seven other occasions in his writings: *Uncollected Prose* (London: Macmillan, 1975), 116; *Essays and Introductions* (London, Macmillan, 1961), 296, 469; *A Vision*, 42; *Mythologies* (New York: Macmillan, 1959), 368; *Prefaces and Introductions* (London: Macmillan, 1988), 112, 156.

18 Members of a paramilitary force recruited in Britain and sent to Ireland as part of the Royal Irish Constabulary to suppress the Irish rebellions of 1919–21.

19 Charles Maurras (1868–1952) was a French journalist and critic who became increasingly monarchical and anti-democratic; his intemperate attacks resulted in his being imprisoned twice. The "Blue Shirts" was the colloquial name for the Army Comrades' Association, which was established in Ireland in February 1932. In July 1933, the group was renamed the National Guard, and it adopted marches, flags, and salutes based on those of the German Nazi Party. In addition to fighting against left-wing groups in Ireland, the Blue Shirts also fought for the Nationalist Army during the Spanish Civil War, and during the Second World War they negotiated with politicians in Germany about the possibility of undertaking a policy of sabotage against the British. While Yeats's association with the Blue Shirts was brief, it was closer than he let on: he composed three marching songs for the group and met several times with its leaders. But he promptly left the organization when he realized that it had little or no regard for education and culture, and was unlikely to ever deliver the kind of independent Ireland in which he was interested. See Bernard G. Krimm, *W.B. Yeats and the Emergence of the Irish Free State, 1918–1939: Living in the Explosion* (Troy, N.Y.: Whitstone Publishing, 1981), 139–76; and Elizabeth Cullingford, *Yeats, Ireland and Fascism* (New York: New York University Press, 1981), 197–214.

20 After "follows it," *UTQ* ends the sentence with "the existence of which Yeats's 'instructors' appear to have overlooked."

21 Yeats wrote *The King's Threshold* in 1904, but revised the ending in 1922 (see n. 37, below).

22 Freud acknowledged the resemblance of his theories of psychoanalysis to the philosophy of Schopenhauer, but he claimed that his ideas developed independently (a claim disputed by most students and scholars of his work). Freud writes: "The large extent to which psycho-analysis coincides with the philosophy of Schopenhauer—not only did he assert the dominance of the emotions and the supreme importance of sexuality but he was even aware of the mechanism of repression—is not to be traced to my acquaintance with his teaching. I read Schopenhauer very late in my life." See Sigmund Freud, *An Autobiographical Study* (New York: Norton, 1963), 114.

23 Butler writes: "There is no living organism untenanted by the Spirit of God, nor any Spirit of God perceivable by man apart from organism embodying and expressing it. God and the Life of the World are like a mountain, which will present different aspects as we look at it from different sides, but which, when we have gone all round it, proves to be one only. God is the animal and vegetable world, and the animal and vegetable world is God." See Samuel Butler, *God the Known and God the Unknown* (London: A.C. Fifield, 1909), 54–5.
24 The doctrine of the *amina mundi* ("World Soul" or "Universal Mind") holds that all life and matter in the universe is part of a single living order or intelligence. The concept can be traced as far back as Plato's *Timaeus.* It attained philosophical currency with the advent of Neoplatonism during the Renaissance, and returned to prominence in the late nineteenth and early twentieth centuries through the writings of mystagogues like Madame Blavatsky and the depth psychology of C.G. Jung.
25 Quoted by Yeats in *The Trembling of the Veil*, bk.1, sec. 19. See *Autobiographies*, 175.
26 See *Mythologies*, 343.
27 The Buddhist concept of Bardo, the state of spiritual limbo after death but before subsequent reincarnation, fascinated NF throughout his life. His diaries record his desire to write a novel set in Bardo, and his "Third Book" notebooks are peppered with references to it. For a thorough discussion of NF's interest in Buddhism and the Bardo state, see Robert Denham's "Frye and the East," in *Northrop Frye: Eastern and Western Perspectives*, ed. Jean O'Grady and Wang Ning (Toronto: University of Toronto Press, 2003), 3–18. See also Michael Dolzani's "The Book of the Dead: A Skeleton Key to Northrop Frye's Notebooks," in *Rereading Frye: The Published and Unpublished Works*, ed. David Boyd and Imre Salusinszky (Toronto: University of Toronto Press, 1999), 19–38.
28 Sally Rand was a famous fan dancer and one of the stars of the 1933 Chicago World's Fair, which NF attended in June–July 1933.
29 After "accurate text," *UTQ* completes the sentence with, "and neither of these young men—both were in their twenties—had any real knowledge of editing."
30 William Blake, *The Works of William Blake: Poetic, Symbolic, and Critical*, vol. 1, ed. Edwin J. Ellis and William Butler Yeats (London: Bernard Quaritch, 1893), 313.
31 "Edmund Spenser," in Yeats's *Essays and Introductions*, 382.
32 Spengler, *The Decline of the West*, trans. Charles Francis Atkinson (New York: Alfred A. Knopf, 1932), 206.
33 "Reveries over Childhood and Youth," in *Autobiographies*, 15.
34 Yeats writes, "We make out of the quarrel with others, rhetoric, but out of

the quarrel with ourselves, poetry." See *Per Amica Silentia Lunae*, in *Mythologies*, 331. In his personal copy of this book (in the NFL), NF writes at the end of Yeats's excursus on this subject, "This section, which is all about belief and sincerity, has been written without much of either. It's rhetoric."

35 *UTQ* adds here "Lawrence's primitivism."

36 Sidney's exact words are that the poet "nothing affirms, and therefore never lieth." Philip Sidney, "An Apology for Poetry," in *The Critical Tradition*, ed. David H. Richter (New York: Bedford, 1998), 149.

37 NF's syntax here obscures the chronological order of Yeats's revisions to *The King's Threshold*. In the original conclusion of the play, written in 1904, the poet starves. In the rewritten conclusion of 1922, the king concedes the authority of the poet and gives him his crown. See *The Variorum Edition of the Plays of W.B. Yeats*, 309–10.

24. The Betjeman Brand

1 The reference is to Joseph Hilaire Pierre Belloc (1870–1953), the English writer and politician of French birth. A prolific poet, essayist, satirist, and historian, he frequently approached subjects from a Roman Catholic perspective.

25. Edith Sitwell, *The Shadow of Cain*

1 The left-leaning *Reynolds News* published a review of *Edith Sitwell's Anthology* after its appearance in 1940 which referred to Sitwell and her brothers Osbert and Sacheverell as "among the literary curiosities of the 1920s," and suggested that their "energy and self-assurance [had] push[ed] them into a position which their merits could not have done." The Sitwells were particularly offended at the article's suggestion that "oblivion has claimed them and they are remembered with a kindly if slightly cynical smile." See *Reynolds News*, 14 February 1940. The Sitwells sued *Reynolds News* for libel and in 1941 were awarded £350 each. See also Geoffrey Elborn's *Edith Sitwell: A Biography* (London: Sheldon Press, 1981), 142, 147.

2 It should be noted that NF's praise for Edith Sitwell was not proffered in a vacuum. In the 10 October 1947 issue of *The Spectator*, Sitwell reviewed *FS*, stating that it is a "book of extraordinary importance, not only for the light it throws on Blake, but also philosophically and religiously . . . . It is a book of great wisdom, and every page opens fresh doors on to the universe of reality and that universe of the transfusion of reality which is called art." NF wrote Sitwell a thank-you note in January 1948, and the poet sent him a copy of *The Shadow of Cain* with her reply, which NF reviewed in this single paragraph, which Ayre suggests was "quickly inserted" into that month's

Canadian Forum (Ayre, 205). Several months later, NF wrote a second letter to Sitwell, complimenting her on her "very lovely, haunting, and almost unbelievably suggestive poem," which he said took "a contemporary situation" and expanded it, "by way of certain human archetypes, into . . . a kind of miniature epic." Sitwell responded with a letter stating that "it was exciting for [her] to know that at last we have the critic we have been waiting for," and that NF would "also prove to be the religious teacher we have been waiting for." See NFF, 1990, box 2, file 1, and 1991, box 11, file 1.

26. For Tory and Leftist

1 NF is referring here to Max Beerbohm's popular caricature "Parerga of Statesmanship." See Max Beerbohm, *Observations* (London: William Heinemann, 1925), 1.
2 "Oh, too lucky for words, if only he knew his luck, is the countryman" (*Georgics*, 2.l.458–9).
3 The poet Edmund Blunden was NF's tutor at Merton College, Oxford University in 1936–37 and 1938–39. See Ayre, 129–30, 134, and *NFHK*, vol. 2, passim.

27. Virginia Woolf

1 *The Common Reader* (London: Hogarth Press, 1925), and *The Common Reader*, 2nd ser. (London: Hogarth, 1932).

28. Four Short Reviews

1 NF appears to be quoting from the dust jacket, back cover, or some other ancillary material appended to this book. This text is not in the book itself.
2 The name of Holland M. Smith's "ghost writer" is given on the book's title page as Percy Finch.

29. Ezra Pound

1 After moving to Italy in 1924, Pound developed Fascist sympathies and became an enthusiastic supporter of Mussolini. While he mostly addressed artistic and cultural topics, anti-democratic and anti-Semitic remarks began to appear in his writings and speeches, and by the outbreak of war he had become a significant propagandist for the Axis powers. He was arrested in May 1945 by Italian partisans, and later turned himself over to American forces. Incarcerated at a U.S. Army detention camp outside Pisa, Pound spent twenty-five days in an open cage before suffering a nervous break-

down and being moved to a tent. It was there that he drafted *The Pisan Cantos*. After World War II, Pound was returned to the United States to face charges of treason, but was declared unfit to face trial by reason of insanity (although most scholars and biographers believe that he was of a merely unconventional, rather than an unsound, mind). In 1946, he was committed to St. Elizabeth's psychiatric hospital in Washington, D.C., where he was allowed occasional visits from friends, scholars, politicians, and other poets. In 1949, Pound was awarded the inaugural Bollingen prize, an annual (and after 1965 a biennial) award for excellence and achievement in poetry given by the Bollingen Foundation, for his *Pisan Cantos*. The award was met with controversy as many journalists, reviewers, and politicians objected to such a prestigious award going to an apparent madman and enemy of the state (see no. 32, n. 5). After a concerted campaign from his friends and fellow poets, Pound was released in 1958. He returned to Italy, and while his writings of this period suggest his cultural and political certainties had failed him, some contemporaneous letters suggest that he was unrepentantly anti-Semitic. He died in Venice in 1972. See John Tytell, *Ezra Pound: The Solitary Volcano* (New York: Anchor Press, 1987); and Humphrey Carpenter, *A Serious Character: The Life of Ezra Pound* (London: Faber & Faber, 1988).

2 "Lord Haw-Haw" was the nickname of William Joyce, the announcer of an English-language Nazi propaganda radio program that was broadcast to audiences in Great Britain and the United States from 1939 to 1945. Joyce was hanged for treason in January 1946. "Axis Sally" was the nickname of Mildred Gellars, a radio personality who sought to demoralize Allied troops through broadcasts on Radio Berlin in 1944–45. She was imprisoned from 1949 to 1962 on charges of treason.

3 Eliot dedicated his poem *The Waste Land* to Ezra Pound, referring to him in its epigraph as *il miglior fabbro* ("the better craftsman"). Among other comments, Yeats called Pound a "solitary volcano," crediting him with a singular influence in the advent of literary modernism.

30. George Orwell

1 NF is referring obliquely to *The God That Failed* (New York: Harper, 1949), a collection of essays by influential ex-Communists edited by British MP Richard Crossman. The book includes essays by Louis Fischer, André Gide, Arthur Koestler, Ignazio Silone, Stephen Spender, and Richard Wright.

2 George Orwell, *Animal Farm* (New York: Harcourt Brace, 1946), 112.

31. Novels on Several Occasions

1 "They became what they beheld" is a frequent refrain in William Blake's

Jerusalem: The Emanation of the Giant Albion, a somber warning not to give attention and devotion to unworthy things.

2 For an excursus by NF on the work of Charlie Chaplin, see *NFMC*, 98–102.

3 The complete sentence reads, "The poet makes himself a *visionary* through a long, immense and reasoned derangement of all the senses." Arthur Rimbaud in a letter to Paul Demeny (15 May 1871). See Arthur Rimbaud, *Complete Works*, trans. Paul Schmidt (New York: Harper & Row, 1975), 102.

32. Phalanx of Particulars

1 Kenner paraphrases the meaning of the Chinese ideogram as "the purification of the word" (53).

2 "To make a study of blank verse alone would be to elicit some curious conclusions. It would show, I believe, that blank verse within Shakespeare's lifetime was more highly developed, that it became the vehicle of more varied and more intense art-emotions than it has ever conveyed since; and that after the erection of the Chinese Wall of Milton, blank verse has suffered not only arrest but retrogression." T.S. Eliot, "Notes on the Blank Verse of Christopher Marlowe," in *The Sacred Wood* (London: Methuen, 1920), 87.

3 See no. 29, n. 1.

4 In Pound's long poem *Hugh Selwyn Mauberley*, the character Nixon warns "Don't kick against the pricks, / Accept opinion. The 'Nineties' tried your game / And died, there's nothing in it" (*Hugh Selwyn Mauberley*, sec. 9, ll. 22–4).

5 Robert Hillyer, a professor of literature at Harvard University and winner of the Pulitzer prize for poetry in 1934, was the most prominent and outspoken voice to criticize the awarding of the Bollingen Prize to Ezra Pound in 1949. He objected on both aesthetic and political grounds to the honouring of *The Pisan Cantos*, and in two lengthy articles made the somewhat extravagant claim that the *Cantos* and the award were evidence of a complex conspiracy against American ways of life and tastes in literature. See Karen Leick, "Ezra Pound v. *The Saturday Review of Literature*," *Journal of Modern Literature*, 25, no. 2 (Winter 2001/2002): 26. See also no. 29, n. 1.

33. Quest and Cycle in *Finnegans Wake*

1 There are two annotated editions of *Finnegans Wake* in the NFL: New York: Viking Press, 1939, and London: Faber & Faber, 1964. The former contains extensive marginalia. The two editions have almost identical pagination, but references to *Finnegans Wake* in this volume are keyed to the 1939 edition, with parenthetical citation of page number and line number separated by a colon.

2 This phrase is Thomas Hardy's. See *Tess of the d'Urbervilles*, chap. 59.
3 The subtitle of chap. 7 of Lewis Carroll's *Through the Looking Glass*.
4 This occurs, famously, on the opening page of *Finnegans Wake*, with an unpronounceable hundred-letter word: "bababadalgharaghtakamminarronnkonnbronntonnerronntuonnthunntrovarrhounawnskawntoohoohoordenenthurnuk" (3:15–17).
5 The subtitle of chap. 6 of *Finnegans Wake*.
6 NF has misquoted slightly, probably because he was quoting from memory. The phrase is "cold mad feary father." *Finnegans Wake* (628:2).
7 Four recurring characters in *Finnegans Wake*—Matthew Gregory, Mark Lyons, Luke Tarpey, and Johnny MacDougal—who reappear as the Four Evangelists, the Irish historians of The Annals of the Four Masters (see n. 8, below), the four provinces of Ireland, and, according to some critics, various other sets of four.
8 The four authors of The Annals of the Four Masters, the great history of medieval Ireland. The Annals were compiled in the Franciscan monastery of Donegal by Michael, Conary, and Cucogry O'Clery, and by Ferfesa O'Mulconry, who are now commonly referred to as the Four Masters. They began their work in 1632, and completed it in 1636. The Annals were translated from old Irish into English and published in 1854.
9 Bergson's term for perceived or continuously experienced time (duration), as distinct from empirically measured or "clock time." See Bergson's *Duration and Simultaneity* (Indianapolis: Bobbs-Merrill, 1965).
10 NF has conflated two separate quotations from *Finnegans Wake* (the latter of which is a typically Joycean portmanteau with multiple resonances), "vicious circle" (98:19) and "vicous cicles" (134:16).
11 W.B. Yeats, *A Vision* (London: Macmillan, 1937), 213.
12 The faithful young woman who waits during the hero's wanderings in Ibsen's *Peer Gynt*.
13 "The book of Doublends Jined" [20:15–16] is a pun which Joyce seems to intend as a description of *Finnegans Wake* itself. The phrase simultaneously suggests "double-ends joined" and "Dublin's giant." Beside this phrase in one of his annotated copies of *Finnegans Wake*, NF writes "cyclic vision identified with apocalyptic-sided book," and beneath it he writes, "He's trying to tell us how to read his book." At the bottom of the page, he records his observation of the two meanings of the phrase.

34. Graves, Gods, and Scholars

1 See pp. 59, 64, above.
2 See the opening paragraph of the "Author's Prologue" of Rabelais's *Gargantua and Pantagruel*.

3 The allusion is to bk. 4, chaps. 34–48 of *Gargantua and Pantagruel*.
4 The reference is to Samuel Butler's *Evidence for the Resurrection of Jesu Christ*.

35. Nature and the Psyche

1 The reference is to the series of investigations of the scientific validity of extrasensory perception (ESP) conducted by Joseph B. Rhine at the parapsychology laboratory at Duke University, which began in 1931 and continued in various forms until Rhine's retirement in the early 1970s. Jung repeatedly refers to Rhine's experiments in *The Interpretation of Nature and the Psyche*, and substantial correspondence between the two can be found in Jung's *Letters, Vol. 1: 1906–1950*, ed. Gerhard Adler and Aniela Jaffé, trans. R.F.C. Hull (Princeton: Princeton University Press, 1992), and *Vol. 2: 1951–1961*, ed. Gerhard Adler, trans. Jeffrey Hulen (Princeton: Princeton University Press, 1976). Further correspondence was published in Victor Mansfield et al., "The Rhine–Jung Letters: Distinguishing Parapsychological from Synchronistic Events," *The Journal of Parapsychology* 62 (March 1998): 3–25.
2 In his personal copy of *The Interpretation of Nature and the Psyche* (in the NFL), NF responds in marginalia to Jung's suggestion that time, space, causality, and synchronicity form a quaternity with the remark, "these are really two: causality-time and synchronicity-space."
3 As with Rhine (see n. 1, above), Jung was a long-time correspondent of Wolfgang Pauli. See *Atom and Archetype: The Pauli/Jung Letters, 1932–1958*, ed. C.A. Meier, trans. David Roscoe (Princeton: Princeton University Press, 2001).

36. Poetry of the Tout Ensemble

1 See editor's introduction, n. 28.
2 NF is referring to the fact that René Char was active in the French Resistance, leading a group against the Nazi forces occupying the Vaucluse area. In fact, Char wrote much of *Hypnos Waking* during this time (1943–44).
3 John Stuart Mill, *Autobiography*, in *Autobiography and Literary Essays*, 153 (chap. 5).
4 NF has misquoted slightly here, perhaps intentionally to suit his context. The line as written by René Char reads: "Gratitude to Georges de la Tour, who overpowered the Hitlerian night with a dialogue between human beings" (151).
5 Originally the name for the brush-covered high ground of southeastern France, the Maquis was the colloquial name for the French Resistance in World War II.
6 NF is referring to an infamous claim of T.S. Eliot's, which yielded an oft-

repeated catchphrase in modernist criticism: "In the seventeenth century a dissociation of sensibility set in, from which we have never recovered." T.S. Eliot, "The Metaphysical Poets," *Selected Essays* (London: Faber & Faber, 1951), 247.

37. The Realistic Oriole: A Study of Wallace Stevens

1 *An Ordinary Evening in New Haven*, sec. 28, ll. 11–12 (*CP*, 486).
2 NF is referring to Eliot's notion of the "objective correlative," a theory suggesting that poetry communicates by finding external objects or situations that adequately symbolize abstract human emotions and thoughts. See Eliot's "Hamlet," in *Selected Essays*, 145.
3 *The Man with the Blue Guitar*, sec. 22, l. 1 (*CP*, 176).
4 *So-And-So Reclining on Her Couch*, ll. 18–20 (*CP*, 295).
5 *Notes toward a Supreme Fiction: It Must Be Abstract*, sec. 4, ll. 13–14 (*CP*, 383).
6 *Of Modern Poetry*, l. 28 (*CP*, 240).
7 *The Idea of Order at Key West*, l. 52 (*CP*, l. 130).
8 *Anecdote of the Jar*, l. 1 (*CP*, 76).
9 Samuel Taylor Coleridge, *Biographia Literaria*, chap. 13.
10 Written in 1913–14 and published posthumously in 1924, T.E. Hulme's essay "Romanticism and Classicism" was, like some of T.S. Eliot's essays (see no. 6, n. 1), an influential critique of the "excesses" of Romanticism. See *The Collected Writings of T.E. Hulme*, ed. Karen Csengeri (Oxford: Oxford University Press, 1994), 59–73.
11 *The Pediment of Appearance*, l. 3 (*CP*, 361).
12 NF's original page citation here refers to two passages in Stevens's poetry: "The basic slate, the universal hue" (*Le Monocle de Mon Oncle*, sec. 6, l. 3; *CP*, 15), and "Through all its purples to the final slate" (*The Man Whose Pharynx Was Bad*, l. 11; *CP*, 96).
13 *The Auroras of Autumn*, sec. 1, l. 10 (*CP*, 411).
14 Stevens writes: "It is important to believe that the visible is the equivalent of the invisible; and once we believe it, we have destroyed the imagination; that is to say, we have destroyed the false imagination, the false conception of the imagination as some incalculable *vates* within us, unhappy Rodomontade" (*NA*, 61).
15 *Jumbo*, ll. 16–17 (*CP*, 269).
16 In *Prelude to Objects* Stevens's phrase is pluralized to "nigger mystics" (sec. 1, l. 22; *CP*, 195), and in *The News and the Weather* he speaks of "a nigger fragment, a *mystique* / For the spirit left helpless by the intelligence" (ll. 21–2; *CP*, 265). Beside the first passage in his well-annotated copy of Stevens's *Collected Poems* (in the NFL), NF writes "ego is the domination of black." Further in the poem, Stevens calls upon the poet to "conceive for the

courts / Of these academies, the diviner health / Disclosed in common forms. Set up / The rugged black, the image." (*Prelude to Objects*, ll. 26–9; *CP*, 195). Beside this passage, NF writes "the rugged black is the opposite of abstract black or nigger mysticism." See also n. 17, below.

17 Stevens writes: "Reality is things as they are. The general sense of the word proliferates its special senses. It is a jungle in itself. As in the case of a jungle, everything that makes it up is pretty much of one color" (*NA*, 25–6).

18 *An Ordinary Evening in New Haven*, sec. 6, l. 2 (*CP*, 469).

19 *An Ordinary Evening in New Haven*, sec. 6, l. 1 (*CP*, 469).

20 *The Poems of Our Climate*, sec. 3, l. 4 (*CP*, 194).

21 *Connoisseur of Chaos*, sec. 1, ll. 1, 2 (*CP*, 215).

22 *Study of Images I*, l. 7 (*CP*, 463).

23 *Large Red Man Reading*, ll. 14–15 (*CP*, 424).

24 *Things of August*, sec. 3, l. 7 (*CP*, 490).

25 *The Comedian as the Letter C*, sec. 2, l. 44 (*CP*, 31).

26 *Examination of the Hero in a Time of War*, sec. 7, l. 12 (*CP*, 276).

27 *Anything Is Beautiful If You Say It Is*, l. 2 (*CP*, 211).

28 NF is referring here to Stevens's essay "The Noble Rider and the Sound of Words" (*NA*, 1–36), the title of which itself recalls the famous figure from Plato's *Phaedrus*.

29 *In the Element of Antagonisms*, ll. 5–6 (*CP*, 426).

30 "An age is green or red" (*Description without Place*, sec. 2, l. 8; *CP*, 340).

31 Stevens's line actually reads "There was a bright *scienza* outside of ourselves, / A gaiety that is being" (*Of Bright and Blue Birds and the Gala Sun*, ll. 12–13; *CP*, 248).

32 The title of Stevens's poem *Lebensweisheitspielerei* (*CP*, 504) is derived from a German term which compounds the words *leben* ("life" or "living"), *weisheit* ("wisdom"), and *spielerei* ("play" or "game"). "The World Is Larger in Summer" is the title of sec. 2 of *Two Illustrations That the World Is What You Make of It* (*CP*, 514).

33 *The Brave Man*, l. 1 (*CP*, 138).

34 NF's original page citation here refers to Stevens's poem *Tea at the Palaz of Hoon* (*CP*, 65).

35 *The Latest Freed Man*, l. 8 (*CP*, 204).

36 *Evening without Angels*, l. 16 (*CP*, 137).

37 *Theory*, l. 1 (*CP*, 86).

38 *Anecdote of Men by the Thousand*, ll. 1–2 (*CP*, 51).

39 *A Dish of Peaches in Russia*, ll. 3–4 (*CP*, 224).

40 *New England Verses*, sec. 1, l. 2 (*CP*, 104).

41 NF's original page citation here (*CP*, 33 ff.) seems to refer to the relationship between secs. 2 and 3 of *The Comedian as the Letter C*.

42 *Homunculus et La Belle Étoile*, l. 2 (*CP*, 25).

43 NF's original page citation here seems to refer to *Valley Candle* (l. 1; *CP*, 51) and *A Quiet Normal Life* (l. 15; *CP*, 523).
44 *The Candle a Saint*, l. 14 (*CP*, 223).
45 *Description without Place*, sec. 1, l. 10 (*CP*, 339).
46 *The Hermitage at the Center*, l. 2 (*CP*, 505).
47 *Final Soliloquy of the Interior Paramour* (*CP*, 524).
48 NF is interpreting Stevens's use of the word "anima" as related to C.G. Jung's. The line simply reads: "His anima liked its animal / And liked it unsubjugated" (*Esthétique du Mal*, sec. 10, l. 5; *CP*, 321).
49 *The World as Meditation*, l. 5 (*CP*, 520).
50 NF's original page citation here suggests that by "the eternal Eve or naked bride" he is referring to the female figure of Steven's *Hand of Being* (*CP*, 271) and the "spouse" of *Notes toward a Supreme Fiction: It Must Change*, sec. 8, l. 4 (*CP*, 395), respectively.
51 NF's account of Stevens here is somewhat unclear. NF's phrase "major imagination" is interpreting Stevens's repeated references to a "major man" in *Notes toward a Supreme Fiction: It Must Be Abstract* (*CP*, 387–8). NF's annotation of this passage in Stevens's *Collected Poems* refers to *Paisant Chronicle* (ll. 1, 13; *CP*, 334, 335), where the figure (pluralized as "major men") also appears.
52 NF is referring to *Tea at the Palaz of Hoon* (*CP*, 65) and "that mountain-minded Hoon" of *Sad Strains of a Gay Waltz* (l. 8; *CP*, 121).
53 *Credences of Summer*, sec. 3, ll. 1–5 (*CP*, 373).
54 NF's original page citation here indicates he is referring to *A Rabbit as King of the Ghosts* (*CP*, 209) and *The Candle a Saint* (*CP*, 223).
55 *Like Decorations in a Nigger Cemetery*, sec. 25, l. 2 (*CP*, 154).
56 As in *The Comedian as the Letter C* and *Peter Quince at the Clavier*.
57 *Sea Surface Full of Clouds*, sec. 5, ll. 12, 14 (*CP*, 102).
58 *Like Decorations in a Nigger Cemetery*, sec. 35, l. 3 (*CP*, 156).
59 The reference is to Stevens's *The Dwarf* (*CP*, 208).
60 The reference is to *Lunar Paraphrase* (*CP*, 107).
61 The reference is to *No Possum, No Sop, No Taters* (*CP*, 293) and *Two Illustrations That the World Is What You Make of It* (*CP*, 513).
62 *Esthétique du Mal*, sec. 8, ll. 1–2 (*CP*, 319).
63 *Colloquy with a Polish Aunt*, l. 4 (*CP*, 84).
64 *A Thought Revolved*, sec. 2, l. 13 (*CP*, 185).
65 *The Man with the Blue Guitar*, sec. 5, ll. 9–10 (*CP*, 167).
66 *Extracts from Addresses to the Academy of Fine Ideas*, sec. 3, l. 2 (*CP*, 254).
67 *Earthy Anecdote*, l. 3 (*CP*, 3).
68 NF's citation here also directs the reader to *Esthétique du Mal*, sec. 6, as well as to *The Jack-Rabbit*, (*CP*, 50; cf. 318).
69 *Peter Quince at the Clavier*, sec. 4, l. 16 (*CP*, 92).

70 *Final Soliloquy of the Interior Paramour*, ll. 4, 12 (*CP*, 524). In a commentary on this point at the bottom of this page in his annotated copy of Stevens's poems, NF writes: "When Everyman is dying, reality will make some excuse. Only the imagination will go with him and be his guide."
71 *The Comedian as the Letter C*, sec. 4, ll. 92–5 (*CP*, 39).
72 The reference is to Stevens's poem *Imago* (*CP*, 439). NF is interpreting Stevens's use of the word as connected with Sigmund Freud's, although the poem contains no explicit reference to Freud.
73 *Things of August*, sec. 8, l. 22 (*CP*, 494).
74 NF's page citation here indicates that he is referring to Stevens's poem *The Irish Cliffs of Moher* (*CP*, 501).
75 *Metaphor as Degeneration*, ll. 8–9 (*CP*, 444).
76 The reference is to Stevens's poem *Like Decorations in a Nigger Cemetery* (*CP*, 150). See also n. 16, above.
77 See Wallace Stevens, *Opus Posthumous* (New York: Alfred A. Knopf, 1957), 139.
78 NF's syntax here obscures Stevens's: "[Poetry] is an illumination of a surface," Stevens writes, "the movement of a self in the rock" (*NA*, viii).
79 *The Rock*, sec. 3 (*CP*, 528).
80 See *Saint John and the Back-Ache* (*CP*, 437).
81 See *The Countryman* (*CP*, 428).
82 *The River of Rivers in Connecticut*, l. 18 (*CP*, 533). NF is obviously echoing Revelation 21:1: "And I saw a new heaven and a new earth: for the first heaven and the first earth were passed away; and there was no more sea."
83 *Montrachet-le-Jardin*, l. 93 (*CP*, 263).
84 *Peter Quince at the Clavier*, sec. 4, l. 6 (*CP*, 92).
85 *Not Ideas about the Thing But the Thing Itself*, l. 18 (*CP*, 534).
86 *Celle Qui Fût Héaulmiette*, l. 16 (*CP*, 438).
87 *Opus Posthumous*, 132.
88 *Arcades of Philadelphia the Past*, l. 1 (*CP*, 225).
89 *Peter Quince at the Clavier*, sec. 4, l. 2 (*CP*, 91).
90 *The Rock*, sec. 3, l. 17 (*CP*, 528).
91 Jerusalem, pl. 77; E231.
92 *An Ordinary Evening in New Haven*, sec. 28, l. 16 (*CP*, 486; cf. 198–9).
93 *An Ordinary Evening in New Haven*, sec. 15, l. 7, and sec. 9, ll. 4–5 (*CP*, 476, 471).
94 Cf. *Thirteen Ways of Looking at a Blackbird*, sec. 4, ll. 3–4 (*CP*, 93).
95 *Things of August*, sec. 8, ll. 17–18 (*CP*, 494).
96 *CP*, 429. NF's original parenthetical citation here also directs the reader to *Contrary Theses (II)* (*CP*, 270) and *The Candle a Saint* (*CP*, 223).
97 The reference is to the subtitle of the first part of *Notes toward a Supreme Fiction: It Must Be Abstract* (*CP*, 380).

98 *Esthétique du Mal*, sec. 7, ll. 1–4 (*CP*, 318–19).
99 *Montrachet-le-Jardin*, ll. 67, 68 (*CP*, 262).
100 *Chocorua to Its Neighbor*, sec. 21, l. 4 (*CP*, 301).
101 *Montrachet-le-Jardin*, l. 69 (*CP*, 262).
102 *The Surprises of the Superhuman*, l. 3 (*CP*, 98).
103 NF's original parenthetical citation refers the reader to *Examination of the Hero in a Time of War*, sec. 15 (*CP*, 280).
104 See n. 51, above.
105 *Asides on the Oboe*, sec. 1, l. 12 (*CP*, 250).
106 *Thinking of a Relation between the Images of Metaphors*, ll. 15–16 (*CP*, 357); cf. *The Dove in the Belly* (*CP*, 366–7).
107 *Chocorua to Its Neighbor*, sec. 11, l. 2 (*CP*, 298). See also *Final Soliloquy of the Interior Paramour*, l. 16 (*CP*, 524).
108 See *A Primitive Like an Orb*, sec. 6, l. 1, sec. 7, l. 1 (*CP*, 441–2).
109 *A Pastoral Nun*, l. 12 (*CP*, 378).
110 *A Primitive Like an Orb*, sec. 12, ll. 1–8 (*CP*, 443).
111 *Prologues to What Is Possible*, sec. 2, l. 5 (*CP*, 516).
112 *The Man with the Blue Guitar*, sec. 15, l. 4 (*CP*, 173).
113 NF's original page citation here directs the reader to *Chocorua to Its Neighbor*, sec. 5 (*CP*, 297).
114 NF's original page citation here indicates he is referring to *Things of August*, sec. 2, l. 1 (*CP*, 490).
115 *A Pastoral Nun*, l. 3 (*CP*, 378).
116 *Two Illustrations That the World Is What You Make of It*, sec. 2, ll. 8–9 (*CP*, 514). NF's original page citation also refers to *NA*, 49.
117 *So-And-So Reclining on Her Couch*, ll. 23–4 (*CP*, 296).
118 *Description without Place*, sec. 3, ll. 11–18 (*CP*, 341).
119 *Description without Place*, sec. 6, l. 1 (*CP*, 344).
120 *Description without Place*, sec. 6, ll. 9–12 (*CP*, 345).
121 *An Ordinary Evening in New Haven*, sec. 5, ll. 10–18 (*CP*, 468–9).
122 Yeats's exact words are "Man has created death." *Death*, l. 12.
123 Rainer Maria Rilke, letter to Ellen Delp, 27 October 1915. See *The Wartime Letters of Rainer Maria Rilke, 1914–1921*, trans. M.D. Herter Norton (New York: Norton, 1964).M. D. Herter
124 *The Bouquet*, sec. 2, l. 3 (*CP*, 448).
125 *Notes toward a Supreme Fiction: It Must Be Abstract*, sec. 10, ll. 20–1 (*CP*, 389).
126 Eliot writes: "Immature poets imitate; mature poets steal; bad poets deface what they take, and good poets make it into something better, or at least something different. The good poet welds his theft into a whole of feeling which is unique, utterly different from that from which it was torn; the bad poet throws it into something which has no cohesion. A good poet will usually borrow from authors remote in time, or alien in language, or

diverse in interest." See Eliot's "Philip Massinger," in *The Sacred Wood*, 125.

127 *The Prejudice against the Past*, l. 18 (*CP*, 369).

128 A famous dictum of Pound's, pronounced most notably in his collection of that title, *Make It New: Essays* (New Haven: Yale University Press, 1935).

129 In his *Song of the Exposition*, Whitman asks the Muse to "migrate from Greece and Ionia; / Cross out, please, those immensely overpaid accounts," because "a better, fresher, busier sphere—a wide, untried domain awaits" (ll. 12–18).

130 *Reply to Papini*, ll. 9–10 (*CP*, 446).

38. Religion and Modern Poetry

1 See no. 23, n. 36.

2 See William K. Wimsatt and Monroe C. Beardsley, "The Intentional Fallacy," *Sewanee Review*, 54 (Summer 1946): 468–88. Revised and republished in *The Verbal Icon: Studies in the Meaning of Poetry* (Lexington: University Press of Kentucky, 1954): 3–18.

3 See *John Milton*, ed. Stephen Orgel and Jonathan Goldberg (Oxford: Oxford University Press, 1994), 250.

4 NF is referring to the general influence of Confucius on Pound's poetry, and particularly to Pound's translation of Confucius. See Pound's *Confucius: The Unwobbling Pivot and The Great Digest* (Norfolk, Conn.: New Directions, 1947).

5 Yeats writes: "I am very religious, and deprived by Huxley and Tyndall, whom I detested, of the simple-minded religion of my childhood, I had made a new religion, almost an infallible Church of poetic tradition, of a fardel of stories, and of personages, and of emotions, inseparable from their first expression, passed on from generation to generation by poets and painters with some help from philosophers and theologians" (*Autobiographies*, 115–16).

6 NF quotes these words by Erasmus in *GC* (18/36), the note for which directs the reader to Roland H. Bainton, *Erasmus of Christendom* (New York: Scribner's, 1969), chap. 6 (p. 140).

7 See T.E. Hulme, "Romanticism and Classicism," in *The Collected Writings of T.E. Hulme*, ed. Karen Csengeri (Oxford: Clarendon, 1994), 62.

8 NF has slightly misquoted Dylan Thomas here. The lines read, "it was all / Shining, it was Adam and Maiden" (*Fern Hill*, ll. 29–30).

39. The Nightmare Life in Death

1 Samuel Beckett, *Proust* (New York: Grove Press, 1931).

2 See Marcel Proust, *In Search of Lost Time*, vol. 1, *Swann's Way*, trans. C.K. Scott Moncrieff and Terence Kilmartin, rev. D.J. Enright (New York: Random House, 1992). The two "epiphanies" to which NF refers, the most significant of several in Proust's novel, reverberate and in fact constitute much of the narrative. NF is referring to the reputation of these episodes as the best-known literary depictions of the psychological experience of involuntary (or "Proustian") memory, a phenomenon in which inanimate objects or physical stimuli are said to prompt spontaneous recollection and/or sustained reverie.
3 Samuel Beckett, *Murphy* (New York: Grove, 1938), 9.
4 *Murphy*, 78, 112.
5 *Murphy*, 181.
6 *Murphy*, 82.
7 *Murphy*, 250.
8 Samuel Beckett, *Krapp's Last Tape and Other Dramatic Pieces* (New York: Grove, 1960), 27.
9 Samuel Beckett, *Watt* (New York: Grove, 1959), 247.
10 *Watt*, 221.
11 Samuel Beckett, *Waiting for Godot: A Tragicomedy in Two Acts* (New York: Grove, 1954), 13.
12 *Waiting for Godot*, 25.
13 *Waiting for Godot*, 51.
14 *Finnegans Wake*, 403–554 (chaps. 13–15).
15 Ibid., 474–554 (chap. 15).
16 *Proust*, 16–17.
17 *Murphy*, 167.
18 The reference is to the so-called Peripatetic Axiom: *Nihil est in intellectu quod non prius fuerit in sensu* ("Nothing is in the understanding that was not earlier in the senses"). Recognized as the first principle of most empirical philosophy, the axiom is often attributed to Thomas Aquinas, but its *locus classicus* is Aristotle's *De Anima*, bk. 3, chap. 8.

40. Comment

1 See Norbert Weiner's *The Human Use of Human Beings: Cybernetics and Society* (New York: Doubleday, 1954).
2 John Livingston Lowes, *Geoffrey Chaucer and the Development of His Genius* (Boston: Houghton Mifflin, 1934).
3 Kenneth Burke, "The Vegetal Radicalism of Theodore Roethke," *Sewanee Review*, 58 (Winter 1950): 68–108; reprinted in Burke's *Language as Symbolic Action: Essays on Life, Literature, and Method* (Berkeley: University of California Press), 254–80.

4 Alfred B. Lord, *The Singer of Tales* (Cambridge, Mass.: Harvard University Press, 1960).
5 The paper referred to is "Academy without Walls," an address to the Canadian Conference of the Arts (May 1961), published in *Canadian Art*, 18 (September–October 1961): 296–8; reprinted in *NFMC*, 126–33.
6 In his *A Short View of Tragedy* (1692), Thomas Rymer referred to Shakespeare's *Othello* as "a bloody farce without salt or savour."

41. *T.S. Eliot*

NOTE: The abbreviated titles listed below, which are those given by NF at the start of *TSE* with the addition of *CPP*, have been used in references for this item only. NF also observes after giving the list that "A few of the longer titles have also been abbreviated in the text; thus *Prufrock* for *The Love Song of J. Alfred Prufrock*, etc." References to Eliot's plays are cited by part, act and/or scene, where possible, and by page number in *The Complete Poems and Plays of T.S. Eliot*, preceded by *CPP*. NF's references to secondary sources have been filled out from his bibliography where possible.

ASG *After Strange Gods: A Primer of Modern Heresy*. London: Faber & Faber, 1934.
CPP *The Complete Poems and Plays of T.S. Eliot*. London: Faber & Faber, 1969.
FLA *For Lancelot Andrewes: Essays on Style and Order*. London: Faber & Faber, 1928.
ICS *The Idea of a Christian Society*. London: Faber & Faber, 1939.
NDC *Notes towards a Definition of Culture*. London: Faber & Faber, 1948.
OPP *On Poetry and Poets*. London: Faber & Faber, 1957.
SelE *Selected Essays*. London: Faber & Faber, 1951.
SW *The Sacred Wood*. London: Methuen, 1950.
UPUC *The Use of Poetry and the Use of Criticism*. London: Faber & Faber, 1933.

1 The 1st ed. reads, "had come in the seventeenth century from East Coker, in Somerset, to New England."
2 See "Modern Education and the Classics," *SelE*, 509–10.
3 This sentence and the preceding are one sentence in the 1st ed.: "Eliot's main academic interest was in philosophy, and though he wrote poetry and was 'Class Odist' of his year, he was not especially precocious as a poet." Eliot had objected that "My academic interest was not in philosophy but in literature." For this and other objections, see his memorandum, forwarded by his publisher on 24 June 1963, in NFF, 1988, box 61, file 5. The file also contains a letter of 12 June 1963 from Eliot to his publisher suggesting that perhaps NF "would have done better not to have undertaken the task."

4 *ASG*, 40. [NF]

5 In the 1st ed. this sentence reads, "It may be significant that Eliot's doctoral thesis (accepted, but not presented for the degree) was on F.H. Bradley, at that time the leading philosophical opponent of pragmatism." Eliot had objected that "To speak of F.H. Bradley simply as being 'the leading philosophical opponent of pragmatism' is to display complete ignorance of Bradley."

6 In the 1st ed. this sentence begins, "Meanwhile he had discovered the French *symboliste* poets, especially Baudelaire and Laforgue." Eliot had objected that "Baudelaire was not a *symboliste* but the fore-runner of the *symbolistes*."

7 "Yeats," *OPP*, 252. [NF]

8 *Ezra Pound: His Metric and His Poetry* (New York: Knopf, 1917).

9 See Eliot's *Homage to John Dryden: Three Essays on Poetry of the Seventeenth Century* (London: Hogarth, 1924), which contained his essays "John Dryden," "The Metaphysical Poets," and "Andrew Marvell." These were later reprinted in *SelE*, 305–16, 281–91, 292–304.

10 *NDC*, 117. [NF]

11 Some original drafts of *The Waste Land*, along with Ezra Pound's annotations and edits, were eventually made available. See *The Waste Land: A Facsimile and Transcript of the Original Drafts Including the Annotations of Ezra Pound*, annotated and edited by Valerie Eliot (London: Faber & Faber, 1971). Eliot had objected that Pound's editing improved the poem and that there were no grounds for suggesting that he made it more enigmatic, but NF did not alter his judgment here.

12 "Thoughts after Lambeth," *SelE*, 368. [NF]

13 The 1st ed. reads, "joining the Anglo-Catholic wing of the Church of England in 1927." Eliot had objected that "one does not join an Anglo-Catholic wing!"

14 The 1st ed. reads, "and became a director before his retirement," to which Eliot had objected.

15 Eliot writes, "The struggle of our time is to concentrate, not to dissipate; to renew our association with traditional wisdom; to re-establish a vital connection between the individual and the race. It is, in a word, a struggle against Liberalism" (*ASG*, 53).

16 The word "especially" is an addition in the 2nd ed.

17 In the 1st ed. the two preceding sentences read, "During the 1930s also Eliot wrote *Four Quartets*, so far the summing up of his nondramatic poetry. The first Quartet, *Burnt Norton*, was published in 1934; the last, *Little Gidding*, was completed while the Nazi bombs were falling in London."

18 "Poetry and Drama," *OPP*, 84. [NF]

19 The 1st ed. adds, "chiefly of an academic nature," to which Eliot had objected.

20 Pound refers to Eliot as "Possum" in *Canto* 81, l. 43. The 1st ed. had claimed that the nickname "derived from the preface to *For Lancelot Andrewes*." In this preface Eliot writes, "I have made bold to unite these occasional essays merely as indication of what may be expected, and to refute any accusation of playing 'possum'" (vii). However, Eliot objected that "How Professor Frye could make this derivation from the preface to FOR LANCELOT ANDREWES is more than human ingenuity can explain."

21 This sentence is, of course, an addition in the 2nd ed.

22 This paragraph (with the exception of the common concluding sentence) is a completely rewritten version of the paragraph in the 1st ed.: "Besides *On Poetry and Poets, The Complete Poems and Plays* (1950), which contains the poetry and plays up to *The Cocktail Party*, and the third edition of *Selected Essays* (1951) are essential for Eliot's reader. These however do not contain everything that a student of Eliot would want. There are many uncollected and fugitive pieces in both poetry and criticism, and many prefaces to books. Some of the books are important works of contemporary literature, including the poems of Ezra Pound, Djuna Barnes's *Nightwood*, and the English translation of Valéry's critical essays, *The Art of Poetry*. Others are items of Lenten reading with such titles as *Thoughts for Meditation* and *Testament of Immortality*."

23 At the end of this sentence the 1st ed. adds, "which attempts to give the central facts about Eliot, in four chapters, as a man of letters, a critic, a satiric poet, and a devotional poet and dramatist."

24 This last paragraph is missing in the 1st ed. Instead, after "allusions" in the preceding paragraph, the paragraph and chapter conclude with the following: "I often think of a student who once asked me to translate for him the passage from the *Inferno* at the beginning of *Prufrock*, with the comment: 'The book I read says this stuff here's the key to the whole thing, but what the hell good's that when you don't know what it says?' This implies a critical principle that could be extended to much more of Eliot than his untranslated mottoes, and is the principle I have tried to keep in mind throughout."

25 *The Decline and Fall of the Roman Empire*, vol. 6 (London: J.M. Dent, 1960), 553.

26 *OPP*, 165–6.

27 See no. 23, n. 15. This view, which NF calls in the next paragraph "the bobsled or 'down we went' theory," he elsewhere calls the "butterslide" theory. See, e.g., *EICT*, 177–8.

28 "What is a Classic?" *OPP*, 61. [NF]

29 See *Canto* 45, passim.

30 "Modern Education and the Classics," *SelE*, 514. [NF]

31 *OPP*, 57.

32 "Thoughts after Lambeth," *SelE*, 387.
33 *NDC*, 108.
34 Henry Adams, *The Education of Henry Adams*, chaps. 24 and 25, respectively.
35 *NDC*, 48. [NF]
36 *NDC*, 52. [NF]
37 *NDC*, 57.
38 *ASG*, 16.
39 *ASG*, 20.
40 "Rudyard Kipling," *OPP*, 250. [NF]
41 *ASG*, 63.
42 Edmund Burke, *Appeal from the New to the Old Whigs*, in *The Works of the Right Honourable Edmund Burke* (London: Oxford University Press, 1906–7), 5:101.
43 *NDC*, 27. [NF]
44 *ASG*, 18. [NF]
45 "Second Thoughts About Humanism," *SelE*, 485. [NF]
46 *NDC*, 31. [NF]
47 *ICS*, 61. [NF]
48 *NDC*, 34. [NF]
49 Both Eliot and NF have altered Emerson's line slightly. The sentence reads "An institution is the lengthened shadow of one man." See Ralph Waldo Emerson, "Self-Reliance," in *"Essays" [and] "Essays: Second Series,"* 2 vols. republished as one (Columbus, Ohio: Charles E. Merrill, 1969), 50.
50 *NDC*, 48. [NF]
51 "The Social Function of Poetry," *OPP*, 18. [NF]
52 "Johnson as Critic and Poet," *OPP*, 191. [NF]
53 *NDC*, 67. [NF]
54 *NDC*, 75. [NF]
55 *ICS*, 46. [NF]
56 "Goethe as the Sage," *OPP*, 219. [NF]
57 See Coleridge's *On the Constitution of the Church and State*, ed. John Colmer (Princeton: Princeton University Press, 1976), vol. 10 of *The Collected Works of Samuel Taylor Coleridge*), passim.
58 *ICS*, 35. [NF]
59 *ICS*, 49. [NF]
60 See Newman's *The Idea of a University* (London: Longmans, 1907), 208.
61 Matthew Arnold, *Culture and Anarchy*, in *Poetry and Criticism of Matthew Arnold*, ed. Dwight Culler (Boston: Houghton Mifflin, 1961), 426 (chap. 1).
62 "Tradition and the Individual Talent," *SelE*, 21.
63 "Imperfect Critics," *SW*, 31. [NF]
64 "Dante," *SelE*, 275. [NF]
65 "William Blake," *SelE*, 321–2.

66 "Dante," *SelE*, 240.
67 "Second Thoughts about Humanism," *SelE*, 488. [NF]
68 Preface to Wilson Knight, *The Wheel of Fire: Interpretations of Shakespearian Tragedy* (London: Oxford, 1930), xv. [NF]
69 "Four Elizabethan Dramatists," *SelE*, 114, 117. [NF] Eliot is here quoting William Archer, *The Old Drama and the New* (London: Heinemann, 1923), 110.
70 "Dante," *SelE*, 252. [NF]
71 "'Rhetoric' and Poetic Drama," *SelE*, 39.
72 "Hamlet and His Problems," *SelE*, 143.
73 "Four Elizabethan Dramatists," *SelE*, 116n. 1. The "two grinning footnotes" to which NF refers are here and in "Hamlet," *SelE*, 141, n. 1.
74 Preface to Wilson Knight, *The Wheel of Fire*, xix.
75 "Niccolo Machiavelli," *FLA*, 49, 52. [NF]
76 In the preface to *For Lancelot Andrewes*, Eliot announced that he had three "small volumes" in preparation, entitled *The School of Donne*, *The Outline of Royalism*, and *The Principles of Modern Heresy*. None of these were ever published, though the title of the last is echoed in the subtitle of *After Strange Gods: A Primer of Modern Heresy*.
77 "John Bramhill," *SelE*, 360. [NF]
78 "Milton II," *OPP*, 148. [NF]
79 "Milton I," *OPP*, 144. See also no. 32, n. 2.
80 "Milton II," *OPP*, 155.
81 "Notes on the Blank Verse of Christopher Marlow," *SW*, 90.
82 "The Possibility of Poetic Drama," *SW*, 66.
83 "Johnson as Critic and Poet," *OPP*, 167.
84 "Andrew Marvell," *SelE*, 296.
85 "Ben Jonson," *SelE*, 160.
86 "Milton I," *OPP*, 142.
87 "Shelley and Keats," *UPUC*, 89.
88 "Shelley and Keats," *UPUC*, 89.
89 "Byron," *OPP*, 201.
90 "Shelley and Keats," *UPUC*, 99. [NF]
91 "Religion and Literature," *SelE*, 396.
92 *ASG*, 60.
93 *ASG*, 60. [NF]
94 *ICS*, 20. [NF]
95 *ICS*, 79; "The Modern Mind," *UPUC*, 134. [NF]
96 *NDC*, 105. [NF]
97 "The Frontiers of Criticism," *OPP*, 106. [NF]
98 "The Metaphysical Poets," *SelE*, 290. [NF]
99 *ASG*, 38.

100 "Dante," *SelE*, 251.
101 "Sir John Davies," *OPP*, 134.
102 "What is a Classic?" *OPP*, 53; cf., however, "The Modern Mind," *UPUC*, 129. [NF]
103 "Milton II," *OPP*, 159.
104 "What is a Classic?" *OPP*, 64. [NF]
105 "What is Minor Poetry?" *OPP*, 47; "Andrew Marvell," *SelE*, 292. [NF]
106 "Introduction," *SW*, xiii. [NF]
107 *ICS*, 30.
108 Cf. "Thoughts after Lambeth," *SelE*, 368. [NF]
109 *ASG*, 25. [NF]
110 "Tradition and the Individual Talent," *SelE*, 14. [NF]
111 "Philip Massinger," *SelE*, 206. [NF]
112 "Ubi sum? Sub ortu solis, an sub cardine glacialis ursae?" ("Where am I? Under the rising of the sun or beneath the wheeling course of the frozen bear?"). Seneca, *Hercules Furens*, l. 1138.
113 Grover Smith, *T.S. Eliot's Poetry and Plays: A Study in Sources and Meaning* (Chicago: University of Chicago Press, 1974), 254 (the fullest treatment of Eliot's sources). [NF]
114 *Murder in the Cathedral*, pt. 2, *CPP*, 272.
115 "Matthew Arnold," *UPUC*, 113. [NF]
116 "The Three Voices of Poetry," *OPP*, 97–8. [NF]
117 "The Music of Poetry," *OPP*, 38. [NF]
118 "Conclusion," *UPUC*, 146. [NF]
119 "Philip Massinger," *SelE*, 217.
120 "Swinburne as Poet," *SelE*, 327. [NF]
121 See Ezra Pound, *The Spirit of Romance* (Norfolk: New Directions, 1952), 5.
122 "Andrew Marvell," *SelE*, 297.
123 This famous phrase occurs in "Hamlet," *SelE*, 145. [NF] Cf. also no. 37, n. 2.
124 "Matthew Arnold," *UPUC*, 119. [NF]
125 "Andrew Marvell," *SelE*, 303; cf. preface to Valéry, in *The Art of Poetry*, trans. Denise Folliot, vol. 7 of *The Collected Works of Paul Valéry* (New York: Pantheon, 1958), xxiii. [NF]
126 "Dante," *SelE*, 268.
127 "The Metaphysical Poets," *SelE*, 287. [NF]
128 "Matthew Arnold," *UPUC*, 118–19. [NF]
129 "Rudyard Kipling," *OPP*, 238. [NF]
130 "Johnson as Critic and Poet," *OPP*, 169. [NF]
131 "The Metaphysical Poets," *SelE*, 286, 288, 298. [NF]
132 "The Metaphysical Poets," *SelE*, 289.
133 See no. 36, n. 6.

134 *The Confidential Clerk*, act 1, *CPP*, 451.
135 "Philip Massinger," *SelE*, 206–17.
136 "Imperfect Critics," *SW*, 31. [NF]
137 "Swinburne as Poet," *SelE*, 326.
138 "Swinburne as Poet," *SelE*, 327.
139 "Dante," *SelE*, 242.
140 "Rudyard Kipling," *OPP*, 238. [NF]
141 "Conclusion," *UPUC*, 151. [NF]
142 "Yeats," *OPP*, 255. [NF]
143 "What is a Classic?" *OPP*, 63. [NF]
144 "Charles Whibley," *SelE*, 501; cf. *OPP*, 89. [NF]
145 "Conclusion," *UPUC*, 151. [NF]
146 "A Dialogue on Dramatic Poetry," *SelE*, 56. [NF]
147 Cf. "The Music of Poetry," *OPP*, 37. [NF]
148 "The Music of Poetry," *OPP* 32. [NF]
149 "Rudyard Kipling," *OPP*, 251. [NF]
150 "Byron," *OPP*, 201.
151 "The Music of Poetry," *OPP*, 31. [NF]
152 "Poetry and Drama," *OPP*, 82; cf. Helen Gardner, *The Art of T.S. Eliot* (London: Cresset, 1949), 46 ff. [NF]
153 *The Cocktail Party*, act 1, sc. 3, *CPP*, 386.
154 *Murder in the Cathedral*, pt. 1, *CPP*, 240–1.
155 "Dante," *SelE*, 262.
156 This is the first sentence of Rymer's *A Short View of Tragedy* (1692). Cf. also no. 40, n. 6.
157 "Thomas Heywood," *SelE*, 175. [NF]
158 "Ben Jonson," *SelE*, 157. [NF]
159 "The Three Voices of Poetry," *OPP*, 97.
160 "John Marston," *SelE*, 232. [NF]
161 "Conclusion," *UPUC*, 153. [NF]
162 "Goethe as the Sage," *OPP*, 211.
163 "Goethe as the Sage," *OPP*, 226.
164 "Second Thoughts about Humanism," *SelE*, 485n. [NF]
165 "Shakespeare and the Stoicism of Seneca," *SelE*, 131. [NF]
166 "Dante," *SelE*, 250. [NF]
167 See *Chandogya Upanishad*, 6.8.7, chiefly.
168 See *Heraclitus*, ed. Philip Wheelwright (Princeton: Princeton University Press, 1959), 90 (fragment 108).
169 "Dante," *SelE*, 250.
170 "Poetry and Drama," *OPP*, 86.
171 "Lancelot Andrewes," *SelE*, 351.

172 "Poetry and Drama," *OPP*, 87. [NF]
173 "Tradition and the Individual Talent," *SelE*, 17. [NF]
174 "Shakespeare and the Stoicism of Seneca," *SelE*, 135.
175 "William Blake," *SelE*, 322.
176 "What is Minor Poetry?" *OPP*, 50. [NF]
177 "Ben Jonson," *SelE*, 158; "John Ford," *SelE*, 203. [NF]
178 W.B. Yeats, "Discoveries," in *Essays and Introductions* (New York: Macmillan, 1961), 294.
179 *The Family Reunion*, pt. 2, sc. 3, *CPP*, 343.
180 "Matthew Arnold," *UPUC*, 106. [NF]
181 *The Confidential Clerk*, act 2, *CPP*, 472–4.
182 *The Family Reunion*, pt. 2, sc. 2, *CPP*, 335.
183 "Dante," *SelE*, 273. [NF]
184 *Murder in the Cathedral*, pt. 2, *CPP*, 270.
185 *Murder in the Cathedral*, pt. 2, *CPP*, 271; *Burnt Norton*, l. 45.
186 "Hamlet," *SelE*, 144.
187 See George Bernard Shaw's play *Saint Joan* (stage direction of the opening of scene 1).
188 *The Cocktail Party*, act 3, *CPP*, 437. The quotation is from *Prometheus Unbound*, ll. 191–9.
189 *The Family Reunion*, pt. 1, sc. 1, *CPP*, 288.
190 *The Elder Statesman*, act 2, *CPP*, 553.
191 "What is a Classic?" *OPP*, 62. [NF]
192 Cf. "John Ford," *SelE*, 194. [NF]
193 In his essay "Characters of Dramatic Writers, Contemporary with Shakespeare," Charles Lamb compares *Call for the robin redbreast and the wren* from Webster's play *The Duchess of Malfi* to *Full fathom five* from Shakespeare's *The Tempest*: "I never saw anything like the funeral dirge in this play for the death of Marcello, except the ditty which reminds Ferdinand of his drowned father in *The Tempest*. As that is of the water, watery; so this is of the earth, earthy. Both have that intenseness of feeling, which seems to resolve itself into the element which it contemplates." *The Works of Charles Lamb*, ed. Thomas Hutchinson (London: H. Milford / Oxford University Press, 1924; vol. 1 of *The Works of Charles and Mary Lamb*), 64.
194 Beside this passage of *The Waste Land* (ll. 307–11) in his annotated copy of Eliot's *Collected Poems and Plays, 1909–1950* (in the NFL), NF writes, "Augustine and the Buddha have the same relation to Madame Sosostris that some Xy [Christianity] has to occultism in *The Dry Salvages*."
195 The editors have been unable to verify or locate this note by Joyce. NF confessed in a letter that this reference "was a somewhat irresponsible one, having been quoted orally from someone who was working on the Joyce papers at [the State University of New York at] Buffalo. I ought to resist the

temptation to introduce such things when I haven't checked them myself. But this one seemed too good to pass up." See NFF, 1988, box 12, file h6.

196 In his annotated copy of Colin Still's *Shakespeare's Mystery Play* (London: Cecil Palmer, 1921), beside a reference to act 1, sc. 2 of *The Tempest* (p. 161), NF writes "Cf. *The Waste Land*. Eliot seldom acknowledges when he really steals."

197 Cf. Jeremiah 22:29; Isaiah 35:1; Ezekiel 37; Micah 6:3; Exodus 17:6; Judges 15:19. [NF]

198 Leonard Unger, *T.S. Eliot: A Selected Critique* (New York: Rinehart, 1948), 357. [NF] Unger is the editor of this collection as well as the author of the self-titled article in which this observation is made.

199 *The Family Reunion*, pt. 1, sc. 1, *CPP*, 289.

200 *The Family Reunion*, pt. 2, sc. 2, *CPP*, 335. Cf. "What might have been and what has been / Point to one end, which is always present" (*Burnt Norton*, ll. 9–10, 47–8).

201 A remark attributed to American transcendentalist Margaret Fuller. See Paula Blanchard, *Margaret Fuller: From Transcendentalism to Revolution* (New York: Dell, 1978), 87.

202 *The Trembling of the Veil*, bk. 1, sec. 19, in *Autobiographies*, 158.

203 *Heraclitus*, ed. Wheelwright, p. 68 (fragment 66).

204 "What is a Classic?" *OPP*, 70. [NF]

205 Cf. "Virgil and the Christian World," *OPP*, 131. [NF]

206 *Murder in the Cathedral*, pt. 2, *CPP*, 272.

207 *Murder in the Cathedral*, pt. 1, *CPP*, 257.

208 *Murder in the Cathedral*, pt. 1, *CPP*, 244.

209 *Murder in the Cathedral*, pt. 1, *CPP*, 246.

210 *Murder in the Cathedral*, pt. 1, *CPP*, 248.

211 *Murder in the Cathedral*, pt. 1, *CPP*, 258.

212 *The Family Reunion*, pt. 1, sc. 1, *CPP*, 294.

213 *The Family Reunion*, pt. 2, sc. 2, *CPP*, 331.

214 See n. 189, above.

215 *The Family Reunion*, pt. 2, sc. 2, *CPP*, 339.

216 "Poetry and Drama," *OPP*, 84. [NF]

217 *The Family Reunion*, pt. 2, sc. 3, *CPP*, 344.

218 *The Cocktail Party*, act 3, *CPP*, 438.

219 *The Cocktail Party*, act 3, *CPP*, 440.

220 Oscar Wilde, *The Importance of Being Earnest*, act 1, ll. 172–3.

221 "Christopher Marlowe," *SelE*, 123. [NF]

222 *The Confidential Clerk*, act 2, *CPP*, 474.

223 *The Confidential Clerk*, act 3, *CPP*, 502.

224 *The Elder Statesman*, act 2, *CPP*, 549.

225 *The Elder Statesman*, act 1, *CPP*, 537.

226 *The Elder Statesman*, act 3, *CPP*, 573.
227 *The Elder Statesman*, act 3, *CPP*, 582.
228 NF misquotes here, perhaps purposefully. The line reads: "The word within a word, unable to speak a word" (*Gerontion*, l. 18).
229 *The Family Reunion*, pt. 2, sc. 3, *CPP*, 345.

42. Tribute to John Crowe Ransom

1 In act 4 of George Bernard Shaw's *The Doctor's Dilemma*, Ridgeon remarks that "the most tragic thing in the world is a man of genius who is not also a man of honour."

43. The Rising of the Moon: A Study of *A Vision*

1 Swedenborg's conception of correspondence and his interpretation of the Bible are articulated most fully in his *Arcana Coelestia* (New York: Swedenborg Foundation, 1965 [orig. pub. 1747–56]). Yeats also refers to Swedenborg's five-volume *Spiritual Diary* (London: James Speirs, 1883–1902 [orig. writ. 1747–63]). See also Yeats's "Swedenborg, Mediums, and the Desolate Places," *Explorations*, 30–70.
2 "It [cosmology] belongs to a department of literature remarkable for its persistence and astonishing in its variety; cosmology is one of the most ancient literary forms." See Paul Valéry, "On Poe's *Eureka*," trans. Malcolm Cowley and James R. Lawler, in *The Collected Works of Paul Valéry*, vol. 8: *Leonardo Poe Mallarmé* (Princeton: Princeton University Press), 170.
3 Henry Crabb Robinson writes: "Jacob Boehme was spoken of as a divinely inspired man. Blake praised, too, the figures in Law's translation as being very beautiful. Michel Angelo [*sic*] could not have done better." See *Diary, Reminiscences, and Correspondence of Henry Crabb Robinson*, ed. Thomas Sadler (London: Macmillan, 1872), 9. In *A Vision*, Yeats refers to "the diagrams in Law's *Boehme*, where one lifts a flap of paper to discover both the human entrails and the starry heavens. William Blake thought those diagrams worthy of Michel Angelo, but remains himself almost unintelligible because he never drew the like" (23–4).
4 One might infer from NF's remark that Yeats was unimpressed by or critical of the level of contribution made by Ellis to their edition of Blake, but this is not the case. Yeats does state in his letters that Ellis is "useless through lack of mystical knowledge" and recalls Ellis's confession that he "didn't understand 'the doctrine of the four Zoas,'" but he also claims that Ellis "knows Blake much better than I do, or anyone else perhaps" and frequently praises Ellis's work and leadership. NF's remark seems rather

to be taking stock of the many times that Yeats's letters mention working on interpretative articles, essays, and diagrams for the edition, which ultimately formed the bulk of the edition's analysis and commentary and were (as NF mentions) testing ideas later articulated in *A Vision*. See *The Letters of W.B. Yeats*, ed. Allan Wade (London: Rupert Hart-Davis, 1954), 112, 163, 475.

5 *Purgatorio*, canto 28, ll. 88–120. For further commentary by NF on this passage, see *RT*, 398–9.

6 See no. 23, n. 33.

7 *An Honoured Guest* has "In actual count there are one or two more."

8 The real echo is from the final chorus of Shelley's *Hellas*. [NF] The Yeats line is from *Two Songs from a Play*, l. 9.

9 *The Letters of W.B. Yeats*, 904.

10 This essay is by some years the earliest writing in the book, and the view taken here of Poe's *Eureka* is not one that I would endorse now. [NF]

11 Yeats writes: "My 'private philosophy' is the material dealing with individual mind which came to me with that on which the mainly historical *Vision* is based. I have not published it because I only half understand it. . . . In my own philosophy the sensuous image is changed from time to time at predestined moments called *Initiatory Moments* . . . . One sensuous image leads to another because they are never analysed. At *The Critical Moment* they are dissolved by analysis and we enter by free will pure unified experience. When all the sensuous images are dissolved we meet true death." See *The Letters of W.B. Yeats*, 916–17.

12 Spengler writes: "Second Religiousness . . . appears in all Civilizations as soon as they have fully formed themselves as such and are beginning to pass, slowly and imperceptibly, into the non-historical state in which time-periods cease to mean anything. . . . [It] consists in a deep piety that fills the waking-consciousness . . . . But neither in the creations of this piety nor in the form . . . is there anything primary or spontaneous. Nothing is built up, no idea unfolds itself—it is only as if a mist cleared off the land and revealed the old forms, uncertainly at first, but presently with increasing distinctness. The material of the Second Religiousness is simply that of the first, genuine, young religiousness—only otherwise experienced and expressed. It starts with Rationalism's fading out in helplessness, then the forms of the Springtime become visible, and finally the whole world of the primitive religion, which had receded before the grand forms of the early faith, returns to the foreground." See Spengler's *The Decline of the West*, trans. Charles Francis Atkinson (New York: Alfred A. Knopf, 1932), 310–11.

13 *The Letters of W.B. Yeats*, 211.

14 Yeats writes, "Again and again with remorse, a sense of defeat, I have failed when I would write of God, written coldly and conventionally." See "Pages

from a Diary Written in Nineteen Hundred and Thirty" (sec. 21), in *Explorations*, ed. Mrs. W.B. Yeats (London: Macmillan, 1962), 305.
15 "Estrangement" (sec. 32), in *Autobiographies*, 482.
16 After "predecessor," *An Honoured Guest* concludes the sentence with "perhaps to get it more exactly into his own time."
17 *Two Songs from a Play*, pt. 2, l. 4. See also *A Vision*, 268.
18 *An Honoured Guest* adds "in practice" at this point.
19 Sec. 5 of the essay "Private Thoughts" was excised from "On the Boiler" when it was republished in the collection *Explorations*. The omitted passage to which NF refers reads: "I detest the Renaissance because it made the human mind inorganic; I adore the Renaissance because it clarified form and created freedom. I too expect the counter-Renaissance, but if we do not hold to freedom and form it will come, not as an inspiration in the head, but as an obstruction in the bowels." NF recopied the omitted passage on page 437 of his annotated edition of *Explorations*, now in the NFL. See "On the Boiler," in *The Collected Works of W.B. Yeats*, vol. 5, *Later Essays*, ed. William H. O'Donnell (London: Charles Scribner, 1994), 239, 490.
20 *An Honoured Guest* reads "anxious as it was."
21 See Yeats's note to *The Hosting of the Sidhe*, in *The Collected Poems of W.B. Yeats*, ed. Richard J. Finneran (New York: Macmillan, 1989), 454.
22 *The Letters of W.B. Yeats*, 256.
23 "Samhain 1904: The Dramatic Movement," in *Explorations*, 132.
24 *The Letters of W.B. Yeats*, 733.
25 "Samhain 1904: First Principles," in *Explorations*, 149.
26 "J.M. Synge and the Ireland of His Time," in *Essays and Introductions*, 339.
27 Lady Gregory, *Our Irish Theatre: A Chapter in Autobiography* (New York: G. Putnam's Sons, 1913), 121.
28 The title of a play by Yeats published in 1894.
29 "The Golden Age," in *The Celtic Twilight*. See *Mythologies*, 104.
30 See no. 23, n. 25.
31 *The Collected Plays of W.B. Yeats* (London: Macmillan, 1952), 301.
32 Yeats writes that, "because it came when my wife's growing fatigue made communications difficult and because of defects of my own, ["The Soul in Judgment"] is the most unfinished of my five books" (*A Vision*, 23).
33 See "Discoveries: In the Serpent's Mouth," in *Essays and Introductions*, 287.
34 "The Trembling of the Veil" (bk. 2: "Ireland after Parnell," sec. 14), in *Autobiographies*, 246.
35 "Gods and Fighting Men," in *Explorations*, 24.
36 *Dramatis Personae* (sec. 22), in *Autobiographies*, 457.
37 "A General Introduction for My Work," in *Essays and Introductions*, 509.
38 *The Letters of W.B. Yeats*, 728.
39 *Per Amica Silentia Lunae*, in *Mythologies*, 356n. 1.

40 See no. 23, n. 17.
41 "The Tablets of the Law," in *Mythologies*, 300.

44. Foreword to 1984

1 In an oft-quoted obituary, V.S. Pritchett referred to Orwell as "the wintry conscience of a generation." See V.S. Pritchett, "George Orwell," *New Statesman*, 28 (January 1950): 96.
2 See "George Orwell," *LS*, 140–3. See also no. 30, p. 87
3 The first line of chap. 7 of *1984* tells of how Winston Smith records this sentiment in his diary, and he recalls it periodically in the novel.

45. The Top of the Tower: A Study of the Imagery of Yeats

1 See Yeats's introduction of his play *The Words upon the Window-Pane*, in *The Variorum Edition of the Plays of W.B. Yeats*, 970.
2 Frazer, J.G., *The Golden Bough: A Study in Magic and Religion*, pt. 7, *Balder the Beautiful*, vol. 1 (London: Macmillan, 1913), 281. In abridged editions of *The Golden Bough*, the passage is found in chap. 62, pt. 8.
3 The "twisted, echo-harbouring shell" of Yeats's *The Song of the Happy Shepherd* (l. 36).
4 See Yeats's introduction of his play *The Words upon the Window-Pane*, in *The Variorum Edition of the Plays of W.B. Yeats*, 968.
5 "The Mandukya Upanishad," in *Essays and Introductions*, 474.
6 *The Cap and Bells* [ll. 29–32], from *The Wind among the Reeds* (1899). [NF]
7 *Those Images* [l. 16], in *Last Poems* (1939). [NF]
8 Thomas Browne, *Religio Medici* (pt. 2, sec. 6). See *The Works of Thomas Browne*, vol. 1, ed. Geoffrey Keynes (London: Faber & Faber, 1964), 79.
9 See "Swedenborg, Mediums, and the Desolate Places," in *Explorations*, 39.
10 *The Pilgrim* and *The Wild Old Wicked Man* are the titles of poems by Yeats.
11 The opening paragraph of Porphyry's *Life of Plotinus* tells of how Plotinus was reluctant to sit for a painter or sculptor, embarrassed to possess material form.
12 NF may be referring to the third part or "Third Bardo" of the Buddhist text *The Tibetan Book of the Dead*, which instructs souls on how to select an appropriate womb through which to be reincarnated.
13 See no. 43, n. 28.
14 See Yeats's note to *Crossways* and *The Rose*, in *The Collected Poems of W.B. Yeats*, ed. Richard J. Finneran (New York: Macmillan, 1989), 453.
15 See *AC*, 203–6/189–92, 237/222, 292/273, 299/280, 321/301.
16 "If youth only knew, if age only could."
17 NF is referring to Yeats's play *The King of the Great Clock Tower* (1935).

18 NF is referring to Yeats's play *A Full Moon in March* (1935), in addition to the passages from *A Vision*.
19 Yeats found it distasteful to observe the growing Irish-nationalist fervour and the concomitant poor fortunes of his friends Maud Gonne and Eva and Constance Gore-Booth. The sentiment is expressed in poems such as *No Second Troy*, *In Memory of Eva Gore-Booth and Con Markievicz*, and *Easter, 1916*.
20 *To Ireland in the Coming Times* [ll. 6–8], from *The Rose* (1893). [NF]
21 See "The Philosophy of Shelley's Poetry," in *Essays and Introductions*, 86–8.
22 See no. 23, n. 17.

47. Wallace Stevens and the Variation Form

1 See no. 37, n. 2.
2 Stevens writes: "The mind has added nothing to human nature. It is a violence from within that protects us from a violence without. It is the imagination pressing back against the pressure of reality" (*NA*, 36).
3 See no. 37, n. 14.
4 *The Comedian as the Letter* C, sec. 1, l. 69 (*CP*, 29). "Dich an sich" (German, "things in themselves") is a phrase that occurs throughout Immanuel Kant's writings, particularly his *Critique of Pure Reason*, in reference to his principle that objective reality is inaccessible and that only our perceptions of reality can be queried.
5 NF's original page citation here refers to *Description without Place*, sec. 1. Cf. ll. 3–4, "What it seems / It is and in such seeming all things are" (*CP*, 339).
6 *So-And-So Reclining on Her Couch*, ll. 22–6 (*CP*, 296).
7 *Not Ideas about the Thing but the Thing Itself*, ll. 9, 18 (*CP*, 534).
8 *The Idea of Order at Key West*, l. 52 (*CP*, 130).
9 Stevens writes that "there are degrees of the imagination, as, for example, degrees of vitality and, therefore, of intensity. It is an implication that there are degrees of reality" (*NA*, 7).
10 See no. 37, nn. 16 and 17.
11 *Le Monocle de Mon Oncle*, sec. 6, l. 3 (*CP*, 15).
12 *The Pediment of Appearance*, l. 3 (*CP*, 361).
13 See Sartre's *Being and Nothingness: An Essay in Phenomenological Ontology*, trans. Hazel E. Barnes (New York: Citadel Press, 1965).
14 *The Snow Man*, ll. 14–15 (*CP*, 10).
15 *Sunday Morning*, l. 16 (*CP*, 67).
16 *Oak Leaves Are Hands*, l. 15 (*CP*, 272).
17 The distinction between "imagination" and "fancy" is found in Coleridge's *Biographia Literaria*, chap. 13. See also I.A. Richards, *Coleridge on Imagination* (London: K. Paul, Trench, Trubner, 1934).
18 *The Pediment of Appearance*, l. 18 (*CP*, 362).

19 *The Poems of Our Climate*, l. 21 (*CP*, 194).
20 *Mrs. Alfred Uruguay*, ll. 35–6 (*CP*, 250).
21 *Final Soliloquy of the Interior Paramour*, l. 14 (*CP*, 524).
22 Later printings of *OP* point out (see p. vii) that the essay in which this quotation appears ("On Poetic Truth") was not actually by Stevens: it was written by H.D. Lewis and copied out by him. The editors thank Dr. Eleanor Cook for drawing this to our attention.
23 *Theory*, l. 1 (*CP*, 86).
24 *Colloquy with a Polish Aunt*, l. 4 (*CP*, 84).
25 *Sad Strains of a Gay Waltz*, l. 27 (*CP*, 122).
26 See no. 37, n. 70.
27 *Notes toward a Supreme Fiction: It Must Be Abstract*, sec. 8, l. 17 (*CP*, 387).
28 *Asides on the Oboe*, ll. 15–16 (*CP*, 250).
29 NF's original page citation here refers to *A Weak Mind in the Mountains* (*CP*, 212). Cf. ll. 16–20.
30 *A Pastoral Nun*, l. 12 (*CP*, 378).
31 *The Winter's Tale*, 4.4.102–11.
32 *A Primitive Like an Orb*, l. 1 (*CP*, 440).
33 *Peter Quince at the Clavier*, l. 54 (*CP*, 92).
34 *Peter Quince at the Clavier*, ll. 51–3 (*CP*, 91).
35 See Samuel Alexander, *Space, Time, and Deity: The Gifford Lectures at Glasgow, 1916–18*, 2 vols. (London: Macmillan, 1966), annotated copy in the NFL; and Alfred North Whitehead, *Science and the Modern World* (New York: Macmillan, 1929), annotated copy in the NFL. The "great passage" to which NF refers is found on p. 133.
36 "Eliot and I are dead opposites," Stevens writes in one of his letters; "I have been doing about everything that he would not be likely to do" (*L*, 677). There are implicit and explicit criticisms of Eliot throughout Stevens's letters.
37 *Thirteen Ways of Looking at a Blackbird*, ll. 13–17 (*CP*, 93).
38 This phrase appears in *Finnegans Wake* as "the seim anew" (215:23).
39 *Prologues to What Is Possible*, l. 28 (*CP*, 517).
40 *Not Ideas about the Thing but the Thing Itself*, ll. 1, 18 (*CP*, 534).
41 *Description without Place*, l. 14 (*CP*, 341).
42 *Things of August*, ll. 17–18 (*CP*, 490).

48. Aldous Huxley

1 Although Huxley maintained that the character of Rampion was "just some of Lawrence's notions on legs," most critics regard the character of Rampion as being modelled outright on D.H. Lawrence. Interestingly, NF's statement in his next response that Huxley's characters are "puppets" seems to

accord more with the author's claim. See *The Letters of Aldous Huxley*, ed. Grover Smith (London: Chatto & Windus, 1969), 340; and Brad Buchanan, "Oedipus in Dystopia: Freud and Lawrence in Aldous Huxley's *Brave New World*," *Journal of Modern Literature*, 25 (Summer 2002): 75–89. After Lawrence's death, Huxley also edited an edition of Lawrence's correspondence. See Lawrence's *Letters*, ed. Aldous Huxley (London: Heinemann, 1932).

2 After moving to Hollywood in 1937, Huxley became interested in the principal branch of Hindu philosophy known as Vedanta. He joined the Vedanta Society of Southern California and became a major contributor to its journal *Vedanta and the West*.

49. Rolls Royce

1 *The Garden of the Finzi-Continis*, trans. Isabel Quigly (London: Faber & Faber, 1965); *Behind the Door*, trans. William Weaver (New York: Harcourt, Brace, Jovanovich, 1972).

2 A poem and a collection by Layton. See Irving Layton, *For My Brother Jesus* (Toronto: McClelland & Stewart, 1976).

50. Cycle and Apocalypse in *Finnegans Wake*

1 The French critic and poet Nicolas Boileau speaks of "le clinquant du Tasse à tout l'or de Virgile," or "the tinsel of Tasso and the gold of Virgil" (Satire 9, verse 76).

2 *The Collected Works of Samuel Taylor Coleridge*, vol. 4: *The Friend* (vol. 1), ed. Barbara Rooke (London: Routledge & Kegan Paul, 1969), 20–1.

3 Byron's translation of the first canto of *Morgante Maggiore* by Luigi Pulci (1432–84) was published in the *Liberal*, no. 4, 30 July 1832.

4 Lines 78–149 of Eliot's *Little Gidding*, the infamous "compound ghost" sequence, are written in a modified *terza rima* form in imitation of metre of Dante's *Divine Comedy*.

5 See Joyce's *Ulysses* (New York: Random House, 1934), 22. Stephen Dedalus's remark is a reference to *The Servant of Two Masters*, a play by the Italian dramatist Carlo Goldoni (1707–93).

6 Mary T. Reynolds, *Joyce and Dante: The Shaping Imagination* (Princeton: Princeton University Press, 1981).

7 See Giordano Bruno, *The Expulsion of the Triumphant Beast*, trans. Arthur D. Imerti (New Brunswick: Rutgers University Press, 1964); and *The Heroic Frenzies*, trans. Paul Eugene Memmo, Jr. (Chapel Hill: University of North Carolina Press, 1966). An annotated copy of the first of these is in the NFL. Chapel Hill : University of North Carolina Press, c1966 Chapel Hill : Univer-

sity of North Carolina Press, c1966 Chapel Hill : University of North Carolina Press, c1966.

8 Samuel Beckett, "Dante . . . Bruno. Vico . . . Joyce," in *Our Exagmination Round His Factification for Incamination of Work in Progress* (Paris : Shakespeare, 1929), 3–22.

9 NF is referring to Clive Hart's *Structure and Motif in "Finnegans Wake"* (Evanston, Ill.: Northwestern University Press, 1962). An annotated copy of this book is in the NFL.

10 "The Day of the Rabblement," in *The Critical Writings of James Joyce*, ed. Ellsworth Mason and Richard Ellmann (New York: Viking, 1959), 69.

11 James Joyce, *Letters of James Joyce*, ed. Stuart Gilbert [and Richard Ellman, 3. vols.] (New York: Viking Press, 1957[–66]), [1:]224–5. [NF]

12 *Letters of James Joyce*, [1:]241. [NF]

13 See Richard Ellman's *James Joyce* (New York: Oxford University Press, 1959), 351.

14 The volume to which NF refers is his heavily annotated Viking Press edition of 1939 (see no. 33, n. 1). The number "98" is scrawled in pencil on the rear fly-leaf. In regard to the event NF describes here, John Ayre writes: "[NF] had looked over a copy [of *Finnegans Wake*] which Mike Joseph had bought in Oxford when it first came out and his interest was renewed soon after the war started when Helen noticed the original edition for 89¢ at Eaton's College St. store. When Frye rushed over to buy it, the clerk confessed she thought it a bad bargain" (Ayre, 165). Ayre appears to be mistaken about or has misprinted the price of the book.

15 T.S. Eliot, "The Frontiers of Criticism," in *On Poetry and Poets* (London: Faber & Faber, 1957), 108.

16 *Ulysses*, 35.

17 *Finnegans Wake*, 20:15–16. See also no. 33, n. 13.

18 *Finnegans Wake*, 8:9. Joyce refers to the "Willingdone Museyroom" as housing the "triplewon hat of Lipoleum" (8:10, 15–16).

19 Near the end of George Bernard Shaw's play *Man of Destiny*, Napoleon remarks: "Yes: I forgot the Irish. An English army led by an Irish general: that might be a match for a French army led by an Italian general." See *Plays: Pleasant and Unpleasant* (New York: Brentano, 1905), 213.

20 *The Autobiography of Giambattista Vico*, trans. Max Harold Fisch and Thomas Goddard Bergin (Ithaca, N.Y.: Great Seal, 1963).

21 Hugh Kenner, *Dublin's Joyce* (Boston: Beacon Press, 1962), 323–4.

22 Adaline Glasheen, *A Second Census of "Finnegans Wake": An Index of Characters and Their Roles* (Evanston, Ill.: Northwestern University Press), 124.

23 See Swift's *Journal to Stella*, letter 10 (25 November 1710).

24 The editors have been unable to locate the quotation to which NF refers. It may be a similar case to the one described in no. 41, n. 195.

25 Samuel Butler, *The Way of All Flesh* (New York: Three Sirens, 1935), 344.
26 *The Way of All Flesh*, 371.
27 See no. 23, n. 23.
28 Giordano Bruno, *The Expulsion of the Triumphant Beast*, trans. Arthur D. Imerti (New Brunswick: Rutgers University Press, 1964), 242
29 A phrase used repeatedly by Blake, e.g., *The Four Zoas: Night the Fourth*, p. 56, l. 13; E337, and *Milton*, pl. 15; ll. 39, 46; E110.
30 Thomas De Quincey, *Confessions of an English Opium-Eater and Other Essays* (Oxford: Oxford University Press, 1985), 212.
31 The reference is to the 1882 murder of two officials of the British government of Ireland, Thomas Henry Burke and Lord Frederick Cavendish. In 1887 Parnell had been accused in the *Times* of condoning the murders.
32 NF is referring to a view expressed frequently in the writings of Jacques Lacan and proponents of his theories. See Jacques Lacan, *The Language of the Self: The Function of Language in Psychoanalysis*, trans. Anthony Wilden (New York: Delta, 1968).
33 See Samuel Butler, *Life and Habit* (London: Cape, 1935), particularly chap. 1, "On Certain Acquired Habits," and chap. 2, "Conscious and Unconscious Knowers." See also Butler's *Unconscious Memory* (London: Jonathan Cape, 1922), an annotated copy of which is in the NFL.
34 *All Religions Are One* (epigraph); E1. Blake is of course echoing Mark 1:3.
35 NF is referring to the diary entries that constitute the final pages of *The Portrait of the Artist as a Young Man*, in which Stephen refers to Cranly as "the precursor."
36 The line actually reads "the seim anew" (215:23).
37 NF is speaking of his essay "Charms and Riddles" (*SM*, 123–47 and *CPCT*, 369–90).
38 See no. 36, n. 6.
39 Arielle Saiber translates this Latin phrase as "There is cheerfulness in sadness, sadness in cheerfulness." See Arielle Saiber, *Giordano Bruno and the Geometry of Language* (Burlington, Vt.: Ashgate, 2005), 84.
40 NF is misquoting slightly. The phrase actually reads "Till thousendsthee" (628:14–15).
41 See Dorothea Waley Singer, *Giordano Bruno: His Life and Thoughts with Annotated Translation of His Work On the Infinite Universe and Worlds* (New York: Henry Schuman, 1950), 232. Here Bruno writes: "FIFTHLY, Aristotle's definition of position is unsuited to primal, vast, universal space and it befitteth not to take the surface nearest and adjoining the content or other such foolishness which would regard space as mathematical and not physical, not to mention that between the containing surface and the content which moveth therein, there is always and inevitably an intermediate space which should rather be named position; and if we wish only to take the surface of space, we need to go seeking a finite position in the infinite." A note explains that

the word "position" translates Bruno's *loco*, and the word "space" translates Bruno's *spacio*. "The meaning seems to be," the note continues, "that Aristotle wrongly reduces the Greek word *χώρα* to signify a space which occupies a definite position where it should be used for the infinite immensity of physical space." In his annotated copy of this book (in the NFL), NF writes "space is place" and "*χώρα* still means place: Bruno is right."

42 See Eugene Jolas, "My Friend James Joyce," in *James Joyce: Two Decades of Criticisms*, ed. Seon Givens (New York: Vanguard, 1963), 8.

43 See Richard Ellmann, James Joyce (New York: Oxford University Press, 1959), 179. Blavatsky is also mentioned in *Ulysses* (p. 110).

44 See Eugene Jolas, "My Friend James Joyce," in *James Joyce*, 15.

45 Joyce in a letter to Harriet Shaw Weaver, 4 February 1921. See *Letters of James Joyce*, 1:156. See also Hugh Kenner, *The Pound Era* (Berkeley: University of California Press, 1973), 45, 505. Annotated copies of both texts are in the NFL.

51. Henry James and the Comedy of the Occult

1 The editions to which NF refers are: *The Ivory Tower* (London: Collins, n.d.), and *The Sense of the Past* (London: Collins, n.d.).

2 According to his notebooks, NF at one point debated entitling this paper "Time & Identity in H[enry] J[ames]" (*LN*, 131).

3 *The Wings of the Dove* (Harmondsworth: Penguin, 1971), 161–6.

4 *What Maisie Knew* (London: John Lehmann, 1947), 21.

5 *The Wings of the Dove*, 74.

6 *The Ambassadors* (New York: Harper & Brothers, 1930), 93.

7 "Mr. Bennett and Mrs. Brown," in *The Essays of Virginia Woolf*, 3 vols., ed. Andrew McNeillie (San Diego: Harcourt Brace Jovanovich, 1986–88), 3:384–9.

8 See *The Letters of William James*, ed. Henry James (Boston: Little Brown, 1926), 277–8.

9 *The Wings of the Dove*, 91–2.

10 *The Golden Bowl* (New York: Scribner, 1923), 2:94.

11 E.M. Forster, *Howards End* (New York: Knopf, 1944), 33 (chap. 4). A copy of this edition is in the NFL.

12 *The Other House* (London: Rupert Hart-Davis, 1948), 218.

13 *The Ivory Tower* (London: Collins, n.d.), 284–5.

14 *The Princess Casamassima* (New York: Harper & Row, 1968), 52.

15 *The Wings of the Dove*, 5.

16 In his notes to the unfinished *The Ivory Tower*, James writes: "By the blest operation this time of my Dramatic principle, my law of successive Aspects, each treated from its own centre, as, though with many qualifications, *The Awkward Age*, I have the great help of flexibility and variety; my persons

in turn, or at least the three or four foremost, having control, as it were, of the Act and the Aspect, and so making it *his* or making it *hers*" (268). Beside this passage in his annotated copy (in the NFL), NF writes "dr[amatic] pr[inciple], turned inside out, as in *The Ring and the Book*."

17 T.S. Eliot, "On Henry James," in *The Question of Henry James: A Collection of Critical Essays*, ed. F.W. Dupee (New York: Holt, 1945), 110.

18 NF misquotes James here. The line reads "I have never entertained an idea. Ideas often entertain *me*." *The Europeans* (New York: New American Library, 1964), 90.

19 See Henry James, *Fourteen Stories*, ed. David Garnett (London: Rupert Hart-Davis, 1948), 36.

20 *The Great Short Novels of Henry James*, ed. Philip Rahv (New York: Dial, 1944), 338.

21 *The Portrait of a Lady* (New York: Modern Library, 1936), 71 (vol. 2, chap. 34).

22 *Fourteen Stories*, 149.

23 See *Henry James: Stories of the Supernatural*, ed. Leon Edel (New York: Taplinger, 1980), 424. Beside this passage of *The Friends of the Friends* in his annotated copy of this anthology (in the NFL), NF writes, "like the governess in TS [*Turn of the Screw*], she's as batty as a Kentucky cave. And like the governess, she is an unconscious agent of the evil (the dead husband who beat his wife) she thinks she's resisting."

24 See *Henry James: Stories of the Supernatural*, 535.

25 Ibid., 529.

26 Ibid., 550.

27 Ibid., 529.

28 In what was something of a controversy in Henry James criticism, Wilson put forth this view in an essay published in 1934, and was later forced to recant it when presented with counter-arguments by other critics. See Edmund Wilson, "The Ambiguity of Henry James," in *The Question of Henry James* (see n. 17, above), 160–90.

29 See n. 23, above.

30 NF is referring to Balzac's novel *Louis Lambert* (1832).

31 *The Sacred Fount* (New York: Grove Press, 1953), 296.

32 See *The Great Short Novels of Henry James*, 560.

33 Ibid., 562.

34 *Ten Short Stories of Henry James*, ed. Michael Swan (London: John Lehmann, 1948), 86.

35 James's precise remark is that "a story-teller who aims at anything more than a fleeting success has no right to tell an ugly story unless he knows its beautiful counterpart." See James's *Notes and Reviews* (Cambridge, Mass.: Dunster House, 1921), 226.

36 See no. 50, n. 29.

Emendations

page/line

26/10–11	Sewell Stokes *for* G.W. Stokes
26/14	G.W. Stonier *for* He (sentiment mistakenly attributed to Stokes)
30/1	we find this in E.J. Pratt's *for* we find this is E.J. Pratt's
30/11	one reads *for* we read
30/35	says is strikingly acute *for* says in strikingly acute
46/14	T.F. Powys of *for* T.F. Powys or
48/3	The satire of the episode *for* the satire on the episode
58/11	"climbing moon" *for* "brilliant moon" (see no. 23, n. 9)
68/11	"Any student of occultism . . . should especially notice" *for* "The student of occultism . . . should particularly notice" (as in source)
80/27	subtlety and delicacy exist *for* subtlety and delicacy exists
96/12–13	newly created *for* new created
109/3–4	which exists *for* and exists
109/30	to the four evangelists *for* the four evangelists (for parallelism)
126/11	waking consciousness *for* making consciousness
135/27–8	"the comic sum" *for* "the comic sun"
136/22	Of empty heaven" *for* "Of empty heavens"
136/3–4	but itself a part *for* but as itself a part
151/14	"Every thing possible to be believ'd" *for* "Whatever is possible to be believed" (as in E)
152/28	and that are indifferent *for* and are indifferent
173/26–7	Canadian Conference of the Arts *for* Canadian Conference Arts
174/32	days and hours and seasons *for* days and hours of seasons
182/13	*Notes towards the Definition of Culture for Notes towards a Definition of Culture*
189/30–1	differences of religious and political views *for* difference of religious and political views (as in Eliot)

208/35–6	*logos koinos* (*κοινός*) *for logos κοινός*
218/34	*Mélange adultère de tout* for *Mélange adultère du tout*
234/34–5	visions of loss and despair *for* vision of loss and despair
238/34–5	for the sunflower *for* or the sunflower
246/36	humility and innocence make *for* humility and innocence makes
278/15	*A Clergyman's Daughter* for *The Road to Wigan Pier* (corrected by NF in a letter to Bellhaven House, NFF, 1988, box 61, file 2)
290/27	Shakespeare's *The Phoenix and Turtle for* Shakespeare's *The Phoenix and the Turtle*
291/11–12	the first *Winding Stair* poem *for The Winding Stair* (disregarded correction by NF for paperback version of *StS*)
292/35	Congal *for* Conchubar (disregarded correction by NF for paperback version of *StS*)
305/35	new psychological discoveries in the work of Freud *for* new psychological discoveries into the work of Freud
306/25	smaller and less populous communities *for* the smaller and less populace communities
310/28	socialist realism *for* social realism
316/3–4	*OP*, 220 *for NA*, 220
319/15	"the inhuman making" *for* "the non-human making"
323/15	*"A Collect of Philosophy" for "A Collect for Philosophy"*
333/20	previously . . . in English literature *for* previously . . . in English literature before
336/38	that lend *for* providing (as in *Vico and Joyce*; to avoid repetition)
340/11	"a triumph of female imbecility" *for* "a perfect triumph of female imbecility"
342/28	*God the Known and God the Unknown for God the Known and Unknown*
344/32	instant *for* instance (as in *Vico and Joyce*)
347/18	Virgin in Yeats *for* Virginian Yeats (as in *MM*)
355/5	hundreds of pages *for* hundred of pages

Index

NOTE: Dates of works are for first publication in the language of the title, unless otherwise noted. Those for the works of Yeats, which are taken from Allan Wade's bibliography, may be for publication in a periodical or under a different title.

www.ingramcontent.com/pod-product-compliance
Lightning Source LLC
LaVergne TN
LVHW040154080826
844660LV00014B/955/J